CAMBRIDGE STUDIES IN
PUBLISHING AND PRINTING HISTORY

GENERAL EDITORS

Terry Belanger and David McKitterick

TITLES PUBLISHED

*The Provincial Book Trade in
Eighteenth-Century England*
by John Feather
Lewis Carrol and the House of Macmillan
edited by Morton N. Cohen & Anita Gandolfo
The Correspondence of Robert Dodsley 1733–1764
edited by James E. Tierney
Book Production and Publishing in Britain 1375–1475
edited by Jeremy Griffiths and Derek Pearsall

TITLES FORTHCOMING

The Making of Johnson's Dictionary, 1746–1773
by Allen Reddick
*Before Copyright: the French
book-privilege system, 1498–1526*
by Elizabeth Armstrong
*The Commercialization of
the Book in Britain, 1745–1814*
by James Raven

BOOK PRODUCTION AND PUBLISHING IN BRITAIN
1375–1475

EDITED BY

JEREMY GRIFFITHS

St John's College, Oxford

AND

DEREK PEARSALL

Professor of English, Harvard University

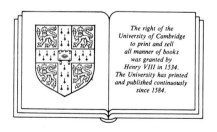

The right of the
University of Cambridge
to print and sell
all manner of books
was granted by
Henry VIII in 1534.
The University has printed
and published continuously
since 1584.

CAMBRIDGE UNIVERSITY PRESS

CAMBRIDGE
NEW YORK   PORT CHESTER
MELBOURNE   SYDNEY

Published by the Press Syndicate of the University of Cambridge
The Pitt Building, Trumpington Street, Cambridge CB2 1RP
32 East 57th Street, New York, NY 10022, USA
10 Stamford Road, Oakleigh, Melbourne 3166, Australia

First published 1989

Printed in Great Britain at the University Press, Cambridge

British Library cataloguing in publication data

Book production and publishing in Britain 1375–1475
1. Great Britain. Manuscript books.
Production, 1375–1475
1. Griffiths, Jeremy. 11. Pearsall, Derek.
686'.0941

Library of Congress cataloguing in publication data

Book production and publishing in Britain, 1375–1475 /
edited by Jeremy Griffiths and Derek Pearsall.
p.   cm. – (Cambridge studies in publishing and printing history).
Includes bibliographies and indexes.
ISBN 0 521 25736 0
1. Books – Great Britain – History. 2. Scriptoria – Great Britain –
History. 3. Manuscripts, Medieval – Great Britain – History.
4. Book industries and trade – Great Britain – History. 5. Publishers
and publishing – Great Britain – History. 6. Great Britain –
Intellectual life – Medieval period, 1066–1485.
1. Griffiths, Jeremy. 11. Pearsall, Derek Albert. 111. Series.
Z8.G7B66   1989
070.5'0941 – dc19   88–25892   CIP

ISBN 0 521 25736 0

CE

CONTENTS

List of illustrations and figures   *page* vii
List of contributors   xi
Acknowledgements   xiv
List of abbreviations   xv
List of works cited in short form   xvii

Introduction *Derek Pearsall*   1

THE BOOK

1 Materials: the paper revolution *R. J. Lyall*   11
2 Design, decoration and illustration *Kathleen L. Scott*   31
3 English decorated bookbindings *Mirjam M. Foot*   65

BOOK PRODUCTION

4 Evidence for the study of London's late medieval manuscript-
   book trade *C. Paul Christianson*   87
5 Publication by members of the religious orders *A.I. Doyle* 109
6 Lollard book production *Anne Hudson*   125
7 The production of books of liturgical polyphony
   Andrew Wathey   143

PATRONS, BUYERS AND OWNERS

8 Patrons, buyers and owners: the evidence for ownership, and
   the rôle of book owners in book production and the book trade
   Kate Harris   163
9 Patrons, buyers and owners: book production and social status
   Carol Meale   201
10 Books and book owners in fifteenth-century Scotland
   R. J. Lyall   239

THE CONTENTS OF BOOKS

11   The manuscripts of the major English poetic texts
     A.S.G. Edwards and Derek Pearsall   257
         Appendix: Some statistics for manuscripts containing major
                 literary texts   270
12   Anthologies and miscellanies: production and choice of texts
     Julia Boffey and John J. Thompson   279
13   Vernacular books of religion *Vincent Gillespie*   317
14   Scientific and medical books *Linda Ehrsam Voigts*   345

AFTERMATH

15   Manuscript to print *N.F. Blake*   403
         Appendix A: Caxton prints for which a copytext survives or
                 which were used as a copy   409
         Appendix B: Rejected Caxton examples   425
         Appendix C: Other incunabula copied into manuscripts or
                 for which manuscript copytexts exist in
                 England   426
         Appendix D: Rejected example   429

Index of manuscripts   433
General index   445

ILLUSTRATIONS AND FIGURES

ILLUSTRATIONS

1 Berkeley, California, University of California, MS 150, Heller Hours, c. 1470–80, fols. 11v–12r   *page* 34

2a New York, Pierpont Morgan Library, MS Glazier 9, Hours and Psalter, c. 1460: fol. 14v   36

2b London, British Library, MS Egerton 1991, John Gower, *Confessio Amantis*, early 15th century, fol. 7v   36

3a Oxford, Bodleian Library, MS Don.d. 85, Psalter, c. 1410–15, fol. 58v   37

3b New York, Pierpont Morgan Library, M 893, Hours and Psalter, before 1446, fol. 182v   37

4a London, British Library, Add. MS 29301, John Arderne, *Chirurgia* and *Fistula in Ano*, c. 1420–30, fol. 3r   40

4b Cambridge, St John's College, MS H.1 (204), *Dialogus inter Militem et Clericum*, early 15th century, fol. 1r   40

5a As plate 3b, fol. 12r   41

5b London, British Library, Add. MS 42131, Hours and Psalter, c. 1420, fol. 122r   41

6a Oxford, Bodleian Library, MS Bodley 183, Wycliffite Bible, early 15th century, fol. 1r   44

6b Cambridge University Library, MS Kk.2.7, Psalter and Hours, c. 1480, fol. 9r   44

7 A plate of tools: nos. 1–9 unlocated bindery; nos. 10–15 previously unrecorded   69

8 A plate of tools: nos. 1–2 from Oxford, Bodleian Library, MS Bodley 460; nos. 3–7 previously unrecorded   71

9 Terence, *Vulgaria* (London, c. 1483): a London 15th-century binding   75

10 Bookmen's London in the fifteenth century   90

11 Robert Treswell, 'West-Cheap as it appeared in 1585'   95

12 British Library MS Egerton 2820, early 15th century, fols. 41v–42r (anonymous sermon)   127

vii

13   Oxford, Bodleian Library, MS Bodley 665, New Testament in
      the Later Version of the Wycliffite Bible, early 15th century,
      fol. 1r   130
14   Ibid., fol. 84r   130
15   London, British Library, Add. MS 41175, Glossed Gospels, c.
      1400, fol. 59   133
16   Cambridge, Pembroke College, MS 307, John Gower, *Confessio
      Amantis*, early 15th century, fol. 125r   171
17   Cambridge, Trinity College, MS O.4.16 (1247), Psalter, fol. viii
      verso, mid-15th century addition to a late 13th-century psalter   176
18   London, Lambeth Palace Library, MS 265. *The Dicts and Sayings
      of the Philosophers*, 1477, fol. vi verso   210
19   London, British Library, MS Harley 326, *The Three Kings' Sons*,
      c. 1480, fol. 102r   210
20   Ibid., fol. 117v   211
21   London, The Skinners' Company, Book of the Fraternity of Our
      Lady's Assumption, c. 1470 onwards, fol. 34v   214
22   Ibid., fol. 41r   214
23   Warminster, Wiltshire, Longleat House, MS 258, second half of
      15th century, fols. 137v–138r   282
24   Cambridge, Trinity College, MS R.3.19 (599), end of 15th
      century, fols. 161v–162r   289
25   Edinburgh, National Library of Scotland, MS Adv. 19.3.1, late
      15th century, fols. 29v–30r   296
26   Oxford, Bodleian Library, MS Ashmole 61, end of 15th century,
      fols. 16v–17r   299
27   Oxford, Bodleian Library, MS Douce 25, first half of 15th
      century, fol. 72r   320
28   Cambridge University Library, MS Add. 6578, Nicholas Love's
      Mirrour of the Blessed Lyf of Jesu Christ, late 14th or early 15th
      century, fol. 2v   323
29   Oxford, Bodleian Library, MS Bodley 3, *Pore Caitif*, early 15th
      century, fol. 63r   329
30   London, British Library, MS Harley 2409, *Contemplations of the
      Dread and Love of God*, first half of 15th century, fols. 1v–2r   331
31   Oxford, Bodleian Library, MS Bodley 446, *Speculum Vitae*, first
      half of 15th century, fols. 126v–127r   334
32   Los Angeles, Library of Irwin J. Pincus, M.D., Pincus *horae*, late
      14th or early 15th century, fol. 31v   346
33   London, British Library, MS Egerton 847, middle of first half
      of 15th century, fol. 55r   349
34   London, British Library, MS Sloane 213, late 14th or early 15th
      century, fol. 124r   349

35 Oxford, Bodleian Library, MS Digby 235, end of 15th and beginning of 14th century, fols. 248v–249r — 354

36 Oxford, Bodleian Library, MS Digby 98, middle of first half of 15th century (in a late 12th century manuscript), fols. 103v–104r — 355

37 Oxford, Bodleian Library, MS Ashmole 6, first half of 15th century, fol. 13v — 357

38 Cambridge, Trinity College, MS O.1.57, middle of 15th century, fol. 10v — 358

39 London, British Library, MS Sloane 1, middle of 15th century, fol. 313r — 359

40 Oxford, Bodleian Library, MS Bodley 676, middle of 15th century, fol. 156v — 359

41 London, British Library, MS Harley 3719, beginning of 15th century, fol. 175v — 360

42 London, Wellcome Institute, MS 552, beginning of 15th century, fol. 35r — 361

43 Oxford, Bodleian Library, MS Digby 97, late 14th or early 15th century, fol. 280v — 361

44 Cambridge, University Library, MS Ee.3.61, end of 15th century, fol. 62r — 362

45 Ibid., fol. 108v — 363

46 London, British Library, MS Harley 3719, beginning of 15th century, fol. 156 — 364

47 Cambridge, Trinity College, MS R.15.18, middle of 15th century, p. 31 — 364

48 Oxford, Bodleian Library, MS Laud misc. 657, end of 14th century, fol. 48r — 365

49 Oxford, Bodleian Library, MS Digby 77, end of 14th century, fol. 36v — 366

50 Cambridge, Trinity College, MS O.1.57, middle of 15th century, fol. 83r — 367

51 Cambridge University Library, MS Kk.6.30, middle of second half of 15th century, fol. 11v — 368

52 Ibid., fol. 17r — 368

53 Oxford, St John's College, MS 205, middle of first half of 15th century, fol. 60r — 369

54 London, British Library, MS Harley 3719, beginning of 15th century, fol. 245 — 369

55 Oxford, Bodleian Library, MS Digby 97, late 14th or early 15th century, fols. 142v–143r — 370

56 Oxford, Bodleian Library, MS Digby 98, first half of 15th century, fol. 135v — 371

57 London, British Library, MS Sloane 6, early 15th century, fol. 177v   374

58 Cambridge, Emmanuel College, MS 69, early 15th century, fol. 93v   375

59 London, British Library, MS Sloane 2320, dated 1454, fol. 4v   376

60 Oxford, Bodleian Library, MS Laud misc. 558, dated 1459, fol. 262r   377

61 Cambridge, University Library, MS Kk.6.30, middle of second half of 15th century, fol. 14r   378

FIGURES

1 and 2   Drawings of binding designs   67
3   Diagram showing the position of sheets in a gathering   408

CONTRIBUTORS

NORMAN F. BLAKE is Professor of English Language and Pro-Vice-Chancellor of the University of Sheffield. Before coming to Sheffield in 1973 he was Lecturer and Senior Lecturer in the Department of English Language at the University of Liverpool. Professor Blake has written widely on the Later Medieval period. Among his recent publications are *The Textual Tradition of the Canterbury Tales* (1985), and *William Caxton, a Bibliography* (1985). He was also an editor of *Index of Printed Middle English Prose* (1985).

JULIA BOFFEY is Lecturer in the Department of English at Queen Mary College, University of London; author of *The Manuscripts of English Courtly Love Lyrics in the Later Middle Ages* (1985).

C. PAUL CHRISTIANSON is Mildred Foss Thompson Professor of English at the College of Wooster (Ohio). He is the author of *Memorials of the Book Trade in Medieval London: The Archives of Old London Bridge* (1987) and *A Directory of London Stationers and Book Artisans 1300–1500* (forthcoming).

A.I. DOYLE is Honorary Reader in Bibliography and former Keeper of Rare Books in the University of Durham. He is a contributor to the Pelican Guide to English Literature, vol. 1, *The Age of Chaucer* (1954); co-author of *Manuscript to Print: Tradition and Innovation in the Renaissance Book* (1975) and of the Palaeographical Introduction to the facsimile of the Hengwrt Manuscript (1978); author of the Introduction to the facsimile of the Vernon Manuscript (1987).

A.S.G. EDWARDS is Professor of English, University of Victoria. He is General Editor of the *Index of Middle English Prose*, author of *Stephen Hawes* (1983), *John Skelton: The Critical Heritage* (1981), *Index of Printed Middle English Prose* (with N.F. Blake and R.E. Lewis, 1985).

MIRJAM M. FOOT is Deputy Director, West European Branch, British Library (Department of Printed Books). Publications include two volumes of *The Henry Davis Gift* (Volume 1, *Studies in the History of Bookbinding*, 1979;

Volume 2, *A Catalogue of North European Bindings*, 1983), a short book on *Pictorial Bookbindings* (1986), and numerous articles on the history of book-binding, of book structures, and of decorated papers.

Vincent Gillespie is a Fellow of St Anne's College, Oxford, and Lecturer in English in the University of Oxford. He has published articles on catechetic and pastoral materials, mystical writing and the circulation of religious books.

Jeremy Griffiths was previously Lecturer in English at Birkbeck College in the University of London and at St John's College, Oxford.

Kate Harris was formerly Lady Margaret Research Fellow in English at New Hall, Cambridge, and is now Librarian and Archivist at Longleat House. Her articles include a study of Cambridge University Library MS Ff.1.6 and she is currently completing a study of the reception of Gower's *Confessio Amantis*.

Anne Hudson is University Lecturer in Medieval English and Fellow of Lady Margaret Hall, Oxford; editor of *Selections from English Wycliffite Writings* (1978), and of *English Wycliffite Sermons* I (1983); author of *Lollards and their Books* (1985) and of *The Premature Reformation: Wycliffite Texts and Lollard History* (1988).

R. J. Lyall is Lecturer in the Department of Scottish Literature at the University of Glasgow.

Carol Meale teaches at the University of York. Publications include studies of manuscript and early printed copies of Middle English romances, and an investigation of patronage in relation to Malory. Forthcoming: *John Colyns and BL MS Harley 2252: a London Merchant and His Book* (Boydell & Brewer); *Generides: an Edition of the Romance from PML MS M 876* (Garland).

Derek Pearsall is Gurney Professor of English at Harvard University; was previously Professor of English and Co-Director of the Centre for Medieval Studies at the University of York.

Kathleen L. Scott is an independent scholar, working in the production and decoration of the manuscript-book in late medieval England. Previous publications include *The Caxton Master and his Patrons* (1976), *The Mirroure of the Worlde* (1980). Forthcoming: *Later Gothic Manuscripts 1385–1500*, vol. VI of *A Survey of Manuscripts Illuminated in the British Isles*, ed. J. J. G. Alexander.

JOHN J. THOMPSON is Lecturer in English at the Queen's University of Belfast, and author of a monograph on *Robert Thornton and the London Thornton Manuscript* (1987).

LINDA EHRSAM VOIGTS is Curators' Professor of English, University of Missouri–Kansas City; and was Visiting Fellow, Clare Hall, Cambridge, in 1987. Publications include *A Latin Technical Phlebotomy and its Middle English Translation* (with Micheal McVaugh), Transactions of the American Philosophical Society 74 (1984); *A Handlist of Middle English in Harvard Manuscripts*, vol. 33 of the *Harvard Library Bulletin* (1985).

ANDREW WATHEY is a Fellow of Downing College, Cambridge. His article on 'Dunstable in France' (*Music and Letters*, vol. 67, 1986, pp. 1–36) won the 1986 Westrup Prize.

ACKNOWLEDGEMENTS

Acknowledgement is made for permission to reproduce the following photographs: to the Syndics of Cambridge University Library, for plates 6b, 28, 36–40; to the Master and Fellows of St John's College, Cambridge, for plate 4b; to the Pierpont Morgan Library, for plates 2a, 3b and 5a; to the Library of the University of California, for plate 1; to the Folger Shakespeare Library, for plate 11; to the Master and Fellows of Pembroke College, Cambridge, for plate 16; to the Master and Fellows of Trinity College, Cambridge, for plates 17, 24, 33–35; to His Grace the Archbishop of Canterbury and the Trustees of Lambeth Palace Library, for plate 18; to the Skinners' Company, London, for plates 21 and 22; to the Trustees of the British Library, for plates 2b, 4a, 5b, 12, 15, 19, 20, 30, 41–48; to the Bodleian Library, for plates 3a, 6a, 13, 14, 26, 27, 29, 31, 50–59; to the Master and Fellows of Emmanuel College, Cambridge, for plate 32; to the Wellcome Institute Library, London, for plate 49; to the President and Fellows of St John's College, Oxford, for plate 60; to Irwin J. Pincus, M.D., of Los Angeles, for plate 61.

ABBREVIATIONS

Abdn. Reg.	*Registrum Episcopatus Aberdonensis*, ed. C. Innes, 2 vols. (Edinburgh, 1845)
APS	*Acts of the Parliament of Scotland*, ed. T. Thomson and C. Innes, 2 vols. (Edinburgh, 1844)
BJRL	*Bulletin of the John Rylands Library* (Manchester)
BL	British Library (London)
BLJ	*British Library Journal*
BLR	*Bodleian Library Record*
BN	Bibliothèque Nationale (Paris)
BQR	*Bodleian Quarterly Record*
BRS	British Record Society
BRUC	*A Bibliographical Register of the University of Cambridge to 1500*, by A.B. Emden (Cambridge, 1963)
BRUO	*A Bibliographical Register of the University of Oxford to 1500*, by A.B. Emden, 3 vols. (Oxford, 1957–9)
CPR	*Calendar of Patent Rolls*
CUL	Cambridge University Library
DNB	*Dictionary of National Biography*
EETS, ES, OS	Early English Text Society, Extra Series, Original Series
EHR	*English Historical Review*
ELN	*English Language Notes*
GEC	*The Complete Peerage*, by G.E.C.[ockayne], rev. ed., Hon. Vicary Gibbs, 13 vols. (London, 1910–40)
Glas. Mun.	*Registrum Episcopatus Glasguensis, Munimenta Ecclesie Metropolitane Glasguensis*, ed. C. Innes, 2 vols. (Edinburgh, 1843)
Glas. Reg.	*Ibid.*
GUL	Glasgow University Library
HLQ	*Huntington Library Quarterly*
HMC	Historical Manuscripts Commission
IMEV	*Index of Middle English Verse*, by C. Brown and R.H. Robbins (New York, 1943). With *Supplement* by R.H. Robbins and J. Cutler (Lexington, Ky., 1965)

JWCI	*Journal of the Warburg and Courtauld Institutes*
LSE	*Leeds Studies in English*
MLN	*Modern Language Notes*
MLR	*Modern Language Review*
MP	*Modern Philology*
NLS	National Library of Scotland (Edinburgh)
NLW	National Library of Wales (Aberystwyth)
NM	*Neuphilologische Mitteilungen*
NQ	*Notes and Queries*
NS	New Series
NYPL	New York Public Library
PBSA	*Papers of the Bibliographical Society of America*
PML	Pierpont Morgan Library (New York)
PMLA	*Publications of the Modern Language Association of America*
PRMA	*Proceedings of the Royal Musical Association*
PRO	Public Record Office (London)
PSAS	*Proceedings of the Society of Antiquaries of Scotland*
PUL	Princeton University Library
RES	*Review of English Studies*
RMS	*Registrum magni sigilli regum Scotorum* (Register of the Great Seal), ed. J.M. Thomson and J.B. Paul, 2 vols. (Edinburgh, 1882, 1912)
Rot. Parl.	*Rotuli Parliamentorum*, ed. J. Strachey. 6 vols. (London, 1767–77)
s.in., s.ex., s.med.	of the beginning / end / middle of the century (*saeculi ineuntis / exeuntis / medii*)
SB	*Studies in Bibliography*
SC	*Summary Catalogue of Western Manuscripts in the Bodleian Library at Oxford*, by F. Madan *et al.* 7 vols. in 8 (Oxford, 1895–1953)
SRO	Scottish Record Office
STC	*Short Title Catalogue of Books Printed in England, Scotland and Ireland . . . 1475–1640*, by A.W. Pollard and G.R. Redgrave, 2 vols. (London, 1926)
STS	Scottish Text Society
TCBS	*Transactions of the Cambridge Bibliographical Society*
TCC	Trinity College, Cambridge
TCD	Trinity College, Dublin
TEBS	*Transactions of the Edinburgh Bibliographical Society*
TRHS	*Transactions of the Royal Historical Society*
UL	University Library

WORKS CITED IN SHORT FORM

Alexander, 'Painting and Manuscript Illustration': J.J.G. Alexander, 'Painting and Manuscript Illustration for Royal Patrons in the Later Middle Ages', in Scattergood and Sherborne, pp. 141–62.

Alexander, 'William Abell': J.J.G. Alexander, 'William Abell "lymnour" and 15th Century English Illumination', in *Kunsthistorische Forschungen: Otto Pächt zu seinem 70. Geburtstag*, ed. A. Rosenauer and G. Weber (Salzburg, 1972), pp. 166–72.

Bennett, 'Production and Dissemination': H.S. Bennett, 'The Production and Dissemination of Vernacular Manuscripts in the Fifteenth Century', *The Library*, 5th series, 1 (1947), 167–78.

Benskin and Samuels: M. Benskin and M.L. Samuels (eds.), *So Meny People Longages and Tonges: Philological Essays . . . Presented to Angus McIntosh* (Edinburgh, 1981).

Bühler, *The Fifteenth-Century Book*: C.F. Bühler, *The Fifteenth-Century Book: The Scribes, The Printers, The Decorators* (Philadelphia, 1960).

Deanesly, 'Vernacular Books': M. Deanesly, 'Vernacular Books in England in the Fourteenth and Fifteenth Centuries', *MLR*, 15 (1920), 349–58.

Doyle, 'English Books In and Out of Court': A.I. Doyle, 'English Books In and Out of Court from Edward III to Henry VII', in Scattergood and Sherborne, pp. 163–81.

Doyle, 'The Manuscripts': A.I. Doyle, 'The Manuscripts', in *Middle English Alliterative Poetry and its Literary Background*, ed. D. Lawton (Cambridge, 1982), pp. 88–100.

Doyle, 'Reflections': A.I. Doyle, 'Reflections on Some Manuscripts of Nicholas Love's *Myrrour of the Blessed Lyf of Jesu Christ*', *LSE*, NS, 14 (Essays in Memory of Elizabeth Salter) (1983), pp. 82–93.

Doyle, *Survey*: A.I. Doyle, *A Survey of the Origins and Circulation of Theological Writings in English in the 14th, 15th and Early 16th Centuries with special Consideration of the Part of the Clergy therein* (unpublished Ph.D. dissertation, Cambridge, 1954).

Doyle, 'Vernon and Simeon Manuscripts': A.I. Doyle, 'The Shaping of the Vernon and Simeon Manuscripts', in *Chaucer and Middle English Studies in honour of Rossell Hope Robbins*, ed. B. Rowland (London, 1974), pp. 328–41.

Doyle, 'William Ebesham': A.I. Doyle, 'The Work of a Late Fifteenth-Century English Scribe, William Ebesham', *BJRL*, 39 (1957), 298–325.

Doyle and Parkes: A.I. Doyle and M.B. Parkes, 'The production of copies of the *Canterbury Tales* and the *Confessio Amantis* in the early fifteenth century', in *Medieval Scribes, Manuscripts and Libraries: Essays presented to N.R. Ker*, ed. M.B. Parkes and A.G. Watson (London, 1978), pp. 163–210.

Edwards, *Middle English Prose*: A.S.G. Edwards (ed.), *Middle English Prose: A Critical Survey of Major Authors and Genres* (New Brunswick, N.J., 1984).

Edwards and Pearsall: A.S.G. Edwards and Derek Pearsall (eds.), *Middle English Prose: Essays on Bibliographical Problems* (New York and London, 1981), pp. 115–27.

Guddat-Figge: G. Guddat-Figge, *Catalogue of Manuscripts containing Middle English Romances* (Munich, 1976).

Hammond, *Chaucer*: E.P. Hammond, *Chaucer: A Bibliographical Manual* (New York, 1908).

James, *Manuscripts of Trinity College*: M.R. James, *A Descriptive Catalogue of the Western Manuscripts in the Library of Trinity College, Cambridge*, 4 vols. (Cambridge, 1900–4).

Jolliffe: P.G. Jolliffe, *A Check-list of Middle English Prose Writings of Spiritual Guidance* (Toronto, 1974).

Ker, *Medieval Libraries*: N.R. Ker, *Medieval Libraries of Great Britain: A List of Surviving Books* (2nd edn, London, 1964).

Lawton, 'The Illustration of Late Medieval Secular Texts': Lesley Lawton, 'The Illustration of Late Medieval Secular Texts, with Special Reference to Lydgate's Troy-Book', in Pearsall, *Manuscripts and Readers*, pp. 41–69.

Lewis and McIntosh: R.E. Lewis and A. McIntosh, *A Descriptive Guide to the Manuscripts of the Prick of Conscience*, Medium Aevum Monographs, NS, 12 (Oxford, 1982).

Madan, *Summary Catalogue*: F. Madan *et al.*, *Summary Catalogue of Western Manuscripts in the Bodleian Library at Oxford*, 7 vols. in 8 (Oxford, 1895–1953).

Manly and Rickert: J.M. Manly and E. Rickert, *The Text of the Canterbury Tales, edited on the basis of all known manuscripts*, 8 vols. (Chicago, 1940).

Pächt and Alexander: O. Pächt and J.J.G. Alexander, *Illuminated Manuscripts in the Bodleian Library, Oxford*, 3 vols. (Oxford, 1966–73).

Parkes, 'Literacy of the Laity': M.B. Parkes, 'The Literacy of the Laity', in *Literature and Western Civilization: The Medieval World*, ed. D. Daiches and A.K. Thorlby (London, 1973), pp. 555–77.

Parkes, '*Ordinatio* and *Compilatio*': M.B. Parkes, 'The Influence of the Concepts of *Ordinatio* and *Compilatio* on the Development of the Book', in *Medieval Learning and Literature: Essays presented to R.W. Hunt*, ed. J.J.G. Alexander and M.T. Gibson (Oxford, 1976), pp. 115–41.

Pearsall, *Manuscripts and Readers*: D. Pearsall (ed.), *Manuscripts and Readers in*

Fifteenth-Century England: The Literary Implications of Manuscript Study (Cambridge, 1983).

Pollard, 'Company of Stationers': G. Pollard, 'The Company of Stationers before 1557', and 'The Early Constitution of the Stationers' Company', *The Library*, 4th series, 18 (1937), 1–38, 235–60.

Robinson, 'The Booklet': P.R. Robinson, '"The Booklet": A Self-Contained Unit in Composite Manuscripts', *Codicologica*, 3 (1980), 46–69.

Salter, 'The Manuscripts': E. Salter, 'The Manuscripts of Nicholas Love's *Myrrour of the Blessed Lyf of Jesu Christ* and Related Texts', in Edwards and Pearsall, pp. 115–27.

Scattergood and Sherborne: V.J. Scattergood and J.W. Sherborne (eds.), *English Court Culture in the Later Middle Ages* (London, 1983).

Scott, *The Caxton Master*: K.L. Scott, *The Caxton Master and his Patrons*, with a Preface by J.A.W. Bennett, Cambridge Bibliographical Society Monographs, 8 (Cambridge, 1976).

Scott, 'Lydgate's Lives': K.L. Scott, 'Lydgate's Lives of SS Edmund and Fremund: A Newly Discovered Manuscript in Arundel Castle', *Viator*, 13 (1982), 335–66.

Scott, 'A Mid-Fifteenth-Century English Illuminating Shop': K.L. Scott, 'A Mid-Fifteenth-Century Illuminating Shop and Its Customers', *JWCI*, 31 (1968), 170–96.

Scott, *Mirrour of the Worlde*: K.L. Scott, *Introduction (The Physical Composition, Decoration and Illustration) to the Mirrour of the Worlde: MS Bodley 283*, Roxburghe Club (Oxford, 1980).

Warner and Gilson: G.F. Warner and J. Gilson, *British Museum Catalogue of the Western Manuscripts in the Old Royal and King's Collections*, 4 vols. (London, 1921).

INTRODUCTION

DEREK PEARSALL

In the present state of scholarship, any book on publishing and book-production in England in the century before the introduction of printing is bound to be limited in its ambitions, tentative in its statements, and, to some extent or in some ways, premature. The primary research which would clarify the view of the subject has been done only in part – one is reminded of the caveats of Dom David Knowles before entering on the fifteenth-century volume of his history of the religious orders in England[1] – and there is the strong possibility that, when all the evidence that is to be gathered is gathered, some important matters will remain obscure. Given the impossibility of a definitive and comprehensive book on the subject, it has still seemed to us important to ask a number of scholars to make at least interim statements on the area of their specialisation, and we have been encouraged to think that the time is opportune by a number of developments: the newly concentrated attention directed to fourteenth- and fifteenth-century vernacular English manuscript books as *books* that has inspired or followed on from the publication of a comparatively large number of facsimiles in the last fifteen years;[2] the explorations of a number of scholars in fields of provenance, patronage and workshop practice;[3] and the recognition by the two most active and distinguished palaeographical experts on manuscripts produced in the British Isles during the period of the wider significance, for the study of both book-production and literary culture, of their narrower specialisation.[4] In our response to what we see as these stimuli, we have made an attempt to 'cover' the subject, but we are aware that there are gaps, and that there will remain dark patches. The best expectation we have is that these essays will make clear what has been done in particular areas, identify the questions that need further to be asked, and thus point the way for future research. If this book provides some rungs on a ladder which can later be kicked away as obsolete, it will have served its purpose.

To the question that will be asked concerning the appropriateness of a book on 'publishing' in England in the pre-printing era, and the particular reason for a book on the subject dealing only with the century before printing, it is possible to return some answer. Setting aside those forms of written text which are not regarded as the subject-matter of this book, such as documentary records and private letters,[5] and concentrating on manuscript-books (*codices* or *libri manuscripti*), it may be useful to think of book-production and publishing as a process or activity that may be initiated in three ways: by the author, by the consumer, or by the producer. The producer may of course be the author, in the case of autograph manuscripts of the author's own work, and he may be the consumer too, if the book he is copying is for his own use, or a 'commonplace book'; the producer may likewise be the consumer in the case of works copied in a monastery's own scriptorium for the use of the monastery's inmates. However, neither the amalgamation of functions in such cases, nor the absence of the function of 'author' in certain kinds of book, such as liturgical and legal books, impedes the perception of the distinctness of the function, nor the value of that perception.

The characteristic form of author-initiated production is the copy made at the author's instigation for circulation among friends or for presentation to a patron; the characteristic form of consumer-initiated production is the copy made by the consumer himself, or to the order or commission of a customer, whether acting as an individual or as an institution (such as a monastery). These forms of production are well evidenced in the Middle Ages. The third form of production, that initiated by the producer or entrepreneur, is crucially important to the history of book-production and most obviously coincides with our notion of 'publishing'. Much of the present book necessarily addresses itself to the question of the extent to which speculative, entrepreneur-initiated production, as distinct from commissioned or bespoke production, was regular practice in the last century of the manuscript era in England.

That the other forms of production were still widespread, indeed dominant, is clear, and early glimpses of an incipient 'trade' in new books (the second-hand market, though important to the study of publishing and book-production, is not strictly speaking part of it) should not be used as the basis for any simple account of the displacement of one mode of production by another. So Gower, as author, seems to have played some part in the supervision and production of correctly spelt and handsomely presented manuscripts of his works, including a manuscript of the *Confessio Amantis* (the 'Stafford' MS, Huntington Library MS EL 26.A.17) that may well be a presentation copy (to Henry, earl of Derby).[6] Likewise Hoccleve, in an attempt to win himself patronage and preferment, makes a formal dedication of his own autograph copy of his poems (in Durham University Library, MS Cosin v.III.9) to the countess of Westmorland.[7] As for customers, there is unusually full evidence for both commissioning procedure and payment in instances as far apart as 1324, when the countess of Clare had a scribe resident in her household for sixteen weeks so that he might copy for her the *Vitas Patrum*,[8] and 1468, when Sir John Paston gave William Ebesham his instructions for the making of his 'Grete Boke'.[9]

It is also clear, however, that the character of print technology necessarily brought in a dominantly producer-initiated form of book-production, or at least one that was bound to develop in this direction. Caxton spoke in the old terms and cultivated the old manners, but meanwhile calculated what he thought would sell to the particular audiences he saw himself catering for.[10] Their tastes, in the manner which we now regard as 'natural' to the book-trade, were predicted and shaped and nurtured by the producer. What Caxton did, however, in this as in much else, was not new: he merely built upon practices of systematic and commercial book-production that had become vigorous during the century before. A sketch of the background to these developments will provide a preliminary context for the present book.

One might find a beginning for the history of medieval book-production in the monasteries, which maintained a virtual monopoly on all aspects of book-production in western Europe until the twelfth century. All four, for instance, of the major codices of Old English poetry are from monastic scriptoria, and most of the manuscript-books produced in England before 1300, more especially those in Latin, but also those in the English and Anglo-Norman vernaculars, are of monastic provenance. Professional scriveners, illuminators and binders began to cut into the monasteries' monopoly in the twelfth century (somewhat later in England), particularly with the establishment of the commercial book-trade in university towns. Monastic scriptoria continued, of course, to be active, particularly in the production of service-books and theological and devotional writing in Latin, and there would be many areas of cooperative activity with the more recently established secular ateliers, as for instance in the case of the group of late thirteenth-century Fenland manuscripts written by monastic scribes and illustrated by an itinerant professional group of artists.[11] The vigour of monastic book-production in the late fourteenth and fifteenth centuries, albeit in more restricted fields and to some extent out of the main stream, should not be underestimated. Vigorous activity, as well as the existence of an extensive network for the circulation of exemplars, presumably mainly monastic, is implied in the existence of the Vernon manuscript (Bodleian MS English Poetry a.1), itself of monastic provenance, with its vast range of texts and access to exemplars.[12]

The beginning of a commercial book-trade is commonly associated with the growth of the universities in the twelfth and thirteenth centuries. The demand of teachers and students for texts, commentaries and reference books could be partly met by borrowing (for instance, from monastic libraries) and the second-hand trade, but there was much need, in university towns such as Paris, Oxford and Bologna, of new copying. 'Stationers' (*stationarii*) acted as the entrepreneurs in the production of these new copies: they would receive authorised and corrected exemplars of the 'set books' on loan from the university authorities, and have copies made by professional scriveners (or free-lance part-timers such as students or other clerics) at a fixed price. They would work mostly to order, but presumably would not be reluctant to build up a small stock of new copies of standard texts. Stationers could also loan out corrected exemplars piecemeal in quires (*pecia*) to students, for them to copy or have copied on their own behalf, and so build up their own complete copy of the exemplar. From the stationer's point of view, the system contributed to a more rapid turnover and a more economic use of exemplars.

There is good evidence of the *pecia* system for Oxford,[13] as well as for the development of other commercial book-trade enterprises such as are indicated by a professional scribe's advertisement, with specimens, of his skills as a specialist in liturgical book-writing.[14] But it was Paris that was regarded as the centre of the international book-trade, where the stimulus first given by university demand led to the establishment of systematic modes of general book-production as well as the development of that uniformity of format and layout, for the convenience of readers, especially of glossed books of the Bible, that marks the emergence of 'the book' as we would understand it.[15] Richard de Bury, bishop of Durham 1333–45, who gives an account of his zeal as a book-collector in his *Philobiblon*, and who had his own staff of copyists, correctors, illuminators and binders, as well as booksellers all over Europe under his instructions, speaks of Paris as the great source of books and home of scribes and booksellers.[16] Much of this has to do with the trade in second-hand books: Peter of Blois had spoken long before, in the twelfth century, of the many books offered for sale by the Parisian book-dealers,[17] and certainly then referred to the second-hand trade. But there is a fourteenth-century French poem giving a rather fancy description of the wares of a Parisian bookseller which suggests that some were produced to have in stock,[18] and there is other evidence too of speculative production. It is not just a matter of commercial production and of the growth of secular workshops to satisfy the increasing demand for books from general readers: the evidence is firm here for the early establishment of ateliers of secular artists to illustrate the copies of romances that were being produced in large quantities in France in the thirteenth century,[19] and there is the strong suggestion too that scribes (who needed of course less organisation than artists and who could work on a more individual, *ad hoc* and private basis) were coming to be similarly organised. It has been argued that some thirteenth-century copies of French *chansons de geste* were produced in multiple copies in workshops and that certain surviving copies may be traceable to the same workshops,[20] and a similar case has been made for 'the existence of a lay establishment specialising in the copying and illustration of secular Anglo-Norman literature in the second quarter of the thirteenth century'.[21] What is more significant, though, is the evidence that booksellers were beginning to commission works on their own initiative, which may be taken to be an important stage in the development of what we are accustomed to call publishing. In 1403, to take one notable instance, the duc de Berry bought a book of prose Arthurian tales from a bookseller, Raoul de Mortet, a purchase that has been taken as 'proof that the clientele with a taste for de luxe editions was large enough for a stationer to order a manuscript to be prepared at considerable expense (it was sold for 300 gold *écus*) without a definite buyer in view'.[22]

Discussion of the development of book-production during the fourteenth century should not neglect, however, the important and increasing role of the new breed of non-clerical authors in initiating production. The best evidence comes from Italy, from the letters of Boccaccio and Petrarch.[23] Boccaccio, for instance, sends a letter to Maghinardo dei Cavalcanti to accompany a presentation copy of the *De Casibus Virorum Illustrium*: uncertain, he says, whom to dedicate it to, he dismissed various princely possibilities, while the work lay on his hands, and finally decided on his old friend, whom he begs to receive it, correct it, share it with friends, and 'finally send it forth to the public [*emittas in publicum*] under your name'.[24] A similar letter to Madonna Andrea Acciaioli accompanies the *De Claris Mulieribus*. This was the act of 'publication': the preparation of the copy at the author's expense, with or without the promise of remuneration, and then the placing of the copy in the hands of the 'patron', under whose auspices, if he chooses, it then goes forth. It was a decisive moment in the history of a literary work, and Petrarch frequently shows himself unwilling to take this final step of formal publication. Even after reading a poem aloud or having it circulated among his friends with requests for criticism, he would often return to it to make major additions and corrections before sending it forth *in publicum*. He also describes the care he takes in personally revising the scribe's copy,[25] most notably how he and Boccaccio worked together on the exemplars of the *Bucolics* at the time of publication, with Boccaccio reading from the original exemplar and Petrarch proof-reading the copies made from it. It looks as though an 'edition' of several exemplars was being prepared, to be sent simultaneously to various friends and potential patrons. The possibility always existed, of course, that a work might be pirated by unscrupulous friends or scribes, who might publish on their own account unauthorised and uncorrected copies. This was Petrarch's experience with a copy of part of his *Africa*, and Boccaccio's too with the *De Genealogia Deorum*. Deguileville's complaints about the unauthorised publication of the first version of his *Pèlerinage de la Vie Humaine* refer to a similar insecurity or 'leakiness' in the publication process, and Pecock speaks likewise of writings he intended to correct being loosed into circulation by indiscreet friends and copied against his will.[26]

France was perhaps more old-fashioned, in that here still it would more often be the great patrons who initiated production, as Charles V for instance asked Nicole Oresme in 1369 to make a translation of Aristotle for the benefit of royal officials and advisers.[27] Here too, however, authors would often initiate production: Machaut and Christine de Pizan supervised the preparation of presentation copies of their poems, and the latter comes close to being a 'professional' author and book-producer, publishing her works in multiple copies for royal and other readers and making a living from their patronage.[28] The presentation by Froissart of a beautifully bound copy of his poems to Richard II in 1395 is a classic instance of a presentation copy prepared as a bid for patronage.[29] English authors were beginning to make similar moves: Chaucer's reference to his poem of *The Legend of Good Women* being given, when complete, to Queen Anne (Prologue, F.496–7) is presumably to some kind of presentation copy, while the transfer of dedication of Gower's *Confessio Amantis* from Richard II to Henry, earl of Derby, may have something to do with the latter's willingness to act as a patron for publication as well as with his political views.

On the continent, the fifteenth century saw a considerable increase in the commercialisation and specialisation of book-production. Scribes, rubricators, illuminators and binders worked together, even if not on the same premises, in an organised production process, carrying out a series of commissions. Nor was it always bespoke production: a document survives from 1437 in Flanders, referring to a bookseller's order to the chief copyist in a workshop for 200 copies of the Seven Penitential Psalms, 200 of Cato's *Distichs*, and 400 prayerbooks.[30] A bookseller in Lille in the mid-fifteenth century commissions scribes to write manuscripts for his stock, in the firm expectation that he will be able to sell them without difficulty.[31] Against this, it needs to be asserted, as Bühler insists, that most production was still in the hands of amateur scribes, that the trade in books was still largely a second-hand trade, and that most new books were produced on commission.[32]

The picture in fifteenth-century England is patchier and needs even more qualification. The claims that have been made for the existence of a London bookshop in the 1330s, on the evidence of collaborative activity in the Auchinleck manuscript,[33] are probably exaggerated, and Doyle and Parkes are justifiably sceptical of the existence of any such 'bookshops' before the mid-fifteenth century.[34] By that time, or soon after, as Kathleen Scott has shown, there were groups of scribes and artists working together, even if not on the same premises (the question of physical location is not vital), on the production of numbers of books, including multiple copies and probably copies done 'on spec'.[35] But progress towards this type of organised production was slow, and in the meantime the emphasis must be, except for special cases like the regular workshops that must have been responsible for the copying of texts of the Lollard sermon cycle[36] and the increasingly systematic production of texts of Chaucer, Gower and Lydgate in London, on the scattered and limited nature of book-production in England. Pollard's cautious account of the early history of the Company of Stationers suggests that the important stages in the development of the book-trade come in the years after 1403, when the two gilds of the Textwriters and the Lymners ask to be amalgamated.[37] The petition speaks of 'folks of trades of text letter, lymenours, and other folks of London, *usantz auxi de lyer & vendre livres*' (Pollard, p. 14), and the variety of nomenclature in the following years suggests that 'the leading members of the Company were shopkeepers employing a number of craftsmen in the different stages of book-production' (Pollard, p. 15). Such shopkeepers, or stationers, might have carried a certain amount of stock, including new books of the kind in constant demand – smaller service books for the laity such as were now being imported in quantity from Flanders, and school text-books like the Donatus – but there is no evidence, says Pollard, 'to show that before printing there was any wholesale dealing in such books as were sufficiently standardized to be kept in stock' (p. 16).

It is important to remember that books were still quite rare, and still 'essentially a luxury commodity'.[38] Prices mean very little, but it has been pointed out that the value of the 'twenty bookes, clad in blak or reed', that Chaucer's Clerk of Oxford owned or would like to have owned (*Cant. Tales*, 1.294) would be about sixty times his annual income, while Jankyn's 'book of wikked wyves' (*Cant. Tales*, III.685) would have been a treasure worth several pounds[39] (and all the more annoying to have it vandalised by the outraged Wife). With the exception of bibliophiliacs like Richard de Bury, who owned perhaps 1,500 volumes, eminent churchmen would rarely have owned more than a hundred books,[40] and aristocratic owners, to judge from their inventories, many fewer.[41] Sir John Paston, by chance one of the best-known collectors of the fifteenth century, owned only about twenty books or so.[42] In an examination of 7,568 wills of the fourteenth and fifteenth centuries, Margaret Deanesly found mention of only 338 books, which, whatever qualification is made of the value of the evidence, is a remarkably small number.[43] There was an increase in the demand for, availability and ownership of books of all kinds in the fifteenth century, but one is still struck by the comparatively unsophisticated nature of production, the importance of patrons and commissions, and the lack of evidence for any such exchange of information or exemplars between producers as would have eliminated the multiple independent English translations that were made, not always in widely dispersed geographical locations, of works in great demand such as Mandeville's *Travels*[44] or the pseudo-Bonaventuran *Meditationes Vitae Christi*.[45] The changes that were introduced into what was in England essentially a cottage industry by the increased use of paper (brought into Europe in the thirteenth century but rarely used in England for books before the middle of the fifteenth), and then by the invention of printing, were at first changes only in scale in the activity of publishing and book-production, but they were bound to bring in changes in the nature of the activity.

NOTES

1 Dom D. Knowles, *The Religious Orders in England*, 3 vols., Vol. II: *The End of the Middle Ages* (Cambridge, 1955), p. viii: 'The monastic historian of the later Middle Ages cannot expect to enter in upon a harvest which others have prepared'.

2 Among those that might be mentioned are the facsimile reproductions of well-known anthologies and miscellanies such as Lincoln Cathedral Library MS 91 (the Thornton MS), Edinburgh, NLS, Advocates 19.2.1 (the Auchinleck MS), CUL MSS Ff.1.6 (the Findern MS) and Ff.2.38, Bodleian Library MSS Bodley 638, Fairfax 16, Tanner 346, and Eng. poet. a.1 (the Vernon MS), and BL MS Add. 60577 (the Winchester anthology); and, of Chaucer's works, Cambridge, Corpus Christi College, MS 61, Cambridge, St John's College, MS L.1, Aberystwyth, National Library of Wales MS Peniarth 392D (the Hengwrt MS), CUL MS Gg.4.27, and Cambridge, Magdalene College, MS Pepys 2006.

3 The work of Kathleen L. Scott might be singled out for special mention, e.g. 'A Mid-Fifteenth-Century English Illuminating Shop', *The Caxton Master*, *The Mirroure of the Worlde*, and 'Lydgate's Lives' (see above, List of works cited in short form).

4 See Doyle and Parkes, and Parkes, '*Ordinatio* and *Compilatio*'.

5 This distinction is the one made in an essay by L.M.J. Delaissé, 'Towards a History of the Mediaeval Book', *Divinitas*, 11 (1967), 423–36, which is of great historical importance in having helped to initiate the modern movement towards 'le science codicologique', the study of the manuscript-book as a total study, from all aspects. A remarkable recent example is C. Bozzolo and E. Ornato, *Pour une histoire du livre manuscrit au Moyen Age. Trois essais de codicologie quantitative* (Paris, 1980).

6 See Doyle and Parkes, p. 200, and, for the 'Stafford MS', *The Complete Works of John Gower*, ed. G.C. Macaulay, vols. II and III: *The English Works* (Oxford, 1901), II, pp. clii–cliii.

7 See H.C. Schulz, 'Thomas Hoccleve, Scribe', *Speculum*, 12 (1937), 71–81, at 71–6.

8 See H.E. Bell, 'The Price of Books in Medieval England', *The Library*, 4th series, 17 (1936–7), 312–32, at 313, 316.

9 See G.A. Lester, *Sir John Paston's 'Grete Boke'* (Woodbridge, 1984); Doyle, 'William Ebesham'.

10 See N.F. Blake, *Caxton and his World* (London, 1969), ch. 4, 'Choice of Texts', pp. 64–78.

11 See L.F. Sandler, *The Peterborough Psalter in Brussels and other Fenland Manuscripts* (London, 1974).

12 See A.I. Doyle, 'Vernon and Simeon Manuscripts', pp. 332–3.

13 Though G. Pollard, 'The *Pecia* System in the Medieval Universities', in *Medieval Scribes, Manuscripts and Libraries: Essays presented to N.R. Ker*, ed. M.B. Parkes and A.G. Watson (London, 1978), pp. 145–61, suggests it was dying out in Oxford (and in northern Europe generally) in the fourteenth century (p. 149).

14 S.J.P. van Dijk, 'An Advertisement Sheet of an Early Fourteenth-Century Writing Master at Oxford', *Scriptorium*, 10 (1956), 47–64.

15 Parkes, '*Ordinatio* and *Compilatio*'; C.F.R. de Hamel, *Glossed Books of the Bible and the Origins of the Paris Booktrade* (Woodbridge, 1984).

16 See R. Irwin, *The Heritage of the English Library* (London, 1964), p. 189; Richard of Bury's *Philobiblon*, ed. and trans. E.C. Thomas (London, 1888), ch. VIII, p. 69.

17 G.H. Putnam, *Books and their Makers during the Middle Ages*, 2 vols. (1896–7, repr. New York, 1962), I, p. 256.

18 R. Hirsch, *Printing, Selling and Reading 1450–1550* (Wiesbaden, 1967), pp. 61–2.

19 See M.A. Stones, 'Secular Manuscript Illumination in France', in *Medieval Manuscripts and Textual Criticism*, ed. C. Kleinhenz, North Carolina Studies in the Romance Languages and Literatures (vol. 173), Symposia, no. 4 (Chapel Hill, 1976), 83–102. For an example of some mid-fourteenth-century French MSS of secular writings illustrated by the same group of artists, see D.J.A. Ross, 'Methods of Book Production in a XIVth Century French Miscellany (London, B.M. MS Royal 19.D.i)', *Scriptorium*, 6 (1952), 63–75.

20 M. Tyssens, 'Le style oral et les ateliers de copistes', in *Mélanges de Linguistique Romane et de Philologie Médiévale offerts à M. Maurice Delbouille*, ed. J. Renson, 2 vols. (Gembloux, 1964), II, 659–75, at 664–5.

21 D.J.A. Ross, 'A Thirteenth-Century Anglo-Norman Workshop Illustrating Secular Literary Manuscripts?' in *Mélanges offerts à Rita Lejeune*, 2 vols. (Gembloux, 1969), I, 689–94, at 694. The argument seems a little strained if it is held to refer to any more than an organisation of artists, since only two MSS are discussed, and the scribes are different.

22 M. Thomas, 'Manuscripts', in L. Febvre and H.-J. Martin, *The Coming of the Book: The Impact of Printing 1450–1800*, trans. D. Gerard (London, 1976), pp. 15–28, at 25–6.

23 See R.K. Root, 'Publication before Printing', *PMLA*, 28 (1913), 417–31.

24 Root, 'Publication before Printing', p. 419. Very clear evidence of the persistence of the same tradition in fifteenth-century France exists in the dedication of the *Champion des Dames* by Martin le Franc to Philip of Burgundy: see S. Moore, 'General Aspects of Literary Patronage in the Middle Ages', *The Library*, 3rd series, 4 (1913), 369–72, at 379.

25 It should be remembered that both Boccaccio and Petrarch also themselves transcribed copies of their own works, including the longer ones. See Root, 'Publication before Printing', p. 425; V. Branca and P.G. Ricci, *Un Autografo del Decameron* (Padua, 1962).

26 See H.S. Bennett, *English Books and Readers 1475–1557* (1952; 2nd edn Cambridge, 1969), pp. 2–3.

27 Thomas, 'Manuscripts', p. 25.

28 J. Lough, *Writer and Public in France, from the Middle Ages to the Present Day* (Oxford, 1978), pp. 23–6. For Christine, see especially S. Hindman, 'The Composition of the Manuscript of Christine de Pizan's Collected Works in the British Library: A Reassessment', *BLJ*, 9 (1983), 93–123.

29 See the discussion of 'Publication and Circulation', ch. VI in H.J. Chaytor, *From Script to Print: An Introduction to Medieval Literature* (Cambridge, 1945), p. 134.

30 Thomas, 'Manuscripts', p. 28.

31 Bühler, *The Fifteenth-Century Book*, p. 27.

32 *Ibid.*, pp. 23, 33, 27. Considerable scepticism concerning the existence of 'commercial scriptoria' anywhere in Europe during the Middle Ages is expressed by E.L. Eisenstein, *The Printing Press as an Agent of Change: Communications and Cultural*

Transformation in Early-Modern Europe, 2 vols. (Cambridge, 1979), I, 12–14. This is in the face of some sweeping generalisations made by earlier scholars. She even tends to play down the role of the Italian *cartolai* of the fifteenth century, and asserts that the famous Florentine book-merchant, Vespasiano da Bisticci, never ran 'a wholesale business' (I, 48). Her emphasis throughout is on the massive nature of the changes introduced by printing. Oddly enough, Eisenstein accepts the poor evidence for systematic commercial publication in England (the Auchinleck MS; John Shirley): this reflects the general and perhaps understandable neglect of English conditions in general surveys of continental evidence.

33 L.H. Loomis, 'The Auchinleck Manuscript and a Possible London Bookshop of 1330–1340', *PMLA*, 57 (1942), 595–627.

34 Doyle and Parkes, p. 199.

35 Scott, *Mirrour of the Worlde*, pp. 2–7; 'Lydgate's Lives'.

36 See A. Hudson, 'Middle English', in *Editing Medieval Texts English, French and Latin Written in England*, ed. A.G. Rigg (New York and London, 1977), pp. 34–57, at p. 47, and the essay by the same author in the present volume, pp. 125–42.

37 Pollard, 'The Company of Stationers', p. 9.

38 Bell, 'Price of Books', p. 332.

39 W.L. Schramm, 'The Cost of Books in Chaucer's Time', *MLN*, 48 (1933), 139–45, at 144–5. It is usually assumed that books were too expensive for students to be able to afford them – they copied their own: see C.H. Talbot, 'The Universities and the Mediaeval Library', in *The English Library before 1700: Studies in its History*, ed. F. Wormald and C.E. Wright (London, 1958), pp. 66–84, at p. 73. Chaucer's mention (*Legend of Good Women*, Prologue, G version, 273) of his having sixty books of classical stories of women, *alone*, is not to be taken seriously (Schramm unfortunately does, p. 144).

40 Irwin, *The Heritage of the English Library*, pp. 195–6.

41 See the inventories of Simon Burley, of Thomas of Woodstock, duke of Gloucester, and of Archbishop Scrope of York, and the discussion in Elizabeth Salter, *Fourteenth-Century English Poetry: Contexts and Readings* (Oxford, 1983), pp. 34–45.

42 A complete list of John Paston's books is given in *The Paston Letters*, ed. J. Gairdner, 4 vols. (London, 1900), III, 300–1 (item 869).

43 Deanesly, 'Vernacular Books'. See also Chaytor, *From Script to Print*, p. 108.

44 See Bennett, *English Books and Readers*, p. 1.

45 See Salter, 'The Manuscripts', pp. 126–7.

1 · MATERIALS: THE PAPER REVOLUTION

R.J. LYALL

T HE REVOLUTION which affected the production of books in later medieval Europe came in two stages, the first of which is more properly the concern of the present collection. In many respects, the actual process of making-up and writing manuscripts remained unchanged even though the social and economic realities of the book trade were fundamentally transformed through the progressive displacement of parchment by paper in the course of the fifteenth century; and it is important to remember – as evidence in subsequent pages of this volume will illustrate – that the availability of printed books in the latter part of the century could be a stimulus to the production of manuscripts rather than an alternative.[1] Scribes still prepared their inks from carbon compounds or, more usually, from powdered oak galls; they still pricked and/or ruled their folios in order to ensure a neat layout on the page; rubricators and, in the case of the better-quality manuscripts, illuminators still decorated the written product, making it more pleasing to the eye and easier to read. Yet in subtle and important ways the book trade was radically changed by the economic revolution which paper certainly represented, and by the end of the fifteenth century its impact was felt throughout Britain.

The skins of a variety of animals, but principally sheep and cattle, had been employed in the manufacture of books since the early Middle Ages. Techniques of preparation, involving the treatment of the skins with a lime solution to remove all traces of hair, successive stages of soaking and stretching, degreasing and bleaching, created excellent writing surfaces,[2] and it is not surprising that there was some doubt among scribes that paper could provide a satisfactory substitute. The economic factor was, however, in the end decisive: even as early as the close of the fourteenth century, a quire of paper (twenty-five sheets) cost no more than the average skin, but it gave eight times as many leaves of equivalent size.[3] The growth of the paper trade in the course of the fifteenth century, moreover, brought about a steady reduction in prices, so that they had in effect halved by the middle of the century and then halved again by 1500.[4] In such circumstances, the appeal of paper must have been considerable, and it is not surprising that its use spread

Table 1.1.

	Parchment				Paper and parchment*				Paper			
	BL	Oxf	Total	%	BL	Oxf	Total	%	BL	Oxf	Total	%
1401–1425	6	13	19	70.4	1	1	2	7.4	1	5	6	22.2
1426–1450	9	31	40	81.6	—	3	3	6.1	1	5	6	12.2
1451–1475	10	49	59	79.8	2	—	2	2.7	5	8	13	17.5
1476–1500	5	7	12	50.0	—	1	1	4.1	6	5	11	45.8

*This small group includes examples of two types of manuscript: those in which different sections are written on the two kinds of material and those in which paper quires are encased in a parchment leaf, presumably for strength. In some of the latter instances, the central bifolium of the quire is also of parchment.

steadily throughout the market, influencing record-keeping, various private purposes and the commercial production of books.

It is possible to establish, in general terms, the pace of the process by which paper displaced parchment in English manuscript production. One guide is the catalogues of dated manuscripts recently compiled by Andrew Watson, which together contain 174 volumes produced in England in the course of the fifteenth century.[5] Although this is a small (and not, perhaps, entirely representative) sample,[6] a fairly clear pattern emerges from Table 1.1. A larger sample of English manuscripts derived from Neil Ker's *Medieval Manuscripts in British Libraries* essentially confirms this picture; because most of these manuscripts are undated, we must accept the judgments offered by Dr Ker, but it does seem probable that the overall picture given in Table 1.2 is essentially correct. Taken together, these two sets of figures indicate that the use of paper was very rare (but not entirely unknown) about the turn of the fifteenth century, that the proportion of all manuscripts written on paper rose to about 20 per cent by about 1450, and that it had reached 50 per cent or more by the final decades of the century.

But a careful analysis of the evidence reveals a great deal more, for the acceptance of paper was not uniform throughout the book-trade. Liturgical manuscripts, to take the most obvious example, continued to be written on parchment, usually of the best quality, throughout the period, and the percentages in Table 1.2 in particular are certainly affected by the number of volumes of this kind represented in each part of the sample. Similarly, the copies of the Statutes which continued to be produced in fairly large numbers into the early sixteenth century were generally made of parchment. But by the beginning of the Tudor period, the use of parchment for other manuscripts was certainly exceptional, and those that survive are generally of a de

Table 1.2.

	Parchment		(including liturgical manuscripts)		Paper and parchment		Paper	
	No.	%	No.	%	No.	%	No.	%
Early (xv$^{in.}$)	49	90.7	(7	13.0)	2	3.7	3	5.5
First half (xv^1)	53	79.1	(12	18.0)	2	3.0	12	17.9
Middle (xv$^{med.}$)	38	82.6	(16	34.8)	2	2.2	7	15.2
Second half (xv^2)	37	54.4	(9	13.2)	6	8.8	25	36.8
Late (xv$^{ex.}$)	6	40.0	(0	0.0)	2	13.3	7	46.7

luxe character, often with court associations. At the other end of the scale, it is evident that some contexts and/or kinds of material were particularly favourable to the adoption of paper. The new medium was quickly accepted in the universities – where, even in the fifteenth century, the cost advantages may have been particularly significant – and the survival of several relatively early paper manuscripts with a Bristol provenance suggests that such a mercantile environment, too, may have favoured paper.[7] Among its earliest applications throughout Britain was in the keeping of town records, and the merchants and tradespeople who acquired paper for these purposes would naturally have extended its use into the devotional and other books which they were increasingly coming to own.

Two related factors, then, can be seen at work in the choice of material for the making-up of fifteenth-century books: the type of volume, and the audience for which it was intended. There is scope for a good deal of research in this area, and the generalisations which we can at present make must be framed with caution. It seems, for example, that manuscripts with monastic connections, whether evidently the work of the religious themselves or commercially produced for a monastic client, are much more likely than other categories to be written on parchment; and yet it is striking to find more than one member of the house at Westminster, quite early in the fifteenth century, using paper for theological or philosophical works.[8] Collections of medical recipes and other practical manuscripts are likely to be on paper, at least from about 1450 or so, and from this date it is also not unusual to find a copy of Ovid, Boccaccio, or even Xenophon on the same material.[9]

Examination of the traditions of particular texts can also provide valuable insights. Of the manuscripts of *Mandeville's Travels* listed by M.C. Seymour,[10] more than two-thirds are entirely on parchment, while the proportion of those written after 1450 is less than a half. The earliest copies of Hoccleve's *Regiment of Princes* are similarly on parchment, but after the middle of the century, 40 per cent are on paper.[11] In both cases, more work is necessary on the provenance of the manuscripts, and the circumstances in which they were written. It is possible to distinguish four main kinds of context for scribal activity in the later Middle Ages: the production of commissioned works by professional scribes; the commercial production of books on a speculative basis; copying of books within religious houses for the use of the religious themselves; and the private production of books for the writer's own use. Volumes in the first category are obviously likely to be of high quality, especially where the patron is a prince or magnate, as is clearly the case with the early presentation copies of the *Regiment of Princes*, and it is no doubt significant that at least five of the early parchment texts of Mandeville were apparently commissioned.[12] A quite different social context clearly existed for a work like *The Prick of Conscience*, a religious manual of which more manu-scripts survive than of any other Middle English text.[13] Where it is possible to establish an original provenance for these manuscripts, it is often of a clerical character, and many copies were probably made by parish priests and members of religious orders for their own use, while others may have been produced by local scribes for pious laypeople.[14] Here the distinction in materials seems to be primarily chronological: all but three of the manu-scripts written before 1450 are wholly on parchment, while nearly 40 per cent of those written after that date are on paper. A more puzzling – and possibly revealing – example is the *Piers Plowman* tradition, where manuscripts of the A-Text are not uncommonly written on paper (seven out of eighteen copies listed by Kane are on this material), while it is almost unknown for the B- or C-Texts to be written on paper.[15] The explanation in this case does not seem to be entirely to do with the dates of the surviving copies; and it may be that the difference is indicative of the respective audiences of the various recen-sions of the poem. But this, too, is a matter for careful and detailed investi-gation.

Although parchment is much less informative for the codicologist than paper is, it is possible to use the evidence it provides to gain greater understanding of the book trade, and of the ways in which scribes worked. It is, for example, apparent that a number of different grades of processed skin were available, and that the nature of a manuscript and its audience influ-enced the choice of material. Any study of the fine Chaucers, Gowers and Lydgates produced in London in the first half of the fifteenth century cannot but impress upon the reader the fine quality of the parchment which was used for the best books, and the substantial quantity of relatively large sheets which was evidently available.[16] At the lower end of the market, we do encounter many manuscripts written on coarse and unprepossessing forms of parchment, where the clear difference between the whiteness of the flesh side and the yellowish character of the grain side reveals the use of mature sheep.[17] It is difficult, on the whole, to distinguish among parchments of reasonable quality those made from the skins of sheep, goats and calves; but it is often possible to draw inferences about the market from the fineness of the parchment and the care with which it was prepared.

The progressive introduction of paper in the course of the fifteenth century, however, brings real gains for the student of the manuscripts of the period. It is true that the evidence provided by the paper is not always easy to analyse, that there are both theoretical and practical difficulties associated with it, and that the problems and the possibilities are only just beginning to be understood. In order to make sense of paper evidence, we must understand that it is the individual mould upon which the sheets were made which is the key, since each mould has individual peculiarities which enable paper made upon it to be distinguished from that made on any other, even very similar, mould. Since the moulds continued in use for relatively short periods, often as little as twelve to eighteen months and seldom more than a very few years, the manufacture of paper on a single mould (or pair of moulds, since they were usually alternated in the process of manufacture and thus produce two types of paper, with very similar marks, within a single stock) was necessarily confined within these limits; and this obviously has enormous possibilities for the dating of works written upon that stock. There is, of course, no guarantee that any scribe actually used all the paper available to him within a few months of acquiring it, and this is frequently raised as an argument against the application of paper evidence to the dating of manuscripts; but we can in general say that the larger a stock of paper the more recently it is likely to have been purchased, and where we can check the time-lag (as, for example, in the case of dated manuscripts) the evidence seems to be fairly reliable.[18]

We may also be helped by the fact that few manuscripts of any size are written on a single stock of paper from one pair of moulds, and the evidence of several types of watermark taken together will often give a clear indication of date. By way of illustration, we can consider CUL MS Gg.2.6, the unique copy of the Middle Scots *Saints' Lives*. Although the text itself was produced towards the end of the fourteenth century, this manuscript (which, since it was made up by folding the sheets parallel to the shorter sides and then again in the same direction to create a tall, narrow volume 99 mm × 220 mm, we might call a 'vertical quarto')[19] is evidently nearly a century later than the translation. No fewer than six stocks of paper are represented, although three of them occur only briefly and without any corresponding twin. The basic types are marked with two varieties of Gothic 'p', a huge family of marks widespread in much of western Europe in the second half of the fifteenth century; of these, the first to appear, occurring for the first time at fol. 22 and running through the next seven quires, is a long form, 100–103 mm in height, with a lateral stroke across the descender and a rather angular quatrefoil, of the type of Briquet 8665 and of Piccard, *Buchstabe p*, VII, 671–81,[20] recorded between 1481 and 1487. The second kind, which is interspersed with the first and eventually takes over from it, has a trefoil and an exaggeratedly calipered descender: there is no example of the type in either Briquet or Piccard, but there will be no mistaking them if they do turn up elsewhere. A much more significant mark, at least in the present state of our knowledge, is the form of Bull's Head which occurs at three points in the manuscript, and which can, on the basis of its straight horns, distinctive nostrils and generally elongated appearance, be identified with some confidence with Piccard, *Ochsenkopf* VII, 707 and 708, occurring in the northern Rhineland and the Low Countries between 1477 and 1486; one of the pair also turns up, in a late and defective state, as Briquet 15080.[21] This latter example is dated 1468 from the Brussels paper collection, but since all Briquet's other examples fall between 1477 and 1479, it is probable that this is a mistake (perhaps for 1478). Heitz records the frequent use of paper from these moulds in books printed in Strasbourg up to 1484, and they also occur in the edition of John of Hildesheim printed at Cologne in 1478.[22] Most tellingly of all, 707 is found in another Scottish manuscript, the Newburgh Burgh Court Book of 1460–81, now among the muniments of the University of St Andrews.[23] Careful comparison leaves no doubt that this is indeed paper from one of the same moulds, although the sheets in the Cambridge manuscript may represent a later state. At any rate, the relevant leaves of the Newburgh records were written in the latter part of 1479, and it is hard to believe that the *Saints' Lives* manuscript was made up more than a very few years after this date. On the basis of the paper evidence, we can with fair degree of confidence assign it to 'c. 1480–85'.[24]

It seems probable that the Cambridge manuscript of the Scottish *Saints' Lives* was made up as a single unit, although miscellaneous sheets from a number of stocks were certainly used. Where a manuscript is composite, consisting of several units or 'booklets',[25] the evidence of the paper can assist us in understanding the process by which it was compiled as well as giving an indication of date. We may even be able to perceive more clearly the relationships between the parts of two separate manuscripts, as in the case of the two large anthologies compiled by Robert Thornton in the second quarter of the fifteenth century. The value of such evidence in the analysis of manuscript structure can be illustrated by reference to some of the volumes copied by the London scribe John Shirley a little earlier in the century. One of them is now BL MS Add. 16165, a composite manuscript which can, on the combined evidence of the quiring, watermarks and treatment of the texts, be divided into three principal units. The first of these, containing a copy of Chaucer's *Boece* and Trevisa's translation of the *Gospel of Nicodemus* and consisting of nine quires, is made up of paper from five stocks, as follows:

1^{14}, 2^{12} (mark a), 3^{12} (mark b), 4^{12}–5^{12} (mark c), 6^{12} (mark d), 7^{12} (mark e), 8^{12} (mark f), 9^{12} (mark e).

The absence of any mixing of stocks within quires perhaps suggests that Shirley acquired his paper essentially in this form, rather than making his quires up from a stock of loose sheets. Despite a number of changes of ink (e.g. fols. 54r–v) and other signs of separate stints, it seems likely that at least the first text, and quite probably both, were written within a relatively short space of time, and that Shirley must therefore have purchased these five stocks more or less together. The marks are as follows:

a.   *Tower*, of the type of Briquet 15864 (Italian, 1415 × 1422), and of Piccard, *Turm*, II, 503–4 (1420 × 1421).[26] It is the latest examples recorded by Briquet, dating from 1422, which most nearly resemble Shirley's stock.

b.   *Cross and Mounts*, type of Briquet 11685 (Italian, 1405 × 1415), one of a very large family of marks which continue in use throughout the fifteenth century.

c.   *Crown*, type of Briquet 4634 (Italian, 1421 × 1426), and Piccard, *Krone*, I, 331 (1420 × 1426).[27]

d.   *Cross and Mounts*, distinguishable from *b* by the longer stem of the cross (45–46 mm as against 32–37 mm) and more bulbous mounts, resembling Briquet 11700 (1433 × 1434) but very probably earlier.

e.   *Bull*, type of Briquet 2775 (Swiss, 1426 × 1438).

f.   *Bow*, of a large family (Briquet 779–97), current for a century or so from 1335 to about 1435. Cf. Briquet 793 (Italian, 1424 × 1427).

Wherever this evidence gives a specific guide to the date of this unit, it strongly suggests that Shirley assembled and wrote this part of the manuscript in the mid-1420s, early enough to explain the presence of the Tower paper (which was becoming obsolete by 1423 or 1424) but late enough to account for the use of the Bull. On balance, it would seem safe to assign the unit to a year or so either side of 1425.[28]

The second unit, fols. 115–200, is made up of seven quires, arranged as follows:

$10^{12}-14^{12}$ (mark *g*), 15^{12} (mark *f*), 16^{12} (mark *e*).

Here, then, the pattern is different, with a basic stock of paper, different from all six stocks represented in the first unit, making up the first five of the unit's seven quires. The layout of fol. 115r, at the beginning of *The Maystre of the Game* by Edward, duke of York (d. 1415), strongly suggests that this was originally conceived by Shirley as a separate volume; but the occurrence of single quires of the Bow and Bull papers, already found in the first unit, argues for a reasonable proximity in date. The mark on the basic stock is

g.   *Bull's Head with Septfoil*, of the large Briquet family 14741–71 and *very* close, perhaps identical, to 14750 (Vicenza 1423); similar (but not identical) to Piccard, *Oschenkopf*, XII, 448 (1424 × 1425).

This evidence is therefore rather uncertain: if Briquet 14750 is indeed one of Shirley's moulds, *The Maystre of the Game* unit is likely to be almost exactly contemporary with the *Boece/Nicodemus* unit, but Piccard's dates would suggest that this second group of quires was written up to ten years later. There could be no better illustration that the identification of watermark *types* can at best only be broadly indicative where we cannot find evidence of the same *moulds*, and such general evidence can often be downright misleading. But at any event, the text of the *Maystre* continues through to fol. 190, the second leaf of the sixteenth quire, and Shirley then completed the unit with a copy of Lydgate's *Complaynt of an Amorouse Knyght*.

Although the relationship between these two units is not entirely clear, their size and shape is beyond question. The latter parts of MS Add. 16165 are somewhat more problematical. The collation is as follows:

17^{12} (mark *h*), 18^{10} (mark *i*), 19^{12}–20^{12} (mark *j*), 21^{12} (12 missing) (mark *g*).

Three stocks, then, are found only in this part of the manuscript: the final gathering comes from the same stock as the greater part of unit II. Fols. 201r–206r contain the *Regula Sacerdotalis*, a short treatise on the duties of priests which was, according to Shirley's concluding note, promulgated (*divulgata*) in Parliament before both Lords and Commons. Then, on fol. 206v, Shirley begins a copy of Lydgate's *Temple of Glas*, which continues through to fol. 241v. The remainder of the twenty-first quire and all of the twenty-second contain a miscellany of pieces, principally by Chaucer and Lydgate (including a somewhat confused transcription of the *Complaint of Anelyda*) but also by several more minor writers. Many of these pieces are inherently undatable, but there is no good reason to place any of them later than the mid-1420s, consistent with the evidence supplied by the presence of mark *g*. The other three marks are:

h.   *Three Circles* within a larger Circle [a sign of the Trinity?], very like Briquet
      3238 (Palermo 1406);
i.   *Cross and Mounts*, distinct from both *b* and *d*, but closer to the latter: of Briquet's
      published examples, closest to 11722 (Savoy 1413 × Reggio d'Emilia 1439);
j.   *Cherries*, type of Briquet 7423–26 (Catania 1422 × Naples 1430), closest to 7423
      (Catania 1422 × Babenhausen 1430); cf. Piccard, *Frucht*, II, 355–70, esp. 356
      (Frankfurt 1424) and 360–3 (Frankfurt and Friedburg 1428–29).[29]

In general, this evidence also points to the mid- to late 1420s; but there is a distinct possibility that the paper of the seventeenth quire is a good deal earlier than the rest of the manuscript. Briquet found only one instance of this mark, and it is, of course, conceivable that further examples await discovery. But the slim evidence we have suggests that this portion of the manuscript is likely to have originated before 1410 rather than in the mid-1420s, and that it may belong to the earliest period of Shirley's association with the earl of Warwick.[30] Much may hinge upon the date and occasion of the *Regula Sacerdotalis* which quire 17 contains: this text has hitherto received little attention, but it seems clearly to be associated with Lollard agitation in the first decade of the century. Its three chapters provide Biblical and patristic support for the propositions that priests should not be temporal lords, that they should not hold secular office, and that they should be subject to correction by the laity; this looks very like an intellectual equivalent to the 'Lollard' petitions heard by Parliament in 1406 and/or 1410–11.[31] It is striking that Shirley's hand is much more formed and regular in this text than elsewhere in the manuscript, and that the ink is different from that used for the vernacular verse texts which surround it. Everything supports the suggestion that this quire represents the earliest phase of Shirley's surviving scribal work, and that he returned to add *The Temple of Glas*.

This analysis of the paper structure of MS Add. 16165, then, allows us to infer a good deal about Shirley's procedures in writing it. It is, on the whole, a product of the mid-1420s, although there are some grounds, certainly deserving further investigation, for believing that the seventeenth quire may represent a much earlier phase of copying. We can also conclude that there is a close relationship between the *Boece/Nicodemus* unit and the *Maystre* unit, since two stocks of paper are represented in both. The most likely sequence, on the present evidence, seems to be that of the manuscript, with *Boece* and *The Gospel of Nicodemus* copied first, and Shirley then adding a quire of Bull's Head/Septfoil paper in order to make up a large enough unit to take *The Maystre of the Game*. He would then seem to have returned to an old quire, already containing a copy of the once-topical *Regula Sacerdotalis*, in order to begin *The Temple of Glas*. Why he chose to include this controversial Latin text in an otherwise uncontentious vernacular manuscript remains a problem, but the codicological evidence does not seem to invite debate.

If an analysis of MS Add. 16165 requires the separation of distinct elements of a composite manuscript, other parts of the Shirley corpus present the opposite problem. It has previously been recognised that Sion College MS Arc. L40.2/E.44, Cambridge, Trinity College, MS R.3.20 (James 600), and possibly part of BL MS Harley 78, are related, and may be fragments of a much larger manuscript which can to some extent be reconstructed on the basis of surviving quire-signatures.[32] It is, at any rate, striking that while the first four of the twelve quires of the Sion College MS, a copy of Lydgate's translation of *The Pylgrymage of the Lyfe of Man*, are numbered i–iv, the present numbering of the Trinity MS begins at xiv, continuing to xxxvi. If these two fragments did indeed belong together, it would have been as part of a volume of some 300 folios in quires of eight, and it is not surprising that it was broken up at some point in its history. But the watermark evidence does lend support to the theory that this material was copied at about the same time, and – although it is difficult to see where such a small fragment fits into the overall pattern – it is just possible that fols. 80–83 of MS Harley 78 once formed part of the same whole.

The Sion College MS is written on two stocks of paper:

a. *Cross and Mounts*, different from all three stocks of such paper in the Add. MS, with the stem of the Cross 40–42 mm high; the A mark[33] (e.g. fol. 4) has pronounced warp in the chainline above the mark. These moulds resemble

> Briquet 11689 (Florence 1411 × Pisa 1416), but too much significance should not be read into this parallel.
>
> b. *Bull's Head with Septfoil*, different from mark *g* in the Add. MS, distinguishable by the fact that the chain-spaces are 41–42 mm as against 44 mm. Nothing closely approximating this pair is evident in Piccard's numerous examples of the type.

The same stocks occur in the Trinity MS, thus confirming the view that they may once have formed part of a single manuscript. The collations are as follows:

Sion: (two lost quires), 1^8–4^8 (mark *a*); 5^8–12^8 (12^8 wanting) (mark *b*).
Trinity: 1 (xiv)^8–2 (xv)^8 (mark *a*); 3 (xvi)^8–6 (xix)^8 (mark *b*); 7 (xx)^8 (mark *a*); 8 (xxi)^8–9 (xxii)^8 (mark *b*); 10 (xxiii)^8–22 (xxv)^8 (mark *a*); 23 (xxxvi)^8 (mark *b*); 24^4 (24^4 wanting).

The quantities of paper involved here are, by fifteenth-century standards, not trivial: Shirley has used eighty sheets of mark *a* and sixty of mark *b*. This contrasts with his practice in the Add. MS, where the most substantial stock present, that of mark *g*, is represented by only thirty-six sheets, and a total of ten different stocks are used.[34]

Careful examination of the Trinity MS reveals more about the copying process in this case, for another sequence of quire-numbers begins at the tenth quire of the present volume, written in brown ink overwritten in the black ink in which Shirley eventually numbered the quires of his completed manuscript. It would seem, therefore, that fols. 145–352 originally formed, or were intended to form, a separate unit, and very probably represent the earliest stage of the composition of the whole. This unit cannot have been written earlier than the latter part of 1430, since it contains a copy of *The Lyfe of Seynte Margarete*, translated by Lydgate 'at þe request of my lady of Huntyngdon some time þe Countase of þe March, anno 8 Henr. 6'.[35] Several of the Lydgate pieces, indeed, belong to about this date, and it is not improbable that Shirley collected this material early in the 1430s. This is consistent with the evidence of the paper, and with the presence in the first (and, by this argument, more recent) part of 'A Roundell which my lord of Suffolk made after his comyng oute of prysoune', which cannot have been copied before 1432.[36] Although the presence of two interwoven stocks of paper throughout the Trinity MS, and indeed in the Sion College MS as well, argues for no very great delay in the period of compilation of the manuscript, it seems most likely that Shirley began by collecting the Lydgate pieces which now comprise fols. 145–352, and then added the various items – many of which are again by Lydgate, but which include seven French *ballades* and *rondeaux* by the earl of Suffolk – which make up the first 144 folios.

The evidence of reorganisation of his materials which Shirley has given us through his alteration of the quire-numbers in the Trinity MS is repeated in Bodleian MS Ashmole 59, the other manuscript which is (as far as fol. 134) entirely in his distinctive hand. In this case, however, Shirley has clearly extracted part of a larger manuscript rather than the reverse: although the quires in his hand, comprising fols. 1–26, are now numbered i–xi on the final verso of each quire, a previous sequence of numbers (xiij–xxiij) has been cancelled, demonstrating that the text of Lydgate's version of the *Secreta Secretorum* which begins on the present fol. 1r was once preceded by twelve other gatherings. It is, of course, just possible that it was the Sion *Pylgrymage* which occupied this position, but the watermark evidence suggests that these two elements, whatever their intervening circumstances, did not originally belong together. For the paper of Ashmole 59 consists of two stocks of 'BHX' paper (marked with a Bull's Head surmounted with a diagonal cross), which on the evidence of numerous examples collected by Briquet and Piccard could scarcely have been produced earlier than 1440, and more probably after 1445.[37]

The techniques of analysis illustrated so far are important for the fairly precise dating of manuscripts, and for the examination of their structure in relation to the sequence and system of a scribe's activity. There is, however, a further, and potentially even more significant, application of paper evidence. As Stephen Spector has recently pointed out,[38] the patterns of symmetry created by conjugate leaves can be used, even where the original collation has become unclear as a result of the mounting of detached leaves during rebinding, to establish many facts about the original structure of paper books. This technique was used in the past by a few bibliographers,[39] but its value has not been widely recognised and the precision which it permits has been neglected by successive generations of codicologists. The principles are very simple: in a folio arrangement, each watermarked leaf should have an unmarked conjugate, while the mould side of the sheet, which received the direct impression of the wires on the paper-maker's mould and which is usually distinguishable by the reasonably skilled eye, will occur on the recto of one leaf and the verso of the other. There is unfortunately no generally agreed convention of notation for these patterns: Paul Needham has recently compared the three alternative methods currently in use.[40] My own preference is for the system employed by Theo Gerardy,[41] which reflects the actual distribution of the paper in the book, but a simple conversion table makes the three codes mutually intelligible:[42]

Gerardy/Lyall	Z	A
Needham	mL	mR
Ziesche/Schnitger	b	a

Gerardy's method records the orientation of the paper when the marked leaf is positioned the right way up and on the verso (left hand side) of the opening. If the visible side of this marked leaf is the mould-side, the sheet is described as a 'Z' sheet (from German *zugewandt*, lit. 'turned towards'), while if the mould-side is on the recto and the felt-side is visible, the sheet is an 'A' sheet (*abgewandt*, 'turned away'). The natural conjugates in a folio arrangement, therefore, will be nA/–Z and nZ/–A, where 'n' represents the watermark and '–' its absence. A difficulty arises where a sheet is inverted in the made-up book, since this will be recognised in the case of the marked leaf but not in that of its conjugate, which will be described upside-down: I therefore indicate the inversion of a watermarked leaf with an asterisk, and we can accept as alternative patterns of symmetry nA*/–A and nZ*/–Z. These basic rules will thus produce quiring patterns such as the following:

Fol.	1	2	3	4	5	6	7	8	9	10	11	12	13	14	15	16
Mark	–A	–Z	–Z	nA*	nA*	nA*	nA*	–Z	nZ*	–A	–A	–A	–A	nZ*	nA	nA*

The integrity of this quire is apparent from other evidence, but it could certainly have been inferred from the paper evidence alone had the manuscript now consisted of a series of singletons.

These fundamental principles of symmetry apply equally, of course, to quarto arrangements, although here the watermark, being positioned on its side and in the inner margin or gutter, can be difficult to deal with. If we describe the upper and lower sections of the watermarked half of the sheet as nuA and nlA (nuZ and nlZ) respectively, then we would expect to encounter the following symmetrical patterns:

Fol.	1	2	3	4
Mark	nuA	–Z	–A	nlZ
			or	
	nuZ	–A	–Z	nlA

accepting, of course, that the respective positions of the marked and unmarked parts of the sheet may be reversed. The technique of analysis can be illustrated by reference to BL MS Harley 2386, a conflation of two manuscripts, the latter a copy of *Mandeville's Travels*. Since both parts of the manuscript now consist entirely of singletons mounted on guards, M.C. Seymour observes simply 'collation: unknown'.[43] In fact, establishing the original quiring is straightforward, at least for the main body of the volume. Part 2, the Mandeville, is written on a single stock of paper, a pair of French Royal Arms marks of the type of Briquet 1697 and of Piccard, *Lilie*, III, 1426–34, manufactured in the early and mid-1470s.[44] Beginning with the text itself, and disregarding for the moment five preliminary leaves, we can readily identify four quires:

Quire	74	75	76	77	78	79	80	81	82	83	84	85	86	87
1	–Z	–Z	auA	–A	alZ	alA	–Z	–A	auZ	auA	–Z	alZ	–A	–A

	88	89	90	91	92	93	94	95	96	97	98	99	100	101	102	103
2	alZ	–A	–A	alZ	–A	alZ	–A	alZ	auA	–Z	auA	–Z	auA	–Z	–Z	auA

	104	105	106	107	108	109	110	111	112	113	114	115	116	117	118	119
3	alA	–Z	alA	–Z	alZ	–A	–A	alZ	auA	–Z	–Z	auA	–A	auZ	–A	auZ

120	121	122	123	124	125	126	127	128	129	130	131	132	133	134	135
4	auA	–Z	–A	alZ	–A	alZ	–A	alZ	auA	–Z	auA	–Z	auA	–Z	–A	alZ

Apart from the apparent cancellation of a watermarked half-sheet corresponding to fols. 74 and 87, the patterns of symmetry are here perfect, as one would expect where the scribe has made up his quires by the usual 'multifolding' method.[45] This enables us to conclude without hesitation that the original collation was

$a^{14} b^{16}$–d^{16}.

This, however, leaves the problem of the preliminary and final leaves, which are arranged as follows:

69	70	71	72	73
alA	auA	–Z	–A	alZ

136	137	138	139
–A	alZ	auZ?	–A

It is far from easy to distinguish mould- and felt-sides of fols. 136–9, but if my assessment of them is correct they could represent two regular half-sheets from a quire of eight or more folios, the latter part of which has either been cancelled or lost. The present preliminary leaves (fols. 69–73) contain miscellaneous sixteenth-century pen trials, accounts and so on, but are from the same stock of paper as the rest of the Mandeville. The most likely explanation is that they are part of the cancelled portion of the sixth quire: we would then have accounted for nine of what must once have been at least twelve folios. The full collation of the Mandeville section of Harley 2386 would therefore be:

[five leaves] a^{14}, b^{16}–d^{16}, e at least 12 (5–? missing)

Even when a manuscript has suffered quite radical damage, it is possible to employ the symmetries of the paper in effecting a reconstruction. A *Piers Plowman* manuscript, BL MS Harley 6041, affords an illustration of the difficulties which can attend the codicologist in this regard, and of the possibilities of paper evidence: this volume has evidently been subjected to a good deal of ill-treatment in the past, and now consists of 102 single leaves, four of which are fragmentary, all mounted on modern paper guards. Professor Kane has attempted a collation on the basis of scribal catchwords and early signatures, and proposes a^{12}–c^{12} (c^{10} wanting), d^{4}, e^{8}, f^{12}–j^{12}, k (seven leaves).[46] This is, however, admittedly conjectural, and there is some conflict between the catchwords and the signatures, particularly in Kane's quires d and e. A further problem is the lacuna which follows the last line of fol. 51v (xv 201 of the C Text): the first line of fol. 52r is xvii 24, so that 370 lines of the text are missing. Does this mean that a substantial part of the Harley MS is missing, or that this lacuna was inherited from the exemplar? Professor Kane leans towards the latter explanation, but adds that:

> this cannot be conclusively shown, for although the signature v occurs on fol. 52a as if the quire were intact, signatures were added in this manuscript after copying, and the loss may have intervened between the two processes. The trimming of inner edges deprives us of the evidence of the watermarks on this point.

The last remark indicates that Kane is aware that watermarks can indeed assist with problems of collation; but the damage caused to the marks in the course of trimming and mounting the individual leaves of this quarto manuscript has been considerable, and it is understandable that he despaired of getting help from that quarter.

It is also true that the two stocks of paper represented in MS Harley 6041 are not particularly easy to work with. Even where parts of the marks survive they are frequently indistinct, and it is not always possible to distinguish mould-side from felt-side even on the watermarked half of the sheet. The first mark, which occurs in fols. 1–47 (Kane's quires a–e), is a version of the common Mounts and Cross mark (Briquet 11851–97), a representation perhaps of Calvary, which was produced in an Italian mill or mills between about 1376 and 1490. The stem of the cross coincides with a chainline and is not always easy to see, and the relation between the position of the mark and the trimming of the paper means that the top half of the watermarked side of the sheet is not always recognisable. The chainlines are, however, a tell-tale guide, for the measurements between them are as follows:[47]

A sheet (mark left)
24 38 <u>28 32</u> 37 36 29 [. . .] 24 38 37 37 38 38 9

Z sheet (mark right)
 8 38 37 37 37 38 26 [. . .] 29 36 37 <u>32 28</u> 38 25

The narrower spaces are, therefore, an infallible guide to the original presence of a mark, even where the mark itself is no longer visible. Using this information, we can test Kane's collation against the evidence of symmetry.

In the case of fols. 1–47, the distribution of the Cross and Mounts paper can be reconstructed as follows:

Quire	1	2	3	4	5	6	7	8	9	10	11	12
a	–	au	al	–	al	–	–	au	–	au	al	–

	13	14	15	16	17	18	19	20	21	22	23	24
b	al	–	–	au	–	au	al	–	al	–	[torn]	

	25	26	27	28	29	30	31	32	33		34	35
c	[torn]	al	–	al	–	–	–	au	–	[au]	–	au

	36	37	38	39	40	41	42	43	44	45	46	47
d	–	au	–	au	–	au	al	–	al	–	al	–

Even without the additional evidence of mould- and felt-sides, then, we can see a clear quiring pattern. Kane's conclusion that a leaf is missing after fol. 33 is confirmed: there is no surviving conjugate for fol. 27, which is the upper part of the watermarked half of an A sheet. The division of fols. 36–47 into two quires, proposed by Kane, is a response to the existence of a catchword at the foot of fol. 39v; but it is not consistent with the paper evidence. As the above table shows, fols. 36–47 constitute a regularly symmetrical quire of twelve folios, while fols. 40–47 could not stand on their own as a separate gathering. The integrity of these twelve folios is, moreover, confirmed by the early quire-signatures: fol. 36 is marked 'iij qua*ternus*', and the next two folios are marked [ij] and [iij]. The next such indication to survive is on fol. 48, which is marked [v]. If Kane's collation were correct, fol. 48 would surely have been the start of the sixth rather than the fifth quire.

Symmetry also enables us to determine the original structure of the second part of the manuscript, which is written on paper marked with a pair of prancing Unicorns of the type of Briquet 9956 (1405 × 1417) and of Piccard, *Fabeltiere*, III, 1670–87 (1399 × 1425). It *may* be possible to be more precise than this in dating the Unicorn paper in Harley 6041, but at present the firmest statement we can make is 'first quarter of the fifteenth century'. On the problems of collation, however, the evidence is much less ambiguous. Again ignoring the problematical indication of mould- and felt-side, we can see fairly clearly that the manuscript breaks into quires of twelve leaves:

	48	49	50	51	52	53	54	55	56	57	58	59
e	bl	–	–	bu	bl	–	–	bu	bl	–	–	bu
	60	61	62	63	64	65	66	67	68	69	70	71
f	bu	–	–	bl	bl	–	–	bu	bu	–	–	bl
	72	73	74	75	76	77	78	79	80	81	82	83
g	bl	–	–	bl	–	bl	bu	–	bu	–	–	bu
	84	85	86	87	88	89	90	91	92	93	94	95
h	–	bu	bu	–	–	bl	bu	–	–	bl	bl	–
	96	97	98	99	100	101	102					
	bu	bl	–	bl	–	–	bu					

Not only do quires e–h fall neatly into a symmetrical pattern, but the occurrence of pairs of sheets, more or less alternately marked and unmarked, argues that the quires were made up by 'multifolding'. It is clear, moreover, that – barring a remarkable coincidence in the distribution of the paper – nothing has been lost between fols. 51 and 52, demonstrating that the fifteenth- or sixteenth-century note 'haud deficit' refers to a gap in the exemplar rather than to the loss of part of the present manuscript. It is more difficult to know what to make of the final seven leaves: the conjunction of fols. 96 and 97 indicates a disturbance of the regular pattern, and it is probably significant that the text of *Piers Plowman* concludes on fol. 96r. The verso is blank, and the same hand then continues, in a different ink, with a form of confession. The pattern would be regularised if we supplied a conjectural unmarked folio between fols. 96 and 97, which would make fols. 99–102 the central sheet of an original quire of twelve. There is no way of being certain that this was the structure, but it does seem to be the best interpretation of the available evidence.

Much more work needs to be undertaken before the evidence available to the codicologist as a result of the paper revolution can be properly considered in all its aspects. From the association of individual marks or varieties of marks with particular mills, we can infer much about trading patterns and networks of supply. From gradually accumulating data for the dating of moulds and the paper produced on them, we will be able to be more precise about the date-limits of individual manuscripts, and to investigate how scribes like Shirley and Thornton acquired and used their paper stocks. And from the systematic analysis of the distribution of paper within the manuscript, we will be able to solve many specific problems of collation and to understand more clearly the ways in which composite manuscripts were compiled. Work in these areas is still in its infancy, but at least its potential value is now beyond debate. The introduction of paper transformed the book-trade, bringing the acquisition of manuscripts within the reach of a larger section of society than ever before and paving the way for the new technology of print. But it also provided codicologists with a vital, and so far largely neglected, tool, the possibilities of which are only now beginning to be understood.

NOTES

1 See below, pp. 412–16.
2 There is a useful, succinct account of the technical processes involved in the manufacture of parchment and of related subjects in R. Reed, *Ancient Skins, Parchments and Leathers* (London and New York, 1972), pp. 118–73. Cf. D.V. Thompson, 'Medieval Parchment-making', *The Library*, 4th series, 16 (1935–6), 113–17.
3 For the price of parchment and paper in Paris at the end of the fourteenth century, see L. Febvre and H.-J. Martin, *The Coming of the Book*, trans. D. Gerard (London, 1976), pp. 17–18.
4 Evidence on paper prices is summarised by A. Stevenson, *The Problem of the Missale Speciale* (London, 1967), p. 51; cf. S. Corsten, 'Papierpreise in mittelalterlichen Köln (1371–1495)', in *Bibliothek und Buch im Geschichte und Gegenwart: Festschrift für Friedrich Adolf Schmidt-Künsemüller*, ed. O. Weber (Munich, 1976), pp. 45–61. Very similar conclusions are drawn by C. Bozzolo and E. Ornato, *Pour une histoire du livre manuscrit au moyen âge: trois essais de codicologie quantitative* (Paris, 1983), pp. 31–7.
5 A.G. Watson, *Catalogue of Dated and Datable Manuscripts in the Department of Manuscripts in the British Library, c. 700–1600*, 2 vols. (London, 1979); *Catalogue of Dated and Datable Manuscripts in Oxford Libraries, c. 435–1600*, 2 vols. (Oxford, 1984).

6 The dating of manuscripts, especially through a scribal colophon, was very far from being a universal practice in the late Middle Ages. We must therefore consider the possibility, for example, that scribes who used paper were also more likely to date their productions. This would obviously skew the figures.

7 E.g. Bristol, All Saints' Church, MSS 1 and 2, in N.R. Ker, *Medieval Manuscripts in British Libraries*, vols. I–III, continuing (Oxford, 1969–), II, 183–6.

8 E.g. Westminster Abbey MSS 34/2 and 34/5, ibid., I, 402ff.

9 For an Ovid manuscript on paper, see Cambridge, Magdalene College, MSS F.4.34 and Pepys 2124; for copies of works by Boccaccio see Exeter Cathedral MS 3529 and Norwich Cathedral MS 2; for Xenophon see BL MS Royal 10.B.IX (formerly at Canterbury).

10 M.C. Seymour, 'The English Manuscripts of *Mandeville's Travels*', *TEBS*, 4(5) (1965–6), 167–210.

11 M.C. Seymour, 'The Manuscripts of Hoccleve's *Regiment of Princes*, *TEBS*, 4(7) (1968–71), 255–97. See further the Appendix to Ch. 11 below.

12 E.g. BL MSS Arundel 38, Harley 4866, Royal 17.D.VI.

13 See Lewis and McIntosh.

14 For examples of the former type, see Lewis and McIntosh, pp. 34–5, 59–61, 155–6; for the latter, see perhaps pp. 97, 105–6.

15 For MSS of the A- and B-Texts, see *Piers Plowman: The A Version*, ed. G. Kane (London, 1960) and *Piers Plowman: The B Version*, ed. G. Kane and E. Talbot Donaldson (London, 1975) respectively; MSS of the C Text are summarily listed in *Piers the Plowman*, ed. W.W. Skeat, 2 vols. (Oxford, 1886).

16 In the case of GUL MS Hunterian 5, for example, a copy of Lydgate's *Fall of Princes* originally consisting of 216 folios measuring at least 315 × 430 mm and therefore of 108 sheets measuring 630 × 430 mm, we must allow for at least 54 skins and, since we are here at the absolute upper limit of the size of a half-skin, perhaps as many as 108. Cf. Bozzolo and Ornato, *Pour une histoire*, pp. 40–1.

17 The different characteristics of alternative kinds of parchment are described by Reed, *Ancient Skins*, pp. 127–31.

18 For a fundamental discussion of the problem of time-lag in the dating of paper items, see A. Stevenson, *The Problem of the Missale Speciale* (London, 1967), pp. 48–70. Although Stevenson is concerned with incunabula rather than with manuscripts, the evidence of the dated manuscripts which I have analysed tends to confirm that any significant stock of paper, i.e. one consisting of more than a few isolated sheets, tends to be used within a matter of months rather than years.

19 On the dimensions of fifteenth-century manuscripts, see Bozzolo and Ornato, *Pour une histoire*, pp. 269–87, 310–18; J.P. Gumbert, 'The Sizes of Manuscripts: Some Statistics and Notes', in *Hellinga Festschrift*, ed. A.R.A. Croiset van Uchelen (Amsterdam, 1980), pp. 277–88. I prefer 'vertical quarto' to the more usual term 'holster book', since the latter implies conclusions about the use and sociological context of such manuscripts which may not be supported by any evidence.

20 *Die Wasserzeichenkartei Piccard im Hauptstaatsarchiv Stuttgart, Findbuch IV: Wasserzeichen Buchstabe p*, 3 vols. (Stuttgart 1977).

21 *Ibid., Findbuch II: Wasserzeichen Ochsenkopf* (Stuttgart 1966); C.M. Briquet, *Les Filigranes* (Geneva 1907; 3rd edn, ed. A. Stevenson, Hilversum, 1968).

22 Cf. P. Heitz, *Les Filigranes des papiers contenus dans les incunables strasbourgeois* (Strasbourg, 1903).

23 St Andrews University Muniments, MS B54/7/1, fols. 22–24 (18 November 1479–12 April 1480).

24 A further, inconclusive piece of supporting evidence is found in the single sheet of paper bearing a mysterious monument-shaped mark topped by a cross; although this is not included in Briquet's *Les Filigranes*, a tracing of it appears among the Archives Briquet in the Bibliothèque Universitaire et Publique in Geneva, derived from a copy of Gerson's *Doctrin de bon vivre* (J. Brito: Bruges c. 1477).

25 See Robinson, 'The Booklet'; Ralph Hanna III, 'Booklets in Medieval Manuscripts: Further Consideration', *SB*, 39 (1986), 100–11.

26 *Die Wasserzeichenkartei Piccard im Hauptstaatsarchiv Stuttgart, Findbuch III: Wasserzeichen Turm* (Stuttgart, 1970).

27 Ibid., *Findbuch I: Kronenzeichen* (Stuttgart, 1961).

28 This is, incidentally, consistent with the chronology proposed by A.I. Doyle, 'More Light on John Shirley', *Medium Aevum* 30 (1961), 93–101.

29 *Die Wasserzeichenkartei Piccard im Hauptstaatsarchiv Stuttgart, Findbuch XIV: Frucht* (Stuttgart, 1980).

30 Cf. Doyle, 'John Shirley', 94–5.

31 *Rot. Parl.*, III, 583–4, 623.

32 See Ker, *Medieval Manuscripts in British Libraries*, I, 290–1; the connection is not made by James, *Manuscripts of Trinity College*, II, 75–82.

33 See below, pp. 21–2.

34 On the interpretation of such quantities, see Stevenson, *The Problem of the Missale Speciale*, pp. 71–99. Medieval paper was frequently purchased by the quire of 25 sheets; half a ream (250 sheets) would have been a large quantity for a private scribe to buy.

35 Anne Stafford, widow of Edmund Mortimer, earl of March, married John Holand, earl of Huntingdon by 6 March 1427, and died in September 1432; the eighth year of Henry VI's reign ran from 31 August 1430.

36 On Suffolk, see H.N. MacCracken, 'An English Friend of Charles of Orleans', *PMLA*, 26 (1911), 142–80; MacCracken states that the Shirley MS must be later than 1432 and earlier than 1444, since Suffolk is referred to throughout as earl rather than marquis. The latter argument is undoubtedly correct, and the paper suggests a date earlier rather than later in the period; but Suffolk may well have been released from captivity in France *before* 1432, since he was given royal commissions from early in 1431 (*Cal. Pat. Rolls Henry VI*, II, 111, 126).

37 The Ashmole pair are not among the hundreds of examples given by Piccard, *Ochsenkopf*, VII, but the particular variety is unknown before 1440, and rare before 1445; cf. Briquet 15063 (1450).

38 S. Spector, 'Symmetry in Watermark Sequences', *SB*, 31 (1978), 162–78; 'Paper Evidence and the Genesis of the Macro Plays', *Mediaevalia*, 5 (1979), 217–32.

39 So, for example, J. Young and P.H. Aitken in *A Catalogue of Manuscripts in the Library of the Hunterian Museum* (Glasgow, 1908); the basis of the method is present in R.B.McKerrow, *An Introduction to Bibliography* (Oxford, 1927), and discussed briefly (in the context of printed books) in relation to the identification of cancels.

40 P. Needham, 'Johannes Gutenberg and the Catholicon Press', *Papers of the Bibliog. Soc. of America*, 76 (1982), 367–456, at 453.

41 Dr Gerardy has set out his descriptive method on several occasions, notably in

'Die Beschreibung des in Manuskripten und Drucken vorkommenden Papiers', *Codicologica*, 5 (1980), 37–51; and *Das Papier der Seckelmeisterrechnungen von Freiburg i. Ue. 1402–1465* (Schinznach-Bad, 1980), pp. 72–88.

42 There is, clearly, a great need for an agreed descriptive system for medieval paper; cf. T.G. Tanselle, 'The Bibliographical Description of Paper', *SB*, 24 (1971), 27–67.

43 Seymour, 'The English Manuscripts of *Mandeville's Travels*', pp. 186–7.

45 *Die Wasserzeichenkartei Piccard im Hauptstaatsarchiv Stuttgart, Findbuch XIII: Lilie* (Stuttgart, 1983).

45 The best description of this aspect of scribal activity is still that by G.S. Ivy, 'The Bibliography of the Manuscript Book', in *The English Library before 1700*, ed. F. Wormald and C.E. Wright (London, 1958), pp. 32–65.

46 *Piers Plowman: The A Version*, ed. Kane, pp. 6–7.

47 Cf. (with reference to the detection of cancels), A. Stevenson, 'Chain-Indentations in Paper as Evidence', *SB*, 6 (1954), 181–95.

2 · DESIGN, DECORATION AND ILLUSTRATION

KATHLEEN L. SCOTT

IT SHOULD NOT BE REVOLUTIONARY to say that illustration and decoration were relatively common aspects of the design of late fourteenth- and fifteenth-century English manuscripts; yet the principle is either ignored or accepted reluctantly. This 'relative' frequency of decoration means that, from a count of an estimated 40,000 manuscripts and rolls[1] surviving from the late fourteenth to early sixteenth centuries, at least 1,000 of them were produced with illustrations. No count – even approximate – has ever been undertaken of the number of manuscripts decorated only with borders, even though this feature was intimately allied in the minds of medieval book producers and readers with textual divisions.[2] A conservative estimate would be a further 2,000 books with full borders as the main decorative feature. By this very general reckoning, then, at least one in forty books made in the later Middle Ages in England had illustrations or other pictures, and perhaps one in twenty had framing decorative work at one or more textual units. These proportions – even possibly understated – substantiate a claim for decoration as a significant and signifying element in the production of books of the late medieval period.

The frequency of these larger ornamental features – not to speak of the many types of smaller decorative items – was undoubtedly owing to the function performed by decoration as a quick flip-through method of locating a list of contents, the first text page, the chapters, book divisions, and other units of a text. This service to the reader was, however, couched in such a form – a pleasant growing of vines, flowers, birds, animals and people – that nothing less than delight was meant to be a concomitant effect of the function. If function had been the only reason for the existence of borders, then an unadorned band of red or blue along one margin would have served the same purpose; and pictures might have been entirely unnecessary.

But, as human beings have an urge to embellish, spaces were in fact set aside for illustrations, and marginal areas were filled with attractive motifs rather than plain bands; and it will be the purpose of this study to describe the changing aspect of pictorial and marginal spaces on the pages of later medieval books in England. I shall consider what types of pictorial spaces were used in this period; where they were located with respect to the text

31

area; and what sort of subject-matter was contained in them and, by implication, what was thought desirable as illustrative matter. Because decorative borders had little potential range of movement on the page, we need to inquire less into the location of the space that they occupied than into the generic types of decorative content and referencing between border design and textual division. Necessarily very concise, this survey will not deal with stylistic or iconographic problems, much less with the identification of artistic hands or particular shop production.[3] The survey will moreover not be able to include all aspects of the decorative hierarchy or other elements of page design sometimes ornamented, the initials, titles, line endings, ascenders and descenders, *nota bene* signs, catchwords and ruling;[4] nor can it mention the fundamental but, for this study, more tangential circumstances of book decoration: the potentially complex situation between craftsmen involved in production;[5] the materials used in book decoration; the influence of gild regulations (still largely unknown); or the interrelationship between the working span of a shop and its decorative designs and stylistic evolution.[6] The study will be limited, then, to a discussion of the two major decorative elements and textual divisors, pictures and borders, and to a review of the organisational principles and main themes of illustration and decoration that it seems possible to formulate on the basis of a substantial manuscript sample.

In order to bring some quantitative sense to the type of late medieval reading matter normally furnished with illustration, I have developed a working classification that groups, according to their subject matter, 845 illustrated texts from both manuscripts and rolls. The following fifteen classifications of texts are more refined in some cases (e.g. 'Gower' and 'Lydgate') than in others (e.g. 'Writings in the vernacular, including Chaucer, translations, etc.'); but except for two or three admittedly unwieldy categories, especially Nos. 2 and 5, the classifications are probably precise enough to give both the drift towards and even the firm reality of manuscript couplings of illustration and text. By 'drift', I mean that if even another five hundred illustrated texts were miraculously discovered, they would very likely follow the same pattern or proportion as below. The classification of these 845 texts[7] and the number in each category are as follows:

1.	Medical–astronomical–scientific, including calendars and almanacs[8]	136
2.	Texts in Latin, by known or anonymous authors[9]	114
3.	History, chronicles, genealogical chronicles[10]	104
4.	Books of Hours, manuals, prayerbooks	102
5.	Writings in the vernacular (English and French), including Chaucer, translations, etc.[11]	98
6.	Service books, including missals (41), breviaries (19), etc.[12]	69
7.	Statutes, indentures, ordinances, coronation orders	49

8.	Psalters	48
9.	John Gower[13]	29
10.	John Lydgate[14]	29
11.	Gildbooks, benefactor books, registers, cartularies	16
12.	Prayer and obituary rolls, including *Arma Christi*[15]	15
13.	Governance of Princes, including Thomas Hoccleve and Guido da Columna	15
14.	Saints' lives[16]	11
15.	Texts with heraldic materials[17]	10
		845

Perhaps surprisingly, the classification of 'medical–astronomical–scientific' works outnumbers all types of liturgical books, but *not* the sum of all kinds of books of private devotion (Nos. 4, 8, and 12); one might nevertheless have expected books of Hours alone to head a list of illustrated books. Although the medical category includes texts illustrated only by diagrammatic items, its predominance is still impressive. Another unexpected result is the quantity of historical-chronicle texts that were issued in the later period with pictures, and that these also outnumber books of Hours with pictures. The category of vernacular works and translations would be much larger if *all* texts in the vernacular had been combined into it, that is, if medical texts, manuals and prayer rolls in English, the works of Gower, Lydgate, and Hoccleve, and saints' lives had been included. While the vernacular category still remains very miscellaneous, larger groupings of ten or more vernacular texts were separated out in order to give sharper definition to conclusions about texts illustrated in the later period. Service books – with the exception of missals – proved a disappointing source of illustration. Statutes are a somewhat odd choice for pictorial work but proved a consistent source, if with predictable iconography. Gower and Lydgate ran neck and neck in this sample, and rather disconcertingly, ahead of the illustration of Chaucer's literary works[18] (counted at eight). Gild and benefactors' books are a category that would scarcely have appeared at all in a reckoning of earlier manuscripts; and they are undoubtedly indicative of secular pressure on various aspects of later medieval life. Prayer rolls could have been lumped together with books of Hours and prayerbooks but proved to be revealing in a classification by themselves. The 'Governance-of-Princes' type of text and the saints' lives became separate categories as the count proceeded; they were also among the unexpected revelations. Had manuscripts with only coats of arms as illustration been included – and there is no doubt but that these reproductions have an important relationship with the text (if one occurs) – heraldic texts would have ranked much higher numerically.

In sum, then, although texts with primarily functional pictures, e.g. of Zodiac and Blood-letting men, cautery points, foetal presentations, eclipses, medical instruments, urine samples, maps, and lines of genealogical descent,

1   Berkeley, California, University of California, MS 150, Heller Hours, c. 1470–80, 11v–12r:
full-page frontispiece with mixed English and foreign border; filigree band border on recto; both
borders in pink pen outline.

stand at the head of the list, many texts contained pictorial matter for equally
significant reasons: for emphatic division of the text, for a visual 'parallel
narrative',[19] for the purposes of private devotion (of praying, in some cases,
before an indulgenced image),[20] and for reasons frankly to do with grati-
fication, that is, for satisfaction of ownership or for delight in representation.
The emphatic marking of major textual sections with pictures could of course
be considered a functional use, yet pictures were certainly not the only means
by which texts could be made more readable; borders and large initials were
other efficient options. In order to focus more precisely on the nature of the
relationship between text and picture, we need to take a less than fashionable
approach and start at a rather elementary level – the actual physical place-
ment of illustrations with respect to the text. What amount of space and what
type of space did pictures occupy in late medieval English books; and where
were these spaces generally located?

The largest area potentially occupiable by an illustration on one side of a
folio would be its entire dimensions, or the full page. The term 'full-page'
miniature is, however, something of a misnomer in that the actual picture
space in later English manuscripts seldom occupied the entire page: the

picture took up, more accurately, about two-thirds of the page, the remainder being occupied with, usually, a frame, a border, and a blank marginal area (Ill. 1).[21] This type of pictorial arrangement completely displaced the text. As far as page design – the layout of picture space relative to text space – was concerned, full-page miniatures, like other pictorial formats, performed two main and not exclusive functions: introductory and empathic. As far as the *content* of the text was concerned, pictures might of course also serve other functions: interpretive, didactic, meditative or emphatic. As introduction to the book (and not necessarily always to a text), the full-page picture was usually placed on the verso of the leaf facing the first page of text (Ill. 1) or the table of contents, with the recto often left blank. This position was the most common arrangement in devotional, vernacular and other books with a *single* introductory picture, whether or not other texts were in the book and whether or not other picture-formats, such as historiated initials, were part of the whole book design. The full-page miniature used as frontispiece is found more frequently prefacing books of Hours and vernacular works than before any other type of text (Ill. 1).[22] Variant formats on the single-picture frontispiece were produced infrequently: a few manuscripts have introductory scenes on a double opening;[23] and at least one, which is illustrated throughout, has a sequence of three introductory full-page pictures: a coat of arms before the table of contents, a picture of the author before the prologue, and a representation of the Coronation of the Virgin before the first text page.[24]

A second important design use of the full-page miniature was in a grouping at the front of the main text, usually together with very short units of text. This format may have developed late in the fourteenth or early in the fifteenth century in order to accommodate the contemporary fashion for locating Memorials to saints before the little Hours of the Virgin. In finer books of Hours these prayers were equipped with an image of the saint – probably for use as an object of devotion – resulting in a cluster of full-page pictures at the front of the manuscript. To judge by survival, these clusters of pictures and prayers might comprise anything from three to forty-seven pictures.[25] This practice does not seem, however, to have persisted throughout the fifteenth century; in the second half of the period a book of Hours, such as that in Berkeley, University of California, MS 150, might contain prayers and pictures at the end of the book, after the Jerome Psalter.[26] By contrast with these devotional books, only a very few non-liturgical manuscripts – all of which bear the clear mark of patronal interference – have a group of pictures preceding the first text page (or list of contents); two of these were made under the direction of one patron, Thomas Chaundler, Chancellor of Oxford University.[27] Pictures were also occasionally placed in a cluster – as we do in modern publishing – within the text, especially in a manuscript composed of several texts copied by the same scribe. A fine example of this format,

2a New York, Pierpont Morgan Library, MS Glazier 9, Hours and

2b London, British Library, MS Egerton 1991, John Gower, *Confessio Amantis*, early 15th century, 'a-column' miniature

3a Oxford, Bodleian Library, MS Don.d. 85, Psalter, c. 1410–15, 58v: historiated-initial format with priests chanting ('Cantate Domino') and with illusionistic scrollwork beside; bar-frame border with acanthus clusters at corners, etc.

3b New York, Pierpont Morgan Library, M 893, Hours and Psalter, before 1446, 182v: half-page miniature of priests chanting and King David praying at right; bar-frame border with vine and leaf roundels and full spraywork.

in BL Add. MS 29301, has eight pages of drawings of herbs between two texts; and the drawings are not evidently related to either text.[28] Grouping leaves with pictures within the text may have been looked upon as a convenience in medical manuscripts.[29]

The final possible location for a full-page single illustration – aside from random insertion – was in the position facing a book division, chapter opening, or other chief section of the text. Once again, many surviving examples of this siting of pictures occur in books of Hours;[30] but almanacs and some medical manuscripts were also often produced with full- or near full-page pictures of Zodiac or Blood-letting Men in the text.[31] The full-page illustration of the Crucifixion, designed as the opening opposite the 'Te igitur' page of the missal, should also be remarked on as a consistent pictorial element in the layout of this type of liturgical book.[32] Vernacular books were, on the other hand, rarely produced with full-page pictures at divisions within the text; the copy of Nicholas Love's *Myrrour of the Blessed Lyf of Jesu Christ* in the National Library of Scotland is an outstanding exception to the normal practice.[33] Occasionally full-page illustrations were inserted in an existing text as a means of up-grading a book of good commercial quality to an even more affluent appearance;[34] this option was of course not open to most of the other picture formats, e.g. to half-page scenes or historiated initials. Full-page miniatures within a text or in an introductory position may have been considered as a balancing piece to the division, the ultimate functional and aesthetic emphasis (Ill. 1).

The half-page miniature is another inexact term; it is here employed to denote a picture space that lies full across the top or bottom of the justification (whether ruled for single or double columns) and that may range in height anywhere from one-third to three-quarters of the justification (Ills. 2a, 3b, 5a). This format seems, in a considerable number of manuscripts, to have been regarded as virtually the equal in decorative status to a full-page miniature. In particular, books of Hours of moderate to expensive quality were often laid out with a half-page miniature at the text divisions.[35] Whereas the half-page format had the advantage of achieving a balanced and compact page design for picture, text and border (Ills. 3b, 5a), it involved the disadvantage of forcing a planning decision from the outset and probably of adding to the production time: unlike full-page pictures, half-page scenes could not be made simultaneously with the scribal process. A few psalters[36] made use of this layout (Ill. 3b), as did a considerable number of vernacular and non-liturgical Latin texts. These two last types of text, whose picture cycles were usually briefer than those in Hours and psalters, employed the half-page format for the introductory scene and sometimes at successive major book divisions,[37] or, in books containing more than one text, at text divisions.[38] A few vernacular texts were, however, designed with an extensive cycle of half-page pictures throughout the text;[39] and a few employed half-page scenes at introductory and sometimes other divisions together with a different size or type of picture elsewhere in the text.[40] An arched or rounded top to a half- or full-page picture was used infrequently in English book illustration and mainly under foreign or patronal influence. Even within a single text, a rounded upper frame might not be used consistently: in PML M 893, for instance, nine of the twenty-two half-page scenes have a small rounded area at the top, not always serving a necessary function (e.g. 17r).

The version of the half-page miniature that occupied less than half or even less than one-third of the total written space on a page may be described as a 'column' picture or miniature (Ill. 2b). This format was planned for no more than the width of one column of text in a two-column format and normally, if not always, for less than one-half the height of the text column. This picture format seems to have been particularly used in large-sized manuscripts containing vernacular texts and especially in works of Gower and Lydgate, who were, as we have seen, the two most illustrated of contemporary writers.[41] With a two-column text format the rectangular column-miniature gave a sense of occasion without the expense of a full-page scene; and it eliminated the extra trouble of allowing for a half-page picture across two columns of text. In planning for a column-sized miniature the scribe could simply leave blank a previously decided number of lines at the head of any division to be illustrated; the picture space then simply followed the course of the copying and fitted into its natural pauses.[42] The column-miniatures could, like the full- and half-page picture, separate and formalise textual divisions with more authority than the historiated initial but with less difficulty in planning than the other two types of rectangular picture space.

Without resorting to a formal count, one would be tempted to state that the historiated initial – a picture located within the first letter of the first word of a text division – was the most commonplace picture format in fifteenth-century English manuscripts (Ills. 3a, 4b, 5b). It was used in nearly every circumstance: singly in a manuscript at the prologue or at the text opening; for an extensive sequence of illustrations; with every type of textual matter (liturgical, medical, vernacular, historical, legal and regulatory, collegiate, religious and theological);[43] and in the most and least costly types of book.[44] Where only one picture was to illustrate a book, it was most frequently an historiated initial; and with some texts, the historiated-initial format dominated the design of the copies produced. In fifteenth-century psalters, for instance, this lay-out was so prevalent that on one occasion when the artist was apparently commissioned to make half-page pictures in a psalter, he clearly struggled to fill out the extra space available (compare Ills. 3a and 4b).[45]

Because most English border decoration was joined structurally with the stems of the first letter of the text and because the historiated initial was ruled into the text space (e.g. Ill. 4b), any scene within the first letter is physically and aesthetically more intimately connected to the surrounding border and to

4b Cambridge, St John's College, MS H.1 (204), *Dialogus inter Militem et Clericum*, early 15th century, 1r: historiated initial with figures of *personae*, the soldier and the cleric; bar-frame border with vine roundels at corners and illusionistic designs in roundels beside initial.

4a London, British Library, Add. MS 29301, John Arderne, *Chirurgia* and *Fistula in Ano*, c. 1420–30, 3r: marginal pictures of a medical instrument and two flasks.

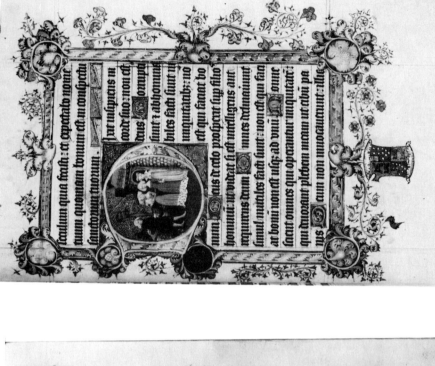

5a New York, Pierpont Morgan Library, M 893, Hours and Psalter, before 1446, 12r: half-page miniature; full trellis border with figures and with heads in roundels; dense spraywork in an 'understood' space outside.

5b London, British Library, Add. MS 42131, Hours and Psalter, c. 1420, 122r: historiated initial with life of David scene; full monochrome band border infilled with illusionistic scroll and acanthus work and with illusionistic designs in roundels.

the text space than is true of full- or half-page pictures; these stand more apart from the text (Ills. 1 and 2a). The historiated initial was thus less formal and created less of a full-stop for the reader: its normally smaller size may also have meant a less inhibiting effect on the movement of the eye down the page. With a larger pictorial space the reader could be expected to dwell longer (cf. Ills. 2b and 4b). It is unlikely that contemporary designers of books did not recognise a substantial difference in the effect on the reader between a framed scene surrounded by a border, perhaps on a separate page, and a diminutive scene within a letter.[46] Presumably, however, the ultimate decision for the type of illustrative format would, for reasons of cost, have remained with the patron, not with the book designer.

Some five other types of picture space or format were used in later medieval books and rolls; all arrangements are relatively rare, but a few have the interesting facet that they can be associated with a particular text. The roundel was the format – in smaller and larger sizes – used almost exclusively in roll and roll-codex genealogical chronicles,[47] whether written perpendicular to or down the length of the roll. The circular form may have been held appropriate as a shape to contain the human heads or busts which were frequently the subject-matter of these illustrations; and the roundels with heads may then in turn have influenced the format of narrative scenes in the chronicles, such as Adam and Eve or Noah's Ark, perhaps causing them also to be placed in roundels. The period in which the use of roundels with genealogical descents became fixed has not been precisely identified; but a late fourteenth-century English roll containing Peter of Poitiers' *Compendium Historiae in Genealogia Christi*[48] was laid out with a mixture of rectangular and round picture spaces used for the narrative scenes, suggesting that the circular format established itself somewhat later. There may also have been some association made between the circular shape of the roll and the roundel as pictorial space.

Copies of the *Speculum Humanae Salvationis* also had to have an individual solution for a design problem raised by the contents of the text. As the prototype work had been composed, so later manuscripts had to be designed to align textual and pictorial renderings of Old Testament archetypes with a New Testament type. In some English manuscripts[49] the relationship was set up at a double opening, with one rectangular picture, roughly one-quarter the size of the ruled space, positioned in the upper right-hand corner of the ruled space of both verso and recto; the type and archetype in text and picture were thus arranged to face each other, forcing a certain comprehension of events upon the reader. This format might be considered a variation of the small-miniature (see below), but the *Speculum* pictures were not a movable feast: unlike the small-picture format, they were fixed in an unvarying position. Another individual pictorial format was employed with a few texts written in roll form horizontally to the length of the roll: with the Rous Rolls and one copy of *Verses on the Kings of England* a single standing figure, unframed, was drawn atop a single column of the relevant text.[50]

Although cyclical illustration of stanzaic poetry was not particularly common, a method for integrating pictures within verse was developed for the design of at least one text, John Lydgate's *Lives of Saints Edmund and Fremund*; and this layout was then imitated in other later copies of the same poem. By using a page blocked into three seven-line stanzas for, roughly, a quarto-sized leaf (with two blank lines between each stanza), the designer could have either a stanza or an oblong picture inserted in the space, and, at special divisions or moments in the narrative, the picture could be doubled to the height of two stanzas plus four lines.[51] The rime-royal stanzas in Thomas Hoccleve's *De Regimine Principum* were, by contrast, consistently placed four to a page and issued without any – or with very few – miniatures.[52]

One of the more interesting kinds of picture space – because of its ostensibly spontaneous and unplanned nature – is the marginal scene, figure, or object (Ill. 4a). This type of representation, which stood completely apart from the text space and required no special ruling or planning except an adequate blank margin, was generally unframed: hence the lingering sense that marginal pictures were additions or a productional afterthought, even if contemporary. Once more it is possible to isolate connections between pictorial format and type of text; but with this format the range of textual matter involved is less precisely definable. One general type of text with which marginal figures or scenes might be used was the vernacular narrative. Unframed, single figures, whether standing, seated or mounted, may occur in the margins of texts composed of a series of narratives and may represent either the narrators of tales or the central figure in the narrative. The selection of pictorial subjects would in these cases seem to derive from a reading or an approach to the text (discussed further below) rather than from any necessity created by or related to the design of the page, except for one consideration: that a single standing figure would have been wasteful of material if ruled into the text space. A copy of the *Mirroure of the Worlde* (in Bodleian Library, MS Bodley 283) is an exceptional instance where single figures of the Apostles – and even these were seated – were situated within the justification, forcing the pen artist to fill side spaces with long scrolls.

Texts surviving with pictures in the marginal format are, as instances, the *Canterbury Tales*, *Piers Plowman*, and the *South English Legendary*.[53] Texts with excerpts from ancient philosophers would have been ideal for this handling, but in fact the standing figures in one group of manuscripts were placed unframed, within part of the text space, and only one copy of the *Turba Philosophorum* is known with free-standing figures in the margins.[54] Two manuscripts[55] of John Lydgate's works also attracted marginal scenes and figures; each of these has an extensive sequence of narrative scenes in the margins (also including one or more pictures ruled into the text space);

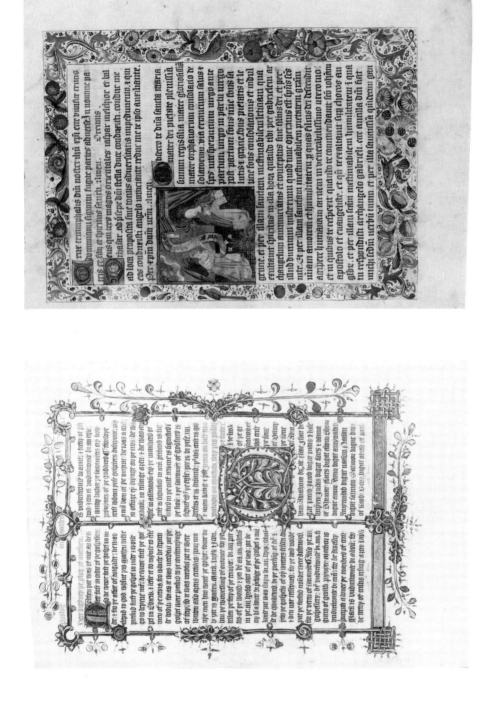

6a Oxford, Bodleian Library, MS Bodley 183, Wycliffite Bible, early 15th century, 1r: mixed bar frame and filigree band border with interlaces at lower corners.

6b Cambridge University Library, MS Kk.2.7, Psalter and Hours, c. 1480, 9r: small-miniature format, with full foreign-style border in a pink pen outline.

somewhat surprisingly, they were not produced in the same scribal or illuminating circumstances, and were not a copy of the same text. The deciding factor in the pictorial format of each was probably less the nature of the text than its length and the large number of pictures that would have had to be anticipated and prepared for within the text. Quite apart from the considerable effort involved in planning for as many as 69 or 157 pictures, as in these manuscripts, the added cost of material and labour might have made such a commission prohibitive for some patrons.

Medical and scientific treatises were another category of text sometimes designed with marginal pictures (Ill. 4a). Here a functional purpose of a different sort was served: by delineating next to the text a relatively obscure object or process that might not be comprehended by naming or verbal description alone, the author and subsequent producers of the text could hope to be understood – apart from the inherent dangers of recopying an unknown object. A vivid case in point is John Arderne's *Chirurgia* and *Fistula in Ano*, many copies of which illustrate everything from clyster-pipes to points of incision.[56] Treatises with heraldic information are another type of text having marginal representations of a functional nature. Here is another circumstance in which it was desirable to set a coloured diagram next to the text and impractical to rule space for each coat of arms or even for a row of arms within the justification.[57]

One last, seldom-found format for pictures is a small rectangular space, less than a column in width, whose location and size corresponds perhaps most closely to the historiated initial (Ill. 6b). In a manuscript where no border had been planned for the pages with miniatures or where a foreign-style border had replaced the conventional English type, it may have been more convenient or appropriate to use a framed scene rather than the first initial letter. Other influences, such as provincial origin or minor trends in fashion in the second half of the century, may also prove to account for the use of this picture format. This small format is not evidently associated with any particular type of text.[58]

In contrast to the shape and location of late fourteenth- and fifteenth-century English pictures, the thematic matter of English illustration might at first appear to be an intractable subject. Nonetheless, some formulations can be made as a starting point for discussion about the content of pictures: not the relationship of a particular picture to a particular text but about the type of pictorial themes, abstracted from individual representations, that were the implicit or explicit subjects of miniatures. The pictorial materials of English book illustration are divisible, with some overlapping between them, into the following types: narrative, static, and utilitarian. Both narrative and stati-cally depicted scenes or figures could on one level also be considered utili-tarian, that is, as having introductory or emphatic functions with regard to page design and text divisions, whereas many utilitarian pictures, such as those of urine bottles or coats of arms, are in no way narrative, nor even 'static', in the sense defined below. The themes or subjects (i.e. the event or single figure) chosen for pictorial representation and the form in which they were represented (i.e. active or static) may moreover indicate a late medieval mind-set or approach to a given text,[59] particularly if a choice for the illustration of a given text could have been made between a narrative scene and a static figure.

By narrative subject-matter, I mean scenes that depict an event or a moment in the action of a story, life, chronicle, service or account. Narrative would seem to be the very stuff that book illustration is made of,[60] but in fact relatively few manuscripts containing tales or chronicles are actually illustrated by a corresponding pictorial account of the narrative events. The works illustrated by narrative scenes in the later period can almost be encompassed by the following list (and several of these survive in only one copy): lives or miracles of the Virgin;[61] *Livres du Graunt Caam* and *Alexander*, in same MS;[62] *Gawain*, *Pearl*, and related alliterative texts, in same MS;[63] Nicholas Love, *Myrrour of the Blessed Lyf of Jesu Christ* (and the closely related *Privity of the Passion*);[64] John Gower's *Confessio Amantis* (Ill. 2b);[65] *Romance of the Three Kings' Sons*;[66] Stephen Scrope's translation of the *Épître d'Othéa*;[67] Thomas Chaundler's *Liber Apologeticus*;[68] lives of Edward the Confessor;[69] John Mandeville, *Travels*;[70] *The Pageants of Richard Beauchamp, Earl of Warwick*, in one MS;[71] Guillaume de Deguileville's *Pilgrimages*, in translation;[72] and, above all, the works of John Lydgate, whose manuscripts received more extensive narrative illustration than any other author of the later period in England.[73] It is however remarkable that liturgical and devotional texts with no narrative content were produced with pictorial narratives more often than any type of true narrative: these, of course, were: (1) books of Hours, with scenes from the life or passion of Christ integrated into and identified with the eight services of the liturgical day – in which simple diurnal time sustained the historico-religious events of Christ's life (e.g. figs. 2a, 5a); (2) the missal, with an illustrative sequence compiled from a mixture of narrative subjects from the Old Testament, the life of Christ, the life of the Virgin, and the performance of the ritual, together with non-narrative representations of saints;[74] and (3) psalters, with a sequence of narrative pictures arising from the first words of a text division (Ill. 3a),[75] or based on events from the life of King David that are related not in the psalms but elsewhere in the Bible (Ill. 5b). On the other hand, texts such as the *Canterbury Tales* and the *Brut* chronicles, where one might expect to see narrative illustration, were either not illustrated or were illustrated with non-narrative scenes;[76] and texts such as the bible, apocalypses, and romances, which in previous centuries had received much narrative illustration, were either not illustrated or not produced at all in the later period.[77] One cannot argue that long narrative picture cycles were not supported by fifteenth-century English patronage; it is rather that the interest of patronage had shifted to books for private devotion and related teachings (e.g. the *Pilgrimages*), to local or contemporary authors (Gower and Lydgate), and to the life of Christ (as in books of Hours and prose treatises); and that later patronage otherwise sponsored only sporadic or one-off items with extensive narrative illustration.

The second term 'static', used above to denote a type of pictorial content in English illustration, is less self-explanatory than the term 'narrative'. This designation includes the numerous late medieval pictures of a single human figure, whether standing, seated[78] or mounted, as a torso or head, including authors, narrators, *personae* (Ill. 4b), scribes, saints, kings, philosophers, donors, personifications, planetary figures and historical personages. This kind of pictoral theme – or, actually, approach to the text – occurs in a wide range of works: in secular narrative texts, in books of Hours (with the Memorials to saints), in books of statutes, in verse or prose chronicles, in astrological treatises, in monastic registers of donors, in selections of philosophical works, in genealogical chronicles, and in any text where the author was known or thought to be known.[79] Some static figures had, relative to the textual matter, an iconic function, e.g. the Virgin and Child or Man of Sorrows;[80] others were more or less meant to be resemblances, e.g. pictures of Ranulf Higden or Thomas Netter of Walden;[81] others served as guides through a complex genealogical descent;[82] others, however finely wrought, were a hook on which to hang emblems and attributes;[83] and yet others, e.g. pictures of philosophers and Chaucer's pilgrims,[84] fulfilled equally notational and pleasurable functions. All have in common that they do not depict an event. This frequent selection for representation of an author, narrator or main character over an event from a story or life is of singular importance for an understanding of the late medieval approach to narrative materials. This type of pictorial choice indicates an attitude in which the author or narrator, etc., rather than the fictional or historical events of the narrative, was viewed as the authority or embodiment of truth, even though the narrative events might depict Christian truth in action. It was a state of mind which perceived the speaker as more significant than the marvels of which he spoke. In consequence, if a non-liturgical manuscript was to be illustrated with only one picture,[85] it was very often a representation of the author[86] or main actor; and at the head of a sequence of narrative pictures, the preferred choice was the author or the author in a presentation scene, even if chronologically after the fact. The author, narrator or main character – not the entertainment – was the 'place' in the text, to paraphrase Kolve,[87] that 'exerted the greatest pressure'. Applied to non-narrative works, such as those of Augustine and Jerome,[88] such an attitude or pictorial selection seems of course quite reasonable; but, otherwise, shop practice, individual artistic personalities, transfer of models, content of text – all of this was secondary to the almost puritanical mind-set that favoured the austerity and authority of the teller over the tale.

Relatively little of the pictorial content of later English book illustration was, moreover, symbolic or allegorical in nature. We have a few sequences of the vices, some Apocalypse illustrations in copies of Nicholas de Lyra, a number of representations of Dame Fortune, one copy of *Piers Plowman* illustrated with personifications, mythographic illustrations in astrological treatises, a few marginal owls, peacocks, and pigs, and, in more abundance, symbols of the Passion, often with a picture of the wounds of Christ. The visually symbolic language that we have been urged to learn in order to give us access to Chaucer's imagery will not as a rule be found in fifteenth-century English illustration. Other areas of the visual arts and crafts, such as corbels, misericords, tiles and stained glass, may provide a more rewarding source of this kind of image.

The third thematic type in late medieval pictures is the illustration entered in books for purely functional or utilitarian reasons: these pictures are usually of objects (Ill. 4a) or diagrams but can be of animals, plants or even human figures. Medical books and scientific treatises, with their depictions of anatomical figures, parts of the body, foetal positions, herbs, diseases, instruments, equipment and eclipses, are a virtual cornucopia of such illustration; and even pictures containing human figures acting out a sequence of events, such as clystering or blood-letting, are essentially demonstrations of a medical process and may be looked upon as utilitarian rather than narrative.[89] Other texts of a different nature were also produced with utilitarian illustration, some regularly: processionals with diagrammatic stages of the mass;[90] the *Polychronicon* with two versions of Noah's Ark;[91] chronicles with maps, pictures of cities, temples, etc.;[92] books of hunting, with identifications of species;[93] the single fifteenth-century copy of *Liber de Bestiis*;[94] and at least one illustrated copy of Mandeville's *Travels* that depends heavily on functional pictures.[95] Utilitarian scenes, moreover, occur frequently with a cycle of narrative pictures; in Bodley 264, the famous English sequence of Marco Polo's *Travels*, scenes of cities and peoples visited by Polo are interspersed regularly with narrative scenes of his adventures.[96]

The next aspect of decoration to be discussed in this study is borderwork made of gold and pigments – much more common in the design of late medieval English books than illustration but more 'invisible' to the modern user of manuscripts. An enormous number of English books were produced with full or partial illuminated borders and yet virtually no scholarly work has been undertaken concerning either their design or their relationship with each other.[97] The second of these objectives is patently impossible in this study – and indeed in any single study – but one can at least begin on the first task by differentiating the more important kinds of full border design and their uses.

The bar-frame border (Ills. 3a, 3b, 4b) was painted and gilded on the pages of more fifteenth-century English manuscripts than any other design of full border. It was used at both introductory and subsidiary textual divisions. This 'everyman's' design can be identified by the following six elements, usually present:

(1) a basic frame of two bars side by side, one usually in gold, the other alternating in rose and blue;

(2) heavy decorative emphasis at the four corners of the frame, and usually at two and sometimes three mid-points on the bars, the emphasis being expressed as interlaces (fig. 6a bottom), acanthus clusters (Ill. 3a), or roundels of vines and leaves infilled with leaves (often trifoliate) (Ill. 4b); aroid flowers (Ill. 3b); monochrome designs (Ills. 4b top; 5b), coats of arms, or historiations (i.e. faces, figures: Ill. 5a, and rarely scenes); with the mid-points used as the starting place for spraywork (Ills. 4b, 5b);

(3) similar decorative emphasis next to the large introductory initial (Ill. 4b);

(4) further but attenuated designs halfway between the corners and the mid-points (Ill. 4b);

(5) sometimes another subdivision of two or three sides of the bar frame into eights, as it were, by minor motifs, such as single leaves, vine stubs, or pen squiggles (Ill. 6a), and

(6) the initial side of the bar frame[98] showing a staggered design (relative to the opposite vertical frame) and less decoration (Ills. 3a, 4b).

In the late fourteenth century the bar-frame border was sparse and self-contained, with a design that focussed on the bars, the corners and the initial, with only minor invasion of the blank marginal areas. There was some experimentation with semi-circular breaks in the straight bar frame[99] and with one side, usually on the right, made of vines developed from the top and bottom bars;[100] neither of these designs was widely used. Early in the century, c. 1410, the approach to the bar-frame design began to change: instead of being a modestly decorated enclosure for the text, the bar-frame and its appendages came to fill more and more of the available marginal or empty area around the text (Ills. 3a, 4b). Emphasis began to shift to decorative elements and motifs attached to the *outside* of the frame – and at this point sprays came into their own (Ill. 3b). Sprays consist of straight or curling feathering, that is, pen lines and green lobes, from which gold motifs and coloured leaves or flowers appear to grow (e.g. Ills. 4a, 5b). This type of augmentation of the basic bar frame was put to use extensively throughout the century, often reducing the bar frame to a barely visible support for the feathering (Ill. 3b).[101] A second, less common development saw decoration at the frame corners and centrepoints become massive – with one bizarre pseudo-flower developing into another – leaving a much smaller space for spraywork between them (Ill. 2a).[102] In the third and fourth quarters of the century, and perhaps under continental influence, the previously 'free' sprays were enclosed in a pen frame, often drawn in pink; this rectangular space for sprays was sometimes used with a bar frame, and sometimes not (Ill. 6b).[103]

From the earliest use of sprays there had, however, been an 'understood' border space, that was sometimes delineated by ruling as part of the preparation of the leaves but that was afterwards usually erased when the border was finished (Ill. 3b). Later in the century, the pink pen outline or frame merely made the thought explicit. Only very late on – and again under strong foreign influence – did the bar frame disappear completely (Ill. 6b)[104] or leave only vestigial fossil traces.[105]

The next two significant types of English border design were usually placed in an introductory position in later English books; and through the presence of their design they almost certainly alerted the medieval reader to the fact that he had arrived at the first text page.[106] Occasionally, in a more lavish manuscript (with or without pictures), these borders were also entered as visual signs at other textual divisions. The first of these designs, the trellis border, was formed by separating the two bar frames to form a relatively broad area that was then filled with vine and leaf or flower work. The vine-work might be contained within the bars,[107] or loop back and forth between the bars, sometimes forming roundels that in turn enclosed leaves, flowers and, more seldom, historiations (Ill. 5a).[108] Probably by analogy with the bar frame, the trelliswork border sometimes retained decorative emphasis at corners and mid-points, and, less often, at quarter-points; occasionally, the bars were completely displaced by the intertwining leaves and vines (Ill. 5a).[109] Trellis borders were employed with every kind of text,[110] and variations on the trellis theme – achieved through colouring and composition – were as numerous as they are attractive.

The other border type used in an introductory position and elsewhere, possibly more frequently than the trellis, was the band border. This design was based either on an expansion of the bar frame to create a long strip or panel suitable for decoration (Ill. 5b) or by the addition of a strip along the outside of the bar frame. Most commonly the space was rendered in a monochrome pink, blue, orange or green with scrollwork or elongated acanthus leaves twisted illusionistically around an imaginary centre (Ill. 5b).[111] Another kind of band border was developed from strips of coloured ground – usually dark rose or dark blue – superimposed with gold filigree-work or white designs (Ills. 1, 6a).[112] Filigree band borders were produced mainly in the early fifteenth century, a survival from a fourteenth-century fashion of border decoration, whereas monochrome bands were used, after hesitation in the first decade, throughout most of the century.[113] The first text page was signalled not only by the (possible) use of one of these three types of border designs but also often, especially later in the century, by the appearance of a 'master' artist, whose borderwork occurred only on the first page or in the first quire, with other borders being entered by an associate hand.[114]

These four English border types inevitably became muddled, and a final, catch-all term is appropriate: the 'mixed' border which is a combination usually of the bar frame with either the trellis, monochrome or filigree band (Ill. 6a), but which may be made up of as many as three of these designs.[115] The mixed designs, especially the slender bar frame with the broader panels, were not always successfully balanced, yet, while still creating emphasis at important text divisions, they may have been somewhat less expensive for the patron.

This swift survey of border designs will take one almost to the end of manuscript production with decoration in the English Gothic style. In the very last period, from about 1490 to 1540, English borders – when they were used at all – were based on the bar frame and not as a rule on the other kinds. The bar frame survived, where the trellis and band borders[116] virtually disappeared, probably because the bar design was more adaptable to other influences: by two simple methods, either by omitting English motifs and adding others (Ill. 2a) or by omitting the entire English spray (Ill. 1, left), a border artist could insert various kinds of foreign motifs – animals, grotesques or strewn branches of flowers – and give an up-to-the-minute look to his old-fashioned border design.[117] Some borders in the late English manuscripts took the fashion even further and substituted entire foreign borders for the conventional insular work (Ill. 6b).[118]

From a conceptual point of view, the English framing border – in its various manifestations – was more than adequate for the functions that it had to perform: to contain and decorate the text; to support the introductory initial; to form, when necessary, a satisfying adjunct to a half-page picture; to act as a receptacle for pictorial comment or ownership devices in the roundels at its corners and mid-points; to remain attractive even in its simpler forms, which were especially useful for large-format manuscripts;[119] or to sustain an extremely ornate expansion either of itself or of motifs developed from it. The deliberate differentiation of framing borders was probably a common device and more apparent to contemporary readers than to modern eyes. One may point to the differencing by border type in an early fifteenth-century illustrated Missal[120] where a varied border design was drawn at each main division; or to a Psalter[121] of the second quarter of the century, in which nearly every section containing sprays was ornamented with different leaves or pseudo-flowers: a motif might be re-used on another page but seldom on the same page. Whereas the former type of differencing would have promoted more immediate referencing to the text, the latter was probably worked in as a visual consideration to the reader.

The relationship of the conventional English bar-frame border to the lines of text was on the whole two-dimensional. The border framed the text in the same two planes as the script was written and usually made no pretence of doing anything else. But certain border designs, especially the bar frame and monochrome band, contained 'black holes' or small areas that became sudden entries into a third dimension of space, just as the historiated initial was a pictorial entry sunken in the text space. These three-dimensional areas on the frame happened mainly within corner or initial roundels (Ill. 5a), within monochrome bands (Ill. 5b), and sometimes at scrollwork twisted around the bar frame (Ill. 3a). For English illuminators of the late fourteenth and fifteenth centuries, preliminary skirmishes with perspective, modelling, and illusionistic handling of pigment may have taken place in these roundels (and in small initials). The earliest roundels of this kind apparently were made in the late fourteenth-century Carmelite Missal, whose decorators used two types of this work: modelled human heads and monochrome leaves and scrollwork in initial stems.[122] These three-dimensional insets were afterwards used in border designs by various English artists and shops throughout the century, largely without further exploration of the possibilities. From a spatial point of view, the illusionistic cameo – with a frame as the starting plane – went back into the depth behind the page, away from the reader; by contrast, the strewn borders used by later continental-influenced illuminators contained objects that seemed to lie on top of the page surface, and that were spatially on the reader's side of the page. Borders as a whole were however not treated in an illusionistic manner (the 3-D elements or areas were held by two-dimensional frames: see Ill. 5b), nor was a coherent programme of illusionistic work developed relative to the text. But the fact that an initial infilled with illusionistic motifs or with illusionistic letter stems (Ills. 2a, 3b, 5a–b) ranked higher in the decorative hierarchy than a gold letter with a foliate or filigree infilling may perhaps be explained by its three-dimensional content: a letter with this type of shading may have been more valued than the plain gold letter on a parti-coloured ground.

Whether or not one believes that the fourteenth-century written and decorated page had 'begun to disintegrate' and was no longer an 'artistic unit',[123] English page design had reconstituted itself by the turn of the century, and its parts again fitted together more rationally perhaps than in the previous century. In fifteenth-century border design the intimate connection of initial and border elements, the development of parts of the border from each other, the reinforced strength of borders at corners, the integration of the half-page picture and the historiated initial with the border, and the *lack*, as a rule, of historiations in the border, with the picture space remaining the site of illustration – all of these aspects of typical English design led to a cohesiveness, balance and unity of pattern, and offered the reader a satisfying, non-distracting frame for a textual division. In terms of fifteenth-century book aesthetics, some fourteenth-century pages were wild excesses – and perhaps elicited a reaction in the next century; the later English borders seem to have assumed a conscious air of decorum. They became completely serviceable, if less fun.

This widely ranging survey of the number, size, location and decorative value of English illustration and borderwork has not failed if it brings some coherence to the apparently amorphous survival of later illustrated and illuminated English manuscripts. We have seen that the number of manuscripts ornamented with either pictures or borders was probably high relative to the total surviving; that four precisely defined types of texts – medical, historical, vernacular and private devotional – were the books most frequently illustrated; and that borders were even more widely used for structural emphasis in page design than pictures. We have reviewed the most common types of formats used for illustrations, and their positions on the page and within the book as a whole; we have seen certain formats preferred together with certain texts; we have proposed a grouping for the thematic content of later English illustration with a view to understanding late medieval approaches to text illustration; and finally we have tried to differentiate types of full-border designs and their use within a text. This study represents a certain state of knowledge and experience: the descriptions and proposals can – and should – be more finely worked for an even more enlightened appreciation of contemporary uses of and attitudes towards decoration and page design.

NOTES

1 An estimate made by Dr A.I. Doyle and Professor M.B. Parkes at the York Manuscripts Conference in 1983.

2 See S. Hindman and J.D. Farquhar, *Pen to Press: Illustrated Manuscripts and Printed Books in the First Century of Printing* (University of Maryland and The Johns Hopkins University, Exhibition, 1977), pp. 72–75. The use of colours and decorated initials as apparatus was discussed in the important article by Parkes, '*Ordinatio* and *Compilatio*'. See also Doyle and Parkes, p. 186.

3 As in Scott, 'A Mid-Fifteenth-Century English Illuminating Shop', and 'Lydgate's Lives'.

4 For ruling as decoration, see Hindman and Farquhar, *Pen to Press*, p. 53.

5 Doyle and Parkes, pp. 167, 194–5, 192, 196–7, 199–200; Scott, *Mirroure of the Worlde*, pp. 50, 53–4, 56–8.

6 This sort of information will be an interesting by-product of C.P. Christianson's research on the book-trade in London; see his preliminary study 'A Century of the Manuscript-Book Trade in London', *Medievalia et Humanistica*, ns, 12 (1984), 143–65, e.g. pp. 148–9, and pp. 87–108 below.

7 The count does not include all illustrated English books of the later period. Manuscripts not included in this count but which were included in the 'at least 1,000' mentioned in the text are the following: (1) those manuscripts whose representational matter was in flourished or calligraphic initials (e.g. profile faces), in catchwords, or as grotesques in borders (although of art historical interest and an aspect of decoration, they are rarely relevant to the textual matter); and (2) manuscripts with added drawings, whether marginal or full-page, not made to illustrate the original text. If only one text in a composite volume was illustrated,

only that text was included in the count (e.g. Hatfield House CP 308, prayers, psalter, with only the prayers illustrated). If a manuscript contained two important texts with illustrations, such as a book of Hours and a psalter, each text was counted separately in its own classification (e.g. BL Add. MS 42131, Bedford Hours and Psalter; Oxford, University College, MS 85, with an Alain Chartier translation and a *Secret of Secrets*). Fragments with pictures (not identified as separated from a known surviving manuscript) were counted as an independent text. No attempt was made for the purpose of this count to undertake a comprehensive search of all British library collections, or of sale catalogues. Because of the series by Otto Pächt, Jonathan Alexander and Elźbieta Temple, the Bodleian Library and Oxford college libraries are reasonably completely represented in the count; and the author has covered most Cambridge libraries and many other smaller collections in England and the United States. The existence of pictures in those manuscripts not seen by the author (e.g. Australia, New Zealand, South Africa) has been verified through catalogue descriptions or photography, or else not counted. This sample of illustrated texts is sufficiently large to indicate the major trends both numerically and by subject-matter. It will of course be aggravating to the reader not to know by shelfmark which manuscripts have been included in the count; such a listing may come in due course in the form of an independent monograph or of an appendix to my forthcoming *A Survey of Manuscripts Illuminated in the British Isles*, ed. J.J.G. Alexander, VI: *Later Gothic Manuscripts*. John Harthan (*An Introduction to Illuminated Manuscripts* (Victoria and Albert Museum, 1983), pp. 11–13) divides 'illuminated' books into two basic groups, religious and secular.

8 Many of these illustrations are diagrammatic in nature, e.g. palms of the human hand (e.g. Edinburgh, Royal Observatory, MS Cr.1.2, 107v–108r), urine bottles (e.g. Durham, University Library, MS Cosin. v.III.10, 9r–13v), or eclipses (e.g. San Marino, Huntington Library, HM 39465, 18r–19r), or are of equipment (as in many copies of John Arderne and in Chaucer's *Treatise on the Astrolabe*, e.g. Cambridge, Trinity College, MS R.15.18, 5r–79r). The most common figural representations in this group are the Zodiac Man and Blood-letting Man. Texts of the *Secreta Secretorum* were included here with pictures of philosophers, as were pictures of physicians. A recent survey of medical illustration, based on manuscripts mainly in the British Library and Wellcome Institute for the History of Medicine, is by P.M. Jones, *Medieval Medical Miniatures* (London, 1984), with a useful select bibliography. See also L. MacKinney, *Medical Illustrations in Medieval Manuscripts*, Publications of the Wellcome Historical Medical Library, NS, 5 (1965), which does however not indicate the place of origin of the illustrated manuscript.

9 This category, the least helpful of any, includes anonymous texts such as the *Speculum Humanae Salvationis*, the *Biblia Pauperum*, and *Pupilla Oculi*, and such miscellaneous authors as Augustine, Duns Scotus, Jerome, Stephen Langton, Nicholas de Lyra, Bartholomaeus Anglicus, Nicholas Upton, Petrus Carmelianus and Johannes de Giglis.

10 This classification includes such texts as Ranulf Higden's *Polychronicon*, the *Scala Mundi*, Peter of Poitiers' *Compendium Historiale*, as well as the many surviving genealogical chronicles in roll or roll-codex form, many of which are listed in A. de la Mare, compiler, *Catalogue of the Collection of Medieval Manuscripts bequeathed to the*

Bodleian Library, Oxford, by James P.R. Lyell (Oxford, 1971), No. 33, 80–5. See also A. Allan, 'Yorkist Propaganda: Pedigree, Prophecy and the "British History" in the Reign of Edward IV', in *Patronage, Pedigree and Power in Later Medieval England*, ed. C. Ross (Gloucester, 1979), pp. 171–92, with many manuscripts noted but without reference to their illustration. Maps were counted here as an item of illustration.

11 This category includes Chaucer, William Langland, Nicholas Love, Stephen Scrope, John Mandeville, John Mirk, Alain Chartier, Christine de Pizan, Guillaume de Deguileville (but not Lydgate's translation), and Vegetius, as well as such texts as the *Cursor Mundi, Prick of Conscience, Master of Game, Romance of the Three Kings' Sons*, and *Arma Christi* texts not in roll form. Only the English works of writers such as Richard Rolle and John Capgrave were included here.

12 Also including pontificals (3), gospel books (3), antiphonaries (2), lectionaries (1), epistle books (1), graduals (1), processionals (1), choirbooks (1). Missals were a much favoured object of illustration in the late fourteenth and early fifteenth centuries in England.

13 See J.J.G. Griffiths, K. Harris, and D. Pearsall, *Catalogue of Gower MSS* (forthcoming), for a complete list of illustrated manuscripts of the *Confessio Amantis*; and for the *Vox Clamantis*, G.C. Macaulay, ed., *The Complete Works of John Gower*, IV (Oxford, 1902), pp. lix–lxx.

14 For groupings of illustrated Lydgate manuscripts, see Doyle and Parkes, p. 201 and nn. 100, 103; Scott, 'Lydgate's Lives', and Lawton, 'The Illustration of Late Medieval Secular Texts'.

15 R.H. Robbins, 'The "Arma Christi" Rolls', *MLR*, 34 (1939), 415–21, with interesting discussion of the use of these pictures; R. Berliner, *'Arma Christi'*, *Münchener Jahrbuch der bildenen Kunst*, 3 Folge, 6 (1955) 35–152; C. Bühler, 'Prayers and Charms in Certain Middle English Scrolls', *Speculum*, 39 (1964), 270–8, with earlier bibliography but little mention of illustration; J. Krochalis, 'God and Mammon: Prayers and Rents in Princeton MS. 126', *The Princeton University Library Chronicle*, 44 (1983), 209–21, the first in her investigations of late medieval literary rolls; R. Dennis, *The Heraldic Imagination* (New York, 1975), pp. 96–8, with mention of the *Arma Christi* in heraldic rolls.

16 These texts include both well-known manuscripts, such as the *South English Legendary* in Bodleian Library, MS Tanner 17, and lesser-known lives of individual saints, such as Edward the Confessor and Katherine (as in Bodleian Library, MS Laud misc. 501; and Cambridge, Gonville and Caius College, MS 196).

17 This does not include heraldic texts illustrated solely with coats of arms rather than with representational figures or scenes. A study of these might begin with A.R. Wagner, *A Catalogue of English Mediaeval Rolls of Arms, Aspilogia I* (Oxford, 1950); R. Dennis, *The Heraldic Imagination*; and R. Marks and A. Payne, eds., *British Heraldry from its Origins to c. 1800* (London, 1978).

18 The *Treatise on the Astrolabe* was listed under the 'Medical–astrological–scientific' grouping.

19 A phrase used by Lawton, 'Illustration of Late Medieval Secular Texts', p. 50.

20 See S. Ringbom, *Icon to Narrative: The Rise of the Dramatic Close-up in Fifteenth-century Devotional Painting*, Acta Academiae Aboensis, Series A (1965, 2nd edn, 1983), pp. 23–30. For illustrations with both structural and devotional purposes in a Middle English poem on the Litany (in Cambridge, Fitzwilliam Museum, MS

14–1950, Beauchamp Hours), see D. Gray, 'A Middle English Illustrated Poem', *Medieval Studies for J.A.W. Bennett Aetatis Suae LXX* (Oxford, 1981), pp. 185–205, esp. pp. 188–9.

21 There are not many exceptions to this type of arrangement; one is in New York, PML M 775, which has four miniatures worked out to the edge of the page and even more bizarrely a three-quarter picture painted to the edge, yet with five lines of justified text above it.

22 Examples of devotional books with a full-page frontispiece are: Dublin, Trinity College, MS B.3.3., Psalter, 1v (damaged); the Saxby Hours and Psalter, 7v (Sotheby's, *Catalogue of Western Manuscripts and Miniatures*, 13 July 1977, lot 81); New York, PML, MS Glazier 9, 11v; Oxford, Keble College, MS 14, 7v; BL MS Arundel 203, 8v; and Liverpool Cathedral Library, MS 6, 5v, all books of Hours; see also Ill. 1. Examples of vernacular manuscripts with a frontispiece, whether added or not, are Bodleian Library, MS Bodley 263, Lydgate, *Fall of Princes*, page 7; Bodl. MS Laud misc. 658, *Three Kings of Cologne*, 1v; Bodl. MS Fairfax 16, miscellany, 14v; BL MS Harley 2278, Lydgate, *Lives of SS. Edmund and Fremund*, 1v; BL MS Harley 4826, 1r, added to texts by Lydgate and Hoccleve; BL MS Harley 629, Lydgate, *Life of Our Lady*, 1v; New York, PML, M 775, chivalric miscellany, 2v; Cambridge, Corpus Christi College, MS 61, Chaucer, *Troilus and Criseyde*, Iv; Oxford, Queen's College, MS 357, Pilgrim's Narration, 8v; and BL MS Royal 17.B.XLIII, St Patrick's Purgatory, 132v (added). (See also n. 32.) The following are examples of non-vernacular and non-devotional books with frontispieces: CUL MS Gg.6.5., *Liber de bestiis*, 2v; BL MS Sloane 2002, John Arderne, 24v; BL MS Cotton Faustina B.VII, 72v, and Bodleian Library, MS Lyell 22, 6v: copies of the Register of the Honour of Richmond, and BL MS Stowe 594, Bruges' Garter Book, 5v; Edinburgh, University Library, MS 169, medical texts; and Paris, BN MS lat. 6276, Placentius, *De optimo fato*, 1r. I have not listed any full-page depictions of coats of arms, but I should say that I consider them, if not precisely illustrative of content or wording of a text, to be illustrative of the nature of a given copy and decidedly an introduction to it. Whether or not a full-page picture was originally with or added to a text is in the context of this essay irrelevant in that the addition was conceived *at some point* in the fifteenth century to be a suitable part of the book design.

23 E.g. BL MS Cotton Faustina B.VI, *Desert of Religion*, 1v–2r; Add. MS 37049, religious miscellany, 1v–2r. The opening scenes in Bodleian Library, MS Douce 18, 10v–11r, a small psalter, belong with this group, even though 11r was made with eight lines of text below the picture.

24 In Edinburgh, NLS, Advocates' MS 18.1.7, Nicholas Love, *Mirror of the Blessed Life of Christ*, respectively, 5v, 8v and 12v. The famous MS Bodley 264 has a sequence of two (1v, 2v) frontispieces separated from their relevant text of c. 1400–5 by 200 folios of an earlier Flemish copy of the *Romance of Alexander*.

25 See York, Minster Library, MS Add. 2, with 47 pictures at the front; Boulogne-sur-Mer, Bibliothèque Municipale, MS 93, with 23; Brussels, Bibliothèque Royale, MS IV.1095, with 21; Rennes, Bibliothèque Municipale, MS 22 and its detached part in BL MS Royal 2.A.XVIII, with 16; BL Add. MS 65100 (formerly Upholland College, MS 42), with 15; Hours of the Duchess of Clarence (whereabouts unknown), with 8; Cambridge, Fitzwilliam Museum, MS 3–1979 and

NLW, MS 17520, both with 7; and Cambridge, Trinity College, MS B.11.7, with 3. Oxford, Bodleian Library, MS Lat. Liturg. f.2 has a group of six full-page miniatures at the front and five Memorials with pictures at the end as part of additional material to a Franco-Flemish core text.

26 Janet Backhouse notes that in 'early English books [of Hours] the Memorials to saints sometimes followed after Lauds' (*Books of Hours* (British Library Publications, 1985), p. 73).

27 Oxford, New College, MS 288 and Cambridge, Trinity College, MS R.14.5. Another example is Bodleian Library, MS Bodley 546, *Master of Game*, with a full-page coat of arms followed by five full-page illustrations relating to the text.

28 The contents of BL Add. MS 29301 are mentioned on p. 45 above. An earlier version of these drawings and texts is in BL MS Sloane 335; I am indebted to Peter Murray Jones for my knowledge of this copy. A group of twelve pages of coloured drawings of the life of Edward the Confessor also stands without text at the end of a late fourteenth-century Apocalypse (Cambridge, Trinity College, MS B.10.2, 39r–44v; see Scott, *Survey*, forthcoming).

29 See Bodleian Library, MS Laud Misc. 724, 94r–97v; BL MS Sloane 6, 175r–177v, with text; and London, Wellcome Historical Medical Library, MS 290, 49v–53v.

30 E.g. Berkeley, California, University of California, MS 150 (Ill. 1); CUL MS Ii.6.7 and Trinity College, MS B.11.20; Bodleian Library, MS Liturg. 9; Edinburgh, University Library, MS 308; Philadelphia, Museum of Art, MS 45–65–6.

31 It should suffice to give only a few examples of these very common representations: Brussels, Bibliothèque Royale, MS 4862–9, 66v, 67r; Boston, Countway Library of Medicine, MS DeRicci 23, 57v; BL MS Harley 5311, sheets A and F; New York, PML, MS Glazier 47, 6r and 6v. The full-page Zodiac and Blood-letting Men were usually designed with labelling or with text on the same page. John Foxton's *Liber Cosmographia* has a series of twelve full-page astrological figures within the text (Cambridge, Trinity College, MS R.15.21).

32 Rather than list the many instances in fifteenth-century missals of a full-page Crucifixion in this position, I note instead the few exceptions, where the Crucifixion scene is half-page: Dublin, Trinity College, MS 83, 97v; BL Add. MS 25588, 109v; Bodleian Library, MS Don.b.6, 156v. In Cambridge, Fitzwilliam Museum, MS 34, a missal made c. 1470 for Richard Fitzwilliam, the Crucifixion page (3r) was used as a frontispiece opposite a patron-page (2v).

33 See Edinburgh, NLS, MS Adv.18.1.7. The *Liber Regalis* (Westminster Abbey MS 38, late fourteenth century), in Latin, contains a full-page frontispiece and two other full page scenes within the text. BL MS Cotton Nero A.x, the *Gawain* manuscript, was probably not designed to include full-page pictures, but it is important for the history of vernacular book design that they were added, apparently shortly after production. Bodleian Library, MS Ashmole 764, Foundation of the Office of Arms, with a frontispiece and two full-page pictures within the text, and BL Add. MS 10302, Norton's *Ordinall of Alchemy*, with a frontispiece and four other pictures, are two later fifteenth-century instances of a vernacular text planned with full miniatures.

34 E.g. Bodleian Library, MS Lat. liturg. f.2 and BL Harley MS 2887, both books of Hours.

35 See Cambridge, Trinity College, MS B.11.7; BL Add. MS 50001; San Marino,

Huntington Library, HM 19913, Miller Hours; New York, PML, M 893, Hours and Psalter of Henry, duke of Warwick (Ills. 3b + 5a); and Manchester, John Rylands/University Library, MS Lat. 165, prayers of Abbot Islip; and others. The half-page format was used freely together in the whole design of a book with historiated initials and full-page pictures.

36 London, Victoria and Albert Museum, MS Reid 42; Oxford, St John's College, MS 293, together with historiated initials; and NYPL, MS Spencer 3.

37 E.g. BL MS Harley 326, *Romance of the Three Kings' Sons*, changing to a smaller picture size later; and Bodleian Library, MS Digby 233, Aegidius de Columna, *De Regimine Principum*.

38 E.g. Oxford, University College, MS 85, p. 1, Alain Chartier, *Quadrilogue* and p. 70, *Secret of Secrets*.

39 E.g. Cambridge, Trinity College, MS B.10.12, *Privity of the Passion*; New York, PML, M 648, Nicholas Love, *Mirror of the Blessed Life of Christ*.

40 E.g. Bodleian Library, MS Bodley 264, *Livres du Graunt Caam*, 218r–274r (in French); BL Harley MS 1766, Lydgate, *Fall of Princes*; Manchester, John Rylands/University Library, MS Eng. 1, Lydgate, *Fall of Princes*.

41 For illustrated copies of Lydgate's works in the two-column format, see e.g. Bodleian Library, MSS Digby 232 and Rawl. C.446; BL MSS Cotton Augustus A.IV and Royal 18.D.II, and Cambridge, Trinity College, MS O.5.2, all of the *Troy Book*; and San Marino, Huntington Library, HM 268, and Philadelphia, Rosenbach Museum, MS 439/16, *Fall of Princes*. For Gower's works, see the forthcoming study by Griffiths, Harris and Pearsall (n. 13 above). Probably because of its immense size, a three-column format (with column-sized pictures) was used for Bodleian Library, MS Eng. poet. a.1, the Vernon MS. Other vernacular works designed with column-miniatures are: BL MS Cotton Claudius B.I, Brigittine *Revelations*; Bodleian Library, MS Bodley 264, *Alexander and Dindimus* and *Livres du Graunt Caam*.

42 J.J. Griffiths ('*Confessio Amantis*: The Poem and its Pictures', in *Gower's Confessio Amantis: Responses and Reassessments*, ed. A.J. Minnis (Cambridge, 1983), pp. 163–77) discusses connections and discontinuities that may be revealed through a study of the positioning of miniature spaces in textually similar manuscripts. His conclusion that 'there need be no similarity of art, layout, or text between manuscripts that can be associated by their positioning of spaces or miniatures' (p. 168) is of unusual importance not only for a study of textual descent but also for pictorial genealogy. Lawton 'Illustration of Late Medieval Secular Texts', discusses the content and location of pictures in the manuscripts of Lydgate's *Troy Book*, pp. 54–69.

43 E.g., respectively: BL Add. MS 42131, Bedford Hours and Psalter; Paris BN MS anglais 25, Guy de Chauliac, *Chyrurgie*; NLW MS 21242C, Lydgate, *Life of Our Lady*; London, College of Arms, MS Arundel 3, Chronicle of St Albans; BL MS Hargrave 274, *Nova Statuta*; London, PRO, H.C.A. 12/1, Black Book of the Admiralty; Cambridge, Sidney Sussex College, MS 2, Statutes of Jesus College, Cambridge; Durham, University Library, MS Cosin.v.III.5, John Mirk, *Festial*; and Oxford, Magdalen College, MS 153, Thomas Netter of Walden, *De Doctrinale Fidei Catholicae*.

44 For luxury manuscripts illustrated in the picture-initial format, see, e.g., London, Lambeth Palace, MS 69, Chichele Breviary; BL MS Royal 1.E.IX, Big Bible; BL

Add. MS 42131, Bedford Hours and Psalter (Ill. 5b); Paris BN MS lat. 1196, Prayerbook of Charles d'Orléans; and Nottingham, University Library, Wollaton Antiphonal.

45 In New York, PML, M 893, the Warwick Hours and Psalters, the 'Cantate Domino' scene – invariably of priests chanting – needed to have a figure of David praying at a *prie-Dieu* added rather strangely at the right (Ill. 3b); and a number of other scenes in the psalter show the stress of expansion, in the form of unusual or unnecessary figures.

46 For the ways in which a letter might be drawn with respect to its historiation, see Margaret Rickert, *The Reconstructed Carmelite Missal* (London, 1952), pp. 61–2.

47 Many illustrated roll-chronicles have been located: see de la Mare, *Catalogue*, and A. Allan, 'Yorkist Propaganda', especially nn. 3, 4, 5, 6, 8 and 15. An unusual roll with large rectangular picture spaces is in BL MS Harley 7353, a typographical life of Edward IV, and undoubtedly a one-off design. A rare example of the roundel format used within a codex is the sequence of astrological pictures in Cambridge, Emmanuel College, MS 1.3.18.

48 York Minster Library, MS Add. 256, membrane 1.

49 E.g. Oxford, Corpus Christi College, MS 161; New Haven, Yale University, Beinecke Library, MS 27; Chicago, Art Museum, MS 23.420.

50 The anonymous *Verses on the Kings* is in BL MS Cotton Julius E.iv, art. 1 (the other illustrated copy shows each king holding a placard inscribed with verses, too eccentric a format to be noted separately). The Rous Rolls are in BL Add. MS 48976 and London, College of Arms, 'Warwick MS' (no shelfmark).

51 The earliest and perhaps the original of this text–picture format occurs in BL MS Harley 2278, made c. 1434 for presentation to Henry VI; the later copies (after 1461) are in BL MS Yates Thompson 47 and Arundel Castle, Library of His Grace the Duke of Norfolk: see Scott, 'Lydgate's Lives', figs. 1–3 and 8 for the one-stanza format, and figs. 5–7 for the two-stanza format. Another form of blocking the page into three pictures and three stanzas is described by D. Gray ('A Middle English Illustrated Poem', p. 189) relevant to a poem on the Litany. Some similar type of decision concerning design may have taken place with respect to a group of manuscripts of the prose *Pilgrimage of the Soul* produced in the same locale in eastern England; the flattened picture space in these books looks as if an arbitrary number of (too few) lines had been designated whenever a picture had to be inserted (see BL MS Egerton 615 and Bodleian Library, MS Laud misc. 740).

52 See, e.g., BL MSS Arundel 38, Harley 4866 and Royal 17.D.vi; and Edinburgh, University Library, MS 202; even though apparently written by different scribes, these copies have a very similar page design and style of decoration. Bodleian Library MS Selden supra 53 also was made according to the four-stanza format. Two manuscripts containing the *Desert of Religion* (BL MS Cotton Faustina B.vi, Pt ii, and the later version in Add. MS 37049, 46r–66v) have an unusual two-column lay-out, with one column of text beside an elongated, column-high miniature. This page design may originally have been devised in order to economise on materials by using the space at the right side of the verse stanzas.

53 See San Marino, Huntington Library, EL 26 C 9, Chaucer; Bodleian Library, MS Douce 104, *Piers Plowman*; and Bodl. MS Tanner 17, *South English Legendary*.

54 For examples of the *Dicts and Sayings of the Philosophers*, see Bodleian Library, MS

Bodley 943 or CUL MS Dd.9.15. The *Turba* is in Cambridge, St John's College, MS G.14.

55 These copies are Manchester, John Rylands/University Library, MS Eng. 1, *Troy Book*, with 69 miniatures, and BL MS Harley 1766, *Fall of Princes*, with 157 miniatures. The unframed scenes in BL MS Cotton Tiberius A.vii make use of the marginal area, sometimes extensively (e.g. 75r), but on the whole the scenes are accommodated within the justified text space.

56 See, for example, the fine copy in BL Add. MS 29301 (Ill. 4a). Many other Arderne manuscripts survive; they are being studied by Peter Murray Jones, of King's College, Cambridge. From time to time, other types of scientific drawings were located in the marginal area, e.g. CUL MS Ee.3.61, 8v–9r, sometimes in an ingenious manner.

57 Cases in point are Bodleian Library, MS Laud misc. 733, *De Arte Heraldica* with a Brut chronicle, e.g. 29r; Cambridge, Fitzwilliam Museum, MS 329, Thomas Anlaby Collection, e.g. fol. ix (in this manuscript vertical ruling was actually made for the marginal diagrams).

58 Examples are in Paris, BN MS lat. 13285, Matins and Hours, late fourteenth century, 7r; BL Add. MS 30946, Nicholas Upton, *De Officio Militari*, dated 1458; CUL MS Kk.2.7, Psalter and Hours, 3rd–4th quarter fifteenth century (Ill. 6b).

59 See also Lawton, 'Illustration of Late Medieval Secular Texts', pp. 59, 61; Griffiths, '*Confessio Amantis*', p. 175. Doyle and Parkes, pp. 187, 190–1, discuss the tendency of pictures to reinforce the structure rather than the narrative of a work.

60 For the manner in which narrative scenes and cycles might be constructed from stock figures, objects, and landscapes, see M.A. Stones, 'Secular Manuscript Illumination in France', *Medieval Manuscripts and Textual Criticism* ed. C. Kleinhenz, North Carolina Studies in the Romance Languages and Literatures, No. 173 (Chapel Hill, 1976), 83–102; E. Salter and D. Pearsall, 'Pictorial Illustration of late Medieval Poetic Texts: The Role of the Frontispiece or Prefatory Picture', in *Medieval Iconography and Narrative; A Symposium*, Proceedings of the Fourth International Symposium (Odense, 1980), pp. 103–4; and Lawton, 'Illustration of late Medieval Secular Texts', pp. 65–6 and n. 67.

61 Bodleian Library, MS Eng. poet. a.1, Vernon MS, 124r–166v; MS Bodley 596, 86r–104r.

62 Bodleian Library, MS Bodley 264.

63 BL MS Cotton Nero A.x.

64 Edinburgh, NLS, MS Advocates' 18.1.7 and New York, PML, M 648; and Cambridge, Trinity College, MS B.10.12.

65 This text is usually illustrated with one or two scenes from the dramatic framework for the tales, but two copies were produced with further narrative scenes: Oxford, New College, MS 266 and New York, PML, M 126.

66 BL Harley MS 326.

67 New York, PML, M 775, 200r–274r; Cambridge, St John's College, MS H.5 (208).

68 Cambridge, Trinity College, MS R.14.5.

69 Cambridge, Trinity College, MS O.9.1, 102r; and MS B.10.2, 39r–44v.

70 BL MS Harley 3954. Another copy in Royal 17.C.xxxviii has in the lower margins about 110 pictures that are mainly static in nature rather than narrative (see below).

71 BL MS Cotton Julius A.iv, art.6.

72 E.g. NYPL MS Spencer 19, *Pilgrimage of the Soul*; Bodleian Library, MS Laud misc. 740, *Pilgrimage of the Life of Man*.

73 *Lives of SS. Edmund and Fremund*: BL MS Yates Thompson 47 and Arundel Castle, Library of His Grace the Duke of Norfolk; *Fall of Princes*: e.g. BL MS Harley 1766 and San Marino, Huntington Library, HM 268; *Troy Book*: e.g. Manchester, John Rylands/University Library, MS Eng. 1. Salter and Pearsall 'Pictorial Illustration' have a similar list of illustrated narrative texts (p. 104); and Lawton ('Illustration of Late Medieval Secular Texts') mentions some 'texts which seem to have been viewed as illustrated books'; my list includes items that were singletons and further texts that were clearly viewed as 'illustratable', i.e. Mandeville and Nicholas Love.

74 A full but typical sequence of pictures from a missal is as follows: priest and acolyte at a lectern; priest at altar with an infant; Nativity; Adoration of the Magi; a baptism ceremony; Christ in Judgment; a priest and acolyte; Sacrifice of Isaac; Resurrection; Ascension; Pentecost; Trinity; Corpus Christi procession; Dedication of a Church; Martydom of St Andrew; Presentation in the Temple; St John the Baptist; SS. Peter and Paul; Assumption of the Virgin; Nativity of the Virgin; All Saints; a saint; marriage ceremony (from Biblioteca Apostolica Vaticana, MS Pal.lat.501, late fourteenth century; to be discussed in Scott *Survey*, forthcoming).

75 Some of the commonly illustrated incipits with narrative implications are: Psalm 26, 'Dominus illuminatio mea' = David (or sometimes a nondescript male) pointing to his eyes; Psalm 38, 'Dixi custodiam vias meas' = David, etc., pointing to his mouth; Psalm 68, 'Salvum me fac' = David in the waters. Cambridge, Gonville and Caius College, MS 148/198 has a sequence of this type; and BL Add. MS 42131, the Bedford Psalter, is illustrated with scenes from the life of David (Ill. 5b).

76 V.A. Kolve has already made the point with respect to the *Canterbury Tales*: 'no surviving manuscript of [Chaucer's] work illustrates the narrative action of any of his poems' ('Chaucer and the Visual Arts' in *Writers and their Background: Geoffrey Chaucer*, ed. D.S. Brewer (Ohio University Press, 1975), p. 293). Even so, we can learn a good deal about the medieval approach to a text, whether or not the pictures are narrative, whether or not they are 'crude', and even whether or not standard models or a pre-existing pattern was used. In the Hoccleve manuscripts with an illustration of Chaucer, for instance, the *fact* or presence of those portrait-like pictures is at least as significant as the origin of the model. Salter and Pearsall ('Pictorial Illustration') recognise that the figures of the pilgrims in the Ellesmere Chaucer represent a reading of the *Tales*, showing 'a recognition of the dramatic structure of the *Canterbury Tales*, as a whole' (p. 105).

77 Only one Bible and one Bible Concordance seem to have been made with pictures in the later period: BL MS Royal 1.E.ix and Cambridge, King's College, MS 40 (damaged). CUL MS Dd.1.27 contains a Bible with small scenes from Genesis in the left-hand border of 1r. One illustrated Apocalypse (Cambridge, Trinity College, MS B.10.2) has survived from the later fourteenth century, and none from the fifteenth.

78 F.P. Pickering in *Literature and Art in the Middle Ages* (Coral Gables, Florida, 1970) discusses one type of seated figure: the male with bowed head, seated on a rock or mound (pp. 92–114).

79 I question whether the presentation scene – of an author giving a book to a patron

or of a patron commending himself to a religious image – should not also be in this category, that is, whether the presentation scene is not the embodiment of a conceptual idea or action rather than a genuine narrative incident; but, because the surface reading of these scenes is that of an event, real or not, I have omitted them from this category.

80 See, e.g. Oxford, Keble College, MS 14, 42r; and Edinburgh UL MS 308, 109v.

81 E.g. Aberdeen UL MS 21, *Polychronicon*, 12r; and Oxford, Merton College, MS 319, *Doctrinale Fidei Catholicae*, 2r.

82 E.g. Cambridge, Mass., Harvard University, Widener Library, bMS. Typ. 40; and see de la Mare, *Catalogue*, and A. Allan, 'Yorkist Propaganda'.

83 Cambridge, Trinity College, MS R.15.21, John Foxton, *Liber Cosmographia*.

84 E.g., respectively, Bodleian Library, MS Bodley 943; and San Marino, Huntington Library, EL 26 C 9.

85 E.g., Cambridge, St John's College, MS 23, Richard Rolle, with his picture at the head of two different texts, 11r and 41r; BL MS Lansdowne 851, *Canterbury Tales*, 2r; and New York, PML, M 817, *Troilus and Criseyde*, 2r. Sometimes it is not evident whether the figure represents author or dramatic *persona*, e.g. Oxford, Bodleian Library, MS Bodley 686, *Canterbury Tales*, 1r.

86 For a *distinctio* of the guises in which an author might be represented in an introductory picture, see Salter and Pearsall, 'Pictorial Illustration', pp. 115–16.

87 See Kolve, 'Chaucer and the Visual Arts', p. 293.

88 E.g. Oxford, Merton College, MS 23, Jerome, Commentary on the Minor Prophets.

89 See n. 8 above; and Jones (*Medieval Medical Miniatures*) reproduces medical preparations and procedures (figs. 41, 50, 56), instruments (figs. 49, 50), urine bottles (pl. III, fig. 28), foetal presentations (figs. 19–20), and alchemical apparatus (fig. 42) from fifteenth-century English manuscripts.

90 E.g. BL Add. MS 57534, with four full-page tinted drawings of the stations of participants (indicated by a tonsure) and equipment (candles, books, chalices) for various ceremonies, such as Palm Sunday and Baptism. The fragment in London, College of Arms, MS B.2.9, fol. 20, may represent a fine lost copy.

91 E.g. San Marino, Huntington Library, HM 132, 48r; Aberdeen, University Library, MS 21, 56v.

92 E.g. Dublin, Trinity College, MS 505, *Brut*, p. 86; Bodleian Library, MS Laud misc. 730, 10r.

93 E.g. Bodleian Library, MS Douce 335, *Master of Game*, in which animals are depicted for the purpose of future recognition in the field.

94 CUL MS Gg.6.5.

95 BL MS Royal 17.C.xxxviii.

96 For further discussion of other aspects relating to pictures in manuscripts, such as costing based on miniature size, the rôle of patterns in creating illustrations for books, the adaption of iconographies, and methods of transferring designs to the picture space, see Hindman and Farquhar, *Pen to Press*, pp. 77–86.

97 The important exception is Margaret Rickert, who discussed the partial borders in manuscripts of the *Canterbury Tales*, in Manly and Rickert, 1, 561–605.

98 The bar frame can also be viewed as developing or 'growing' from the large initial

on the page; see Rickert, pp. 565, 569–70; Harthan, *Introduction to Illuminated Manuscripts*, p. 8.

99 E.g. Cambridge, Trinity College, MS B.11.3, Leventhorpe Missal, 34v, late fourteenth century; San Marino, Huntington Library, HM 19920, Statutes, 227r, c. 1413. Ill. 3a shows a curved break in the left-hand bar, here almost certainly due to an over-large flourished initial.

100 E.g. GUL MS Hunterian 270, *Dives and Pauper*, 11r; Bodleian Library, MS Barlow 5, Missal, 1r.

101 E.g. Cambridge, Fitzwilliam Museum, MS McClean 90, Hours, 17r.

102 E.g. New York, Public Library, MS Spencer 3, Hours.

103 E.g. New York, PML, M 1033, Hours, 64v.

104 E.g. CUL MS Kk.2.7, Hours, 9r (Ill. 6b).

105 E.g. Leeds UL, Brotherton Collection, MS 15, Hours, 24r.

106 This fact may not always have been obvious in, for instance, a composite volume or one with a text preceded by a lengthy table of contents or by prayers, etc.

107 E.g. London, Lambeth Palace, MS 23, Alexander Neckham, *Super Cantica*, late fourteenth century, 1r; BL MS Harley 7334, *Canterbury Tales*, early fifteenth century, 1r; Cambridge, Trinity College, MS B.11.13, Gospel Book, 2nd quarter fifteenth century, 6r.

108 Durham, Cathedral Library, MS A.1.3, Nicholas de Lyra, *Postilla in Pentateuch*, dated 1386, 1r, with leaves and flowers; New York, PML, M 893, Hours and Psalter, 12r, with figures in the trelliswork (Ill. 5a).

109 E.g. BL Add. MS 50001, Hours of Elizabeth the Queen, 7r.

110 E.g. books of Hours: Cambridge, Trinity College, MS B.11.7, 7r, and as in n. 108; *Canterbury Tales*: n. 107; Matthew Paris, *Flores Historiarum*: BL MS Cotton Claudius E.viii, 1r; Nicholas de Lyra, *On Moses*: Durham, Cathedral Library, MS A.1.6, 1r; Alexander Neckham: n. 107; charters: Bodleian Library, MS Ashmole 1831; psalters: BL MS Royal 2.B.x, 8r; gospel book: n. 107.

111 E.g. BL Add. MS 27944, Bartholomaeus Anglicus, *De Proprietatibus Rerum*, 8r; Cambridge, Emmanuel College, MS I.4.13, Hours, 7r; and Firle Place, Library of Lord Gage, book of Hours, in which the rationale of design was to use a monochrome band border with every large historiated initial or half-page picture. M. Rickert (pp. 82, 90) described the innovative use of this shading in the Carmelite Missal (see n. 46).

112 E.g. CUL MS Mm.3.14, sermons, late fourteenth century, 9r; Urbana, University of Illinois, DeRicci MS 70, *Speculum Humanae Salvationis*, 2r (I am indebted to J.B. Friedman for my knowledge of this manuscript); Cambridge, Trinity College, MS B.11.7, Hours, e.g. 32v.

113 The English illuminator's model-book in BL MS Sloane 1448A, described in the *British Library Journal* for 1975 by Janet Backhouse, demonstrates in a skeletal way most of the border types named here. In the section with drawings of borders, the illuminator has depicted: (1) two styles of bar frame (18v, 19r); (2) a band border with scrollwork around a central stem (18r); (3) a plain band, probably for filigree work (21r); and (4) leaves curled within a band, one type of trelliswork border (19v). Only a true looped trellis is lacking. Unfortunately no surviving costing in an English manuscript distinguishes between types of border designs:

the only known Middle English or other term for a full border is 'vinet' or 'hole vinet'; English costings do however differentiate between various initial types.

114 See Oxford, Bodleian Library, MS Hatton 10, *Nova Statuta*; Bodl. MS Bodley 263, Lydgate, *Fall of Princes*; Leeds, Brotherton Library, MS 15, Hours; CUL MS Kk.2.7, Hours (Ill. 6b); or New York, PML, M 126, Gower, *Confessio Amantis*.

115 E.g. BL MS Royal 2.B.x, Psalter, 8r, a bar frame with two sides of trelliswork; CUL MS Ii.2.24, Ranulf Higden, *Polychronicon*, 13r, a bar frame with a trellis at the bottom and a band with white designs at the right side; and Bodleian Library, MS Bodley 277, Wycliffite Bible, 167r, bands of monochrome scrollwork and a trellis mixed. Other types of border designs appear from time to time, but are rare on the whole and probably indicative of a relatively isolated workshop or person, or of foreign influence; see, for example, the bars completely wrapped in scrollwork in Oxford, Merton College, MS 319, Thomas Netter, *Doctrinale fidei*, 2r, 41r.

116 A rather ugly version of the monochrome band border from the 4th quarter of the century is in the Bray Antiphoner in Westminster Abbey, Cathedral Library, MS 43, 170v, etc.

117 E.g. Bodleian Library, MS Hatton 10, *Nova Statuta*, 188r and 210r, or Oxford, St John's College, MS 196, Psalter, 8r, for motifs added to existing sprays and for foreign-type sprays substituted for English designs; see Oxford, Merton College, MS 297B, *Nova Statuta*, 331r, for a magpie and grapebranch instead of the usual acanthus cluster.

118 E.g. BL Add. MS 27924, book of Hours, *passim*; even the initials in this book are foreign in style.

119 E.g. BL MS Royal 1.E.ix, Big Bible; Bodleian MS Bodley 264, Marco Polo, 218r; Bodl. MS Laud misc. 609, Gower, *Confessio Amantis*, 1r.

120 Oxford, Oriel College, MS 75.

121 Malibu, California, John Paul Getty Museum, MS Getty 17.

122 Rickert, *Carmelite Missal*, pls. I, VIII, XVIIb, XVIII, XIXb, etc.

123 Elizabeth Salter, 'Medieval Poetry and the Visual Arts', *Essays and Studies*, 22 (1969), p. 27.

3 · ENGLISH DECORATED BOOKBINDINGS

MIRJAM FOOT

THE PERIOD from 1375 to 1475 is not propitious for the study of decorated English bookbindings. Much earlier, during the second half of the twelfth century and the beginning of the thirteenth, splendidly tooled leather bindings were produced in Winchester, London and probably Durham,[1] and the earliest known European decorated leather binding, which may be as early as the seventh century, comes from Northumbria.[2] There is however a notable gap in the production or survival of tooled leather bindings during the fourteenth and the first half of the fifteenth centuries. It is just possible that the binding covering Stephen Langton, *Super Ecclesiasticum*, a manuscript in Durham Cathedral Library dating from the first half of the thirteenth century, was made in the thirteenth or fourteenth century;[3] but, though the tools used to decorate this binding have an archaic look, their arrangement has more in common with that found on bindings made during the second half of the fifteenth century. Another binding in Durham University Library decorated with Romanesque type tools in an unusual arrangement may date from the end of the thirteenth century.[4]

The scarcity of decorated leather bindings dating from before 1450 may be due to the fact that the grandest medieval bindings were made of precious metals or rare fabrics. Practically no English silver-gilt or silver bindings have survived,[5] the majority having been melted down during the Reformation, and most of the fabric bindings of this period have suffered from the ravages of time and moths. Nevertheless, there is a certain amount of documentary evidence for the one-time existence of medieval treasure bindings as well as for textile bindings made during the fourteenth and fifteenth centuries.[6] The only surviving early English embroidered binding, now inlaid in eighteenth-century calf, is that on the fourteenth-century Felbrigge Psalter. The upper cover, which is still remarkably fresh, shows the Annunciation, while the lower cover shows a rather worn representation of the Crucifixion.[7]

Apart from references to, and a few remains of, what must have been the top end of the market, a fair number of plain leather medieval bindings made for more general use survive, but they are very difficult to date.

There seem to be only minor variations in the way English binders of the fifteenth century chose and handled their materials.[8] Most bindings of this period are sewn on alum-tawed, sometimes on tanned leather thongs; the thongs are laced into the wooden boards, lie in grooves on the inside of the boards and are secured by square or round pegs, sometimes in a staggered pattern.[9] In some cases there are traces of a whitish clay-like substance covering the exposed thongs, presumably used to make an even surface for the vellum paste-downs. The boards themselves are made of wood, usually oak,[10] frequently finished with a slight bevel – sharply bevelled boards, commonly found in Germany and sometimes in the Netherlands, are unusual. Headbands have in many cases not survived. Those that have withstood the wear and tear of use are frequently sewn in white, or blue and white, thread over an alum-tawed, sometimes a tanned leather core, and are either laced in in tunnels on the inside of the boards and pegged like the thongs, or are brought over the outside of the boards and then disappear into holes in the wood. Sometimes the headbands are covered with the spine leather. The boards are often cut flush with the edges of the leaves, though I have equally often found them flush at the fore-edge and with slight protruding squares at the top and tail. Clasps, normally two, are commonly used and have leather thongs, almost invariably hinging on the upper cover.[11] Chain marks, signs of an occasional later addition, occur from time to time, often at the bottom right-hand corner but also in the centre of the top edge of the upper cover. End-leaves are usually of vellum and in many cases the paste-downs, once secured to the inside of the covers, have now been lifted. Neil Ker has shown that manuscript paste-downs were commonly used in Oxford during the late fifteenth and sixteenth centuries.[12] They were already in use there in the 1470s and though they are also on occasion found in bindings produced elsewhere, they seem indeed to turn up most frequently in Oxford bindings.

During the fifteenth century and at the beginning of the sixteenth, the book trade in England was much influenced by imports and immigrants from the Continent. I have tried to show elsewhere[13] that the binding trade during this period owed much both to immigrant binders and to the importation of binding designs, tool designs, and decorative panels, especially from the Low Countries. Low Country influences on binding technique are also discernible. Plaited headbands such as occur on bindings from the Low Countries were unusual in England. However, the Greyhound binder who possibly worked in Oxford or London in the 1490s occasionally used them. Pink plaited headbands are found on bindings by the Lily binder, who also used sharply bevelled boards, put metal shoes on the edges of the boards (a habit more common in the Low Countries than in England), and on occasion put the clasps on his bindings with the hinges on the lower cover. As a rule the spines of English bindings were left undecorated or were decorated with a few blind lines, either running vertically down the spine or forming a saltire between horizontal lines in each compartment. Three binders who occasionally put tools on the spines of their bindings, a German habit, are the Unicorn binder,

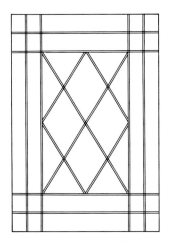

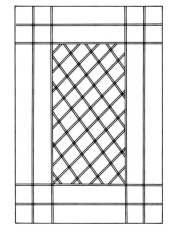

Fig. 1 Drawing of binding design: see also Oldham, *EBSB*, pl. II, no. 1; pl. IV.

Fig. 2 Drawing of binding design: see also Oldham, *EBSB*, pl. II, no. 3; pl. XII.

the Indulgence binder, and the Fruit and Flower binder. Several German and Flemish binders were in the habit of putting a square stamp in sideways, and a number of English binders, such as the man who worked for Caxton, the Antwerp binder, the Scales binder, and some Oxford binders, occasionally did the same.

Two binding designs, widely used on both sides of the Channel, show a frame of intersecting fillets around fillets forming a diamond and a saltire (see Fig. 1), or fillets dividing the centre into smaller diamond-shaped and triangular compartments (see Fig. 2). The design formed by the arrangement of small stamps in rows, frequently found in Oxford and sometimes in London, is also found in France.

The design of the small hand tools used to decorate English bindings of the second half of the fifteenth century equally shows strong Low Country influence. Many of the motifs, such as dragons, fighting cocks, double-headed eagles, various kinds of monster, pelicans, lambs-and-flags, roses, fleurs-de-lis, and pineapples, are found in abundance in the Netherlands as well as in England, and a great deal of attention to detail is necessary in order to distinguish certain types of tools used in both countries.

The surviving tooled leather bindings produced in England during the second half of the fifteenth century have been the subject of study by a number of binding historians. Of these G.D. Hobson, J.B. Oldham and more recently Graham Pollard have been most prolific, and their work has been the starting point for this chapter.[14]

Though tooled bindings were produced in monasteries in Canterbury, Jervaulx, Tavistock and at Osney Abbey near Oxford, and in towns such as Winchester and possibly also Salisbury, the main centres of bookbinding during the second half of the fifteenth century were London, Oxford and Cambridge.

Fewer than a dozen binderies are known to have started work before 1475 and possibly the earliest of these is that of the Scales binder. He worked in London from the 1450s until after 1481 and his work, which can be divided into two distinct groups, has been discussed in detail by Nicolas Barker.[15] The most characteristic feature of this bindery is that it practised the technique of cutting the leather with a knife to effect part of the design, a habit otherwise unknown in England, though popular in German-speaking countries during the fifteenth century. The Scales binder also used thirty-six decorative stamps (from one of which, a pair of scales, he gets his name), and a total of twenty bindings from his shop are known to have survived: thirteen produced before 1465 and seven between 1466 (or later) and 1481.

A binder of whose work only two examples are now known, who used a square tool with four flowers very similar to that used by the Scales binder, may also have worked in London. He bound a fifteenth-century manuscript of Albertus Magnus, *De caelo et mundo*, now at Pembroke College, Cambridge,[16] and a copy of the Middle English Brut Chronicle, c. 1450–75, which was lot 12 in the Bute sale at Sotheby's on 13 July 1983.

A third binder who may have been located in London and who worked before 1474 was christened by Graham Pollard the Sheen binder. Three bindings from this shop are known, decorated with characteristic bird, animal, and monster tools arranged in concentric frames.[17]

Another early bindery that arranged its tools in concentric frames, also achieving an all-over style of decoration, was at work possibly between 1460 and 1463 and had strong connections with Salisbury. It bound two manuscripts written by Herman Zurke for Gilbert Kymer, physician to Humphrey, duke of Gloucester, twice Chancellor of the University of Oxford, and treasurer and later dean of Salisbury cathedral.[18] The Register of Vallis Scholarium at Salisbury and a manuscript volume of Coluccio Salutati's treatises that belonged to William Witham, Dean of the Arches and canon of Wells, were also bound in this shop.[19] The bindings that cover the manuscripts written for Gilbert Kymer are decorated with a set of word-stamps forming the phrases 'mon bien mon/dain', 'ladi help', and 'ih[es]u m[er]cy', as well as with pictorial stamps showing a flower vase, a small dog with an erect tail, a square tool with a double-headed eagle and another depicting a fleur-de-lis. The double-headed eagle and fleur-de-lis tools form the link with the other two bindings of this group, which in turn are also decorated with tools attributed by J.B. Oldham to his binder I.[20] Oldham's binder J,[21] whom he tentatively placed in Salisbury, is said by Graham Pollard (who gave the location of this workshop as uncertain) to have been responsible for four bindings.[22] A fifth binding belongs to this group. It covers a translation (1488) by William Sellyng, prior of Canterbury, of a sermon by St John

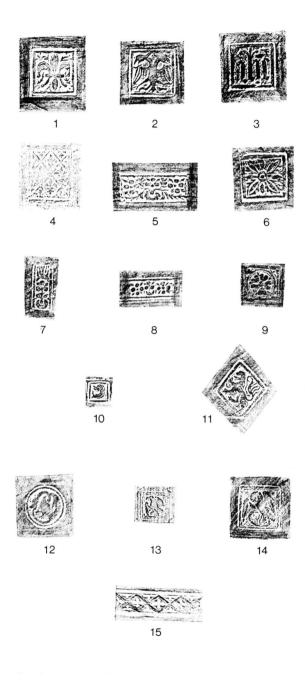

7 A plate of tools: nos. 1–9 unlocated bindery, compare Oldham's binder J; nos. 10–15 previously unrecorded tools from the Oxford quasi-romanesque group.

Chrysostom and other works in an early sixteenth-century manuscript.[23] The tools illustrated by Oldham clearly come from Salisbury MS 99 and though they are extremely similar to those on the other bindings in this group (Add. MSS 6173, 15673; MS Laud Misc. 701 and MS Douce 246), I believe them to be different. It is highly probable that Oldham saw only Salisbury MS 99, and it would be wiser to attribute the other four bindings to a separate unlocated workshop (Ill. 7, nos. 1–9).[24] The two other small groups established by J.B. Oldham which may have started work before 1475 are his binders K and L.[25] Binder K arranged his tools in horizontal rows within a frame composed of individual stamps on Burlaeus, *De vita et moribus philosophorum* (Cologne, 1472). The spine of this binding has been lined with strips cut from an English manuscript which makes reference to St Albans and Chelsmford.[26]

Of the work of binder L also only one example seems to have survived. It covers a collection of religious and other treatises, the last item of which is a suit in the Consistory Court of Exeter between the abbey of Tavistock and others, and Thomas Ralegh, rector of St John's-by-Anthony, 1422–7. The original covers, now onlaid on later brown sheep, are decorated in blind with diagonal fillets dividing the covers into diamonds and triangles, filled with rose and fleur-de-lis tools.[27]

A bindery located in Oxford, which may have been at work already during the 1450s, uses six imitation romanesque tools. Strickland Gibson illustrated several examples from this group, as well as detailed drawings of the majority of the tools used to decorate these bindings (Ill. 7, nos. 10–15).[28] G.D. Hobson identified twenty-two bindings belonging to this shop, Graham Pollard and Nicolas Barker have contributed one each, and nine or ten more can now be added.[29] Graham Pollard attributed three bindings from this group to Thomas Hokyns of Oxford, who worked from 1438 to 1465, ten to his successor John More, who worked from 1439 to 1472, and an unspecified number to Thomas Hunt, who worked from 1473 to 1492.[30] Apart from the fact that Thomas Hokyns is recorded as a bookbinder who worked in Oxford when the earliest bindings in this group may have been produced, and that at the time of this death in 1465 his goods were in the house of the University Stationer, John More, and that the University Stationer, Thomas Hunt, was still alive when the last bindings of this group may have been made, there is no reason to attribute any bindings in this group to any of these three men. The thirty-four bindings now known cover manuscripts and books dated between c. 1450 and 1489; the tools used to decorate them link them together and indicate that they were the work either of one shop or possibly of two shops of which the second bought or inherited the tools of the first. They display a variety of designs, ranging from all-over and central-block designs to circle and diaper designs. Not too much importance should be attached to a variation in design, as designs, though influenced by habit and fashion, are easy to copy.

It is just possible that the Fishtail binder, who worked in Oxford from

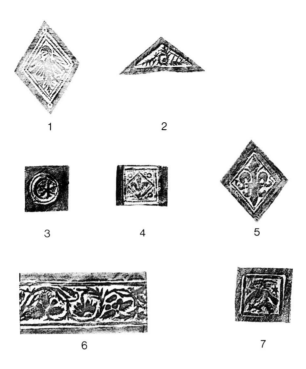

8 A plate of tools: nos. 1–2 from MS Bodley 460; nos. 3–5 previously unrecorded tools belonging to the Fishtail binder; no. 6 previously unrecorded tool belonging to the Demon binder; no. 7 previously unrecorded tool belonging to the Lattice binder.

c. 1473 to c. 1500, acquired two tools that occur on bindings of this Oxford quasi-romanesque group. The large fleur-de-lis that is found on MS Bodley 460[31] in combination with Gibson tools 10 and possibly 6, as well as two tools that are neither in Gibson nor in Oldham (Ill. 8, nos. 1–2), may be identical with that on BL Add. MS 34807, bound by the Fishtail binder, though I am not absolutely certain that this is so. A better case can be made for the curly-tailed monster[32] that occurs on the binding of Leonardus de Utino, *Sermones quadragesimales de legibus*, (Paris, 1477) in combination with Gibson's tools 55, 73 and 79.[33]

J.B. Oldham knew thirteen examples of the Fishtail binder's work, covering manuscripts and books printed between 1473 and 1498.[34] Graham Pollard mentioned seventeen known bindings and suggested that the Fishtail binder's name was Christopher Coke, a bookbinder recorded in Oxford from 1484 who died in 1501.[35] I have seen nineteen or twenty examples altogether with the same or possibly a slightly extended range of imprints[36] and three tools can now be added to this shop's decorative material (Ill. 8, nos. 3–5).

Two more pre-1475 binderies can be identified: the Demon binder who

worked in Cambridge, possibly between c. 1473 and c. 1497, and the Winchester Virgin and Child binder, whose bindings cover manuscripts and
books with imprints between 1474 and 1497.

In *Bindings in Cambridge Libraries*[37] G.D. Hobson identified nine bindings
from a Cambridge binder whom he christened the Demon binder. J.B.
Oldham found two more examples[38] and another three, two of which are
recent acquisitions by the British Library, can now be added. One covers
three incunabula printed between 1488 and 1494 and bound together,[39] the
second covers Cicero, *Epistolae ad familiares* (Venice, 1494)[40] and displays a
new floral tool not found in Oldham (Ill. 8, no. 6). The Virgin and Child
binder was discovered and discussed by Neil Ker,[41] Graham Pollard added
four to Ker's seven known examples,[42] and the British Library acquired
about nine years ago an anthology of Middle English verse, a Winchester
manuscript of c. 1487, bound in the same shop.[43]

During the last quarter of the fifteenth century, a variety of binderies
emerged that were engaged in the production of decorated leather bindings.
A certain amount has been written about these shops and their products, and
I propose to present the state of knowledge, bring it up to date where possible,
and, in a few cases, make some different suggestions.

Some of these shops can be located and most can be given approximate
dates for the span of their working life, with the dated manuscripts and the
imprints of the books providing at least a *terminus post quem* for the bindings.
As was the case for the earlier fifteenth-century bindings, the majority of the
bindings that can be located were made in London, Oxford or Cambridge. I
have mentioned Salisbury and Winchester as other possible centres; A.I.
Doyle has made a good case for a small group of late fifteenth-century
bindings to have been produced in or near Durham;[44] and a group of eleven
decorated bindings can be assigned to Canterbury. G.D. Hobson published a
list of six bindings made there, and J.B. Oldham brought the number up to
eleven.[45] The bindings show different designs on each cover, often incorporating one or two circles and chequered areas made by using square or
triangular hatched tools side by side with plain ones. Other characteristic
stamps depict running hares, stags, flowers and word-stamps forming the
phrase 'time deum'. Graham Pollard described how he rediscovered that the
binder responsible for this set of bindings was John Kemsyn, who worked for
the churchwardens of St Andrews, Canterbury, during the 1480s and 90s.[46]

The only pre-1500 British binder who signed his bindings with his full
name was Patrick Lowes, a Scot, who bound and signed the Haye manuscript, a translation of three medieval French treatises into Scots by 'Gilbert
of the Haye, knycht', dated 1456. The binding, which is probably about thirty
years later than the manuscript, shows a central-block design built up of
round and square tools, depicting roses, animals, including unicorns, and a
variety of saints, as well as lamb-and-flag tools, decorative stamps and

word-stamps forming the names 'ihesus', 'maria', 'iohannes', and the legend 'patricius lowes me ligavit'. Several of the tools, including the lamb-and-flag tool and a stamp showing a dog fighting a lion, occur also on a binding in Aberdeen University Library.[47]

Notwithstanding the impressive number of names of bookbinders who worked in London during the fourteenth and fifteenth centuries discovered by Paul Christianson,[48] the groups of bindings that can be attributed to London are but few. I mentioned earlier the Scales and the Sheen binders, as well as the binder of Pembroke MS 204 who may have been a Londoner; for the later part of the fifteenth century only four or possibly five shops can be added. In *Bindings in Cambridge Libraries* G.D. Hobson discussed the Indulgence binder,[49] so named because of the discovery by Henry Bradshaw of two different indulgences printed by John Lettou that were found lining the quires of a two-volume Latin Bible (Cologne, 1480) in Jesus College, Cambridge. *In Blind Stamped Panels in the English Booktrade*, Hobson listed fifteen bindings from this shop, placed it in London, and adopted Bradshaw's suggestion that Lettou may have been the binder.[50] Graham Pollard added two more bindings to the list and attributed the whole group with increasing conviction to Lettou.[51] Recently two other bindings from this shop have come to light, one covering Aegidius Carlerius, *Sporta fragmentorum* (Brussels, 1478), the other Littleton, *Tenores novelli* (c. 1482);[52] close inspection of the latter raises the suspicion that this may have been a remboîtage. Meanwhile, William Ward and Christopher de Hamel have found strips of indulgences printed by Lettou and by Caxton used to strengthen the spines of bindings from the Rood and Hunt binder, who worked in Oxford and to whom I shall return later.[53] The discovery of indulgences printed by two different printers, one working in London, the other in Westminster, in a binding by an Oxford binder shows that such fragments cannot be used as proof either of the place of binding or of the identity of the binder. All we can say at this point is that the unfortunately named Indulgence binder worked from c. 1475 to c. 1480 or possibly c. 1482, and that the location of his shop is still uncertain.

We are on firmer ground with the binder who worked for William Caxton and Wynkyn de Worde. Thirty-nine examples from this shop are now known, covering manuscripts and books printed between [1477] and 1511.

Howard M. Nixon has conclusively proved that, though the bindings can be divided into five groups, they all come from one or possibly from two shops; that the binder or binders worked in close relationship with William Caxton and after his death with his successor Wynkyn de Worde; and that the documentary evidence does not justify the identification with any named individual.[54] Two of the Caxton binder's designs, Nixon's types A and B, show Low Country influence, and two of his tools in particular (the triangular stamp with a dragon and the fleur-de-lis tool) look like straightforward copies of Netherlandish examples. They are indeed so closely similar that Graham

Pollard believed them to be identical with those used on two Flemish manuscripts in the Bodleian Library.[55] Close inspection shows small differences, but this type of tool was much in use in the southern Netherlands and particularly in Bruges.[56]

Three more examples from Caxton's bindery have emerged since Nixon wrote his articles. One covers Reuchlin's *Vocabularius* (Basel, 1481), another St Augustine, *Confessiones* (Cologne, 1482).[57] Both are now in the British Library. A third, a fifteenth-century manuscript *Formula Novitiorum* in English, is at Queens' College, Cambridge (MS 18).

A binder who used a rebus stamp, identified by G.D. Hobson as Henry Cony, worked in London until after 1503. Ten examples of his work are known, covering books printed between 1483 and 1492.[58]

The Crucifer binder, of whose work ten examples are known, covering manuscripts and books dated between [1476] and 1507, worked in London and was probably employed by Richard Pynson,[59] a stationer and printer who also probably owned a bindery. He came to England before 1491. During a long-drawn-out quarrel with Russhe's executors he was called a bookbinder. He was appointed Printer to the King in 1508, and died in 1530.[60]

On the binding of Lord Newton's copy of the 1487 Sarum *Missal* one of the Crucifer binder's tools occurs in combination with two tools that belonged to J.B. Oldham's binder A. This binder also bound four other books printed between 1480 and 1488.[61]

One of Pynson's two rose panels (Oldham, *Panels* RO1), both found in combination with the Crucifer binder's square floral tool on the indenture (1503) made between Henry VII and Thomas Silkesteade, prior of Winchester (now at Windsor Castle),[62] also occurs alone or together with one of Pynson's two signed panels (Oldham MISC. 14). as well as the two Rose panels (Oldham RO1 and 2) and the two signed panels (Oldham MISC. 4 and 14), Pynson used a panel depicting St John the Baptist (Oldham ST 18). These panels are found alone or in various combinations on eleven bindings.[63]

There are a few instances of panels being used before 1500. The famous trio of Dutch panels found, together with some tools belonging to the Indulgence binder, on the first volume of a six-volume set of Vincent of Beauvais's *Works* (c. 1473–8) at Corpus Christi College, Oxford, were discussed with much ingenuity by G.D. Hobson, who attributed the binding to William de Machlinia and dated it c. 1482–7. Graham Pollard suggested that the volume was bound by Pynson in a consciously archaic style as late as c. 1515.[64] As these arguments were to a large extent based on the probably false assumption that John Lettou was the Indulgence binder, the question as to the owner of the panels and the date of their use in England remains unresolved.

It seems likely that the earliest use of a panel in London dates from c. 1494. Howard M. Nixon showed that an animal in foliage panel (Oldham AN 17)

9   Terence, *Vulgaria*, [London, c. 1483]: a London 15th-century binding with quasi-romanesque tools. IA 55454.

which was used on a presentation binding of a [1494] Sarum *Horae* at Lambeth Palace was also used by Caxton's binder.[65]

It is possible that a small panel depicting St George (Oldham ST 10) which belonged to the Cambridge binder WG, and which is found on three books with the imprint dates of 1490, 1491, and 1494,[66] was used earlier than the Caxton binder's panel. Another small panel, this time showing the English Royal arms (Oldham HE 5), may also have been used before 1500. It is found on a book at Westminster Abbey, probably originally a blank book, which now contains some manuscript prayers of Erasmus written some time after the book was bound. This panel belonged to the Half-Stamp binder and there is no reason to believe that it was used before 1495.[67]

With the subject of panel stamps we move decidedly into the sixteenth century, and this is not the place for further discussion.

We must return to London, where the last bindery to be discussed that may have been located there was at work at the very end of the fifteenth century and at the beginning of the sixteenth. It used curious romanesque type tools, like the Oxford quasi-romanesque bindery mentioned above, and it arranged them, at least on one occasion, in a typical romanesque design. Only two examples from this shop are known. One covers Terence, *Vulgaria* (London, c. 1483) and shows the tools arranged in a large circle between two horizontal rows of large stamps (Ill. 9), [68] the other is on Marsilio Ficino, *Epistolae* (Venice, 1495). The latter binding has been lined with leaves from a book printed by Pynson in 1502 and is now at Westminster Abbey Library.[69]

To our knowledge of the binders who worked in Cambridge during the end of the fifteenth century and the first decade of the sixteenth only very little can be added.

J.B. Oldham divided a large group of bindings produced in Cambridge into the work of the Pre-Unicorn binder and that of the Unicorn binder. He attributed to the first five bindings executed between 1480 and 1485.[70] Seven of his ten tools are found on bindings by the Unicorn binder, whose shop was discovered and described by G.D. Hobson,[71] who knew of forty-four examples of his work. J.B. Oldham brought the number up to seventy-three and Graham Pollard, who did not make the distinction between the Unicorn binder and the Pre-Unicorn binder, stated that 'nearly 100 bindings by the Unicorn binder' are known; they cover books dated from 1478 to 1507.[72] Since Graham Pollard wrote this, the British Library has acquired a copy of M.A. Sabellicus, *Rerum Venetarum decades* (Venice, 1487) from this shop. G.D. Hobson suggested in his Sandars Lectures that the Unicorn binder may be Walter Hatley, University Stationer, who worked in Cambridge from 1484/5 to 1504 or possibly 1508, but Graham Pollard has pointed out that Hatley's dates also coincide with those of another Cambridge binder who goes by the nickname of the Heavy binder.

A bindery that used two stamps very similar to those belonging to the Unicorn binder, and that owned a fleur-de-lis tool found together with tools from the Unicorn bindery on the work of yet another binder, used a signed tool with the monogram WG. The same shop also owned a roll with two monograms WG and IG and two panels signed IG. Oldham has shown that the output of this bindery, which covers books printed between 1478 and 1533, can be divided into three groups, linked by either the WG stamp or by the WG–IG roll, and he has suggested that it was run by two generations, father (WG) and two sons (the elder WG, and the younger IG). The first group, which is the only one to contain bindings produced before 1500, covers the period 1478 to 1507 and consists of over one hundred bindings.[73]

Three binders who used tools belonging to the Unicorn binder, as well as having other tools in common, are the Lattice binder, the Heavy binder and the Monster binder, and much more research is needed before any firm conclusions can be drawn about these shops. J.B. Oldham suggested[74] that they were three different binders: the Lattice binder, who worked from 1485 to 1511 and who acquired six tools from the Unicorn bindery; the Heavy binder, who worked from 1485 to 1505 and who used the same lattice tool (Oldham 72) as the Lattice binder and the Unicorn binder; and the Monster binder, whose bindings cover books printed between 1481 and 1505, but who seems to have acquired one of his tools from the Heavy binder, two from the Lattice binder and nine from the Unicorn binder. Only the monster tool seems to have been used by no one else. If this is the case, he probably did not start work until c. 1505. Of these binders' work, forty-four examples made by the Lattice binder were mentioned by Oldham and Pollard,[75] and two were recently acquired by the British Library, a *Homeliarius Doctorum* (Nuremberg, 1494) with one unrecorded tool (fig. 8, no. 7) and one volume of Gerson's *Opera* (Strasburg, 1494).[76] Seventeen come from the Heavy binder's shop, and only four specimens of the Monster binder's output have been recorded.

In addition to an 'unnamed' Cambridge binder of whose work only one book in three volumes is known to exist, J.B. Oldham has made a tentative case for Cambridge as the home of both the Athos binder and the Antwerp binder.[77] The first was active at the end of the fifteenth century, and six examples of his craft are known to have survived; the second produced twenty-two bindings now known, and he seemed to have worked during the last two decades of the century. Recently, the Pierpont Morgan Library acquired a binding by the Antwerp binder covering St Augustine, *Explanatio Psalmorum* [c. 1485?].[78]

In a fascinating lecture delivered to the Bibliographical Society on 15 April 1969[79] Graham Pollard displayed the results of years of searching the archives of the colleges, the university and the city of Oxford. He found a number of named bookbinders whose activities in the way of binding books, exercising the office of University Stationer, receiving money, hiring houses, owing rent, being sued in court, dining and dying he recorded, and whose dates he linked with those postulated for the work of several binders hitherto only known by nicknames. There are no cast-iron proofs for any of these identifications but some sound highly probable.

The largest and most interesting of the binderies that worked in Oxford during the last quarter of the fifteenth century is that which for generations has been called the Rood and Hunt bindery.[80] This shop bound books printed by early Oxford printers, among whom was Theodoric Rood, as well as books imported from the continent which may have been for sale through Thomas Hunt's bookshop.

In 1483 the Louvain printer John of Westfalia and Peter Actors, later the Royal Stationer, called on Thomas Hunt and arranged for him to take a consignment of books on the basis of sale or return. Dr D.E. Rhodes[81] has shown that books of John of Westfalia's press sold well in Oxford, and several of these were bound there at the time by the Rood and Hunt binder. He decorated them either to a central-block design with horizontal rows of stamps, or with the stamps arranged in concentric frames, or, less frequently, to a diaper design. The stamps themselves bear a very close resemblance to tools used in the Netherlands and especially to those employed in Louvain by Ludovicus Ravescot, an illuminator, printer and bookbinder who worked from c. 1473 until after 1501 and who is known to have bound for John of Westfalia. Another Louvain binder who worked on occasion for the printer Johan Veldener also used tools closely similar in design.[82]

No up-to-date list of bindings by the Rood and Hunt binder has been published. Gibson listed twelve examples (mostly with now obsolete press-marks).[83] Graham Pollard said that he knew of twenty-three bindings, covering manuscripts and printed books dated between 1478 and 1482;[84] Christopher de Hamel has identified two more, one an odd volume of Nicholas de Lyra's Bible Gloss (Venice, 1481) at Dunedin, the other a canon law text printed in Padua in 1476 at All Souls.[85] Dr Lotte Hellinga has reported another example on a 1482 Lathbury in the Folger Library in Washington; a copy of Petrus de Alliaco, *De imagine mundi* [Louvain, c. 1483] bound in this shop was sold at Christie's on 24 July 1970 (lot 3), and is now in Mr Otto Schaefer's library at Schweinfurt.[86] Pollard pointed out that the dates 1478–1482 fit neither Rood nor Hunt, but do fit a certain Nicholas Bokebynder who lived in Cat Street, was paid for binding in 1478 and 1483, and who seems to have left Oxford by the end of 1483 owing rent and 'taking his tools with him'.[87] There is, alas, one snag. The Rood and Hunt binding at Stonyhurst College covers a copy of Petrus Lombardus, *Sententiarum libri IV*, printed at Basel by Nicolaus Kesler on 8 March 1486, and it cannot have reached Oxford and received its binding until three years after Nicholas Bokebynder appears to have left.

A group of bindings which may be of earlier date than the work of the Rood and Hunt binder is that of Oldham's binder C.[88] Graham Pollard reported but did not list eleven bindings on books printed between 1475 and c. 1485.[89] Binder C may be connected with the group of Oxford quasi-romanesque bindings, but as the linking tool is the large fleur-de-lis, and as a number of variants of this tool exist, I am not yet convinced that this is so. Another binder who may have started work in Oxford in the late 1470s is the Floral binder. J.B. Oldham listed twenty-two examples of this binder's work, and Graham Pollard mentioned 'some thirty books' bound by him with dates ranging from 1476 to 1496, identifying him with Thomas Uffyngton, book-binder, who appears in the Oxford records between 1479 and 1496.[90]

The Dragon binder was discussed in turn by G.D. Hobson, J.B. Oldham, and by Graham Pollard, who identified him with Thomas Bedford who bound for Magdalen College in 1487, and who succeeded Christopher Coke as University Stationer. His own successor was appointed in 1507. The forty-seven examples of the Dragon binder's work cover books with imprints between 1486 and 1506.[91]

The bindings produced by the Fruit and Flower binder cover books printed between 1491 and 1512. J.B. Oldham knew seventeen examples from this shop and Graham Pollard more than forty. If Pollard is right in identifying this binder with George Chastellaine (before 1502–13), he falls outside the period covered in this chapter.[92]

The Half-Stamp binder, who owned a small panel with the English royal arms, also possessed a set of hand stamps, including a hand with a pointing finger and an easily recognisable heart tool. His work, consisting of twenty-three known bindings, covers books with imprint dates between 1491 and 1511. J.B. Oldham was not certain of his location, but Graham Pollard placed him in Oxford on the basis of the discovery in one of his bindings of several leaves from the accounts for 1459 of an Oxford Stationer.[93]

We are left with three small groups, probably produced in Oxford, which do not seem to connect with any of the groups discussed thus far. In the *Book Collector* for 1975 David Rogers published an Oxford binding on a Boccaccio manuscript of c. 1480 and connected it with a binding on J. Nider, *Consolatorium timorate conscientie* (Paris, 1478) [and other works] and with a manuscript of Alexander Hales written in 1477 at All Souls (MS 322).[94] The dolphin tool also occurs on a detached cover which J.B. Oldham saw in Durham Cathedral in 1951.[95] A second group of four bindings, three with a diaper design and the fourth with a rather clumsily filled panel (all decorated with Gibson's tools 22–26, 38), cover books printed between 1478 and 1487.[96]

A third group of six bindings, two with a central circle design on one cover and a central diamond on the other cover, and four with diaper designs, covering manuscripts and books printed in 1482 and 1483, display Gibson's tools 60–71.[97] Seven groups of uncertain location remain to be discussed and there is very little if anything that I can add to the work published by Hobson, Oldham and Pollard.

The Huntsman binder, who owes his name to his most distinctive tool, a finely engraved image of a behatted figure holding a spear and standing among trees, bound one manuscript and books printed between 1477 and 1498. J.B. Oldham listed ten examples, and the British Library acquired a few years ago a 1498 Basel (Froben) Bible in two volumes from this shop.[98]

I commented above on the un-English technical habits of the Lily binder, and the designs of some of his tools also show Low Country influence. J.B. Oldham listed eighteen examples of his work covering books printed between 1481 and 1504, there is a copy of J. Beets, *Expositio decalogi* (Louvain, 1486), bound by him at Cambridge University Library, and Bartolus de Saxoferrato's *Digestum novum* (Venice, 1493) may also have come from this bindery.[99]

Of the work of the Bat binder only three examples were listed by J.B.

Oldham, one on a manuscript and two on books printed in 1486 and 1489;[100] a fourth covering Alexander de Villa Dei, *Doctrinale* (Paris, 1489) was sold at Christie's in New York on 8 April 1981 (lot 118).

Oldham's binder E bound books printed between 1486 and 1491, and two examples of his work came to Cambridge University Library with the books from Peterborough Cathedral.[101]

J.B. Oldham recorded ten examples of the work of the Octagonal Rose binder, covering books printed between 1489 and 1496, and Graham Pollard saw eleven bindings from this shop.[102] A larger group of bindings has survived that can be attributed to the Foliaged Staff binder. J.B. Oldham and Graham Pollard both mention thirty-eight examples but do not list them. They are said to cover manuscripts and books printed between 1489 and 1502.[103]

The last group to be mentioned was produced by the Greyhound binder. G.D. Hobson first distinguished this binder; J.B. Oldham listed ten examples of his work and suggested Oxford as a probable place of their production. He seemed to have worked during the 1490s, and Graham Pollard, who placed him among the unlocated binderies, has pointed out that of the ten volumes known to have been bound by him, six were given by Bishop Richard Fox to Corpus Christi College, Oxford.[104]

It will be clear from this survey that, although a great deal of valuable work has been done in the field of fifteenth-century English bookbinding, much more research is needed to establish whether the binderies whose tools seem to link were in fact more than one shop, whether the many small groups are in all cases the products of as many separate establishments, and whether the still uncertain origin of many of the groups of bindings cannot be more firmly determined. Especially, more data are necessary in order to come to any firm conclusions about the identity of the nameless binders. Archive research as carried out by Graham Pollard and Paul Christianson is extremely valuable, but, unless an unambiguous fact, such as a binder's signature, a contemporary note on the original endleaves, or a bill for binding an identifiable book, connects the man with the object, identification, based on the availability of a name on the one hand and a group of bindings on the other, even with matching dates for both, remains conjectural.

NOTES

1 G.D. Hobson, *English Binding Before 1500* (Cambridge, 1929); *idem*, 'Further Notes On Romanesque Bindings', *The Library*, 4th series, 15 (1934–5), 161–210; *idem*, 'Some Early Bindings and Binders' Tools', *The Library*, 4th series, 19 (1938–9), 202–49; H.M. Nixon, 'The Binding of the Winton Domesday', in M. Biddle (ed.), *Winchester in the Early Middle Ages. Winchester Studies* 1 (Oxford, 1976), pp. 526–40; C. de Hamel, *Glossed Books of the Bible and the Origins of the Paris Booktrade* (Woodbridge, Suffolk, 1984), pp. 64–86; M.M. Foot, 'Bindings', in *English Romanesque Art 1066–*

1200. Catalogue of an exhibition at the Hayward Gallery, London, 5 April–8 July 1984 (London, 1984), pp. 342–9.

2 T.J. Brown (ed.), *The Stonyhurst Gospel of St John* [with a technical description of the binding by Roger Powell and Peter Waters] (Roxburghe Club, 1969).

3 MS A.III.28; Hobson, *Before 1500*, pp. 34–5, pl. 31; A.I. Doyle, 'Medieval Blind-Stamped Bindings Associated with Durham Cathedral Priory', in G. Colin (ed.), *De libris compactis miscellanea. Studia Bibliothecae Wittockianae*, 1 (Brussels, 1984). I am most grateful to Dr Doyle for showing me this article in proof.

4 MS Cosin v.II.8; Hobson, 'Some Early Bindings', 242–2; Doyle, *Wittockiana*.

5 For early examples see P. Needham, *Twelve Centuries of Bookbinding* (New York and London, 1979), pp. 33–8; H.M. Nixon, Lyell Lectures, Oxford, 1979, Lecture 1 (publication forthcoming).

6 Nixon, Lyell Lecture 1.

7 BL MS Sloane 2400; C. Davenport, *English Embroidered Bookbindings* (London, 1899), p. 3.

8 Graham Pollard has written about the construction of medieval bindings and changes in binding techniques in 'Some Anglo-Saxon Bookbindings', *The Book Collector*, 24 (1975), 130–59; 'The Construction of English 12th-Century Bindings', *The Library*, 5th series, 17 (1962), 1–22; 'Describing Medieval Bookbindings', in J.J.G. Alexander and M.T. Gibson (eds.), *Medieval Learning and Literature. Essays presented to R.W. Hunt* (Oxford, 1976), pp. 50–65; 'Changes in the Style of Bookbinding, 1530–1830', *The Library*, 5th series, 11 (1956), 71–94. See also B. Middleton, *A History of English Craft Bookbinding Technique* (2nd edn, London, 1978).

9 I have seen a few cases where pairs of thongs have been laced in to form a large V-shape, alternating with single thongs.

10 For two examples of leather boards see Pollard, 'Construction of English 12th-Century Bindings', 13, and J.B. Oldham, *English Blind-Stamped Bindings* (Cambridge, 1952), p. 31 (quoted as Oldham, *EBSB*).

11 Oldham, *EBSB*, p. 8, first noted this habit of English (and French) binders; the clasps on German and Dutch bindings hinge on the lower cover.

12 N.R. Ker, *Early Pastedowns in Oxford Bindings* (Oxford, 1954).

13 M.M. Foot, 'Influences from the Netherlands on Bookbinding in England during the Late Fifteenth and Early Sixteenth Centuries', *Actes du XIᵉ Congrès International de Bibliophilie* (Brussels, 1979), pp. 39–64 (with literature).

14 Hobson, *Before 1500*; Oldham, *EBSB*; G. Pollard, 'The Names of Some English Fifteenth-Century Binders', *The Library*, 5th series, 25 (1970), 193–218 (quoted as Pollard, 1970).

15 N.J. Barker, 'A Register of Writs and the Scales Binder', *The Book Collector*, 21 (1972), 227–44, 356–79. One more can be added: *Liber assisarum*, MS c.1460, with one unrecorded tool; acquired by the British Library, 1988.

16 MS 204; Hobson, *Before 1500*, p. 53, pl. 38.

17 MS Bodley 117, Manchester, John Rylands University Library, MS Lat. 211, Oxford, Magdalen College, MS 145; Pollard, 1970, pp. 201, 211, pl. II. The binding of Magdalen College, MS Lat. 196 can still not be linked with any known binding or group of bindings.

18 Oxford, Merton College, MS 268 (Hobson, *Before 1500*, pl. 34); Bodley, MS Laud misc. 558.

19 BL Add. MS 28870 and Manchester, Chetham's Library, Mun. A.3.131 (MS
    27929). All four bindings are discussed in Pollard, 1970, pp. 204, 212. It is possible
    that these bindings were made in Oxford.

20 Oldham, *EBSB*, pl. xxvii, nos. 402–5, p. 31, note 1.

21 *Ibid.*, nos. 406–10, p. 31, note 1.

22 Pollard, 1970, p. 212 (iic). They are: Bodleian, MS Laud misc. 701; Bodleian, MS
    Douce 246; BL Add. MS 6173; and Salisbury Cathedral, MS 99.

23 BL Add. MS 15673.

24 This shop may link with the Crucifer binder and Pynson. The fleur-de-lis tool
    found on Bodleian, MS Laud Misc. 701 and on MS Douce 246 (Ill. 7, no. 1) seems
    to be identical with the fleur-de-lis tool found on the Indenture at Windsor (see
    p. 74) and on a Henry VII deed in Bremen Town Library (see J.B. Oldham,
    Blind Panels of English Binders (Cambridge, 1958), RO1. I have not seen this book).

25 Oldham, *EBSB*, pl. xxvii, nos. 411–18, p. 31 note 1.

26 Bodleian, MS 4° B 1 Art. Seld. All tools on this binding are upside down. The book
    does not appear to have been re-sewn.

27 BL Add. MS 24057.

28 S. Gibson, *Early Oxford Bindings* (Oxford, 1903), (quoted as Gibson), pls. i, ii, iii,
    iv, v, viii, xii, xiii, xiv, xvii, xxxi; tools 1–18, 27–32, 52–9, 72–81. This bindery (or
    these binderies) used seven more tools not in Gibson: one is Oldham, *EBSB*, tool
    159; for the other six see Ill. 7, nos. 10–15.

29 Hobson, *Before 1500*, p. 48, pls. 35–6; Pollard, 1970, pl. iv (All Souls MS 82); N.J.
    Barker, 'Quiring and the Binder', in *Studies in the Book Trade in Honour of Graham
    Pollard* (Oxford, 1975), p. 15: Bodley, MS Lyell 16 (Barker's attributions of these
    bindings are based on Pollard's work: see below). The additional attributions are:
    Chronica (MS 15th cent.), Lambeth, MS 340; *Liber precum* (MS 15th cent.), Lord
    Middleton, now on deposit in Nottingham University Library, MS MiLM 11;
    P. Nicolettus, *Summa naturalium* (Venice, 1476), Ripon Cathedral, XVIII.H.9 (I
    owe this reference to Nicolas Barker); Leonardus de Utino, *Sermones quadragesimales
    de legibus* (Paris, 1477), Leicester, Wyggeston Hospital; Jacobus de Theramo,
    Consolatio peccatorum (Gouda, 1481), Shrewsbury School, B.iii.24 (Oldham, *Shrews-
    bury School Library Bindings* (Oxford, 1943), pl. 1, quoted as Oldham, *Shrewsbury*);
    Nicolaus de Lyra, *Super libros Salomonis et Prophetas* (Nuremberg, 1481), Durham
    Cathedral, Inc.1.f; Magninus (Mediolanensis), *Regimen sanitatis* (Louvain, 1482),
    Gloucester Cathedral, Sel. 3–21; Michael of Hungary, *Sermones* (MS Oxford,
    c. 1470–83), Sotheby's, 6th December 1983, lot 64; G. Lyndewode, *Constitutiones
    Provinciales* [Oxford, 1483], BL IC 55322 (Goff L 413, Proctor 9753. I am not sure
    that this binding belongs to this group; the binding is very worn and the tools are
    difficult to identify); Antonius de Butrio, *Speculum de Confessione* [Louvain, after
    1483] [and seven other tracts], Lambeth, 1483.3. For MS Bodley 460 see the
    Fishtail binder (p. 71). I do not think that MS Bodley 95 belongs to this group (see
    Barker, 'Quiring', p. 24). The tools on this binding are similar to, but not identical
    with Gibson, tools 12, 68, 79.

30 Pollard, 1970, pp. 201–3, 212 (Pollard's unidentified group iii ii a also belongs to
    this Oxford quasi-romanesque group). The date of the start of this shop is still
    uncertain (see Barker, 'Quiring', p. 14).

31 Attributed to the Fishtail binder by Barker, 'Quiring', p. 28.

32 Oldham, *EBSB*, pl. xviii, no. 159.

33 See note 29 above, list.

34 Oldham, *EBSB*, p. 22, note 4, lists ten examples. See also pls. xvi, xviii. Thirteen are noted but not listed in J.B. Oldham, 'English Fifteenth-Century Binding' in *Festschrift Ernst Kyriss* (Stuttgart, 1961), p. 170. H.M. Nixon has told me that the date of printing of no. v of Oldham's list (CA 43 in Westminster Abbey Library) is [1498].

35 Pollard, 1970, pp. 210, 213 (iv c 2).

36 As well as the bindings mentioned by Oldham, (*EBSB*, p. 22, note 4): T. Valois and N. Trivet, *Commentarius in S. Augustini libros de civitate dei* (MS 15th cent.), Bodleian, MS Laud misc. 128; Bartholomeus de Urbino (MS 15th cent.), MS Bodley 460 (I am not sure that the attribution of this binding to the Fishtail binder is correct); Theological tracts (MS 15th and early 16th cent.), BL Add. MS 34807; Cicero, *De Senectute* [and other works] (Deventer, n.d.), CUL Inc. 4.E.4.1 (Oates 3447); Leonardus de Utino, *Sermones* (Paris, 1477), Leicester, Wyggeston Hospital (see above, n. 29); Johannes Salesberiensis, *Policraticus* [and other works] (Cologne, 1480), Lincoln Cathedral, SS 3.19; Laurentius Valla, *Elegantiae* (Paris, 1491), BL IA 40179 (BMC viii, 145); Thomas Aquinas, *Catena aurea super quattuor Evangelistas* (Venice, 1493), Reigate Church; *Sermones super orationem dominicam* [and other works] (Paris, 1494), BL IA 40664 [etc.] (BMC viii, 29; viii, 27/8; viii, 106). Cato, *Disticha de moribus* (Deventer [between 1492 and 1500]), and four other educational works, [Cologne, c. 1480]; [Southern Netherlands, not before 1491]; Paris, 1491; [Paris, c. 1478–82], BL IA 47755 [etc.] (GW 6293; Vouilléme (Köln) 417; Campbell 21; Copinger 5229; Hain 14635).

37 G.D. Hobson, *Bindings in Cambridge Libraries* (Cambridge, 1929), pl. xiii.

38 Oldham, *EBSB*, p. 18, note 3, pl. xiv.

39 Boethius, *De consolatione philosophiae* (Cologne, 1488), IB 3600 (Goff B 783); Boethius, *De disciplina scholarium* (Louvain, 1485), IB 49177a (BMC ix, 143); J. Versor, *Quaestiones super libros Ethicorum Aristotelis* (Cologne, 1494), IB 4880 (Goff v 256).

40 IB 22910 (BMC v, 443). Dr. A. I. Doyle has reported a third binding from this shop in the New York Public Library (MS 121).

41 N.R. Ker, 'The Virgin and Child Binder, LVL, and William Horman', *The Library*, 5th series, 17 (1962), 77–85. A.G. Watson (ed.), *Books, Collectors and Libraries* (London, 1985), pp. 100–10.

42 Pollard, 1970, pp. 208, 213. See also E. Wilson, *The Winchester Anthology: a facsimile of B.L. Add. MS 60577* (Cambridge, 1981), p. 7 (with a correction to Pollard's list).

43 Add. MS 60577.

44 Doyle, *Wittockiana*.

45 Hobson, *Before 1500*, pl. 33, p. 15, note 6. Oldham, *EBSB*, p. 24, note 15 (lot 123a in Sotheby's sale on 22 May 1950 is now in the British Library as part of the Henry Davis Gift: see M.M. Foot, *The Henry Davis Gift*, vol. 2 (London, 1983), no. 2, pl. xx).

46 Pollard, 1970, pp. 204–5, 212.

47 J.H. Stevenson, *The Fifteenth Century Scots Binding of the Haye Manuscript* (Edinburgh, 1904); G.D. Hobson, 'Further Notes on the Binding of the Haye Manuscript', *Papers of the Edinburgh Bibliographical Society*, 14 (1930), 89–97; W.S. Mitchell,

'Scottish Bookbinding' in A. Kent, H. Lancour and J.E. Daily (eds.), *Encyclopedia of Library and Information Science*, vol. 27: *Scientific and Technical Libraries to Slavonic Paleography* (New York and Basel, 1979), pp. 117–19.

48 P. Christianson, 'Early London Bookbinders and Parchmeners', *The Book Collector*, 32 (1985), 41–54, and 'Evidence for the Study of London's Late Medieval Book-trade', Chapter 4 below. I am most grateful to Dr Christianson for showing me both articles in typescript.

49 Hobson, *Cambridge*, pl. IX; *Before 1500*, p. 20.

50 G.D. Hobson, *Blind-Stamped Panels in the English Book-Trade* (London, 1944), pp. 21–2. See also J.B. Oldham, *Blind Panels of English Binders* (Cambridge, 1958), Rel 2, AN 3, AN 4.

51 Pollard, 1970, pp. 195, 207, 212, 214, 215.

52 The first is Bodleian Library, Auct. Q.1.3.10; the other Heritage Bookshop, Catalogue 144, March 1982, item 248, previously sold at Sotheby's, 23 February 1959, lot 57.

53 [W. Ward in] Sotheby's catalogue, 16 October 1979, lot 253 (this binding is now BL IB 55317a); C. de Hamel in an unpublished paper read to the Oxford Bibliographical Society on 1 December 1982. I am very grateful to Dr de Hamel for showing me the typescript of his paper.

54 H.M. Nixon, 'William Caxton and Bookbinding', *Papers Presented to the Caxton International Congress 1976*, *Journal of the Printing Historical Society*, 11 (1976/7), 92–113; 'Caxton, his Contemporaries and Successors', *The Library*, 5th series, 31 (1976), 305–26.

55 Pollard, 1970, p. 205.

56 Foot, 'Influences', pp. 48–9

57 IB 37262A (BMC III, 746) and IA 3941 (BMC I, 241).

58 Hobson, *Before 1500*, p. 23; *English Bindings 1490–1940 in the Library of J.R. Abbey* (London, 1940), p. 185. See also Oldham, *EBSB*, pp. 27–8, pl. XXI, and *Kyriss Festschrift*, p. 164. Pollard, 1970, p. 207 (with further literature), p. 213.

59 M.M. Foot, 'A Binding by the Crucifer Binder, c. 1505', English and Foreign Bookbindings 11, *The Book Collector*, 28 (1979), 554–5.

60 H.R. Plomer, 'Two Lawsuits of Richard Pynson', *The Library*, NS 10 (1909), p. 116; E.G. Duff, *The Printers, Stationers and Bookbinders of Westminster and London from 1476 to 1535* (Cambridge, 1906).

61 Oldham, *EBSB*, pl. XXVI, p. 31, note 1. They are: Westminster Abbey, CC.41(1) [Deventer, ? 1480]; Leicester, Guild Hall 15/59 (n.p., 1488); Hereford Cathedral, MS H.2.19 (Louvain, 1488); Ushaw College, XVIII. c.5.17 [Basel, 1489/90]. I have only seen J.B. Oldham's rubbings of these bindings. It is possible that the large fleur-de-lis tool found on Leicester Guild Hall 15/59 is that used by binder C (Oldham, *EBSB*, tool no. 360) who in turn links with the Oxford quasi-romanesque group. However, this is a relatively common tool and the one used by binder A may well be a variant.

62 The fleur-de-lis tool on this binding also occurs on two bindings at the Bodleian Library, MS Laud misc. 701 and MS Douce 246, which belong to the group of four unlocated bindings (see p. 70). Oldham has found this fleur-de-lis together with Pynson's panel RO1 on the binding of a Henry VII deed in Bremen Town Library (see note 24 above).

63 Oldham, *Panels*, RO1, MISC 4, MISC 14 lists nine. One was sold at Christie's, 12 November 1974, lot 149 (previously sold at Sotheby's, 31 May 1960, lot 9) (RO2 and MISC 14) and one is BL Add. MS 59862 (RO1).

64 Hobson, *Panels*, pp. 19–23; Pollard, 1970, pp. 214–15. Vol. 1 is Oxford, Corpus Christi College, φ. A.4.1.

65 Nixon, 'William Caxton and Bookbinding', p. 102; *idem*, Lyell Lecture 1.

66 Oldham, *Panels*, ST 10; Pollard, 1970, pp. 216–18.

67 Hobson, *Before 1500*, p. 25, pl. 55; Nixon, Lyell Lecture 1; see also above, p. 79.

68 BL IA 55454 (Goff T 111).

69 Hobson, *Before 1500*, p. 24, pl. 54.

70 Oldham, *EBSB*, pp. 18–19, pl. xi.

71 Hobson, *Cambridge*, pls. xiv, xv; *Before 1500*, pp. 21–2, pls. 47–9.

72 Oldham, *Shrewsbury*, pp. 52–5; *idem*, 'Note on Some New Tools Used by the "Unicorn Binder"', *The Library*, 5th series, 2 (1948), 283–4; *idem*, *EBSB*, p. 17, pl. xi; *idem*, *Kyriss Festschrift*, pp. 169–72; Pollard, 1970, pp. 208, 212, 213. As Pollard does not list the additional ? 27 bindings I am not sure whether the recent BL acquisition (IC 21646; BMC v, 308/9) was known to him. As this binding once belonged to Major Abbey, he probably did know it.

73 Oldham, *EBSB*, pp. 16–17, pl. x; *idem*, *Shrewsbury*, pp. 58–64. See also Hobson, *Cambridge*, pp. 46–7; *idem*, *Before 1500*, pp. 22–3, pl. 51; Pollard, 1970, pp. 208, 213.

74 Oldham, *Shrewsbury*, pp. 7–12; *idem*, *EBSB*, pp. 18–19, pl. xi.

75 *Ibid.*, p. 18; Pollard, 1970, p. 213.

76 Respectively IB 7480a (BMC ii, 439) and IB 2178a (BMC i, 153).

77 Oldham, *EBSB*, pp. 19–20, pl. xiv; *idem*, *Kyriss Festschrift*, pp. 172–3. See also Pollard, 1970, p. 213.

78 GW 2908. Dr Doyle reports that Durham Cathedral, Inc. 32–34 are bound by this binder.

79 Printed in *The Library*, 5th series, 25 (1970), 193–218.

80 W.H.J. Weale, *Bookbindings and Rubbings of Bindings in the National Art Library*, 2 vols. (London, 1898, 1894; Gibson, nos. 17–20; W.H.J. Weale and L. Taylor, *Early Stamped Bookbindings in the British Museum* (London, 1922); Hobson, *Before 1500*, pl. 37, p. 17.

81 D.E. Rhodes, 'Account of Cataloguing Incunabula in Oxford College Libraries', *Renaissance Quarterly*, 29 (1976), 1–20. See also his *Catalogue of Incunabula in all the Libraries of Oxford University outside the Bodleian* (Oxford, 1982).

82 Foot, 'Influences'.

83 Gibson, nos. 17–20 (with note).

84 Pollard, 1970, pp. 209, 212.

85 In his paper to the Oxford Bibliographical Society (see note 53 above). The All Souls pressmark is SR.58.g.1.

86 I owe this information to Dr de Hamel.

87 Pollard, 1970, p. 209.

88 Oldham, *EBSB*, pl. xxvi, p. 31, note 1. See also my note 61 above.

89 Pollard, 1970, p. 212.

90 Oldham, *EBSB*, p. 22, note 6, pl. xviii; Pollard, 1970, pp. 210, 213.

91 Hobson, *Before 1500*, p. 24, note 1, pl. 52; Oldham, *Shrewsbury*, pp. 46–9; *idem*, *EBSB*, pp. 21–2, pl. xv; *idem*, *Kyriss Festschrift*, p. 168; Pollard 1970, pp. 210–11,

213. Dr Doyle has reported one more example at Upholland College, Lancs.

92 Oldham, *EBSB*, p. 23, pls. XVII, XVIII; *idem, Kyriss Festschrift*, p. 168; Pollard, 1970, pp. 211, 213.

93 Oldham, *Shrewsbury*, pp. 36–8; *idem, EBSB*, pp. 29–30, pls. XXIV, XXV; Pollard, 1970, pp. 196, 213.

94 D. Rogers, 'An Unpublished Early Oxford Binding', *The Book Collector*, 24 (1975), 65–9.

95 Inc.4A. J. Duns Scotus, *Quaestiones super libro quarto sententiarum* (Strassburg, 1474).

96 M.M. Foot, 'An Oxford Binding, *c.* 1480. English and Foreign Bookbindings 30', *The Book Collector*, 33 (1984), 332–3.

97 Littleton, *Tenores novelli* (MS 15th cent.), Cambridge, St John's College, C.13 (Gibson, no. 24); *Summa Theologiae*, 4 vols. (Nuremberg, 1482), Oxford, Brasenose College, UB/S.I.16; Lathbury (Oxford, 1482), BL, IB 55317 (Proctor 9749); Bertachinus, *Repertorium iuris* (Nuremberg, 1483), 2 vols. (II, III) Oxford, New College, Founders Library, A.9.5.6; Peter Carmelianus (MS in or after 1486), BL Add. MS 33736; *Biblia* [Nuremberg, 1487], Worcester Cathedral, Inc. 8.

98 Oldham, *EBSB*, p. 30, note 7, pl. XXV; BL IB 37895a (BMC III, 791/2).

99 Oldham, *EBSB*, p. 29, note 5, pl. XXIII. CUL Inc. 3.F.2.8 (3284) (Oates 3814); BL IC 21428 (Goff B 220) (the binding is very worn).

100 Oldham, *EBSB*, p. 28, note 7, pls. XXII, XXIII.

101 Oldham, *EBSB*, p. 31, note 1, pl. XXVI. CUL Pet.Q.2.7 (Oates 3093.5 and 3093.7); CUL Pet.G.1.12 (Oates, 4007.2, 249.5, 3779.5 and 1118.5). To the remaining groups of binders whom Oldham (*EBSB*, p. 31, note 1) simply indicated by a letter, i.e. binders B, D, F, G, and H, and who worked during the 1480s and 90s, I have at present nothing to add.

102 Oldham, *Shrewsbury*, p. 56; *EBSB*, p. 30, note 5, pl. XXV; Pollard, 1970, p. 213.

103 Oldham, *EBSB*, p. 30, pl. XXVI; Pollard, 1970, p. 213.

104 Hobson, *Cambridge*, pl. xv (p. 49); *Before 1500*, p. 24, pl. 53; Oldham, *EBSB*, p. 21, note 3, pl. xv; Pollard, 1970, p. 213.

4 · EVIDENCE FOR THE STUDY OF LONDON'S LATE MEDIEVAL MANUSCRIPT-BOOK TRADE

C. PAUL CHRISTIANSON

AT A REMOVE of well over five hundred years, the earliest stages of the English book trade have long been the subject more of speculation than of clear documentation. This has been especially true for the commerce in manuscript books that developed in London during the century leading up to the introduction of print technology in 1476. Facts discovered about the early London trade have been few, the most important of which attest to the organisation of a common mistery or gild of book artisans in 1403, uniting separate fourteenth-century gilds of manuscript artists and textwriters; the appointment of gild wardens in various years between 1393–1441; the attempt at regulation of the book trade by church constitutions of 1409; and, much later, the encouragement of trade from abroad by specific provision of Parliament in 1484, particularly aimed at printed books.[1] Beyond these data, little information has been forthcoming, inasmuch as the gild's records before the sixteenth century do not survive. As for individual artisans' identities and activities, the habit of deliberate anonymity regularly adopted for craftwork done has meant that only incidental facts have emerged, usually tied to the close study of specific surviving books.[2] What Graham Pollard once remarked when speaking of English binding in the fifteenth century thus could apply to the entire trade throughout the period: 'It is a strange world . . . it has no real people in it . . . it lacks the co-ordinates of place and time.'[3] Despite such loss of direct documentation, certain information about London's medieval book trade survives in other kinds of records, particularly in archival documents related to the City. The purpose of this essay is to indicate what such data may reveal.

Among printed records found most useful for this study are the calendars of the plea and memoranda rolls [1323–1482] and the letter-books of the City [1275–1498], which cover transactions in the Mayor's Court and matters of civic administration; the indexes of early Chancery proceedings [1385–1529] and the calendars of the close rolls [1227–1509], which often reveal ordinary citizens' relations to the central administration; and the indexes to testaments and wills, especially those available for London residents.[4] Other archival records do not exist in printed form and yet are essential for further inquiry into the book trade. Among these documents, most use has been made of file copies of probate wills proved in the Prerogative Court of Canterbury and in three London courts, the Archdeaconry, the Commissary, and the Hustings. Extensive use has also been made of the journals of the City's Common Council covering the years 1416–1527, which until 1495 contain proceedings of both the Court of Aldermen and that of the Council; and the recognizance rolls of those gaining freedom of the City by redemption, which run from 1437 to 1493.[5]

Perhaps the most valuable set of unpublished records used, significant for showing rental of shops to book-trade members and periodically the commissioning of work by them, is that once kept by the wardens of old London Bridge. These documents include the deeds of properties bequeathed to the Bridge (most of them prior to the sixteenth century), the Bridgemasters' account rolls [1381–1405], the Bridge House account books [1404–1525], and the books of expenditures of the Bridge [Series 1 and 2, 1404–45 and 1505–38].[6]

Close study of all these public records permits discovery of certain facts from which gradually a composite picture of the manuscript-book trade begins to emerge, the most basic feature of which is simply the size of the trade group. Thus far, my study has identified at least 254 citizens who were professional manuscript-book craftsmen and stationers at work in London between 1300 and 1520. Since London citizenship depended on craft membership, such affiliations were often carefully noted in many of the public records kept. These 254 artisans, therefore, are identified consistently in records by one or more craft designations: textwriter, limner, bookbinder, parchmener, stationer, apprentice, or servant. Specifically, 117 artisans are identified only as stationer, with no other book-craft designation (although one stationer was also a grammar school teacher, five were notaries, two, haberdashers, two, drapers, and one, a legal scrivener). In other categories, thirty-five are identified as limners (including ten also listed as stationer); thirty are identified as textwriters (including six also listed as stationer, three as legal scrivener, one as draper, one as parish clerk, and one as clerk of the chapel on London Bridge); six are identified both as limners and textwriters; forty-four are identified as bookbinders (including eighteen also listed as stationer, four as scribe, and one as both textwriter and notary); twelve are identified as parchmener (including two also listed as stationer, one as haberdasher, and one as bookseller); four are identified only as servants (three to stationers and one to a textwriter); six are identified only as apprentices (one to a stationer, three to limners, and two to textwriters). It should be noted that, with the exception of bookbinders, 'stationer' became the predominant tag for all book craftsmen after the 1440s, at about the same time when the 'Mistery of Stationers' became the prevailing name for the common craft gild; in London records examined, 'lymnour' last occurs in 1461, 'tixtwriter', in 1465.[7]

Exclusions from this list of book artisans must also be noted. It does not include, when they appear near the end of the period studied, printers or importers of printed books.[8] Nor does it include a group of at least seventy-two fifteenth-century painters in London, some of whom may have worked as limners.[9] Also excluded are fourteenth- and fifteenth-century Writers of the Court Letter (a separate gild of legal writers, the forebear of the Scriveners' Company) and other clerical scriveners (both groups together numbering over 295 writers), some of whom presumably worked as occasional text-writers, as did no doubt certain lesser clerks in the central administration (such as Hoccleve), including those in Chancery.[10]

It must always be borne in mind that the compilation of names of pro-fessional book-trade people, identified as such primarily by their craft desig-nations, becomes at best only a relative guide, given the fugitive nature of surviving records. Distortions are bound to occur, for many of the archival data are limited both in the span of years covered and in the completeness of information given for specific events. Notwithstanding these restrictions, the decade 1380–9 shows the first sizeable group of book artisans appearing in the records examined: sixteen were working London during this ten-year period, an increase of ten over the previous decade. By the next decade, 1390–9, the number of artisans had jumped to thirty-four, and by the first decade of the fifteenth century to forty-four. Thereafter, the number continues fairly stable decade by decade until the end of the century: 1410–19 (40); 1420–9 (34); 1430–9 (42); 1440–9 (40); 1450–9 (47); 1460–9 (48); 1470–9 (50); 1480–9 (39); 1490–9 (41). In the following decade, 1500–9, the number drops to twenty-eight; and in 1510–19 to twelve. From such evidence it would appear that the period of greatest commercial activity in making and selling manu-script books ran almost precisely for a century, from the 1390s to the 1490s. Once the printing press had arrived and wholesale trade from abroad was encouraged, the number of book artisans begins to decline by the early sixteenth century.[11]

Beyond the question of aggregate number and relative concentration at various points in time, the data gathered reveal another feature in the composite picture, that of the main location of the book trade within the City. Records of property transactions (including the rental of shops) and of parish membership or residence offer topographical identification of 144 of the 254 book artisans working in London, 136 of them located, at least at certain points in their careers, in parishes whose churches stood within five hundred yards of the crossing of St Paul's (including sixty-one craftsmen who rented one or more shops from the wardens of London Bridge, fifty-six craftsmen working out of shops in Paternoster Row alone). Certain parishes, moreover, had large concentrations of book artisans: St Faith the Virgin by St Paul's (60); St Michael le Querne (12); St Botolph without Aldersgate (11); St Nicholas at the Shambles (11); St Sepulchre without Newgate (10); St

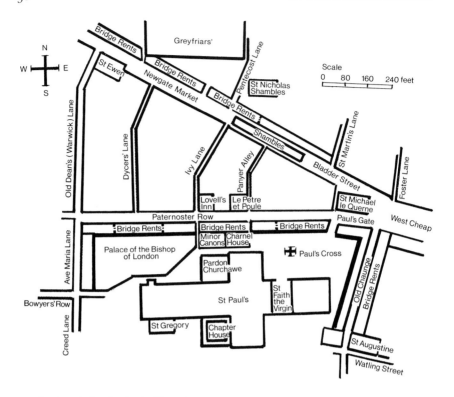

10   Bookmen's London in the fifteenth century.

Augustine near St Paul's (8); St Bride Fleet Street (7) (see Ill. 10). Clearly, the area immediately surrounding St Paul's, especially to the north, northwest, and east, was from the beginning a craft neighbourhood, a fact long guessed at (given later concentration of print trade in the area) and now certainly documented.

Such congregation of trade members within a very small part of the City would seem to suggest a parallel concentration of professional and personal associations within the group. Other records bear this out. The examination of fifty-eight surviving wills of book artisans and stationers (all but five before 1500), including those of forty craftsmen living within five hundred yards of St Paul's, shows that thirty-eight fellow trade members were named as executor, overseer, witness, or beneficiary. In various other records examined, forty-eight craftsmen are specifically identified as members of the book-trade gild between 1393 and 1464 (nineteen of whom can be located in the area around St Paul's, and twenty-one of whom are also mentioned in artisans' wills), named as gild wardens, as stationers entering the mistery and taking up freedom of the City by redemption, or as members standing surety for these new stationer-citizens. Such evidence, it may be argued, attests not only to long-standing personal relationships, but perhaps also to craft affiliations.

If vocational ties seem to be signalled by place and patterns of association, they are only one part of the picture. Book craftsmen were also active as freemen of London, frequently in contact with other members of the mercantile community, or with its political and religious leaders, with whom presumably trade was periodically generated and whereby a livelihood for these artisans was assured.[12] Thus, for example, on eighty-one occasions in the years 1431–83, various members of the trade are recorded as entering into pledge actions, the chief means of debt transaction in a largely cashless society whereby lines of credit were extended by the making of a symbolic gift of goods and chattels. On twenty-two occasions, seventeen craftsmen gave such gifts; on fifty-five occasions, thirty-four received them; and on four occasions, four served as witness. One may surmise that a number of these transactions represented specific instances of financing book-trade activities.[13]

Records of other kinds of transactions identify specifically the times when trade members had additional first-hand contact with fellow citizens. On thirty-nine occasions between 1337 and 1444, thirty served as mainpernors in legal cases; eight times between 1370 and 1544 seven were named as guardians or gave surety for inheritance; nine times between 1380 and 1455 twelve were named in dispute arbitrations; sixteen times between 1415 and 1479 fourteen served as witness or gave surety in debt or property suits; and four times between 1438 and 1493 four stood surety for non-book-trade craftsmen gaining freedom of the City. Book-trade members also were parties in various cases in different courts: twenty-seven were named in suits brought before the King's Bench on fifty-one occasions between 1486 and 1505; twenty were named in Chancery suits on twenty-seven occasions between 1404 and 1538; and fourteen appeared on sixteen occasions between 1416 and 1481 in the Court of Common Council. While such activities were no different from those of other Londoners at the time, they nonetheless identify a series of relationships (involving over 1,200 people) on which artisans might have based promotion of trade in books.

Such records of the working lives of book-trade members thus document their participation in London life throughout more than a century and a half. Yet statistics based on such data give no indication of individual lives. To see these in detail, it is useful to turn to a specific artisan whose example shows the kind of documentation that close study of public records can reveal.

William Abell was a manuscript artist whose working career in London may be traced over a period of at least twenty-eight years, from 1446 to 1474. Facts about him are few in number and yet are significant for what they reveal. First notice appears in 1447 when he was paid £1 6s 8d for work done the year before on the consolidation charter of Eton College, a document that still survives.[14] The following year, in 1448, as a member of the Mistery of Stationers, Abell, along with three other members, William Childern, Robert Chirche, and Edward Cok, served as surety for a foreign stationer, John Corbet, gaining freedom of the City by redemption (RR 17 3). In 1450, Abell, identified as 'lympnor', that is, limner, was named as supervisor of the will of another London 'lympnor', Thomas Fysshe, from whom he received rights to the unexpired terms of two apprentices, Robert Fitzjohn and William Buttler (GL 9171/5 (Sharp) 8v). Fysshe was, therefore, presumably also Abell's former master. In 1452, and again in 1470, one of the churchwardens at St Nicholas at the Shambles was a William Abell, almost certainly the same man.[15] In 1459, William Abell, 'lymnour', participated in a debt transaction, receiving, along with the fruiterer James Molett, the gift with warranty of the goods and chattels of a London butcher, Richard Kylfoull (CCR 1454–61, 359). Finally, between 1469 and 1474, the year of his death, Abell rented one, then two, and ultimately three adjoining shops in Paternoster Row in a building owned by the wardens of London Bridge (BHA 1460–84, 162, 168, 174, 188, 203, 219, 235).

In all, only these six facts remain to document the life of this fifteenth-century London limner – a small measure of anyone's existence. And yet if one examines the facts in light of comparable evidence for other craftsmen, a somewhat fuller account emerges. Perhaps the most useful fact is the record of Abell's shop rentals, here pinpointing his business premises and 'atelier' in Paternoster Row, at least late in his career. The concentration of the book trade in the area of St Paul's, particularly in Paternoster Row, has been noted above. Yet who were these neighbouring craftsmen and stationers, and where precisely were these rental shops? To answer such questions, one must look briefly at the parallel growth of two London institutions, St Paul's itself and old London Bridge. Both were dominant London landmarks; each in its way also served as a powerful focus for the City's civic life.

When the Bridge, newly built in stone, was completed in 1209, King John set the precedent that endowment and upkeep of the structure would be met by gifts and by rental profits from buildings to be erected on the Bridge itself (ultimately there were 139 of them), but also by rents from tenements built in other vacant places in the City. The first of these constructions elsewhere in the City was the Stocks market in Cornhill Ward, beside St Mary de Wolchurchawe, erected in 1282 by the Mayor Henry le Waleys.[16] To provide additional funds to combat the damage and decay already occurring to the fabric of the Bridge (Stow, p. 24), Waleys began to build other rental property in the following year, 1283, notably in the area of St Paul's.

One row of shops built by Waleys lay to the east of St Paul's, along the small street called Old Chaunge, the buildings (eventually encompassing 28 shops) running between West Cheap on the north and St Augustine at the corner of Watling Street on the south (Stow, p. 289; BHD F 48; see Ill. 10). At the same time, Waleys also built another row of shops in Paternoster Row, immediately to the north of the churchyard wall and extending along Paternoster Row between the gate and lane leading to the cathedral's north transept and, farther west, the gate and lane leading to the centre of the cathedral nave (Stow, p. 302; see Ill. 10). This row of shops stood directly to the north of Pardon Churchawe and of the charnel house (Stow, p. 294), a juxtaposition that soon led the Archdeacon Robert de Ros and other canons to complain that the shops' height exceeded that of the wall surrounding the close, that tenants threw dirt out of windows into the churchyard, and that the bishop, dean, and chapter were prevented from building tenements within their close because they could make no doorways to Paternoster Row (LB A 213–14). The expedient solution was to build a chapel to the Virgin Mary over the charnel house, to be supported in part from rental income from the shops. Waleys also agreed to certain restrictions on who could be shop tenants:

> We shall nott permite butchers, poticaris, gouldsmithes, cookes or comon women, to dwell in the same shopps by whose noyse or tumulte or dishonestee the quietness or devotion of the ministers of the churche may be troubled, nor also shall suffer those which shall dwell in the said shopps to burne any seacooles in the same, or such other thinges which doe stinke.[17]

At the outset, rentals of these shops were taken over by the Bridge wardens; presumably, in later years when book-trade artisans were tenants, they were found to be the quiet and honest sort of shop-keepers desired.

Eventually, the wardens of the Bridge acquired or built other rental properties along Paternoster Row. In 1388, for example, they paid £17 in part payment of a sum of £40 for construction of a house with shops in it immediately beside Paul's Gate, across the road from St Michael le Querne (BAR 7 m. 11); the following year, they paid £53 6s 8d for five additional shops adjoining this house (BAR 9 m. 11; 10 m. 7). In later years, this property was probably the building rented (1519–36) by the printer John Rastell and called by him the 'Mermaid'.[18] In 1409, shops in a tenement built in 1358 (LB G 132; BHD G 44 and G 65), located at the opposite end of Paternoster Row abutting the palace of the bishop of London, yielded 40s yearly for the Bridge (BHA 1404–21, 12). In 1454, income from shops across the road, at the northwest corner of Paternoster Row and Panyer Alley, in the tenement 'le Petre et Poule', was left to the Bridge wardens for ten years by the building's owner, the bookbinder and stationer Peter Bylton (BHD I 22). Similar rental properties had been built in the immediate area by the Bridge wardens earlier, in 1391, namely, a row of twenty-seven shops on three storeys in a tenement northwest of the gate leading to Greyfriars' Church, facing on Newgate Market (BHD I 11; BHA 1404–21, 4v). Other nearby properties already acquired for the Bridge as early as 1404 lay within the parishes of St Michael le Querne (a tavern with the sign 'The Raven'), St Nicholas at the Shambles (two tenements, one with the sign 'The Bell,' as well as six shops and a brewhouse), and St Ewen, near Greyfriars' Church (twenty-seven shops and eight cabins) (BHA 1404–21, 3v–4; BAR 15 m. 9; see Ill. 10).

The location of shops, many of them (especially in Paternoster Row) rented to members of the book trade, is not the only matter of interest. One would also like to have some estimation of the size of these shops. Were these large, centralised workshops where limners, textwriters, and binders worked together, or was the process of manufacture a more decentralised activity, with independent artisans working in small shops on jobs farmed out to them by an entrepreneur?[19]

Some indication of the size of such establishments may be gained from the rental properties held by the Bridge wardens. Returning to the row of shops in the centre of Paternoster Row built by Henry le Waleys in 1283, one discovers that in 1388 (and in the years immediately following) these shops were completely rebuilt, at about the same time when, on the other side of the churchyard wall, the minor canons of St Paul's were building their hall and houses. The site is precisely described in an agreement finally reached in 1408 concerning run-off water from the two new sets of buildings:

Composition between the Mayor, Drago Barantyn, the aldermen and the commonalty of London and the Warden and Minor Canons of St Paul's touching the carrying off of rain water, etc., from the shops newly erected to the use of London Bridge on land situated between the wall enclosing the houses of the said warden and canons on the south and Paternoster Row on the north and the gate of the cathedral opposite Ivy Lane on the west and a gate in the little lane leading from 'le northdore' of the cathedral into Paternoster Row on the east.[20]

Four years earlier, in 1404, the first volume of the Bridge House Accounts begins its listing of rental records with this recently rebuilt row of shops: 'In Paternoster Row is one great messuage and thirty shops with solars which are let as follows' (BHA 1404–21, 3). Here, for the first time, the exact number of fifteenth-century units in this property parcel is identified, and if one estimates the distance available along Paternoster Row for these shops, one discovers that the frontage could not have been more than about 160–5 feet (Paternoster Row itself was approximately nine hundred feet long).[21] Given this restricted site, there could not have been thirty shops in a row, for that would make each of them only five feet wide. But thirty shops could have been accommodated on two storeys, if each shop was ten to eleven feet wide (or on three storeys, if sixteen feet wide).

Such dimensions are confirmed by records of other shop constructions in the immediate area at the time. In 1369, for example, the carpenters Roger Fraunkeleyn and John Page were engaged by the dean and chapter to build a row of twenty shops on the south side of the cathedral near the chapter

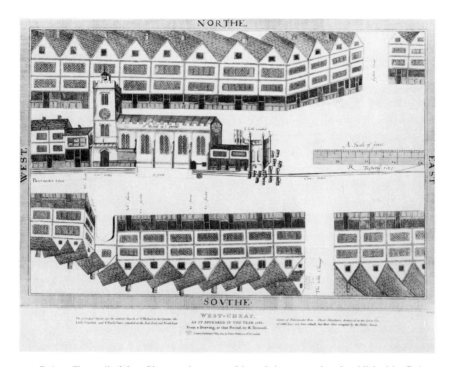

11   Robert Treswell, 'West-Cheap as it appeared in 1585', engraved and published by Robert Wilkinson, *Londina Illustrata* (London, 1819–25).

bakehouse on a frontage of eighty-six yards (RCHM 50). These shops, therefore, would have been about twelve feet wide. A year later, in the same area, a row of eighteen shops was commissioned by the dean and chapter, and here the dimensions were specified: each shop was to measure eleven by twenty-five feet, with each unit to be divided into two rooms, with ten chimneys to be built for the shops, eight of them double, that is, shared along the common dividing walls (RCHM 12). Other shops were even smaller. The twenty-seven rental units constructed for the use of the Bridge in 1391 by Greyfriars' Church, for example, were built above a cellar site 95 by $7\frac{1}{2}$ feet. Shops thus created were only $10\frac{1}{2}$ feet wide and ten feet deep (on the first two storeys) or $11\frac{1}{2}$ feet deep (on the third), the larger dimensions accommodated by overhanging jetties.[22]

If these dimensions are comparable, then the thirty Paternoster Row shops recently built and now rented by the Bridge wardens in 1404 would have been comparatively small, each with two rooms in a space about ten by twenty-five feet, if arranged with fifteen shops on the ground floor of the row and fifteen on the floor above.[23] However small such shop-rental units were, nonetheless as many as eighteen of the fifty-seven tenants occupying them at various times in the years 1404–10 covered by the record entries appear to have been book-trade artisans, eight of them later to become wardens of the trade gild. Although tenants are seldom identified by craft in the rental accounts, sixteen names correspond with those of individuals identified as book-trade members in other contemporary records. The group includes three stationers, Edmund Cok, Edward Cok, and John Robert; three bookbinders, Peter Bylton, Roger Dunce, and Richard More; three textwriters, John Boys, Thomas Marleburgh, and John Roulande; and seven limners, John Anys, Thomas Bowland, John Broune, Thomas Fysshe, Thomas Hyhelm, John White, and Roger Ybott. Two other names are of interest, John Hun and Herman Skereueyn, both of whom were, successively, tenants in the same shop. In light of so many other shop rentals to book artisans, especially to limners, one might argue that John Hun was possibly the elusive 'Johannes', who decorated and signed Oxford, Bodleian Library, MS Bodley 264, thought to have been made in London c. 1400. And Herman Skereueyn may have been the now-famous London-based foreign limner Herman Scheerre, who decorated and signed London, British Library, Add. MS 1698 and Add. MS 42131, and Lambeth Palace, MS 69, all of which have been dated as early fifteenth-century work.[24]

Such attestation of sixteen, and perhaps eighteen, book-trade artisans in these small Paternoster Row shops thus supports an hypothesis that the mode of manufacture for manuscript books in fifteenth-century London was quite different from that practised in monastic scriptoria. Instead of labouring in large workspaces, many artisans may have worked independently in small quarters, not in concert in a single shop, and a book was therefore presumably created on many different sites, none of them, however, any great distance apart, perhaps many of them separated by only a few yards or a flight of stairs.

It is unfortunate that the Bridge records of shop rentals break off in 1410 and do not resume until 1460, for it would seem likely that in the intervening years, as was the case for the remainder of the century, a sizeable number of book-trade artisans continued to rent shops in Paternoster Row. Equally unfortunate is the fact that after 1460 the rental accounts do not indicate precise shop locations other than by street (e.g., Paternoster Row) or by parish. Nonetheless, Abell's rental of small business premises from the Bridge wardens (1469–74) would seem to be typical of many other members of the trade, both early and later in the century. His rental of as many as three such small shops is more problematic, although one might argue that this fact suggests more readily the idea of expansion of work in his single craft than it does his accommodation, as stationer, of all the book crafts in one business operation and site, for which there is no evidence.

Details of Abell's other known activities illustrate additional features typical of the trade, one of which is proximity to other book artisans in their daily business. During the course of the twenty-eight years, from 1446 to 1474, in which Abell's name appears in the documents examined, he could have had contact with as many as a hundred other book-trade members, all of whom were active in London, most of them in his neighbourhood, in the 1440s, 50s, 60s, or 70s. One presumes, for example, that he knew fellow tenants in the Bridge properties along Paternoster Row, a group that between 1469 and 1474, just the period of his documented tenancy, included ten stationers: William Barwe, William Kendall, John Lidston, Robert Multon, Richard Rider, William Scotte, Nicholas Silverton, the textwriter William Childern, the bookbinder John Barell, and the limner Richard Elys. In addition, as an active member of the Mistery of Stationers, Abell would presumably have known well other members whose activities in the gild are recorded during Abell's gild tenure, a group of twenty-nine craftsmen and stationers, including seven wardens of the mistery.[25]

Among this group of gild members are five prominent limners, all of them older than Abell, all well-established London book artists. These men are (1) Abell's presumed master Thomas Fysshe, who earlier, in 1423, had served as warden of the craft gild, along with the textwriter Thomas Marleburgh (to whom Hoccleve once dedicated a poem);[26] (2) the limner Thomas Tresswell (perhaps related to a contemporary Oxford limner and a forebear of a sixteenth-century London artist),[27] who, along with the bookbinder Thomas Broke, had witnessed Fysshe's will; (3) the limner William Barough, warden of the gild in 1433, along with the stationer Robert Chirche; (4) the limner Gilbert Melton, warden in 1426, along with the bookbinder Peter Bylton; (5) the limner Richard Okewell, warden in 1439, along with stationer Richard Infeld. From these instances one might infer, in addition to Abell's general trade associations, his more particular craft association with a group of older fellow artists, some of whom may have had an influence on his artistic development. Since all of them lived in the immediate neighbourhood, Abell might well have been familiar with their work. More directly, however, one could argue that Abell's master and hence main teacher had been Thomas Fysshe. A concern for such tutelage may be seen in Fysshe's own words, as recorded in English in his will of 1450:

I ordeyn and maak William Abel lympnor of London superviser of this my present testament and last will and y bequeth to hym for his labour xl*s* allso y gyve and bequeth vnto þe said William Abell all the termys of apprentishod þat I haue in Robert ffitz John myn apprentice and William Buttler myn apprentice after the strength virtue & effect of the Endenture of apprentishode maad betwene me & þe said Robert ffitz John and William Buttler. The said William Abell to teche Enforme and fynd þe said Robert and William Buttler as y þe said Thomas am bound to tech Enforme and fynd by þe vertue of þe said Endenture (GL 9171/5 (Sharp) 8v).

If Abell had himself been apprenticed to Thomas Fysshe, one may also wish to work backward, in an attempt to trace Fysshe's own early influences. Hypothetically, such a line goes back at least as far as 1404–10 when, as noted earlier, Fysshe's name appears among those of seven (nine, if Hun and Skercueyn are included) limners renting shops in Paternoster Row. Of this group, Fysshe may have had particular association with two, Thomas Bowland and Thomas Hyhelm: at some point before 1410, Fysshe took over the shop previously rented by Bowland, who in turn took up tenancy in a shop previously held by Hyhelm. In 1417, Bowland was to serve, along with the limner John Asshe, as warden of the craft gild, and earlier, in 1394, Hyhelm had served, along with Roger Horsle, as warden of the old single-craft Mistery of Limners.[28] From such contiguity, of shop location and professional gild association, it is possible, at least in theory, to weave a network of craft connections, presenting circumstantial evidence for tracing mutual influence among a group of nineteen manuscript artists, most of them located in Paternoster Row or in the immediate area and many of them active in the craft gild, over a period of eighty years, from 1394 to 1474.[29]

In a parallel argument about William Abell and artists associated with him, Jonathan Alexander has identified a group of eighteen manuscripts, all falling within the years c. 1440–65 and thus compatible with documented dates of Abell's activity in London, that may be attributed to Abell on the basis of stylistic similarities with his one attested work, the consolidation charter of Eton College of 1446.[30] Alexander then notes what appear to be stylistic connections between certain work in one of the manuscripts he attributes to Abell (the so-called 'Warwick Hours', New York, Pierpont Morgan Library, MS M 893) and the work of another artist, the 'Trinity Master' (in Cambridge, Trinity College, MS B.11.7). The 'Trinity Master', in turn, appears to have been influenced by one of the artists making London, Lambeth Palace, MS 69 (the so-called 'Nevill Hours'), which was illuminated by various artists in the workshop of Herman Scheerre, including Scheerre himself.[31] Alexander (pp. 169–70) also suggests that Abell may have been influenced by the work of two other older artists, the first whose work survives in BL Royal MS 2.B.I and in a patent of arms granted to the Drapers' Company in 1439; and a second artist, whose work survives in Edinburgh, NLS, MS Adv. 18.1.7, in Manchester, John Rylands University Library, MS Eng. 1, and in Oxford, Bodleian Library, MS Laud misc. 733.

Certainly one cannot at this stage of reconstructing the work relations among London artists supply with any confidence names for those limners whose work Alexander has identified, and yet the possibility remains that the 'Trinity Master' was Thomas Fysshe and that the two other older artists influencing Abell were two of the limners named earlier. To be sure, problems in the use of circumstantial evidence drawn from archival records for positive identification of unsigned work remain great. Eventually, however, the case for possible cause and effect in the development of London-based manuscript art in the fifteenth century may be aided by the clearer record of known artisans working there at the time, such information heretofore unavailable.

Other professional associations Abell may have had can be guessed at from the fact of his serving as churchwarden at St Nicholas at the Shambles, in 1452 and again in 1470. He may have known the scribe John Harpenden and the bookbinder Thomas Holywode, who in 1454 were hired to write and bind the church accounts.[32] Abell would certainly have known a group of younger stationers who were members of the same congregation: Thomas Eglyston, John Rowland, John Hotersall, and William Brereton.[33] Abell may also have known the book craftsmen who lived in five nearby parishes, each less than three hundred yards from St Nicholas: at St Sepulchre without Newgate, the stationer Henry Hutton and the stationer John Barkeby, who was also a grammar school teacher at St Bartholomew's Hospital and eventually at St Paul's School;[34] at St Botolph without Aldersgate, the stationer Thomas Hert and the parchmener Geoffrey Sprottesburgh, master of the popular Fraternity of St Trinity at the church;[35] at St Augustine near Paul's Gate (near Watling Street), the stationers Richard Darby, John Pye, and Robert Frosten;[36] at St Faith the Virgin by St Paul's, the stationer Edmund Cok, who had been a fellow Bridge property tenant as well as fellow parishioner of Abell's presumed master Thomas Fysshe, and whose wife Margaret Cok left the bulk of her estate to the Mistery of Stationers;[37] and at St Michael le Querne, the stationer Robert Chirche and the limner Richard Okewell, already mentioned in connection with the trade gild, and the stationer John Multon, who may be identified with the writer of a sizeable number of surviving manuscripts.[38]

The concurrence of various associations Abell may have had, the result of fellow book craftsmen's parish residence, business address, gild activity, and testamentary comity, illustrates well, therefore, a point to be emphasised, namely, the physical proximity and the consequent possibility of actual collaboration or influence that characterises the book trade in fifteenth-century London. The world of books and their makers was undoubtedly a small one, but it was not thereby necessarily simple or unimportant. The makers of books occupied – in a sense both figurative and literal – a place of central importance in the manuscript culture of late medieval London.

London's literary culture, however, depended on a larger community – of book readers, owners, and customers. Although many details about that literate society remain to be discovered, it is clear that one important part of book commerce involved not only private patrons but also corporate bodies. One indication of this may be seen in surviving records of payments to members of the trade for work done. On forty-five occasions, thirty-three artisans were paid for binding, limning, or writing books, for valuing or purchasing them, or for supplying parchment and paper. Almost all of these payments involved service to royal commissions, schools, churches, or civic and governmental accounts. Such jobs could range widely in size and importance. In 1467, for example, churchwardens at St Michael Cornhill paid 'to

Robert Burton stacyoner for new byndyng & new helyng of a grayell and an antyphoner of the chirche xvjs iiijd . . . for new byndyng and new helyng of the new prikked song boke ijs viijd'.[39] In contrast, in 1421, the stationer John Robert, whose shop in Paternoster Row was rented from the Bridge wardens, was paid £12 8s from Exchequer accounts for his work in writing twelve books on hunting for the use of the king, Henry V.[40]

Here, the significance of the Bridge records should once again be noted, not only for rental of shops to craftsmen, but also, on at least twenty-nine occasions, for commissioning their work. In 1414, for example, the limner John Walcote was paid 11s 4d for his work in decorating the *temporale* and *sanctorale* of a *Legenda*, recently purchased for the Chapel of St Thomas on the Bridge (BHE 1412–21, 126). In 1421, 'Petro Bylton bokebynder' was paid 3s 4d for binding a large paper book of expenditures; the following year he was paid 7s 4d for binding two such large paper books, as he was again in 1431, when he was paid 6s 8d for his work (BHE 1421–30, 7, 24; 1430–45, 36v).

In a later example, again from the Bridge accounts, the wardens in 1510 paid 'to Thomas Symond stacyoner . . . for byndeng gluyng pastyng and coueryng of two antyphoners w'yn the sayd chapell [on the Bridge] fyndeng to the same stuf and workmanship xvjs xd' (BHA 1509–25, 30). Here, an early use of glue in the binding process is worthy of note. Another entry in these accounts suggests that craftsmen submitted written, itemised bills for their work: in 1490, Bridge wardens paid the bookbinder William Barell 40s 'for writing & noting of certain masses bynding & repairing of diuers bokis in the saied chapel [on the Bridge] As by his bille thereof made the parcellis particulor remembring' (BHA 1484–1509, 117v). Finally, the transition to print culture should be noted, when Bridge accounts record the first purchases of printed books: in 1509, 'to Rychard Pynson prynter for ij proccessioners of parchemyne a ijs viijd'; in 1514, 'to Raynold Blake for ij processyoners in prynte for the . . . chapell ijs' (BHA 1509–25, 12, 104).

Of equal if not greater importance to the study of actual book commerce is the incidence of surviving manuscript books that may be associated with known London book-trade members, whether through signed or attributed work or through records of possession or sale; in some instances, the purchaser is also known. Two examples may be cited here. The first involves the bookbinder and stationer Peter Bylton, a prominent member of the trade whose career is well documented in various surviving records over a span of fifty years, from 1404 to 1454, all of which was spent in Paternoster Row, working out of shops rented from London Bridge or, after 1450, in his own building, 'le Petre et Poule', which stood at the corner of Panyer Alley. In his will in 1454, Bylton instructed his executors, the textwriter John Taillour, Richard Joly, and the parchmener Richard Collop, 'to selle alle my bokes . . . of dyvynyte matter in scole or in lawe' (BHD I 22). Two of these books were bought in 1455 'ab executore petri Bylton' by Richard Hopton, a fellow of Eton at the time (and later rector of St Alban in Wood Street), as indicated in notes written in the surviving books, now in the Eton Library. One, a fourteenth-century volume of works by St Augustine, sold for 56*s*; the other, a thirteenth-century volume of works by St Bernard, for 20*s* (Eton MSS 101, fols. i, 1–182, and 39). These surviving manuscripts suggest that Bylton also dealt in older books, if they were not in fact part of his own private collection or books kept as exemplars for copying.

The second example is that of the stationer John Pye. Pye's career in London may be traced over a period of at least 30 years, from 1433 to 1463, and records show him to have been perhaps an even more prominent stationer than Bylton. At the time when William Abell was working on the Eton College charter, 1446–7, for example, Pye was being recommended as agent in securing books for the libraries of Eton and of King's College. He was described as one of those who 'ben connyng and have undirstonding in such matiers'.[41] Altogether, seven books survive that contain records of having passed through Pye's hands as a London stationer, all of them religious or theological in character. In contrast to Bylton's books, all but one of Pye's books were made in the fifteenth century (although of course not necessarily supervised by Pye himself). The notes in these books vary a good deal: two show purchasers' names, three cite prices paid, four identify Pye as seller, and three simply identify Pye by name.[42]

Such incidental information in surviving manuscripts, often incomplete or inconclusive, is illustrative, pointing to the problem of trying to match books (and their owners) to identifiable London craftsmen and stationers. Such connections are not easily made without collateral evidence provided by the close study of a manuscript's history and its ordonnance, artwork, and handwriting. Insofar as these critical forms of inquiry come together (and here I owe many debts to the work of others), at least sixty-seven manuscripts and books may be associated with twenty known London book artisans. Of these twenty, three are textwriters[43] and five are limners[44] whose work may be documented or attributed with a high degree of probability. The remaining twelve are all stationers who owned or sold surviving books, eight of them involved with the sale of older manuscripts not of their own making and four involved with sale or possession of fifteenth-century books.[45]

Until a good deal more information is brought together, however, including those records of signed contributions by artisans and of payment for scribal, art, and binding work to be found in surviving books, as well as a fuller account of early trade patronage and book ownership,[46] the information reported in this essay is of necessity incomplete. Also needed is a clearer understanding of the early book trade outside London and the influence of the capital on provincial book commerce,[47] and the fate of manuscript books and their makers in the dawning age of print.[48] Notwithstanding such

desiderata, the evidence available in public records identifying members of
the London trade is a necessary component of this larger study. As this essay
has attempted to show, in this body of data lies significant information that
may eventually support not only attribution of craftsmen's work, influence,
and association, but also critical inquiry into many other aspects of the early
trade. In its own right, moreover, the evidence here summarised establishes
an unmistakable fact heretofore not fully acknowledged, namely, the vital
presence of a flourishing book trade in London during the century leading up
to Caxton.

NOTES

1 The ordinance merging the limners' and textwriters' gilds in 1403 was the result of
   a petition by those 'of the trades of writers of text-letter, *lymenours*, and other folks of
   London who are wont to bind and to sell books'. For full text, see H.R. Riley, ed.
   Memorials of London and London Life in the XIIIth, XIVth, and XVth Centuries (London,
   1868), pp. 557–8. The term 'stationer' does not appear in this petition; its first
   recorded use for the gild occurred in 1417 when it was called the 'Mistery of
   Scriveners, Limners, and Stationers'. See G. Pollard, 'The Company of
   Stationers'. See also H.W. Winger, 'Regulations Relating to the Book Trade in
   London from 1357 to 1586', *The Library Quarterly*, 26 (1956), 157–95, esp. 162–3.

2 See, for example, Doyle and Parkes; Scott, 'A Mid-Fifteenth-Century English
   Illuminating Shop'.

3 'The Names of Some English Fifteenth-Century Binders', *The Library*, 5th series,
   25 (1970), 193–218, esp. 193.

4 *Cal. of Plea and Memoranda Rolls*, ed. A.H. Thomas and P.E. Jones (Cambridge,
   1926–), hereafter cited as CPMR, with volume dates; *Cal. of Letter-Books of the City
   of London*, ed. R.R. Sharpe (London, 1889ff.), hereafter cited as LB, with volume
   letter; *An Index of Persons named in Early Chancery Proceedings*, ed. C.A. Walmisley, 2
   vols. (London, 1927–8); *List of Early Chancery Proceedings* (London, 1901–), part of
   Public Record Office Lists and Indexes, vols. XII (1385–1467), XVI (1467–85), XX
   (1485–1500), XXIX (1500–15), XXXVIII (1515–29); *Cal. of the Close Rolls* (London,
   1892–1963), hereafter cited as CCR, with volume dates; J. Challenor C. Smith,
   Index of Wills Proved in the Prerogative Court of Canterbury 1383–1558, 2 vols. (London,
   1893, 1985); *Index to Testamentary Records in the Archdeaconry Court of London*, vol. I, ed.
   M. Fitch (London, 1979); *Index to Testamentary Records in the Commissary Court of
   London*, vol. I *1374–1488*, vol. II, *1489–1570*, ed. M. Fitch (London, 1969, 1974); *Cal.
   of Wills Proved and Enrolled in the Court of Hustings*, ed. R.R. Sharpe, 2 vols. (London,
   1889, 1890).

5 London, PRO, MS PROB 11, Probate Wills Proved in Prerogative Court of
   Canterbury, hereafter cited as PROB 11; MS Early Chancery Proceedings.
   London, Guildhall Library, MS 9051/1, Registered Copy Wills (Archdeaconry
   Court) 1393–1415, Calendar 1368–1421; MS 9168, Probate and Administration
   Act Books, Commissary Court, London; MS 9171, Register of Wills, Probate Acts,
   and Acts of Administration, Commissary Court, London, hereafter cited as GL
   9171. Corporation of London Records Office, MS Hustings Rolls Deeds and Wills,

hereafter cited as HDW; MS Journals of the Court of Common Council, vols. I–XII, hereafter cited as JCCC; MS Recognizance Rolls (Freemen and Their Sureties), hereafter cited as RR.

6 Corporation of London Records Office, MS Ancient Deeds Among Bridge House Records; hereafter cited as BHD; MS Bridgemasters' Account Rolls, 17 rolls; hereafter cited as BAR; MS Bridge House Accounts, vols. I–V; hereafter cited as BHA, with volume dates; MS Expenditures of the Bridge, Series 1 and 2, hereafter cited as BHE, with volume dates.

7 Richard Elys, 'lymnour' (BHA 1460–84, 21v); John Taillour, 'tixtwriter' (HDW 195, 32–3).

8 The fullest treatment of early printers is found in E. Gordon Duff, *A Century of the English Book Trade* (London, 1905, 1948), hereafter cited as Duff. See also H.R. Plomer, 'The Importation of Books Into England in the Fifteenth and Sixteenth Centuries', *The Library*, 4th series, 4 (1923–4), 146–50, and 'The Importation of Low Country Books and French Books Into England', *The Library*, 4th series, 9 (1928–9), 164–8; N.J.M. Kerling, 'Caxton and the Trade in Printed Books', *The Book Collector*, 4 (1955), 190–9; E. Armstrong, 'English Purchases of Printed Books from the Continent 1465–1526', *EHR*, 94 (1979), 268–90; H.S. Bennett, *English Books and Readers 1475–1557* (Cambridge, 1952).

9 Records examined reveal several connections between painters and book artisans. In 1434, the painter Guy Lyncoln, along with the goldsmith William White, gave surety for the stationer John Pye on a loan default (CMPR 1413–37, 280). In 1440, the textwriter and stationer William Childern was named, along with the painter Richard Salle, in a suit brought before the Common Council (JCCC 3, 42v). In 1446, Childern made a gift of his goods to the painter John Body (CCR 1441–47, 431–2). In 1455, the limner Thomas Cok, along with the alderman William Morise, was appointed to examine the Bill of the Mistery of Painters to report as to its conformity to reason (JCCC 5, 225). London, BL Add. MS 19909 contains (fol. 1) the name 'Johannes Kale', who may be the London painter John Keyle (CCR 1435–41, 329), elected master of the Mistery of Painters in 1433 (LB K 150).

10 A list of 210 members and apprentices of the scriveners' gild between 1392 and 1500 may be found in the *Scriveners' Company Common Paper 1357–1628*, ed. Francis W. Steer (London, 1968). For discussion of the role of Chancery in training writers, see J.H. Fisher, 'Chancery and the Emergence of Standard Written English in the Fifteenth Century', *Speculum*, 52, 4 (1977), 870–99; M. Richardson, 'Henry V, the English Chancery, and Chancery English', *Speculum*, 55, 4 (1980), 726–50. For Hoccleve's work as occasional textwriter, see Doyle and Parkes; H.C. Schultz, 'Thomas Hoccleve, Scribe', *Speculum*, 12 (1937), 71–81.

A portion of Oxford, Bodleian Library, MS Rawl. C.86 is signed (fol. 186), 'Explicit Per Johannem Reve ffree.' Reve may possibly be identified with the legal scrivener Johannes Reve, admitted to the Scriveners' Company in 1505 (Steer, 24; see J.J. Griffiths, 'A Re-examination of Oxford, Bodleian Library, MS Rawlinson, C.86', *Archiv*, 219 (1982), 381–8, at 387 and n. 14). In the will of Henry Kays, keeper of the Hanaper, proved in 1426, he left a book of statutes and a book of medicine 'quem Swetenham michi scripsit' (PROB 11/3 (Luffenham) 6). Swetenham may have been a legal scrivener or minor Chancery clerk (I am indebted to

Malcolm Richardson for this reference). A book of charters of 20 July 1463 was signed by the scribe, 'Spayne' (Sotheby's Sale Cat., 14 July 1981, lot 67). Spayne may have been the legal scrivener Robert Spayne who signed the Common Paper of the Scriveners' Company upon admission in 1445 and who was still active in London in 1478 (Steer, 11, 12, 22).

11 For a convenient overview of current Caxton studies, see L. Hellinga, *Caxton in Focus* (London, 1982). Of equal importance to the introduction of the printing press into England was the opening up of foreign import and wholesale trade in printed books and materials, specifically encouraged by Parliament in a statute of January 1484 (see Duff, pp. xi–xii). Because established stationers were not only craftsmen but booksellers as well, there could have been few in the decades closing the fifteenth century and opening the sixteenth who did not realise the market value of printed books. For examples, see E. Gordon Duff, 'Early Chancery Proceedings Concerning Members of the Book Trade', *The Library*, 2nd series, 8 (1907), 408–20, and 'Notes on Stationers from the Lay Subsidy Rolls of 1523–4', *The Library*, 2nd series, 9 (1908), 257–66.

12 Oxford, Bodleian Library, MS Ashmole 1827, a fifteenth-century collection of medical texts, contains verses (fol. 173v) by John Somerset (d. 1455), physician to Henry VI. Somerset had associations with a number of book artisans and stationers. In 1431, he acquired the tenement, 'le Petre et Poule', in Paternoster Row, which he sold in 1450 to the bookbinder Peter Bylton and the stationer John Taillour. Witnesses to the earlier transaction were Bylton, the stationer John Robert (see n. 40 below), and the bookbinder Richard More; witnesses to the later sale to Bylton included the stationer Robert Chirche and the limner Thomas Tresswell (BHD H 58, 81, 83). In 1458, Thomas Fawkys, rector of St Bride Fleet Street, left a bequest in his will of 'unum vetus missale emptum de Scotte stacionario' (PROB 11/4 (Stokton) 17), a reference to the stationer John Scot. In 1444, the grocer John Walden brought a complaint against the stationer John Pye for a debt of eight marks owed to the parish of St Botolph near Billingsgate for a missal (Corp. of London Records Office, MS Files of Original Bills, Mayor's Court 3. 328; I am indebted to A.I. Doyle for this reference).

For discussion of a number of London tradesmen who owned and signed surviving books, see K. Scott, *Mirrour of the Worlde*, p. 9. One of these books, now London, BL MS Harley 273, was owned by the grocer and apothecary John Clerk, temp. Edward IV; he may be the John Clerk associated with the stationer William Chaunt in 1458 (CCR 1454–61, 340). Another of these books, now CUL MS Gg.I.34.2, dated after 1472, was owned by the grocer Richard Walker, who may have been related to the grocer Thomas Walker, involved in a debt transaction with the stationer Robert Burton in 1478 (CCR 1476–85, 124).

13 The stationer John Pye was involved with a number of such pledge actions. In 1439, he made a gift of his goods and chattels by delivery of a 'Masboke' to a turner and a tailor. He made a similar gift in 1457, to John Wakeryng, master of St Bartholomew's Hospital, and the stationer John Taillour, along with others, by delivery of a 'prymer' (CPMR 1437–57, 161; CCR 1454–61, 256).

14 Alexander, 'William Abell', p. 166, n. 1.

15 Wardens' accounts, cited in Norman Moore, *The History of St. Bartholomew's Hospital*, 2 vols. (London, 1918), esp. II, 215.

16 John Stow, *The Survey of London* (New York, 1912, repr. 1980), pp. 23, 202; hereafter cited as Stow. See also LB E 186.

17 *Ninth Report of the Royal Commission on Historical Manuscripts*, Part I (London, 1883), pp. 50–1, citing a sixteenth-century translation; hereafter cited as RCHM. See also Gwyn A. Williams, *Medieval London: From Commune to Capital* (London, 1963), pp. 86–7; Corp. of London Records Office, MS Bridge House Estates Deeds: Small Register, fol. 149.

18 H.R. Plomer, 'John Rastell and His Contemporaries', *Bibliographica*, 2 (1896), 437–51, esp. 438–9; BHA 1509–25, 179.

19 See Doyle and Parkes, and Scott, 'A Mid-Fifteenth-Century English Illuminating Shop', who argue for the latter case.

20 BHD I 5; see also Stow, p. 293. Records of demolition and reconstruction of these shops may be found in BAR 6 m. 11; 7 ms. IV and 8; 8 m. 9; 9 ms. 6–7; 10 ms. 7–8.

21 For scale maps, see 'London in the Fifteenth Century', in C.L. Kingsford, *Prejudice and Promise in Fifteenth Century England* (London, 1962); M.B. Honeybourne, *A Sketch Map of London Under Richard II*, London Topographical Society Publ. no. 93 (London, 1960).

22 E. Rickert, *Chaucer's World*, ed. C.C. Olson and M.M. Crow (New York, 1948), p. 9; BHD I 11. For additional examples of contemporary shop dimensions, see S.L. Thrupp, *The Merchant Class of Medieval London* (Ann Arbor, 1948, 1962), pp. 130–1 and n. 83.

23 For purposes of comparison, see Ill. 11, the 1585 drawing by Robert Treswell of the corner of Paternoster Row by St Michael le Querne, showing later shop buildings sixteen feet wide, with three storeys plus a garret, as well as one older building next to the church with two storeys, only twelve feet wide.

24 The argument for dating Scheerre's English work in the years 1403–19 is summarised by G.M. Spriggs, 'The Nevill Hours and the School of Herman Scheerre', *JWCI*, 37 (1974), 104–30.

Bridge accounts showing rentals between 1404 and 1410 are listed in BHA 1404–21, 3–3v and take a simple form with little commentary. Tenants' names are merely listed, and when vacancies occurred, the name of the first tenant in 1404 is crossed out and that of the next occupant written in, with change in rent, if any, noted. Changes in tenancy are only infrequently dated, as, for example, when Roger Cornewalle took over the shop vacated by the limner John Anys at Easter 6 Henry IV. If tenants rented more than one shop, this was also noted, as in the case of the bookbinder Peter Bylton, who rented four shops, or Thomas Marleburgh, who rented two. No other book-trade member rented more than one shop. Dates when Skereueyn succeeded Hun are not indicated. The rent for their single shop, as for others, was 26s 8d yearly.

Among other tenants at the time, the following may be identified: the haberdasher Thomas Glym, the draper Richard Martyn, the waxchandler Simon Prentot, the tallowchandler Thomas atte Wode, the coppersmith Nicholas Peeke, the barbers John Lymnour and William Wodehouse, the apostolic notary John Yonge, the goldsmiths Thomas Glade and Solomon Oxneye and the scriveners Thomas Charlton, William Kyngeston and John Bracy.

25 John Acastre (fl. 1441), John Aleyn (fl. 1441), John Barell (fl. 1460–95), John Barker (fl. 1450), William Barough, warden (fl. 1430–53), John Bellervu (fl. 1449),

William Burgham (fl. 1445–75), Robert Burton (fl. 1464–80), Peter Bylton, warden (fl. 1404–54), William Childern (fl. 1436–70), Robert Chirche, warden (fl. 1433–59), Robert Church (fl. 1445–47), Edmund Cok (fl. 1404–50), Edward Cok (fl. 1404–49), John Corbet (fl. 1448), Richard Eston (fl. 1449–57), Thomas Fysshe, warden (fl. 1404–50), Robert Hamer (fl. 1464), Marmaduke Howton (fl. 1448–55), James Lacy (fl. 1465), Thomas Lesyngham (fl. 1436–51), Gilbert Melton, warden (fl. 1424–55), Richard Okewell, warden (fl. 1439–46), John Pye, warden (fl. 1433–63), John Scot (fl. 1450–8), Nicholas Silverton (fl. 1448–72), Thomas Swertbreke (fl. 1448), Thomas Tresswell (fl. 1441–50), John Wellewyk (fl. 1440). For a complete list of known wardens of the gild, see Pollard, 'Stationers' Company', pp. 36–7.

26 Now San Marino, Calif., Huntington Library, MS HM 744; see Doyle and Parkes, p. 198.

27 In 1463 and again in 1466, records of the Chancellor of Oxford name a Thomas Tresawell, 'illuminator librorum de Catstrete'. See H.E. Salter, *Registrum Cancellarii Oxoniensis 1434–1469* (Oxford, 1932), vol. II, pp. 123–4 and 188. The sixteenth-century artist, Robert Treswell, who made a drawing of Paternoster Row in 1585 (see Ill. 11), may have been a descendant.

28 Pollard, 'Stationers' Company', pp. 36–7.

29 William Abell, John Anys, John Asshe, William Barough, Thomas Bowland, John Broune, William Buttler, Richard Elys, Robert Fitzjohn, Thomas Fysshe, Roger Horsle, John Hun (or Johannes), Thomas Hyhelm, Gilbert Melton, Richard Okewell, Herman Skereueyn (or Scheerre), Thomas Tresswell, John White, Roger Ybott.

30 Alexander 'William Abell', pp. 166–8; for a list of some of these manuscripts, see n. 44 below.

31 Noted by G. M. Spriggs; see n. 24 above.

32 Moore, *St. Bartholomew's*, II, 215.

33 Church membership for these four men is documented as follows: London, BL Cotton Vitellius MS F.ix; GL 9171/8 (Harvy) 207; GL 9161/8 (Harvy) 46v–7v; GL 9171/7 (Lichfield) 128–9. In his will of 1493, Hotersall made bequests of 'a boke callid gesta Romanorum wᵗ other contentes' and 'my boke of constitutionis provincialis', as well as requesting the 'sale of my bokys and pamflettes'. In his will of 1485, Brereton left his son William 'alle such bookes of myn as he woll chese hym selfe and specially my boke of Guy of Warewyk written on parchment & bounde in bourdes'.

34 See GL 9171/8 (Harvy) 92v; BHA 1460–84, 307v, 323v, 340, 358, 377.

35 See London, BL MS Add. 37664 32–2v (ed. P. Basing, *Parish Fraternity Register* (London, 1982)); GL 9171/5 (Sharp) 25v.

36 See GL 9171/6 (Wilde) 109; Moore, *St. Bartholomew's*, II, 78; PROB 11/7 (Logge) 19).

37 See GL 9171/5 (Sharp) 14v, 34v.

38 See GL 9171/4 (Prowet) 191v; GL 9171/5 (Sharp) 281; GL 9171/6 (Wilde) 178v. For manuscripts attributed to Multon, see n. 43 below. See also A.I. Doyle, 'An Unrecognized Piece of *Piers the Ploughman's Creed* and Other Works by Its Scribe', *Speculum*, 34 (1959), 428–36, and 'English Books In and Out of Court', p. 177,

n. 42; R.F. Green, 'Notes on Some Manuscripts of Hoccleve's *Regiment of Princes*', *BLJ*, 4 (1978), 37–41; E. Hammond, 'A Scribe of Chaucer', *MP*, 27 (1929), 27–33.

39 W.H. Overall, ed., *The Accounts of the Churchwardens of* ... *St. Michael Cornhill 1455–1608* (London, 1871), pp. 35–6.

40 Frederick Devon, *Issues of the Exchequer* ... *from King Henry III to King Henry VI Inclusive* (London, 1837), p. 368, cited in S.H. Cavanaugh, 'A Study of Books Privately Owned in England: 1300–1450', diss., Univ. of Pennsylvania, 1980 (Ann Arbor, Univ. Microfilms, 1980), p. 413.

41 A.N.L. Munby, 'Notes on King's College Library in the Fifteenth Century', in *Essays and Papers* (London, 1977), p. 28. Pye was to work with the chaplain Richard Chestre 'to laboure effectually in quere and diligently in serche in all place that ben under your [Henry VI] obeysaunse to gete knowleche where suche Bokes Onourmentes and other necessaries for your said Colages may be founden'.

42 Oxford, Bodleian Library, MS Bodley 110 (bought by W. Cleue from Pye as stationer for 20s), MS Laud misc. 414 (contains a reference to Pye's family and others named Lye, Insall, Pratt, and Bentley); BL MS Royal 5.C.III (bought by T. Eyburhale from Pye for 27s 6d), MS Royal 8.D.x (bought from Pye as stationer for 20s); Cambridge, Gonville and Caius College, MS 247/473 (bought from Pye as stationer); London, Gray's Inn, MS 8 (contains Pye's name); Lancashire, Stonyhurst College, MS *Summa de Officiis Ecclesiasticis* (contains Pye's name).

43 Ricardus Franciscus: BL MSS Harley 2915 and 4775; New York, PML MS M 126; Oxford, Bodleian Library, MS Ashmole 765 and MS Laud misc. 570; University College, MS 85; Philadelphia, Rosenbach Foundation, MS 439/16; and others.

    John Multon: Cambridge, Trinity College, MS R.14.52 and R.3.21, fols. 34–49v; BL Add. MS 34360, MS Arundel 59, MS Cotton Claudius A.VIII, fols. 175–97, MSS Harley 78, fol. 3r and 2551, MS Royal 17.D.xv, fols. 167–301, Royal College of Physicians, MS 13; Oxford, Bodleian Library, MS Rawl. D.913, fol. 43; Worcester Cathedral, MS F.172.

    John Preston: London, Westminster Abbey, MS Lytlington Missal.

    Other London-based scribes who wrote manuscripts are here excluded, for they cannot be shown to have been professional members of the book-trade. These include T. Werken (see R.A.B. Mynors, 'A Fifteenth-Century Scribe: T. Werken', *TCBS*, 1 (2) (1950), 97–104); William Ebesham (Westminster) (see A.I. Doyle, 'William Ebesham'); Richard Frampton (see R. Somerville, 'The Cowcher Books of the Duchy of Lancaster', *EHR*, 51 (1936), 598–615); and the amateur scribe and book collector John Shirley (see A.I. Doyle, 'More Light on Shirley', *Medium Aevum*, 30 (1961), 93–101, and 'English Books In and Out of Court' pp. 176–8; R.F. Green, *Poets and Princepleasers* (Toronto, 1980), pp. 130–2; C. Greenberg, 'John Shirley and the English Book Trade', *The Library*, 6th series, 4 (1982), 369–80).

44 William Abell: Cambridge, King's College, MS Charter ... 16 March 1446, St John's College, MS 208 (H.5); Eton College, MS Consolidation Charter; BL MS Royal 2.A.xvIII (cf. Scheerre), Company of Mercers, MS Ordinances, Company of Tallow Chandlers, MS Patent of Arms; New York, PML, MS M 893; Oxford, Bodleian Library, MS Digby 227; and others (see Alexander, 'William Abell').

Richard Elys: San Marino, Calif., Huntington Library, MS HM 39465.

'Johannes': BL Add. MSS 50001 and 42131 (cf. Scheerre); Oxford, Bodleian Library, MSS Bodley 264 and 902 (cf. Scheerre), MS Don. d.85.

Thomas Rolf: London, Westminster Abbey Library, MS Lytlington Missal (?).

Hermann Scheerre: Gloucester, Berkeley Castle, MS 'Book of Hours'; BL Add. MSS 16998, 42131, 58078, MS Arundel 38, MS Egerton 1991, MSS Royal 1.E.ix and 2.A.xviii, MS Stowe 16, Lambeth Palace, MS 69; Oxford, Bodleian Library, MSS Bodley 294, 693, 902, MS Gough liturg. 6, MS Lat. liturg. f.2, MS Laud misc. 609; Paris, Bibliothèque Nationale, MS lat. 1196.

Excluded from this list of London artists is the Dominican artist John Siferwas.

45 Peter Bylton: Eton College Library, MSS 101.B1.10 and 39. Bk.4.3.

Robert Chirche: BL MS Sloane 3481.

Edmund Cok: BL MS Harley 641.

Richard Collop: London, Lambeth Palace, MS 472.

John Elys: CUL MS Dd.8.2.

Thomas Lokton: Cambridge, Gonville and Caius College, MS 23/12.

David Lyonhill: Cambridge, Corpus Christi College, MS 164.

Thomas Marleburgh: Cambridge, Gonville and Caius College, MS 492/261.

William de Nessefylde: Cambridge, Gonville and Caius College, MS 17/133.

John Pye: see n. 42 above.

John Sampson: Oxford, Bodleian Library, MS Rawl. C.86 (?).

Thomas Veysy: Cambridge, Bodleian Library, MS Auct. D.4.5, University College, MS 91.

46 A large amount of information, drawn from printed wills and other records relating to various sites in England, may be found in S.H. Cavanaugh, 'A Study of Books Privately Owned in England'.

47 For a selective comparison of manuscript books in English produced in London and in other parts of the country, see A.I. Doyle, 'English Books In and Out of Court'.

48 See J.B. Trapp, ed., *Manuscripts in the Fifty Years After the Invention of Printing* (London, 1983); especially note L. Hellinga, 'Manuscripts in the Hands of Printers', pp. 3–11. For general views, see E.L. Eisenstein, *The Printing Press as an Agent of Change* (Cambridge, 1979).

If stationers began to deal with printed books as well as with manuscript books, retail of both was also probably true for early printers, Caxton being a prime example. See N.F. Blake, *Caxton and His World* (London, 1969), esp. pp. 74–8; see also J.A.W. Bennett, 'Preface', in Scott, *The Caxton Master*, pp. ix–xvii, esp. p. xi.

5 · PUBLICATION BY MEMBERS OF THE RELIGIOUS ORDERS

A.I. DOYLE

T<small>HROUGHOUT</small> the fourteenth and fifteenth centuries the members of the religious orders (monks, regular canons, mendicant friars and nuns) were a large, if relatively declining, part of the more educated population – probably about a third of all the clergy (which was perhaps about a tenth of the men literate in some sense) and somewhat fewer than the numbers of the beneficed secular clerks.[1] Their initial literary schooling was not essentially different from that of the latter, but their subsequent careers were more extensively and more constantly directed by and to books than that of any other social group, except possibly the less permanent body of university teachers and students, of whom more than a proportionate part were regular clergy (monks and canons as well as friars), especially among those taking degrees in theology, and those of whom there is record as authors.[2] In every religious order and community in addition to the daily, weekly and seasonal round of public readings in the liturgy, refectory and chapter, times were prescribed and books provided for private study, while duties of teaching, preaching, counsel or administration involving the use of books were assigned to individuals.[3] In attempting to assess the roles of the religious as authors, translators, compilers, copyists, patrons, purchasers, and users of books, or of portions of books, we must allow for the effects on the evidence of, positively, their maintenance of communal collections and records up to the dissolution of their houses and, negatively, the differing degrees of survival or identifiability of the remains thereafter. We must also bear in mind that while *esprit de corps* may have ensured the recording of the connections of particular members in one capacity or another with its books, there were also religious traditions discountenancing self-advertisement, to reinforce the prevalent medieval practice of anonymity. But, apart from cases in which a personal name, house and status are specified, there are others when one of the latter is at least indicated, and more where associations may support guesswork. Nonetheless, very many cases of authorship are wholly undetermined, and the great majority of manuscripts still want attachment to particular circumstances of origin and early ownership. What we would like to be sure of, yet can only sample, is how large a share the religious, and which of them, had in the writing, copying and circulation of various kinds of literature, and what part their peculiar modes of life played in these activities.

We are here concerned with authorship only so far as it is one of the processes involved in the publication and production of books. In any era the *production* of books will consist of, on one hand, a range of recent compositions and compilations or fresh versions and translations and, on another, simply new copies of earlier ones. Fresh authorship in itself does not entail *publication*, which must comprise, at least, communication (not necessarily by the author) of a piece to another person or persons, with leave (perhaps tacit) or motivation to pass it on to others; which *may* be preceded or followed by the growth of knowledge of its existence and interest, rousing a desire for further copies, consequent reproduction and gradual dissemination to a greater or lesser extent.[4] There are therefore different degrees of intended and eventual publication, and, before the introduction of printing required the simultaneous display, advertisement and wide distribution of unprecedented numbers of copies of the same piece in order to recoup heavy speculative outlay, commercial participation in the processes of publishing was generally secondary, supplying single copies on request until it was clear that there was a very steady market for more, and doing little (so far as is evident) towards promoting widespread demand.[5] That non-commercial factors exerted more influence on the fortunes of many works is an impression which future research could well modify, however.

The aims and reach of new writings by religious (as of any other class of author) have to be assessed from, first, the author's words, in which we may be able to discern the range of audience or readership he envisaged, and, second, from the known copies and references to the work, how far in fact it got, by what agencies and in what conditions. The various facets of the monastic, canonical and mendicant vocations and their relationships to other social groups led to a variety of types of composition with quite widely differing purposes and outcomes. Regular religious traditions, training and facilities were particularly conducive to literary activity, up from informal annotation, through rapiaria of extracts, or indexing of books, to fresh expression in a few or many words, for the writer's own benefit, or his colleagues, or for one or more readers or listeners outside that community or order.

Writing for any purpose in principle required the command or permission of the religious superior, and in practice it must have usually involved an understanding that the product would be communicated (perhaps after scrutiny and amendment) either only to members of the same community or order, unless or until someone else should learn enough about it to ask after it; or else direct to an outsider or outsiders, with prospects thereafter, depending on its reception and the milieu, of more or less unlimited diffusion. Of these two courses only the latter can be thought of as actively ventured publication, but the former almost passively could sometimes have similar results in the long run. Apart from the encouragements to authorship, there were practical advantages in the fellowship of religious houses and orders for the spread of knowledge of new texts, not only those by their own members but also ones of interest to them, the in-house reproduction and inter-house conveyance of copies, and the multiplicity of persons and places whence response might arise.[6]

A very large amount of writing by religious, perhaps the majority, must have been, so far as one can see, limited in audience or readership to the immediate brethren or pastorate of the authors, and to their successors through the inheritance of their manuscripts. It is apparent that certain kinds of composition, such as academic exercises and occasional sermons, written down before or after delivery (a form of publication), were not copied much beyond a small circle of individuals and institutions closely concerned.[7] It is clear from prefaces or epilogues (when they exist), internal references, contents and extant copies that most of the traditional kinds of monastic historical composition in Latin, whether simple annals or more continuous chronicles, which persisted in the period of survey, although in the latter kind very conscious of a stylistically sophisticated readership, was primarily for a domestic one, and particularly posterity, within the house of origin and its dependencies.[8] Almost all the surviving manuscripts (and history was a category better preserved than most after the Dissolution) are apparently autographs or apographs, rough and fair, often with corrections and continuations of domestic interest: those of Henry Knighton of Leicester (Augustinian), the Westminster chronicler (Benedictine), Thomas Burton of Meaux (Cistercian), Thomas Elmham of St Augustine's Canterbury (Benedictine), John Strecche of Kenilworth (Augustinian), John Wessington of Durham (Benedictine), from the late fourteenth and early fifteenth century.[9] Among the rather more numerous copies of the St Albans (Benedictine) chronicles attributable to Thomas Walsingham, the majority from the unusually well-testified scriptorium there under his direction in the same period, and belonging to the mother house or its cells, there is evidence of external transmission in two closely similar handsomely produced manuscripts containing the shorter chronicle (dating from about 1388), which both bear the arms of Norwich Cathedral Priory, though one must have been very soon procured by Thomas, duke of Gloucester, and given to the college he founded at Pleshey (Essex) in 1393, by the time of his death in 1397. It may not be a coincidence that in the same span of years Walsingham was prior of the St Albans dependency of Wymondham near Norwich (also a Benedictine priory).[10] Yet the relatively limited character of that circulation contrasts with that of the work to which the St Albans chronicle in the Norwich and Pleshey manuscripts is only a continuation, the mid-fourteenth-century *Polychronicon* of Ranulph Higden, Benedictine of Chester, a much more ambitious world history which had already established itself as a standard work in various monasteries (for Knighton's and other chronicles were also conceived as its continuations) and the author's successive revisions were disseminated through much of England, presumably commencing at Chester Abbey, where a repeatedly altered autograph remained.[11] Yet versions of Walsingham were used by the anonymous chronicler of Westminster Abbey (Benedictine) in the 1390s, and in the fifteenth century by the supposedly northern Thomas Otterburne, in which the St Albans cell of Tynemouth may have helped, and by John Capgrave, Augustinian friar of Lynn (Norfolk), where there was also a cell of Norwich Cathedral Priory.[12] These could be instances of the privileged provision of texts or access to them rather than traces of so wide a circulation as the *Polychronicon* attained.

The sources of copying texts and the agencies of dissemination are often plainer to discern for shorter pieces associated in collective volumes than for longer works occupying single volumes each. Separate quires or booklets quickly and cheaply copied and easily transported could also easily be bound up with other sections of similar character, and subsequently small groups repeated in other collective volumes. The treatises of controversial and speculative theology by Uthred of Boldon, Benedictine monk of Durham (d. 1397), from his time as an Oxford doctor in the 1360s, though there and then attracting academic attention, seem to have survived only in one, two or three copies, chiefly in one mid-fifteenth-century collection. His treatises on monastic rules and history, written possibly on his return to Durham and its nearby cell of Finchale in the later part of his life, interspersed with participation in ecclesiastical business elsewhere, are not extant in many more, and those mostly in manuscripts from his mother house and connected with provincial chapters of his order.[13] However, eight copies of his *Meditatio Devota* are known, only two of which are from Durham, the other copies all being of a variant text mentioning St Albans saints, one of them for its abbot, two probably from a Canterbury monastic source, of which one is in a manuscript made for Charles d'Orléans while prisoner in England from 1415 to 1440; one was copied by a Carthusian of Hinton (Somerset), and another was given to Sheen Charterhouse (Surrey, founded 1415) by an Austin friar of the Clare convent (Suffolk), both in the middle of the fifteenth century, while one was given to the Brigittine brethren's library of Syon Abbey (Middlesex, also founded 1415) at a later date;[14] copies are also recorded at Farne Island (a dependency of Durham) and at Reading Abbey (also Benedictine). A parallel can be observed in the writings of one of Uthred's contemporaries at Oxford, William Rymyngton, Cistercian of Sawley (W. Yorks.). His attacks on Wycliffe are again recorded in single copies,[15] yet his *Stimulus Peccatoris* or *Meditationes ad quemdam monachum anachoritam* is known now from nineteen of the whole or parts – two in volumes with Uthred's *Meditatio* for Durham Priory and Charles d'Orléans, the latter copied selectively at his direction from a manuscript belonging to his brother Jean (also an English prisoner 1412–45), and related in contents to a lost one in the Syon brethren's library; Syon also had the piece in a volume given by Simon Wynter, one of the earlier members of the house and spiritual counsellor of the duchess of Clarence who was responsible for the Orléans brothers in the 1420s. Other copies were given to the Charterhouses of Witham (Somerset) and Sheen by clerical sympathisers in the second half of the fifteenth century. One bears the arms of the Fortescue family (perhaps for Sir John, the judge, d. 1476), another was at Evesham Abbey (Benedictine) by the early sixteenth century, and one was in the catalogue of Leicester Abbey (Augustinian canons) by the same date.[16] As most lack the introductory verses which intimate the author's name and the tripartite structure, and as there is an alternative at one point for a secular reader instead of a monk, the text was probably given to other people besides the first recipient and thereafter spread by more than one route, under its own momentum, so to speak, one ascription to Rolle being in effect a tribute of worth. It looks nevertheless from the surviving copies that the most responsive milieu continued to be the monastic.

Many pieces of spiritual counsel were customarily addressed by religious or different orders (and no doubt by some secular clergy) as epistles to individuals at a distance, and the forms in which we have them, whether Latin or vernacular, may either imply or invite broader currency, among people in similar circumstances or else in different ones. Even the *Cloud of Unknowing* and the related epistles address more than a single reader, though the author's and readers' scruples are probably reflected in a seemingly slow and tight diffusion through the Carthusians and other contemplative communities and individuals.[17] The several Latin epistles of Walter Hilton, Augustinian canon of Thurgarton (Notts.), some perhaps from his own spell as a solitary, and what were apparently the two separately published books of the *Scale of Perfection*, allow for recipients in distinct conditions of life and for different extents of circulation, reflected in the rates of survival of copies, as they stemmed from the author or the addressee. The best-surviving epistle, that to Adam Horsley, a royal clerk who became a Carthusian, was obviously circulated within and by the latter order, as were the others to a lesser extent.[18] There is a want of positive evidence that Hilton's own order, the Austin canons (whose houses were autonomous like the Benedictines', subject to only occasional provincial chapters), did much towards the early diffusion of his writings, but the exceptionally cohesive organisation of the Carthusians played a major role in the transmission and conflation of the *Scale* in the fifteenth century, commending it also probably to the Brigittines and the devout laity of the court and metropolis.[19] Although the Latin *Scale* was the work of a Carmelite friar, Thomas Fyslake, whose order was very active in contemplative spiritual counsel as well as other fields in this period, and which like all the mendicants had a provincial and international organisation rivalling the Carthusians', the latter are again the most conspicuous in its circulation, extending beyond Britain.[20]

One large compilation of material from native and foreign sources, the *Speculum Spiritualium*, by an early fifteenth-century Carthusian, who characterises it as not only for his own benefit but also for other contemplatives and of use to persons in active life, and invites readers to copy selections,[21] is found in whole or portions in a dozen manuscripts – two from Mountgrace Charterhouse, one belonging to the recluse at Sheen Charterhouse, four in the brethren's library at Syon Abbey, one bequeathed by a London rector who was a benefactor of Syon and Sheen to his brother in 1476, one at Chester Abbey, one at Southwark Priory (Surrey, Augustinian), and one at the secular college at Arundel (Sussex) by the early sixteenth century – not to speak of its subsequent distribution in print.[22] A shorter but still substantial work, the *Donatus Devocionis*, 'compilatus a quodam claustrali', dated 1430, partly derived from the *Speculum*, in two books of which the first, like that of Hilton's *Scale* and possibly for similar reasons of separate issue or differing interest, is not always found with the second, is known in nine manuscripts of English origin and fourteen foreign. Among the former, one was owned by the recluse of Sheen, two by the Syon brethren, one was given by a former royal confessor to Witham Charterhouse, one belonged to Bermondsey Abbey (Cluniac, Surrey), one to unidentified Austin canons and one to Franciscans; one was half written by Jean d'Orléans in England and another copied for Charles in France. The Paris Celestine convent probably got book 1 from them, but the abbey of St Victor (Augustinian) perhaps got its copy from Germany where, possibly by two independent religious channels, copies reached the Carthusians of Cologne, Erfurt, Mainz and Trier, Benedictines and Franciscan nuns also at Trier, and Benedictines at Nuremberg. Both books reached the Franciscans at Landshut (Bavaria).[23] Although some of the English manuscripts of the *Speculum Spiritualium* and *Donatus Devocionis*, like many of Hilton's or Higden's, must be by non-religious copyists, the recurrence of particular religious provenance or associations argues that recourse for exemplars was made via such links and that texts were transmitted from house to house, not always within the same order, as well as to interested non-religious owners, who not infrequently bestowed their acquisitions in time on their source or on like-minded institutions.

A similar contrast to that observed within the writings of Uthred of Boldon and William Rymington may be seen in the evidence of limited circulation of the Latin, academic and controversial works of the late fourteenth-century Carmelites Richard Lavenham and Richard Maidstone in comparison with their English compositions. The first wrote an English treatise on the deadly sins, of which sixteen copies are known, evincing considerable currency and varied ownership in and beyond East Anglia, and the second wrote a verse paraphrase of the penitential psalms, surviving in twenty manuscripts of even broader distribution.[24] These represent the friars' popular orientation, as does Maidstone's Latin set of sermons, *Dormi secure*, for all that they involve (as Lavenham's treatise implies) clerical intermediaries, and it may be to the latter as much as to the Carmelites themselves that the dissemination is owing, though the English pieces must have often become private lay reading. Recognition of this kind of change in the potential public may well be responsible for the impression that in this period the identifiable friar authorship of sermons preserved in writing, singly or in sets, seems to be less than previously. The ingenious series of homilies known as *Jacob's Well* survives unsurprisingly in only one copy,[25] but it may have been conceived for special circumstances of domestic reading, as was surely a lengthy conventional cycle of English postils also known in a single copy,[26] by the anonymous author of *Dives and Pauper*. The latter, an English theological dialogue of remarkable sophistication, is addressed like the postils to a 'dear friend', but it had a considerable diffusion in the eastern counties, including St Albans Abbey and Holy Trinity, Aldgate (London, Augustinian) as well as lay owners. Each of these works has been attributed persuasively to a friar, but we lack any evidence of mendicant promotion, however probable, in the last case.[27]

The regular canons, unlike the monks whom they otherwise largely resembled, took a not inconsiderable part in the lay pastorate. Philip Repingdon, Austin canon and later abbot of Leicester, after abandoning Wycliffitism, and before becoming bishop of Lincoln, wrote an English treatise on the decalogue known in a few copies, and a Latin homily cycle in more. The latter was owned by St Paul's (London) and Wells Cathedrals, King's and Queens' Colleges at Cambridge, and Eton (Berks.), Durham Priory and Syon Abbey, besides two bishops of Norwich and other secular clergy, the predominance of whom is evident.[28] John Mirk, another Austin canon, of Lilleshall (Shrops.), composed his English homily and legend cycle, the *Festial*, almost certainly to compete with the Lollard homily cycles; its spread throughout the northern Midlands and as far as Ireland, shown in the dialects of the thirty copies of all or parts of two recensions of the original and of later adaptations, may have been virtually spontaneous once it was put, as designed, into the hands of parish priests, and also after later modification for lay reading, when it got into the hands of the metropolitan book-trade, becoming an early printed best-seller.[29] Mirk's English verse instructions to parish priests and his Latin *Manuale Sacerdotis*, addressed to a cleric, in comparison had less success, not finding as big a gap as the *Festial*.[30] As with Hilton, there is nothing to show that Repingdon's or Mirk's Austin brethren were active in promoting their writings, though they can hardly have been indifferent.

How the metropolitan book-trade could be brought in to augment other means of diffusion through individual and religious channels may be divined from the characteristics of many of the sixty manuscripts of the *Mirror of the*

Life of Christ based on the pseudo-Bonaventuran *Meditationes Vite Christi* by Nicholas Love, first prior of Mountgrace Charterhouse (N. Yorks.). Written at the request of 'somme devoute soules' who could have been but were not necessarily religious, its proheme opens it also to 'lewed men and wymmen' who could have been both religious and lay. It may have been communicated to a limited number of people and perhaps religious houses before 1410, when it was submitted for approbation by Archbishop Arundel of Canterbury 'antequam fuerit libere communicata', whose action is thus often recorded, together with his mandate that it should be 'publice communicandum' in order to confute the Lollards.[31] It may be significant that the see not of York but of Canterbury was invoked, since not only was it by Arundel's constitutions that the copying and use of scriptural translations had been restricted, against the spread of heresy, but also it was within his province that the chief centres of book production existed. Love's book was explicitly to be published, not, it seems, by the conventions of patronage, but by certification to potential readers and producers, who appear to have responded rapidly and abundantly; yet by no means obviating independent transmission. To emphasise the several factors in Love's success we have in contrast another prose version of the *Meditationes* (with a good deal more matter than in Love's from sources like Suso's *Horologium Sapientie* and the Revelations of St Brigit of Sweden), the *Mirror to Devout People*, by a monk of a south-eastern Charterhouse. At first in ignorance of Love's work, yet encouraged by his prior, he wrote for a religious sister and others ignorant of Latin: his translation is known only from one copy made by a monk for Sheen Charterhouse and another made for John, lord Scrope of Masham (d. 1455, Yorks.), of a family having many ties with Syon Abbey, where the original recipient may have been.[32] Similarly, the epilogue to the English versions of the lives of three Low Countries women religious mystics and a letter about St Catherine of Siena which survive only in one mid-fifteenth-century manuscript from Beauvale Charterhouse (Notts.), says that they were done by a monk at the bidding of his prior and were meant for 'alle men and wymmen þat in happe rediþ or heriþ þis englyshe', though he still apologises for his style to 'letterd men and clerkes'.[33] Whatever the author's and this superior's notions, a new work communicated solely to one confined religious audience, if it did not enlist alternative outlets, might easily fail to reach a more general public. It is in another English piece of hagiography by a religious author, the life of St Jerome by Simon Wynter, Brigittine brother of Syon, addressed to the duchess of Clarence (d. 1439), whose relationship has been mentioned above, that the mode of publication through dedication is best spelled out: 'Wherfore I desire þat hit shulde lyke ȝoure ladyshype first to rede hit and to doo copye hit for ȝoure self and syth to latte other rede hit and copye hit whoso wyl'.[34] The implication in this instance seems to be that the copy supplied by the author was either to serve through his patroness as an exemplar for further copying or to be returned to him, presumably with the same purpose. In fact the small number of manuscripts and the early printed edition suggest that it may have been mostly for religious of his own order, and perhaps of others, that the life was reproduced. The recipient of a dedication, and of a presentation copy to keep (for which at the least some reward in cash or kind must have been expected, though not invariably bestowed), need not have put himself or herself out to commend or lend the work to other potential owners, and in any case they may not have responded. Dedication to a patron, even after a request or encouragement, was thus not necessarily a more effective means of publication than other initiatives of the author or his brethren.

There are not a few examples of dedications that seem to have been abortive for circulation, though not necessarily without other results: William Sudbury's (of Westminster) to Richard II, Thomas Walsingham's to Henry V, and an anonymous religious's to Henry VI[35] are cases where there is little trace of more than a single monastic or the recipient's copy. These are erudite Latin compositions, unlikely to win wide lay interest, in contrast with, say, the translation of Vegetius, *De Re Militari*, done for Thomas, lord Berkeley, probably by John Walton, Austin canon of Osney Abbey (though emancipated from it as a papal chaplain), of which eleven manuscripts are known, or the stanzaic English version of Boethius's *De Consolatione Philosophiae* he did for Berkeley's daughter Elizabeth, of which there are twenty-four.[36] For neither would there be reason to suppose that religious channels played any part in dissemination, though copies belonged to religious; yet as the dedication of the Boethius is found only in one manuscript and the edition printed at the Austin abbey of Tavistock in 1525, it may be that the majority of the other copies do not descend from the patron's but from one or more of the author's independent launching, carried on however through commercial copying.

Many of the poems, longer and shorter, of John Lydgate, Benedictine monk of Bury St Edmund's (Suffolk), were commissioned by members of the upper and middle classes of State and Church, and it is probable from their aspect and associations that the majority (though not all) of the numerous manuscripts of some of the longer poems such as the *Life of Our Lady* and *Troy-Book* for Henry V, and the *Fall of Princes* for Duke Humphrey of Gloucester, were commercial products resulting from interest generated in and about the court and supplied by the metropolitan or provincial book-trade.[37] There was almost certainly a closer concern of his own community with the original and further production of Lydgate's lives of SS Edmund and Fremund, composed as a memento from the abbey to Henry VI, augmented in some copies with later miracles, and with the dedication altered in others to Edward IV, after the author's death; and with certain copies of the *Fall of Princes* which appear to have been made by the same groups of local scribes and illuminators who produced a volume of shorter Lydgate poems for his abbot but who were themselves rather lay professionals than monks.[38] When John Whethamstede, abbot of St Albans, paid in 1439 for the life of St Alban composed for him by Lydgate the sum was enough for a handsome copy, illustrated like those of the Bury saints, but we do not know if the relatively limited subsequent distribution of which there is evidence came from one or both monasteries.[39] We need more comparative studies of the manuscripts containing Lydgate's works before we can know if monastic or other religious connections than those mentioned affected their dissemination, but the indications are that secular contacts and commercial enterprise contributed most to it.

That contrasting degrees of distribution are not solely or mainly a question of language nor of the relatively autonomous or unified organisation of the religious orders concerned is emphasised by the manuscripts of both English and Latin works of John Capgrave, who, as prior of Lynn (Norfolk) and provincial of the Austin friars (1453–7), was particularly well placed to promote diffusion through his order. Yet most of his works in both tongues, like those of the monastic chroniclers already mentioned, survive only in autographs and apographs corrected by himself, with dedications to eminent laypeople (Henry VI, Edward IV, Duke Humphrey and Sir Thomas Tudenham of Norfolk), churchmen (the archbishop of Canterbury and bishop of Ely), other religious superiors (the Premonstratensian abbot of West Dereham, Norfolk, and the Master of the Gilbertine order, for his nuns) and an unnamed lady. Though these all may have retained presentation copies, rewarding Capgrave for his trouble, time and expense, and two or three eventually passed Latin works on to Oxford libraries, there is a lack of evidence of activity either on their part or even on his part towards the further publication which his prologues adumbrate.[40] An exception is his English verse life of St Katharine, undedicated, presented as a communal enterprise ('ȝe þat rede it pray for hem alle þat to þis werk eyther travayled or payde'), for a diverse public ('It schall be know of man, mayde and of wyffe') and alternative ways of communication ('He þat thys lyve wryȝtis, redis or els cuthe here'). From the fact that none of the copies show the author's hand, and that they are of distinctively derivative quality, we may infer that the poem had some success in East Anglia. It was in a popular mode favoured by the friars and its circulation could have been helped by Capgrave's Austin brethren, strong in the area, but positive proof is wanting. At least two copyists were secular priests, one or more of Wisbech (Cambs.), while a sub-prioress gave a copy to the Augustinian nunnery of Campsey (Suffolk).[41]

There are similarities, and some differences, in what we can gather about the English writings of Capgrave's contemporary and confrère, Osbern Bokenham of Clare (Suffolk). A number of his verse lives of saints were composed for but, it seems, not formally dedicated to various noble and gentlewomen and gentlemen of the area, and one for a fellow friar, Thomas

Burgh, between 1443 and 1445. They all survive only (with one exception) in a collective volume made at Cambridge in 1447 for Burgh, at a cost and in a style suggestive of commercial workmanship, yet possibly conventual, to give to a nunnery (with little doubt in East Anglia) where his sister was a nun.[42] Clearly this must derive from the author's retained (perhaps revised) copies of the separate lay-patronised texts, and it shows how relationships within and outside an order, spiritual and personal, might promote extensions of circulation to different publics, though sometimes only short shoots, so to speak. The other pieces attributable to Bokenham are also known from unique copies. The English verse translation of Claudian made in 1445 at Clare for Richard, duke of York, and the verse dialogue on the pedigree of his forebears, patrons of the house, of 1455 or later, both anonymous, were handsomely written and illuminated, presumably for presentation,[43] whereas the acknowledged but undedicated *Mappula Anglie* in English prose, addressed to a general public, with a possible pendant dated 1445, is in a plainer miscellany probably at a further remove from the original, not however far in time or place, but not obviously made by or for Bokenham's brethren.[44] The disappearance of the other lives of saints Bokenham mentions in the *Mappula* (which do not match any known anonymous instances) also suggests that the possibilities of escaping from the limits of a single patronal, local or regional publication by way of the national and international facilities of a religious order were not normally taken advantage of in cases of this sort, namely for vernacular literature of secular interest, as inappropriate. Nor do most of Capgrave's theological works, in Latin or English, long or short, appear to have been pushed in that way.

It was the literature most specifically relevant to the way of life of the regular religious which most clearly found its way from one house and order to another, and beyond to secular clergy and lay-people who were in close sympathy and touch with them. When religious authors treated other topics they did not always have advantages over seculars in the processes of publication, it appears. The fashion for magnates' patronage may have been sometimes something of a sidetrack, perhaps diverting authors from full use of other opportunities for more effective publication, since patronage was in fact so often a purely passive relationship, important for potential benefits of different kinds, while authors were not necessarily over-concerned with reaching a large audience, as we tend to assume they must have been.

1 J.C. Russell, 'The Clerical Population of Medieval England', *Traditio*, 2 (1944), 177–212; J.W. Adamson, *The Illiterate Anglo-Saxon and Other Essays* (Cambridge, 1946), pp. 38–61.

2 W.A. Pantin, *The English Church in the Fourteenth Century* (Cambridge, 1955), pp. 177–22; D. Knowles, *The Religious Orders in England*, II (Cambridge, 1955),

232–3; N. Orme, *English Schools in the Middle Ages* (London, 1973), pp. 1–56, 244–51; T.H. Aston, 'Oxford's Medieval Alumni', *Past and Present*, 74 (1977), 1–40, at 32–5; 'The Medieval Alumni of the University of Cambridge', *ibid.*, 86 (1980), 9–86, at 63–6.

3 Knowles, *Religious Orders*, II, 233–9.

4 Cf. J.H. Harrington, 'The Production and Distribution of Books in Western Europe to the Year 1500', (Columbia Univ. Ph.D. thesis 1956; Ann Arbor, University Microfilms 17057); P.J. Lucas, 'The Growth and Development of English Literary Patronage in the Later Middle Ages and the Early Renaissance', *The Library*, 6th series, 4 (1982), 219–48; P. Bourgain, 'L'Edition des Manuscrits', in *Histoire de l'édition française*, ed. H.J. Martin *et al.*, 1 (Paris, 1982), 49–75.

5 Cf. L. Febvre and H.J. Martin, *L'Apparition du livre* (Paris, 1958, 1971), pp. 165–89, 307–47.

6 E.g. *Documents Illustrating the Activities of the General and Provincial Chapters of the English Black Monks 1215–1540*, ed. W.A. Pantin, III, Camden Soc., 3rd series, 54 (London, 1937), pp. 76–7, letter from Adam Easton (monk of Norwich and agent at the papal court) to the abbot of Westminster asking for copies of Wycliffe's writings from the former's students and offering to pay the costs of copying (1376 ?), pp. 98–9, Thomas Ledbury (monk of Worcester, student at Oxford) sending the abbot of Bury a devotional piece of Lenten reading, in thanks for his help with the costs of his education and his being sent to the Council of Constance (c. 1417–19).

7 E.g. Pantin, *English Church*, pp. 178–85 (Easton and Thomas Brinton); *Three Middle English Sermons from the Worcester Chapter Manuscript F.10*, ed. D.M. Grisdale, Leeds School of English Language Texts and Monographs, 5 (1939); or those in Oxford, Bodleian Library, MS Laud misc. 706, of which five have been ed. P.J. Horner (Albany Ph.D., 1975) and one is by the monk of Gloucester who owned the volume.

8 In nonetheless general terms: e.g. Thomas Burton of Meaux of his predecessors 'laude dignos patrum suorum actus litteris tradere publicis minime curaverunt' and to his public 'Obsecro ergo vos omnes, quicunque hanc qualemcunque chronicam estis lecturi . . . '; ed. E.A. Bond, Rolls Series, 1 (London, 1866), 71–2.

9 Knowles, *Religious Orders*, II, 263–70; A. Gransden, *Historical Writing in England*, II (London, 1982), pp. 157–93, 342–424.

10 V.H. Galbraith, *The St. Albans Chronicle 1406–20* (Oxford, 1937), pp. xxxvi–lxvi; Gransden, *Historical Writing*, II, pp. 118–56; cf. G.B. Stow, 'Bodleian MS. Bodley 316 and the Dating of Thomas Walsingham's Literary Career', *Manuscripta* 25 (1981), 67–75.

11 J. Taylor, *The Universal Chronicle of Ranulph Higden* (Oxford, 1966), pp. 89–133.

12 Gransden, *Historical Writing*, II, 196; *The Westminster Chronicle 1381–94*, ed. and tr. L.C. Hector and B.F. Harvey (Oxford, 1982), p. xix; *John Capgrave's Abbreuiacion of Chronicles*, ed. P.J. Lucas, EETS, os, 285 (Oxford, 1983), pp. lxxvii–lxxxvi.

13 W.A. Pantin, 'Two Treatises of Uthred of Boldon on the Monastic Life', in *Studies in Medieval History Presented to F.M. Powicke*, ed. R.W. Hunt *et al.* (Oxford, 1948); *English Church*, pp. 165–75; Knowles, *Religious Orders*, II, 48–54.

14 Ed. H. Farmer, *Studia Anselmiana*, 43 (Analecta Monastica 5th series, 1958), pp. 187–206, not noticing Paris, BN MS lat. 1201 (for Charles d'Orléans).

15 Cf. J. MacNulty, *Yorks. Arch. Journ.*, 30 (1931), 231–47.
16 Ed. R. O'Brien, *Citeaux*, 16 (1965), 278–304, not noticing BN MS lat. 1201, Durham UL MS Cosin V.v.15, Uppsala UB MS C.193 (prologue), nor M34–35 in the Syon brethren's catalogue, ed. M. Bateson (Cambridge, 1898), pp. 103–4, nor no. 521 in the Leicester catalogue, ed. M.R. James, *Trans. Leics. Arch. Soc.*, 19 (1936–7), 124.
17 'I speke at þis tyme in specyall to þiself, & not to all þoo þat þis writyng scholen here in general . . . If eny oþer be so disposid as þou arte, to whom þis writyng may profit . . . ' (*Privy Counselling*). Cf. A.I. Doyle, *Survey*, I, 276–80.
18 See H.L. Gardner, 'Walter Hilton and the Mystical Tradition in England', *Essays and Studies*, 22 (1936), 103–27, and J.M. Russell-Smith, 'Walter Hilton and a Tract in Defence of the Veneration of Images', *Dominican Studies*, 7 (1954), 180–214, on the genesis of the epistles. M.W. Bloomfield, *Incipits of Latin Works on the Virtues and Vices 1100–1500 A.D.* (Cambridge, Mass., 1979), no. 1658, has only three copies of that 'de ymagine peccati', and, no. 1671, four of that to Horsley, of which I knew respectively four and thirteen, besides extracts from each in the *Speculum Spiritualium* and *Donatus Devocionis*. Two 'de ymagine' occur with Horsley's, and two further epistles are found only with one of the latter and in one other copy each.
19 Doyle, *Survey*, I, 243–75, subject to more recent findings by S.S. Hussey, 'The Text of the Scale of Perfection Book II', *NM*, 65 (1964), 75–92, and in M.G. Sargent, 'Walter Hilton's *Scale of Perfection*: the London Manuscript Group Reconsidered', *Medium Aevum*, 52 (1983), 189–216.
20 S.S. Hussey, 'Latin and English in the *Scale of Perfection*', *Mediaeval Studies*, 35 (1973), 456–76; another copy, Naples, Bib. Naz., MS VII.G.31 was later in Franciscan ownership in Italy.
21 H.E. Allen, *Writings Ascribed to Richard Rolle* (New York, 1927), pp. 405–6; the original index to the Syon catalogue attributes the same four (of its eventual five) copies to each of Adam monachus Cartusiensis and Henricus Domus Cartusiensis de Bethleem (i.e. Sheen), of whom the latter may have only compiled an index to it. One of the Adams of the appropriate period is Horsley himself, who died in 1424 at Beauvale; extracts from his epistle and other works 'venerabilis magistri Walteri Hylton' occur in the *Speculum*.
22 Bloomfield, *Incipits*, no. 512, has only five manuscripts and the printing of 1510. I know of eleven manuscripts of substantial portions and two of extracts. The edition had distinct British and continental issues, from both of which copies survive belonging notably to religious houses.
23 The sources, relationships and dissemination of the *Speculum* and *Donatus* have not yet had the treatment they merit. I am indebted for information to the late Clare Kirchberger, Miss J. Russell-Smith, Dr M.B. Hackett O.S.A., Professor E. Colledge O.S.A., and Dr G. Ouy, and to the University of Durham Research Fund for travel grants.
24 *BRUO*, II (Oxford, 1958), 1109–10, 1204; J.P.W.M. van Zutphen, ed., *A Litil Tretys on the Seven Deadly Sins* (Rome, 1956), to whose list of copies can now be added London, Soc. of Antiquaries 687, pp. 383–411, and BL MS Sloane 3160, fols. 4r–23r (incomplete); 'The Seven Penitential Psalms' in *The Wheatley Manuscript*, ed. M. Day, EETS, os, 155 (London, 1921), xii–xviii, 9–59; *IMEV*, nos. 1961, 2157, 3755, 3824, and *Supplement*.

25 Salisbury Cathedral, MS 103: part I, ed. A. Brandeis, EETS, os, 115 (London, 1900).

26 A. Hudson and H.L. Spencer, 'Old Author, New Work: the Sermons of MS. Longleat 4', *Medium Aevum*, 53 (1984), 220–38.

27 Doyle, *Survey*, I, 93–7; cf. *Dives and Pauper*, ed. P.H. Barnum, I, part I, EETS, os, 275 (London, 1976); Hudson and Spencer, 'Old Author, New Work', 228. Professor C.P. Christianson has told me of another copy left by Robert Rowse, parson of St Stephen Walbrook, London, to Sheen Charterhouse in 1479.

28 *BRUO*, III (1959), 1565–7; the English tract attributed by its scribe in BL MS Cotton Vespasian A.XXIII, fols. 107–115v, occurs also in BL MS Harley 2250 and, imperfectly, in CUL MS Kk.i.3.

29 C. Horstmann, ed., *Altenglische Legenden, Neue Folge* (Heilbronn, 1881), pp. cxii–xv, cxxii; M.F. Wakelin, 'The Manuscripts of John Mirk's Festial', *LSE*, NS, 1 (1967), 93–118; S. Powell, ed., *The Advent and Nativity Sermons from a Fifteenth-Century Revision of John Mirk's Festial*, Middle English Texts 13 (Heidelberg, 1981), pp. 18–32; T.E. Marston, 'An Early English Best-Seller', *Yale Univ. Lib. Gazette*, 46 (1971).

30 *IMEV*, no. 961 (seven copies); Bloomfield, *Incipits*, no. 2787 (eleven copies, Pembroke Cambridge 236 in error; two more can be added).

31 Salter, 'The Manuscripts'; Doyle, 'Reflections', and *Survey*, I, 138–59.

32 *The Speculum Devotorum of an Anonymous Carthusian of Sheen*, ed. J. Hogg, vols. II–III, Analecta Cartusiana 12–13 (Salzburg, 1973–74) (vol. 1 (introduction) not yet published); there are unpublished editions by B.A. Wilsher (London M.A. thesis, 1956) and J. Banks (Fordham Ph.D. thesis, 1959); Doyle, *Survey*, I, 159–61.

33 Ed. C. Horstmann, *Anglia*, 8 (1885), 102–96; G.H. Gerould, *Saints' Legends* (Boston, 1916), p. 289.

34 M. Görlach, *The South English Legendary, Gilte Legende and Golden Legend*, Braunschweiger Anglistische Arbeiten, 3 (1972), pp. 20–1; authorship confirmed by a medieval ascription in Yale UL MS 317. Cambridge, St John's College, MS 250 is part of a dismembered volume by a hand which shares in a definitely Carthusian volume, Bodley 549.

35 For Sudbury see *BRUO*, III (1959), 1813; for Walsingham's *Ypodigma Neustrie*, see Galbraith, *St Albans Chronicle*, pp. lx–lxi; 'Tractatus de Regimine Principum ad Regem Henricum Sextum', in *Four English Political Tracts of the Later Middle Ages*, ed. J.P. Genet, Camden Soc., 4th series, 18 (London, 1977), pp. 40–173.

36 Cf. G.A. Lester, *Sir John Paston's 'Grete Boke'; a Descriptive Catalogue, with an Introduction, of British Library MS Lansdowne 285* (Cambridge, 1984), pp. 159–63; *Boethius De Consolatione Philosophiae*, tr. J. Walton, ed. M. Science, EETS, os, 170 (London, 1927); *IMEV*, no. 1597 and *Suppl.*; *BRUO* III (1959), 1975; Copenhagen, Kon. Bib. Thott 304 fol., which has what look like printer's markings, and a Cornish owner, may have included the dedication before it became defective.

37 Cf. A.S.G. Edwards, 'Lydgate Manuscripts: Some Directions for Future Research' and L. Lawton, 'The Illustrations of Late Medieval Secular Texts with Special Reference to Lydgate's "Troy Book"', in Pearsall, *Manuscripts and Readers*, pp. 15–26, 41–69.

38 K.L. Scott, 'Lydgate's Lives'.

39 *The Life of Saint Alban and Saint Amphibal*, ed. J.E. van der Westhuizen (Leiden, 1974): four complete manuscripts, one extract and a printing at St Albans in 1534.

40 F. Roth, *The English Austin Friars 1249–1538*, Cassiciacum, 6, 1 (New York, 1966), pp. 111–16, 532–8; P.J. Lucas, 'John Capgrave, O.S.A. (1393–1464), Scribe and "Publisher"', *TCBS*, 5 (1969), 1–35; E. Colledge, 'The Capgrave "Autographs"', *TCBS*, 6 (1974), 137–48; C. Smetana, ed., *The Life of St Norbert*, Studies and Texts 40 (Toronto, 1977); P.J. Lucas and R. Dalton, 'Capgrave's Preface Dedicating his Commentary *In Exodum* to Humphrey Duke of Gloucester', *Bodleian Library Record*, 11 (1982), 20–5; P.J. Lucas, ed., *Abbreuiacion of Chronicles*, pp. xv–xxix.

41 *The Life of St. Katharine of Alexandria*, ed. C. Horstmann, with forewords by F.J. Furnivall, EETS, os, 100 (London, 1893); D.A. Pearsall, 'Capgrave's Life of St. Katharine', *Mediaevalia et Humanistica*, ns, 6 (1975), 121–37; William Gybbe, not Sybbe or Tybbe, one of the copyists and owner of Bodleian Lib., MS Rawl. poet. 118, was priest at Wisbech from at least 1443 and long after: P.J. Lucas, 'William Gybbe of Wisbech: a Fifteenth-Century English Scribe', *Codices Manuscripti*, 11 (1985), Heft 2. 'M.R. Englisshe' who wrote BL MS Arundel 20 was also most probably a secular clerk.

42 Roth, *English Austin Friars*, 1, 421–4, 515–17; *Legendys of Hooly Wummen*, ed. M.S. Serjeantson, EETS, os, 206 (1938); A.G. Watson, *Catalogue of Dated and Datable Manuscripts c. 700–1600 in . . . the British Library* (London, 1979), 1, no. 464, 11, pl. 488: the major copyist more expert than the two others each responsible for a single legend, of whom one added the colophon information. *IMEV*, no. 3936 has another copy of lines 1–35 of the life of St Dorothy in BL MS Add. 36983.

43 Watson, *Catalogue*, 1, no. 59, 11, pl. 470; *Catalogue of the Heralds' Commemorative Exhibition* (London, 1936), pl. 42. That Bokenham was alive as late as 1464 was pointed out by Dr M.B. Hackett, *NQ* 206 (1961), 244. Görlach, *South English Legendary*, pp. 82–6, does not accept that Bokenham's lost legends can be those added to the prose *Gilte Legende* of 1438.

44 *Mappula*, ed. C. Horstmann, *Englische Studien*, 10 (1887), 34–41; *Catalogue of the Harleian Manuscripts in the British Museum*, 111 (London, 1808), 103; G.F. Warner, ed., *The Libelle of Englyshe Polycye* (Oxford, 1926), p. liii, dating Harley 4011 to the third quarter of the century. The scribe of the *Mappula*, W. Gravell, uses a Welsh motto and an annotator of another piece mentions the abbot of Lilleshall (Shrops.), but the latter had a house in London and the spelling of the piece following the *Mappula* (written or compiled by William Brewyn ?) has East Anglian traits.

6 · LOLLARD BOOK PRODUCTION

ANNE HUDSON

Books were a matter of life and death of Lollards. From the earliest commissions against the followers of Wyclif in 1382 until the mid-sixteenth century when Lollardy merged, in the eyes of its opponents, with Lutheranism, books had been primary evidence of heresy:[1] ownership of suspicious books, a category which could cover any vernacular scriptures and extend as far as *The Pricke of Conscience* or *The Canterbury Tales*, was sufficient to bring a man or woman to trial;[2] adherence to the views expressed in the theological or polemical volumes owned, or the conviction that vernacular scriptures were legitimate, could be sufficient to bring the arrested person to the stake.[3] Wyclif's works were burnt at Carfax in Oxford in 1410;[4] a similar fate awaited the *libri*, *quaterni* and *schedulae* found in the course of the hunt for heretics in the following hundred years.[5] The extent of the destruction can be partially measured by the fact that, though Thomas Netter had a fairly complete library of Wyclif's theological writings from which he quoted in his *Doctrinale* written in the 1420s, about two-thirds of those texts no longer survive complete in manuscripts in England.[6] Vernacular material probably suffered worse because its owners were more open to the investigations of episcopal authorities. The high value that Lollards set upon literacy, and the lengths that they would go to educate themselves first to read books and then to comprehend their arguments through instruction in their *scholae* and *conventiculae*, emerge through the records of many trials, together with an indication of the extent to which one literate member of a group became the focus of instruction in a community.[7] The sophistication of thought to which Lollards might be expected to attain can be measured from the content of those books that survive; the money and organisation that went into their production can be assessed from the quality of the manuscripts.

An instructive starting point is the account of the London skinner John Claydon, examined for a second time on suspicion of heresy by Archbishop Chichele in August 1415.[8] Claydon was a Lollard of long standing, first apprehended by Bishop Braybrook in London and imprisoned for a period of some five years, but then released after abjuration; on his rearrest he admitted that he had reverted to his old opinions and old associates. Most important evidence against Claydon in this second trial was afforded by his possession of 'plures libros scriptos in Anglicis': his condemnation seems to have been obtained not by inquiry into Claydon's beliefs, but by asking Claydon whether he agreed with the content of the books; when Claydon admitted his complete sympathy with them, a committee of masters, including the canonist William Lyndwood, was set to enumerate the heresies found in these books; the list of heresies found in Claydon's copy of *The Lanterne of Light*, and Claydon's prior admission of sympathy then formed the basis for his condemnation – books and heretic alike were to be burned. In the course of the investigation a number of interesting points emerged about Claydon's acquisition of the books, and about the books themselves. Apart from the *Lanterne of Light*, two other texts are specified: a commentary on the ten commandments, presumably one of the several commentaries tinged in varying degrees by Lollardy,[9] and a sermon preached *apud Horsaldowne* which may be identical with *þe sermoun of þe horsedoun* whose opening survives in Bodleian MS Douce 53.[10] The *Lanterne* was said to be covered in red leather, well bound and written on vellum in a good English hand. The volume had been made to Claydon's commission by John Gryme; Gryme had brought the loose quires to Claydon's house in St Martin's Lane, where he and one of Claydon's servants, John Fuller, had read the material to Claydon, himself illiterate. Two days had been spent 'circa correcionem et lecturam dictorum quaternorum', after which Claydon had expressed himself well pleased with the book. Its binding presumably followed also at Claydon's expense. When it was complete Claydon had spent many hours talking about its content with like-minded friends and servants.

This is a particularly well-documented case of book-production for a Lollard and by his commission. About Gryme we unfortunately know nothing more, though since Claydon was of the parish of St Anne's Aldersgate he could well have come from Paternoster Row, the centre of the London book-trade.[11] It is evident that, despite Claydon's inability himself to read the book, he was prepared to spend a good deal of money on its making and, significantly, was anxious that it should be correct. Claydon's copy of the *Lanterne of Light* inevitably does not survive, but the indication of the *secunda folia* given in the trial suggests that it is likely to have been of the same size as the two manuscripts of the text that do survive.[12] If so the volume was far from being one of the larger or more expensive productions of Lollardy, though its intellectual pretensions, with numerous quotations from patristic writers and the Bible in Latin followed by English translation, were not negligible. As a means of instruction in Lollard belief the *Lanterne* would have been quite efficient, since it is divided into chapters with clear headings and deals explicitly with the differences between the church of Christ and that of antichrist (the established church of the pope and his prelates).

The case of Claydon illustrates the initiative taken by a Lollard layman in the production of books for his own use. Another story shows how on the

12 British Library MS Egerton 2820, fols.41v–42r, anonymous sermon (see p. 127). Note the correction and the precise references within the text and in the margins.

other hand Lollard preachers might organise book-production for the use of those to whom they ministered. A long sermon written before 1413 and probably after 1407 concludes with a passage in which the preacher explains that he will leave a copy of his sermon with the congregation for them to study, exhorting them to note any arguments advanced against him by any enemy who should attempt to confute him, and promising to return to deal with these points and with any doubts that should arise from the study of the text. The sermon survives in three fifteenth-century copies, all of them of the same format and two of them in the same hand.[13] Since the format is pocket-sized it seems reasonable to think that these three volumes are those actually distributed by the preacher. If this is the case, the copies handed out were professional productions of high quality (see, for example, BL MS Egerton 2820 illustrated in Ill. 12). Like the *Lanterne* the sermon is in content ambitious: the congregation was expected to comprehend arguments drawing on grammatical, legal and logical minutiae without full explanation within the text. The study of the text, and of arguments against its tenets, was presumably to occur within the *conventiculae* of which so much is heard in Lollard trials.[14]

These two instances concern the Lollard movement some thirty years after

Wyclif's death, by which time the activity of the establishment to suppress it was, with the enactment of *De Heretico Comburendo* and of Arundel's *Constitutions*, far advanced. Evidence for book production in the years immediately following Wyclif's condemnation in 1382 is unfortunately less prolific. As has been said, books were recognised from the first as a means of dissemination as important as preachers; but details about where or when these books were produced, or who was responsible for their production as scribes or patrons or buyers, are sadly deficient. Only the manuscripts as artefacts, and the nature of their contents, can indirectly offer any enlightenment. From this evidence it is difficult to avoid the conclusion that the earliest Lollard book production was in Oxford, using academic compilers and the professional scribes available in the university. Such must obviously have been the case with Wyclif's own writings, even those issued after his withdrawal from the university to Lutterworth in 1382. At an early stage Wyclif or his disciples realised that it would be helpful to provide summaries, chapter by chapter, of these lengthy works and to furnish indexes, along with the necessary accompanying marginal indexing letters; by these means the texts became more accessible to preachers.[15] How long the copying of Wyclif's works continued in the university is unclear: certainly, however, copies were numerous enough there to justify a bonfire in 1410 and, no doubt more exceptionally, ownership by colleges later than that can be established.[16]

Turning to writings by Wyclif's followers, the Latin language of some of their earliest works points towards production in Oxford, since the outspoken criticism of the monastic and fraternal ways of life seems to preclude the possibility of copying in religious scriptoria. Such a conclusion is amply reinforced by the academic form of the early texts. The most extreme case is the *Floretum*, compiled between 1384 and 1396, a vast set of *distinctiones*, drawing on Wyclif's writings and, often with a tendentious slant, on the Bible, the Fathers, canon law and more recent theologians, each quotation provided with a precise reference that would allow quick verification. Leaving aside the question of the way in which the compilation was put together, the production of a manuscript such as Harley 401, containing 509 *tituli* on over three hundred closely written and heavily abbreviated folios, with the numerous references to patristic sources usually underlined, each entry divided into numbered sections, and preceded by an index giving cross references by *titulus* and section numbers, is an undertaking that would seem to necessitate expertise in the making of academic books.[17] A similar format is found in manuscripts of the *Rosarium*, an abbreviation of the longer compilation but still clearly Lollard, made apparently to facilitate access by preachers to a handbook that they might find useful. Use of the *Floretum* and the *Rosarium*, as sources for authorities that might support Lollard viewpoints and to provide the organising structure for sermons, can be shown from later writings.[18] Their method of citation with precise reference to sources is reflected through a great number of vernacular Lollard writings, even when the intended audience would appear to have been far removed from the academic world. The concern for precision and accuracy is reflected too in the presentation of texts, in the meticulous rubrication and correction of most manuscripts of the long sermon cycle, in the processes of collation and modification that its producers claimed underlay the versions of the Bible translation and to which the manuscripts testify.

It is clear, however, that book production and dissemination fairly rapidly moved outside the university; this was partly the result of increasing hostility to Wyclif's ideas at Oxford, but more importantly because of the relative ease with which heterodoxy could be investigated there and the concentration by the authorities on those investigations. By 1407 when the Czech scholars Mikuláš Faulfiš and Jiři Kněhnič visited England, they started in Oxford but went on to Braybrooke in Northamptonshire and to Kemerton in Gloucestershire to complete their copies of three of Wyclif's theological works.[19] Both places were connected with the Lollard knight, Sir Thomas Latimer. Latimer himself twenty years previously had been ordered to produce to the King in Council the books and quires he owned containing errors contrary to the faith.[20] By 1407 Latimer was dead, but Robert Hook, the incumbent of Latimer's home benefice at Braybrooke since 1401, continued to hold heretical views there until 1425; at various times he was apprehended for heresy, for holding *scolae* and for composing, copying and causing to be copied books of heresy in English and Latin. At the time of the Oldcastle rebellion in 1413 Braybrooke was known as a centre for the dissemination of seditious and heterodox pamphlets in Leicestershire and Northamptonshire.[21] Leicester itself had harboured Lollards who produced heterodox books since the 1380s: in 1389 William Smith admitted assembling and writing books of epistles and gospels in English with commentaries over eight years; though the figure is likely to be an exaggeration, there is no reason to doubt the substance of the account.[22] The surnames of two of the Lollards apprehended the same year as Smith is probably not insignificant: Michael Scrivener and William Parchmener are two early suspects in a line of men associated with the book-trade who appear in investigations of Lollardy in many parts of the country.[23] Unfortunately, however, it is hard to build up a coherent picture of Lollard book-production, partly because the enquirers were more interested in the views of their suspects than in their trade, but more because it is clear that, just as Lollard owners rarely wrote their names in their books, so the producers of the books took good care to conceal their activity.

Before examining the nature of the surviving manuscripts of Lollard compositions in more detail, it may be convenient to consider the case of the Wycliffite Bible translation since this, although the best preserved of texts claiming Lollard origin, constitutes something of a special case in the view of

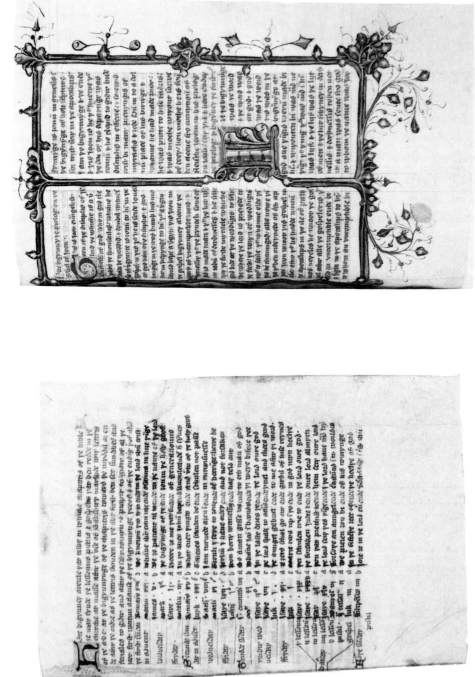

13–14 Oxford, Bodleian Library, MS Bodley 665, fols. 1r and 84r, New Testament in the Later Version of the Wycliffite Bible. Ill. 13 shows the beginning of the table of lessons, with heading explaining how it should be used; Ill. 14 shows the prologue and opening of chapter 1 of St John's certain scholars.[24] There is not space here to outline the processes involved in the translation and, following the production of a first literal version, of its modification to an idiomatic and fluent text: differences between the two texts are not, so far as examination has gone, reflected in differences in the type of manuscript, though copies of the later, idiomatic version outnumber the first stilted translation by about ten to one.[25] Both versions evidently existed by 1407, when Archbishop Arundel forbade the production of biblical translation, and the ownership of existing translations unless they dated from before the time of Wyclif and unless the owner had obtained a licence from the diocesan authorities; these authorities were meant to approve both version and owner. That this legislation continued to be a tool used by investigating authorities up to the 1520s is evident from trial documents.[26] Yet, as has often been observed, copies of the Wycliffite Bible are found in hands of undoubted orthodoxy: whatever the sympathies of Thomas of Woodstock, who owned Egerton 617–618, a copy of the Early Version, it seems impossible to impugn the orthodoxy of Henry VI, who gave the handsome MS Bodley 277, a complete copy of the Later Version, to the London Carthusian house, or of Henry VII who owned MS Royal 1.C.viii of the same version.[27] Doubtless such men could have obtained permission for the ownership of their copies, but it seems rather unlikely that all the owners of the 250-odd manuscripts containing the whole or part of the Wycliffite translation that survive today had been aproved by their diocesans, let alone that, at a time before mass-production of lists made identification of a translation relatively simple, the copies themselves had been checked – if they had, a lot of mistakes were made.

The manuscripts that survive vary in type and quality a good deal less than might be expected given the history of the text; very few indeed seem to be amateur productions. Inevitably copies of the entire translation are larger and more impressive than copies of a single book. But particularly in copies of the complete New Testament, or on a smaller scale of the four gospels, there is a surprising degree of uniformity between the great majority of manuscripts:[28] clear distinction between books and chapters by rubricated headings (and decorated initials in the richer copies), marking off of alternative renderings within the text by underlining, provision of running titles of book and chapter number, indication of subdivision within the chapters by marginal indexing letters. Many copies are provided with lists of gospels, and sometimes epistles, for the temporale and often the sanctorale of the ecclesiastical year; in most of these the biblical reference and indexing letter for the incipit is given, together with the opening and closing words of the lection; these indexing letters correspond to those in the margins of the text, where often also the end of lections is marked by (see Ills. 13 and 14 for a typical example of the features described).[29] It is hard to prove that this laborious procedure bore fruit in the use of the Wycliffite versions for reading in church (though many of the manuscripts are certainly written with sufficient clarity for this to be a feasible use), but this may have been their original intention; in default of this objective, they may well have been used by pious individuals or in Lollard schools for less public reading.[30]

The evident costliness of many of the surviving manuscripts appears to be at odds with the means of most of the suspects who got into trouble with the ecclesiastical authorities for their ownership of vernacular scriptures. Typical of such suspects is William Follegh, a parishioner of Devizes, who in 1434 admitted to the officials of Bishop Nevill of Salisbury that he, along with other heretics, 'was woned an vsed to here in secret place, yn holkys and hyrnes, the redyng of the bybele yn englyssh and to thys redyng gaffe entendance by many ʒerys';[31] equally typical is the later case of Richard Colins of Ginge in Berkshire, detected in 1521 to Bishop Longland of Lincoln as 'a great reader', who as well as a copy of *Wyclif's Wycket*, had possessed at various times books containing the gospels, the epistles and the Apocalypse, probably, to judge by the words of those informing against him, in a series of volumes each containing one gospel or a small group of epistles.[32] A surviving manuscript that contains only the books of Job and Tobit is marked by its original scribe with the price 6s 8d; one branch of the Colins family examined had spent 20s on a Bible.[33] How had relatively poor members of the community found such sums, or purchased the type of manuscript surviving? The easy answer is to say that the surviving manuscripts are not those that were owned by such men, but that their copies were of poorer, less professional quality and were destroyed; or to say that the claims of expense in trials were exaggerated. This is, however, to multiply considerably the number of copies originally made and to suggest improbably that not a single 'cheap' copy has survived. It is much more likely that copies were purchased not by the individual but by the group, conventicle or extended family in which Lollardy flourished, perhaps aided by a sympathetic *scriveyn* or *parchemyn maker*. Alice Sanders of Amersham in 1521 gave sixpence towards an English book that cost five marks, and it is noticeable in the case of Colins that a large number of his family were involved in his proselytising activities.[34] Slightly earlier, in the inquiries made in Coventry during the years 1511–12 it had emerged that there was an effective system of loaning books, not only among Lollards in the town but also between sympathisers there and those in Leicestershire.[35]

If orthodox owners of Wycliffite scriptures are known, it is possible that some if not many of the professional copiers of that forbidden work were likewise orthodox. It is much more difficult to explain the production of expensive manuscripts of other Lollard works in this way, since their heretical content was much more clearly proclaimed. Of the so-called 'Glossed Gospels', a verse-by-verse and often word-by-word commentary on the four gospels using a revised text of the Early Version of the translation,

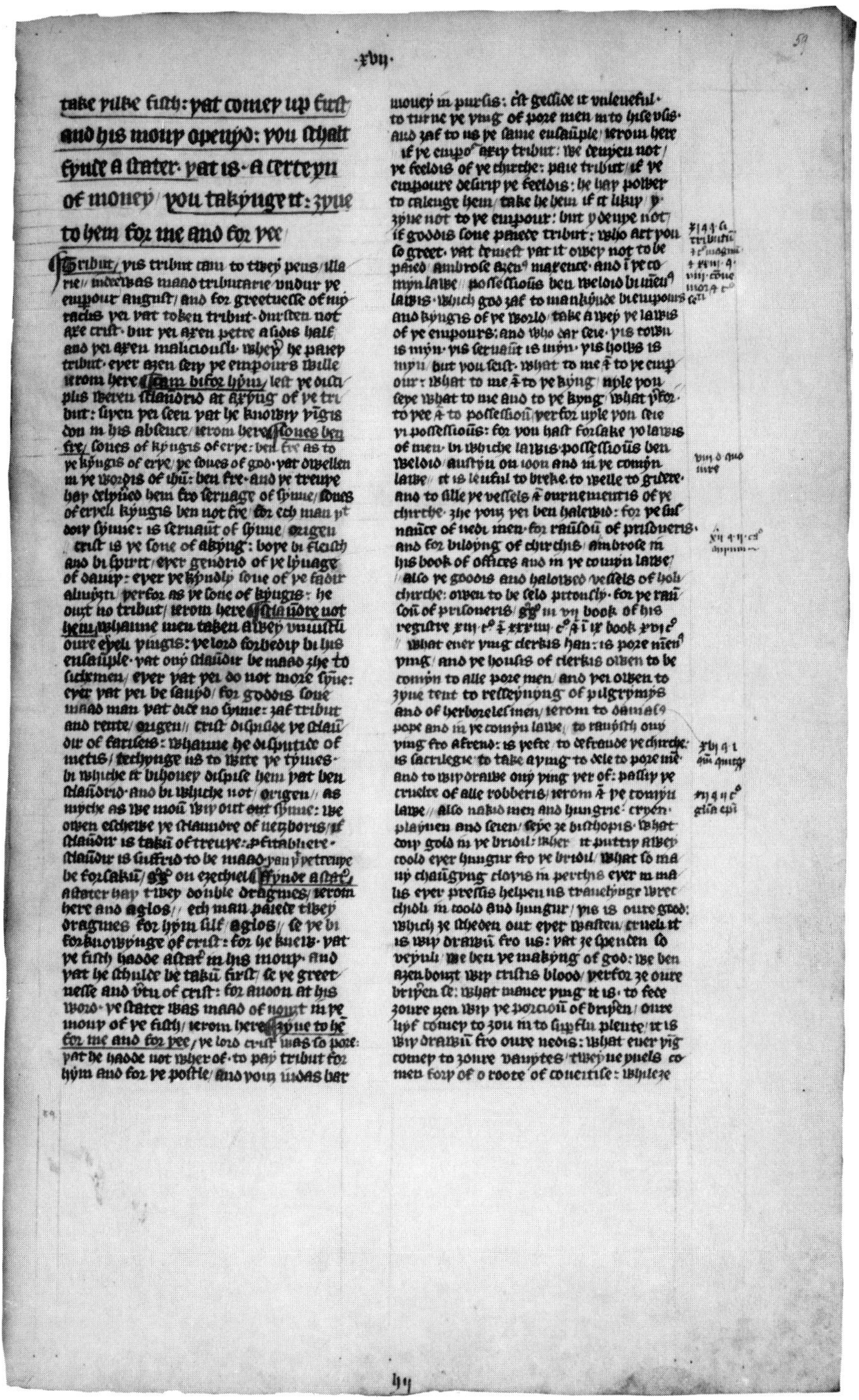

15 British Library, Add. MS 41175, fol. 59, Glossed Gospels. The text, here Matthew 17.27, is set out in display format and underlined (the added gloss excepted), each work or phrase for comment is preceded by a paraph mark and is itself underlined, and the source of the comment is given at the end of each; some extra references are provided in the margin.

with varying amounts of polemical material, most manuscripts are handsome volumes and all differentiate with scrupulous care between biblical translation, lemma for comment, and the commentary itself, each part of which is attributed to its patristic or medieval source (see Ill. 15, BL Add. MS 41175).[36] Equally professional in presentation and layout are the manuscripts of the Lollard revision of Rolle's Psalter commentary, with regular differentiation by means of script or punctuation between Latin verse, English translation of it and commentary.[37] In both cases, gospel and Psalter commentaries, location of a passage is made simpler by the provision of running titles of chapter or psalm number, and by clear rubrication of text. Common to these and to the majority of manuscripts of the long sermon cycle is the evidence from script, rubrication and correction of concern for the precise words of scripture, concern that it should be easily distinguishable from the words of lesser men and therefore subordinate authority, concern for accuracy of rendering, and concern to make the biblical material accessible. The lengths to which these concerns went in copies of the sermon cycle have been examined elsewhere.[38] What emerges from a detailed study of the thirty-one manuscripts of the cycle is the surprising degree of control that must have existed over the scribes producing those manuscripts, since only by that means could the uniformity of text and presentation, alongside permitted variations in the ordering of the sermons, have been achieved. More work remains to be done before similar claims can be made for the production of copies of the commentaries, or of the numerous manuscripts that contain the Later Version translation of the Bible in whole or in part, but the most superficial codicological survey would suggest that conclusions may not be very different.

Of the *schedulae* mentioned in trial proceedings, or of the *billis* or *rollis* mentioned in vernacular accounts, no example survives, though it is certain that the text known as the *Twelve Conclusions of the Lollards* (known to us only in the form in which it was divided up to precede the sections of Dymmock's Latin refutation of them) began life in such a form, and it is probable that other short English tracts now incorporated into anthologies of Lollard writings may well have done.[39] The use of such *schedulae* was evidently sometimes public, as when they were posted on the doors of churches and other public buildings, but often more private, either in attempting to stir up sympathisers, as was declaredly done in Leicester at the time of Oldcastle's rebellion, or in serving as notes for the converted to use when attacked.[40] To recognise the *quaterni* or *quires* mentioned by foes and friends is more difficult: the story of Claydon above reminds us that these might simply be a stage in the production of ordinary books. One example that survives as a single independent quire, containing a dialogue, is now Durham University, MS Cosin V.viii.6: though lacking the rubrication evidently intended to complete it, the script is a professional book-hand, with clear differentiation of the two speakers of its dialogue, and with some marginal annotation of the authorities cited. Despite its limited size, it does not give the impression of having been intended as an ephemeral production.[41]

To generalise about the manuscripts of Lollard writings shorter in length than the Bible translation, scriptural commentaries and sermon cycle is more difficult. Only one entirely informal notebook is known to me, now the first part of Harley 3913; it is a series of passages, mostly in Latin but with some English, on various theological and moral topics, some ascribed to their patristic and later sources, probably put together gradually by its compiler.[42] The first half of Cambridge, Trinity College, MS B.14.50 contains notes to aid a preacher that refer to the *Rosarium*, which are not known elsewhere and could have been a private production, along with Wyclif's own *Descriptio Fratris*. But bound with the quires that contain these texts is a second part in a more formal book hand, containing three Lollard texts and some further quotations from the *Rosarium*. Though an apparently casual assembly, it would be inaccurate to describe the volume as a commonplace book.[43] Anthologies of texts are more frequent: examples are the volumes that are now BL Add. MS 24202, Oxford, Bodleian Library, MS Eng.th.f.39, MS Douce 273–74, Dublin, Trinity College, MSS 244 and 245, and York Minster Library, MS xvi.L.12. But it is clear that these volumes and others like them were planned collections, copied continuously; they are not the outcome of binding together separately written quires or booklets. Uniformity of subject matter was apparently not aimed for: though Add. MS 24202 has some interesting and uniquely preserved texts on ecclesiastical government, or Douce an unparalleled *Tractatus de Regibus*,[44] they both also have other Lollard tracts, on quite unrelated topics. Equally, not all anthologies contain exclusively Lollard texts: MS Eng.th.f.39 contains Wimbledon's sermon, and even Add. MS 24202's tract on miracle plays is not, despite its usual modern title, decisively of heterodox outlook. Conversely, texts of seemingly Lollard origin are found in manuscripts whose main contents appear orthodox: thus the outspoken English *Vae Octuplex* and *Of Ministris in the Church* appear in Cambridge, St John's College, MS G.25 after the orthodox Elucidarius translation, Apocalypse commentary, Clement of Lanthony and a pious meditation on the sacraments,[45] and the Lollard canticle commentaries are appended to the original version of Rolle's Psalter commentary in some manuscripts.[46]

The difficulty that contemporaries might find in distinguishing orthodox from heterodox is well illustrated by the scribe who wrote a verse prologue in Bodleian, MS Laud misc. 286, lamenting that Rolle's Psalter commentary had been 'ympyd in with eresy' by 'yuel men of lollardry', but who then proceeded to follow it by an interpolated version of that commentary with some Lollard views in it. However, despite variations in appearance, one generalisation does seem possible about those manuscripts whose contents are wholly or predominantly Lollard and whose origins must therefore presumably be sought within the movement: this is an unusually persistent interest in the sources and authorities cited, marked by rubrication of such names in the text or by marginal annotation or frequently by both. It is not claimed that this is uniquely a feature of Lollard manuscripts (the case of the *Pore Caitif* discussed below, p. 332, makes that clear), but it is certainly characteristic of them. All of the anthologies mentioned above share it, and it is found, for instance, also in manuscripts of the *Thirty-Seven Conclusions*,[47] in the sermons in BL Add. MS 41321 and Bodleian MS Rawlinson c. 751, and in the account of Thorpe's trial in Bodleian MS Rawlinson c.208.

The importance that Lollards placed upon the words of scripture, and the associated emphasis upon a readily identifiable hierarchy of authority, seem to have led to a corresponding desire for clarity of presentation. The vast majority of Wycliffite bibles are in book-hands of a kind perhaps rather old-fashioned for their date, with few cursive elements; of the sermon cycle, half are in similar text hands, and the remainder with only isolated exceptions in anglicana formata script of great regularity and legibility.[48] Furthermore, though disapproval of the entry of aesthetic considerations into religion (in the form of visually pleasing images or elaborate forms of chant) is rife throughout Lollard compositions, this disapproval was not extended into lack of concern with the appearance of manuscripts. Though figural ornamentation in Lollard books is almost unknown, flourished capitals are ubiquitous, the use of gold leaf for major capitals and of decoration round the margin in leaf-and-spoon or similar styles are common. The wealthy patrons who must have paid for manuscripts such as Lambeth Palace MS 34, Cambridge, Trinity College, MS B.5.25 or BL MS Royal 18.C.xxvi of the Psalter commentary revision, or for BL Add. MS 41175 or MS Bodley 243 of the Glossed Gospels, or for BL Add. MS 40672 of the sermon cycle, clearly expected their costly manuscripts to look splendid as well as to contain edifying matter.

Persecution brought about the destruction of many Lollard books, and even of all copies of some texts such as the Latin *Opus Arduum*, or the vernacular *Wyclif's Wycket*, the *Praier and Complaynte of the Ploweman* and the so-called *Ploughman's Tale*; our knowledge of the first comes from Hussite transcripts, of the rest from printed editions put out by the early reformers.[49] The destruction of Lollard books was often the work of opponents, but equally might be the prudent precaution of a sympathiser unwilling to die for his beliefs: as John Phip commented during Longland's inquiries between 1518 and 1521 'he had rather burn his books than that his books should burn him'.[50] The dangers of persecution also hide from us many of the facts we should like to know about Lollard book production. It was safer for an owner not to write his name in any heterodox books he owned, and it is unlikely to be coincidental that it is the orthodox owners of Wycliffite bibles who are recorded, or that the only copy of the sermon cycle in which a near contemporary set his name was that which belonged to Thomas Dekyn, a Dominican friar attached to the house at Dunstable, now BL Royal MS 18.B.IX.[51] Equally, scribes would be unwise to sign their work, or patrons to seek record in the colophons of manuscripts. On the other hand, trial documents provide evidence of a kind that is generally lacking for orthodox texts; but the evidence is patchy and often hard to interpret. We may hear of a 'librum valde pulcrum de et super noua lege in anglicis traductis',[52] but though we can guess what this might have looked like and even the sort of text it contained, the details are insufficient for identification with any surviving work. Even in a case like Claydon's *Lanterne of Light* where identification is possible, the actual manuscript, which would do so much to clarify the claims made at the trial, is absent. More surprisingly, although the importance of books in spreading the heresy was recognised by the authorities from the start, no records seem to survive to suggest that any move was made to discover the scriptoria from which the books emanated (if such existed), the scribes persistently responsible or the sources of funding for the production of the volumes. Inquiry seems always to have been directed to the books once produced and to those who happened to own them at the time. Despite the apparent success, however, of the persecutors, a large number of Lollard manuscripts survive – more copies of the Wycliffite Bible than of any other medieval work in English, more copies of the standard sermon cycle than of any single version of *Piers Plowman* and nearly twice as many as of *Troilus and Criseyde*. The Lollard writings cover a wide range of topics in the religious and political field, and utilise a number of literary forms. The involvement of professional scribes is certain from the quality of the vast majority of manuscripts, and that involvement necessitates the assumption of considerable sources of funds. All the evidence points to the very high value which the Lollards set upon the written word. Reginald Pecock called them *Bible Men*;[53] it would be equally accurate to describe them as *Book Men*.

NOTES

1 At the two extremes see *Calendar of Patent Rolls 1381–5* (London, 1897), p. 153, dated 13 July 1382, and the lists of 1530 and 1531 printed in D. Wilkins, *Concilia Magnae Britanniae et Hiberniae* (London, 1737), III, pp. 727–39.

2 For these two examples see respectively *The Acts and Monuments of John Foxe*, ed. S.R. Cattley (London, 1837–41), IV, p. 236, quoting a case from 1521 from the investigation of Bishop Longland of Lincoln, and Lincoln reg. Chedworth fol. 62v in a case of 1462.

3 For the first point see the case of Claydon discussed below; for the second see my paper 'Lollardy: the English Heresy?', *Studies in Church History*, 18 (1982), 261–83 (reprinted in Hudson, *Lollards and their Books* (London, 1985), pp. 141–63).

4 See Gascoigne, *Loci e Libro Veritatum*, ed. J.E. Thorold Rogers (Oxford, 1881), p. 116.

5 See for instance Bath and Wells reg. Stafford opening 181a–b (1441), 'quosdam libros siue libellos huiusmodi suspectos tunc repertos per incendium annichilari mandauimus' and the references given in my paper 'Some Aspects of Lollard Book Production', *Studies in Church History*, 9 (1972), 147–57 at p. 148 n. 1 and p. 149 n. 2 (repr. in *Lollards and their Books*, pp. 181–91 at p. 182 n. 1 and p. 183 n. 2).

6 See W.R. Thomson, *The Latin Writings of John Wyclyf: An Annotated Catalog* (Pontifical Institute of Medieval Studies Toronto, Subsidia Mediaevalia 14, 1983), *passim*.

7 See the most important collection of material by Margaret Aston, 'Lollardy and Literacy', *History*, 62 (1977), 347–71.

8 *The Register of Henry Chichele, Archbishop of Canterbury 1414–1443*, ed. E.F. Jacob (Canterbury and York Society, 1938–47), IV, pp. 132–8.

9 The discussions in A.L. Kellogg and E.W. Talbert, 'The Wycliffite *Pater Noster* and *Ten Commandments* with Special Reference to the English MSS 85 and 90 in the John Rylands Library', *BJRL*, 42 (1960), 345–77, and in A. Martin, 'The Middle English Versions of *The Ten Commandments*, with special reference to Rylands English MS 85', *BJRL*, 64 (1981), 191–217 are not in every respect accurate, particularly in regard to the more extreme Lollard versions.

10 MS Douce 53, fols. 30–32v; the sermon takes its name from the place where it was preached, now Horsleydown in the parish of St Olave's Southwark.

11 I am grateful to Professor Paul Christianson for telling me that a scribe John Gryme does not appear in records concerning London book production that he has scrutinised.

12 The text was edited by L.M. Swinburn (EETS, os, 151, 1917) from BL Harley 2324; Swinburn did not know BL Harley 6613, now defective through loss of leaves, and did not use the print by Redman ([1535?], *STC* 15225). The second folio incipit is in the edition p. 3/12.

13 The passage is edited in *Selections from English Wycliffite Writings*, ed. A. Hudson (Cambridge, 1978), p. 96, lines 100–15; evidence for the date will be given in my forthcoming complete edition of the text. The two in the same hand are BL Egerton MS 2820 and CUL MS Dd.14.30(2); the third copy is Huntington Library, MS HM 503.

14 For an example which shows particularly clearly how they functioned see N. Tanner, *Heresy Trials in the Diocese of Norwich, 1428–31* (Camden Society 4th series 20, 1977), *passim* and especially pp. 25–30.

15 A. Hudson, 'Contributions to a Bibliography of Wycliffite Writings', *NQ*, 218 (1973), 445–6 (repr. in *Lollards and their Books*, pp. 4–5).

16 A copy of the *De Mandatis* was accepted as security for a loan by Queen's College in 1401–2. Oriel College 15 was purchased by the college in 1454, and the treasurer's accounts acknowledge that it contained material by Wyclif (his *De Incarnacione Verbi*); the following entries in those accounts record purchases of Wyclif's *De Dominio Civili* and *De Blasphemia* and of a book *cum multis continentis Wycliff*. See L. Minio-Paluello, 'Two Erasures in MS Oriel College 15', *Bodleian Library Record*, 4

(1952–3), 205–7, and N.R. Ker, 'Wyclif Manuscripts in Oxford in the Fifteenth Century', *BLR*, 4 (1952–3), 292–3.

17 See A. Hudson, 'A Lollard Compilation and the Dissemination of Wycliffite Thought', *Journal of Theological Studies*, ns, 23 (1972), 65–81 and 'A Lollard Compilation in England and Bohemia', *Journal of Theological Studies*, ns, 25 (1974), 129–40 (both repr. in *Lollards and their Books*, pp. 13–29 and pp. 31–42). For the term *tituli* see R.H. Rouse and M.A. Rouse, *Preachers, Florilegia and Sermons: Studies on the* 'Manipulus Florum' *of Thomas of Ireland* (Toronto, 1979), p. 29. The *tituli*, or effectively 'chapters', of the *Floretum* are topics of moral, theological or ecclesiastical interest.

18 See C. von Nolcken, *The Middle English Translations of the Rosarium Theologie* (Middle English Texts 10, Heidelberg, 1979), and 'Some Alphabetical Compendia and how Preachers used them in Fourteenth-Century England', *Viator*, 12 (1981), 271–88.

19 The texts are the *De Veritate Sacre Scripture, De Dominio Divinio* and *De Ecclesia*; the copy is now Vienna, Österreichische Nationalbibliothek 1294. See the Thomson, *Latin Writings*, and R.L. Poole's observations in his edition of the second text (Wyclif Society, London, 1890), pp. ix–xii.

20 For Latimer see K.B. McFarlane, *Lancastrian Kings and Lollard Knights* (Oxford, 1972), pp. 139–226, especially pp. 192–6, and Hudson, 'Wycliffite Writings', p. 445.

21 See the details and references given in *English Wycliffite Sermons* ed. A. Hudson, 1 (Oxford, 1983), 197–8.

22 *Chronicon Henrici Knighton*, ed. J.R. Lumby (Rolls Series, London, 1889–95), ii, p. 313; the date of 1392 given there is a mistake. See further J. Crompton, 'Leicestershire Lollards', *Translations of the Leicestershire Archaeological and Historical Society*, 44 (1968–9), 11–44, for more details about the early Leicester group.

23 *Ibid.*, p. 23. Other examples are, in 1414, Thomas Scot of Braybrooke *scriveyn* and William Mably *parchemyner* (PRO KB.9.204/1.111 and 141); in 1428, Robert Dykkes of Bury St Edmund's *skryvaner* (Norwich reg. Alnwick, REG/5.9, fol. 108v); in 1462, Thomas Skryvener of Amersham was amongst those apprehended (Lincoln reg. Chedworth, fol. 62). Cf. the form of abjuration devised about 1428, which commits the suspect to give up all books, quires and rolls of heresy 'quos me scripsisse noui', or 'quos me recipere seu quos ab alijs recipi, scribi seu dictari scire me continget' (see A. Hudson, 'The Examination of Lollards', *Bulletin of the Institute of Historical Research*, 46 (1973), 145–59, at p. 156 (repr. in *Lollards and their Books*, pp. 125–40, at p. 136)).

24 The two versions were printed, along with details of the manuscripts then known, by J. Forshall and F. Madden, *The Holy Bible . . . made from the Latin Vulgate by John Wycliffe and his Followers* (Oxford, 1850), 4 vols.; an edition of the Old Testament in the Early Version, using all copies, has been made by C. Lindberg, *Stockholm Studies in English*, 6 (1959), 8 (1961), 10 (1963), 13 (1965), 20 (1969) and 29 (1973). Lindberg has also printed a fuller list of manuscripts in *Studia Neophilologica*, 42 (1970), 333–47.

25 See most helpfully H. Hargreaves in *The Cambridge History of the Bible*, vol. ii, ed. G.W.H. Lampe (Cambridge, 1969), 387–415. MS Bodley 959 reveals very clearly

some of the processes of revision, and shows that a number of correctors must have worked on the text before the quires were bound up.

26 The Constitutions are printed in *Concilia*, ed. Wilkins, III, pp. 314–19; for some cases that used its terms see my 'Lollardy: the English Heresy?'.

27 See most recently A.I. Doyle, 'English Books In and Out of Court', pp. 168–9.

28 This is noted by Doyle, *ibid.*, p. 169, who suggests that the majority of these manuscripts to a common pattern were produced in London. A palaeographical investigation under way by Steven Halasey of the University of California Los Angeles should when complete cast further light on many of the questions raised by these enigmatic manuscripts.

29 As examples of manuscripts having all or most of these features may be mentioned CUL MSS Dd.1.27, Kk.1.8, Ll.1.13, Mm.2.15, Add. 6684; Cambridge, Magdalene College, MS Pepys 15, 16 and 2073; Oxford, Bodleian Library, MSS Bodley 183, 531, 665, Douce 240, 265, Fairfax 11, Gough Eccl. Top 5, Hatton 111, Junius 29, Lyell 26, Rawlinson c.259, Selden supra 49 and 51.

30 A comparable list of lessons appears in Cambridge, Pembroke College, MS 237, a preliminary quire before the Wycliffite sermon cycle; use of the indexing subdivisions of chapters is found in references in some manuscripts of the sermons (see edition, I, pp. 137–8).

31 Salisbury reg.Nevill II. fol. 57v; the opening stages of the case are on fol. 52. Follegh also went under the name of Wakeham; his trade is not stated, but two of the witnesses who gave evidence against him were weavers.

32 The case appears in the records of Bishop Longland of Lincoln, a summary of which appears in Foxe, IV, pp. 234–40; it is evident that Colins was one of, and possibly the most important of, the ringleaders of the Lollard group in the upper Thames–north Berkshire area. See also C. Cross, *Church and People 1450–1660* (London, 1976), pp. 32–5.

33 For the latter see Foxe, IV, p. 237. The manuscript mentioned is now BL MS Harley 3903, a small volume written in a professional book-hand with elegantly decorated initials at the beginning of each book; a note, 'The prijs of þis book is vi.s & viii.d', appears rather oddly at the foot of the leaf (fol. 46v, leaf 6, quire 6) on which Job ends, but seems to refer to the entire volume as it now stands (quire numbering which appears to be scribal, and is certainly medieval, allows for nothing before the start of Job and there is no reason to think that anything followed Tobit, which ends neatly at the foot of the last leaf of quire 8, with no catchword provided).

34 Foxe, IV, p. 231; the recurrence of the same texts in testimony of various witnesses is also noticeable here, and is implied by the account of the group earlier on the Norfolk–Suffolk border (see Tanner, *Heresy Trials*, pp. 25–30).

35 See J. Fines, 'Heresy Trials in the Diocese of Coventry and Lichfield, 1511–12', *Journal of Ecclesiastical History*, 14 (1963), 160–74, and I. Luxton, 'The Lichfield Court Book: a Postscript', *Bulletin of the Institute of Historical Research*, 44 (1971), 120–5.

36 See H. Hargreaves, 'Popularising Biblical Scholarship: the Role of the Wycliffite *Glossed Gospels*', in *The Bible and Medieval Culture*, ed. W. Lourdaux and D. Verhelst (Louvain, 1979), pp. 171–89; the most professional manuscripts are BL Add. MS

41175 and what is probably its second half, MSS Bodley 243, Bodley 143 and York Minster Library MS xvi.D.2.

37 There are various different versions of the Lollard redaction: a preliminary survey is given by D. Everett in 'The Middle English Prose Psalter of Richard Rolle of Hampole', *MLR*, 17 (1922), 217–27, 337–50 and 18 (1923), 381–93. Examples of the features mentioned here are Cambridge, Trinity College, MS B.5.25; BL MSS Royal 18.C.xxvi and 18.D.i, Oxford, Bodleian Library, MSS Bodley 288, 877, Laud. Misc. 286 and 321, Tanner 16; Lambeth Palace MS 34 and Oxford, University College, MS 74 (this last unfinished by the decorator).

38 See *English Wycliffite Sermons*, ed. Hudson, i, 8–97, 124–202.

39 For the *Twelve Conclusions* see Hudson, *Selections*, no. 3; other texts possibly originally put out in *bill* form are mentioned in my 'Lollard Book Production', p. 149.

40 One of the charges against the suspect John Belgrave in 1395/6 was of placing slanderous pamphlets in a local church (Crompton, 'Leicestershire Lollards', p. 25); Thomas Ile of Braybrooke was said to be a *communis factor billarum* by one witness, and a *compositor ac asportator billarum* by another in the enquiries that followed the revolt (PRO KB.9.204/1.130 and 141); William Taylor at his trial in 1421 'extraxit de sinu suo quasdam auctoritates et dicta doctorum in quadam papiri cedula scripta' (*Chichele reg.* iii. 67). Cf. Aston, 'Lollardy and Literacy', p. 350, n. 11.

41 See more fully A. Hudson, 'A Lollard Quaternion', *RES*, ns, 22 (1971), 435–42 (repr. in *Lollards and their Books*, pp. 193–200).

42 I owe knowledge of this to the kindness of Dr Ian Doyle. The notebook section is fols. 1–111v; the second part, in a different hand and set of quires, contains the orthodox Apocalypse commentary printed by E. Fridner (Lund Studies in English, 29, 1961). Some sections of the notebook have headings or side-notes, but these are not an adequate guide to the contents; many favourite Lollard authors are quoted, including at fol. 73 Wyclif himself.

43 See my 'Lollard Compilation and Dissemination', pp. 77–8 (*Lollards and their Books*, pp. 25–6).

44 Most of the texts in the first manuscript have not been printed; the *Tractatus* is edited by J.-P. Genet, *Four English Political Tracts of the Later Middle Ages* (Camden Society, 4th series, 18, 1977), pp. 5–19.

45 For the Lollard texts see T. Arnold, *Select English Works of John Wyclif* (Oxford, 1869–71), ii, pp. 379–423; for the Apocalypse commentary, see the edition printed by Fridner (Lund Studies in English, 29, 1961).

46 BL Harley 1806, Oxford, Magdalen College, MS 52 and fragment in Bodleian Library, Douce 258.

47 BL MS Cotton Titus D.i and Norwich Castle Museum, MS 158.926.4g3 are copies made by the mid-fifteenth century, MS Bodley 540 comes from the end of that century; Dublin, Trinity College, MS 246 from c. 1600.

48 A good deal more work needs to be done before the claim of M. Benskin and M. Laing ('Translations and *Mischsprachen* in Middle English Manuscripts', in Benskin and Samuels, pp. 55–106, at pp. 90–1) that cursive script fosters dialectal translation can be supported from Wycliffite texts. Cf. P. Saenger, 'Silent

Reading: its Impact on Late Medieval Script and Society', *Viator*, 13 (1982), 367–414.

49 For the first see A. Hudson, 'A Neglected Wycliffite Text', *Journal of Ecclesiastical History*, 29 (1978), 257–79 (*Lollards and their Books*, pp. 43–65); for the rest, '"No newe thyng": the Printing of Medieval Texts in the early Reformation Period', in *Middle English Studies presented to Norman Davis*, ed. D. Gray and E.G. Stanley (Oxford, 1983), pp. 153–74 (*Lollards and their Books*, pp. 227–48).

50 Foxe, IV, p. 237; the friend who reproached Phip for his action estimated the books to be worth a hundred marks.

51 See *English Wycliffite Sermons*, ed. Hudson, I, pp. 60–1.

52 Lichfield Record Office B/C/13, fol. 6.

53 *Repressor of Over Much Blaming of the Clergy*, ed. C. Babbington (Rolls Series, London, 1860), I, p. 36). Many of the texts here mentioned, and some of the issues here raised, are discussed in more detail in my book *The Premature Reformation: Wycliffite Texts and Lollard History* (Oxford, 1988).

7 · THE PRODUCTION OF BOOKS OF LITURGICAL POLYPHONY[1]

ANDREW WATHEY

THE COMMERCIAL PRODUCTION of manuscript books developed gradually in England through the activities of a book-trade based on fixed locations and with a professional identity that was increasingly clearly defined. The thirteenth century saw the establishment of gilds and other incorporated groups of scribes and illuminators in London and York. A close relationship later grew up between the universities and local stationers in Oxford and Cambridge. The members of this profession practised a mainly bespoke trade, so far as complete books were concerned, executing commissions for known buyers. It was thus primarily their skills that they marketed rather than finished objects. In these and other respects there was no fundamental change in the practices of the book-trade before Caxton introduced printing into England, with the 'need to promote sales among a wider clientele and the methods of mass production'[2] that this entailed. Even then, the existing forms of activity were not immediately extinguished, but were slowly transformed in response to the competition offered by the new process.

The contribution of the book-trade to the production of books of liturgical polyphony has not received direct attention. Yet in studies both of musical sources and of lost books traceable from book lists and accounts, the ready availability of these books for purchase and the existence of centres of production have been widely assumed. It has also been thought that the book-trade's practitioners, working singly or in groups, were responsible for the illumination of books of polyphony and sometimes for their script.[3] In a recent study, Reinhard Strohm has suggested that books of polyphony were comparable to other luxury products of the book-trade.[4] They were assumed to have been produced and circulated in similar ways, and thus might readily be commissioned from groups of professional book-makers, be used as gifts or be treated as collectors' items. In this and other studies the production of books of polyphony has been assimilated to patterns of production known for other, superficially similar forms of book. Thus the production and dissemination of choirbooks was equated with that of books of Hours, for which extensive retail and export trades were known to exist.[5] It has similarly been assumed that the production of books of polyphony was comparable to that of standard service-books, mainly because both types of book were used in liturgical celebration.[6] Although a limited number of cases can be identified in which professional illuminators and binders were involved in making books of polyphony, the importance of many of their patterns of activity for the production of these books could be questioned. It is doubtful whether the production of books of polyphonic music involved specialist book-makers, and – by implication – separate groups of producers and consumers, to any extent. The ways in which books were produced, as Carla Bozzolo and Ezio Ornato's recent studies of Bibles and patristic works suggest,[7] were to a large extent dependent on the textual characteristics of their contents. An explanation for the distinguishing features in the production of books of polyphony must be sought in the highly distinctive circumstances for which their contents were designed. The idiosyncrasies of written polyphony and their consequences have received some attention in studies of transmission and the textual status of individual manuscripts;[8] their implications for the production of these books, however, have largely gone unnoticed, as has the place occupied in this process by rolls, quaterns and other written ephemera. To assess the means and patterns of the production of books of polyphony, we shall look first at their general characteristics and distribution in comparison to other forms of book. We shall need then to explain the character of institutional collections of these books. Finally we shall ask how the detailed structure of the surviving books reflects the circumstances under which they were compiled.

The main contrasts between music and literary texts lay in the relative impermanence of musical composition and the small size of its individual units. Single items rarely occupied more than two or three openings, and were frequently accommodated on just one. They were separately composed and copied, and although they were occasionally transmitted in large groups, it is far from clear that this was usually the case. The utility of written copies of musical compositions, to a greater extent than that of other forms of text, was dependent on a knowledge of how they were to be performed. As several writers have pointed out, these features characterised the transmission of music texts, and their consequences are traceable also in the make-up of complete books.[9] The brevity of individual compositions meant that books of polyphonic music were compiled gradually, often from several exemplars. Although the initial phases of their compilation may have been relatively homogeneous, compositions were added as they became available and books thus grew to form unique anthologies. The relatively short life-span of compositions imposed limits on the working lives of books, and as a factor in their survival was markedly more important than physical wear and tear.[10] In 1533 the canons of the collegiate church of St Catherine, Aiguebelle (Savoy) claimed still to be using the service books of Hereford Use brought by their founder in 1264.[11] There is little, however, either from surviving copies or from documentary evidence, to suggest that books of polyphony remained in use for periods longer than thirty or forty years. Only occasionally are copying dates within a single source more widely separated; these cases do not represent continuous musical traditions, and may reflect merely a short-age of readily available parchment when the later items were copied.[12] The extent to which books of polyphony were useful depended on the availability of musical forces and perhaps also specific musical skills. As these forces changed, so too – albeit more gradually – did the repertories that they used. Changing fashion may have played a part in the gradual turnover of reper-tory, but this process was also, up to a point, a natural side-effect of the replacement of existing skills and expertise.

The principal, if not the only, identifiable users of books of liturgical polyphony were the groups of singers working in the greater churches and the household chapels of the king and higher nobility. Outside this sphere evidence for the independent existence of these books is almost entirely lacking. There is little to suggest that the ownership of these books by singers as individuals was related to the musical concerns that they maintained outside the confines of their professional activities. Similarly the autonomous presence of books of polyphony in institutional hands, unconnected with the business of performance, is hard to trace. They are found only exceptionally in the catalogues of library collections.[13] Although written polyphony may have been used for the purposes of study, this did not give rise to separate collections of books. Institutionally owned books used for teaching appear to have been kept with other books of polyphony.[14]

It is important to realise how closely written polyphony was associated with specific groups of singers. The individual members of these groups contributed pieces to, and not infrequently owned, books of polyphony; the collective abilities of the group created unique combinations of technical demands in the repertories that were copied by its members. Since the spheres within which these groups were active were relatively few in number – at least until the mid-fifteenth century – books of polyphony were also strongly tied to specific establishments. These features imposed limitations on the more widespread use of books, inhibiting movement, even though within a single volume there may often have been different layers of repertory that reflected the changing skills of a group of singers. In practice the links between a book of polyphony and a specific church or household chapel were more important than links with singers, who typically joined and left these foundations as individuals. The primary consideration, however, was the continuity of musical abilities. In the few cases where it can be shown that books moved from one foundation to another they were accompanied by sizeable bodies of singers. The fate of the books used in the household chapel of Louis of Luxembourg, bishop of Ely and Henry VI's Chancellor in France, provides a case in point.[15] After Louis's death in 1443 almost all of the clerks of his household chapel were engaged by Gilles de Bretagne, brother of John

IV, duke of Brittany. They took with them a number of the chapel ornaments, and special arrangements were made so that this group could also
retain two books, one beginning with Kyrie settings and the other of 'ymys
and venites'. The repertory of these books, which may have included items of
English origin, no doubt reflected the clerks' capabilities and limitations, and
to this extent remained valuable when they moved as a body to new
employment.

The textual characteristics of polyphonic music are nowhere more evident
than in loose quaterns, pamphlets and rolls.[16] These forms typically contained small numbers of pieces, were easy to compile and were relatively
short-lived. They also played an important part in the compilation of more
substantial and permanent books.[17] They provided a flexible means by which
new compositions could be written down and performed separately, or by
which small numbers of existing pieces could be re-grouped for a temporary
or specialist purpose. The contents of rolls and quaterns were accumulated in
larger choirbooks, and these larger books in turn provided a pool of compositions from which single items might be extracted. Loose quaterns also
contributed physically to complete books; some books were wholly formed
from collections of quires that were formerly independent, and these quires
were added to books as supplements. Some clear evidence for this process and
for the resulting changes in the physical make-up of books can be found in the
lists and inventories of institutional book collections. A parchment book of
polyphony with an added paper quire appears in an inventory of the sacristy
at St Mary's Warwick drawn up in 1464.[18] In a book-list attributed by N.
Denholm-Young to the Cluniac priory of St Saviour at Bermondsey, an entry
recording a number of 'quaterni non ligati de cantu' was later changed to
read 'duo libri'.[19] The physical characteristics of rolls clearly precluded their
amalgamation or absorption within larger compilations. In the main they
contained fewer pieces than loose quaterns, although the form of the surviving examples varies considerably. Some are sizeable and can be compared
with books in the quality of their script and illumination; others are roughly
written, ephemeral compilations.[20] Many of these less extensive rolls were
written on waste parchment drawn from discarded documents, and this is
indicative of the relatively short-term use for which they were intended. The
smaller rolls often contained single pieces or even single voice-parts;[21] up to a
point these can be seen as the physical counterparts of the basic textual unit
in which music circulated.

The extent of the part played in transmission by rolls and quaterns is
unclear, but a measure of textual interdependence can nonetheless be traced
between books and ephemera. The groupings of contents found in complete
books occasionally suggest that they were compiled from a number of smaller
sources. Similarly, a number of the surviving rolls and quaterns appear to
have inherited features of layout and design from exemplars in book form.

The remains of two quaterns, the paper leaves now part of the 'Fountains Fragments'[22] and some leaves in the binding of Lincoln's Inn MS 146, provide relatively clear examples of copying from larger sources. The 'Fountains Fragments' leaves contain a mixed repertory of mass movements and motets, several of which are also known from large and prestigious choirbook sources, including the Old Hall Manuscript (British Library, Add. MS 57950). A single scribe was responsible for most of the quire, and he arranged its contents according to a pattern common in these and other choirbooks. Individual items were grouped by type and these groups placed in a standard order, even though no more than two or three items appear in each section. The crude pen-work initials found in this quire also imitate designs that were current in lavishly produced books. The fragmentary quire now part of Lincoln's Inn MS 146 contains an office of St Anne in which polyphonic items are integrated with plainsong and readings.[23] It may be that this quire was intended as a supplement to a processional or was designed for independent use, like the numerous 'quaterni de servicio sancte Anne' recorded with growing frequency in book lists of the mid- and late fourteenth century. The two types of content in these leaves must have originated in separate sources; both the liturgical and polyphonic items may have been drawn from exemplars in book form. No other source survives from this period in which polyphonic and liturgical items are combined. For special occasions, the commemoration of saints' days and other ceremonies, however, such compilations cannot have been uncommon.

Rolls and quaterns were better suited to use in performance than books, at least partly because they were less cumbersome and because their form afforded greater visibility. From early times their use can be traced in liturgical celebration, and they are also frequently encountered in connection with the performance of drama. What appears to be a single actor's part from the Middle English play 'Dux Moraud' survives as a roll, and a number of other plays are preserved only in this form.[24] The frequency with which rolls were used in performance may also be reflected by their appearance associated with practical contexts in iconographic traditions. Successive generations of initials to psalm 97 ('Cantate Domino') in English psalters portray singers with rolls of music. At least one of these, in the Gorleston Psalter, appears to depict the singing of polyphony.[25] The principal factors that encouraged the use of rolls and quaterns were no doubt portability and economy. These forms were easy to compile and use, and their suitability for performance probably ensured that for the majority of singers they were both familiar and readily accessible. Itinerant performers, as Richard Rouse has suggested, may well have preferred rolls to books because they were easier to carry.[26] It is clear, however, that ephemera enjoyed widespread use, and in late medieval England they were also common among singers working in institutions. Even more perhaps than books, ephemeral compilations were tied to local musical cultures. The repertories that they contained may have precluded their use elsewhere but, more important in this respect, their compilation was a response to short-term needs. Where singers were active as composers, rolls and quaterns were probably the forms in which new pieces were first recorded. One-off celebrations of local importance or convenient arrangements of pieces not present in the available books may also have prompted their compilation. The numbers in which rolls and quaterns were used is obscured by their ephemeral character. By comparison with books a small proportion survives, and relatively few can have been worth recording in the inventories and lists of institutional collections. The compilation and ownership of ephemera frequently fell to individuals, and this is a further reason why they were rarely mentioned in these sources.

Institutions inevitably dominate the history of liturgical music in late medieval England, but – at least until the mid-fifteenth century – it is far from clear that they played an active part in building and maintaining collections of books of polyphony and in encouraging their production. Two principal means by which books of polyphony came into institutional ownership emerge from the evidence of book lists and accounts. They were made by singers, whose costs for materials and labour were met from institutional funds. They were also acquired through gifts and bequests. It cannot be shown conclusively from these materials – and here there is a contrast with service books – that books of polyphony were purchased in a complete form from outside book-makers or from other establishments. Until the end of the fourteenth century, gifts and bequests probably account for the majority of books of polyphony in institutional ownership. Of twenty-four books and rolls of demonstrable origin that are known in the possession of churches and household chapels before 1400, thirteen were gifts or bequests by these institutions' own members.[27] Clerics frequently bequeathed books to the churches where they had served and where they were beneficed. As a result, books of polyphony occasionally came into the possession of smaller foundations and parish churches where there was no provision for the performance of polyphony.[28] For the most part, however, it was the major churches and household chapels that gained from bequests made by singers. Given the strength of the more important establishments' connections with these groups, it was inevitable that they should receive some books of this type. But there is another reason why the disposal of the books owned by singers followed this pattern: frequently they still formed parts of working collections. John Aleyn, a clerk of the royal household chapel and canon of St George's Chapel, Windsor, from 1362, left a roll of polyphony to St George's at his death in 1373; its presence in inventories up to 1410 may suggest that it was used for some time.[29] Robert Wynewyk, master of the Lady Chapel at Westminster Abbey in 1376, bequeathed a book of polyphony to the Abbey in 1383, and here, since new quires were added in 1393/4, it can be demonstrated more conclusively that the book remained in use.[30] Books such as these were difficult to replace, and occasionally steps were taken to prevent their dispersal, or to recover those that had passed into other hands. James Michell, a priest in the service of Edmund Lacy, bishop of Exeter, clearly felt it prudent to add to his will the observation that his bequest to another priest of a quatern 'cum canticis de musyke', used in the bishop's household chapel, had his master's consent.[31] A clearer case of the dependence of institutions on individual singers can be traced from a group of books owned by Henry Brewster, master of the children in the household chapel of Humphrey, duke of Buckingham.[32] In addition to a large choirbook, this collection included several rolls 'of the makyng of the forseide Henry as of other chapelmen' and sets of loose quires, possibly part books, and the items listed here may well have been most of those available for use within the duke's chapel. After Brewster's death in 1517, the books were purchased from his widow by the keeper of the duke's wardrobe. They were delivered to one of the clerks of the chapel, and from this it can be inferred that they were still of use in the chapel's services.

For much of the fifteenth century it is difficult to speak of a steady or sustained growth in institutional collections of books of liturgical polyphony. The activities of singers as composers and performers of polyphony fell largely outside official control,[33] and it seems likely that they themselves provided most of the books that they used. It was mainly the larger books that were acquired at institutional expense. At St George's Chapel, Windsor, in the first half of the fifteenth century, for example, the only payments from the corporate funds were for exceptional items. Parchment was bought for a book of sixty folios in 1416/17, and a book of seventy-two folios was copied in 1449/50.[34] Only in the later fifteenth century are payments found in large numbers or with any continuity. At Magdalen College, Oxford, in 1483, John Claveryng, the instructor of the choristers, supplied a music book for the choir, and in the following year was provided with parchment to write books of 'sett song'. An antiphon and an 'Asperges me' setting were copied in 1486, and in 1491 William Bernard, instructor of the choristers, was paid 3s 4d for new books made for the boys.[35] It can also be shown that other books, not mentioned by the college *Libri computi*, were written during this period.[36] Regular payments for parchment and paper intended for 'cantici' were made at Winchester College from the early 1490s; a more extensive series of payments, providing details of individual pieces, can be traced at Tattershall from the same period.[37] In the space of four years, twenty-one named compositions, two of which may survive, were copied by members of the college, and it is clear that there were others. The payments also mention the ephemeral 'scrowes' and quaterns, whose ownership was more usually the exclusive preserve of individual singers.[38] This denser pattern of institutional provision is found increasingly in the early sixteenth century. A list of music books at Magdalen, made probably in 1524, records – after a number of older items – a total of nine volumes said to have been purchased since 1518: two large books of masses and two large books of antiphons in seven, six and five parts, two small books of Lady masses and two books of antiphons in five and four parts, and one large book 'pro viris tantum vel pueris' containing antiphons, psalms, magnificats and sequences for the Lady mass.[39] The rapid assembly of this collection may suggest that a more calculated plan of acquisition was followed than can be found in earlier periods.

The books of polyphony in the possession of churches and household chapels were frequently administered in conjunction with collections of liturgical books. In the majority of cases they were the responsibility of a sacrist who was charged with their routine upkeep and repair.[40] It was probably through this association with larger collections that books of polyphony were most often brought into contact with professional book-makers. A more extensive similarity with the production of liturgical books is, however, hard to trace. Service books were needed in larger numbers than books of polyphony, and were also more widely distributed.[41] Their contents were highly standardised; the demand for these books thus lent itself more readily to methods of mass production. In-house provision was the most convenient means of acquiring new copies of liturgical books and, especially in the case of large noted volumes, institutional needs were met through the duplication of master-copies. The will of Lewis Charlton, bishop of Hereford (d. 1369) mentions an 'antiquum gradale meum de usu sarum quod fuit exemplar omnium aliorum';[42] payments for correcting newly written books often reveal a similar dependence on older copies in institutional hands. Nonetheless, within the confines of a single foundation, the demand for service books could easily exceed the capacity for provision, and this laid considerable emphasis on external sources of supply. In the major urban centres at least, service books appear to have been readily available for purchase. In new foundations, and elsewhere when demand was heavy and generously financed, books were acquired both from other institutions and, more important, from members of the book-trade. In 1404 several service books, including three antiphoners, were purchased in London for use at Winchester College.[43] At All Souls College, Oxford, in 1448/9, one John 'stationario' was paid for twenty new processionals.[44] Stationers and other members of the book-trade also repaired and main-tained service books, and these activities probably account for most of their dealings with both large and small foundations. Payments to stationers for binding books and adding blank quires are commonly found, and on occasion they also provided written supplements to existing books.[45] A stationer's advertisement sheet, dating from the late fourteenth century, presents a range of sample scripts and formats from liturgical books, and may have been aimed at this trade in incidental tasks as much as at the market for complete books.[46]

The most tangible effects of the workshop production practised by the book-trade were close similarities in the script, format and make-up of manuscripts. It is important to realise, however, that the existence of like-nesses between books was not exclusively tied to direct copying. As Doyle and Parkes have pointed out, the continual copying and imitation of books gave rise to common conventions of design that in time became self-perpetuating.[47] Although standard designs and plans of contents have fre-quently been seen as evidence for organised book production, these features probably arose more often from normative models that existed independently of direct copying. The features shared among the surviving sources of English liturgical polyphony can for the most part be explained in this fashion. Where a number of sources originated from the same institution they are usually dissimilar in appearance; there is little in their design to suggest that they were the products of a single or coherent musical culture. Page layout in particular was standardised through common ruling methods and configur-ations of parts in the repertories copied. The use of nine- and twelve-stave page formats – the most frequently encountered in fourteenth-century sources – was a consequence mainly of copying three-part music written in score. The use of a rastrum to rule staves and of marginal prickings to regulate their spacing gave sources a distinctive appearance.[48] A more extensive generic similarity between sources can be found in the early fifteenth century, although this is not paralleled by a consistent fifteenth-century terminology. For the more sizeable and well-written books, especially those devoted primarily to mass music, a twelve-stave format appears to have become relatively standard. A larger page-size distinguishes these books from their predecessors; within individual sources both the dimensions and the internal organisation of the written space became more consistent. Eight surviving books or parts of books share these features, together with some roughly observed conventions in the arrangement of contents.[49] They nonetheless lack the fixed physical structures and exclusive associations with specific repertories found in later sources.

For two of these early fifteenth-century choirbooks, the Old Hall manu-script and a slightly later group of fragments described by Margaret Bent as the 'Lost Choirbook', a common provenance can be traced.[50] From the authorship of their contents it can be suggested that both of these books were used by the royal household chapel during the 1420s and that the fragment-ary book was very likely copied by its members. The link between Old Hall and the royal chapel, however, derives only from its later parts. The com-poser whose work is most fully represented in the large main corpus of the manuscript, Lionel Power, can be traced as a clerk of the household chapel of Thomas, duke of Clarence. As Roger Bowers has suggested, it may be for this establishment that the book was originally intended.[51] The book probably came into the possession of the royal household chapel after Clarence's death in 1421; its acquisition was no doubt facilitated by the interests held by the

Crown in Clarence's estate and the close political and dynastic ties between these two chapels' masters. This change of ownership can be used to explain the separation in script between the earlier and later parts of the book. Music by two composers, Power and Cooke, appears in both parts of the manuscript, and this may indicate that some continuity existed between the repertories of Clarence's and Henry V's chapels. Before 1421 compositions used in one of these establishments may have been accessible to clerks working in the other; after Clarence's death music by members of his chapel may still have been available for copying into Old Hall from other sources similarly acquired by the clerks of the royal chapel. The composer Cooke may be the John Cooke who was a clerk of the royal household chapel, probably between 1413 and his death in 1419.[52] He may, however, be the Richard Cooke traceable as a clerk of Clarence's chapel in 1420.[53]

Among the surviving sources a close copying relationship can be traced only between the Old Hall manuscript and the fragmentary choirbook. In their present form the fragments share five pieces with Old Hall, drawn from both its earlier and later repertories. The close textual similarities, the small number of variants and the preservation of ligature patterns suggest a measure of dependence between the copies of these items. It may be possible to infer the existence of a closer link, if not a direct copying relationship, from a correction shared by both copies of a Credo setting by Cooke.[54] Although the fragmentary book was a successor to Old Hall, it is unlikely that it was compiled at a much later date; no obvious discrimination between the older and newer music in Old Hall emerges from the main body of its contents. It may well be that Old Hall continued to be used after the later book was written. Any shift in the chapel's repertory is more readily traceable from the additions made to the fragmentary book. A cyclic mass and a four- or five-part 'Gaude flore virginali' setting added to the fragments and dating probably from the mid-century mark the presence of later repertories. The main and subsidiary bodies of contents in the Old Hall manuscript were not so widely separated. In the case of these books, as with others, the structure of repertory reveals more about the continuing use of sources than about their assembly or, in so far as it existed, their original plan. The organisation of pieces could impose a form of structure within a manuscript, but this did not always tally with its layout or with the patterns of physical details generated at an early stage of its compilation.

The structure of the Old Hall manuscript has been studied at length by a number of writers.[55] Through an analysis of repertory, characteristics in the work of individual scribes and the manuscript's principal codicological features, the existence of two independent layers of contents can be demonstrated. The first of these contained a heterogeneous body of pieces of widely differing dates and styles by composers for whom no common sphere of activity can be traced. The second, more coherent, layer contained pieces by composers working largely within the royal household chapel. As Margaret Bent has pointed out, these layers represented first and foremost stages in the copying of the manuscript; it was only as a secondary characteristic that they reflected the date or internal divisions of its repertory.[56] Nor did these layers always correspond closely to the manuscript's physical structure. This feature is demonstrated most clearly in the additions made to the manuscript; second-layer compositions were copied both on blank parchment and on gatherings and single leaves added to accommodate further pieces. A disparity between make-up and content can, however, also be traced within the first layer of the manuscript, usually regarded as structurally unified. From differences in frame ruling patterns, the dimensions of the ruled space and stave gauges, two structural divisions emerge. First, the format of folios 1 and 2 differs in all of these respects from that of the other leaves of the original gatherings of the manuscript; there are also slight, although not consistent, differences in script.[57] It may well be that these leaves, probably representatives of a larger section, originally formed part of another book. Second, through variations in stave gauge, two independent ruling stints can be traced within the manuscript's original gatherings.[58] The boundaries between these stints divide the Gloria, Credo and Sanctus sections of the manuscript; they cannot, however, be exclusively identified with the division – present in each of these sections – between settings written in score and in parts. A larger number of separate ruling stints emerges from what remains of the fragmentary choirbook.[59] At least four can be traced within the original gatherings of the book, and again their pattern is only partially disclosed by the arrangement of contents. These ruling patterns can also be used to distinguish later additions made on blank parchment from those for which structural additions in the form of inserted gatherings were necessary. The relatively late 'Gaude flore' setting appears within one of the original gatherings, and this may suggest that space here was left unfilled for some time. The addition of new leaves or gatherings need not, of course, have been dependent on the exhaustion of existing space.[60]

The arrangement of pieces by format found in these books has been widely thought to show that they were conceived as wholes from the outset and according to some definite plan.[61] The existence of sections devoted to individual mass movements or other items may simply reflect an arrangement of convenience. A division between settings notated in score and in parts, however, was more susceptible to disruption from later additions; the grouping of settings by format could thus suggest that the scribe responsible for the book had a firm idea of its final form before beginning to write. Preliminary plans for these books may well have existed in some form. Their implementation was, however, more flexible than many have suggested, and they were also less dependent on the repertory that the books eventually contained. In the fragmentary choirbook different patterns of stave-ruling and indentation for initials were used to distinguish pages intended for settings in score from those to be used for settings in parts.[62] This scheme therefore anticipated a division by format within the book's principal sections, but at the copying stage its guidelines were not always followed. The second of the two surviving Agnus settings and the motet 'Iste conf[essor]', written in parts, were copied on leaves designed for music in score, with different adaptations of the ruling format to accommodate their initial letters.[63] The first Agnus setting is written in score; further settings of this type had presumably been intended to follow. Settings written in parts may well have been separately catered for. It should not, however, be assumed that no space had been left for additions.[64] A similar discrepancy between the scheme generated by patterns of ruling format and the arrangement of what was copied can be observed in the Old Hall manuscript.[65]

The plans of contents traceable in these books were not designed specifically to facilitate collaborative copying, and in a number of respects they were better fitted to the gradual accumulation of contents. The patterns of ruling most commonly found pre-determined only a limited range of features. This afforded a measure of flexibility not only in the number and distribution of voice-parts but also in the relative ease with which one page design could be converted into another. The arrangement of contents by type and by format was not dependent on the immediate availability of repertory, nor did it predicate the copying of specific pieces. It may thus be questioned whether the presence of these sections alone meant that the scribe of a book 'had the majority of the music in front of him before he began to copy'.[66] The heterogeneous character of these books' ruling structures may also suggest that they were prepared with gradual compilation in mind. By comparison with what is found at a later date, the ruling stints of early fifteenth-century books are relatively short. New gatherings were probably prepared *ad hoc* to meet a developing scheme of contents, and this may suggest that, at the outset, ideas about what the books would contain were relatively fluid. Economy was perhaps the principal reason why larger quantities of parchment were not ruled at once. There may not always have been an assured flow of new compositions, nor can what was available always have found its way into one particular book. BL MS Egerton 3307, dating from the mid-fifteenth century, is the earliest surviving source ruled as a whole. It is striking that more than an eighth of this book, including the whole of the last gathering, remains unused.[67]

It remains to ask how far the members of the book-making profession became involved with books of this type. The Old Hall manuscript and the fragmentary choirbook are both lavishly illuminated, with historiated initials used to begin major sections and elaborate penwork forms in subsidiary positions.[68] The principal initials at least were probably the work of a specialist illuminator, and in the first layer of Old Hall they appear to have been executed in a single stint. This may suggest that an outside illuminator worked with these books *in situ* within the royal household rather than in a separate workshop. Above all, for the Old Hall manuscript and the fragmentary choirbook, as for other books made in small numbers and with limited frequency, this form of collaboration was probably arranged *ad hoc*. The occasional involvement of outside specialists was probably not unusual in making prestigious books of this type; it is unlikely, however, that a very high proportion of choirbooks was illuminated to this standard. Payments made for materials suggest that books were commonly illuminated by their scribes, and this fits well with the modest quality of the decoration found in most of the surviving sources.[69] Two cases can be traced from administrative records in which outside craftsmen worked with institutionally owned books of polyphony. At St Michael's Cornhill in 1466/7 a stationer was paid for 'new helyng and byndyng' a book written by the parish priest in the previous year; a similar task was performed at Magdalen College, Oxford, in 1496/7.[70]

These two books, their make-up and the links between them bear out many of the conclusions that can be drawn from the documentary evidence. The same structural change and piecemeal growth in contents are found here as can be traced from book lists and other administrative sources. The personnel of the royal chapel were intimately involved in these processes; the monopoly that they maintained in copying music for use in the chapel may help to explain why its books of polyphony are mentioned so rarely in royal administrative records.[71] To judge from the relationship between the Old Hall manuscript and the fragmentary choirbook these books relied heavily on their predecessors in both form and content. Behind the Old Hall manuscript, which contains music dating from c. 1370 onwards,[72] there may have been a succession of other books of similar design. Some indication of the circles in which the immediate predecessor of this book was used can perhaps be inferred from the presence in the first layer of Old Hall of music by composers working in the chapel of John of Gaunt and at Westminster Abbey.[73] Both of these establishments were closely related to the Crown, and, as later, this form of connection may have served to underwrite the transfer of books to the royal household chapel.

To a certain extent the groups of singers in the major churches making books for their own use can be thought of as scriptoria. But although this activity exemplifies the persistent collaboration between scribes identified by Doyle and Parkes as the main prerequisite for a scriptorium,[74] its underlying purpose was different. The production of books of polyphony provided receptacles for the developing musical repertories of major churches and household chapels, rather than a means of duplicating texts for wider use. For groups of singers, moreover, the writing of these books did not become an end in itself. Until the second half of the fifteenth century the specialist nature of polyphonic music inhibited the emergence of commercial activity, of distinct groups of producers and consumers, and of the relatively autonomous forms of transmission that the existence of these separate groups entailed. It also restricted the importance of collections of books of polyphony owned by the major churches and the extent to which their growth was institutionally inspired. Only in the late fifteenth and early sixteenth centuries did the provision of books of polyphony change to accommodate more regular forms of demand, a greater availability of repertory and musical abilities and – eventually – the opportunities offered by the new technology of printing.

NOTES

1 An earlier version of this essay was delivered to the Tenth International Medieval and Renaissance Music Conference, Manchester, 1982; for their help at this stage I should like to thank David Fallows and Christopher Page. The present text was substantially completed in 1984 and although revised here may in places not take full account of more recent work. A catalogue of references to written polyphony drawn from administrative sources, formerly an appendix to this essay, from which several items are cited below, is A. Wathey, 'Lost Books of Polyphony in England: A List to 1500', *Research Chronicle: Royal Musical Association*, 21 (1988), 1–19.

2 Doyle and Parkes, p. 201. See generally L.E. Boyle, *Medieval Latin Palaeography: A Bibliographical Introduction*, Toronto Medieval Bibliographies, 8 (Toronto, 1984). See also E.L. Eisenstein, *The Printing Press as an Agent of Change: Communications and Cultural Transformations in Early-Modern Europe*, 2 vols. (Cambridge, 1979), I, pp. 3–159.

3 See F. Ll. Harrison, *Music in Medieval Britain*, 4th edn (Buren, 1980), pp. 157ff.; Dom A. Hughes, 'The Topography of English Mediaeval Polyphony', *In Memoriam Jacques Handschin*, ed. H. Anglès *et al.* (Strassburg, 1962), pp. 127–39; M. Bent, 'The Transmission of English Music 1300–1500: Some Aspects of Repertory and Presentation', *Studien zur Tradition in der Musik: Kurt von Fischer zum 60. Geburtstag*, ed. H.H. Eggebrecht and M. Lütolf (Munich, 1973), pp. 65–84.

4 'European Politics and the Distribution of Music in the Early Fifteenth Century', *Early Music History*, 1 (1981), 315, 317; see also R. Strohm, *Music in Late Medieval Bruges* (Oxford, 1985), pp. 120–3.

5 'European Politics and the Distribution of Music', p. 317. For these books see N.J. Rogers, 'Books of Hours Produced in the Low Countries for the English Market in the Fifteenth Century' (unpublished M.Litt thesis; University of Cambridge, 1982), pp. 1–63, 264–301; see also S. Thrupp, 'The Grocers of London: A Study of Distributive Trade', *Studies in English Trade in the Fifteenth Century*, ed. E. Power and M.M. Postan (Cambridge, 1933), pp. 247–92.

6 For example, Hughes, 'The Topography of English Mediaeval Polyphony', pp. 127–39; Bent, 'The Transmission of English Music', pp. 65–84; Strohm, *Music in Late Medieval Bruges*, pp. 13ff.

7 *Pour une histoire du livre manuscrit au moyen âge: trois essais de codicologie quantitative*, 2nd edn (Paris, 1983), pp. 49, 85, 92, 100ff., 114, 118–19, 364–8; see also C. Bozzolo and E. Ornato, 'Les Fluctuations de la production manuscrite à la lumière de

l'histoire de la fin du moyen âge française', *Bulletin philologique et historique (jusqu'à 1610) du Comité des Travaux Historiques et Scientifiques: année 1979* (Paris, 1981), pp. 51–75. The detailed conclusions of these essays must, however, be treated with caution.

8 See, for example, M. Bent, 'Some Criteria for Establishing Relationships Between Sources of Late-Medieval Polyphony', *Music in Medieval and Early-Modern Europe: Patronage, Sources and Texts*, ed. I. Fenlon (Cambridge, 1981), pp. 296–8; S. Boorman, 'Limitations and Extensions of Filiation Technique', *ibid.*, pp. 320–1, 335ff.

9 See, for example, Bent, 'Some Criteria', pp. 296–8 and her comments (pp. 300–3) on C. Hamm, 'Manuscript Structure in the Dufay Era', *Acta Musicologica*, 34 (1962), 166–84; Boorman, 'Limitations and Extensions of Filiation Technique', pp. 320–1. The brevity of individual textual units is important also in the transmission of letter collections, poetical works and the *pecia*; see Boorman, *ibid.*, p. 320, n. 4, and A. Dondaine, 'Apparat critique de l'édition d'un texte universitaire', *Actes du premier congrès international de philosophie médiévale, Louvain–Bruxelles, 28 Août–4 Septembre 1958: L'homme et son destin d'après les penseurs du moyen âge* (Louvain, 1960), pp. 211–20.

10 See R. Bowers, 'Obligation, Agency, and *Laissez-faire*: The Promotion of Polyphonic Composition for the Church in Fifteenth-Century England', *Music in Medieval and Early-Modern Europe*, ed. Fenlon, p. 13. The Act 'for the Abolishinge . . . of Bookes and Images' (3 & 4 Edward VI c. 10; *The Statutes of the Realm*, ed. A. Luders *et al.*, 11 vols. (London, 1810–28), IV, pp. 110–11) probably accounts for the loss of a smaller proportion of books of polyphony than of other forms of service book.

11 See *Registrum Caroli Bothe, episcopi Herefordensis, A.D. MDXVI–MDXXXV*, ed. A.T. Bannister, Canterbury and York Society, 28 (London, 1921), pp. 273–5; the Hereford Use was retained at Aiguebelle until 1580.

12 For example, Oxford, Lincoln College, MS Latin 124, fols. 222–3; see A. Wathey, 'Newly Discovered Fifteenth-Century English Polyphony at Oxford', *Music and Letters*, 64 (1983), 58–62.

13 A single case is known to me: the 'libri de cantu' included in a library catalogue attributable possibly to Bermondsey Priory. See N. Denholm-Young, 'Edward of Windsor and Bermondsey Priory', *EHR*, 48 (1933), 442–3; Wathey, 'Lost Books', nos. 6–7. For polyphony included in miscellanies see *ibid.*, nos. 13–14, 25.

14 See for example *ibid.*, no. 18; Harrison, *Music in Medieval Britain*, p. 163.

15 Louis of Luxembourg died at Hatfield on 16 September and the clerks of his chapel were engaged by Gilles in the following year; see A. Leroy, 'Catalogue des Prévosts du monastère de Watten, sur la rivière d'Aa, diocèse de Saint-Omer, 1072–1577', *Archives historiques et littéraires du nord de la France et du midi de la Belgique*, NS, 6 (1847), 284, and Valenciennes, Bibliothèque Municipale, MS 660, fol. 227v. For Gilles de Bretagne, see B. Wolffe, *Henry VI* (London, 1981), pp. 178–9; for the books see Wathey, 'Lost Books', nos. 166–7.

16 For rolls see R.H. Rouse, 'Roll and Codex: The Transmission of the Works of Reinmar von Zweter', *Paläographie 1981: Colloquium des Comité International de Paléographie: München, 15.–18. September 1981, Referate*, ed. G. Silagi, Münchener Beiträge zur Mediävistik und Renaissance-Forschung, 32 (Munich, 1982), pp. 107–23; M.T. Clanchy, *From Memory to Written Record: England 1066–1307* (London, 1979),

pp. 105–13. See also, more generally, B. Bischoff, *Paläographie des römischen Altertums und des abendländischen Mittelalters*, Grundlagen der Germanistik, 24 (Berlin, 1979), pp. 48–50. For pamphlets see P.R. Robinson, 'The "Booklet": A Self-Contained Unit in Composite Manuscripts', *Codicologica*, 3 (1980), 46–69.

17 See Hamm, 'Manuscript Structure', pp. 166–9; Bent, 'Some Criteria', pp. 300–3. See also the remarks, based on a comparison with the *pecia* system, in S.J. Williams, 'An Author's Role in Fourteenth-Century Book Production: Guillaume de Machaut's "Livre ou je met toutes mes choses"', *Romania*, 90 (1969), 441–5.

18 See Wathey, 'Lost Books', no. 113; also no. 121.

19 *Ibid.*, no. 6.

20 For example Cambridge, Trinity College, MS O.3.58 and London, PRO LR 2/261. Among numerous others see Berkeley Castle, Select Roll 55; CUL MSS Add. 2764, Buxton 96; PRO E 149/7/23; Oxford, Bodleian Library, MSS Eng. misc. c. 291 and Lat. liturg. b. 19. See also 'Lost Books', nos. 11, 120, 133, 141, 150.

21 For example Arundel Castle, Muniment M 534, and BL Add. MS 39255 (N); see R. Bowers and A. Wathey, 'New Sources of English Fifteenth- and Sixteenth-Century Polyphony', *Early Music History*, 4 (1984), 298–304; *Census Catalogue of Manuscript Sources of Polyphonic Music 1400–1500*, Renaissance Manuscript Studies, 1 (Neuhaussen–Stuttgart, 1979–), II, p. 76.

22 BL Add. MS 40011B, fols. 9–14; see *Census Catalogue*, II, pp. 77–8.

23 See P.M. Lefferts and M. Bent, 'New Sources of English Thirteenth- and Fourteenth-Century Polyphony', *Early Music History*, 2 (1982), 323–9, and n. 62 for similar compilations without polyphony.

24 See *Non-Cycle Plays and Fragments*, ed. N. Davis, Early English Text Society, supplementary ser., 1 (Oxford, 1970), pp. c–ciii, 106–14.

25 BL Add. MS 49622, fol. 126; see further J.W. McKinnon, '*Canticum novum* in the Isabella Book', *Mediaevalia*, 2 (1976), 207–22.

26 'Roll and Codex', p. 120.

27 See Wathey, 'Lost Books', nos. 11, 25, 35, 59–63, 81, 95, 97, 121, 133.

28 *Ibid.*, nos. 11, 25, 81, 97, 109.

29 *Ibid.*, no. 133; for Aleyn see A. Wathey, 'Music in the Royal and Noble Households in Late Medieval England: Studies in Sources and Patronage' (unpublished D.Phil. thesis; University of Oxford, 1987), p. 46, n. 1.

30 Wathey, 'Lost Books', no. 121.

31 *Ibid.*, no. 168.

32 See Longleat House, Archives of the Marquess of Bath, Misc. MS XIII (Wardrobe Account, 1517/8), fol. 10: 'first one great boke of iiij queyers paper Riall with Masses Antemps Exaltavit &c, vij queyers of dyvers masses of v partes and vj partes, iiij queiers of masses of iiij partes upon the playnesong, v queiers of antemps of v partes to be song aftir Evensong, v queires of Antemps to be song aftir masse, iij queyers of the Service yn Lent for En Rex venit, Gloria laus and other, and v queyers of Carolles for the Feast of Christmas all bownde yn Forelles, one masse of φ in oon Cure and dyvers other songes of masses and antemps yn skrowes aswell of the makyng of the forseide Henry as of other Chapelmen yn dyvers partes'.

33 See Bowers, 'Obligation, Agency, and *Laissez-faire*', pp. 8–9, 11–14.

34 'Lost Books', nos. 135, 137.

35 *Ibid.*, nos. 83, 85, 86, 90.

36 *Ibid.*, no. 92, written probably during the period, c. 1490–2, when Davy was *informator choristarum* at Magdalen.

37 *Ibid.*, nos. 129–32, 100–108. For Tattershall see also *Report on the Manuscripts of Lord de L'Isle & Dudley Preserved at Penshurst Place*, 6 vols., Historical Manuscripts Commission, [77] (London, 1925–66), I, pp. 194–7; R. Bowers, 'Choral Institutions Within the English Church; their Constitution and Development 1340–1500' (unpublished Ph.D. thesis; University of East Anglia, 1975), p. A059; D.S. Josephson, *John Taverner: Tudor Composer*, UMI Studies in Musicology, 5 (Ann Arbor, 1979), pp. 20–2.

38 'Lost Books', no. 105.

39 Magdalen College Archives, 219/4, dorse; see Harrison, *Music in Medieval Britain*, p. 431.

40 See, for example, Bowers, 'Choral Institutions', pp. 5049–50; the day-to-day custody of these books was occasionally the responsibility of instructors of choristers (cf. 'Lost Books', no. 88; Harrison, *Music in Medieval Britain*, p. 166).

41 See, for example, the provisions in *Councils and Synods with other Documents Relating to the English Church II: A.D. 1205–1313*, 2 vols., ed. F.M. Powicke and C.R. Cheney (Oxford, 1964), I, pp. 29, 81, 111, 115, 128.

42 See London, Lambeth Palace, Reg. Whittlesey, fol. 102 (23 May 1369; proved 29 June); the book was left to the parish of Tettenhall, formerly held by Charlton (see Emden, *BRUO*, I, p. 391).

43 Winchester College Archives, Muniment 78.

44 All Souls Muniments, Bursars' Account 1448/9, m. 1.

45 See for example G.J. Gray, *The Earlier Cambridge Stationers & Bookbinders and The First Cambridge Printer*, Bibliographical Society Monographs, 13 (Oxford, 1904), pp. 9–17. An early sixteenth-century stationer, John Borell, was paid for 'wrytyng of the feryall letanye' in a small breviary at St Margaret's Westminster, among other tasks (PRO E 101/676/45; see also H.R. Plomer, 'Notices of English Stationers in the Archives of the City of London', *Transactions of the Bibliographical Society*, 6 (1900–2), 20–1).

46 See S.J.P. van Dijk, 'An Advertisement Sheet of an Early Fourteenth-Century Writing Master at Oxford', *Scriptorium*, 10 (1956), 47–64.

47 'The Production of Copies of the *Canterbury Tales* and the *Confessio Amantis*', p. 200, and see their comments (pp. 200–1) on A. Brusendorff, *The Chaucer Tradition* (Oxford and Copenhagen, 1925), and G. Dempster, 'Manly's Conception of the Early History of the *Canterbury Tales*', *PMLA*, 61 (1946), pp. 379–415.

48 For ruling, see J.P. Gumbert, 'Ruling by Rake and Board: Notes on Some Late Medieval Ruling Techniques', *The Role of the Book in Medieval Culture: Proceedings of the Oxford International Symposium 26 September–1 October 1982*, 2 vols., ed. P. Ganz, Bibliologia, 3–4 (Turnhout, 1986), I, pp. 41–54, and more generally L. Gillisen, 'Un élément codicologique trop peu exploité: la réglure', *Scriptorium*, 23 (1969), 150–62.

49 The Old Hall manuscript and a related fragmentary book (now in CUL Add. MSS 4435, 5963; Oxford, Bodleian Library, MSS Don. b. 31, 32; Oxford, Magdalen College, MS 267; Oxford, University College, MS 192; Canberra, National Library of Australia, MS 4052/2); fragments in Cambridge, Pembroke College,

MS 314; Trinity College, MS B.11.34 (in part formerly MS B.10.5); Hertford, Hertfordshire Record Office, ref: 57553; BL Add. MS 49597 (O); Oxford, University College, MS 16; Stratford, Shakespeare Birthplace Trust, DR 37, vol. 41.

50 For the Old Hall manuscript, see A. Hughes and M. Bent, 'The Old Hall Manuscript: A Reappraisal and Inventory', *Musica Disciplina*, 21 (1967), 97–147; M. Bent, 'Sources of the Old Hall Music', *PRMA*, 94 (1967–8), 19–35; M. Bent, 'The Old Hall Manuscript: A Paleographical Study' (unpublished Ph.D. thesis; University of Cambridge, 1968); *The Old Hall Manuscript*, 3 vols., ed. A. Ramsbotham, H.B. Collins and Dom A. Hughes, Plainsong and Mediaeval Music Society (London, 1933–8); *The Old Hall Manuscript*, 3 vols., ed. A. Hughes and M. Bent, Corpus Mensurabilis Musicae, 46 (Rome, 1969–73). For the fragmentary book see M. Bent, 'A Lost English Choirbook of the Fifteenth Century', *International Musicological Society: Report of the Eleventh Congress, Copenhagen 1972*, 2 vols., ed. H. Glahn *et al.* (Copenhagen, 1974), pp. 257–62; M. Bent, 'The Progeny of Old Hall: More Leaves from a Royal English Choirbook', *Gordon Athol Anderson (1929–1981): In memoriam, von seinen Studenten, Freunden und Kollegen*, 2 vols., ed. L. Dittmer, Wissenschaftliche Abhandlungen, 39 (Henryville, Ottawa and Binningen, 1984), pp. 1–54.

51 'Some Observations on the Life and Career of Lionel Power', *PRMA*, 102 (1975–6), 109–10.

52 See PRO E 101/406/21, fol. 27, and *CPR 1416–1422*, p. 219; see also Emden, *BRUC*, p. 157. Another John Cooke was a clerk of the chapel from 1428/9 until April 1455 or after (*CPR 1452–1461*, p. 229). See also Bent, 'The Progeny of Old Hall', pp. 28–9, where it is assumed that Cooke died at a later date.

53 See Westminster Abbey Muniment 12163, fol. 14; Bowers, 'Some Observations', p. 108.

54 No. 92 (*The Old Hall Manuscript*, ed. Hughes and Bent, II, pp. 96–101); see Bent, 'The Progeny of Old Hall', p. 7, n. 16. For the contents of the fragmentary book see *ibid.*, pp. 20–3; 'A Lost English Choirbook', pp. 261–2.

55 See *The Old Hall Manuscript*, ed. Ramsbotham *et al.*, I, pp. xii–xv; III, pp. x–xii; M. Bukofzer, *Studies in Medieval and Renaissance Music* (London, 1951), pp. 73ff.; Bent, 'Sources of the Old Hall Music', pp. 19–22 and *passim*; 'The Old Hall Manuscript: A Paleographical Study, pp. 96–205.

56 'Sources of the Old Hall Music', pp. 26–7.

57 Fols. 3–6 (the remainder of gathering I in Hughes and Bent, 'The Old Hall Manuscript', pp. 136–7) thus formed part of a separate gathering, whose collation can be expressed as: 2^8 (wants 1 and 2 before fol. 3, 4 and 5 before fol. 4). Fols. 1–2 are not conjoint. The collation for fols. 59–79 offered by Hughes and Bent (*ibid.*, pp. 140–3, their Gatherings x–XII; see also Bent, 'The Old Hall Manuscript: A Paleographical Study', pp. 33–44 and Table I, p. 430a) should be revised to read (allowing for an extra gathering at the head of the manuscript) $11^8 + 1$ leaf after 6 (wants 4 and 5 before fol. 62), 12^6, $13^8 + 1$ leaf after 1 (wants 6 before fol. 78). Fols. 61 and 62 are conjoint and fols. 65 and 72, placed by Hughes and Bent in their Gathering XI, must therefore belong respectively to their Gatherings X and XII (here 11 and 13).

58 See *ibid.*, pp. 40–1 for details.

59 Separate stints within the books' original gatherings cover (i) CUL Add. MS 4435,

parts a–c, Oxford, Bodleian Library, MSS Don. b. 31, 32, Oxford, Magdalen College, MS 267, fols. 90–1; (ii) Magdalen College, MS 267, fol. 89; (iii) CUL Add. MS 5963, Oxford, University College, MS 192, fol. 27a; (iv) Add. MS 4435, part d, Canberra, National Library of Australia, MS 4052/2.

60 CUL Add. MS 4435, part d; the cyclic mass, which possibly predates the 'Gaude flore' setting, was written on an inserted gathering (Magdalen College, MS 267, fol. 92; University College, MS 192, fol. 28).

61 Bent, 'Sources of the Old Hall Music', pp. 19, 27, for example.

62 Leaves intended for settings in parts were ruled with indentations one stave deep on the recto and two staves deep on the verso; those intended for settings in score were ruled without indentation. Compare for example the plates in Bent, 'The Progeny', pp. 33–4 and 35–42. See also Bent, 'The Old Hall Manuscript: A Paleographical Study', pp. 182, 198.

64 See the plates in Bent, 'The Progeny', pp. 49–52.

64 *Ibid.*, p. 20.

65 See Bent, 'The Old Hall Manuscript: A Paleographical Study', p. 198.

66 Bent, 'Sources of the Old Hall Music', p. 27; 'The Old Hall Manuscript: A Paleographical Study', p. 183.

67 Fols. 78–88; see *Census Catalogue*, II, pp. 89–90.

68 See M. Bent, 'Initial Letters in the Old Hall Manuscript', *Music and Letters*, 47 (1966), pp. 225–38, and Bent, 'The Progeny', pp. 30–2.

69 See, for example, Wathey, 'Lost Books', no. 134.

70 *Ibid.*, nos. 56, 92. A further case (no. 54) may involve service books for use at the organ.

71 Books of polyphony for use in the chapel appear once, in 1295 (*ibid.*, nos. 155–6). For chapel service books see BL Add. MS 35181, fol. 7 (1334); PRO E 101/393/4, fol. 6v (30 September 1357).

72 See Bent, 'Sources of the Old Hall Music', Table 1.

73 Respectively John Pycard and John Tyes (see Wathey, 'Music in the Royal and Noble Households', p. 46, n. 1; Westminster Abbey, Liber Niger, fol. 86v: 'Anno regni regis Ricardi secundi xxiij°. Isti fuerunt cantores seculares in Ecclesia Westm' scilicet Johannes Byfeld tenor habuit hoc anno pro stipendiis suis x marcas cum ij tunicis et una furrura. Item Johannes Tyes organista habuit absque vestura x li. Item Willelmus Causton habuit x marcas et vesturam et furruram sicut J. Byfeld. Item Johannes Barker treble habuit ix marcas cum vestura et furrura ut supra. Item Johannes Grede treble habuit x marcas absque vestura et furrura. Item Petrus Pleford treble habuit ix marcas cum vestura et furrura ut supra. Item Johannes Browning treble habuit C s. cum j vestura absque furrura.').

74 Doyle and Parkes, p. 201.

8 · PATRONS, BUYERS AND OWNERS: THE EVIDENCE FOR OWNERSHIP AND THE RÔLE OF BOOK OWNERS IN BOOK PRODUCTION AND THE BOOK TRADE

KATE HARRIS

THE PARTIAL NATURE of the evidence for book ownership in late medieval England, rather than any deficiency in the number of facts diligently collected by scholars, ensures that a study of the subject cannot be definitive.[1] If the partiality of the evidence of the extant or the recorded manuscripts on which the study of book ownership relies were merely arbitrary, a matter of incompleteness only, it would be possible to draw generalisations from the surviving evidence, treating it as an unbiassed representative sample; the contrary being the case, it is important that the direction of the bias be acknowledged at the outset. It will be the purpose of this essay first to evaluate the evidence before attempting, within the context of a discussion of the demand for manuscripts and through necessarily less concerted treatment of three main themes (in novel order – second-hand books, royal patronage and imported books), some more incautious assessment of the part played by the late medieval book owner in book production and the conduct of the book trade.

I

It is possible that H.R. Plomer's comment on a projected survey of all books mentioned in medieval wills, 'it is practically certain that the result would be very incommensurate with the labour spent in obtaining it',[2] may be considered more dismissive than is quite necessary. However, it is true that most scholars would now treat all the conclusions drawn by Margaret Deanesly, in her article, 'Vernacular Books in England in the Fourteenth and Fifteenth Centuries',[3] as in need of qualification; Deanesly deduced from the evidence of wills 'the extreme booklessness of the population as a whole, the rarity of vernacular books as opposed to Latin, and the preponderance, among vernacular books, of works of piety or devotion over secular books, such as romances or chronicles'.[4]

The observations that all the books owned by a testator are unlikely to be mentioned in his will, that books which are mentioned may be so imperfectly described as to evade identification and that it is no function of a will (a document requiring only that one manuscript be distinguished from another) to list all the works contained in any particular volume, are commonplaces. Further, the fact that recorded manuscripts cannot be assumed to be new militates against the use of documentary evidence *per se* as a source for a study of actual book production (this is a point which will be raised again later). Where extant and recorded evidence can be compared it is usual for some area of discrepancy to emerge. The will of Sir Thomas Chaworth of Wiverton in Nottinghamshire (dated 16 January and proved 27 March 1459) notices none of the extant manuscripts he is known to have commissioned – Columbia University, MS Plimpton 263 (Trevisa's translation of the *De proprietatibus rerum*), British Library, MS Cotton Augustus A.iv (Lydgate's *Troy Book*) and the Wollaton Antiphonal (now deposited in Nottingham University Library), all bearing his arms. The will of Richard Fox 'of seint Albon simple seruant' (10 May, proved 12 August 1454) includes a numbered list of books: of these the third and fifth ('the 3. begynneth w^t d*omine* ne in furore / . . . The 5. begynneth w^t Elfrede z Alfrede kyngg*es* and so forth croneteles./') are now extant, surviving respectively as CUL MS Kk.I.6 and MS 181 in the duke of Bedford's library at Woburn; both (and this is the fact not made apparent in the will) are partly in Fox's own hand.[5] Of course it is more usual still for the relation of the books mentioned in a will with all those owned by the testator during his lifetime, let alone with the testator's scholarly or literary interests (his lifetime of reading), to remain a matter for conjecture only.

Deficiencies in completeness and in points of detail undermine the use of testamentary evidence as a general basis for an analysis of book ownership, but bias within that evidence actually discredits such a practice. As a factor increasing the likelihood of a book's appearance in a will, intrinsic value is probably outweighed by devotional or liturgical content. The special appropriateness of devotional and liturgical books to the document is signalled by bequests of such manuscripts which are accompanied by the injunction (to which the book is a means) that the recipient pray for the testator's soul.[6] Also appropriate to the document in a special way are the book bequests made by members of the learned professions to their successors or to advance, as places of study, their college and cathedral libraries, as well as bequests extending a form of posthumous patronage to further the career of some protégé – all means of perpetuating the testator's profession and, more personally, his own professional connections.[7] Motivation remains particularly clear in the bequest made in 1500 to King's College, Cambridge, by John Hesewell; he left 'three volumes or books called "Glossa ordinaria super total bibliam", my name to be entered in every book thereof'.[8]

The strength of testamentary convention seems to have been such that the drawing up of a will might itself suggest to the testator the acquisition of books well adapted to the occasion; this passage from the will of Henry, Lord Scrope of Masham (5 August 1415) might be adduced:

Volo quod Executores mei emant omnino Unum Missale, quod detur alicui loco, ubi per Legem cotidie oporteat celebrari, ubi non convenientius Missale non habetur, ut in praedicto loco Celebrantes habeant Animam meam recommendatam in Missis & in Orationibus suis.[9]

The difficulty of deducing a private collection of books from a benefaction to an institutional library, suitable books being likely to be acquired with the benefaction in view, is also apt to be remembered here.[10] Yet to conclude a discussion of wills by emphasising convention rather than the personal religious acts which may operate within the convention is inappropriate. Personal associations are evidenced by references made to a previous owner; John of Gaunt, for instance, refers to the books he leaves his son, Henry Beaufort, bishop of Lincoln, as 'mon messale & mon porthous qe furent a mon seigneur mon frere Prince de Gales qe Dieux assoile'.[11] The terms of a bequest may at once provide a revelation of the testator's religious life and show that he envisaged the bequest extending that life. Chaworth left to his eldest son 'a litel Portose the whiche the saide *sir* Thomas toke w^t hym alway when he rode'. Eleanor Bohun, duchess of Gloucester, left to her daughter, Joan (9 August 1399):

un livre oue le psautier primer et autres deuoc*i*ons oue deux claspes enamaillez oue mes armez quele liure iay pluis usee oue ma beneison . . .[12]

To his chaplain, Robert Blundell, Walter Skirlaw, bishop of Durham, left in his will of 7 March 1404 (proved 21 April 1406), 'parvum meum Missale portatile, et parvum Portiforium, super quo matutinas et vesperas mecum dicere consuevit'.[13] Such personal associations may lie behind the simplest bequest of a single service book in those many wills (often treated as so much statistical chaff by commentators on book ownership) mentioning the one book and no other.

To such patterns of ownership, as to the book provisions of the population at large, inventories, that form of documentary evidence seemingly free from many of the problems of bias inherent in the use of wills, give no access at all. Although inventories may be assumed to present a complete (if not always a detailed or fully accurate) account of books owned, the insignificance of their numbers at this period and their narrow social base, their confirmed tendency to present information about exceptional collections, the libraries of the illustrious, ensure that they too cannot supply a general basis for the study of book ownership.[14] This is not, of course, to detract from the interest of individual documents nor to underestimate the necessity for work on the cruces of interpretation they present (not least the matter of the effect of duress on valuations).[15]

Commenting on 'the fallacious test of surviving books', Neil Ker, in the introduction to his *Medieval Libraries of Great Britain*, argued that it is impossible to infer the size of a medieval library from the evidence of surviving books.[16] Manuscripts now extant, like the documentary evidence, do not provide a true picture of the books in circulation in the medieval period. A work's popularity, the likelihood that it was read to pieces, is probably the factor most frequently mentioned as giving an element of bias to the evidence of surviving manuscripts. The *Index of Middle English Verse* includes a table showing the number of manuscripts in which given texts survive,[17] from which the compilers concluded that (p. xi) 'it is really long books that are found in the largest number of MSS'; pointing to 'the lack of preservation of secular entertainment, namely the romances', they argued that 'small MSS may have been destroyed because of much use'. Professor Pearsall, noting that twelve of the fifteen extant poems of the western and northern alliterative revival survive only in unique copies, adduces secular subject-matter as part of his rationale for the disappearance of an hypothetical corpus of Middle English alliterative poetry of the thirteenth and early fourteenth centuries; he writes: 'Their vulnerability would have been increased by their presumably secular subject-matter, by their regional affiliation, and by the additionally disadvantaged status of English during this period.'[18] Dr Doyle, discussing the same group of manuscripts, sees the issue in more complex light; as well as adducing the likelihood of heavy wear and tear on cheap manuscripts (whether alliterative texts, romances or dramatic works) made for communal entertainment, he mentions 'the factors of obsolescence and revolution in fashions of learning or religion . . . the length of a text, its purport, style, dialect, starting-place and ways of communication', as well as 'the competition of other compositions' as possibly affecting manuscript survival.[19] It was cheap books (followed by small books) which Rudolf Hirsch chose to head his list of twelve categories of fifteenth-century manuscripts especially liable to destruction: the rest of the categorisation is concerned, broadly speaking, with practical, educational and heretical books, and with vernacular and devotional books of a popular kind.[20] Commentators neglect the further possibility that, provoked by the changed status of the language itself, losses among French vernacular manuscripts may have been disproportionately heavy. The continuing allegiance of the bilingual English nobility to earlier French literary forms, and their taste for the fashionable exclusivity of contemporary (largely imported) French culture, only highlight the radical nature of the divorce of that culture, for all its aesthetic (and social) attractions, from the main concerns of the growing reading public.[21]

Secular subject-matter, particularly vulnerable though it may have been to the vicissitudes of changing taste, could have given some immunity against that major revolution in religious thought which decimated the English manuscript collections of the Middle Ages. Even so it is probably reasonable to suggest that it is rather manuscripts produced at the top end of the scale of production (though liable to mutilation for the sake of their miniatures, initials and illuminated borders[22] and, many of them, to destruction in the period of official iconoclasm following the Reformation) which have their chances of survival enhanced, being retained for their obvious intrinsic value when no longer regarded (or legible) as reading matter. The case has been well put by Carla Bozzolo in her study of the French translations of Boccaccio:

La conservation des manuscrits est généralement fonction de leur niveau d'exécution. Il est donc évident que les manuscrits de présentation ou d'apparat destinés à des membres des familles régnates et des Maisons princières, ou de la vieille noblesse nous sont plus fréquemment parvenus.[23]

Ultimately, with some notable exceptions, the substance of a manuscript seems to outweigh its subject-matter as a factor affecting its chances of survival in the Middle Ages and, especially, beyond.

In seeking to define the relation of book owner and production, it is essential that the owner's initiative be proven. Of the recorded evidence Professor Scattergood has written:

wills and forfeitures simply record the ownership of books; it does not follow necessarily that the recorded owners sought to possess the books in question.[24]

The location of the point of acquisition (a phrase involving a useful ambiguity) is at once crucial and, even for surviving manuscripts, rarely possible: it has been said to be easier to detect first-hand ownership in the case of early printed books.[25] Armigerous manuscripts constitute the single most important group containing evidence of the circumstances of their commission.[26] Although a study of such manuscripts can provide only a restricted view of book ownership in the period, a view confined to owners of high social status and, largely, to manuscripts of high quality, I have thought it worthwhile to try to gauge the quantity of such evidence from a survey of armigerous manuscripts produced for English owners between the end of the fourteenth century and the early years of the sixteenth, as recorded in the catalogues of the Royal collection in the British Library and of the illuminated manuscripts in the Bodleian Library, Oxford.[27] The collections were chosen for the very reason that they were likely to yield a significant number of such manuscripts; nevertheless (the study being confined necessarily to those manuscripts in which the arms are an integral part of the original programme of decoration) the Royal collection furnished evidence of only about thirty commissions falling within the relevant period. Of these no fewer than seventeen were ordered by Edward IV in Bruges.[28] It is notable that six, perhaps seven, of the manuscripts were commissioned for, rather than by, the owner, being presentation manuscripts or gifts from those seeking patronage or influence.[29]

A group of manuscripts of similar size is yielded from the study of the third volume of the Bodleian catalogue (*British, Irish, and Icelandic Schools*); again there is evidence of about thirty commissions by English owners during the period – this out of a sample of nearly 550 falling within the period. A further half-dozen manuscripts from the second volume (*Italian School*) may be added to the list, at least half of them commissioned by John Tiptoft, earl of

Worcester, in Padua. The first volume (*German, Dutch, Flemish, French and Spanish Schools*) yields three more manuscripts fulfilling the criteria laid down, that is, if MS Lat. liturg. f 3 (*SC* 29742), a Flemish *horae* produced for Anne of Bohemia, is included.[30] However, in its constituents and in its diversity the Bodleian group of manuscripts differs from the armigerous volumes in the Royal collection, the latter group dominated by prestige copies of secular, vernacular (largely French) texts (even without Edward IV's manuscripts it would be so dominated) and with a significant number of presentation manuscripts. The Bodleian group probably presents a more typical cross-section of armigerous manuscripts, including as it does a sizeable number of Books of Hours and volumes of private prayer, a class of manuscripts which, because of their personal nature and customary high level of production, might be expected to contain a record of the circumstances of their commission in the form of their owners' arms (for a slightly earlier period the same high incidence of psalters in such a sample would be unsurprising). It also includes a dozen or so manuscripts wholly or partly in English, an indication of the prestige of the vernacular at this period.[31] A number of the Bodleian manuscripts were intended as gifts to institutional libraries; they present a group differing from, but not unrelated to, the presentation manuscripts noticed amongst the Royal volumes; in both cases the arms presumably were intended to play some part in the impression created by the benefaction or gift.

A search for armigerous manuscripts amongst the copies of major Middle English texts (a group, the Bodleian sample suggests, not wholly unrepresentative) confirms that only for a very small fraction of the books produced does such evidence of original ownership survive.[32] Of the forty-nine copies of Nicholas Love's *Myrrour of the Blessed Lyf of Jesu Christ* three bear the arms of the original owners.[33] Of the sixteen copies of the *Troilus* he records, R.K. Root lists three as bearing arms.[34] Manly and Rickert describe the same number of manuscripts of the *Canterbury Tales* as including arms.[35] Three of the fifty copies of the *Confessio Amantis* bear coats of arms integral with the decoration (San Marino, Huntington MS EL 26 A 17, BL MS Harley 3490 and Oxford, Christ Church MS 148) but Cambridge, St John's College, MS B.12 (34), in which the top of a shield is just visible in the mutilated lower border of fol. 1r, should also be mentioned.[36] Two of the manuscripts of Hoccleve's *Regiment of Princes* bear the original owners' arms, MS Digby 185 with arms associated with the Hopton family, and BL MS Arundel 38, with arms recently identified as belonging to John Mowbray, the second duke of Norfolk (1392–1432).[37] Out of the nineteen copies described by Henry Bergen in his edition of Lydgate's *Troy Book* (EETS, ES, 126), three are recorded as bearing the arms of the original owner, though Professor Alexander would add a fourth, the profusely illustrated Manchester, John Rylands University Library, MS Eng. 1, to the list, judging the arms of Carent on the singleton fol. 173r to be integral with the rest of the illumination.[38] Out of the thirty he describes, Bergen notices two copies of the same poet's *Fall of Princes* bearing the original owners' arms – one of them, Royal 18.D.IV, was Tiptoft's copy.[39]

Unsurprisingly none of the ninety-seven copies of the Main Version or the eighteen copies of the Southern Recension of the *Prick of Conscience*, significantly more modestly and more often locally produced than most of the manuscripts of the other texts discussed, includes the arms of the original owner.[40] The *Piers Plowman* manuscripts bear comparison here; only one copy includes a coat of arms integral with the decoration – Harley 6041, dating not long after 1425 and bearing the arms of the Hoo family of Bedfordshire.[41] Five of the copies of the *Prick of Conscience*, on the other hand, supply evidence of their origin in the form of an identification of a scribe rather than an owner.[42] Although an investigation into the origins of a series of manuscripts seeks to bring into reciprocal relation the evidence for manufacture and ownership, it has to be said that, for the present purpose, the former does not necessarily supply the crucial indication of the direction of the initiative behind production. This drawback does not apply in the case of manuscripts copied by scribes for their own use, manuscripts like the copy of the *Canterbury Tales* written by the Norwich scrivener, Geoffrey Spirleng, and his son, Thomas (work was completed in January 1476/7), or the copy of the *Confessio Amantis* written by Thomas Chetham of Nuthurst in Lancashire (c. 1533–7), or the copy of Hoccleve's *Regiment* written (before 1446) for his own use by William Wilflete, fellow of Clare Hall in Cambridge.[43] In fact the incidence of named scribes in manuscripts typically produced unsystematically seems to be likely to be particularly high; fifteen of the thirty-six manuscripts David Thomson describes as containing Middle English treatises on Latin grammar (usually produced by schoolboys for their own use) contain notices of named scribes.[44]

Of the necesssity for a reciprocal relation to be drawn between production and ownership in future research on the origins of any given group of manuscripts there can be no doubt; Dr Doyle has put the case for the manuscripts of Love's *Myrrour* as follows:

As we increasingly recognize in them more hands of copyists and limners of other manuscripts we may be able to get nearer to discerning the relative roles of the executants and acquirers of such books and what intermediaries and processes lay between them, which, for want of really explicit evidence, is still so mysterious, both the processes whereby a new work was 'libere communicata' and that by which anyone might obtain a copy of something new to him, through what we call the book-trade.[45]

For vernacular texts another factor may be pertinent: the concurrence of the evidence of dialect and that of provenance, even if the latter evidence is quite late, can sometimes provide the sole proof of provincial production.[46] Generally speaking, however, provenance evidence is not 'improvable': it is the lack of the explicit in the evidence, the depth of the mystery in the relation of owner and production, which should probably be blamed for the more or less confirmed tendency to see provenance evidence as capable of amelioration, evidence for ownership or just association transmutable into evidence for commission, any legible (or nearly legible) name entered in a manuscript capable of generating a handsome book-owning affinity, a new and perverse version of fiction and the reading public.

In his essay 'English Books In and Out of Court from Edward III to Henry VII', Dr Doyle poses and answers in these terms a question about the proliferation of uniform, London-produced books written by scribe D of the Trinity R.3.2.(581) *Confessio* and related copyists:

His and related books by other scribes must have been expensive and fashionable enough for the court to have provided the initial demand, but how far did they continue to work chiefly for such circles? Early evidence is sparse: the paucity of armorial insignia is not conclusive, but the ownership of these books later in the century by country gentry and London citizens perhaps means that their forbears were as active in acquiring them as their betters.[47]

With Dr Parkes he had previously made a similar comment on two copies of Gower's English poem:

Fifteenth-century names – of a Bedfordshire gentleman in Oxford, Bodleian Lib., MS Bodley 902 and a London mercer in Oxford, Corpus Christi Coll., MS 67 – if not early enough to be those of the first owners of these books, may be those of their heirs, or be representative of the kinds of persons who were the first owners.[48]

It is doubtful whether a very rigorous (or very conservative) treatment of provenance evidence would allow of such an, apparently reasonable, hypothesis, fashion dictating that a manuscript's descent in time may be coincident with a descent in the social scale.[49] This point is well illustrated by an early fifteenth-century copy of the *Confessio Amantis*, Cambridge, Pembroke College, MS 307, a manuscript with miniatures closely connecting it with Bodley 902 (*SC* 27573), partly in the hand of scribe D. The manuscript bears early sixteenth-century notes of ownership by the goldsmith Sir John Mundy, alderman of London (d. 1537; Mundy also owned the illustrated *Troy Book*, Rylands English 1); it also bears on three occasions the motto 'sur tous autres' and the signature of Jaquette de Luxembourg, the second wife of John, duke of Bedford (see Ill. 16).[50]

II

Although unsystematically produced books, whether copied for a professional[51] or a literary purpose, are not my main theme, any consideration of the demand for manuscripts cannot ignore the fact that, at this period, the owner could be engaged in independent production. It has also to be said that amateur, vernacular letters are not necessarily to be equated with literary

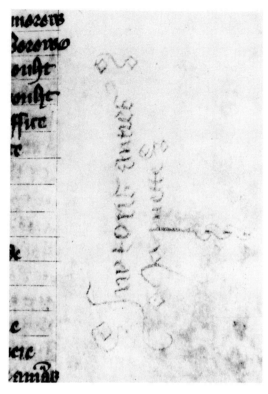

16   Cambridge, Pembroke College, MS 307, John Gower, *Confessio Amantis*, early 15th century, fol. 125r; marginal inscription added by Jaquette de Luxembourg.

backwaters remote from the mainstream of textual transmission[52] and, in another sphere, that the humanist collocation of authorship and the autograph copy probably enhanced the status of the book produced outside the trade, rather than the reverse – the desire for facility in penmanship was, no doubt, promoted by the radical difference of the new script (it would have been a highly visible accomplishment). That ownership was not itself a *sine qua non* for access to books is obvious enough in the case of the resources offered by the institutional libraries; less obvious, as well as much less widespread, was the access provided for the less learned by such intensively used volumes as the Common Profit books, religious texts intended to be passed from hand to hand by successive owners;[53] access by loan generally is hardly quantifiable.

Curt Bühler has asserted:

The trade in books throughout the Middle Ages was largely a second-hand business; only with the invention of printing did a new-book market become commonplace.[54]

Contrasting the 'economy of abundance' establishing itself within the century after the invention of printing, Elizabeth Eisenstein has written of the preceding period:

The production, collection, and circulation of books were subject to an economy of scarcity, and tasks of preservation were naturally of paramount concern.[55]

Granted that one important piece of evidence is missing, evidence of experiment in the rapid multiplication of copies in the period just prior to the invention of printing,[56] it seems next to impossible that the growth in demand which undeniably took place at this time passed unperceived and left no discernible mark on the strategies and practices of those engaged, within this 'economy of scarcity', in the production of manuscripts.

In the years before the invention of printing the issue of the relative importance of the bespoke trade (or the trade in new books generally) and the second-hand trade, coupled with that of the relative value of new and second-hand manuscripts, becomes critical – not least for those observing the market at the time. Source studies always excepted, research tends to be conducted in terms of a manuscript's genesis (emphasising synchronic analysis) and to be confined within the aesthetic 'time capsule' inherent in the concept of 'period', thus making likely an underestimation of the role of earlier manuscripts in the book provision of the late Middle Ages. As a counterbalance, the second-hand trade (the background against which book production itself has to be viewed) is here given precedence.

Taking a broad view first, it is possible that some indication of the sheer numbers of second-hand books available on the market at a given time can be deduced from the policy evolved to establish working collections for the new foundations of Henry VI: in his account of the Cambridge foundation, Munby published a petition from the provosts of Eton and King's asking that men, including Richard Chestre (one of Henry's chaplains) and John Pye ('youre Stacioner of London'), be appointed to search out the necessary books, and that they be given first refusal of all books coming on the market:

The ferste choise of alle suche goodes afore eny other men and in especiall of all maner Bokes ornementes and other necessaries as nowe late were perteyning to the Duke of Gloucestre.[57]

Whether the document was inspired by the difficulty of obtaining the requisite books or by the urgency of obtaining Gloucester's books, it is clear that the inordinate demand on the supply of second-hand manuscripts, occasioned by the establishment of the new libraries, was seen as necessitating a privileged contravention of the normal conduct of the trade.

John Pye (Warden of the Stationers' Company in 1441) was himself part of the established second-hand trade in London, a trade presumably much larger than its provincial counterpart, sustained, like its more specialised equivalent in Oxford and Cambridge, by an assurance of a ready market for the books required for the exercise of, and training in, the learned profes-sions.[58] The comments here on the later medieval life of earlier medieval books are, however, founded not on such contrasts but rather on a sense of the divide between, on the one side, the demands of the professional, academic and clerical book-buying public and, on the other, those of the wider lay public; this is certainly a fundamental distinction but, considering the many finer points of difference existing in this field between categories of reader and between individual texts, it is inevitably a simplification.

In academic circles it was obviously not unusual for books of the twelfth and thirteenth centuries to circulate as current working copies, the enduring traditions of medieval scholarship ensuring the longevity of texts, and the utility of those texts having more consequence to their owners than the age or material aspect of the manuscript containing them.[59] No doubt, in addition, the growth of humanistic studies in fifteenth-century England enhanced the trade in earlier copies of texts otherwise unavailable or rare because outside the traditional curriculum. If the ownership of books like Oxford, Balliol College, MS 183, Bodleian Library, MS Bodley 198 (*SC* 1907), Salisbury Cathedral MS 17 or Victoria and Albert Museum, MS L 2060–1948 by fifteenth-century scholars is in itself well attested,[60] in other cases annotation and, less often, signs of renovation vouch for the continuing or renewed use of a volume. *Olim* Sion College, Arc. L. 40. 2/L. 21, for example, dating from the middle of the twelfth century and containing Suetonius' *De vita Caesarum* with other texts (including Aulus Gellius, genealogies of the Frankish and Capetian kings and of Lothair, as well as Einhard's *Vita Karoli Magni*), bears the annotations of John Gunthorp (he bought it from the Dominican Convent in Northampton). Oxford, Corpus Christi College, MS 82, produced in France in the twelfth century and containing, amongst other texts, Quintus Curtius' *De gestis Alexandri Magni*, Caesar's *De bello gallico* and Paulus Diaconus' *Historia Langobardum*, has a table of contents by John Tiptoft on the front pastedown and annotations in his hand elsewhere. From a different milieu, Oxford, Magdalen College, Cod. Lat. 15, a twelfth-century Horace, includes, in a single fifteenth-century hand, verses on John Seward the London schoolmaster (d. before 14 January 1436), and, scattered throughout the manuscript, notes on metre.[61] The gift or bequest of an earlier manuscript to an institutional library may also provide some assurance of its status as a working copy;[62] Edward IV's gift of MS Bodley 192 (*SC* 2099), a mid-twelfth-century copy of Gregory's *Homilies*, and MS Bodley 729 (*SC* 2706), a late twelfth-century copy of Bede and Rabanus, to the collegiate library of St George's at Windsor, whatever the king's own level of interest in the books, presupposes a confidence in their continued utility elsewhere.[63] Occasionally earlier material is even incorporated in a fifteenth-century volume: Bodleian MS Digby 98 (*SC* 1699) is a composite collection of scientific and mathematical texts, dating from the late twelfth to the early fifteenth centuries, assembled

and partly written in Oxford by Peter Partriche, Chancellor of Lincoln
(d. 1451): in his commonplace book, Dublin, Trinity College, 516, itself
compiled during the 1460s and early 1470s, John Benet, vicar of Harlington
in Bedfordshire, incorporated not only a somewhat earlier copy of John of
Legnano's *De bello* (fols. 76–107) but also (fols. 208–19) an historical collection datable, on the evidence of a list of archbishops of York it contains, to the
early fourteenth century.[64]

The will of the Kingsman William Warmystre, recorded in the *Ledger Book*
of the college under the date 13 October 1457, neatly evokes the certainty of
demand in academic circles; Munby notes that:

He left to the College text-books of Aristotle's logic and natural philosophy, for
distribution, *so long as they lasted*, to the Fellows and Scholars.[65]

Whilst it is easy to imagine circumstances (like dearth) in which *any* manuscript would be at a premium, demand amongst the wider lay public is
probably correctly characterised as more variable and uncertain; it is also,
because more unpredictable, more difficult to analyse (there is no curriculum
to act as a guide).

The niche occupied in the market place by such early fourteenth-century
French vernacular manuscripts as BL Royal 15.D.II, 14.E.III and the
Provençal manuscript, 19.C.I[66] (all with lavish illustrations guaranteeing
against desuetude and destruction, whatever favour their texts might find), or
by the much plainer Harley 273[67] (a composite volume of the thirteenth and
fourteenth centuries) or CUL Add. 7071, is far from clear. All imply the
interest of fifteenth-century readers, be the evidence confined to the addition
of names or of a more conclusive nature, as in the case of the Arthurian
romance manuscripts, Royal 14.E.III with its table of contents possibly in the
hand of Sir Richard Roos (d. 1481), and the Cambridge manuscript with its
programme of renovation (including replacement leaves) undertaken at the
end of the century.[68]

For volumes prized as 'joyaux', the state of the market is more certain and
the connotations of the term 'second-hand' less than appropriate; the small
minority of manuscripts likely to have received contemporary and continuing
recognition as artefacts of exceptional aesthetic character were probably
capable of retaining something of their original status despite changes in
fashion. Manchester, Rylands Latin 22, for instance, a French Psalter
brought to England by Joan of Navarre when she married Henry IV, dates
from c. 1220–30.[69] The sixteenth-century note on fol. 84 of Queen Mary's
Psalter (Royal 2.B.VII) evidences the kind of attitude inspired by such
manuscripts; the note, which probably refers to Thomas Manners, Lord
Roos, the first earl of Rutland of that name (cr. 1525, d. 1543), reads:

This boke was sume tyme the Erle of Rutelands, and it was his wil that it shulde by
successioun all way go to the lande of Ruteland or to him that linyally succedis by
reson of inheritaunce to the seide lande.[70]

The *chefs d'œuvre* of manuscript production might themselves be called on to function as instruments of diplomacy; their ability to cross geographical as well as chronological barriers is something of a characteristic – the repeated voyages over the Channel of the Belleville Breviary (Paris, Bibliothèque Nationale, MS f. fr. 10483–4)[71] come to mind, or the itinerary of the Peterborough Psalter (Brussels, Bibliothèque Royale, 9961–2).[72] Presented in 1318 to the papal nuncio, Cardinal Guescelin d'Euse, by Godfrey of Crowland (abbot of Peterborough), the manuscript appears in the French royal inventories of 1374 and 1411 and the Burgundian inventory of 1467.

The ascription of an antiquarian motive to the conservation of the finest illuminated manuscripts is shown to be dubious by those deluxe volumes containing two programmes of work widely separated in date. (Such manuscripts are in some sense analogous to Digby 98 and Trinity Dublin 516, just discussed.) The psalter begun for the St Omer family of Mulbarton in Norfolk c. 1330 is a case in point – it was then left unfinished but was completed with a fifteenth-century programme of illumination, a programme Margaret Rickert suggested was commissioned by Humphrey, duke of Gloucester, who owned the manuscript at this period. (Among manuscripts of early date in the duke's library were the late twelfth-century bestiary, formerly Sion College Arc. L. 40. 2/L. 28, Matthew Paris' *Historia Anglorum*, Royal 14.C.vii and the exotic curiosity Leiden, Bibliothek der Rijksuniversiteit, Scal. Hebr. 8 (Or. 4725) a mid-twelfth-century Hebrew psalter.)[73] Bodley 264 (*SC* 2462), *Li romans du boin roi Alixandre*, could also be cited; produced in Flanders 1338–44, it contains English metropolitan additions of c. 1400, partly illuminated by Johannes and his school – besides the *Livres du Graunt Chaam* and the extract from the English verse *Alexander and Dindimus* (supplying incidents, as M.R. James noted, not treated in the French text), the additions include, at fol. 2, a replacement frontispiece for the original romance. The manuscript has been identified with one of the volumes in the inventory drawn up after the death in 1397 of Thomas of Woodstock; at the time the additions were commissioned it has to be supposed that it was in the hands of someone, perhaps responsive to the quality of the original, certainly with access to the best metropolitan work of the period; but, by 1466, the book was on the open market, for it was bought in London on New Year's Day by Richard Woodville, first Earl Rivers (d. 1469).[74]

A certain pressure in demand is above all to be expected in the case of service books. This view is endorsed by a number of cases in which fifteenth-century programmes of adaptation and addition are introduced to ensure, through textual and material renovation, the earlier books' sufficiency for later medieval purposes. In her account of the Madresfield Hours, Janet Backhouse stresses that the manuscript was in use from the time it was copied (probably in the third decade of the fourteenth century) until the second half of the sixteenth century; to meet the requirements of an owner, the manu-

17 Cambridge, Trinity College, MS O.4.16 (1247), Psalter, fol. viii verso, mid-15th-century addition to a late 13th-century psalter.

script was adapted at the end of the fourteenth century from its original York Use to that of Sarum; a third professional programme of work, this time of the fifteenth century, is to be found in the Office of the Dead and Commendation of Souls, occupying fols. 123–83. The first identifiable owner, on the evidence of arms added soon after the completion of the manuscript and the mention in the prayers on fols. 94v–95r of 'famula tua matilda', was Maud de Tilliol (d. 1343); in the sixteenth century the manuscript was owned and still used by the family of Ambrose Dauntsey (d. 1555) of West Lavington in Wiltshire.[75] Cambridge, Trinity College, MS O.4.16 (1247), a late thirteenth-century psalter (c. 1300 ?) with twelve fine miniatures at fols. 113v–114r surviving from a larger programme, besides having many historiated initials cut from a thirteenth-century Bible and pasted into its margins, has a number of fifteenth-century additions; fol. 167 is a replacement leaf supplying a deficiency at the end of the litany occurring at fols. 162v–167v; the litany of the Virgin is added at fols. 178r–179v; after the Calendar a bifolium (fols. viii–ix), containing the response 'Regnauit dominus', has been inserted – on fol. viii verso, within a border, framed in gold and under an architectural canopy, appears a miniature showing a man kneeling in prayer, identified in the inscription running round the canopy as 'wyllyam . clarkson ferrar of london' (see Ill. 17).[76] Evidence of continuous use is also provided by the Calendar; obits dating from 1311–40 have been systematically erased, eradicating signs of the manuscript's previous associations (on fol. iii recto the early fourteenth-century obit of 'Margareta. de. ferrar.' survives); fifteenth- and sixteenth-century hands supply the names of additional saints (the sixteenth-century addition on fols. iii verso and vii recto of the deposition and translation of St Erkenwald suggests the manuscript's continued presence in the capital). MS B.11.3 (242) in the same library presents a comparable case; a missal of the second half of the fourteenth century, obits entered in the Calendar evidence its continued use by the Leventhorpe family through the fifteenth century; this evidence is endorsed by a late fifteenth-century programme of work, comprising a replacement leaf (fol. 36) and an additional sequence of masses (fols. 308va–314va).[77]

Belated programmes of embellishment, addition, modification or, at the opposite extreme, incorporation suggest a dynamism fitting uneasily into the constraints of 'period'. Requiring an interpretation of use as well as a study of production, they highlight not just the length of time a medieval manuscript might remain in circulation as a serviceable copy but also promote a perception of a medieval view in which the quality of contemporaneity in a book might actually be protracted, a view special to the era before printing and particularly remote from any sense of the book as an expendable commodity. Eisenstein's emphasis on 'tasks of preservation' as paramount in the period prior to the invention of printing is not misplaced, but neither has it the stature of a generalisation equally applicable to all categories of books.

In the fifteenth century a more 'democratic' element might be said to enter book patronage: the commissions lying behind the *opus* of the illuminator, William Abell, or the vogue scribe, Ricardus Franciscus, seem to be drawn from a much wider social spectrum than would previously have been expected.[78] As attention will be confined here to royal patronage, an area, arguably, quite remote from the broader changes taking place in the production and marketing of books at this time, it is the more important to acknowledge that, although the term 'patron' remains useful, particularly in referring to the bespoke trade where terms like 'client' and 'customer' might blur important distinctions, some modification of the very concepts of protection and deference embodied in patronage is usually needed when dealing with books produced at the end of the Middle Ages.

It is doubtful whether, even with royal patrons (patrons whose ability to manipulate the resources of book production seems undeniable, if not always unrivalled), there was, during this period, a simple linear development towards an increased 'bookishness'. Thus the emphasis that Gordon Kipling has created by placing Henry VII (largely because of his institutionalising of the royal library, his appointment of a royal librarian, his creation of the office of King's Printer) at the end of such a line of development may turn out to be misleading, disguising the personal and varying element in the individual's success in fulfilling the dynastic imperative towards patronage.[79] Rather than a survey of royal commissions,[80] the intention here is to present a modification of this and a related view put forward by Denys Hay in his comparative study 'History and Historians in France and England during the Fifteenth Century', where official historiography (a crucial area of royal patronage) is judged to emerge in England only with the Tudors.[81]

It might be noted first that there is, in Henry VII's reputation as an initiator of manuscript commissions, something of the equivocal: in most of the manuscripts in the present Royal collection bearing Henry's arms, the heraldic insignia are not integral with the original illumination; three of the remaining manuscripts (19.C.VI, 19.C.VIII and 20.E.I–VI) were presentation copies or gifts.[82] The king is usually associated with the lavish programme of Flemish work in Cambridge, Fitzwilliam Museum MS 57, upgrading and updating the original English *horae*; another Book of Hours, Vienna, Österreichische Nationalbibliothek Cod. 1840, combining work of the 'Bedford trend' and Maître François, may be a similar case, patronage again becoming a matter of intervention rather than origination.[83] The second programme in the Fitzwilliam manuscript includes new sections of prayers and *memoriae*,[84] as well as new borders inserted in the earlier English work.[85] It is possible that the programme was not undertaken to meet the requirements of the king himself – several prayers at the beginning of the volume suggest a female owner; the prayer to the Trinity on fol. 9r, for instance, includes the words 'ego ancilla tua te supplex adoro. te laudo. te laudo. te glorifico. te benedico.', that on fol. 7r–v, the words 'mihi peccatrici'. A connection with Elizabeth of York may be implied by the appearance on fol. 31v of a union rose within the initial introducing a prayer to St Elizabeth.[86]

Of the fabric of the late medieval, non-institutional libraries, royal or otherwise, only glimpses remain, brief views, say, of the study constructed for Henry IV at Eltham or (a century later) the Percy libraries at Leconfield and Wressle Castle.[87] Rather more is known about the personnel involved in running the royal collections; several names of custodians of the king's books are recorded well before the appointment of Quentin Poulet – Professor Alexander (though apparently in error) even mentions one Ralph Dunion, Keeper of the King's Wardrobe, as 'custos librorum' to Henry III. Ralph Bradfelde is recorded as keeper of Henry IV's books; John Burnham, one of Henry V's yeomen of the chamber, served that king in the same capacity; according to the *Liber Niger*, one of Edward IV's yeomen of the crown would have been appointed 'to kepe the kinges bookes'.[88] It is probably not the case that Henry VII created a completely new institution but rather that the earlier administration of the royal collections, subsumed as it was into the organisation of the Chamber, the Wardrobe and the Exchequer, is imperfectly understood. That earlier administration is seen in operation in documents like the roll of issues and receipts of the privy wardrobe at the Tower (1322–41), demonstrating the existence of a royal library there of some 160 volumes, the memoranda roll of the time of Richard II, recording eleven books in the custody of the Exchequer (the earlier appearance of a proportion of them in the inventory of 1358, drawn up on the death of Queen Isabella, suggests a certain continuity in the collection), or Henry VI's privy seal warrant of 10 June 1440, directing that twenty-seven volumes of philosophy, theology, canon and civil law be sent from the Exchequer to the newly founded college of All Souls in Oxford.[89]

Although texts furthering current policy were clearly initiated or sponsored by those in authority, the actual manipulation of production for that most obvious purpose, royal propaganda, seems to have been relatively restricted in its use, not so much a trend as a response to crisis. The innovative (and isolated) Yorkist exploitation of official chronicles was prompted directly by the events following Warwick's rebellion of 1469.[90] Unlike the chronicles, the elaborate genealogical rolls which proliferated particularly in the reign of Henry VI (in response to what Professor Anglo has called 'the uncertainties engendered by the rivalry of Henry VI, Richard, duke of York, and Edward IV')[91] were not a Yorkist innovation. Their inherently propagandist nature is, however, clear enough (they trace the venerable ancestry of the reigning monarch back to Creation); equally clear is the Yorkist bias of some of the texts from Edward IV's reign. Dr Alison Allan has concluded that royal initiative may have been behind both the production of multiple, uniform copies and their updating as the king's family increased.[92] This view is supported by the affinities in text, script, layout or ornamentation (or all four) which have been judged to imply that the biblical pedigrees of the second half of the century were the speciality of a single workshop based in London or Westminster.[93] Given the expense of producing simultaneously multiple, near identical copies of such an elaborate, frequently illustrated text, the pedigree rolls seem likely to have been part of a concerted propaganda programme, their distribution never designed to be indiscriminate in the manner of broadsheet propaganda, but their relative number, uniformity and continuity of production supplying evidence of the importance attached to the justificatory role they were intended to play; the manipulation of production to justify Henry VI's removal and buttress the permanent establishment of a (legitimate) Yorkist dynasty seems to supply, in this period, exceptional evidence for the creation, within the sphere of commercial book production, of 'official channels' for the publication of the views of, and propagation of loyalty towards, the ruling house.

Finally it is appropriate that attention (like that of the last medieval kings) should be directed towards books produced abroad, a group providing a focus on the owner's role in book production suitably sharp to serve as a conclusion. While cultural internationalism might reasonably be judged no less than a characteristic of the medieval period, the import of books (granted a certain stimulus in the demand for rare texts created by the growing interest in humanism in the fifteenth century) seems to have been conducted by individuals through personal contacts,[94] until, that is, the advent of printing, necessarily bringing with it a revolution in marketing practice, created a commercially organised, internationally based, wholesale book trade.[95]

Manuscript imports may be seen as reflecting an individual's career or métier, a particular mission or itinerary, or, as Elizabeth Salter put it in a slightly different context, charting 'the errands of war and peace' of the English nobility.[96] (It is not unhelpful to view even the book acquisitions of John, duke of Bedford, Edward IV or William, Lord Hastings,[97] in some such light.) The collection formed by Tiptoft during (and after) his travels in Italy between 1458 and 1461 is a case in point. Sir Roger Mynors, from William Gray's extant books, was able to map out his career both in England and abroad, in Germany and Italy.[98]

Royal 15.E.VI, Talbot's gift to Margaret of Anjou, constitutes a record, rather than just a reflection, of his diplomatic activity in the years 1444–5, activity culminating in the marriage of Henry VI and Margaret at Titchfield Abbey.[99] Further, the Talbot and the Beauchamp Hours (Cambridge, Fitzwilliam Museum, MSS 40–1950 and 41–1950), companion volumes made in France (perhaps at Rouen), in all likelihood for the occasion of Talbot's own marriage with Margaret Beauchamp (6 September 1425), can be associated with a group of French manuscripts produced for patrons among the English occupying forces.[100] New York, Pierpont Morgan

Library, MS M105 (the 'Kildare' Hours), for instance, was illustrated by the Fastolf Master in Rouen c. 1420–5 for Sir William Porter, who had taken part in the siege of the city and was present there intermittently down to 1431.[101] Rather later (c. 1444) is another Book of Hours of Sarum Use, Dublin, Royal Irish Academy, 12.R.31, made in Rouen for Sir Thomas Hoo (later Lord Hoo, he was Chancellor of France and Normandy).[102] Copies of the same text, Victoria and Albert MS Reid 7 and BL Harley 1251 (again illustrated by the Fastolf Master, an artist whose fortunes seem to have followed the English withdrawal from France), are in some sort *memoriae* of the occupation: the former has added to the Calendar notice of the wounding at Orléans on 23 October 1428 of Thomas Montagu, earl of Salisbury, and of his subsequent death on 3 November; in Harley 1251 the obit of the duke of Bedford appears as a contemporary addition to the Calendar (fol. 12v: the duke's badge in the left margin is probably an addition made after the main work on the folio was completed); the miniature preceding the Vigil of the Dead (fol. 148r) in the same manuscript becomes a representation of Bedford's funeral obsequies – his arms appear on the hatchment and again on four shields.[103] A more isolated example of the same process (manuscript commissions traceable to the patron's military, political or, indeed, increasingly at this period, commercial duties abroad) is the copy of *l'Enseignement de Vraie Noblesse*, now Geneva, Bibliothèque Publique et Universitaire, fr. 166, illuminated by Guillaume Vrelant, a Utrecht artist active in Bruges from 1454. The text completed, according to an explicit, on 4 September 1464, the manuscript includes in the base of the border on fol. 3r the arms of Warwick, 'the Kingmaker'; despite wayward dating of the incident to 1469, Aubert was probably right to trace the origins of the commission back to Nevill's involvement in negotiations with Burgundy – unless, of course, it is just to be associated with his captaincy of Calais.[104]

Any argument that manuscript imports were more than a reflection of personal contacts relies on the evidence of the significantly large number of books produced in the Low Countries for the English market – some two hundred Books of Hours made for the English and Scottish markets are extant.[105] Distinguishing between commissioned and speculative work may present some difficulties, but the characteristics discovered in many of the Low Countries books at the end of the Middle Ages, the routine nature of their manufacture, their standard texts, their use of single-leaf miniatures, indicate preparation in advance inspired by confidence in a general market – James Farquhar has commented, 'single-leaf miniatures were by-products of a book-trade rapidly expanding its markets'.[106] Though they may include material specified by the client, it seems clear that such differentiation might occur late in the process of manufacture, the manuscripts produced being like Philadelphia Free Library, MS Widener 3, made in Bruges for John Brown the younger, merchant of Stamford (d. 1476), merely enlarged versions of standard *horae*,[107] or like the De Grey Hours (NLW MS 15537C) in which the material specified by the client is codicologically distinct.[108] Mass production all too obviously lies behind such errors of assembly as appear in the Hours of c. 1500 formerly belonging to St Mary's Episcopal Cathedral in Edinburgh (now in the National Library of Scotland), a manuscript which combines a calendar suitable for north-eastern France with a Sarum text.[109]

The earliest known record of the import of an actual consignment of printed books remains a London customs return for 30 December 1477,[110] but there has recently been some challenge to the accepted view that (much like imported manuscripts) they first arrived singly, 'purchased abroad by English diplomats or sent as gifts to English notabilities' – the earliest instances cited in this case being the purchases made by James Goldwell whilst on embassy in Hamburg in September–October 1465 and by John Russell whilst acting as envoy in Bruges in April 1467.[111] On the evidence of BL IC 56a, a single leaf from the first printed book, the 42-line Bible (formerly bound in a collection of fragments, Sloane 1044), and Lambeth 'MS' 15, a 42-line New Testament, both with (related) English illumination, Ebehard König has conjectured that the commercial importation of consignments of printed books into England for resale can be placed as early as the 1450s.[112] It is the presence of English illumination which leads König to believe that the books were sold in England 'not long after they left the printing house':[113] he suggests that the coincidence of the survival of two copies of English provenance with similar English decoration (Lambeth is the more lavishly decorated) militates against an interpretation which would see the importation of the books as a matter of independent, individual initiative.

Continental presses were beforehand in producing books especially for the English market – the Sarum Breviary (*STC* 15794) is thought to have been printed in the Southern Netherlands c. 1475; by the closing decades of the century English book owners could expect their printed copies of standard works of Latin scholarship, like their printed service books, to come (or, as it must have appeared, to flood in) from abroad, English printing, meanwhile, developing what Dr Lotte Hellinga has called its 'unique national and almost chauvinistic character'.[114] Some inferences about the early printers' perception of their potential mass market can perhaps be drawn from the congruence of the, generally speaking, conservative, firmly unimaginative publishing policy of those same printers with the requirements of both the bookseller holding stock (whether new or second-hand) for retail sale[115] and the stationer involved in the speculative production of manuscripts: all need, if in varying degrees, the assurance of depth or continuity in demand and are likely, in some measure, to exclude (if such a term can be used of the medieval period) the 'avant garde' and the 'recherché'.

The production of multiple copies of the genealogical rolls and the speculative production of *horae* of English Use in the Low Countries have already been mentioned. Other groups of texts are increasingly being noticed by commentators in this connection – copies of the *Nova Statuta*, and, among vernacular English texts, copies of the *Confessio Amantis*, *Troy Book*, *Dicts and Sayings of the Philosophers*, the *Myrrour of the Blessed Lyf of Jesu Christ* and the *Brut*, as well as a number of the manuscripts copied by the Edmund–Fremund scribe.[116] Because the standardisation of layout and decoration frequently noticed in fifteenth-century manuscripts may reasonably be interpreted merely as the means employed by the supervisors of commercial, metropolitan book production to expedite the fulfilment of single commissions, alone (that is, without the textual confirmation that a workshop was either retaining an exemplar to serve as a basis for future copies, or producing at once from a single exemplar several copies for future sale) such standardisation cannot offer proof positive of a new capital-intensive organisation of manuscript production.[117] The occurrence of voids for arms in otherwise completed books, the blanks left for the later insertion of the coats of prospective clients, has, however, been suggested as further evidence of such new organisation.[118]

Although areas of dispute have arisen (for instance as to the level of production to be expected in manuscripts produced as a speculative venture),[119] the consensus seems to be that the new pattern of organisation was established by the 1450s or 1460s.[120] It seems likely that, even before the invention of printing the patron was abdicating his role in 'the sociology of the text',[121] losing his direct influence on the form in which a text is mediated to the reader (form having the potential at once to define as well as to reflect readership); aesthetic initiative, itself closely linked with economic initiative, and decisive in matters of book design and *mise-en-page*, with, in increased measure, intellectual initiative, was beginning to move elsewhere – to the protagonists of the book trade, even (in time and to some extent) to the author, a figure accustomed to see the book, perhaps especially (if ironically) the presentation manuscript, as an object to be created, to a degree now difficult to envisage, in the patron's image.

NOTES

1 The sheer quantity of the evidence is well attested by Susan Hagen Cavanaugh's 'A Study of Books Privately Owned in England 1300–1450' (University of Pennsylvania Ph.D. 1980; Ann Arbor, Univ. Microfilms, 1981; to be published by Boydell & Brewer as Manuscript Studies 4), an index of book owners based on printed sources only which still has to stop short in the mid-fifteenth century, the increasing richness in the evidence coinciding with an abatement in the price of books. For a bibliography, see P.J. Lucas 'The Growth and Development of English Literary Patronage in the Later Middle Ages and Early Renaissance', *The Library*, 6th series, 4 (1982), 219–48; to this add S.G. Bell 'Medieval Women Book Owners: Arbiters of Lay Piety and Ambassadors of Culture', *Signs, Journal of Women in Culture and Society*, 7 (4) (1982), 741–68; C.H. Clough (ed.), *Profession,*

Vocation and Culture in Later Medieval England: Essays dedicated to the memory of A.R. Myers (Liverpool, 1982); J.T. Rosenthal, 'Aristocratic Cultural Patronage and Book Bequests, 1350–1500', *BJRL*, 64 (1982), 522–48; J. Vale, *Edward III and Chivalry: Chivalric Society and its Context 1270–1350* (Woodbridge, 1982); Scattergood and Sherborne, *passim*.

2 'Books Mentioned in Wills', *Transactions of the Bibliographical Society*, 7 (1902–4), 99.

3 Deanesly ('Vernacular Books') studied roughly 7,600 printed medieval wills.

4 *Ibid.*, p. 349. See also the same author's *The Lollard Bible and other Medieval Biblical Versions* (Cambridge, 1920), pp. 391–8. For further studies of book ownership based on significant samples of wills see S.L. Thrupp, *The Merchant Class of Medieval London (1300–1500)* (Ann Arbor, 1962; first published 1948), ch. 4 (Thrupp notes that about 20 per cent of fifteenth-century wills of personal property include notices of books); M.G.A. Vale *Piety, Charity and Literacy among the Yorkshire Gentry 1370–1480*, Borthwick Paper 50 (York, 1976) (a sample of 148 wills is used); Rosenthal, 'Aristocratic Cultural Patronage' (the sample is made up of the 165 extant wills of 435 peers summoned to parliament between 1350 and 1500, with the 86 surviving wills of their wives); J.I. Kermode 'The Merchants of Three Northern English Towns', in *Profession, Vocation and Culture*, ed. Clough, pp. 7–48 (a study of York, Hull and Beverley c. 1390–1500, involving 320 wills); R.G. Davies 'The Episcopate', *ibid.*, pp. 51–89 (using 64 episcopal wills dating from 1375–1461).

5 For Chaworth's will see Borthwick Institute, York, Reg. 20, fols. 274v–277v, *Testamenta Eboracensia*, ed. J. Raine, part 2, Surtees Society 30 (1855), pp. 220–9. See further Manly and Rickert I, pp. 609–10, and Thorlac Turville-Petre 'Some Medieval English Manuscripts in the North-East Midlands', in Pearsall, *Manuscripts and Readers*, pp. 132–3 (for the *Troy Book* and the Antiphonal see pls. 1–2). The description of the manuscript Chaworth left to Robert Clifton as 'a *newe* Boke of Inglisse' presents an exceptional case, to be related specifically to Chaworth's extant commissions. Fox's will survives in the Stoneham Register of wills proved in the Archdeaconry Court of St Albans: Hertford County Record Office, 1 AR fol. 70v. See G.R. Owst 'Some Books and Book-Owners of Fifteenth-Century St. Albans. A Further Study of the Stoneham Register', *St Albans and Hertfordshire Architectural and Archaeological Society Transactions* (1928), 178–88, and J.J. Griffiths, K.D. Harris and D. Pearsall, *A Descriptive Catalogue of the Manuscripts of the Works of John Gower* (forthcoming). That the manuscripts are partly in Fox's hand sheds light on the number of loose quires he mentions, particularly on a 'work in progress' – 'a boke þ' is in quayers .xxv. for þe more parte wryte redy'.

6 See Cavanaugh, 'Study of Books', pp. 10–11, noting that half the books mentioned in the 8,000 printed wills she studied were liturgical or devotional volumes. For such bequests see e.g. the wills of John de Upton, canon of Wells (Plomer, 'Books Mentioned in Wills', p. 114), John Wodecrofe, vicar of Banstead, Surrey (1465, *ibid.*, p. 117) or John Carpenter, town clerk of London (8 March 1441, pr. 12 May 1442: Thomas Brewer, *Memoir of the Life and Times of John Carpenter* (London, 1856), pp. 133–4); see also Oxford, Bodleian Library, MS Douce 372, fol. 163vb for a similar bequest of the *Gilte Legende* by John Burton, citizen and mercer of London, made in 1460.

7 See the bequest made by William Bathcom, vicar of Trinity Church, Cambridge, to Magister Edward Shuldham (pr. 12 October 1487, Plomer, 'Books Mentioned

in Wills', p. 117; the will is notable but not exceptional in that the books concerned are entailed) or the elaborate provisions made for his common and civil law books by John Newton, Treasurer of York, in a codicil to his will of 4 May 1414 (pr. 13 June, *Testamenta Eboracensia*, ed. J. Raine, part 1, Surtees Society 4 (1836), pp. 368–9).

8 A.N.L. Munby, 'Notes on King's College Library in the Fifteenth Century', *TCBS*, 1 (1951), p. 286.

9 Thomas Rymer, *Foedera*, 1740, IX, p. 132b; in the reprint (Farnborough, 1967) the will appears IV, pp. 131–4.

10 R.H. Bartle 'A Study of Private Book Collections in England Between ca. 1200 and the Early Years of the Sixteenth Century with Special Reference to Books Belonging to Ecclesiastical Dignitaries', Oxford, B.Litt., 1956, p. iv, and cf. p. 115: though the writer draws on all available sources, not just wills, he repeatedly remarks on the difficulty of matching an apparently standard collection of books with the testator's known field of interest. Elizabeth Armstrong sees a likeness between the diversity (as opposed to a medical orientation) of the surviving books of John Argentine (d. 1508, Provost of King's, physician and dean of chapel to Prince Arthur) and those customarily selected for presentation to a learned institution ('English Purchases of Printed Books from the Continent 1465–1526', *EHR*, 94 (1979), 284). For the argument that Humphrey, duke of Gloucester, may have acquired some of his collection of texts from Italy with Oxford University in mind see Albinia de la Mare's foreword to A. Sammut, *Unfredo Duca di Gloucester e gli Umanisti Italiani* (Padua, 1980), Medioevo e Umanesimo 41, p. xiii. On Humphrey's activities, see further Ch. 9 below, p. 204.

11 John Nichols (ed.), *A Collection of All the Wills Now Known to be Extant of the Kings and Queens of England* (London, 1780), p. 158 (the will is dated 3 February 1397; Beaufort was translated to Winchester in 1404).

12 Lambeth Palace, MS Arundel, fols. 163r–164r; Nichols, *Collection*, pp. 177–86 (for the quotation see p. 183). Compare the opening of Richard Fox's book bequests 'I bequeth to Iohan my sone goddes blessyng ȝ myn ȝ my lytell primer heled wᵗ rede leder.'

13 *Testamenta Eboracensia*, part 1, p. 311 (for the breviary see also the inventory attached to the will, *ibid.*, p. 319). Compare e.g. the will of John Depden of Healaugh, Yorkshire (Borthwick Institute, Prob. Reg. 3 fols. 88v–89v, 20 August 1402) where the missal he leaves to his parish church is described as the book 'quo utor cotidie in Capella mea'.

14 These limitations do not pertain in later periods: see, for instance, A. Labarre's influential *Le Livre dans la vie Amiénoise du seizième siècle: l'enseignement des inventaires après décès 1503–1576* (Paris and Louvain, 1971), Publications de la Faculté des Lettres et Sciences Humaines de Paris Sorbonne, Série Recherches 66, based on about 4,500 inventories, and P. Clark, 'The Ownership of Books in England, 1560–1640: The Example of some Kentish Townsfolk', in Lawrence Stone (ed.), *Society and Schooling: Studies in the History of Education* (London, 1976), pp. 96–111), based on 2,771 inventories of personal wealth drawn up after the owner's death by appraisers in Canterbury, Faversham and Maidstone.

15 References to the inventories (not all with valuations) of the forfeited goods of the condemned traitors Sir Simon Burley (tutor to Richard II; executed 1388),

Thomas of Woodstock (murdered 1397) and Henry, Lord Scrope of Masham (see above, pp. 164–5), with notice of the inventories of Leo, Lord Welles (drawn up in 1430) and that of John Holland, duke of Exeter (d. 5 August 1447), the inventory of Sir John Fastolf's books 'In the stewe hous' at Caister (1448; Oxford, Magdalen College, Fastolf Papers 43 fol. 11r) and of the two inventories of Sir Thomas Charlton (Speaker of the House of Commons; d. 1465) are collected together in K.B. MacFarlane's *The Nobility of Later Medieval England* (Oxford, 1980 (first published 1973), pp. 237–8). For the Burley inventory and that of the priest, William de Walcote (his goods were confiscated because of debt, 1358) see V.J. Scattergood, 'Two Medieval Book Lists', *The Library*, 5th series, 23 (1968), 236–9. See further e.g. the inventory of Alice de la Pole's goods arriving at Ewelme from Wingfield on 10 September 1466 (HMC Eighth Report Appendix (London, 1881), pp. 628–9); Bodleian Library, Ewelme Muniments VII A 47), the 'Inventory off Englysshe bokis' of Sir John Paston II (d. 15 November 1479; *Paston Letters and Papers*, ed. N. Davis, I (Oxford, 1971), pp. 516–18), the inventory of the goods of Sir Thomas Urswick (Recorder of London, d. 19 March 1479: PRO E 154/2/2; F.W. Steer, 'A Medieval Household: the Urswick Inventory', *The Essex Review*, 63 (1954), 12), and, less well known, the inventory of the widow, Elizabeth Sywardby (1468: *Testamenta Eboracensia*, ed. J. Raine, part 3, Surtees Society 45 (1865), p. 163). Jenny Stratford is currently editing three inventories drawn up by the executors of John, duke of Bedford, 1444–9.

16 *Medieval Libraries*, p. xi: Ker went on to consider (pp. xi–xv) the factors affecting the survival of manuscripts from monastic, cathedral, collegiate and other institutional libraries after the Dissolution, concentrating on the patterns of acquisition of the royal library and of local collectors.

17 *IMEV*, Appendix v, pp. 737–9; and *Supplement*, Appendix D, pp. 521–4.

18 D.A. Pearsall, 'The Alliterative Revival: Origins and Social Backgrounds', in D.L. Lawton (ed.), *Middle English Alliterative Poetry and its Literary Background* (Woodbridge, 1982), p. 44.

19 Doyle, 'The Manuscripts', p. 88.

20 *Printing, Selling and Reading* (Wiesbaden, 1967), p. 11.

21 See further below, p. 174.

22 Such depredations do not necessarily eradicate all evidence of the manuscript's existence; see e.g. M. Rickert, *The Reconstructed Carmelite Missal* (London, 1952). For the practice of dividing manuscripts for the sake of illuminations see A.N.L. Munby, *Connoisseurs and Medieval Miniatures 1750–1850* (Oxford, 1972), pp. 31–2, 65–8, 160, the Sotheby's sale of single leaves and miniatures 25 April 1983 (with introduction noting the fifteenth-century practice of re-using Romanesque miniatures; see below, p. 177, and J.S. Dearden 'John Ruskin the Collector', *The Library*, 5th series, 21 (1966), 127, 134–6, 145, 146, and especially pl. IX, with the letters to *The Times* from Dearden and Sydney Cockerell, 7 and 22 March 1962.

23 *Manuscrits des traductions françaises d'oeuvres de Boccace XVe siècle* (Padua, 1973), Medioevo e Umanesimo 15, pp. 39–40.

24 V.J. Scattergood, 'Literary Culture at the Court of Richard II' in Scattergood and Sherborne, p. 36 (for new books in wills see above, p. 164 and n. 5).

25 The inclusion of date and place of publication perhaps supports this argument. A sanguine account of the uses of provenance study applied to incunables is given in

I.R. Willison's 'The Treatment of Notes of Provenance and Marginalia in the "Catalogue of Books printed in the XVth century now in the British Museum"', in L. Hellinga and H. Hartel (eds.), *Book and Text in the Fifteenth Century. Proceedings of a Conference held in the Herzog August Bibliothek Wolfenbuttel March 1–3 1978* (Hamburg, 1981), pp. 167–77 (especially pp. 171–2: see also Dr Hellinga's introduction, p. 16).

26 For some qualification of this point, see below, p. 183.

27 Warner and Gilson; Pächt and Alexander. For a related survey, based on Leroquais' descriptions of late medieval French missals, see C. de Hamel, *A History of Illuminated Manuscripts* (Oxford, 1986), pp. 191–2.

28 A further half-dozen of the manuscripts originated in France.

29 The manuscripts include Royal 15.E.VI, presented to Margaret of Anjou, probably on her marriage in 1445, by John Talbot, earl of Shrewsbury (Warner and Gilson, II, pp. 177–9); Royal 20.E.I–VI, the *Chroniques de France* given to Henry VII in 1487 by Sir Thomas Thwaytes, Treasurer of Calais (Warner and Gilson, II, pp. 387–8); Royal 19.C.VI, Henry VII's presentation copy of Claude de Seyssel's translation of Xenophon's *Anabasis* (Warner and Gilson, II, pp. 334–5); Royal 18.D.II, Lydgate's *Troy Book* and *Siege of Thebes*, made for Sir William Herbert (afterwards earl of Pembroke) and his wife, Anne Devereux, and said by Warner and Gilson (II, pp. 308–10) to have been intended as a gift to Henry VI or Edward IV (but on this point see Lawton, 'The Illustration of Late Medieval Secular Texts', in Pearsall, *Manuscripts and Readers*, pp. 66–8. On the additions in this MS, see Ch. 9 below, nn. 76–7).

30 Pächt and Alexander, I, no. 299; the *Summary Catalogue* suggests that the manuscript belongs to the period in which the marriage treaty with Richard II was concluded in Flanders, Anne remaining for some time in Brussels.

31 The sample also includes theological texts, a missal, a classical commentary, statutes, chronicles and cartularies. Of the 300 or so English manuscripts of the period recorded in J.J.G. Alexander and Elżbieta Taylor, *Illuminated Manuscripts in Oxford College Libraries, the University Archives and the Taylor Institution* (Oxford, 1985) (a group dominated by the old and new learning and not, typically, lavishly illuminated: see *ibid.*, p. vii), just over thirty bear the arms of the original owner; a further seven produced abroad also include such arms. In each case a disproportionate number (a dozen in all) were commissioned by William Gray, bishop of Ely (1454–78).

32 The remarks which follow refer to complete or nearly complete copies of the texts concerned (the inclusion of extracted texts would significantly alter the profile of the sample). All the manuscripts of the *Confessio Amantis* have been systematically examined with a view to re-evaluating the evidence for their provenance; otherwise this account is largely based on printed sources. In the same sample of texts a search for a point of acquisition in the form of a later purchase of a second-hand copy rather than in the form of a commission draws an almost negligible result.

33 Glasgow University, MS Gen. 1130 (arms of Robert, Lord Willoughby d'Eresby d. 1452); NLS MS Advocates 18.1.7 (arms of Edmund, Lord Grey of Ruthyn and his wife, Lady Catherine Percy, whom he married c. 1460: for this lavishly illuminated copy see J.J.G. Alexander and C.M. Kauffman, *English Illuminated Manuscripts 700–1500* (exhibition catalogue, Bibliothèque Royale Albert Ier) (Brussels,

1973), pp. 113–14, pl. 41); Bodleian Library, MS e Mus.65 (SC 3615, arms of Beaufort and Nevill). This account follows Doyle's *Survey*, 1, pp. 144–56 and the same author's 'Reflections' (see p. 87 for an identification of the arms in e Mus.65); Elizabeth Salter's *Nicholas Love's 'Myrrour of the Blessed Lyf of Jesu Christ'*, Analecta Cartusiana 10 (Salzburg, 1974), pp. 1–22, and the same author's 'The Manuscripts'.

34 *The Manuscripts of Chaucer's Troilus*, Chaucer Society, First Series 98 (London 1914); see Henry V's copy, New York, PML MS 817 (Campsall); Bodleian Library, MS Arch. Selden B 24 (a Scottish manuscript with arms of Sinclair) and BL MS Harley 1239 (with arms not firmly identified) – Dr Windeatt's new edition makes no additions to this list. The absence of such evidence in the lavishly produced (and more lavishly planned) Cambridge, Corpus Christi College, MS 61 has proved tantalising. Compare Scott, 'Lydgate's Lives', where the absence of contemporary coats of arms and notes of ownership in lavishly produced copies of Lydgate's poem is described as 'unfortunate and even puzzling' (p. 365).

35 Manly and Rickert, 1, *Descriptions of the Manuscripts*; see BL Add. MS 5140 (owned by Henry Deane) and Paris, Bibliothèque Nationale, MS fonds anglais 39 (owned by Jean d'Angoulême); the arms in the initial on fol. 70ra of Cambridge, Trinity College, MS R.3.3 (582), though clearly integral, seem to be merely decorative (see further the small black shield on fol. 88ra).

36 The arms in Oxford, New College, MS 326 are additions. A full account of the *Confessio* manuscripts will appear in Griffiths, Harris and Pearsall, *Descriptive Catalogue*.

37 The Arundel manuscript was long associated with Henry V as Prince of Wales; for the identification of the arms see Harris, 'The Patron of British Library MS Arundel 38' *NQ*, 31 (1984), 462–3. For the Hoccleve manuscripts, see below, p. 264. Some comment on the provenance of Rawlinson poet. 168 (SC 14660) appears in Harris, 'John Gower's *Confessio Amantis*: the Virtues of Bad Texts', in Pearsall, *Manuscripts and Readers*, p. 30. For the Digby manuscript, see C. Richmond, *John Hopton: a Fifteenth-Century Suffolk Gentleman* (Cambridge, 1981), p. 131 and n. 108, and the essay by Meale, Ch. 9 below, n. 85.

38 'William Abell', p. 169, n. 35. The three other manuscripts concerned are BL Cotton Augustus A.iv (Chaworth's copy) and Royal 18.D.ii (see above, n. 29), and Cambridge, Trinity College, O.5.2 (1283); for the last see D.A. Pearsall, 'Notes on the Manuscripts of "Generydes"', *The Library*, 5th series, 16 (1961), 205–10.

39 See also PML MS 124, with arms of the Cheney family. Henry Bergen (ed.), *Lydgate's Fall of Princes*, Part IV, EETS, ES, 124 (1927).

40 See Lewis and McIntosh.

41 For the *Piers* manuscripts see G. Kane (ed.), *Piers Plowman: the A Version* (London, 1960), pp. 1–18 (for Harley 6041 see pp. 6–7); G. Kane and E. Talbot Donaldson (eds.), *Piers Plowman: the B Version* (London, 1975), pp. 1–15; W.W. Skeat (ed.), *William Langland The Vision of Piers Plowman*, III, Text C, EETS, OS, 54 (1873), pp. xix–l. Anne Middleton's 'The Audience and Public of "Piers Plowman"' (in *Middle English Alliterative Poetry*, ed. Lawton, pp. 101–23) does not mention Harley 6041 (on the poem's audience see further Robert A. Wood, 'A Fourteenth-Century London Owner of "Piers Plowman"', *Medium Aevum*, 53 (1984), 83–90).

42 BL Add. MSS 11305, 24203, 32578, Bodleian Library, MS Bodley 423 (SC 2322)

and Chicago, Newberry Library, MS 32.9. For *Piers* MSS by named scribes see Digby 145, Rawlinson poet. 137, Bodley 851 (*SC* 1746, 14631, 3401) and San Marino, Huntington Library, HM 137 (for Bodley see A.G. Rigg and C. Brewer (eds.), *Piers Plowman, the Z version* (Toronto, 1983), pp. 3–5).

43 Glasgow, Hunterian MS U.1.1. (197), Manchester, Chetham's Library, MS A.7.48 (6696), Cambridge, Corpus Christi College, MS 496. For Chetham see C.A. Luttrell, 'Three North-West Midland Manuscripts', *Neophilologus*, 42 (1958), 38–50, and Harris, 'John Gower's *Confessio Amantis*', pp. 28–9.

44 *A Descriptive Catalogue of Middle English Grammatical Texts* (New York and London, 1979). One of the manuscripts, BL MS Arundel 249, contains a coat of arms.

45 'Reflections' p. 88; the phrase 'libere communicata', used by Dr Doyle, derives from the Latin *Memorandum* which occurs in many copies of the *Myrrour*.

46 The notice of the gift of CUL MS Dd.12.69, a copy of the *Prick of Conscience*, to a Sussex church, for example, concurs with the dialect of the text, pointing to the manuscript's origins in the same area; in the Taylor copy of this text in Princeton University Library, the note of ownership by John Aston of Cropwell Butler in Nottinghamshire similarly concurs with the dialect evidence. See also e.g. Cambridge, St John's College, MS B.12 (34), St Catharine's College, MS 7 and Oxford, New College, MS 326, all copies of the *Confessio Amantis*.

47 'English Books', p. 171.

48 Doyle and Parkes, p. 209.

49 For qualification of this argument see p. 174 below.

50 For the signature on fol. 125r (written lengthwise in the right-hand margin in plummet) see Ill. 16 (the other two inscriptions have been erased). Compare the signature and motto on fol. 1r of Harley 4431, the autograph copy of Christine de Pizan presented to Isabeau de Bavière (p. 85, fig. 43 in L. Hellinga's *Caxton in Focus* (London, 1982)).

51 See e.g. E.W. Ives, 'The Origins of the Later Year Books', in Dafydd Jenkins (ed.), *Legal History Studies 1972* (Cardiff, 1975), pp. 136–51, and also Ives' 'The Common Lawyers', in Clough, *Profession, Vocation and Culture*, p. 193.

52 See e.g. Harris, 'The Origins and Make-Up of Cambridge University Library MS Ff.1.6', *TCBS*, 8 (1983), especially pp. 307–12.

53 For the Common Profit books see Bennett, 'Production and Dissemination', p. 171, and M.B. Parkes, 'The Literacy of the Laity', p. 568 and n. 77. See also J.A. Hoeppner Moran's article, 'A "Common Profit" Library in Fifteenth-Century England and Other Books for Chaplains' (*Manuscripta*, 28 (1984), 417–25), which places useful emphasis on the 'multiple readership' of medieval manuscripts but extends the usual definition of the Common Profit book.

54 *The Fifteenth-Century Book*, p. 33. Bühler writes from the point of view of the market-place rather than the workshop; the distinction he draws ignores the less typical mode of turning out new manuscripts – speculative production. Viewed from the vantage of the workshop the established and innovatory forms of book production are most likely to be differentiated primarily as bespoke and speculative trades; see, for example, Graham Pollard's opening remarks in the first of his Sandars Lectures for 1959, 'The Rise of the Wholesale Trade' ('The English Market for Printed Books', *Publishing History*, 4 (1978), 9–48)): 'When Caxton set up the first printing press at Westminster in 1476, the book trade, such as it was,

was almost entirely a bespoke trade . . . ' (see also Pollard, 'Company of Stationers', p. 15).

55 'From Scriptoria to Printing Shops: Evolution and Revolution in the Early Printed Book Trade', in Kenneth E. Carpenter (ed.), *Books and Society in History* (New York and London, 1983), p. 30.

56 Comment based on Albert Desrolez's closing remarks at the conference *From Script to Book*, held at Odense University, 15–16 November 1982.

57 'Notes on King's College Library'; for the petition (PRO Chancery Warrant for the Great Seal (c. 81) File 1444, No. 2; endorsed 21 March 1447), see pp. 281–2.

58 Munby 'Notes on King's College Library', p. 281, n. 4) lists four earlier manuscripts sold by Pye to his clerical clientèle; see MSS Bodley 110 (*SC* 1963), Laud misc. 414 (*SC* 836) and Royal 5.C.III and 8.D.X (Warner and Gilson, I, pp. 105–7, 248). For Pye see also Pollard, 'Company of Stationers', pp. 11, 16, 37, Pollard, 'The English Market', *loc.cit*, and Doyle and Parkes, p. 197, n. 88. For Bodley 110 see further Doyle, *Survey*, I, p. 194, II, pp. 272–3. See H.R. Plomer's 'Some Early Booksellers and their Customers' (*The Library*, 3rd series, 3 (1912), 414–16) for citations of New College, Oxford, MS 101 (s. xiii, *Historia Scholastica*) bought by Lewis de Charlton (bishop of Hereford, d. 1369, *BRUO*, I, pp. 391–2) from Richard Lynne, stationer of Oxford University; New College, MS 104 (s. xii, *Historia Scholastica*) bought by Thomas Cranley (archbishop of Dublin, d. 1417, *BRUO*, I, pp. 510–11) from the Oxford stationer, John Brown; Oxford, University College, MS 91 (s. xiii, Peraldus) bought in 1433 by William Palmer (precentor of Crediton) from the London stationer, Thomas Veysey; Cambridge, Corpus Christi College, MS 164 (a composite volume, s. xiii–xv in.) bought by John Gunthorp (dean of Wells *BRUC*, pp. 275–7) from the stationer, David Lyenel. For the dealings of the stationer Thomas Marlburgh (Warden of the Limners and Textwriters' Guild 1423) in second-hand books, see Cambridge, Gonville and Caius College, MS 492/261 (see further Doyle and Parkes, p. 197, n. 88, and p. 198, and Pollard, 'Company of Stationers', p. 37).

59 Sir Roger Mynors (*Catalogue of the Manuscripts of Balliol College Oxford* (Oxford, 1963), p. xxvi) describes twelfth- and thirteenth-century books from monastic scriptoria and books of the thirteenth century and later, written both in English and continental academic centres, as among the stock held by the early fifteenth-century Oxford stationers.

60 Haymo on the Pauline Epistles (Italian, s. xi/xii) owned by William Gray (*BRUO*, II, pp. 809–14; see Mynors, *Catalogue*, pp. xxxv and 185–6); Robert Grosseteste's copy of Augustine's *De civitate dei* and Gregory's *Moralia* (s. xiii, second quarter) owned by Thomas Gascoigne (Chancellor of Oxford 1444, *BRUO*, II, pp. 745–8; see A.C. de la Mare and B.C. Barker-Benfield (eds.), *Manuscripts at Oxford: An Exhibition in Memory of Richard William Hunt* (Oxford, 1980), p. 59, XIII.2, fig. 37); Jerome's letters (s. xii) owned by William Brygon (canon of Salisbury, d. 1469; see R.W. Hunt and A.C. de la Mare, *Duke Humfrey and English Humanism in the Fifteenth Century* (Oxford, 1970) (Catalogue of an exhibition held at the Bodleian Library), p. 35); New Testament (s. xiii^2) pawned by Giles Dent, fellow of Clare College, Cambridge, on October 25 1469 (*BRUC*, p. 183; see Ker, I, pp. 390–1; Bartle ('Study of Private Book Collections', p. 250) records the appearance of thirteenth-century small Bibles in wills as late as the sixteenth century).

61 For the Sion MS see Ker, I, pp. 278–9, and Sotheby's Sale Catalogue, 13 June 1977, lot 70; Gunthorp later gave it to Thomas Cornysh, fellow of Oriel, bishop of Tine (d. 1513, *BRUO*, I, pp. 491–2). For the Corpus MS see de la Mare and Barker-Benfield (eds.), *Manuscripts at Oxford*, pp. 99–100, XXII.7, figs. 70, 71 – Professor de la Mare notes that two fifteenth-century English humanistic manuscripts of Caesar (Vatican Chig. H VII 215 and Vat. lat. 4681) are closely related to and probably dependent on Tiptoft's copy. (For the renovation of manuscripts see Dr Barker-Benfield's account of Clement of Canterbury, the librarian of St Augustine's, *ibid.*, pp. 89–92.) For the Magdalen MS, see V.H. Galbraith, 'John Seward and his Circle', *Medieval and Renaissance Studies*, 1 (1941), 99 and n. 1.

62 See, among the gifts of Walter Crome (*BRUC*, p. 168) to Gonville and Caius, MSS 129/67 and 342/538. Of the manuscripts described in de la Mare and Barker-Benfield (eds.) *Manuscripts at Oxford*, see Oxford, Lincoln College, Lat. 100 (p. 28, v.2) collected by William of Malmesbury in the mid-1120s and given to the college by Robert Flemmyng (*BRUO*, II, pp. 699–700: see further Flemmyng's gift of Lincoln Gr. 82, Hunt and de la Mare, *Duke Humfrey*, p. 37, no. 63); New College 112 (p. 59, XIII.3) bought at Chester from Brother Richard Torbok on 2 July 1408 by Thomas Cranley (see n. 58 above) who presented it to the college (for Cranley's practice of entering the details of his purchases in his books compare New College, MSS 37, 38, 91, 122); see further Oriel MS 42 (p. 29, v.5, fig. 18), and MS Bodley 4 (*SC* 1844; p. 62, XIV.1). See also R.W. Hunt, 'The Medieval Library', in John Buxton and Penry Williams (eds.), *New College Oxford 1379–1979* (Oxford, 1979), pp. 317–45 (especially pp. 324–5, 328).

63 M.R. James, 'The Manuscripts of St George's Chapel Windsor', *The Library*, 4th series, 13 (1933), p. 66.

64 See de la Mare and Barker-Benfield, *Manuscripts at Oxford*, p. 120, XXVI.3, for Digby 98 and *BRUO*, III, pp. 1430–1 for Partriche; the manuscript has a table of contents in his hand fol. 1 verso. For the Dublin manuscript, see G.L. and M.A. Harriss, *John Benet's Chronicle for the years 1400 to 1462*, Camden Miscellany 24, Camden Fourth Series 9 (London, 1972), pp. 153–7, and for Benet, *ibid.*, pp. 157–8; both the added items are in Benet's table of contents and have additions in his hand (the dating of the fourteenth-century item follows M.L. Colker's typescript catalogue of the medieval Latin manuscripts at Trinity; the list of the archbishops ends on fol. 209r with Thomas of Corbridge, d. 1304).

65 'Notes on King's College Library', p. 284. The inscriptions in many of Nicholas Kempston's manuscripts express comparable intent and expectation; that in Longleat MS 9 (Chrysostom s. xiv ex.) directs that the book be passed from priest to priest '*quam diu liber durauerit*' (fol. 21v).

66 Warner and Gilson, II, pp. 171–2, IV pl. 94; II, p. 140, IV, pl. 85; II, pp. 331–2; for 15.D.II see D.D. Egbert, 'The so-called "Greenfield", " La Lumiere as Lais" and "Apocalypse", Brit. Mus., Royal MS. 15.D.II', *Speculum*, 11 (1936), 446–52. Compare the later medieval fate of the Laval–Middleton MS (c. 1275, Nottingham University Library, Mi.LM.6).

67 H.L.D. Ward, *Catalogue of Romances in the Department of Manuscripts in the British Museum*, 1 (1883), pp. 587–9, II (1893), pp. 471–4, III (by J.A. Herbert) (1910), pp. 272–84. The manuscript (including a French psalter, the *Bestiaire d'Amours*, prose *Turpin*, *Purgatoire de Saint Patrice*, *Manuel de Pesches*, recipes, charms and

prayers) was owned by John Clerk, 'grocero ac apotecario regis Edwardi quarti'.
Compare the fifteenth-century provenance of BL Add. 39777.

68 For Add. 7071 see Eugène Vinaver (ed.), *The Works of Sir Thomas Malory*, 2nd edn
(Oxford, 1967), III, pp. 1279–81; pl. VI (fol. 189r, detail) shows a note of s. xvi in.
collating the text with Caxton's edition. See further Carol Meale, 'The Manu-
scripts and Early Audience of the Middle English Prose *Merlin*', in A. Adams, A.
Diverres, K. Stern and K. Varty (eds.), *The Changing Face of Arthurian Romance*
(Woodbridge, 1986), pp. 92–111, for the popularity of Arthurian material in the
early Tudor period. Royal 15.D.II bears the signature of Cecily, daughter of
Edward IV, as does 14.E.III, also signed by Elizabeth Woodville and Elizabeth of
York. Royal 19.C.I (the works of Matfre Ermengau) includes the monogram of
Henry VII.

69 L. Delisle, 'Notice sur un psautier de XIIIᵉ siècle appartenant au Comte de
Crawford', *Bibliothèque de l'Ecole des Chartes*, 58 (1897), 381–93. M.R. James'
description (*A Descriptive Catalogue of the Latin Manuscripts in the John Rylands at
Manchester* (Manchester, 1921), pp. 64–71, pls. 48–50) follows Delisle. See further
Alexander, 'Painting and Manuscript Illumination', p. 148, pl. 6. On fol. 2v of
this, now much mutilated, manuscript appears 'Royne Iahanne'.

70 Warner and Gilson, I, p. 47; George Warner, *Queen Mary's Psalter* (London, 1912),
p. 1.

71 V. Leroquais, *Les Bréviaires Manuscrits des Bibliothèques Publiques de France*, III
(Paris, 1934), pp. 198–210 (see also K. Morand, *Jean Pucelle* (Oxford, 1962),
pp. 43–5). Dating from c. 1323–6 and illuminated by Pucelle, the manuscript was
given by Charles VI to Richard II, and was later sent by Henry IV to Jean duc de
Berry.

72 C. Gaspar and F. Lyna, *Les Principaux Manuscrits à peintures de la Bibliothèque Royale de
Belgique*, part I (Paris, 1937), pp. 114–21 (for the provenance, see pp. 115–16) and
pls. XXIII, XXVI. See also L.F. Sandler, *The Peterborough Psalter in Brussels and other
Fenland Manuscripts* (London, 1974), pp. 108–15. The manuscript was purchased
for Philip IV (1328–50) from the executors of Clement of Hungary; during its stay
in the Louvre library, backgrounds of red and blue charged with gold fleurs de lis
were added; when in the possession of Philippe le Bon, the arms of Burgundy were
added at the base of all pages containing miniatures, and all earlier coats were
replaced with those of the duke's provinces.

73 For BL Yates Thompson 14 (Add. 39810), the St Omer Psalter, see M. Rickert,
Painting in Britain in the Middle Ages, 2nd edn (Harmondsworth, 1965; first
published 1954), pp. 131, 181–2; for the fifteenth-century work see *ibid.*, pl. 182A
(fol. 87r). Professor Jonathan Alexander ('A Lost Leaf from a Bodleian Book of
Hours', *BLR*, 8 (1971), p. 251, n. 7) describes the fifteenth-century borders fols.
154r–167v as close to the Fastolf Master's style. See further Sammut, *Unfredo Duca
di Gloucester*, p. 109, no. 18, and for the other manuscripts cited, *ibid.*, pp. 110–11,
no. 20, p. 106, no. 13, and pp. 101–2, no. 7. For comment on the kind of attractions
the Hebrew psalter would have had for Gloucester, see G.I. Lieftinck, 'The
"Psalterium Hebraycum" from St Augustine's Canterbury rediscovered in the
Scaliger Bequest at Leyden', *TCBS*, 2 (1955), 97–104, pls. VI–VIII.

74 M.R. James *The Romance of Alexander. A Collotype Facsimile of MS. Bodley 264*
(Oxford, 1933) (the facsimile includes only the fourteenth-century work); Pächt

and Alexander, I, no. 297, pl. XXIII, III, nos. 792, 793, pl. LXXV; Doyle, 'English Books', p. 167; fol. 2v is illustrated in R. Marks and N. Morgan, *The Golden Age of English Manuscript Painting 1200–1500* (London, 1981), pl. 35. For the association with Thomas of Woodstock, see W.D. Macray *Annals of the Bodleian*, 2nd, enlarged edn (Oxford, 1890; first published 1868), p. 22, n. 2; see also *SC* and James, *Romance of Alexander*, p. 5. A note recording Rivers' purchase appears on fol. 274r; see James, *ibid.*

75 J. Backhouse, *The Madresfield Hours: A Fourteenth-Century Manuscript in the Library of Earl Beauchamp*, Roxburghe Club (1975), pp. 25–9. Maud de Tilliol was daughter of Roger de Lascelles, who held lands in the Honour of Richmond, and wife of Robert de Tilliol (d. 1321) of Scaleby, Cumberland. Evidence of fifteenth-century ownership survives in the form of the obit of 'Domina Matilda de Neville' in the Calendar and, on fol. 15v, an inscription and coat of arms of the Scrope family. Ambrose Dauntsey was brother of the better-known William Dauntsey, mercer and alderman of London (d. 1543) whose name appears in BL Add. 10340, a copy of the *Canterbury Tales*.

76 See Ill. 17. A second miniature appears on the following recto: at the base of the vinet on this page is a defaced coat of arms; close examination suggests the possible blazon – quarterly 1 and 4 argent on a chief gules three leopard's faces or (Depden), 2 and 3 azure a lion rampant (possibly a griffin segreant) or, a chief argent (alternatively on a chief argent . . .) (Smith of Middlesex?). Netherlandish influence apparent in the naturalistic motifs of leaves and strawberries to the lower right of the border on fol. ixr, confirms a date in the middle of the century.

77 See further e.g. Bodleian, Gough liturg. 18 (*SC* 18332) an early fourteenth-century psalter to which has been added a fifteenth-century calendar for the use of Tynemouth Priory in Northumberland (Pächt and Alexander, III, no. 553 pl. LV) or Longleat House, MS 10 (made for the first earl of Hereford c. 1316–22; see L.F. Sandler, 'An Early Fourteenth-Century English Breviary at Longleat', *JWCI*, 39 (1976), 1–20) in which fifteenth-century additions to the calendar (fols. 115v, 116v, 117v, 119r–v) and sanctorale (fols. 344ra–364vb) adapt the volume for use in Lincolnshire (see also additional prayers and lessons fols. 111va–114rb, 122rb–vb). The appearance in a manuscript of two programmes of work more closely related in date, witnessing to the late intervention of an owner ordering a resumption of production to cater for some personal taste or to meet some current need (or generally to upgrade the quality of the manuscript), unsurprisingly given the nature of the manuscript book, is not particularly rare – see for example MSS Arch. Selden B 10 (*SC* 3356, Pächt and Alexander, III, no. 1117, pl. CIV, and no. 1180), Royal 18.D.II (see n. 29 above), Harley 2887 (Scott 'A Mid-Fifteenth-Century Illuminating Shop', pp. 172–82), Cambridge, Fitzwilliam Museum, MS 57 (see below, pp. 178–9), PML M 775 and M 893 (for the former see (with further bibliography) G.A. Lester, *Sir John Paston's 'Grete Boke'* (Woodbridge, 1984), pp. 31–4, 93–5 and for the latter Alexander, 'William Abell', p. 166 and n. 8, Marks and Morgan, *The Golden Age*, pp. 114–17).

78 For Abell, see Alexander, 'William Abell'. An attempt to outline an identification of the series of patrons commissioning work from Ricardus Franciscus was made in my paper, 'Pierpont Morgan MS M 126: An Occasion for Illustration', read at the New Chaucer Society Conference held at York, 6–11 August 1984.

79 G. Kipling, 'Henry VII and the Origins of Tudor Patronage', in G. Fitch Lytle and S. Orgel (eds.), *Patronage in the Renaissance* (Princeton, 1981), pp. 117–64.

80 For such a survey see Alexander, 'Painting and Manuscript Illumination'. See also Meale, Ch. 9 below, pp. 202–6.

81 *Bulletin of the Institute of Historical Research*, 35 (1962), 111–27.

82 Note also Henry's presentation copy of the Statutes of the Order of the Golden Fleece (Sotheby's Sale Catalogue, 24 June 1986, lot 75). For recent notice of books associated with the king, see also Alexander and Taylor, *Illuminated Manuscripts*, no. 823.

83 Kipling notes the Fitzwilliam manuscript, 'Henry VII', p. 127, n. 36. See M.R. James, *A Descriptive Catalogue of the Manuscripts in the Fitzwilliam Museum* (Cambridge, 1895), pp. 142–9, with plate showing English and Flemish work. For references to the Vienna MS, see M. Meiss, *French Painting in the Time of Jean de Berry. The Limbourgs and their Contemporaries* (New York, 1974), I, p. 368; for work by the later artist in this manuscript, see also PML M 815, an *horae* of Sarum Use belonging to the king.

84 Fols. 7r–36v, 45r–49v, 79r–95v, 111r–126v (see also the miniature on fol. 168v) and 178v–192v.

85 Fols. 37r, 96r, 127r, 169r.

86 This motif appears again only on fol. 120r, where it is supported by Tudor emblems, the white greyhound and red dragon.

87 R. Allen Brown, H.M. Colvin and A.J. Taylor, *The History of the King's Works* (London, 1963), *The Middle Ages*, II, p. 935; *The Regulations and Establishment of the Household of Henry Algernon Percy, the Fifth Earl of Northumberland at his Castles of Wresill and Lekingfield in Yorkshire begun Anno Domini M.D.XII* (London, 1770), pp. 99, 101, 378, 452–3, 460; Royal MS 18.D.II, fol. 195v *et seq.*; Francis Grose, *The Antique Repertory*, IV (London, 1809), pp. 393–421. See further R.F. Green, *Poets and Princepleasers* (Toronto, 1980), pp. 95–6, including notice of the royal library at Richmond in 1501.

88 Alexander 'Painting and Manuscript Illumination', p. 156. R. Kent Lancaster has pointed out that the relevant entry in the close rolls of 1252 should refer to Dunion as 'custos liberorum' (keeper of the king's children) – he is elsewhere described as 'custodius puerorum regis' (see pp. 88–9 in 'Henry III, Westminster Abbey, and the Court School of Illumination', *Seven Studies in Medieval English History and Other Historical Essays presented to Harold L. Snellgrove*, ed. R.H. Bowers (Jackson, Miss., 1983)). For Bradfelde, see Griffiths, Harris and Pearsall, *Descriptive Catalogue*. For Burnham see Green, *Poets and Princepleasers*, p. 96, and N.H. Nicolas, *Proceedings and Ordinances of the Privy Council of England (1386–1542)* (London, 1834–7), III, p. 168. For the *Liber Niger* see A.R. Myers (ed.), *The Household of Edward IV* (Manchester, 1959), p. 116.

89 BL Add. 60584 (J. Vale, *Edward III and Chivalry*, pp. 47–50); PRO E 159/161 (see also Bodleian Eng. hist. C. 775; R.F. Green, 'King Richard II's Books Revisited', *The Library*, 5th series, 31 (1976), 235–9); PRO Privy Seal Office Warrants P.S.O. 1/8/404–5 (N.R. Ker, *Records of All Souls College Library 1437–1600*, Oxford Bibliographical Society, NS, 16 (1971), pp. 1–2, and R. Weiss, 'Henry VI and the Library of All Souls College', *EHR*, 57, (1942), 102–5 with (p. 102 and n. 4) notice

of the presence of royal books in the Exchequer from the reign of Edward II onwards). The size of the royal collection, for want of a full-scale inventory earlier than that of Richmond 1534/5, is a matter for speculation; an ample library is suggested by the will of Henry V (10 June 1421: ed. Patrick and Felicity Strong, *EHR*, 96 (1981), 79–102) – worthy of note are the assumptions behind the form of bequest (italics mine): 'volumus quod omnes libri nostri, cuiuscumque fuerint facultatis aut materie, in nostro testamento aut codicillis non legati, filio nostro remaneant *pro libraria sua*' (*ibid.*, p. 100).

90 C. Ross, 'Rumour, Propaganda and Popular Opinion During the Wars of the Roses', in R.A. Griffiths (ed.), *Patronage, the Crown and the Provinces in Later Medieval England* (Gloucester, 1981), p. 24. For official (commissioned by authority) and quasi-official (written probably to attract patronage and reflecting authority's point of view) chronicles see A. Gransden, 'Propaganda in English Medieval Historiography', *Journal of Medieval History*, 1 (1975), 363–81; for Yorkist chronicles, see pp. 374–5 and, further, J.A.F. Thomson, '"The Arrival of Edward IV" – the Development of the Text', *Speculum*, 46 (1971), 84–93).

91 S. Anglo, 'The "British History" in Early Tudor Propaganda', *BJRL*, 44 (1961), 21: see appendix (pp. 41–8) for a list of manuscripts containing genealogies of the English kings produced *temp.* Henry VI–Henry VIII.

92 'Yorkist Propaganda: Pedigree, Prophecy and the "British History" in the reign of Edward IV', in Charles Ross (ed.), *Patronage, Pedigree and Power* (Gloucester, 1979), pp. 172–5. Allan writes (p. 174) 'It is quite feasible that Edward IV or an adherent, sensible of the example of earlier texts, should order the production of similar manuscripts to demonstrate the new king's title to the throne.'

93 See A.C. de la Mare's description of Lyell 33 in the *Catalogue of the Collection of Medieval Manuscripts bequeathed to the Bodleian Library Oxford by James P.R. Lyell*. Professor de la Mare offers groupings of the text by Roger of St Albans and of the four versions of the Yorkist pedigree (for which see also Allan, 'Yorkist Propaganda', p. 174). To be associated with Lyell is a previously unidentified manuscript, dating after 15 March 1454 and now at Longleat House. For relevant plates, see A.G. Watson, *Catalogue of Dated and Dateable Manuscripts c. 435–1600 in Oxford Libraries* (Oxford, 1984), I, nos. 637, 654, 777, 758, II, pls. 689, 653, 666, 698. Dr Scott has suggested further groupings of the MSS based on illustrations produced from identical models ('Lydgate's Lives', pp. 337, n. 7, and 364, n. 92). (See further the same author's *Later Gothic Manuscripts*, forthcoming.)

94 See particularly Roberto Weiss' stress on the importance of official contacts with the Collectors and envoys sent to England by the Roman Curia for the growth of Gloucester's interest in humanism (*Humanism in England During the Fifteenth Century*, 3rd edn (Oxford, 1967), first published 1941, pp. 39–40), a view endorsed by such related remarks as Sammut's 'in Inghilterra l'umanesimo ebbe origine e si sviluppo sopratutto per mezzo dei contatti con la curia romana' (*Unfredo Duca di Gloucester*, p. 6) or Barker-Benfield's 'the English Renaissance was really no more than a side-effect of the Council of Basel' (review of Sammut, *The Library*, 6th series, 4 (1982), p. 192). For books brought from Italy by the humanists see also generally Hunt and de la Mare, *Duke Humfrey*.

95 Cf. Graham Pollard's comment in 'The Company of Stationers', p. 16: 'The

wholesale book-trade was created by the invention of printing and on an international scale. The amazing speed and elaboration of its growth was no doubt
fostered by the universality of the Latin language.'

96 M.B. Parkes and E. Salter, *Troilus and Criseyde. Geoffrey Chaucer. A Facsimile Edition
     of Corpus Christi College Cambridge MS 61* (Cambridge, 1978), p. 22, citing (n. 26)
     BN MSS f. lat. 1158 and f. fr. 831.

97 For Hastings see D.H. Turner, *The Hastings Hours. A 15th-Century Flemish Book of
     Hours made for William Lord Hastings* (London, 1983), and T. Kren (ed.), *Renaissance
     Painting in Manuscript Treasures of the British Library* (an exhibition held at the Getty
     Museum, Pierpont Morgan Library and British Library) (New York, 1984),
     pp. 21–30, no. 3. See also Ch. 9, below, p. 204.

98 Mynors, *Catalogue*, pp. xxiv–xlv. For Tiptoft's manuscripts see most recently de la
     Mare and Barker-Benfield, *Manuscripts at Oxford*, pp. 99–101, and see also Hunt
     and de la Mare, *Duke Humfrey*, pp. 41–51.

99 See Warner and Gilson, II, pp. 177–9, and for fol. 2v, IV, pl. 96; Ward, *Catalogue*, I,
     pp. 471–87; D.J. Conlon (ed.), *Le Rommant de Guy de Warwik et de Herolt d'Ardenne*,
     University of North Carolina Studies in the Romance Languages and Literatures
     102 (Chapel Hill, 1971), pp. 16–26 – a plate (fol. 227r) precedes p. 57.

100 For Talbot's long career in the French wars see G.E.C. XI (Shrewsbury),
     pp. 698–704. For the manuscripts see F. Wormald and P.M. Giles, *Descriptive
     Catalogue of the Additional Illuminated Manuscripts in the Fitzwilliam Museum acquired
     between 1895–1979*, II (Cambridge, 1982), pp. 441–53 pls. 48–51, and see also
     D. Gray 'A Middle English Illustrated Poem', in P.L. Heyworth (ed.), *Medieval
     Studies for J.A.W. Bennett* (Oxford, 1981), pp. 185–6. For the Talbot Master see
     J. Plummer, *The Last Flowering. French Painting in Manuscripts 1420–1530* (New York
     and London, 1982), no. 24.

101 Alexander, 'A Lost Leaf', p. 251. Plummer, *The Last Flowering*, no. 22, with plate.

102 Hoo's portrait and arms occur on fol. 192r and those of his second wife, Eleanor
     (da. of Lionel, Lord Welles) on fol. 196v. See also G.E.C. VI (Hoo) pp. 561–4,
     and, for a full account of the manuscript, L.L. Williams, 'A Rouen Book of Hours
     of the Sarum Use, c. 1444, belonging to Thomas, Lord Hoo, Chancellor of
     Normandy and France', *Proceedings of the Royal Irish Academy*, 75, Section C (1975),
     189–212, pls. VI–XXI.

103 The duke's badge also occurs on fol. 148r, painted over existing border-work; the
     figure of Bedford kneeling in prayer appears three times in the manuscript (fols.
     41r, 51r, and 109r). For the Reid MS, see Ker, I, p. 379. For another Sarum
     Hours produced in Normandy, see Gough liturg. 10 (*SC* 18336), Pächt and
     Alexander, I, no. 647, and for a prayer roll associated with the English occu-
     pation, Sotheby's sale, 25 June 1985, lot 92.

104 H. Aubert, *Notices sur les Manuscrits Petau Conservés à la Bibliothèque de Genève* (Paris,
     1911), p. 129. For this manuscript see further Bernard Gagnebin, 'L'Enluminure
     de Charlemagne à François Iᵉʳ: Manuscrits de la Bibliothèque Publique et
     Universitaire de Genève', *Genava*, 24 (1976), 155–6, no. 68, with plate showing
     frontispiece miniature.

105 N. Rogers, 'Books of Hours produced in the Low Countries for the English
     Market in the Fifteenth Century' (Cambridge University, M.Litt. 1982). See also
     the same writer's 'The Particular Judgement: Two Earlier Examples of a Motif in

Jan Mostaert's Lost Self-Portrait', *Oud Holland*, 97 (1983), 125–7 (I owe most of the points made here to discussions with the author). See further E. Colledge, 'South Netherlands Books of Hours made for England', *Scriptorium*, 32 (1978), 55–7. For descriptions of such manuscripts citing further examples, see e.g. Ker, I, pp. 46–8 (Dulwich College, 25), p. 382 (Victoria and Albert Museum Reid MSS 44–8), II, pp. 393–5 (Edinburgh University 303) and III, pp. 604–5 (Oxford, Campion Hall 3). For notices with plates, see e.g. J.D. Farquhar, 'Identity in an Anonymous Age: Bruges Manuscript Illuminators and their Signs', *Viator*, 11 (1980), illustrating Reid 45 (p. 378 and figs. 3–4), Liverpool, Merseyside Museum 12009 (p. 379 and fig. 8) and Bodleian, Liturg. Misc. 400 (p. 380 and fig. 12): see also M.M. Manion and V.F. Vines, *Medieval and Renaissance Illuminated Manuscripts in Australian Collections* (Melbourne, London and New York, 1984), pp. 132–3, no. 54, pl. 30, and figs. 112–15, and pp. 135–6, no. 56, pl. 31 and figs. 120–7. For the possibility that a similar, if smaller, export trade in commercially produced *horae* existed at Rouen (from the manuscripts discussed, aimed at the Scottish market) see R. Watson, *The Playfair Hours* (London, 1984), especially pp. 13–14 and 32 (where the trade is related to that in printed books).

106 Farquhar, 'Identity in an Anonymous Age', p. 376, and see also p. 382; see further C.F.R. de Hamel, 'Reflections on the Trade in Books of Hours at Ghent and Bruges', in J.B. Trapp (ed.), *Manuscripts in the Fifty Years after the Invention of Printing* (London, 1983), pp. 29–33. The showy quality of the manuscripts brings to mind the new 'democratic' element in fifteenth-century patronage.

107 Save for the prefatory miniature (fol. 8v – showing Brown and his wife, Agnes) an indulgence and a *memoria* of St Agnes, the manuscript is unexceptional in its contents. Note that Rogers' identification of the owner (followed here) differs from that given in Scott, *The Mirroure of the Worlde*, p. 9, n. 3.

108 See fols. 113–46, five quires containing miscellaneous prayers: compare Farquhar's analysis ('Identity in an Anonymous Age', p. 380) of Baltimore, Walters Art Gallery, MS Walters 239 (an *horae* of Rome Use).

109 See Rogers, 'Books of Hours', p. 39, for this manuscript.

110 PRO E 122/194/22. N.J.M. Kerling, 'Caxton and the Trade in Printed Books', *The Book Collector*, 4 (1955), 191, 192; Kerling's article is based on the London Customs returns for 1460–92. See also the earlier articles of Henry Plomer based on the returns for 1480–1508: 'The Importation of Books into England in the Fifteenth and Sixteenth Centuries: An Examination of some Customs Rolls', *The Library*, 4th series, 4 (1923–4) 146–50, and 'The Importation of Low Country and French Books into England, 1480 and 1502–3', *The Library*, 4th series, 9 (1928), 164–8.

111 Armstrong, 'English Purchases', pp. 268–9, 289. A.I. Doyle's notice of the imported books of the Durham monks has also added to the general picture described by Armstrong: see 'The Printed Books of the last Monks of Durham', *The Library*, 6th series, 10 (1988), 206–7.

112 'A Leaf from a Gutenberg Bible Illuminated in England', *BLJ*, 9 (1983), 32–50. For IC 56a see *ibid.*, figs. 1–2 and for Lambeth figs. 3 and 9. The Lambeth copy is catalogued as a manuscript in Henry J. Todd, *A Catalogue of the Archiepiscopal Manuscripts in the Library at Lambeth Palace* (London, 1812), p. 3. Note that the accounts for 11 July 1466–24 March 1468 kept by Gerhard von Wesel of Cologne

(account keeper for the German trade in London) record two printed Bibles presented to Tiptoft (see Kerling, 'Caxton and the Trade in Printed Books', p. 190).

113 *Ibid.*, p. 43.

114 *Caxton in Focus*, p. 101. For a similar analysis see the opening of the article by G.D. Painter, D.E. Rhodes and H.M. Nixon, 'Two Missals Printed for Wynkyn de Worde', *BLJ*, 2 (1976) 159–71 giving an account of the twelve incunable editions of the Sarum Missal, all but two printed abroad. For Maynyal's editions of the Sarum Missal and *Legenda* see also G.D. Painter, *William Caxton: A Quincentenary Biography of England's First Printer* (London, 1976), pp. 157–60; for service books of English Use printed abroad see Armstrong, 'English Purchases', pp. 278–80; and generally for books for the English market printed abroad E. Gordon Duff, *Fifteenth Century English Books*, Bibliographical Society Illustrated Monographs 18 (Oxford, 1917), pp. 133–6. Of the later 'Latin trade' it is to the point to note that the full range of Latin materials used in upper schools was not printed in England until the second quarter of the seventeenth century (see Pollard, 'The English Market', pp. 21–2).

115 The stock listed in Caxton's *Doctrine to Learn French and English* (*STC* 24865 [1480] – the text has been dated to 1465–6) as belonging to one George, the Bookseller, is often cited in this context (it is dominated by those staples of the medieval trade – school book and service books). For references to the stocklists of a number of early sixteenth-century booksellers see S. Jayne, *Library Catalogues of the English Renaissance* (Berkeley and Los Angeles, 1956), pp. 175–6, to which add D.M. Palliser and D.G. Selwyn, 'The Stock of a York Stationer, 1538', *The Library*, 5th series, 27 (1972), 207–19 (for an edition of a Marian bookseller's accounts by J.N. King, see *BLJ*, 13 (1987), 33–57).

116 For the *Nova Statuta* manuscripts see Scott, *Mirrour of the Worlde*, sections IX and X C and Appendix B; see *ibid.*, p. 2, n. 2, for notice of a group of three *Dicts and Sayings* MSS, and for the manuscripts concerned, see further *The Dicts and Sayings of the Philosophers*, ed. C.F. Bühler, EETS, os, 211 (1941), pp. xx–xxv, and (for their textual affinity), p. xxxii. For the *Confessio* and *Troy Book*, see Doyle and Parkes, p. 201, for copies of Love and the *Brut*, Doyle, 'Reflections', p. 88 and for the speculative production of the Edmund–Fremund scribe Scott, 'Lydgate's Lives', p. 361. Lester (*Sir John Paston's 'Grete Boke'*, pp. 7, 47) has disputed Curt Bühler's claim that Lansdowne 285 and Pierpont Morgan 775 'represent an early instance of 'mass-production' ('Sir John Paston's "Grete Boke", a Fifteenth-Century "Best Seller"', *MLN* 56, 1941, 351): see also Lester, 'Sir John Paston's "Grete Boke": A Bespoke Book or Mass-Produced?', *English Studies*, 65 (1985), 93–104.

117 Doyle and Parkes, pp. 201, 203.

118 *Ibid.*, pp. 209–10; see also Scott, *Mirrour*, p. 58 and n. 3, and, for another example, Doyle, 'Reflections', p. 86 (see further Harley 2985, a Sarum *horae* produced in Bruges in the 1460s with space for arms fol. 42r, and BL Add. MS 22139 (*Confessio Amantis*) fol. 1r). This practice makes the case for the occurrence of arms as evidence of the initiative behind a commission slightly less than watertight (see above pp. 167–9) – the book having been some time completed and a client presenting himself, the arms might be inserted (in a manner

apparently integral with the rest of the illumination) just before it was sold across the board.

119 Compare Scott, 'Lydgate's Lives', p. 361, and Doyle's 'Reflections', p. 88.

120 Doyle and Parkes, p. 201, Scott *Mirrour*, p. 2, n. 2, and 'Lydgate's Lives', p. 364, n. 92.

121 For the theory of the 'sociology of the text', involving acknowledgement of the intimate relationship between the textual, material, economic and social aspects of the book, see D.F. McKenzie, 'Typography and Meaning: The Case of William Congreve', in G. Barber and B. Fabian (eds.), *The Book and the Book Trade in Eighteenth-Century Europe*, Proceedings of the Fifth Wolfenbütteler Symposium, November 1–3, 1977, *Wolfenbütteler Schriften zur Geschichte des Buchwessens* (ed. Paul Raabe), 4 (Hamburg, 1981), pp. 82 and 123, n. 51; and *The Panizzi Lectures 1985: Bibliography and the Sociology of Texts* (London, 1986).

9 · PATRONS, BUYERS AND OWNERS: BOOK PRODUCTION AND SOCIAL STATUS

CAROL M. MEALE

THE QUESTION of the interrelationship between the producers and patrons and/or buyers of books in late medieval England, while central to any understanding of how the book-trade functioned, is by no means an easy one to resolve. It is a commonplace to observe that England did not match other European countries in respect of a continuous output of de luxe manuscripts during this period, and yet the relatively healthy state of the trade as a whole is demonstrated at the lower end of the market, where the combination of ever-cheapening methods of manufacture and an increase in disposable income among the middle classes led the way towards an expansion of the manuscript book-trade upon which the eventual viability of printing in England, in catering for unprecedentedly large audiences, was directly dependent.[1] I intend in this chapter to look at a variety of types of book, devotional and secular, poetry and prose, decorated and more workaday. By considering these books in relation to their owners – men and women drawn from a broad social spectrum – it may be possible to determine the nature and level of buyers' demands, and also to gain an idea of the market choices which were open to them.

Where the production of fine books is concerned, the vital questions would seem to be those of incentives and resources: were the producers inhibited by a lack of interest in books in general, and in English ones specifically, among potential patrons? Or, conversely, was there in fact a demand for high quality books which the domestic trade was either unable, or unwilling, to respond to, thereby forcing buyers to look abroad? Neither proposition, taken singly, would appear to offer a satisfactory explanation.

Certainly a number of English buyers and readers took advantage of the opportunities provided by travel abroad to obtain particular texts and kinds of books which were not available to them in their native country. Indeed, it is possible to trace the major historical movements of the late Middle Ages – from the protracted series of Anglo-French wars to the growth of humanism in Italy – in the activities of contemporary book collectors such as John, duke of Bedford, John Talbot, earl of Shrewsbury, Humphrey, duke of Gloucester, and John Tiptoft, earl of Worcester.[2] But the traffic was not all one way. Alien craftsmen, for example the artists Herman Scheerre, the Fastolf Master

and the Caxton Master, and the scribes Milo de Carraria and Ricardus
Franciscus were presumably encouraged to seek employment in England
(whether by invitation or upon their own initiative) because markets for their
work either existed already, or could be found.[3] By the end of the period with
which we are concerned here, however, the buying public for craftsmen such
as those mentioned was not drawn solely, or even primarily, from the
nobility, as wealthy individuals from the middle classes and corporate bodies
alike came to play an active rôle in the commissioning of books. The broad
social range from which, either by necessity or design, English book producers drew their custom is a pointer to the major difference between the
book-trade in England and that abroad (for instance in fourteenth- and early
fifteenth-century France and later fifteenth-century Burgundy): namely, the
apparent lack of an influential and exclusive network of artistic endeavour
and patronage centred upon the royal court.[4]

It must be acknowledged that this perception is based in large part upon
the evidence presented by extant manuscripts, and it is probable that a
considerable amount of material has simply been lost. Thus, while recog-
nising the importance of the library assembled by Edward IV, which is the
earliest substantial collection of royal books to survive, it would be unwise to
conclude that none of his predecessors were active as patrons. Knowledge of
royal book ownership prior to Edward's reign derives almost entirely from
booklists, in itself a form of evidence which is open to contradictory interpretations. This is nowhere more clearly demonstrated than in the debate which
has raged over the level of literary culture promoted by Richard II. Aside
from a few presentation volumes the only manuscripts known to have been in
his possession are the thirteen secular works – mainly romances – plus two
Bibles, which he inherited from his grandfather, Edward III, and which are
listed together with 'certeins ioialx & veassell' dor & dargent' conveyed to
John Bacon, 'clerc gardein', in the first year of the new king's reign.[5] This
number of books, when compared with the total of over ninety owned by his
uncle, Thomas of Gloucester, and kept at his castle in Pleshey and his
London house, suggests that the degree of interest shown by Richard was low
indeed.[6] However, two caveats must be placed upon this interpretation. To
begin with, the lists of Gloucester's books are part of larger inventories of his
assets made after his death, all of which, due to the charge of treason brought
against him, were confiscate to the crown. The circumstances under which
the records were compiled were thus extraordinary, but it would be hard to
justify the assumption that Gloucester's collection of books was similarly
atypical: a connection between bibliophilia and treason, or accusations of
treason, remains to be proved.[7] The corollary to this is that information
culled from previously unexplored documentary sources is liable to alter the
overall picture significantly.

This has proved to be the case with regard to Edward III's court, where new evidence has established that books circulated extensively.[8] Also, the recovery of a list of manuscripts belonging to Henry IV goes some way towards confirming earlier suggestions as to that monarch's personal interest in books.[9] An entry in the records of the King's Bench presents a charge made against a London stationer, Thomas Marleburgh, to the effect that he, with the assent and connivance of Henry IV's 'Custod*em* libror*um*', Robert Brad-felde 'de Bradfeld in Com*itatu* Berks Gentilman', appropriated nine books which had belonged to the late king and retained them 'ad magnam decep-cio*nem*' of his son, Henry V.[10] The books, valued variously at between 100*s* and ten marks, were two psalters, one glossed; two Bibles, one 'in latinus' and one 'in Engelyssh'; a copy of Gregory the Great's *Moralia* on the book of Job; Johannes Balbus' *Catholicon*; a *Polychronicon*; a 'smale cronykeles'; and 'unu*m* aliu*m* libru*m* voc*at* Gower'. Although the language of the last book is not specified, the volume may in all likelihood be identified as Huntington MS EL.26.A.17, a copy of the *Confessio Amantis*.[11] The reference to the nature of Bradfelde's employment is of note: it is generally assumed that there was no official royal librarian before Henry VII's appointment of Quentin Poulet to the post in 1492, but the fact that at this earlier date a royal servant could have his duties defined so precisely implies that Henry's collection of books was sizeable, and that he took care to see them well looked after.[12]

The list is unrevealing as to Henry's activities as a patron, although there are indications in other administrative records that he and Henry V employed metropolitan scribes to produce official documents, service books, and even secular texts.[13] There is, however, little to suggest that their immediate successors gave any consistent stimulus to the native book-trade. Henry VI, for example, commissioned the artist William Abell to illustrate the charters for his foundations of King's College, Cambridge, and Eton in 1446, and also, perhaps, to decorate a Bible Concordance which was owned by the former institution, but the king was not noted for an interest in books,[14] and the only manuscript in the personal possession of the monarchy which Abell embellished, a prayer roll, now Oxford, Jesus College, MS 124, belonged not to Henry but to his wife, Margaret of Anjou. Abell, arguably the most prominent artist of his time in England, could not have depended upon royal patronage for his livelihood. His career as a whole reflects the broad commercial interests common to a majority of his fellow craftsmen, his customers being drawn from merchant companies and the gentry, as well as the church and aristocracy.[15] Edward IV's library, which forms the core of the present collection of Royal manuscripts in the British Library, seems to have been acquired wholesale from Flemish workshops after the Yorkist monarch's period of exile in Burgundian Flanders during the winter of 1470/1.[16] Moreover, Henry VII, who built upon Edward's achievement, also chose to commission continental artists to produce the few de luxe volumes with which he can definitely be associated.[17] It is possible that Richard III, had he reigned longer, would have been more active in utilising native talents, though, as it is, only one of several manuscripts which are known to have belonged to him was certainly made to his order.[18] This is BL MS Royal 18.A.xii, an English translation of Vegetius' *De Re Militari*, which was copied after his assumption of the throne in 1483. It is a modest volume, in size, and in the quality and extent of its illumination. The style and characteristic motifs of the border decoration link it with other late fifteenth-century manuscripts produced probably in London, among which are Harvard Law School, MS 25, a *Registrum Brevium* dated 5 March 1476, which bears the arms of William, Lord Hastings, chamberlain to Edward IV, on fol. 1r, and the *Book of the Fraternity of Our Lady's Assumption*, dating from a similar period, and made for members of the Skinners' Company.[19]

The reliance of the English court upon foreign centres of production during the fifteenth century can perhaps be better understood by examining the influence of continental ideas and practices respecting 'institutional' libraries annexed to the crown. For example, the greatest architect of the French royal library, Charles V (1338–80), enjoyed a reputation for learning during his lifetime and posthumously, but part of his aim in building up the collection was undoubtedly to enhance the international prestige of France itself.[20] That he was successful in this is evident from the desire of the English, in the person of John, duke of Bedford, regent of France, to acquire the library as one of the country's assets.[21] Again, the collections made by Charles' brothers, Jean, duc de Berri (1340–1416), and Philip the Bold of Burgundy (1342–1404), though less extensive, rivalled his in terms of quality, and Philip's was the foundation of the renowned Burgundian ducal library of the fifteenth century.[22]

The earliest firm evidence we have of a similar outlook on the part of an English royal book collector concerns another of Henry V's brothers and the leader of the pro-war faction at Henry VI's court, Humphrey, duke of Gloucester. In Humphrey's assiduous pursuit of Italian scholars and human-ist texts, and his adoption of the essentially public rôle of university benefac-tor, it is possible to detect a careful fostering of the European renaissance ideal of princely 'magnificence'.[23] The depth of Humphrey's scholarship may be open to doubt – there are indications in contemporary sources that his preferred reading matter was in French rather than Latin[24] – but it is clear that he recognised the status which could accrue in the political sphere from acts of literary patronage.

Whilst Edward IV's pretensions did not lie in the realm of scholarship, it would appear that in collecting the books for his royal library he, too, had an eye to reputation, and in this regard the contrast between the volumes he bought from overseas and those which he owned before he assumed the throne in March of 1460/1 could not be more marked. Neither BL MS Royal 12.E.xv, a thirteenth- to fourteenth-century assemblage of Latin medical

tracts and a copy of the pseudo-Aristotelian *Secreta Secretorum*, nor Harley
3352, a small Latin formulary, are distinguished volumes, and the wear to
which both have been subject emphasises the practical, utilitarian nature of
their contents.[25] His Flemish books, by comparison, are remarkable for their
size and weight: to judge from their pristine condition, which suggests that
they were used as display rather than reading copies, there may be some
justification in the charge that they were ordered by the pound,[26] just as fine
bindings today may be bought by the yard. The prominence given in their
decorated pages to the badges of the house of York, to the arms of Edward
himself and, in some cases, to those of his sons Edward, prince of Wales, and
Richard, duke of York, indicates that behind his acquisitions lay an ambition
to publicise the Yorkist dynasty through artefacts of considerable splendour.
Collectively, the books stand as the fruits of a lesson in cultural propaganda
learnt from Edward's contact with the court of Burgundy.

As events turned out this library served to commemorate, and not cele-
brate, the period of Yorkist rule, and it was left to the first Tudor monarch,
Henry VII, to reap the diplomatic benefits conferred by its possession – or so
it would seem, if the protestations of Claude de Seysel may be taken at face
value. De Seysel, French ambassador to England in 1508, presented a copy of
his translation of Xenophon's *Anabasis* to Henry with a prologue in which he
professed admiration for the king's library and referred to Henry's reputation
as a lover of books, stating that these two factors had inspired the gift.[27]

Yet the question of the extent to which Henry actively assumed the role of a
patron of manuscripts, despite the claims which have recently been made,[28]
remains an open one. His most outstanding achievement was the commissioning of sumptuous books illustrated by one of the foremost Bruges/Ghent
manuscript painters of the time, the so-called Master of the Prayerbooks,
whose other patrons included Count Engelbert II of Nassau and Isabella of
Castille. These are BL MSS Royal 19.C.viii, a copy of the Burgundian
didactic allegory, 'Limagination de vraye noblesse', made by his librarian
Quentin Poulet in 1496; Royal 16.F.ii, a volume of the poems of Charles
d'Orléans and works of princely instruction, written c. 1500, probably for
Prince Arthur; and a book of Hours now in the possession of the duke of
Devonshire, which Henry, 'louyng fadre', gave to his daughter Margaret,
queen of Scotland.[29] At an earlier period he commissioned a small book of
Hours of the Use of Sarum illustrated in Paris by an artist who also carried
out work for members of the French royal family, whom Eleanor Spencer has
called the Chief Associate of Maître François. The borders of this manuscript, PML M 815, abound with Henry's badges, including the dragon of
Cadwaladwr, the Beaufort portcullis, the white greyhound, and the red rose
of Lancaster; Henry himself is depicted kneeling before King David on fol.
153v.[30]

The particular cultural debt which the late medieval English monarchy owed to Burgundian example is clear. Indeed, the idea that the Edwardian and Henrician courts sought to emulate Burgundian fashion – whether in choice of texts, the style and design of books, painting or dramatic spectacle – has become a *sine qua non* for scholars studying the period.[31] While this view should be modified where Henry VII is concerned, in that his patronage of the Chief Associate of Maître François and the Parisian printer Antoine Vérard reveals an equal openness to influence from France,[32] there is sufficient manuscript evidence to suggest that English book-buyers in general responded to the lead set by Burgundy.

During Edward IV's reign courtiers such as Richard Neville, earl of Warwick, and William, Lord Hastings, obtained books from Flanders,[33] and the only non-devotional manuscript which may at present be associated with the Prince of Wales, PUL MS Garrett 168, a French translation of a propagandist newsletter describing the elaborate funeral of Mohammed II, 'empereur des turcs', and the civil strife which followed his death, was made in a Flemish workshop.[34] Among the many examples of Flemish books owned by individuals attached to the court of Henry VII are Stonyhurst College, MS 60, a book of Hours containing the obit of Catherine, wife of Sir Reginald Bray, and Bodleian Library, MS Rawlinson liturg. f.36, a book of Latin and English prayers which belonged to Sir Gilbert Talbot, K.G.;[35] BL MS Royal 16.F.VIII, which contains a number of texts including *Le Régime de Santé* and has the arms of Charles Somerset inserted into the border of fol. 1r;[36] and BL Add. MS 17012, a book of Hours which seems to have circulated widely at the courts of Henry and his son, since it contains autograph inscriptions of various members of royalty, addressed to the anonymous owner.[37]

In a different social sphere altogether, ownership of Lambeth Palace 6, a copy of the *Brut* written in English but with illustrations of Flemish workmanship (perhaps by the Master of Edward IV) has been attributed to William Purches, mercer, merchant adventurer and Lord Mayor of London;[38] and the fine frontispiece to the Guild Book of the Confraternity of the Holy Trinity at Luton (founded in 1474) is apparently the work of a Flemish artist who, it has been proposed, may have been brought to England for the express purpose of fulfilling the commission.[39] Burgundian influence may even be glimpsed in the choices made by those readers who could not afford (or chose not to afford) the original article. The courtly aspirations of John Paston II are seen in the numerous accounts in French and English of Burgundian chivalric display incorporated in his 'grete boke', copied for him in 1468 by the freelance scribe William Ebesham; and his younger brother, John III, owned a newsletter in English describing the diplomatic extravaganza which marked the meeting of Duke Charles the Bold and the Emperor Frederick III at Trier in 1473.[40] A copy of this last item also appears in Manchester, Chetham's Library, MS A.6.31 (8009), a late fifteenth-century paper miscellany of romances and saints' lives possibly compiled for, and certainly later owned by, a citizen of London.[41]

These last examples are a graphic demonstration of the interdependence of cultural, political and economic ties: dynastic alliances and trading agreements ensured a continuous traffic between England and Burgundy and facilitated cultural exchange at all levels. But the readiness with which Burgundian fashions were received in England is also a measure of England's continuing participation in a European culture. Another manifestation of this legacy of internationalism is the hold which French retained as a language for the lay reader, despite the growing status of English as the primary language of government, business administration and entertainment.[42] It is now widely acknowledged that French was the preferred literary medium at the court of Richard II.[43] Fifty years later John Talbot may have presented Margaret of Anjou with a volume of romances and chivalric works in French ostensibly in order that she might not forget her native tongue on her marriage to Henry VI,[44] but foreign diplomats had observed Henry's proficiency in that language many years before,[45] and it would seem that bilingualism, at least with regard to the written word, was not uncommon among several social groupings throughout the fifteenth century.

Annotations and repairs to the fabric of earlier medieval manuscripts of French works, for example, show that certain texts remained in circulation and engaged the active interest of their readers. CUL MS Add. 7071, a fourteenth-century copy of the *Estoire del Saint Graal* and the *Suite du Merlin*, written by an Anglo-Norman scribe, underwent conservation treatment towards the end of the fifteenth century when fols. 269–273, 276 and 335–342 were replaced by new parchment and filled by a scribe who attempted to match his work with that of his predecessor, and a keen interest in the work is elsewhere revealed by a note collating the text with Caxton's edition of Malory's Arthurian compendium.[46] One later medieval owner of another fourteenth-century Arthurian collection, BL Royal 14.E.iii, probably Sir Richard Roos (d. 1481), recorded the contents of the volume on a flyleaf (fol. 2v) observing accurately that 'The bigynnyng of þe firste boke of Sankgrall endureth to þende of þe / iiij^{xx} viij lefe' (fol. 88v), and that of the *Mort Artu*, only 'þe begynnyng ys yn / þis same boke'.[47] The inscription 'Cest lyu*re* est mergeret dame de Roos' appears in a roughly contemporary copy of the *Voeux du Paon* in New York Public Library (Spencer MS 9, fol. ivr) and, given the occurrence of the motto and signature 'A moy le mieulx Roos R' on the same page, it is likely that this Margaret may be identified as Sir Richard's wife.[48] Lower down in the social hierarchy, John Clerk, 'grocero ac apotecario / regis Edwardi quarti postconquestum', was in possession of Harley 273, a composite volume of the thirteenth and fourteenth centuries, the contents of which include a French psalter, Grosseteste's 'les Reules', a prose Charlemagne romance, the *Manuel des Peches*, 'la purgatoire de St Patrice', 'Modus praeparandi Colores diverso', charms, medical recipes and prayers.[49]

It was not only French texts with a well-established appeal which were in demand: the works of contemporary French authors such as Christine de Pizan enjoyed considerable popularity within England.[50] Henry IV's interest attests to Christine's reputation in court circles during her lifetime, and her work continued to find an audience among royalty after her death; the *Epistre d'Othéa* was one of five chivalric texts in a volume copied in Flanders for Edward IV (MS Royal 14.E.II), and Caxton maintained that he received a copy of her *Liure des faiz d'armes et de chevalerie* to translate from Henry VII, through the agency of the earl of Oxford.[51] The occupation of France undoubtedly stimulated English interest in her writing, and several manuscripts which originated on the continent probably found their way into this country as a direct result of the war. The *Faiz d'armes* is the penultimate item in Talbot's magnificent presentation volume made for Margaret of Anjou, perhaps in Rouen, while the lavishly illustrated edition of her collected works made for Isabeau of France, now BL MS Harley 4431, came into the possession of the Wydville family.[52] Among the more modest copies, MS Royal 19.A.XIX, the *Cité des Dames*, contains badges of the house of York inserted into the decoration of its opening page; Bodley 821, another copy of the *Faiz d'armes*, has notes in English on the arms of 'maister Movun' added on fol. 140r; and Westminster Abbey 21, where the *Epistre au Dieu d'Amours* is included in a collection of French lyrics, has flyleaf annotations in English.[53]

Other buyers were sufficiently interested in her work to obtain copies from book producers based in England. Sir John Fastolf could have learnt of Christine while he was resident in France, but his copy of the *Othéa*, MS Laud misc. 570, although made by craftsmen who were probably both foreign, may well have been commissioned after his return home.[54] Harley 219 and Bodley Fr.d.5 which contain, respectively, the *Othéa* and the *Liure des trois vertus* (sometimes known as the *Trésor de la cité des dames*), and Royal 19.B.XVIII and Harley 4605, both of which contain the *Faiz d'armes*, are all of English provenance, although, intriguingly, the latter was copied in London by a Frenchman, who recorded in a colophon the completion of his task on 15 May 1434; the illustrations which accompany the text are by an English artist.[55] There are no clues as to the early ownership of the majority of these manuscripts, but the names of two more of Christine's medieval readers are known: Alice de la Pole, duchess of Suffolk, owned a copy of the 'Citee de Dames couered with rede lether clasped with laton' newe'; and Anne, widow of John, fifth Lord Scrope of Bolton, in 1498 bequeathed 'to my lorde of Surrey a Frenche booke called the Pistill of Othia'.[56]

Access to contemporary, or near-contemporary French writing was not, however, restricted to the nobility. The book collection of Thomas Kebell, 'the kynges seriaunt at Lawe', who died in 1500, is remarkable for the breadth of interest it displays. In addition to printed books of English and continental provenance, Kebell owned several manuscripts of French texts, amongst them René d'Anjou's *L'Abuse en Court*; Froissart's *Chronicles* (which he left to Lady Hungerford); and 'a Feyre book of Frenche wreton in parchement de Jehan de Boccace'.[57] Knowledge of law French was essential for anyone engaged in legal practice during the Middle Ages, but it seems from Kebell's choice of books that he viewed the language as one apt for recreation and enjoyment, as well as for professional purposes.[58]

French texts and books produced abroad have figured large in this discussion so far, as is commensurate with the attention accorded them by those who were in a position to exercise choice in the purchase of books. But it must be admitted that the state of our knowledge concerning English secular and devotional manuscripts is still far from complete, and if more information were available regarding the provenance of a number of handsome books which are known to have been produced in this country, we would have a clearer understanding of their status relative to those which originated on the continent.

A striking illustration of this point is provided by Lydgate's *Fall of Princes*. The presentation of the text in several of the manuscripts is exceptionally elaborate. Harley 1776, for instance, has 157 miniatures; Rosenbach MS 439/16 in Philadelphia has seven miniatures and over 200 illuminated initials; and the Huntington/Sloane copy fifty-eight miniatures (with spaces left for others which were never completed) in addition to extravagantly decorated borders in which oversized flowers and fruit-trees, mermaids and musicians, exotic birds and animals run riot.[59] Yet in spite of the courtly context affirmed for the work by Lydgate in his references to Humphrey of Gloucester's rôle as patron, none of these copies can be assigned a courtly provenance, and no presentation copy is extant.[60] An equally puzzling instance of an unplaced de luxe book is a late fifteenth-century *Alexander* manuscript in the National Library of Wales, MS Peniarth 481D. The volume contains Benedict Burgh's *Cato Major*, followed by an interpolated recension of the *Historia de Preliis*; the latter is illustrated by a unique cycle of twenty-six miniatures derived from a variety of sources, the style of which recalls contemporary Flemish workmanship.[61]

It is to be hoped that the problems posed by manuscripts such as these will eventually be resolved, as the investigation of the activities of identifiable scribes, illustrators and decorators leads to a better understanding of patterns and methods of production, and suggests ways in which these were tailored to meet the demands of potential patrons and buyers. This process is under way with regard to Harley 1776, which has been attributed to a centre, possibly based in Suffolk, which seems to have specialised in issuing Lydgate's poems in copies ranging from the luxurious to the more routine; and to Rosenbach 439/16, which has recently been added to the *œuvre* of Ricardus Franciscus.[62]

18   London, Lambeth Palace Library. MS 265. *The Dicts and Sayings of the Philosophers*, 1477, frontispiece, fol. vi verso.

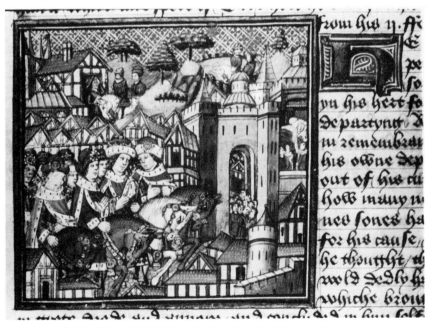

19   London, British Library, MS Harley 326, *The Three Kings' Sons*, c. 1480, fol. 102r.

20   London, British Library, MS Harley 326, *The Three Kings' Sons*, c. 1480, fol. 117v.

It is also now possible to offer further information on another artist probably based in London, whose only previously known work is the frontispiece to Lambeth 265, Anthony Wydville's translation of the *Dicts and Sayings of the Philosophers*, in which the author is depicted presenting his book to Edward IV (Ill. 18).[63] On the basis of technique and the recurrence of common motifs and figure-types it may be concluded that this artist was responsible for illustrating Harley 326, the unique copy of the English translation of the mid-fifteenth-century Burgundian romance of *The Three Kings' Sons*[64] (Ills. 19, 20). Details of costume indicate that this manuscript, like Lambeth 265, was made towards the end of Edward's reign, c. 1480. The programme of twenty-two miniatures is relatively sophisticated and is unparalleled in the extant copies of the French text, none of which is illustrated.[65] It may be that the artist's exemplar is now lost, but even allowing for the possibility that the cycle is derivative, the quality of production singles out Harley 326 from the majority of Middle English romance manuscripts,[66] and suggests that it was made to the order of a discriminating patron. Regrettably, heavy cropping of the pages has virtually destroyed the numerous annotations made by early readers of the romance, and what was possibly an ownership inscription at the end of the text, on fol. 123v, has been erased.

Those few cases of manuscripts in which both the place of origin and the identity of the patron are known are of obvious value in establishing points of reference for future research.[67] One such is Part II of NYPL MS Spencer 3, named the Wingfield Hours after its early sixteenth-century owner, Sir Richard Wingfield, which is one of a number of manuscripts in which Kathleen Scott has detected the influence of an artist whom she calls the Caesar Master. Its six fine miniatures are set within decorated borders notable for their exuberance and vitality; among the motifs are birds (including a delightful green parrot, fols. 47v, 68v), butterflies, a cat holding a mouse in its mouth (fol. 68v), cornflowers, columbines and roses. The presence of various badges of the Stafford family, together with the fact that some of the prayers were adapted for the use of a woman named Anna or Anne, indicate that the book was made for Anne Neville, wife of Humphrey Stafford, earl of Stafford (d. 1460), presumably before her second marriage, to Walter Blount, first Baron Mountjoy, in 1467.[68]

Aside from any spiritual benefits derived by Anne Neville from her possession of Spencer 3, its very luxuriousness was a comment upon her social standing. But it was not only members of the nobility who perceived the value of books in asserting or confirming status, and who found the resources of the native book-trade sufficient to meet their needs. The two large folio manuscripts containing the statutes and membership lists of the fraternities of Corpus Christi and Our Lady's Assumption, which were compiled for the Skinners' Company during the second half of the fifteenth century, demonstrate the wealth and social prestige which these organisations had gathered to themselves by the late Middle Ages.[69] Among those enrolled were royalty, nobility, and prominent City governors from companies other than Skinners. The book which was made for the Fraternity of Our Lady's Assumption is particularly interesting. Although this was a yeoman fraternity, founded by and for the members of the Company who were less powerful and prosperous than the governmental élite of the livery, who formed the association of Corpus Christi, two queens of England – Elizabeth Wydville and Margaret of Anjou – were patrons, and their rôle is commemorated by portrait miniatures on fols. 32v and 34v.[70] In the former, Edward IV's queen is shown in full coronation regalia standing on a grassy hillock surrounded by an extra-ordinary profusion of flowers – roses and gilly-flowers in dusky pink and white, picked out with gold.[71] The miniature of Margaret of Anjou, 'sumty = / me wyff and spowse to kyng / harry the sexthe', appropriately enough, is smaller and less ostentatious (Ill. 21). Dressed in an ermine-lined hooded cloak and accompanied by a lady-in-waiting, Margaret kneels in prayer at a desk on which lie an open book and a crown and sceptre; the diaper-patterned background is powdered with marguerites, presumably in compliment to the one-time queen.[72] Later in this volume is a full-page miniature of the Assumption (fol. 41r; Ill. 22). Here gold is used extravagantly in the nimbus surrounding the figure of the Virgin, and in the clothing of the Trinity. Ermine, the most expensive commodity of the Skinners' trade, lines Mary's cloak and ornaments the hem of her gown, and this overt double reference to the Virgin's regal status and to mercantile aspiration is echoed in the ermine cap, one of the Company's symbols, which an adoring angel holds out.[73] Together the two manuscripts reflect a similar awareness of the Company's importance in civic life which, earlier in the century, had occasioned the commissioning of Lydgate's expository verses on the 'precessyoun of þe feste of corpus cristi', held annually in London under the auspices of the Skinners.[74]

A comparable understanding of the value of de luxe books for self-promotional or even propagandist purposes can be found in the celebrations of the lineage and achievements of individual families. One of the most outstanding illustrated English books of the period (and one for which there is no continental parallel) is the Beauchamp Pageants (BL MS Cotton Julius E.IV, art. 6), which depicts the chivalric exploits of Richard Beauchamp, earl of Warwick. The volume was evidently made for one of his descendants, perhaps, it has been suggested, for another Anne Neville, Beauchamp's daughter, in an effort to win back her inheritance and social position following the disaffection and death in 1471 of her husband, Richard Neville.[75] The emphasis which is placed in the series of drawings on Beauchamp's devoted service to the young Henry VI would certainly seem to support the idea that political considerations lay behind this act of patronage. Various manuscripts owned by the Percy family also simultaneously reflect a proud heritage and

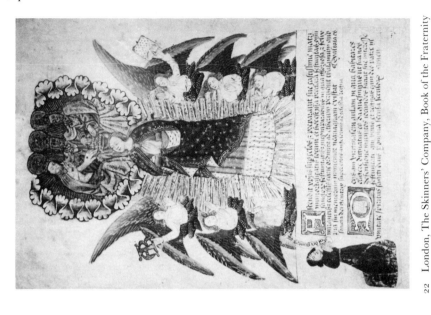

22   London, The Skinners' Company, Book of the Fraternity of Our Lady's Assumption, c. 1470 onwards, fol. 41r.

21   London, The Skinners' Company, Book of the Fraternity of Our Lady's Assumption, c. 1470 onwards, fol. 34v.

proclaim the family's loyalty to the reigning monarch – an astute enough move, bearing in mind the charges of rebellion which document the reversals of Percy fortunes in the fifteenth century and later. MS Royal 18.D.II, for instance, the nucleus of which is formed by Lydgate's *Troy Book* and *Siege of Thebes*, copied for William Herbert and his wife Ann Devereux, was considerably augmented during the lifetime of their grandson, Henry Percy, fifth earl of Northumberland, and among the additions were Skelton's poem 'vpon the dolorus dethe and muche lamentable chance' of the fourth earl, who was killed in Yorkshire in 1489 while collecting taxes for Henry VII; Lydgate's verses on the kings of England, continued to include Henry VIII; and a verse chronicle on the Percy family written by 'William Peeris clerke and preste secretary' to the fifth earl.[76] Besides the efforts made by Skelton and Peeris to underline the strength of the fourth earl's support for the crown, which led directly to his death, his son's sense of duty to the young Henry VIII is stressed by an emblematic drawing and verses in Latin and English.[77] In another Percy manuscript, an elaborate genealogy (Bodley Rolls 5), the line of descent of the family is shown, as is usual in such documents, in tandem with that of the English monarchy (the latter running in unbroken sequence from Adam). The quality of production is high: the text is calligraphically embellished and interspersed with pen and ink drawings and painted shields and badges.[78]

Genealogical rolls made for those who could command fewer resources reveal an equal sense of pride, even where this is regrettably unmatched by the standard of execution. NYPL MS Spencer 193, for example, detailing the history of the Boteler/Sudeley house of Gloucestershire from the reign of Edward the Confessor down to the time of Henry VI, is a singularly unimpressive roll, and the crudeness of the drawings of the English kings is complemented by the uneasy craftsmanship of the accompanying verses.[79]

While families and other well-defined social groups were striving to establish pedigree and reputation through the commissioning of commemorative records, it could be argued that there was a broader movement within England to consolidate a sense of national identity through historical writing. A measure of this ambition to come to terms with the present through knowledge of the past was the translation of the *Brut d'Engleterre* into English around the end of the fourteenth century.[80] The *Brut*, with at least 169 surviving manuscripts, may be judged to have been the most widely circulated secular text of the Middle Ages, apparently exceeding even the homiletic verse treatise *The Prick of Conscience* in popularity.[81] The level of interest which the text generated is shown by the extensive annotations which appear in many of the manuscripts: the *Brut* was a work which invited a committed response on the part of its readers.[82] The evident demand for copies has led to the suggestion that it may have been one of the few texts to be produced speculatively by stationers or booksellers.[83] Confirmation of this will have to await further investigation of its immensely complex textual history, but in the meantime it may be remarked that extant manuscripts show that it was available in a range of materials and formats designed to suit the pockets of a variety of customers drawn from different levels of society.[84]

The Flemish-produced Lambeth 6, mentioned above, is notable for its opulence, and other handsome (if scarcely comparable) copies include Digby 185, possibly made for Sir William Hopton, treasurer to Richard III, which has the arms of the Hoptons and related families painted on decorative shields at the beginning of each item in the book;[85] and Harvard University, Houghton Library, Richardson 35, a paper and parchment folio volume which is adorned by an entertaining series of marginal vignettes and grotesques, and contains the near-contemporary signature (?) of 'Richard Thomas / of Nethe' (fol. 183r).[86] Sir Thomas Bourchier, son of Henry Bourchier, first earl of Essex, owned PUL Garrett 150, a late fifteenth-century parchment manuscript which, although now badly worn, retains something of its original attractiveness.[87] Going slightly down-market, Sloane 2027, a large paper miscellany written by one scribe probably during the 1460s or 70s, contains, in a neat hand of the second half of the fifteenth century, the inscription 'Wylliam Braundon of knolle in the Counte of waryke' (fol. 96r), which is repeated with variations on several blank pages.[88] The other items in the book are Vegetius' *De Re Militari*, John Russell's *Boke of kerving and nurtur* and Lydgate and Burgh's 'booke Off the gouernaunce off kyngis & pryncis' (otherwise known as 'Secrees of Old Philosoffres'), and the thematic consistency of this material gives a comparatively rare insight into the tastes of minor provincial landowners of the time. Lambeth 491, on the other hand, was probably read in an urban milieu. Compiled during the second quarter of the fifteenth century, this smaller paper and parchment codex was written by a scribe from Essex who was regularly employed in the book-trade, perhaps, as Dr Doyle suggests, in London; other secular miscellanies which he copied either wholly or in part are Huntington HM 114 and Harley 3943.[89] Names added in the margins indicate that the manuscript did not travel far from its place of origin, one note stating that a late medieval owner dwelt 'in the tone of barakyng' (fol. 22v.).

The urge towards self-definition through the reading of history is perhaps characteristic of societies in a state of flux, and one factor which undoubtedly contributed to the pre-eminence of the *Brut* amongst English secular works during the fifteenth century was the spread of what Malcolm Parkes has called 'non-pragmatic' literacy amongst the middle classes.[90] Those who, whether members of the gentry, or professional or mercantile classes, had previously acquired the skills of reading and writing in order to conduct their business affairs with greater efficiency, were now increasingly directing those same skills to other ends, using the written word for edification and entertainment.[91]

The growth of this sector of the potential market was in part dependent upon and in part encouraged by changes which were occurring within the book-trade: as paper replaced parchment as the staple material for the copying of plain reading texts, so books came within the reach of a wider public.[92] This broadening of the readership seems to have had an immediate effect on the kinds of texts which were copied commercially. It has been observed, for example, that of the ninety-five surviving Middle English verse romances, less than a third are found in codices which date from before c. 1440, even though around two-thirds of the total were probably composed before or during the fourteenth century.[93] Making due allowance for the fact that some of the extant romance manuscripts are 'home-made' miscellanies (in itself an indication of the general increase in literacy),[94] and for the possibility that fewer copies have survived from the earlier than the later part of the period,[95] it is clear that professional book producers responded to a demand for texts of this type. Many romances were issued in booklets – an economical mode of production which also gave the customer the freedom to select as many, or as few, texts as he or she required;[96] whilst others either formed part of anthologies designed to exemplify certain thematic interests;[97] or were of sufficient bulk to constitute substantial volumes by themselves.[98]

Many of these works were, of course, based upon French originals, and it could be argued that translations were made to satisfy the tastes of those who, newly literate in the native vernacular, did not have the ability to read in any other language. There is probably a degree of truth in this although, as remarked earlier, knowledge of French was more widespread than has perhaps always been supposed. But at the same time English was coming into its own as a literary language, and the level of sophistication to which the writers of English romances could aspire is shown in the early fifteenth-century *Sowdone of Babylon*, which derives from two French Charlemagne romances, and which is embellished with passages of lyrical description inspired by Chaucer's *Canterbury Tales* and *Anelida and Arcite*.[99] The success of this undertaking may, in critical terms, be debatable, but the unique manuscript, PUL MS Garrett 140, dating from after 1450, gives some assurance of the modest prestige which attached to its ownership.[100] The volume is of parchment, and no great effort has been made to economise on the use of this more expensive material: the romance is copied in single-column format, in an attractive and competent mixed hand in which secretary forms predominate; the frequent spaces left for rubricated initials have never been filled, but some thought has evidently been given to the lay-out of the text on the page. The work concludes with an explicit written in an elaborate display script, the ascenders of the first line being decorated with strapwork calligraphy. In short, although the manuscript is by no means an exceptional production, it is pleasant to look at, and to handle.

The deliberate invocation of a Chaucerian poetic in this romance, clumsy as it may be, testifies to Chaucer's contribution to the higher status which English writing came to enjoy in the fifteenth century, a status which was further enhanced by the work of his followers, and in particular, of John Lydgate.[101] It is perhaps no exaggeration to suggest that possession of a Chaucerian text was seen as a gauge of an individual's fashionable tastes, irrespective of that individual's position within society. The attractively produced volume of shorter poems by Chaucer, Lydgate and their courtly imitators commissioned by John Stanley of Hooton, now Bodleian Library MS Fairfax 16, might be seen as an appropriate choice for one whose connections with the court are well documented, and the full-page fronti-spiece illustrating *The Complaint of Mars and Venus* – evidently added in a metropolitan shop to upgrade the compilation – adds to the impression that it was a treasured book.[102] But the contents of Fairfax 16 are to some extent paralleled in a much cheaper paper codex, Cambridge, Magdalene College, MS Pepys 2006, owned by 'Will'mo ffetypace mercerij lond'', later in the century; and the apparently routine production of texts by Chaucer, Lydgate and Hoccleve by metropolitan scribes during the 1460s and 70s argues for an extensive audience drawn from the same social sphere as Fetypace.[103] Equally, Lydgate, although he took pains to cultivate a reputation at court, appealed to a wide readership. His *Troy Book* was dedicated to Henry V, and expensive copies were owned by Lady Margaret Beaufort, William Herbert, earl of Pembroke, and the well-to-do families of the Chaworths, Carents, and Thwaites/Knyvets,[104] but it also found a public amongst the mercantile classes: Digby 232, another extensively illustrated book, has the arms of the Vintners' Company added into the border decoration of its opening page; and Harvard f. MS Eng.752, a paper folio book copied by two scribes who are not noted for the care with which they approached their task, bears the often-repeated inscription 'John Burner vintner' in a hand of c. 1500.[105]

The status of English prose, too, rose in the fourteenth and fifteenth centuries. Some indication of its renewed vitality has been given earlier, in the discussion of the *Brut*. At the most profound level, however, the *Brut* is a popular work, and it is to other translations – especially those sponsored by aristocratic or noble patrons – that we must look to understand the evolution of English into a prestigious medium for secular writing.[106] An apt illustration of the process is provided by Vegetius' *De Re Militari*.[107] This classical Latin treatise on warfare circulated extensively throughout western Europe during the medieval period, and several copies in the original language are known to have been produced and/or owned in England from the twelfth century onwards.[108] The text was eventually translated into all the major European languages, and in various French versions it featured in many royal and noble libraries, including those of Charles V of France, Jean, duc de Berri, Charles d'Orléans, Philip the Good of Burgundy and Louis of Bruges, seigneur de Gruthuyse; and in England, of Edward III, Thomas, duke of Gloucester, Humphrey, duke of Gloucester, Sir John Fastolf and Edward IV.[109]

The earliest, and apparently most widely disseminated of the English translations was that now generally attributed to John Walton, canon of Oseney, who made it, according to the colophon, for Thomas, Lord Berkeley, in 1408.[110] Several of the surviving manuscripts perpetuate the aristocratic associations established by the translator. The most luxurious of them is Digby 233, a massive illustrated volume which opens with Trevisa's translation of Giles of Rome's *De Regimine Principum*, also carried out at the behest of Lord Berkeley, in 1402.[111] The identity of the first owner, or commissioner, is obscure, but the manuscript bears the inscription 'loyallte me ley / Mary hastyngys hungreford / bottreaux mollens and Mulles / god help me' on fol. 228r, and Mary (to whom Thomas Kebell left his Froissart) was daughter-in-law of Edward IV's chamberlain, Lord Hastings.[112] Less ostentatious are Richard III's copy (Royal 18.A.xii, discussed above); Douce 291, made, almost certainly in London, for the Chalons of Devon c. 1445–47; and PML M 775, the composite parchment book which was early in the possession of Sir John Astley, whose arms have been added to the opening page of the Vegetius. It seems that this last manuscript continued in circulation at court, since the names 'Thomas fytzhugh', 'Bryan Tunstall' and 'Thomas Tunstall' occur on a flyleaf, fol. 2r.[113] Add. 14408, Lansdowne 285 and Sloane 2027, on the other hand, are all paper copies owned by members of the middle ranks of society, the last two by John Paston II and William Brandon of Knowle, respectively.[114] The Additional manuscript was probably made in 1473 for 'Nycolas de Saint lo Cheualier', of Somerset, whose *ex libris* is found on fol. 73r. Its other contents are Lydgate's and Burgh's *Governance of Kings and Princes* and an English translation of the *Consilia Isidori*.[115] The volume is the work of one scribe, who writes in a large and rather ugly anglicana, and decoration is limited to rubricated initials. In the case of Laud 416, a slightly more ambitious production, we know the name of the scribe. This paper miscellany, which contains, in addition to the Vegetius, didactic texts, Lydgate's *Siege of Thebes* and *Governance of Kings and Princes*, and Chaucer's *Parliament of Fowls*, bears an inscription on fol. 226v, at the end of the *De Re Militari*, which reads 'scriptus Rhodo per Johannem Neuton die 25 octobris 1459'.[116] Later in its history this copy, like Digby 233, seems to have come into the hands of a female reader, for on the rear pastedown is the name 'syster Anne colvylle', together with a request for prayers. Anne Colville was a nun at Syon in the early sixteenth century and her name also occurs, with perhaps rather more decorum, in Harley 933, a 'common profit' volume of Walter Hilton's *Scale of Perfection*.[117]

The diverse nature of the extant manuscripts of the *De Re Militari* attests once more to the resourcefulness of professional book producers, in their ability to cater to the requirements of individual commissioners and buyers. Yet this very diversity highlights some of those fundamental questions concerning the relationship between the producer and the consumer with which this chapter began. Did customers have a free hand in deciding upon the content, format and design of the books they bought? Were they restricted in their choice of texts to what was available in their immediate locale, be it provincial or metropolitan; or could they on occasions provide professional scribes with exemplars which they had obtained from elsewhere?

Conclusive evidence on these points is not easy to come by, but from John Paston's 'grete boke' it is possible to gain an idea of the control which a buyer could exert over the making of a book. The financial terms upon which Paston employed William Ebesham are known, and it may be assumed that Sir John specified both the texts and the amount of decoration he wanted: he was charged 3s 4d by Ebesham 'for the Rubrisshyng of All the booke', although this sum did not necessarily cover the flourishing of initials.[118] It is even possible that Paston supplied copy for his manuscript. Recent research stresses the textual similarities between items in Lansdowne 285 – among them the Vegetius – and PML M 775 and, given that Paston and Sir John Astley both attended the court of Edward IV (Astley was created K.G. in 1461) it is a plausible theory that personal contact and recommendation played a role in the transmission of these particular works.[119] Such well-documented instances of book production are, however, rare (although a contemporary example which may be cited is the bill for the making of a psalter paid in 1467 by John Howard, later duke of Norfolk, to Thomas Lympnour of Bury).[120] In the main, investigation of the make-up of manuscripts provides the most reliable evidence concerning the choices open to buyers. The recurrence of the same texts within the component booklets of a volume, for example, as in William Fetypace's book, where there are duplicate copies of Chaucer's *Complaint of Mars* and *Complaint of Venus* and other of his shorter poems, suggest that scribes and/or stationers increasingly came to rely upon reproducing a set combination of texts within units which, although self-contained and relatively inexpensive to produce, could be collected together by a purchaser to create a more substantial 'library'.[121] This move towards speed and efficiency of production is paralleled by a tendency towards standardisation of format, whether in the presentation of secular poetry, as in some of Lydgate's work, or of genealogical rolls, or books of statutes.[122] Such anticipation of the economic rationale of printing, whilst benefiting the reading and buying public at large by reducing costs, inevitably lessened the opportunities for the exercise of individual preference.

NOTES

1 On changes in manuscript production and the subsequent effect on readership see M.B. Parkes, *English Cursive Books Hands, 1250–1500*, 2nd edn (London, 1979), p. xvi; and Parkes, 'The Literacy of the Laity'.

2 On Bedford, see M.J. Barber, 'The Books and Patronage of Learning of a Fifteenth Century Prince', *The Book Collector*, 12 (1963), 308–15, updated and corrected in the light of new research by Jenny Stratford, 'The Manuscripts of John, Duke of Bedford: Library and Chapel', *England in the Fifteenth Century: Proceedings of the 1986 Harlaxton Symposium*, ed. D. Williams (Woodbridge, 1987), pp. 329–50; and on Talbot's French manuscripts, M.R. James, *A Descriptive Catalogue of the Second Series of Fifty Manuscripts . . . in the Collection of Henry Yates Thompson* (Cambridge, 1902), pp. 218–38, N.R. Ker *Medieval Manuscripts in British Libraries*, 2 (Oxford, 1977), pp. 113–18, and Douglas Gray, 'A Middle English Illustrated Poem', in *Medieval Studies for J.A.W. Bennett*, edited by P.L. Heyworth (Oxford, 1981), pp. 185–205. (Cf. the discussion of Talbot's presentation volume for Margaret of Anjou, below). On Humphrey of Gloucester, see A. Sammut, *Unfredo Duca di Gloucester e gli Umanisti*, Medioevo e Umanesimo 41 (Padua, 1980); Roberto Weiss, *Humanism in England during the Fifteenth Century*, 3rd edn (Oxford, 1967); K.H. Vickers, *Humphrey Duke of Gloucester* (London, 1907), ch. 10 and Appendix A. For details of Tiptoft's activities, see R.J. Mitchell, *John Tiptoft* (London, 1938), and 'A Renaissance Library: The Collection of John Tiptoft, Earl of Worcester', *The Library*, 4th series 18 (1937), 67–83; Weiss, *Humanism in England*, ch. 7, and 'Another Tiptoft Manuscript', *BQR*, 8 (1935–8), 157–64, 234–5; and *Manuscripts at Oxford: R.W. Hunt Exhibition*, ed. A.C. de la Mare and B.C. Barker-Benfield (Oxford, 1980), pp. 99–101. On the importation of books by individuals for their own use, see also Ch. 8 above, pp. 180–3.

3 See, on Scheerre and the Fastolf and Caxton Masters, G.M. Spriggs, 'Unnoticed Bodleian Manuscripts Illuminated by Herman Scheere and his School', *BLR*, 7 (1964), 193–203, and 'The Nevill Hours and the School of Herman Scheere', *JWCI*, 37 (1974), 104–30; J.J.G. Alexander, 'A Lost Leaf from a Bodleian Book of Hours', *BLR*, 8 (1967–72), 248–51; and Scott, *The Caxton Master*. Milo de Carraria is discussed in R.W. Hunt and A.C. de la Mare, *Duke Humfrey and English Humanism in the Fifteenth Century* (Oxford, 1970), pp. 13–14, and in Scott, *The Mirroure of the Worlde*, pp. 41, 43. The work of Ricardus Franciscus is noted in Scott, 'A Mid-Fifteenth Century Illuminating Shop', p. 170, n. 3; J.J.G. Alexander, 'William Abell', p. 170, n. 37; and '*Sixty Bokes Olde and Newe': Manuscripts and Early Printed Books from Libraries in and near Philadelphia Illustrating Chaucer's Sources, his Works and their Influence*, etc., ed. D. Anderson (Knoxville, 1986), pp. 105–10.

4 For the most recent summary of the evidence see the essays in Scattergood and Sherborne, and compare the comparative survey of European manuscript illumination by A. Stones, 'Secular Manuscript Illustration in France', in *Medieval Manuscripts and Textual Criticism*, North Carolina Studies in the Romance Languages and Literatures 173, ed. C. Kleinhenz (Chapel Hill, 1976), pp. 83–102. On French court patronage see, e.g., L. Delisle, *Récherches sur la Librairie de Charles V*, 2 vols. (Paris, 1907), and Millard Meiss, *French Painting in the Time of Jean de Berry*, 2 vols. (London, 1968, 1974); and see J. Plummer, *The Last Flowering: French Painting*

in Manuscripts 1420–1530, from American Collections (New York and London, 1982), p. xi, on the 'decentralising of artistic patronage' following the English occupation of France in 1415. On Burgundian patronage see, e.g., F. Winkler, *Die Flämische Buchmalerie des XV. und XVI. Jahrhunderts* (Leipzig, 1925); G. Doutrepont, *Inventaire de la Librairie de Philip le Bon* (Brussels, 1906; rpt Geneva, 1977), and *La Littérature Française à la Cour des Ducs de Bourgogne* (Paris, 1909); O. Pächt, *The Master of Mary of Burgundy* (London, 1948); A. van Buren, 'The Master of Mary of Burgundy and His Colleagues: The State of Research and Questions of Method', *Zeitschrift für Kunstgeschichte*, 38 (1975), 286–309.

5 Oxford, Bodleian Library, MS Eng. hist. c.775, fols. 6, 12. I am indebted to Dr Andrew Wathey for this reference. For discussions of these books (based upon their itemisation in a later document of 1384–5) see E. Rickert, 'King Richard II's Books', *The Library*, 4th series, 13 (1933), 144–47; R.S. Loomis, 'The Library of Richard II', in *Studies in Language, Literature and Culture of the Middle Ages and Later*, ed. E. Bagby Atwood and A.A. Hill (Austin, Texas, 1969), pp. 173–8; and R.F. Green, 'King Richard II's Books Revisited', *The Library*, 5th series, 31 (1976), 235–39. The volumes presented to Richard are most fully discussed by V.J. Scattergood, 'Literary Culture at the Court of Richard II', in Scattergood and Sherborne, pp. 29–43, at pp. 33, 41–2.

6 Viscount Dillon and W.H. St John Hope, 'Inventory of Goods . . . Belonging to Thomas, Duke of Gloucester', *Archaeological Journal*, 54 (1897), 275–308, and *Calendar of Inquisitions Miscellaneous (Chancery): preserved in the Public Record Office*, VI (1392–99) (London, 1963), pp. 223–5; also A. Goodman, *The Loyal Conspiracy: The Lords Appellant under Richard II* (London, 1971), pp. 74–86.

7 A point made by K.B. McFarlane, *The Nobility of Later Medieval England* (Oxford, 1973), p. 237; and see the comments on the impossibility of using inventories of this sort as an impartial evidential source made by M.V. Clarke, in *Fourteenth Century Studies*, ed. L.S. Sutherland and M. McKisack (Oxford, 1937), pp. 116–18. See also Ch. 8 above, p. 165.

8 J. Vale, *Edward III and Chivalry* (Woodbridge, 1982), pp. 49–52 and Appendices 9 and 10.

9 See J.W. Thompson, *The Medieval Library* (Chicago, 1939), p. 401, for an account of time spent by Henry in the library of Bardney Abbey during a visit; and *The History of the King's Works*, vol. 2, *The Middle Ages*, ed. R. Allen Brown, H.M. Colvin and A.J. Taylor (London, 1963), p. 935, for a description of the alterations made by the king to his palace of Eltham, which included the construction of a study, provided with two desks; the second of these was to be of two stages 'to keep the king's books in'.

10 London, PRO KB 27/632 Rex. m. 4 Easter 7 Hen.V; the charge was brought on 25 June 1413. I am grateful to Dr Charles Kightley for informing me of this document and giving me his notes on it; the present account is based on my transcription. On Marleburgh see Doyle and Parkes, p. 198 and n. 91.

11 *The English Works of John Gower*, ed. G.C. Macaulay, EETS, ES, 81 (1900), pp. clii–cliii; A.I. Doyle, 'English Books In and Out of Court', pp. 169–70.

12 On Poulet see Warner and Gilson, I, p. xiii and G. Kipling, *The Triumph of Honour: Burgundian Origins of the Elizabethan Renaissance* (Leiden, 1977), ch. 2. J.J.G. Alexander cites the example of Henry III's Keeper of the Wardrobe, who was also

described as 'custos librorum': see 'Painting and Manuscript Illustration', p. 142. John Fleet, Keeper of the Wardrobe at the Tower during the early years of Edward III's reign, was also in charge of the king's books; see Vale, *Edward III and Chivalry*, p. 49.

13 For the employment given to the scribe Richard Frampton by the two Henrys, see R. Somerville, 'The Cowcher Books of the Duchy of Lancaster', *EHR*, 51 (1936), 598–615, and A.I. Doyle, 'The Manuscripts', pp. 93–4 and n. 19. In 1422 Henry V commissioned a Bible from John Hethe, a clerk of the Privy Seal, and a year earlier he ordered twelve books on hunting (perhaps Edward of York's translation of Gaston Phebus' *Livre de la Chasse*, which was dedicated to the king) from one John Robard; see Alexander, 'Painting and Manuscript Illustration', p. 158. The latter is a puzzling instance of patronage, and invites speculation as to the use to which the books were to be put: the most likely explanation is that they were intended as gifts, which in itself is indicative of the status which books had for this monarch. Another secular text which he may have owned is New York, PML M 817, Chaucer's *Troilus and Criseyde*, but it is uncertain whether he would have ordered this himself; see Doyle, 'English Books In and Out of Court', p. 172.

14 This despite his educational foundations: see B. Wolffe, *Henry VI* (London, 1981), pp. 144–5. None of the books associated with Henry VI seems to have been acquired on his own initiative; his mother, Catherine of Valois, probably gave him his psalter, now BL MS Cotton Domitian A.xvii, and various manuscripts were presented to him by authors or others with special cases to plead. Among these were Lydgate's *Lives of Saints Edmund and Fremund*; the anonymous work of advice on statecraft and conduct, *De regimine principum ad Regem Henricum Sextum*; and John Harding's *Chronicle*; the presumed presentation copies are now BL MSS Harley 2278, Cotton Cleopatra A.xiii and Lansdowne 204. See Wolffe, *Henry VI*, pp. 14, 19–20, 36, 62–3 and references cited there. The dedication copy of Tito Livio Frulovisi's *Vita Henrici Quinti* is now Cambridge, Corpus Christi College, MS 285/1; see *Duke Humfrey and English Humanism in the Fifteenth Century*, p. 3. Other books which Henry inherited from his father (on which see P. Strong and F. Strong, 'The Last Will and Codicils of Henry V', *EHR*, 96 (1981), 79–102, at p. 100) he gave away, for example to King's College (see Alexander, 'Painting and Manuscript Illustration', p. 159); and is the early fifteenth-century Wycliffite Bible, now Bodley 277, given by him to the London Charterhouse, the 'bible in Engelyssh' owned by Henry IV? For a description of Bodley 277 see *Wyclif and his Followers: An Exhibition to Mark the 600th Anniversary of the Death of John Wyclif*, ed. J. Catto, P. Gradon and A. Hudson (Oxford, 1984), pp. 47–8 and plate. Perhaps the most magnificent volume which Henry owned was BL Add. MS 18850, the Bedford Hours, given to him by the duchess of Bedford, but its subsequent history – it remained in France and on the fall of Rouen in 1449 was absorbed into the French royal library – scarcely argues that it was a treasured possession; see E. Carleton Williams, *My Lord of Bedford* (London, 1963), p. 250.

15 Alexander, 'William Abell'. But see the introduction to the facsimile of *Bodleian Library MS Fairfax 16* (London, 1979) by J. Norton-Smith for the suggestion that Abell was not solely responsible for all this work, but was, perhaps, head of a 'school' of illuminators (p. xii).

16 M. Kekewich, 'Edward IV, William Caxton, and Literary Patronage in Yorkist

England', *MLR*, 66 (1971), 481–87; Alexander, 'Painting and Manuscript Illumination', pp. 152–3; and J. Backhouse, 'Founders of the Royal Library: Edward IV and Henry VII as Collectors of Illuminated Manuscripts', *England in the Fifteenth Century*, ed. Williams, pp. 23–41.

17 See the discussion on p. 205, and references cited in nn. 29 and 30.

18 P. Tudor-Craig, *Richard III*, catalogue of an exhibition held at the National Portrait Gallery (London, 1973); Carol M. Meale, 'The Middle English Romance of *Ipomedon*: a Late Medieval "Mirror" for Princes and Merchants', *Reading Medieval Studies*, 10 (1984), 136–91. To the manuscripts listed here should be added a copy of Guido delle Colonne's *Historia Troiana* now in the Saltykov–Shahedrin Library, Leningrad, which bears the signature 'Ricardus Rex'; see *The Book Collector*, 4 (1955), p. 107 and plate. I am grateful to Professor A.S.G. Edwards for this reference. The books collected by Richard while duke of Gloucester offer an interesting insight into a 'private' royal library; the contents tally almost exactly with Hoccleve's list of recommended reading which he presented to Sir John Oldcastle in his *Remonstrance*; see *Hoccleve's Works: The Minor Poems*, ed. F.J. Furnivall and I. Gollancz, rev. J. Mitchell and A.I. Doyle, EETS, ES, 61, 73 (1897, 1925; rpd in 1 volume, 1970), pp. 14–15.

19 On these manuscripts see S. de Ricci, *Census of Medieval and Renaissance Manuscripts in the United States and Canada*, 1 (New York, 1935), p. 1027; and J.F. Wadmore, *Some Account of the Worshipful Company of Skinners* (London, 1902), pp. 26–42. The motifs which are common to these books (see BL Royal 18.A.XII, fol. 98r, Harvard Law School 25, fol. 1r and the *Book of the Fraternity of Our Lady's Assumption*, fol. 32v) are distinctively painted gilly-flowers with fleshy stems and leaves, and flat, many-petalled roses. I think, however, that the three books were illustrated by different artists and decorators. What is perhaps the original of the gilly-flower motif may be seen in a manuscript in the Pierpont Morgan Library, Glazier 9, which was produced in southern England c. 1440–50, and partly illustrated by the Fastolf Master; see. e.g., Plummer, *The Last Flowering*, plate 23b. Kathleen Scott has listed other volumes which are linked to Glazier 9 in their style of decoration in *The Mirroure of the World*, p. 43, n. 1; also p. 40, n. 2. I am grateful to the Clerk of the Skinners' Company for permission to study the fraternity book, and its companion piece, the *Book of the Fraternity of Corpus Christi*, produced around the same time; the manuscripts are discussed further on pp. 212–13.

20 Delisle, *La Librairie de Charles V*; and for discussion of Christine de Pizan's written celebration of Charles V's intellectual leanings and his foundation of the royal library (to which she may have had access), see C.C. Willard, *Christine de Pizan: Her Life and Works* (New York, 1984), pp. 21–3, 28–30, 126–7.

21 Stratford, 'The Manuscripts of John, Duke of Bedford'; Alexander, 'Painting and Manuscript Illumination', p. 161.

22 See the references in n. 4 above; also M.J. Hughes, 'The Library of Philip the Bold and Margaret of Flanders, first Valois duke and duchess of Burgundy', *Journal of Medieval History*, 4 (1978), 145–88.

23 On the concept of 'magnificence' see P.J. Lucas, 'The Growth and Development of English Literary Patronage in the Later Middle Ages and Early Renaissance', *The Library*, 6th series, 4 (1982), 219–48, at 225–7.

24 See B.C. Barker-Benfield, review of Sammut, *Unfredo Duca di Gloucester*, *The Library*, 6th series, 4 (1982), 191–4.

25 Warner and Gilson, II, pp. 54–5; C.E. Wright, *Fontes Harleiana* (London, 1972), p. 143.

26 Warner and Gilson, I, p. xi.

27 The book is now BL Royal 19.C.VI; see Warner and Gilson, II, pp. 334–5. Janet Backhouse, however, in 'Founders of the Royal Library', pointed out that similar comments were made by De Seysel concerning the library of his monarch, Louis XII, so the remark may have been little more than a rhetorical flourish, designed to flatter the recipient.

28 E.g. by Kipling, *The Triumph of Honour*, and by the same author, 'Henry VII and the Origins of Tudor Court Patronage', in *Patronage in the Renaissance*, ed. G. Fitch Lytle and S. Orgel (Princeton, 1981), pp. 117–64; Roy Strong, *The English Renaissance Miniature* (London, 1983), pp. 12–15. On Henry VII as a patron, see also Ch. 8 above, pp. 178–9.

29 On the Master of the Prayerbooks see, most recently, T. Kren, 'Flemish Manuscript Illumination 1475–1550', in *Renaissance Painting in Manuscripts: Treasures from the British Library* (New York, 1983), pp. 49–58; also *Medieval and Early Renaissance Treasures in the North-West*, catalogue of the exhibition held at the Whitworth Art Gallery, University of Manchester (Manchester, 1976), p. 31, no. 55; O. Pächt, *Flemish Art, 1300–1700*, Royal Academy of Arts exhibition catalogue (London, 1953), p. 164, no. 615; and Winkler, *Die Flämische Buchmalerei des XV. und XVI. Jahrhunderts*, p. 175. The little-known Chatsworth manuscript is illustrated in F. Thompson, 'The Devonshire Collection at Chatsworth', *Studio*, 144 (1952), 169. There is no thorough account in any of these sources of the miniatures painted by this Master in Henry VII's books, but I note from my own examination of the manuscripts that the first two illustrations in Royal 16.F.II are not by his hand. Backhouse, in 'Founders of the Royal Library', suggests that the production history of this last volume is more complex than hitherto supposed. The fact that this artist worked on manuscripts owned by readers throughout western Europe makes it most unlikely that he followed Quentin Poulet to England and operated from an atelier based at Richmond, as suggested by Kipling, *The Triumph of Honour* and 'Henry VII and the Origins of Tudor Court Patronage'.

30 On other manuscripts illustrated by the Chief Associate of Maître François see Plummer, *The Last Flowering*, pp. 68–70 and plates 89–91a. The notes kept with this manuscript at the Library mention another volume which 'tradition' has associated with Henry VII, Vienna, 1840 [Theol. 496], written c. 1420–2, the miniatures of which were completed sixty years later; see H.J. Herman, *Beschreibendes Verzeichnis der illuminierten Handschriften in Österreich, 3. Französische und Iberische MSS*, Band VII (Vienna, 1938), pp. 129–37. Henry's association with other manuscripts is also traditional rather than proven: on a book of Hours, now dismembered, illustrated by Jean Bourdichon see J. Backhouse, 'Hours of Henry VII', in *Renaissance Painting in Manuscripts*, pp. 163–68; on MSS Royal 15.E.v, 19.E.II and 19.E.III, a copy of the Burgundian romance of *Perceforest*, H.L.D. Ward, *Catalogue of Romances in the Department of Manuscripts in the British Museum*, vol. 1 (London, 1883), pp. 377–81; and on a chansonnier, Cambridge, Magdalene College, MS Pepys

1760, probably a diplomatic gift to Henry VIII, I. Fenlon, *Cambridge Music Manuscripts 900–1700* (Cambridge, 1982), pp. 123–6. A volume which may have been commissioned by Henry is MS Royal 20.A.xix, an office of the mass of the Immaculate Conception of the Virgin; see Warner and Gilson, II, p. 33; it contains a miniature of indifferent execution portraying the Conception, and Henry, kneeling at a desk.

31 See, e.g., D. Bornstein, 'William Caxton's Chivalric Romances and the Burgundian Renaissance in England', *English Studies*, 57 (1976), 1–10; Kipling, *The Triumph of Honour* and 'Henry VII and the Origins of Tudor Court Patronage'. On the triptych now in the National Portrait Gallery, London, depicting John Donne and his wife Elizabeth, sister of William, Lord Hastings, see K.B. McFarlane, *Hans Memling* (Oxford, 1971).

32 On his purchase of books from Vérard see H.R. Plomer, 'Bibliographical Notes from the Privy Purse Expenses of King Henry the Seventh', *The Library*, 3rd series, 4 (1913), 291–305; L.G. Clark, *Collectors and Owners of Incunabula in the British Museum: Index of Provenances from Books printed in France, Holland and Belgium* (Bath, 1962).

33 Warwick's book, *L'enseignement de vraie noblesse*, is now Geneva, Bibliothèque de la Ville, MS fr.166; see H. Aubert, 'Notices sur les manuscrits conservés à la Bibliothèque de Genève', *Bibliothèque de l'Ecole des Chartes*, 72 (1911), 298–302; also Ch. 8 above, p. 181. On Hastings's devotional manuscripts, Add. 54782 and Madrid, Museo Lazaro-Galdiano 15503, see D.H. Turner, *The Hastings Hours* (London, 1983), and T. Kren, 'Hours of William Lord Hastings', in *Renaissance Painting in Manuscripts*, pp. 21–30; and on the volume of Froissart's *Chroniques*, Royal 18.E.I, which bears the unpainted arms and crest of Hastings, see Warner and Gilson, II, p. 314.

34 B. Quaritch, *A Catalogue of Illuminated and Other Manuscripts* (1931), pp. 95–7; C.A.J. Armstrong, 'A Present for a Prince: The Survival of a Newsletter, Constantinople, in 1481', *The Times*, 23 May 1936, p. 15. Add. 54782, Hastings' Hours, may originally have been intended for Edward: the history of the manuscript has been discussed most recently by P. Tudor-Craig, 'The Hours of Edward V and William Lord Hastings', *England in the Fifteenth Century*, ed. Williams, pp. 351–69.

35 *Medieval and Early Renaissance Treasures in the North-West*, p. 30, n. 53; Pächt and Alexander, I, no. 389 (see also no. 390, Gough liturg.7, prayers written for George Talbot, earl of Shrewsbury).

36 Warner and Gilson, II, pp. 205–6. There is a coincidence in the contents, script and illustrations between this volume and Royal MSS 19.B.x and 20.B.ix, which suggests that they were produced in the same Flemish atelier, and the first of these was certainly in England at an early stage in its history: see Warner and Gilson, II, pp. 327, 344.

37 *Catalogue of Additions to the Manuscripts in the British Museum, 1846–47* (London, 1864), pp. 316–17; *The Prymer or Lay Folks' Prayer Book*, ed. H. Littlehales, vol. I, EETS, os, 105 (1895), Plate II.

38 E.G. Millar, 'Les Principaux Manuscrits à peintures du Lambeth Palace à Londres', *Bulletin de la Société Française de Réproductions des Manuscrits à Peintures*, 9e année (Paris, 1925), pp. 5–19 and plate XLIV; Pächt, *Flemish Art 1300–1700*, p. 156, no. 583. On the affiliations of the illustrator see P.W. Parshull, 'A Dutch Manuscript of c. 1480 from an atelier in Bruges', *Scriptorium*, 32 (1969), 333–7 and plate

113b. Millar, 'Les Principaux Manuscrits', p. 15 and n. 1, was the first to attribute the arms in Lambeth 6 – quarterly 1 and 4 argent on a fess sable three bezants or, 2 and 3 argent a lion rampant azure langued gules – to Purches, noting their similarity to those of Purches' descendants, argent, a lion rampant azure, over all a fess sable three bezants or. In J.W. Papworth, *An Alphabetical Dictionary of Coats of Arms . . . forming an extensive Ordinary of British Armorials* (London, 1874), p. 795, the latter coat is stated to be that of Sir William himself; a search through Papworth has revealed no other immediately likely candidate for ownership of the Lambeth MS. No books are mentioned in either Sir William's will (reg. F at Canterbury, fols. 202r–205r, proved 6 April 1503), or that of his wife, Margaret (PRO Prob.11/ 17 fols. 30r–30v, proved 17 November 1511), but there is solid evidence for assuming that he moved in book-owning circles. He left money 'towarde the promocion' of poor scholars at the universities of Oxford and Cambridge; one of his executors and legatees was 'Master Edward Charnebroke clerke', who may be identified with the 'm edward shernbroke p'st', whose signature appears above that of Gerald Fitzgerald, ninth earl of Kildare, in Bodley 690, fol. iiiv; and both he and his wife name 'William Grosen' as arbiter in case of dispute over their respective wills. On Sharnebrook, who was a canon of St Paul's Cathedral, see *BRUO*, I, p. 520; and on Grocyn, who was vicar of St Lawrence Jewry, Purches' parish of residence, *BRUO*, II, pp. 827–30, and Weiss, *Humanism in England*, Ch. XII. Among the other executors and overseers nominated by the testators were both bachelors and doctors of divinity, and Margaret made a bequest to Master Thomas Lovell, her cousin, who was at one time Vicar General to the bishops of Bath and Wells. Another of Sir William's executors was Avery Rawson, mercer, one of whose descendants was apparently in possession of Oxford, Corpus Christi College, MS 67, Gower's *Confessio Amantis*; see *The English Works of John Gower*, ed. Macaulay, vol. 1, p. cxlviii.

39 Sotheby's sale catalogue, *The Bute Collection of Forty-Two Illuminated Manuscripts and Miniatures*, 13 June 1983, p. 85.

40 G.A. Lester, *Sir John Paston's 'Grete Boke': A Descriptive Catalogue, with an Introduction, of B.L. MS Lansdowne 285* (Woodbridge, 1984); *Paston Letters and Papers of the Fifteenth Century*, ed. N. Davis, vol. 1 (Oxford, 1971), p. 592.

41 Meale, 'The Middle English Romance of *Ipomedon*', pp. 138, 146. The London provenance of the manuscript would seem to be confirmed by the appearance of the hand of the principal scribe of Chetham (*ibid.*, plates 4, 8) in PML MS Bühler 5, John Harding's *Chronicle*: this is a paper manuscript copied by several hands, which contains contemporary inscriptions made by various citizens of London. For additional evidence of Burgundian tastes being adopted in England, see the discussions below of NLW MS Peniarth 481 D, and the romance of *The Three Kings' Sons*; also Scott, *The Caxton Master*, and Backhouse, 'Founders of the Royal Library'.

42 See H. Suggett, 'The Use of French in England in the Later Middle Ages', in *Essays in Medieval History*, ed. R.W. Southern (London, 1968), pp. 213–39; E. Salter, *Fourteenth Century English Poetry: Contexts and Readings* (Oxford, 1983), Ch. 2. Compare, however, the impact on production of an expanding reading public for English books, discussed on pp. 216–18.

43 Scattergood, 'Literary Culture at the Court of Richard II'.

44 'I l'a fait faire ainsi que entens / Afin que vous y passez temps / Et lors que parlerez

anglois / Que vous noublier le francois . . . ' Royal 15.E.VI, fol. 2v, col. 2, lines 1–4. For descriptions of this manuscript see Warner and Gilson, II, pp. 177–9 (and IV, plate 96); *Le Rommant de Guy de Warwik et de Hérolt d'Ardenne*, ed. D.J. Conlon, University of North Carolina Studies in the Romance Languages and Literatures 102 (Chapel Hill, 1971), pp. 16–26.

45 Wolffe, *Henry VI*, pp. 13, 70; R.A. Griffiths, *The Reign of Henry VI; The Exercise of Royal Authority, 1422–1461* (London, 1981), p. 241.

46 *The Works of Sir Thomas Malory*, ed. E. Vinaver (2nd edn, Oxford, 1967), 3, pp. 1279–81 and plate IV; W. Matthews, *The Ill-Framed Knight* (Berkeley and Los Angeles, 1966), pp. 108–13. Matthews associates CUL Add. 7071 with the Mauleverer family of Ribston in Yorkshire, but the name does not appear amongst the numerous signatures on fol. 158r.

47 It is difficult to be sure that these notes are in the hand of Sir Richard Roos, who writes his name in a more formal script. For a description see Warner and Gilson, II, p. 140.

48 See plate (c) facing p. 81 in Ethel Seaton, *Sir Richard Roos* (London, 1961), for Sir Richard's signature. Seaton assumes that Spencer 9, and the other fragment of the *Voeux du Paon* in the BL, Add. MS 30864, belonged to Sir Richard.

49 Ward, *Catalogue of Romances in the British Museum*, 1, pp. 587–89; 2 (London, 1895), pp. 471–4, and 3, by J.A. Herbert (London, 1910), pp. 272–84. Attempts to trace this John Clerk have been unsuccessful. It is not certain whether he came from London, but even if it may be assumed that he did, the wills of eleven men of this name were proved at the Prerogative Court of Canterbury between 1466 and 1500; see *Index of Wills proved in the Prerogative Court of Canterbury 1383–1558*, ed. J.C.C. Smith, BRS, *The Index Library*, 10 (London, 1893), p. 124. Several John Clerks are mentioned in C.H. Talbot and E.A. Hammond in *The Medical Practitioners in Medieval England* (London, 1965), but again no satisfactory identification of the owner of Harley 273 may be offered.

50 P.G.C. Campbell, 'Christine de Pisan en Angleterre', *Revue de Littérature Comparée*, 5 (1925), 659–70, updated by A.J. Kennedy, *Christine de Pizan: A Bibliographical Guide* (London, 1984). Christine's popularity did, of course, extend to translations of her work being made in England: see Kennedy for the fullest information, though it should be noted that the evidence for the attribution of one translation of the *Epistre d'Othéa* to Anthony Babyngton (pp. 82–3, and cf. Willard, *Christine de Pizan*, p. 217) rests on uncertain grounds: see *The Epistle of Othea to Hector: a 'Lytil Bibell of Knyghthod'*, etc., ed. J.D. Gordon (Philadelphia, 1942), pp. xxxi–xxxvii. It would also be worth investigating the reception of Alain Chartier's works in England. A number of manuscripts of his texts now in British libraries seem to have entered England during the medieval period: see, e.g., J. Boffey, *Manuscripts of English Courtly Love Lyrics in the Later Middle Ages* (Woodbridge, 1985), p. 79; also J.C. Laidlaw, 'The Manuscripts of Alain Chartier', *MLR*, 61 (1966), 188–98. Several of his works were translated during the course of the fifteenth century: see, for *La Belle Dame Sans Merci*, *The Complete Works of Geoffrey Chaucer*, ed. W.W. Skeat, (Oxford, 1897), pp. li–liii and 299–326; *Le Traité de l'Esperance and Le Quadrilogue Invectif*, ed. Margaret S. Blayney, 2 vols., EETS, os, 270, 281 (1974, 1980); and *The Curial made by maystere Alain Charretier*, translated by Caxton, ed. P. Meyer and F.J. Furnivall, EETS, es, 54 (1888).

51 J.C. Laidlaw, 'Christine de Pizan, The Earl of Salisbury and Henry IV', *French Studies*, 36 (1982), 129–43; Warner and Gilson, ii, pp. 139–40; *The Book of Fayttes of Armes and of Chyualrye*, ed. A.T.P. Byles, EETS, os, 189 (1932), pp. 291–2.

52 On Harley 4431 see S. Hindman, 'The Composition of the Manuscript of Christine de Pisan's Collected Works in the British Library: A Reassessment', *BLJ*, 9 (1983), pp. 93–123, and for the Wydville signatures, L. Hellinga, *Caxton in Focus* (London, 1982), plate 43.

53 Warner and Gilson, ii, pp. 322–3; Madan, *Summary Catalogue*, ii, pt 1, p. 506; G. Paris, 'D'un recueil manuscrit de poésies françaises du XIII⁰ au XV⁰ siècle, appartenant à Westminster Abbey', *Bulletin de la Société des Anciens Textes Français*, 1 (1875), 25–49.

54 K. Chesney, 'Two Manuscripts of Christine de Pisan', *Medium Aevum*, 1 (1932), 35–41; C.F. Bühler, 'Sir John Fastolf's Manuscripts of the *Epître d'Othéa* and Stephen Scrope's Translation of the Text', *Scriptorium*, 3 (1949), 123–8; Pächt and Alexander, i, no. 695. An inventory of Fastolf's books kept 'In the Stewe hous' at Caister Castle, made *c.* 1450, consists entirely of French titles, including chronicles of France and of England; *Titus Livius*; an account of 'Jullius Ceser'; astronomical treatises; a 'liber de Roy Artour'; a *Roman de la Rose*; a *Brut*; Vegetius' *De re militari*; and didactic and devotional works; see HMC, 8th Report, App. 268 (London, 1881).

55 Harley 219 also contains the Latin *Gesta Romanorum*; 'le liure de gouuer/nement des Roys et des Princes'; and a Latin and English gloss of French vocabulary; on fol. 153r is the late fifteenth-century signature, 'John Bartolot'. On the other manuscripts see Pächt and Alexander, iii, no. 1099; Warner and Gilson, ii, p. 331; and M. Rickert, *Painting in Britain: The Middle Ages*, 2nd edn (London, 1965), pp. 182–3 and plate 182b. Is it possible that Royal 19.B.xviii was the copy of the text given to Caxton to translate? The manuscript has an incomplete royal coat of arms inserted on fol. 4r, and the modern editor of Caxton's text, A.T.P. Byles, notes its close correspondence with the printed edition, using it as the basis for collation; see *The Book of Fayttes of Armes*, p. xviii.

56 Bodleian Library, Ewelme Muniments vii.A.47 (3); *Testamenta Eboracensia*, iv, SS 53 (1868), pp. 149–54.

57 E.W. Ives, 'A Lawyer's Library in 1500', *Law Quarterly Review*, 85 (1969), 104–16, and *The Common Lawyers of Pre-Reformation England – Thomas Kebell: A Case Study* (Cambridge, 1983), pp. 362–67 and Appendices A and B. It is possible that the volume 'de Jehan Boccace' was the *Cas de Nobles Hommes et Femmes*, rather than the *Decameron*, as Ives suggests. On the professional and recreation reading interests of lawyers in general, see Ives, 'The Common Lawyers', in *Profession, Vocation and Culture*, ed. C.H. Clough (Liverpool, 1982), pp. 181–217.

58 Surviving manuscripts and wills provide a considerable amount of information concerning the circulation of French texts in late medieval England, detailed collation of which would be useful. For example, Matilda Roos, daughter of Thomas Roos, sixth Lord Clifford and wife of Richard, earl of Cambridge, bequeathed a 'Gyron le Curtesse' in two volumes (*Testamenta Eboracensia*, ii, SS 30 (1855), no. 97); Sir John Scrope (d. 1405) left his daughter Johanna 'unum librum de gallico vocatum Tristrem' (*Testamenta Eboracensia*, i, SS 4 (1836), pp. 383–89); a fragmentary early fourteenth-century copy of *Ipomédon*, Dublin, Trinity College, MS 523 (E.1.39), is prefaced by a series of coats of arms of fifteenth-century

knights, both gentry and aristocracy; Royal 20.D.xi, chansons of the cycle of Guillaume d'Orange, has English names of the fifteenth/sixteenth centuries added on fol. 317v (Warner and Gilson, ii, pp. 384–7); and see C.M. Meale, 'Caxton, de Worde and the publication of romance in late medieval England', in *From Manuscript to Printed Book*, ed. S.M. Horrall and M.W. Driver (forthcoming), for other instances of French romances in English ownership. Amongst other secular works Royal 20.B.i, a copy of Vegetius, has a fifteenth-century abstract of chapters appended on fol. 31v (Warner and Gilson, ii, p. 359); and Bodleian e Mus. 65, a *Roman de la Rose*, dating from c. 1390, belonged to the Courtenay family in the early sixteenth century (Pächt and Alexander, i, no. 612). And for bequests of devotional treatises in French, see the wills of Walter, Lord Hungerford, dated 1 July 1449 (N.H. Nicolas, *Testamenta Vetusta*, 2 vols. in 1 (London, 1826), pp. 257–9); and of Agnes Stapilton, widow of Sir Brian Stapilton of Carlton, Yorkshire, dated 27 March 1448 (*North Country Wills*, SS 116 (1908), pp. 48–9). On the French texts owned by John Shirley see Boffey, *Manuscripts of English Courtly Love Lyrics*, p. 16, n. 28. On the evidential value of wills generally, see Ch. 8 above, pp. 163–5.

59 For descriptions of these manuscripts see *Lydgate's Fall of Princes*, ed. H. Bergen, 4, EETS, os, 124 (1927), pp. 30–51, 88–92, 99–103; and also on the last of these A.S.G. Edwards, 'The Huntington *Fall of Princes* (HM 268) and Sloane 2452', *Manuscripta*, 16 (1972), 37–40.

60 A similar situation exists with regard to Lydgate's *Troy Book*, dedicated to Henry V; no presentation copy apparently survives, but for ownership of the text amongst the nobility see below, p. 218, and A.S.G. Edwards, 'The Influence of Lydgate's *Fall of Princes* c. 1440–1559: A Survey', *Medieval Studies*, 39 (1977), 424–39, at p. 429. Hoccleve's *Regiment of Princes* was also dedicated to Henry, and on the manuscript once thought to be the presentation copy see K. Harris, 'The Patron of BL MS Arundel 38', NQ 31 (1984), 462–3.

61 See D.J.A. Ross, *Alexander Historiatus: A Guide to Medieval Illustrated Alexander Literature* (London, 1963), p. 51, and *Illustrated Medieval Alexander-Books in Germany and the Netherlands: A Study in Comparative Iconography* (Cambridge, 1971), p. 18 and figs. 377, 385, 411; G. Cary, *The Medieval Alexander* (Cambridge, 1956), pp. 43–4. Burgh's text and the *Historia* survive in a contemporary binding together with a copy of John of Hildesheim's Latin *Historia Sanctorum Trium Regum*, probably written and illuminated in Cologne; the binding bears the embossed initials 'MC'. I am indebted to Dr Ceridwen Lloyd-Morgan of the National Library of Wales for her assistance with my queries concerning this volume.

The most famous example of a sumptuous book with no known patron is Cambridge, Corpus Christi College, MS 61, of Chaucer's *Troilus and Criseyde*: see the facsimile with introduction by M. Parkes and E. Salter (Cambridge, 1978).

62 Scott, 'Lydgate's Lives', pp. 336, 342, 346, 355–56, 361 and figure 4; also A.S.G. Edwards, 'The McGill Fragment of Lydgate's *Fall of Princes*', *Scriptorium*, 28 (1974), 75–7; '*Sixty Bokes Olde and Newe*', ed. Anderson, pp. 106–7.

63 A.I. Doyle suggests that the scribe of Lambeth 265, one Haywarde, may have been resident at the hospital of St James in the Fields, Westminster: see 'English Books In and Out of Court', p. 181, n. 54.

64 *The Three Kings' Sons*, ed. F.J. Furnivall, EETS, es, 67 (1895); H. Grinberg, '*The Three Kings' Sons* and *Les Trois Fils de Rois*', *Romance Philology*, 28 (1975), 521–9.

Since I arrived at this conclusion the unpublished dissertation by Henry Grinberg, '*The Three Kings' Sons*: Notes and Critical Commentary' (New York University, 1968), has come to my attention. Here, the possibility that the illustrations in Harley 326 are by the artist of Lambeth 265 is raised, only to be dismissed in favour of the theory of common workshop provenance; see pp. 10–12. Grinberg does not note the occurrence of a similar figure in the frontispiece to the *Dicts* (the courtier who stands immediately to the left of Anthony Wydville) and the miniature on fol. 102r of Harley (the second figure from the right, on horseback); see Ills. 18 and 19. The attitudes of these two figures and the disposition of their hands are identical. Aside from this, compare pictorial details such as the round-headed lattice windows in Harley, fols. 8r, 117v and in Lambeth; and the design, in red and gold, on the hanging of the chamber in Lambeth with that on fol. 9r of Harley (and compare the background to the miniatures on fol. 77r and the bed-hangings on fol. 117v); and the floor rushes in Lambeth – green, highlighted with gold – with those in the miniature on fol. 117v of Harley. I also note the following correspondences of technique: the painting of faces in the two manuscripts is similar – there is little modelling, noses are always drawn in profile and the underlip is strongly marked – and there is on occasions a comparable carelessness in the painting of hair, whereby lines marking individual strands continue beyond the block of colour (e.g. the male figures on fol. 9r of Harley; Lambeth, the figure of Anthony Wydville).

It is probable that the scribe of Harley also worked in London. A.I. Doyle, cited by Grinberg, '*The Three Kings' Sons*', notes four other manuscripts written by this hand: Plimpton 256 in Columbia University Library (see C.F. Bühler, 'Notes on the Plimpton Manuscript of *The Court of Sapience*', *MLN*, 59 (1944), 5–9, and *The Court of Sapience*, ed. E.R. Harvey (Toronto, Buffalo and London, 1984), pp. xii–xiii); BL Cotton Faustina B.ix, fols. 41ff., the English version of *The Book of the Foundation of St. Bartholomew's Church in London* (see the edition by S.N. Moore, EETS, os, 163 (1923)); Bodleian, Fairfax 4, Roger of Waltham's *Compendium Morale* (Pächt and Alexander, iii, no. 1098 and plate civ); and Bodleian, Digby 235, Roger Bacon's *Opus Major*. Harley 326 is the only one of the manuscripts at present known to have been written by this scribe which is illustrated, although Grinberg states that the decorated initials in Harley and Plimpton 256 are identical (pp. 15–16).

65 On the French manuscripts see Grinberg, '*The Three Kings' Sons* and *Les Trois Fils de Rois*', pp. 526–9; also B. Woledge, *Bibliographie des Romans et Nouvelles en Prose Française antérieurs à 1500* (Genève, 1975), pp. 131–2.

66 See, e.g., the survey by Guddat-Figge.

67 Hence, perhaps, the emphasis which has been given to the artist William Abell and his *œuvre*; see the references in n. 15 above.

68 Scott, 'A Mid-Fifteenth Century Illuminating Shop', p. 193, n. 130, and *The Mirroure of the Worlde*, p. 43, n. 1. For descriptions of Spencer 3, see M.R. James, *A Descriptive Catalogue of Fifty Manuscripts from the Collection of Henry Yates Thompson* (Cambridge, 1898), pp. 130–8 and *Illustrations from One Hundred Manuscripts in the Library of Henry Yates Thompson*, 4 (London, 1914), pp. 45–7 and plates lxxvii–lxxxii. This example of patronage suggests that further investigation of women's book-owning and commissioning activities would be worthwhile; a

preliminary study is that by S.G. Bell, 'Medieval Women Book Owners: Arbiters of Lay Piety and Ambassadors of Culture', *Signs*, 7 (1982), 742–68.

69 E.M. Veale, *The Fur Trade in the Late Middle Ages* (Oxford, 1966), pp. 105–15; S.L. Thrupp, *The Merchant Class of Medieval London 1300–1500* (Ann Arbor, 1948), p. 31. On the origins and development of fraternities see also G. Unwin, *Guilds and Companies of London* (London, 1908), pp. 110–26; and C.M. Barron, 'The Parish Fraternities of Medieval London', in *The Church in Pre-Reformation Society*, ed. C.M. Barron and C. Harper-Bill (Woodbridge, 1985), pp. 13–37.

70 The miniature of Elizabeth Wydville is on the opposite page to that containing entries made during 11 Edward IV (1471), but the mention of 'Dame Elizabeth gray' as an entrant in 4 Edward IV (1465), fol. 29r, might imply that she joined the fraternity at this earlier date, perhaps shortly after her secret marriage to Edward in May of 1465.

71 The miniature is reproduced in black and white in C. Ross, *The Wars of the Roses* (London, 1976), p. 69. On the background decoration see n. 19 above.

72 Margaret's entry into the fraternity on 20 July 15 Edward IV (1475) is somewhat puzzling: after the Lancastrian defeat at Tewkesbury in 1471 she was placed in the custody of Alice de la Pole, duchess of Suffolk, at Wallingford; she was removed from there in July 1475, and finally returned to France in November of that year.

73 The date at which this miniature was painted is not clear; the facing verso page records entries for 5 and 6 Henry VII (1489/90), but there is no necessary reason to suppose that the picture was completed at this late date. There are certain stylistic affinities between this miniature and those in Pt II of Spencer 3.

74 *John Lydgate: The Minor Poems*, ed. H.N. MacCracken, 1, EETS, ES, 107 (1911), pp. 35–43; Stow's *Survey of London*, ed. C.L. Kingsford (Oxford, 1908), 2, pp. 230ff.; Derek Pearsall, *John Lydgate* (London, 1970), p. 188.

75 Scott, *The Caxton Master*, pp. 61–5. The manuscript has often been reproduced, but see Viscount Dillon and W.H. St John Hope, *Pageants of the Birth, Life and Death of Richard Beauchamp, Earl of Warwick, K.G., 1389–1439* (London, 1914).

76 On this manuscript see, most recently, Lawton, 'The Illustration of Late Medieval Secular Texts', pp. 41–69 and plate 4, and, for a full description, Warner and Gilson, II, pp. 308–10. On the fate of the fourth earl, see M.A. Hicks, 'Dynastic Change and Northern Society: The Career of the Fourth Earl of Northumberland, 1470–89', *Northern History*, 14 (1978), 78–107.

77 A.G. Dickens, 'The Tudor–Percy Emblem in Royal MS 18.D.II', *Archaeological Journal*, 112–13 (1955–6), 95–9. Dickens cites parallels to the drawing in contemporary Plea Rolls of the King's Bench.

78 Pächt and Alexander, III, no. 1121 and plate CV.

79 This roll is discussed briefly by A. Gransden, *Historical Writing in England*, II, *c. 1307 to the Early Sixteenth Century* (London, 1982), p. 253, and see additional bibliography cited there. The standard of the verses is well represented by the following extract relating to Henry IV: 'a douȝty man / At westmynster crouned he was / where of al Engelond mad solas / In his tyme was a blasyng sterre / þat alle men myȝt see hit ryȝt ferre . . . '. See also the reference below, n. 113, to a copy of Vegetius belonging to the Chalons family of Devon (Douce 291), which opens with a pedigree.

80 *The Brut*, ed. F.W. Brie, EETS, OS, 131, 136 (1906, 1908); L.M. Matheson,

'Historical Prose', in *Middle English Prose*, ed. Edwards, pp. 209–47; Gransden, *English Historical Writing*, II, ch. 8; C.L. Kingsford, *English Historical Literature in the Fifteenth Century* (Oxford, 1913), ch. 5.

81 For the *Brut* manuscripts see L.M. Matheson, 'The Middle English Prose *Brut*: A Location List of the Manuscripts and Early Printed Editions', *Analytical and Enumerative Bibliography*, 3 (1979), 254–66; R.E. Lewis, N.F. Blake and A.S.G. Edwards, *Index of Printed Middle English Prose* (New York and London, 1985), no. 374. On the *Prick of Conscience* see Lewis and McIntosh. Matheson makes the point that the number of manuscripts in which the *Brut* survives is exceeded only by that of Wycliffite translations of the Bible (p. 210).

82 See, e.g., MS Harley 53, which has the arms of the Stokes family on fol. 13v (Kingsford, *English Historical Literature*, p. 125, n. 4); MS Royal 17.D.xxi (see n. 84 below); MS Digby 185, in the possession of the Hopton family (see further p. 216 and n. 85); Harvard, Houghton Library, MS 587; Huntington MS HM 131.

83 A.I. Doyle, 'Reflections', p. 88. Doyle suggests that Love's *Myrrour* itself may have been 'so well-known and frequently in demand that it was worth a stationer's paying for costly copies in advance of actual purchasers'. For further information see also Salter, 'The Manuscripts'. Compare the discussion of *Nova Statuta* manuscripts in K.L. Scott, 'A Late Fifteenth Century Group of *Nova Statuta* Manuscripts', in *Manuscripts at Oxford*, ed. de la Mare and Barker-Benfield, pp. 102–5, and *The Mirroure of the Worlde*, pp. 45–50.

84 Matheson, 'A Location List', p. 265, gives some details of owners, including religious. For a fuller description of MS Royal 17.D.xxi, a copy probably owned by the Augustinian priory of St Bartholomew's in Smithfield, see Warner and Gilson, II, pp. 257–8.

85 *King Ponthus and the Fair Sidone*, ed. F.J. Mather Jr, PMLA 12 (1897), pp. i–lxvii; Guddat-Figge, pp. 255–7. On Sir William, son of John Hopton, see C. Richmond, *John Hopton: A Fifteenth Century Suffolk Gentleman* (Cambridge, 1981). M.C. Seymour, 'The Manuscripts of Hoccleve's *Regiment of Princes*', *TEBS*, 4 (1974), 253–97, at p. 277, suggests that the Hoccleve texts may have been copied from those in Royal 17.D.vi, owned by William FitzAlan, earl of Arundel, and his wife, Joan Neville; if this is so, it may indicate a metropolitan provenance for Digby.

86 See L.E. Voigts, *A Handlist of Middle English in Harvard Manuscripts*, Harvard Library Bulletin, 33 (1) (1985), pp. 60–2. The last eleven folios of the volume contain a neat series of contemporary coats of arms in varying stages of completion; the names of the owners and blazons are written in the hand of the scribe of the *Brut*.

87 Matheson, 'A Location List', p. 265, states that it is Thomas Bourchier, archbishop of Canterbury, whose name occurs in the manuscript, but the identification advanced here is confirmed by the presence of the signature of 'John Sulyerd' (rear flyleaf iiv): Anne, widow of Sir John Sulyard (d. 1488), Justice of the King's Bench, married, as his second wife, Sir Thomas Bourchier.

88 The manuscript is composed of paper bearing a watermark which is very close to no. 9481 in C.M. Briquet, *Les Filigranes*, Jubilee Edition, with introduction by A.H. Stevenson (Amsterdam, 1968), which appears on documents dated between 1461 and 1474. It is probable that William Brandon was a descendant of the Nicholas Brandon who, together with his heirs, received rents resolute from the College of

Knowle (*The Register of the Guild of Knowle, the County of Warwick, 1451–1535* (Walsall, 1894), pp. xxiii, xxx). A 'Nicolaus Brawndon' of nearby Sheldon, and his wife 'Elena', were entered as members of the Guild of St Anne at Knowle in 1 Henry VII (1485/86) (and see City of Birmingham Reference Library A663, A664, for land transactions involving this couple), but I have found no other record of William. Other names which occur in Sloane 2027 are those of 'Rychard proctor', 'John prouctor' and 'John osbvrn' (the latter with the date 1547).

89 A.I. Doyle, 'The Manuscripts', p. 94, and references cited in nn. 22, 23. For descriptions of Lambeth 491, see *The Awntyrs off Arthure at the Terne Wathelyne*, ed. Ralph Hanna III (Manchester, 1974), pp. 4–6; Guddat-Figge, pp. 226–7.

90 Parkes, 'The Literacy of the Laity'.

91 On the classical origins of these two terms (otherwise translated as profit and pleasure) and for their application to literature of the Middle Ages see G. Olson, *Literature as Recreation in the Later Middle Ages* (Ithaca and London, 1982). On social structures in the fifteenth century see, e.g., F.R.H. Du Boulay, *An Age of Ambition: English Society in the Late Middle Ages* (London, 1970); S.L. Thrupp, 'The Problem of Conservatism in Fifteenth Century England', *Speculum*, 18 (1943), 363–8 and *The Merchant Class of Medieval London*. The use of the written word as a confirmation of social standing can also be seen in the proliferation of copies of London chronicles, reflecting the commercial and governmental concerns of citizens; see Kingsford, *English Historical Literature*, ch. 4, and Gransden, *English Historical Writing*, II, pp. 227–48. However, religious concerns undoubtedly impelled others towards literacy: see M. Aston, 'Lollardy and Literacy', *History*, 62 (1977), 347–71.

92 On prices of books see, e.g. W.L. Schramm, 'The Cost of Books in Chaucer's Time', *MLN*, 48 (1933), 139–45; H.E. Bell, 'The Price of Books in Medieval England', *The Library*, 4th series, 17 (1936), 312–32; and *Paston Letters*, ed. Davis, II, pp. 391–2, 386–7.

93 D. Pearsall, 'The English Romance in the Fifteenth Century', *Essays and Studies* (1976), 56–83 (pp. 57–8). It may be remarked that, of the thirty romances recorded by Pearsall as surviving in early manuscripts, fourteen are found in a single codex, the Auchinleck manuscript, National Library of Scotland 19.2.1; see the facsimile with introduction by D. Pearsall and I.C. Cunningham (London, 1977).

94 See, e.g., the so-called Findern anthology (see the facsimile with introduction by R. Beadle and A.E.B. Owen (London, 1977), and K. Harris, 'The Origins and Make-up of Cambridge University Library MS Ff.1.6', *TCBS*, 8 (1983), 299–333); and Robert Thornton's collection, Lincoln Cathedral 91 (see the facsimile with introduction by D.S. Brewer and A.E.B. Owen (London, 1977), and J.J. Thompson, 'The Compiler in Action: Robert Thornton and the "Thornton Romances" in Lincoln Cathedral MS 91', in Pearsall, *Manuscripts and Readers*, pp. 113–24).

95 But see Pearsall's comment in 'The English Romance in the Fifteenth Century', pp. 58–9, that many of these late copies show signs of oral rather than written transmission. A convincing example of this pattern of preservation is *Torrent of Portyngale* which survives uniquely in Chetham's Library, A.6.31 (8009); see the edition by E. Adams, EETS, ES, 51 (1887).

96 Robinson, 'The Booklet'; N.F. Blake, review of the facsimile of MS Tanner 346 with introduction by P.R. Robinson, *English Studies*, 63 (1982), 73. Romance

manuscripts which are made up of booklets include MS Harley 2252 (the fifteenth-century core, containing *Ipomydon* B and the stanzaic *Morte Arthur*); Chetham's Library, MS A.6.31 (8009); Lambeth MS 491 (where the *Awntyrs off Arthure* is in the same unit as the book on hunting attributed to Dame Juliana Berners); and MS Douce 324, also containing the *Awntyrs*, which once formed part of a large collection (see K.L. Smith, 'A Fifteenth Century Vernacular Manuscript Reconstructed', *BLR*, 7 (5) (1966), 234–41, and Doyle, 'The Manuscripts', p. 97 and n. 34).

97 See, e.g., the Ireland/Blackburn manuscript, part of the collection of the late Mr R.H. Taylor, deposited at Princeton University Library, which contains the *Awntyrs off Arthure, Sir Amadace* and the *Avowinge of Arthur* (Phillipa Hardman, 'The Unity of the Ireland Manuscript', *Reading Medieval Studies*, 2 (1976), 45–62); and Longleat MS 257, containing Lydgate's *Siege of Thebes*, Chaucer's Knight's and Clerk's Tales, *Ipomedon* C and verse paraphrases of Old Testament stories (Meale, 'The Middle English romance of *Ipomedon*', pp. 147–50).

98 See, e.g., the prose *Merlin* (CUL MS Ff.3.11); *Partonope of Blois* (BL Add. MS 35288, Bodleian MS Rawl.poet.14, Oxford, University College, MS 188).

99 *The Romance of the Sowdone of Babylone*, ed. E. Hausknecht, EETS, es, 38 (1881); *A Manual of Writings in Middle English 1050–1500*, 1, ed. J.B. Severs (New Haven, Conn., 1967), pp. 82–4; Pearsall, 'The English Romance in the Fifteenth Century', p. 63. Pearsall gives other examples of romances which were influenced by the aureate poets, including *Partonope*, and John Metham's *Amoryus and Cleopes* (which survives only in PUL Garrett 141, the manuscript miscellany made for his patrons, Sir Miles Stapleton and his wife Catherine de la Pole). The increased confidence with which fifteenth-century romance writers approached their task is reflected in the absence of the aggressively patriotic linguistic justification which characterised some early fourteenth-century works, such as *Arthour and Merlin* and *Richard Coeur de Lion*; see the editions by O.D. Macrae-Gibson, EETS, os, 268, 279 (1973, 1979) and K. Brunner, Wiener Beiträge zur Englischen Philologie, Band 42 (Vienna, 1913).

100 The final lines of the romance indicate the status of this copy as a reading text: 'bringe here soules to goode reste / That were so worthy in dede / And gyf vs ioye of the beste / That of here Gestes rede' (compare Pearsall, 'The English Romance in the Fifteenth Century', p. 61). Guddat-Figge, p. 301, reads the early Tudor ownership inscription on p. 81 as 'This is John Eteyes boke / witness by John staff', but the first name could perhaps be 'Edeyes' or 'Eleyes'.

101 Pearsall, *John Lydgate*, pp. 49–51.

102 See Norton-Smith, introduction to the facsimile of Fairfax 16, p. xiii.

103 On MS Pepys 2006 see Manly and Rickert, 1, 406–9; M.R. James, *Bibliotheca Pepysiana: A Descriptive Catalogue of the Library of Samuel Pepys*, 3 (London, 1923), pp. 60–3; and the fascimile, vol. 6 in *The Fascimile Series of the Works of Geoffrey Chaucer*, with introd. by A.S.G. Edwards (Norman, Oklahoma, and Woodbridge, 1985). On the manuscripts copied by the so-called Hammond scribe see, most recently, Doyle, 'English Books In and Out of Court', p. 177, and references cited in n. 42.

104 Lady Margaret Beaufort bequeathed 'a greatte volume of velom of the siege of Troye yn Englissh' to her son, Henry VII: see C.H. Cooper, *Memoir of Margaret*

Countess of Richmond and Derby (Cambridge, 1874), p. 132; and on the other four codices – MSS Royal 18.D.II, Cotton Augustus A.IV, Manchester, John Rylands University Library, English 1 and Cambridge, Trinity College, O.5.2 – *Troy Book*, ed. Bergen, 4, pp. 15–19, 1–4, 29–36, 19–21, and Lawton 'The Illustration of Late Medieval Secular Texts', pp. 53–4; on the Trinity manuscript, see also D. Pearsall, 'Notes on the Manuscript of *Generydes*', *The Library*, 5th series, 16 (1961), 205–9.

105 These volumes are described by Bergen, *Troy Book*, 4, pp. 6–10, 43–6. Lydgate's *Siege of Thebes* had a similarly broad readership: Longleat 257 belonged to Richard III while he was duke of Gloucester; Arundel 119 has the arms of William and Alice de la Pole, duke and duchess of Suffolk, on its opening page; and Laud 557 belonged to Roger Thorney, mercer of London.

106 N.F. Blake makes the point that English enjoyed a different and well-established popularity as a vehicle for devotional writing: see 'Middle English Prose and Its Audience', *Anglia*, 90 (1972), 437–55.

107 The text is at present unedited. See C.R. Shrader, 'A Handlist of Extant Manuscripts Containing the *De re militari* of Flavius Vegetius Renatus', *Scriptorium*, 33 (1979), 280–305; J.A. Wisman, 'L'*Epitoma rei militaris* de Végèce et sa fortune au Moyen Age', *Le Moyen Age*, 85 (1979), 13–31; D. Bornstein, 'Military Manuals in Fifteenth Century England', *Medieval Studies*, 37 (1975), 469–77. John Trevisa's writings could also be considered in this context, although much research remains to be carried out: see the survey by A.S.G. Edwards, 'John Trevisa', in *Middle English Prose*, ed. Edwards, pp. 133–46; and on the audience for his translation of Bartholomeus Anglicus (mainly university and clerical), M.C. Seymour, 'Some Medieval English Owners of the *De Proprietatibus Rerum*', *BLR*, 9 (1974), 156–65. An additional indication of the status of English is the number of translations made into this language by educated members of the nobility. Edward, duke of York, translated Gaston Phebus' *Livre de la Chasse*; John Tiptoft, earl of Worcester, is credited with a reworking of Cicero's *De Amicitia*; and the *Dicts and Sayings of the Philosophers* and *Cordyale* of Anthony Wydville, second Earl Rivers, were both taken from French originals.

108 Shrader, 'Handlist of Extant MSS'; N.R. Ker, *Medieval Libraries*.

109 See on Charles V's and Jean de Berri's books, Delisle, *Recherches sur la Librairie de Charles V*, 1, pp. 273–4 and 2, p. 253; on the copies belonging to Charles d'Orléans and Louis of Bruges, Delisle, *Le Cabinet des Manuscrits de la Bibliothèque Imperiale*, 1 (Paris, 1868), pp. 143, 106; and on Philip the Good's two extant MSS, Shrader, 'Handlist', p. 300. For the texts belonging to Thomas of Gloucester and Fastolf see the references in nn. 6 and 54 above. Edward III's copy, issued from the wardrobe to Isabella of France, is mentioned by Vale, *Edward III and Chivalry*, p. 50; Humphrey of Gloucester's and Edward IV's MSS are, respectively, CUL Ee.2.17 and Royal 17.E.v.

110 Three copies survive of the verse translation attributed to Robert Parker, royal servant and priest of Calais; see *Knyghthode and Bataile*, ed. R. Dyboski and Z.M. Arend, EETS, os, 201 (1935), and D. Pearsall, *Old English and Middle English Poetry* (London, 1977), pp. 240–2.

111 Pächt and Alexander, III, no. 815 and plate LXXV.

112 See Doyle, 'English Books In and Out of Court', p. 173, for the suggestion that this volume could have been produced in a regional centre, perhaps Bristol.

113 On Douce 291, which is well decorated but not illustrated, see Pächt and Alexander, III, no. 910 and plate LXXXVI. PML M 775 contains a number of miniatures, though none illustrates the Vegetius; see the descriptions by Viscount Dillon, 'On a MS. Collection of Ordinances of Chivalry of the Fifteenth Century, belonging to Lord Hastings', *Archaeologia*, 57 (1900), 29–70, and G.A. Lester, 'Sir John Paston's "Grete Boke": A Bespoke Book or Mass-Produced?', *English Studies*, 66 (1985), 93–104. Thomas Fitzhugh may probably be identified as the fourth son of Thomas Fitzhugh, Lord Fitzhugh, and Alice Neville (*GEC*, pp. 432–3); Thomas Tunstall may be the man of that name of Thurland castle in Lancashire, whose eldest (illegitimate) son was Cuthbert Tunstall, master of the rolls and bishop, successively, of London and Durham; and Brian Tunstall may be Cuthbert's younger brother, who was killed at Flodden in 1513 (*DNB*, XIX, 1237–42). I am not convinced that these names are signatures. Sir John Astley (d. 1486) acquired the core of the MS before 1461 (Lester, 'Paston's "Grete Boke"', p. 101), but the incremental nature of its composition is indicated by other notes of ownership: 'R Page' is written in a late medieval hand on fol. ir at the end of a series of verses in French, and under ultra-violet light the inscription 'Cest liuer est' tien Page' emerges on fol. 283r, the first page of a calendar, which forms a discrete unit within the volume as it now stands.

114 On the books belonging to Paston and Brandon see nn. 40 and 88 above.

115 *Fragments of an Early Fourteenth Century Guy of Warwick*, ed. M. Mills and D. Huws, Medium Aevum Monographs, NS, 4 (1974), pp. 1–4.

116 H.O. Coxe, *Laudian Manuscripts*, in *Bodleian Library Quarto Catalogue*, 2, 1, reprinted from the edition of 1858–95 with corrections, additions and historical introduction by R.W. Hunt (Oxford, 1973), p. 306. A John Neuton, prior of Battle Abbey, owned University of Chicago MS 254, a *Brut* (Matheson, 'A Location List', p. 265), and Professor A.S.G. Edwards informs me that he may also be associated with Sloane 4031, Lydgate's *Fall of Princes* and TCC B.14.17, a twelfth-to thirteenth-century manuscript of 'Hieronymus super Ieremiam; super Danielem' (see M.R. James, *Trinity College MSS*, vol. 1, pp. 154–5). It is not clear whether the scribe of Laud 416 may be identified as this John Neuton.

117 Michael G. Sargent, 'Walter Hilton's *Scale of Perfection*: The London Manuscript Group Reconsidered', *Medium Aevum*, 52 (1983), 189–214, at p. 206.

118 Davis, *Paston Letters and Papers*, 2, pp. 386–7, 391–2 for the letters and bill which Ebesham sent to Paston, and see also vol. 1, p. 409; A.I. Doyle, 'William Ebesham', p. 303.

119 Lester, *Sir John Paston's 'Grete Boke'*, pp. 31–4, and 'Sir John Paston's "Grete Boke": A Bespoke Book or Mass-Produced?'. See also Doyle, 'William Ebesham', p. 306, n. 1. Another text which may have been copied by a professional scribe from an exemplar supplied by a patron is *The Awntyrs off Arthure*, now Douce 324: here the northern dialect of the romance contrasts with the predominantly southern character of the other texts which once made up a large volume; see Doyle, 'The Manuscripts', p. 97.

120 J. Fenn, *Original Letters written during the reigns of Henry VI, Edward IV and Richard*

III, etc., 2 (London, 1787), pp. 16–17; Abbot Gasquet, 'Books and Bookmaking in Early Chronicles and Accounts', *Transactions of the Bibliographical Society*, 9 (1906), 15–30, at pp. 28–30.

121 See the references to Pepys 2006 cited in n. 103 above. John Paston himself had duplicate copies of *La Belle Dame Sans Merci* and 'þe Parlement off Byrdys' in separate small anthologies: see Davis, *Paston Letters and Papers*, 1, p. 517; see also the discussion of books of this kind below, Ch. 12.

122 Scott, 'Lydgate's Lives', pp. 364–6, n. 92.

10 · BOOKS AND BOOK OWNERS IN FIFTEENTH-CENTURY SCOTLAND

R.J. LYALL

By comparison with England, evidence of book production and book ownership in later medieval Scotland is fragmentary and scattered. Not a single medieval Scottish library has remained intact, and only in the case of King's College, Aberdeen, is there anything like continuity in the possession of a few manuscripts and printed books from 1500 to the present day.[1] Yet it is clear that Scotland, while it was a relatively poor country on the fringes of Europe, was in no sense culturally isolated. Fifteenth-century inventories of books in the cathedral libraries of Glasgow and Aberdeen reveal both quantity and quality; there is, naturally, a preponderance of Bibles and liturgical books, but there are also some traces of wider reading among the canons of these establishments.[2] There is no reason to suppose that the house of Augustinian canons who served the cathedral of St Andrews, the most important ecclesiastical institution in Scotland, was less well supplied, although no catalogue has survived. Only a tiny handful of extant manuscripts can, however, be assigned with any probability to these cathedral libraries, and the volumes listed in the medieval inventories seem, almost without exception, to have vanished without trace.[3] The same applies to the books which are ascribed to Scottish houses in the proto-Union catalogues which have come down from the Middle Ages, while the volumes which we know to have been donated to the nascent university libraries of St Andrews and Glasgow in the later fifteenth century have similarly disappeared – or, at least, not yet been identified.[4]

More informal evidence of later medieval Scottish libraries can be gleaned from an examination of the sources used by those Scottish writers whose works survive from the latter part of the fourteenth century onwards: John of Fordoun, for example, clearly had access to copies of a variety of chroniclers including Paulus Diaconus, Bede and Geoffrey of Monmouth (although there is a fifteenth-century tradition that some at least of his sources were found during research visits to England and Ireland),[5] while Andrew Wyntoun, lamenting the paucity of his source materials, nevertheless acknowledges his debt to

> Part of the Bibill, with that at Peris
> Comestor ekit in his 3eris,

239

> And Orosius and Frer Mertyne
> With Scottis and Inglis storyis syne . . . [6]

As a canon of St Andrews, Wyntoun would obviously have had access to the library there, and it would indeed be surprising if such basic works as these had not been among its collections. The anonymous translator of the Scottish saints' lives, who may well have had access to the cathedral library at either Elgin or Aberdeen,[7] was likewise able to make use, a little before 1400, of a copy of Jacobus de Voragine's *Legenda aurea*, Vincent of Beauvais' *Speculum historiale*, and a variety of other hagiographical works.[8] It may, therefore, be taken for granted that the most important works of the Latin Middle Ages were to be found in one or more Scottish libraries, even if no surviving copy can be shown to have a Scottish provenance.

It is obvious that at least the initial copies of all such texts must have been imported, either from England or from the continent. The ample evidence which we have of Scottish students in continental universities, both before and after the foundation of the universities of St Andrews (1410–13) and Glasgow (1451),[9] and of churchmen travelling to the Papal court on ecclesiastical business, provides a sufficient explanation of such imports, and there are some fifteenth-century instances, such as the manuscripts copied by William Elphinstone the elder while a student at Louvain in the early 1430s, of books which are known to have come to Scotland in this way.[10] We have, too, a few English books which were certainly in Scotland at an early date: the copy of Gower's *Confessio Amantis* which is now BL Add. MS 22139, written in England in 1432, has some fifteenth-century corrections and additions which reveal a Scottish orthography, while Boston Public Library, MS f.med.94, containing Lydgate's *Siege of Thebes*, was owned by Marion Lyle of Houston at this early period.[11] There is plenty of internal evidence that Robert Henryson and his contemporaries were thoroughly familiar with the poetry of Chaucer, Gower, Hoccleve and Lydgate, and we do not need the survival of a manuscript such as Bodleian MS Arch. Selden B.24, of which we shall have to take notice below, to demonstrate the availability to Scottish scribes of English exemplars.

For all this evidence, direct and indirect, of the existence of a fairly wide range of manuscript books in fourteenth- and fifteenth-century Scotland, there is not much to show of the *production* of literary manuscripts before the last quarter of the fifteenth century. Again, it is easy to justify the inference that there was an indigenous book trade of sorts: the extant later copies of Fordoun's and Wyntoun's chronicles, of Barbour's *Brus* and of the saints' lives, of the *Kingis Quair* and of miscellaneous moral works such as those preserved in CUL MS Kk.1.5 must all have derived from early exemplars. Yet the only surviving copies of the *Brus* are dated 1487 and 1489, more than a hundred years after the composition of the poem; the unique manuscript of the saints' lives can, as we have seen above, be assigned on the basis of its paper to c. 1480–5, again around a century later than the work was written;[12] the earliest surviving copies of Fordoun's and Wyntoun's chronicles appear to be respectively seventy-five and fifty years later than the making of these compilations;[13] the only surviving manuscripts of Gilbert Haye's *Buke of King Alexander the Conquerour*, translated in the middle of the fifteenth century, are of sixteenth-century date; and the anonymous *Buik of Alexander*, datable on internal evidence to 1438, does not exist in manuscript at all, suriving only in a unique copy of Alexander Arbuthnot's edition, printed around 1580. Of over eighty non-liturgical manuscripts which can be shown to have been written in Scotland in the fifteenth century, at least fifty were written after 1470, and only eight can be assigned with any great degree of probability to the first half of the century. Either manuscripts of the earlier period must have perished in disproportionately large numbers, or there was a radical change in the rate of production from about 1470.

To some extent, both conclusions may in part be justified. Many of the surviving books were owned by one of a small group of influential collectors, and were in some instances written for them; and it is likely that such works had a better chance of survival through the vicissitudes of the sixteenth and seventeenth centuries, partly because they had often found their way into the library of a scholarly protector such as Henry Sinclair or James Balfour of Denmilne.[14] Equally, the presence of men like William Scheves, archbishop of St Andrews, whose library was favourably commented upon in his own day, Archbishop Whitelaw and William Elphinstone the younger must have stimulated the production of manuscripts, and we shall have cause below to remark upon the work of particular scribes in their circles. It is seldom easy in such circumstances to distinguish cause from effect, and it is possible that the increasing professionalisation of scribal activity which can be discerned in Scotland in the second half of the fifteenth century was in part a response and in part a stimulus to the commissioning of the copies of the Scottish chronicles and of other works, sometimes from printed books, which took place. Economic factors may also have played a part: I have argued above that the increasing availability of paper at progressively lower prices made the purchase of books of all kinds possible for a larger segment of society, and while this may not have made much difference to a Scheves or an Elphinstone, it probably accounts for the higher level of book ownership among their humbler contemporaries.

It would, on the other hand, be unwise to claim that the corpus I have just described comprises an exhaustive list of surviving Scottish manuscripts, for there are formidable difficulties in identifying provenances for many medieval books. Where there are no distinctively Scottish texts to point the way, the location of manuscripts written north of the border can be troublesome. As we have already seen, the fact that a volume had an early Scottish owner does not necessarily mean that it was written in Scotland, and few scribes sign

their work to bring comfort to the codicologist. In the case of Scottish copies
of vernacular English works, distinctive orthographic features, such as *quh-*,
-i- as a lengthening symbol in vowels, *-it* as the ending of past tenses and past
participles and *-is* as the ending of plural nouns may enable us to infer a
Scottish origin: thus, it seems clear that Scottish Record Office, MS GD
112/71/1(1), containing a short prose chronicle of the reign of Edward II of
England and a copy of Lord Rivers' *Cordiale*, written about 1480 and preserved among the Breadalbane muniments, was produced in Scotland,[15]
while the same *may* apply (although the orthographic evidence is here not so
certain) to the Hunterian copy (GUL MS Hunt.400) of Hardyng's chronicle.[16] Latin manuscripts, of course, offer no such help, and a fully comprehensive list of surviving books produced in Scotland will be possible only
when we have a much clearer understanding of the distinctive characteristics
of fifteenth-century Scottish hands. In the meantime, we can be fairly certain
that the corpus is skewed towards copies of Scottish texts and away from
works in general European circulation.

It is, nevertheless, possible to offer some generalisations about the
fifteenth-century Scottish book-trade. At no time does Scotland appear to
have had an organised centre of book production comparable with the
London ateliers which were responsible for the fine Chaucers, Gowers and
Lydgates described elsewhere in these pages, or even with the more important English provincial centres. In the same way that the smaller Scottish
market was unable to sustain a stable printing industry until almost the end
of the sixteenth century, so the production of manuscripts seems to have
remained rudimentary by comparison with the industry which flourished in
southern England. Yet there was in the course of the fifteenth century a
remarkable growth in the scribal profession, which ultimately had its effect
upon the copying of literary texts. The key to this process was the emergence,
towards the end of the fourteenth century, of a cadre of highly skilled notaries
public, who came to assume a much greater significance in the legal and
economic life of Scotland than was ever enjoyed by their English counterparts.[17] Their staple trade was the preparation of the instruments of sasine
which became the basic document in the transfer of land, and of other
instruments recording judicial decisions, agreements of purchase or loan, or
any other transaction requiring formal authentication. It was the reliability of
the notary as an exponent of legal formulae and as a copyist which consti-
tuted his *raison d'être*, and as the profession developed in the first half of the
fifteenth century we see a growing preoccupation with the appearance of the
instrument, including the stylisation of the handwriting. There does not seem
to have been a formal organisation of notaries public, comparable for
example with the Scriveners' Company in London, but there is a good deal of
evidence of the existence of something like an apprenticeship system which
enabled prospective members of the profession to acquire the necessary

skills.[18] It is certainly true that by about 1450 there is a recognisable family of 'notarial' hands, and that it is most probably through this means that many of the characteristics of continental 'secretary' hands find their way into Scottish scribal tradition.[19]

It is clear to anyone who systematically compares manuscripts written in Scotland with those produced in England that the scribal traditions of the two countries were in many respects distinct. In particular, the specific developments which led in England to the use of anglicana scripts, as documented by Malcolm Parkes,[20] seem never to have taken place in Scotland; while the close links between the Scottish intellectual community and the continent were no doubt responsible for the much stronger continental influence discernible in Scottish hands. This distinctive history can be traced through three principal styles of hand which predominated in Scotland in the second half of the century: one comparable to Bastard Anglicana in its assimilation of cursive features, its pointedness and preference for broken strokes; one, evidently derived from certain types of clerical hand much used in the Rhineland and the Netherlands at this period and characterised by its employment of unlooped ascenders in **b**, **h** and **l**, which might, from its use in universities on both sides of the North Sea, be termed Academica; and a highly cursive style, the direct ancestor of sixteenth-century Secretary hands, developed by notaries public from about 1480 and therefore appropriately called Notariensis.[21] Many scribes, of course, combine features appropriate to more than one type of hand, and their currency overlapped to a considerable degree. But each of the three has a recognisable history, and each was carried to a high level of performance by a substantial number of professional scribes.

This professionalisation of scribal practice can be traced in two related corpora of material: the records of the burghs, and the legal texts which were copied with increasing frequency during the century and which provide some of the earliest examples of indigenous Scottish manuscripts. Where we have early sets of burgh court records, as in the case of Aberdeen (where the series begins in 1396) and Ayr, the hands are initially relatively crude, in a square, partially cursive vernacular tradition which appears to be an amateur version of the hands in which the few surviving Scots charters of the fourteenth century are written.[22] Gradually, however, these irregular and inelegant forms of 'Scoticana' give way to hands which are evidently similar, or perhaps identical, to the even, cursive hands of contemporary notarial instruments; this is scarcely a surprising development, since we now begin to find notaries who describe themselves as *scriba commune* or *scriba curie burgi*.[23] The same pattern applies to the various legal manuscripts in the *Regiam Majestatem* tradition, many of which have burghal provenance. Fragments apart, the earliest is the so-called Bute manuscript, which contains the *Regiam* itself and a number of other Latin texts together with a Scots version of the *Leges*

Burgorum and some other vernacular items, and which was bought by Duncan Parker, burgess of Dundee, from its Edinburgh owner on 20 January 1425.[24] Like the majority of contemporary burgh records, the Bute MS is written in a squarish, uneven Scoticana hand, little marked by Secretary features. By contrast, the copy of *Regiam* which is now National Library of Scotland, MS Adv. 25.4.13, most of which was complete by 17 December 1439,[25] was written by a scribe who had absorbed, however inconsistently, many features of Continental cursive script, including long, splayed descenders and a clear preference for broken strokes.

Some nineteen manuscripts in this legal tradition survive from the fifteenth century, all of them bearing the unmistakable signs of being functional volumes, prepared by or for practising lawyers in the developing Scottish legal system. Almost without exception they are written on paper; some rubrication is the most they have to offer by way of decoration. The writing is often hurried, and little attention has been given in most cases to the design of the page. And yet the professional competence of the scribes, most of whom were in all probability notaries public, is seldom in question. It is true that the neat appearance of NLS MS Advocates 25.4.10, written by Alexander Foulis, burgess and notary public of Linlithgow between 1454 and c. 1480,[26] is evidence of unusual care, but the long period during which the manuscript was produced indicates that the texts were probably being copied for Foulis' own use. Other *Regiam* manuscripts tend to be less painstaking, but nevertheless competently produced. An interesting exception is BL Add. MS 18111, the only member of the class to have been written on parchment. Unlike the rest, too, it is for the most part in a formal bookhand, although a second hand, which takes over at fol. 116r, more closely resembles the notarial scripts of the middle part of the century. Some terse annals on fols. 153v–154r give some clues to its origins: the most recent event mentioned is the coronation of James III (1460), there is a longish note about the disputed succession to the earldom of Mar and the claim of the Erskine family up to '*Schir* Robert lorde of Erskin that last deit',[27] and there are references both to the consecration of Richard Bothwell, abbot of Dunfermline, in 1445 and to a disastrous fire in the burgh in 1455. It seems fairly certain that the manuscript has a Dunfermline provenance; and it may have originated in the abbey itself, which would explain the unusual reliance on parchment and the nature of the script. We shall need to return in due course to the question of Dunfermline as a centre of book production.

The manuscripts we have so far been considering were probably written by practising lawyers, most of them notaries public, for their own use. But the growing influence of notaries as professional penmen clearly permeated the book-trade in Scotland during the second half of the fifteenth century. One of the earliest examples is the copy of Durandus' *Rationale Divinorum Officiorum* (now Bodleian MS Laud misc. 100) written by Robert Kinghorn, chaplain and notary public, and completed on 12 November 1470.[28] Carefully written in two columns, this volume was apparently prepared for a religious house, since fol. 1r bears the remnants of the ownership mark 'Liver *con*uentus de . . .'. It is interesting that a monastic institution should have contracted out the copying of a manuscript, but this is not the only such example in Scotland. There is, as we shall see, good reason to believe that the Augustinian house at Scone employed the services of a notary for one of its books, while the copy of *Regiam Majestatem* once owned by the Carthusian house at Perth (NLS MS Advocates' 25.5.10) may also be a notarial production. We may be justified in concluding that Scottish monastic houses did not involve themselves greatly in the actual production of manuscripts, apart perhaps from the chronicles which were compiled within their walls.

The best example of a notary public moving seriously into the commercial production of manuscripts is Magnus Makculloch, who wrote at least three commissioned manuscripts between 1481 and 1487. Two are copies of the same text, the *Scotichronicon* of Walter Bower:[29] the so-called Brechin Castle manuscript, now SRO MS GD45/26/46, written in 1481, and BL MS Harley 712, written in 1483-4 for William Scheves, archbishop of St Andrews, whose 'familiar clerk' Makculloch acknowledges himself to be. A further connection with the Scheves household is indicated by the rubric in the SRO manuscript, stating that it was 'illuminated' (which appears to mean rubricated, since there are no illuminations) by James Gray, who certainly acted, a few years later at least, as Scheves' secretary.[30] It is this manuscript which was probably written for the Augustinian canons of Scone. The evidence for the attribution is circumstantial but fairly conclusive: the library of the University of St Andrews appears to have owned in the seventeenth century a copy of the *Scotichronicon* written by Makculloch and formerly at Scone, but it was missing by the time the antiquarian Thomas Innes investigated Scottish chronicle manuscripts in 1701.[31] It was probably borrowed by the earl of Dalhousie of the day, with the intention of publishing it, and seems never to have been returned.[32] Both Makculloch's *Scotichronicon* manuscripts are in a two-column format, written in a rapid, current version of a notarial hand. Makculloch's habit of dating his colophons at intervals throughout the text gives us an unusually clear view of his progress: in the SRO manuscript, he had reached the end of Book II (fol. 30r) on 9 January 1481 and the beginning of Book VI (fol. 104v) on 30 January, an average of 3.5 folios per day. He began Book XIV (fol. 322v) on 31 March, which represents a very slight acceleration; but the prospect of completing his task seems to have acted as a spur, since he was at fol. 354v only two days later. The writing of the second copy of Bower's substantial chronicle took more than a year, for Makculloch recorded the commencement of Book III (on fol. 40v) on 10 October 1483, completing the index (fol. 276r) on 7 October 1484. There are three intermediate reference points: Book VIII was completed (fol. 150v) on 13 March (an average of less than 1.5 folios per day) and Book XIV at fol. 245v at the feast of St Giles (that is, 1 September, giving an average of little more than half a folio, one page, per day). Makculloch then accelerated slightly, and the next book was finished on fol. 257v only seven days later, on the eve of the Nativity of the Virgin. But the remaining nineteen folios took him, as we have noted, until 7 October. The importance of Makculloch's patron evidently did not prevent him from writing the Harley copy of Bower much more slowly than the earlier SRO text: perhaps his other tasks in Scheves' household took priority, or perhaps the task of writing out Bower's voluminous chronicle twice in less than four years was simply too daunting.

Like MS Harley 712, Makculloch's other extant manuscript, a copy of Magninus' *Regimen sanitatis*, was written for a prominent member of the court of James III. John Ramsay, who had been created Lord Bothwell in February 1484, was certainly one of the king's favourites, and it is therefore not surprising to find him commissioning a manuscript from Scheves' 'familiar clerk'. Now National Library of Medicine, MS 512, his copy of Magninus was completed by Makculloch at Leith on 12 April 1482, just fourteen months before Bothwell's royal patron was assassinated and he himself forced into exile in England. It is in a much smaller format than the Bowers, arranged as a quarto by contrast with their folio, two-column format. But it resembles them in its thoroughgoing professionalism. Each of these three works is written predominantly on paper from a single stock, although in each case this basic paper is supplemented by material from another stock: in the SRO manuscript, all but the last four quires are made up of Anchor paper, augmented by a quantity of French Royal Arms; Harley 712 is made up of a mixture of Hand paper and a Gothic 'q'; while the Magninus consists mainly of a pair of BHX marks (one of which is identical with Briquet 14243), supplemented by just one sheet of Dog paper. The total number of sheets involved in the Magninus volume is relatively small, but the homogeneity of the large quantities of paper required for the Bowers – both of which are written, moreover, on the more unusual large-format sheets – indicates that Makculloch was able, on occasions at any rate, to buy fairly substantial stocks.

William Scheves, Makculloch's principal patron and one of the most significant figures in the administration of James III, clearly owned an important library. Jaspar Laet of Borchloen, who complimented him upon it during his residence at Louvain in 1491, had been told that its main strengths were in science and medicine;[33] but it is also apparent that Scheves had a more than passing interest in Scottish history. In addition to the Bower which Makculloch prepared for him, he owned a copy of Fordoun's chronicles (BL MS Cotton Vitellius E.XI) which must have been written, in part at least, before 1450,[34] and he also commissioned a copy of the so-called *Liber Pluscardensis*, an adaptation of Bower's work which was closely associated with Dunfermline.

This latter volume, now GUL MS Gen. 333, actually provides the only fully attested example of a product of a monastic scriptorium in Scotland, for a colophon on fol. 299v tells us that the manuscript was written for Scheves of Dunfermline 'de mandato *domini* Thome Monymelle monachi & sacri*ste* euisde*m* loci'. Monimail was sacrist from 1477 until his death in 1490, while Scheves was provided to the archbishopric on 11 February 1478.[35] The paper evidence, however, permits us to be much more accurate in dating the Glasgow manuscript, for the sum total of the eight stocks represented points with remarkable consistency to a date around 1478–80, at the very beginning of Scheves' archiepiscopal career.[36]

Analysis of the structure of the manuscript enables us to establish the way in which Monimail went about meeting the commission, and suggests that the monks of Dunfermline were far from practised in the workings of a scriptorium. Three (or perhaps four) hands are involved, two of which occur in two separate stints; while the physical structure of the volume can be divided into four units which do not altogether correspond either to the scribal stints or to the division of the text into eleven books. Two of the hands, moreover, also turn up in contemporary sections of the Dunfermine Cartulary (now NLS MS Advocates' 34.1.3[A]), and can therefore safely be regarded as belonging to monks of the house.[37] Hand I is responsible for the first few folios, breaking off partway through fol. 6v and giving way to Hand II, reappearing on fol. 8or, at the beginning of the tenth quire, to copy Books v and vI of the text. This latter stint occupies four quires, two of fourteen leaves and two of twelve. Hand II, taking up the copying of Book I on fol. 6v, continues through several quires of very uneven size and uncertain structure to the end of Book II on fol. 43v. The presence in this section of two fragmentary quires of three and four singletons suggests a certain lack of confidence in the arrangement of the volume; there is much more evenness in Hand II's other stint, running from fol. 131r to the end of the manuscript and containing the final five books of the text. Some of the most curious codicological problems, however, arise from the remaining section, fols. 44–79. The hand or hands here differ profoundly from those of the other scribes, resembling one another in their neat, pointed character with frequent broken strokes. Neil Ker believed that two scribes were responsible for these four quires,[38] and it is indeed true that the hand of fols. 44r–59v is much more compressed than that of fols. 6or–79v, fitting in about sixty-two lines to the page as against about fifty. Then again, the initials are treated differently in the two sections, being omitted in the first with spaces left for rubrication, and simply written in larger characters by the second; there is, moreover, a change from fol. 6or to a much blacker ink, and the decorative strapwork which is a feature of the first two quires is less evident in the latter two. Close examination of the letter-forms, however, leaves a strong impression of identity, and the four quires share a remarkable feature: in every case the scribe has filled the last line of a chapter with a formulaic phrase, usually a variation upon the invocation *Maria memento serui/famuli tui Johannis* but sometimes taking the form *vnde uersus*, and once (fol. 59v) occuring as *vnde uersus quod my awne mastir the sacristain*. Since these distinctive formulae are common to the two styles of hand, and since the form *Johannis* on fol. 48r is echoed by *famuli tui J etc etc* on fol. 78r, it is difficult to resist the conclusion that all four quires are in reality the work of a single scribe. It is difficult to see why such a radical restyling should have been necessary, but it confirms the sense that the Dunfermline monks were scarcely well practised in the ways of a scriptorium.

These three historical manuscripts are the only surviving items from Scheves' collection which seem clearly to have been written in Scotland: his three other extant volumes, on medical and scientific subjects, were probably written on the continent, and may have been acquired during Scheves' absence from Scotland in the 1460s.[39] The pattern of his extant manuscripts makes an interesting contrast with that of the books owned at the same period by Scheves' contemporary in royal service, Archibald Whitelaw, who was employed as secretary from 1462 until 1493. The subject emphasis is strikingly different: Whitelaw appears to have been interested in Roman history rather than that of Scotland, and in canon law rather than in medicine and astronomy. As in the case of Scheves, six of his manuscripts survive; one of these, Aberdeen UL MS 257, was certainly written abroad.[40] The origins of NLS MS Advocates' 18.4.8 are more problematical: evidence of Whitelaw's possession of this manuscript is confined to marginal notes on fols. 57r and 68r, and the volume's rather disparate contents, including the 1478 Cologne edition of John of Hildesheim's *Liber de gestis ac translatione trium regum* as well as various texts in at least three different hands, were not necessarily brought together before the sixteenth century.[41] Whitelaw's notes occur beside a copy of *Ilias Latina* written on a single stock of paper marked with a Pot very similar to Briquet 12482, of French, probably *troyen*, manufacture and in use between about 1474 and about 1480.[42] The hand is curious: it has several humanist features, but the form of certain letters (**d**, 2-shaped **r, l**) suggests imitation of humanist norms by a scribe whose usual hand is closer to a Scottish Academica, and this is confirmed by the cursive Secretary character of the inter-linear gloss. The same sort of pattern occurs in the next section of the manuscript, a copy of Antonio Beccaria's translation of Dionysius Periegetes' *De situ orbis habitabilis* written on five different stocks of French paper;[43] but here the superficiality of the humanist features is even more apparent. We cannot be certain that these texts were copied in Scotland, but on the whole it seems likely that they were.

This conjecture is supported by a much more substantial manuscript, the copy of Cicero's philosophical works which is now St Andrews UL MS PA6295.A2A00. Whitelaw probably owned this book before 1482, for the ownership note on fol. 1r, which originally read 'Liber Archibaldi quhitelaw Archidia*coni sancti* andre*e* infra partes laudonie', has been augmented with the words 'ac subdecani glasguensis'; Whitelaw was provided to this office in August 1482.[44] Two hands are responsible for this manuscript: fols. 1r–80v and 264r–280v are in a fairly straightforward Bastard Scoticana, but the rest is in a hand in which, as in the sections of Adv. 18.4.8 discussed above, humanist features seem to have been introduced into an altogether different script. These forms (distinctively humanist types of **g**, **p** and final **s**, along with unlooped ascenders in **b**, **l**, and **h**, and an enclosed **e**) predominate in the early folios written by Scribe II, but they gradually give way to traditional Scottish alternatives, and the duct simultaneously changes from an upright, stilted character to a sloped, pointed Bastard Scoticana. Interestingly, there is a reversion to the quasi-humanist style at fol. 153r, the opening of *De fato*, but the scribe's natural style quickly reasserts itself. This rather curious tension can best be explained, perhaps, as an unsuccessful attempt to assimilate the demands of a patron whose taste for a new style of hand could scarcely be satisfied in fifteenth-century Scotland.

The introduction of such new forms is a recurrent feature of Whitelaw's surviving manuscripts. A similar process of 'slippage' or reversion from a quasi-humanist norm to something apparently closer to the scribe's own natural hand is found in NLS MS Advocates' 18.3.11, a copy of Suetonius, and again, as in Adv. 18.4.8, the hand which gradually asserts itself is a kind of Academica. A different relationship occurs in NLS MS Advocates' 18.3.10: the latter part, containing the index to the *Commentarii* of Caesar compiled by Raimundus de Marliano at Louvain some time between 1465 and 1477, has Whitelaw's marginalia; it is again not certain that the two sections of this manuscript were associated in his day, although both bear the signature of Robert Braidfut, who may be the scribe and who was apparently a member of the Whitelaw household.[45] The other part of Adv. 18.3.10, a copy of the translation by Paulus Diaconus of Eutropius' *Historia romana*, is in a highly cursive, somewhat slanted Academica, while the hand of the Raimundus has that intrusion of humanist forms we have observed in Adv. 18.4.8 and the St Andrews manuscript.[46] Yet another combination of Academica and quasi-humanist hands occurs in Aberdeen UL MS 214, which was, according to a note on fol. 202v, written for Whitelaw. Like Adv. 18.3.10 the Aberdeen manuscript contains historical works, in this case Orosius, Lucius Annius and Cornelius Nepos;[47] here a single Academica hand is responsible for all the texts, but the titles of the various books and a short poem on fol. 158r are in a more calligraphically formed quasi-humanist style, apparently adopted here as a display script.

The bulk of Whitelaw's manuscripts, then, are distinguished not only by their owner's classical interests but also by a steady, if halting, introduction of a few features apparently intended to give a humanist appearance to the text.

These are never more than superficial, and we have observed the difficulties they evidently presented for the scribes; but they suggest the beginnings of a change in taste which would become much more significant in the first half of the sixteenth century. Another indication of this shift is the appointment as first Principal of the University of Aberdeen, founded in 1494, of the Paris-educated Ciceronian Hector Boece; but the surviving books of William Elphinstone, the bishop of Aberdeen whose influence helped to shape the new institution, do not reveal him as a man of classical interests in the same sense as Whitelaw.[48] Of the fifteen volumes from Elphinstone's library now preserved in Aberdeen, three were written by the bishop's father during his studies at Louvain in the 1430s.[49] The bulk of the remainder are works of canon law, more than half written by a scribe who signs himself 'R de S', at Paris during the younger Elphinstone's residence there. The only text with humanist associations is found in Aberdeen UL MS 222, a copy of Valla's *Elegantiae* which was probably made in either France or Scotland about 1470. More characteristic of Elphinstone's interests is Aberdeen UL MS 201, containing Jacobus de Imola's *Commentarium in Clementinarum*, which seems on the basis of its paper to have been written c. 1473–5, shortly after its owner's return to Scotland and provision as official of Glasgow.[50]

These three notable collectors were, of course, all ecclesiastics, and their libraries are, in different ways, clerical and scholarly in character. There is a good deal less evidence of book ownership by laymen, but among the few exceptions is one of the most important of all fifteenth-century Scottish manuscripts, one which illustrates both the capabilities and limitations of the book trade in Scotland towards the close of the century. This is Bodleian MS Arch. Selden B.24, the well-known *Kingis Quair* manuscript. The association of this volume with the Sinclair family is clear enough: it was owned in the later sixteenth century by Sir William Sinclair of Roslyn, and at an earlier date by Henry, Lord Sinclair (c. 1460–1513). Its date has been a matter of some conjecture, although the presence on fol. 120r of a note about the birth of James IV has suggested that it was written in or after 1488.[51] The watermark evidence offers some help on this question, and suggests quite strongly that the manuscript was assembled in its present form very soon after James IV's accession; but it also hints that its early history may have been a little more complex than is apparent at first glance. Seven stocks of paper occur in the Selden MS:

a. *Star* with eight straight points, of the type of Briquet 6056 (Fleurus 1481 × Brussels 1502) – fol. 1; fols. 213–30

b. *Gothic y*, with a tightly curled trefoil tail and surmounted by a cross, of the type of Briquet 9198 (Lille 1462 × Bruges 1474) – fols. 2–15; 31–62 (apart from fols. 52–57)

c. *French Royal Arms* with quatrefoil of the distinctive type represented by Briquet

1808 (Troyes 1479 × Düsseldorf 1489) and by Piccard, *Lilie* III, 1742–80 (1483 × 1515) – fols. 16–30 (apart from fols. 21–24)

d. *French Royal Arms*, crowned with 't' below, of the type of Briquet 1739–41 (Paris 1458 × Amsterdam 1482) and of Piccard *Lilie* III, 1553–1640 (mainly of the 1460s and 1470s) – fols. 21–24, 52–57

e. *Dog with quatrefoil*, close to Briquet 3627 and of the type of 3628–9 (Wittlich 1483 × Middelburg 1494; the conjectural date for 3627 [1466] seems clearly wrong) – fols. 63–78, 83–90. The A sheet of the pair, occurring for example on fol. 63, appears to be identical to the mark found by Briquet in the Hauptstaatsarchiv in Cologne, in letters dated 1485.[52]

f. *Crowned Heart with 'j b'*, close to Briquet 4324 (Dôle 1482 × Utrecht 1498) – fols. 79–82, 91–118

g. *French Royal Arms* of the distinctive type represented by Briquet 1806 (Utrecht 1485 × Maastricht 1490) and Piccard, *Lilie* III, 1745–51 (1486 × 1489) – fols. 119–212

On this evidence, MS Arch. Selden B.24 breaks into two clear parts: that containing Chaucer's *Troilus and Criseyde* (fols. 1r–118v), written essentially on five separate and partially intermixed stocks of paper, and the remaining, miscellaneous texts which are, paradoxically, written on only two stocks. With the exception of fol. 1, there is no mixing of stocks between the two parts.

As I have indicated above, categorical statements about the dating of paper can only be attempted where we are dealing with particular moulds.[53] Nevertheless, some conclusions can be drawn from the evidence of the paper in the *Kingis Quair* MS. The inference from the note about the nativity of James IV, that the MS is not earlier than 1488, is supported by the presence of several stocks of paper which seem to belong to the later 1480s, and especially of stock g, which could scarcely have been available before 1485. But there is, on the other hand, a certain amount of paper which looks earlier: the trefoil tail of the Gothic 'y' of stock b, for example, is characteristic of the period 1460–75, as its presence in Bodleian MS Laud misc. 100 (1470) and Aberdeen UL MS 201 (c. 1473) confirms. The miscellaneous nature of the paper used for copying *Troilus and Criseyde*, indeed, is one of the most striking features of the manuscript: the scribe has used twenty-three sheets of Gothic 'y', twelve each of Dog and Heart, seven of French Arms (Br. 1808) and four of French Arms with 't'. Given that the text seems to have been copied as one continuous process, the eight quires involved were presumably made up at about the same time; so that we must conclude that some of the paper used, and particularly the Gothic 'y', came from old stocks. That the paper employed for the remainder of the texts was of more recent manufacture is confirmed by the larger amount of French Arms (Br. 1806) which was available – forty-eight sheets in all. There is, however, another curious feature of the paper structure: the intrusion into the first quire of a single sheet of stock *a*, apparently lacking a conjugate and certainly the only piece of this stock to occur in the first part of the manuscript. It is significant that the ink on this leaf is quite different from that on fol. 2 and subsequent folios, leaving no doubt that the opening of the *Troilus* was recopied for some reason at a late stage in the production of the manuscript. From the fact that fols. 14 and 15 seem likewise to lack conjugates, moreover, we can infer that two leaves have been lost from the opening of the quire; it is possible that they became detached in the course of the manuscript's production, or the first leaf of the text may have been recopied for some other reason.

It may well be, in fact, that the replacement of fol. 1 is closely linked to the early history of MS Selden B.24. Considerable care was evidently taken with its presentation: it is not, by English standards, a particularly elegant object, but the presence of at least twenty-one illuminated initials and borders suggests a much more elaborate production than was usual in Scotland.[54] Since fol. 1 has such decoration on both recto and verso, in the same style as the rest, it seems clear that the recopying of that leaf must have preceded the process of illumination, and it may have been caused by the need to create space for the work to be done, or to replace some existing decoration. Fol. 1r is particularly elaborate, with a miniature apparently showing a meeting between Troilus and Criseyde. That the illumination was intended for a specific owner is suggested by the inclusion on fol. 118v, at the end of the *Troilus*, of the illuminated arms of Henry, Lord Sinclair, whose ownership mark occurs on fol. 230v. The Selden manuscript is unusual in another respect as well: no other Scottish manuscript of this date brings together courtly, amatory texts with such consistency, suggesting a clear thematic focus on the part of the scribe – and perhaps of the prospective owner. The unanimity of paper evidence and the scribe's note on fol. 120r is, therefore, all the more interesting when we observe that Lord Sinclair was given, on 4 December 1488, a regrant of his father's lands, jointly with his wife Margaret Hepburn.[55] This transaction may have been brought about by the accession of James IV, but it is equally likely that the occasion was Sinclair's marriage, which may well have taken place shortly before.[56] Special care was certainly taken with the manuscript's preparation, and apparently with the choice of contents. The adjustment to fol. 1 may suggest that the *Troilus* text was not originally intended for Sinclair, but it seems consistent with the single-minded pursuit of the theme of love throughout the manuscript that the compilation as a whole was prepared for such an occasion.

The existence of MS Arch. Selden B.24 reveals that by the closing years of the fifteenth century there was a demand on the part of some lay patrons for books which were well produced and secular in content. This is confirmed by other items, such as the recopying, perhaps by one of the scribes of the Selden MS, of the prose translations of Gilbert Hay.[57] Again, the purchase in reasonably large numbers of printed books from the continent and from

England seems initially to have encouraged the copying of texts in manuscript, and at least two extant volumes (Whitelaw's St Andrews Cicero and SRO MS GD 112/71/1(1)) seem to have been copied from printed works. As we noted earlier, the technology of print was slow to establish itself in Scotland, and the press which was set up in Edinburgh by Walter Chepman and Andrew Myllar about 1507 was short-lived. The production and circulation of manuscript books therefore continued well into the sixteenth century, and it was only after the Reformation in 1560 that a really marked shift away from the scribal craft took effect. As in many other fields, the religious upheavals of the mid-sixteenth century revolutionised the Scottish book trade, bringing to an end a small but distinguished tradition in the production of the manuscript book.

NOTES

1 See M.R. James, *A Catalogue of the Medieval Manuscripts in the University Library, Aberdeen* (Cambridge, 1932), and the printed books listed by J. Durkan and A. Ross, *Early Scottish Libraries* (Glasgow, 1961), e.g. under William Elphinstone, bishop of Aberdeen, Hector Boece, and John Vaus.

2 Inventories of Aberdeen cathedral library in 1436 and 1464 are printed in *Abdn Reg.*, II, 127–38, 154–9, while the latter is reprinted by M.R. James, *Aberdeen Catalogue*, pp. 80–5. For a Glasgow inventory of 1432, see *Glas. Reg.*, II, 334–9.

3 The only known surviving volume from the Aberdeen inventories is Bodleian MS Ashmole 1474: see Ker, *Medieval Libraries*, p. 1. Nothing survives from Glasgow: *ibid.*, p. 90.

4 Establishment of a library at St Andrews seems to have been triggered by Allan Cant's donation of 'unum notabilem librum scilicet Magnorum Moralium' in 1456; this gift was matched by three books from John Dunning, vicar of Perth, consisting of Aristotle's *Logic*, Aquinas' commentary on the *Ethics*, and 'unam lecturam super Ethicam yconomicam et polemicam' (*St Andrews Acta*, 114–15). Duncan Bunch and John Brown, early teachers at Glasgow, and John Brown, bishop of Glasgow, made significant donations of books to the new university; see *Glas. Mun.*, II, 403–4; III, 404–5.

5 Two manuscripts of Fordoun claim that he had travelled in England and Ireland; see *Chronica Gentis Scotorum*, ed. W.F. Skene, 2 vols. (Edinburgh, 1871–2), I, pp. xlix–li.

6 Wyntoun, *Original Chronicle*, ed. F.J. Amours, 6 vols., STS (Edinburgh, 1903–14), II, p. 11; cf. I, pp. lxviii–lxxv.

7 The north-eastern origin of the translator of the saints' lives is indicated by his inclusion of the life of Machar, to whom the cathedral at Aberdeen was dedicated, and by the inclusion in the life of Ninian of a local anecdote from Elgin: *Legends of the Saints*, ed. W.M. Metcalfe, 3 vols. STS (Edinburgh, 1896), II, 343–5. For the suggestion, plausible but not supported by any evidence, that he may be identified with William Spyny, see J. Barbour, *Bruce*, ed. M.P. McDiarmid and J.A.C. Stevenson, 3 vols., STS (Edinburgh, 1980–5), I, pp. 24–6.

8 *Legends of the Saints*, ed. Metcalfe, I, xviii–xix.

9   The period up to the beginning of the fifteenth century is comprehensively covered
    by D.E.R. Watt, *A Biographical Dictionary of Scottish Graduates to AD 1410* (Oxford,
    1977); for some specific contacts during the rest of the century, R.J. Lyall, 'Scottish
    Students and Masters at the Universities of Cologne and Louvain in the Fifteenth
    Century', *Innes Review*, 36 (1985), 55–73.

10 L.J. Macfarlane, 'William Elphinstone's Library', *Aberdeen Univ. Review*, 37
    (1957–8), 253–71.

11 Fol. 75v.

12 See above, p. 16.

13 The early copies of Fordoun, BL Add. MS 37223 and Wolfenbüttel, Herzog
    August-Bibliothek, Cod. Helmstedt 538, are on parchment, but seem from their
    hands to be from 1450 or a little later. The earliest Wyntoun MSS, BL MSS Cotton
    Nero D.xi and Royal 17.D.xx, can be dated from their paper c. 1470 and c. 1480
    respectively.

14 On Sinclair's library, see H.J. Lawlor, 'Notes on the Library of the Sinclairs of
    Rosslyn', *PSAS*, 32 (1897–98), 90–120. Balfour of Denmilne's collections formed
    the basis of the library of the Faculty of Advocates, and hence of the National
    Library of Scotland.

15 I am indebted to Dr Sally Godman for drawing my attention to this MS.

16 The general character of the hand is consistent with Scottish provenance, and a
    sprinkling of *-is* and *-it* endings, *sch-* forms and the like, suggests the possibility of a
    Scottish scribe working from an English exemplar. The presence of Hardyng's
    itinerary of Scotland would explain such interest, but the early ownership marks,
    relating to a Thomas Pycmore, indicate that the MS was later in England; see J.
    Young and P. Henderson Aitken, *A Catalogue of Manuscripts in the Library of the
    Hunterian Museum* (Glasgow, 1908), pp. 319–20.

17 For the importance of notaries public in Scotland, see J. Durkan, 'The Early
    Scottish Notary', in *The Renaissance and Reformation in Scotland*, ed. I.B. Cowan and
    D. Shaw (Edinburgh, 1983), pp. 22–40.

18 Much remains to be done on the documentation of this and other aspects of the
    notarial profession in later medieval Scotland, but the evidence of clerks, them-
    selves subsequently notaries in the same locality, copying instruments for estab-
    lished notaries suggests the existence of an apprenticeship system, at least in the
    larger centres.

19 Cf. G.C. Simpson, *Scottish Handwriting 1150–1650* (Edinburgh, 1973), pp. 8–16.

20 M.B. Parkes, *English Cursive Book Hands 1250–1500*, 2nd edn (London, 1979).

21 No systematic descriptive classification of Scottish hands has so far been
    published: the terms employed here represent an attempt to characterise the main
    varieties of script which existed in fifteenth-century Scotland.

22 E.g. William Fraser, *The Book of Menteith*, 2 vols. (Edinburgh, 1880), II, 260–1;
    National MSS. of Scotland, II, no. 47.

23 Among the earliest are William Farnely, burgh clerk of Edinburgh from at least
    1457 (*St Giles Reg.*, p. 109) and Robert Seres, *clericus communitatis* in Dundee by
    1478 (*RMS*, II, no. 1456).

24 *APS*, I, vii.

25 Fol. 164r: Expliciunt leges burgorum xvij. die mensis decembris Anno domini mo
    ccccо xxx nono. Deo gracias.

26 Fol. 30r: Explicit Regiam maiestatem scriptus per manum Alex' de foulis vj. die mensis aprilis anno domini mo cccco liiijto. The paper of fols. 49–80, however, containing the *Quoniam attachiamenta* and other legal texts, seems more likely to belong to the 1480s than to 1454. Foulis was still scribe to the burgh court of Linlithgow in 1487 (*RMS*, ii, no. 1672).

27 Sir Robert Erskine died in 1452, certainly by 6 November and probably by 26 August (*The Scottish Peerage*, ed. J. Balfour Paul, 9 vols. (Edinburgh, 1904–14), v, 604).

28 See Parkes, *English Cursive Book Hands*, p. 13. Two original instruments by King-horn are preserved among the Lockhart of Lee writs (NLS Acc. 4322, Box 27).

29 There is a useful summary description of the Bower MSS in D.E.R. Watt, 'Editing Walter Bower's *Scotichronicon*', in *Proceedings of the Third International Conference on Scottish Language and Literature (Medieval and Renaissance)*, ed. R.J. Lyall and F. Riddy (Stirling and Glasgow, 1981), pp. 161–76; cf. now the introduction to Bower, *Scotichronicon*, viii, ed. D.E.R. Watt (Aberdeen, 1987).

30 NLS MS Adv. 34.7.3, fols. iv, 23v, 31v.

31 Edinburgh UL, MS Laing, iii, 513, vol. v, fol. 285v.

32 Cf. R.J. Lyall, 'The Medieval Scottish Coronation Service: Some Seventeenth-Century Evidence', *Innes Review* 28 (1977), 3–21, at 12–13.

33 Jaspar Laet de Borchloen, *De eclipsi solis* (Gerard Leeu: Antwerp, 1491).

34 The very miscellaneous stocks of paper which make up quires 1–6 (Human Head, 'lorgnette'-type Bull's Head, Grapes, Mounts in Circle) all point to a date of compilation around 1450; the other stocks, corresponding to the change of hand at fol. 84r, are evidently somewhat later.

35 For Scheves' provision, see D.E.R. Watt, *Fasti Ecclesiae Scoticanae Medii Aevi*, 2nd draft (Edinburgh, 1969), p. 295; Monimail was competing for the sacristy of Dunfermline by May 1477 (*Cal. Papal Letters*, xiii, 577), and was dead by 5 November 1490 (Vatican Archives, Reg. Supp. 926, fol. 153r–v).

36 The most decisive conjunction is that of the first two quires (Gothic 'y', close to Briquet 9188, 1470 × 1477) with that of the last two (Fleur-de-lys and 'j b', close to Briquet 7064–5 (1471 × 1490) and to Piccard, *Lilie*, i, 748–9 (1479), while the pair of Bull's Heads on fols. 72–3 are identical to Briquet 14239 (1478 × 1483) and Piccard, *Ochsenkopf*, ix, 192 (1477 × 1479) and (?) ix, 187 (1478 × 1480).

37 For Hand i, see fols. 99v–100r; Hand ii occurs on fol. 93r–v.

38 Ker, *Medieval Manuscripts in British Libraries* (Oxford, 1969–), ii, 908.

39 Scheves was certainly absent from Scotland on 5 October 1468 (SRO, B65/22/50), but reappeared in the Faculty of Arts at St Andrews in March 1470.

40 Ker, *Medieval Manuscripts*, ii, 18. On the basis of references to Brussels and the diocese of Liège, Ker suggests that the MS was written in the southern Nether-lands, but the paper is of a kind commonly found in the Rhineland, consistent with Whitelaw's having acquired it while teaching at Cologne.

41 Cf. I.C. Cunningham, 'Latin Classical Manuscripts in the National Library of Scotland', *Scriptorium* 27 (1973), 64–90, at 75–6.

42 Briquet cites other members of the same group (12481–6) occurring between 1476 and 1482.

43 They are: a pair of Unicorns, one of which is very close to Briquet 10191 (Caen 1491); a pair of Gothic 'p' with crossed descender, difficult to identify; Arms with a

Fleur-de-lys and Dolphin Quarterly, of the type of Briquet 1655 (1477 × 1493); a Cup, very like that occurring in MS Adv. 25.4.10 and close to Briquet 4587 (Darmstadt 1483 × Grammont 1485); and French Royal Arms with Quatrefoil above and 't' below, one of a large family occurring from 1480 onwards and including Briquet 1743–6 and Piccard, *Lilie*, III, 1633–1703.

44 *Cal. Papal Letters*, XIII, 817.

45 Braidfut repeatedly occurs in Whitelaw documents, e.g. Edinburgh City Archives, Misc. Charters A.2 (18 November 1490), *RMS*, II, no. 2154 (1 June 1493), Glasgow University Archives, No. 16380 (6 June 1495).

46 There is a further link between Adv. 18.3.10 and 18.4.8 in the presence, in each of the third and fourth quires of the Paulus Diaconus, of a single sheet of Gothic 'p' paper from the same stock as one of those occurring in fols. 87–9 of 18.4.8. While this is scarcely conclusive, it argues powerfully for the production of parts at least of these MSS within the same milieu.

47 See James, *Aberdeen Catalogue*, pp. 59–60.

48 But cf. L.J. Macfarlane, *William Elphinstone and the Kingdom of Scotland 1431–1514* (Aberdeen, 1985), pp. 36–7.

49 Macfarlane, 'William Elphinstone's Library'.

50 None of the four stocks of paper used, French Royal Arms of the type of Briquet 1790 and Piccard, *Lilie* III, 1426–36, Arms with a Key and Sword in Saltire and a Crosier in Pale of the type of Briquet 1160, Gothic 'y' with Trefoil Tail very close to Briquet 9198, and a 'lorgnette'-type BHX like Briquet 14194, occurs much later than 1475; the latest stock is probably the first, which is found between 1473 and 1477.

51 Cf. *The Kingis Quair*, ed. John Norton-Smith (Oxford, 1971), pp. xxxiii–xxxiv.

52 Geneva, Bibliothèque Universitaire et Publique, Archives Briquet. Briquet's reference is to 'Arch. Cologne', Letters 34 and 35 (Cologne 1485).

53 See above, p. 15.

54 For another example of a manuscript illuminated in Scotland, see G. Hay and D. McRoberts, 'Rossdhu Church and its Book of Hours', *Innes Review*, 16 (1965), 3–17. But most liturgical books seem to have been produced abroad.

55 *RMS*, II, no. 1804.

56 Cf. *Scottish Peerage*, VII, 571.

57 Cf. Ker, *Medieval Manuscripts*, II, 1–2. Attempts have been made (e.g. by Norton-Smith, *The Kingis Quair*, pp. xxxii–xxxiii) to identify this hand with that of James Gray, a suggestion refuted by Ker.

11 · THE MANUSCRIPTS OF THE MAJOR ENGLISH POETIC TEXTS

A.S.G. EDWARDS AND DEREK PEARSALL

In the history of publishing and book production in England in the hundred years before the invention of printing, the early years of the fifteenth century play a decisively significant part, introducing what seems to be a new phase in the development of routine commercial production of English vernacular literature.[1] Even the most cursory comparison of the seventy-five years periods on either side of 1400 reveals a spectacular transformation: in broad figures, one is speaking of the difference between a rate of production that leaves extant about thirty manuscripts and one that leaves extant about six hundred.[2] Prior to 1400, with some notable exceptions, production of books of vernacular writing is largely devoted to religious material, and was probably dominated by the religious establishment. Although firm evidence is lacking, it seems reasonable to assume that the texts of the *South English Legendary*, the *Northern Homily Cycle* and the *Prick of Conscience* made before 1400 were mostly done in religious houses.[3] The Vernon manuscript (Bodleian MS English Poetry a.1) may be taken as the climax of this phase of production (c. 1390).[4] The much smaller number of manuscripts containing secular or 'literary' works are, by contrast, oddities and exceptions: British Library, MS Harley 2253, with its famous lyrics, was done by a Ludlow scrivener for an aristocratic Shropshire family in the 1330s;[5] Cambridge, King's College, MS 13, the unique copy of the alliterative romance *William of Palerne*, said by its author to have been commissioned by Humphrey de Bohun, earl of Essex, was produced in or near Gloucester;[6] BL MS Cotton Nero A.x, containing unique copies of *Sir Gawain and the Green Knight* and the other three poems attributed to its author, was written down by a scribe who came from the borders of Cheshire and Staffordshire[7] and was probably fully intelligible only to people from the same quarter. The Auchinleck Manuscript (NLS, MS Advocates' 19.3.1) seems at first to suggest more organised forms of secular book production: a London manuscript, large, carefully decorated and produced, it contains the texts of fifteen romances, many unique, as well as other works of a largely didactic cast, and is clearly the product of collaborative activity.[8] However, the suggestion that it is the routine production of a 'London bookshop' of c. 1330–40 lacks supporting evidence, and it is perhaps best to regard it as 'an exceptional effort' rather than as 'the sole survivor of routine commercial production'.[9]

It seems from such evidence that the production of books of vernacular poetry was primarily a provincial phenomenon, peripheral to the mainstream of metropolitan literary culture in the fourteenth century.[10] The reasons for the change in the patterns of book-production, which during the years 1390–1410 sees a shift from isolated and scattered production in different parts of the country, and the beginnings of routine commercial production in London, in standardised dialect, spelling, script and format, can be sought in a variety of quarters.[11] The re-expansion of English into the areas of court-based literary culture previously occupied by French and Anglo-Norman is one. If it were asked what the more courtly class of customer for texts of the *Confessio Amantis* in 1425 were buying a century before, the answer is that they were probably buying and reading texts of *Tristan* and *Lancelot* made in France.[12] Another reason for the expansion, centralisation and commercialisation of book production is the general increase in literacy which led to a new demand for English texts and a consequent increase in the copying of manuscripts,[13] though this is a broad development and not one that can be specifically associated with a particular decade or two nor with 'literary' works. The decisive reason might be that there was now, with the mature English writing of Chaucer and Gower (and, in a somewhat different context, Langland), vernacular poetry, in quantity, of a kind capable of attracting paying customers, customers themselves representative of a wider range of the literate public than the traditional court-based literary culture.

There is evidence that efforts were being made to meet this demand by the last decades of the fourteenth century, even though there is nothing among the English writers to compare with the systematic arrangement for 'publication' made by Boccaccio and Petrarch and by some French writers.[14] The manuscripts of Gower's *Confessio* seem to have circulated through some form of organised dissemination of copies, apparently under the author's supervision.[15] Although we lack fourteenth-century copies of any of Chaucer's works, it seems that some must have circulated. Thus Usk's borrowings in his *Testament of Love* (1388) from Chaucer's *Troilus, House of Fame* and *Boece* (as well as possibly from *Piers Plowman*) cannot be convincingly explained as simply memorial retention.[16] And by c. 1400 *Troilus* had circulated sufficiently widely to find its way into devotional compilations.[17] Chaucer's *Envoy to Bukton*, with its exhortation 'The Wyf of Bathe I pray that ye rede / Of this matere . . . ' seems to suggest at least a form of coterie circulation of some parts of the *Canterbury Tales*. And the evidence of Lydgate's *Temple of Glas* (with extensive echoes from the *House of Fame*) and the Prologue to Edward, duke of York's *Master of Game* (which quotes from the Prologue to the *Legend of Good Women*) indicates that copies of these works were circulating in the early years of the fifteenth century, earlier than surviving copies.

Similarly, manuscripts of *Piers Plowman* were clearly circulating before the end of the fourteenth century. Apart from the copy in the Vernon manuscript, several manuscripts of the B Text derive from an early workshop.[18] And some copies were in private hands by the 1390s.[19]

What is unclear is the extent to which this circulation constitutes a form of commercial activity. We still lack any clear sense of the relationship between the processes of composition and those of dissemination. Chaucer, for example, tells us a little about his practice of composition in his poem *Adam Scriveyn*. From this we learn that Chaucer had the *Boece* and *Troilus* professionally copied, and that the copy (with exemplar) was then returned to him so that he could correct it, and that this procedure might be repeated with the same scribe.[20] His complaints about the scribe's carelessness are probably as well justified as they are traditional (Cicero and Petrarch make similar complaints), though one might consider the genuine difficulties a scribe may have had with the author's original, written cramped to save space and spattered with corrections and insertions. Chaucer's purpose was presumably to have a fair copy available for his own use, or for circulation among his friends, or possibly for delivery to a patron (for 'publication') in the classic manner. His corrected version of the scribal copy would supersede his own autograph; it would contain the 'mistakes' (i.e. scribal and original errors unnoticed by the author in revision) that constitute the reason for distinguishing, in textual criticism, between scribal archetype and author's text. It may be that the scribe, at the time of copying, would take a further copy from the author's exemplar, which he then used, with or without the author's permission, and whether or not in part-payment, as the basis for further copies, to be offered for sale. Such a procedure would explain some of the kinds of textual variation that are found among surviving manuscripts of *Troilus* and the *Canterbury Tales*, especially the 'leaking' of subsequently corrected early draft ('first shots') into the manuscript tradition.[21] It would also, elsewhere, explain the complaints of piracy made by Boccaccio, Petrarch, Deguileville and Pecock.[22]

Other writers seem to have acted in a directly entrepreneurial way, in forms that were probably adaptations of traditional modes of production. Thus we can see the continuing tradition of book production by the Austin friars embodied in John Capgrave's activity as scribe and publisher.[23] Thomas Hoccleve also seems to have acted as his own publisher, circulating his own copies of his works and possibly also enlisting his colleagues at the Privy Seal to assist in making copies, just as he helped out with the copying of a Gower manuscript.[24] But the existence of commercial scriptoria, operating directly in collaboration with the author to market his works, is not yet a proven hypothesis. There is some evidence that this happened with Lydgate, both in his relations with the still enigmatic figure of John Shirley, who may have been a London 'publisher',[25] and with a scriptorium, possibly at Bury St

Edmunds, in his later years.[26] And it remains a possibility that some of his
more popular works, which lack a named patron, may have been produced
directly for the book-trade. Certainly a number of early copies of the *Troy
Book*, *Siege of Thebes* and *Life of Our Lady* appear to be high quality metropolitan products.[27]

But this is to raise questions about the organisation of the book-trade that
need some clarification. The development of methods of book-production
that would cater for the demands of this new book-buying public was still in
its early stages. The picture that we tend to have of 'commercial production'
is of a large workshop with many scribes working away at their desks, as in a
monastic scriptorium (or a modern typing-pool), the supervisor moving
among them, tweaking a careless ear here and there. As Bennett puts it: 'The
"corrector" was a familiar figure in any big scriptorium.'[28] It is probably best
to get rid of this picture completely as far as early fifteenth-century England is
concerned, and to modify it considerably even for the later decades. It is true
that there is an impressive consistency in text and layout in large numbers of
copies of the *Confessio Amantis*, especially the large-format 46-line double
column manuscripts, where for long stretches text, layout and minor details
of *ordinatio* such as paragraph-marking will agree minutely.[29] The contrast
with *Canterbury Tales* manuscripts, where there is much variation, and even
more with *Piers Plowman*, suggests that the availability of carefully prepared
and corrected exemplars was the important factor here, not the mode of
production.[30] The impression of consistency that is further obtained, from the
widespread use by professional scribes copying these texts of a notably clear
and regular variety of anglicana, is likewise striking, but it is a general scribal
tendency and not an aspect of workshop production.[31] The more likely
picture of the trade in the new vernacular books in the early part of the
century is of bespoke and *ad hoc* production, in which a bookseller or stationer
(who might himself be a scribe)[32] would take an order from a customer and
then himself supervise the production process. In the simplest cases, this
would be a matter of supplying paper, commissioning a scribe, and having
the written pages bound. More elaborate and expensive manuscripts would
require the attention of rubricators, illustrators and illuminators, who might
work in loose collaboration with groups of scribes in the book production
district of London, and in adjacent premises, but who would be separately
hired by the stationer.[33]

Such a picture fits what we know of the production of manuscripts of
Chaucer, Gower and Langland in the first half of the century. The vast
majority are on vellum (paper only begins to be used to any extent in the third
quarter of the century), though it must be remembered that vellum could
vary greatly in quality and expensiveness. The great majority are written
throughout by a single scribe, and most of the texts (especially the longer
ones: that is, the complete manuscripts of the *Tales*, *Confessio*, *Troy-Book* and

Fall) occur alone, or with only minor addenda.[34] Within the group, however, there are some important distinctions. The manuscripts of the *Confessio* are often significantly grander, as a whole, than those of any other of these works: larger in format, on finer vellum, with more elaborate layout and decoration, often carried out according to a systematic model. The stimulus and precedent given by fine exemplars may be as important as the demand of a particular class of customer.[35] Among the manuscripts of the *Tales* there are few that are so ostentatiously grand, but there are many that are expensively produced, including some that are representative of the best English manuscripts of the period[36] as well as a great many more modestly produced ones; on the whole, it is the variety of kinds of book-making that is remarkable in manuscripts of the *Tales*, reflecting in part at least the geographically diversified centres of production for copies. *Troilus*, unexpectedly, is usually put out in fairly modest form, and in six cases the decoration or flourishing is left incomplete.[37] It may be that the poem was reckoned to be too short to warrant great expense – a defect that Lydgate was quick to remedy in his *Troy-Book*. *Piers Plowman*, more predictably, is published in generally still smaller format, often with other religious or didactic pieces, and rarely with more than minimal decoration;[38] more manuscripts come from outside London.[39]

Manly and Rickert are prepared to identify certain manuscripts of the *Tales* as the product of 'shops', on the evidence of what looks like supervisory annotation or correction,[40] but it has to be said that the existence of these 'workshop supervisors', acting as proof-readers, is shadowy. Corrections are generally done by the scribe himself, and those done by other hands, including the annotation 'ex' (*examinatur*) in the Cardigan MS and Egerton 2726, may as well be the work of the stationer. Certainly there is no reason to doubt the very high quality of editorial attention given to the preparation of exemplars for copying, whether by the scribe, his employer or literary 'advisers' brought in from outside, in manuscripts like the Ellesmere MS of the *Tales* or Huntington MS 137 of *Piers Plowman*, where no question of a 'shop' has usually arisen. Manly and Rickert also allocate certain groups of manuscripts to the same 'shop' on the evidence of resemblances in decoration: here they may be on firmer ground, at least in identifying groups of artists, if not scribes, working together.[41] Kane and Donaldson associate three manuscripts of the B-text of *Piers Plowman*[42] with the same workshop on the basis of identity of layout and text: here the possibility of circulation of exemplars among stationers and scribes has to be allowed as an alternative explanation.

Some scepticism concerning the existence of organised production workshops in the early decades of the fifteenth century is necessary, given the findings of the important article by Doyle and Parkes, already alluded to, dealing with a manuscript of the *Confessio Amantis* written by five scribes,

Cambridge, Trinity College, MS R.3.2. Doyle and Parkes produce here, in their analysis of the work of 'Scribe D', who was responsible for six further copies of the *Confessio* and a portion of a seventh, two copies of the *Tales*, the 'Ilchester' MS of *Piers Plowman*, and part of a manuscript of Trevisa's translation of the *De Proprietatibus Rerum*,[43] striking evidence of full-time professional activity in the production of copies of poetic texts in the early years of the fifteenth century, over a period of some thirty years. However, they also demonstrate that the activity of collaboration in the Trinity MS was so unsystematic and disorganised that it can hardly have taken place on the same premises under supervision. They thus blow a large hole in the 'work-shop' theory, and conclude:

> We can find no evidence for centralized, highly organized scriptoria in the metropolis and its environs at this time other than the various departments of the central administration of government, and no evidence that these scriptoria played any part – as organizations – in the copying of literary works. We believe that it is wrong to assume the existence of scriptoria or workshops without evidence of persistent collaboration. (p. 199)

What we have, in fact, is a group of professional scribes, used to working independently, perhaps in adjacent premises, brought together to execute a specific commission. It may be presumed that this was an expedient to which stationers occasionally resorted when a customer was in a hurry or when an exemplar, for whatever reason, was available only for a limited period. The exemplar was split up and circulated in quires for simultaneous copying. The practice was well known in monastic scriptoria,[44] and has some resemblance to the university *pecia* system, but it was evidently a ticklish operation in the hand-to-mouth world of the London book-trade, which is perhaps why it was so rare.[45]

The absence of evidence for dictation for simultaneous multiple copying, whether external evidence or internal (the latter in the form of identical texts varying persistently in minor auditory errors),[46] is a further minor argument against the existence of 'mass-production' workshops in fifteenth-century London. There is good evidence for the practice on the continent in this period,[47] and in legal and notarial circles,[48] and it seems, on the face of it, an obvious means of making several copies quickly. The one reference to the practice as current is therefore, in the absence of other evidence, rather odd. It comes from Lydgate, who speaks of himself, in a love-poem, knowing as little of love as the 'skryvener' knows of what he writes,

> But as his maister beside doth endyte.[49]

One can only assume that Lydgate is using a conventional, non-contemporary allusion as a topos of ignorance.

It would be interesting to know more about the professional scribes who turned their hands to the production of these new books in the vernacular.

One thing that can be generally affirmed is that they were or had been used to copying Latin: their confidence with conventional Latin abbreviation is often remarkable, especially by contrast with their frequent hesitancy with English.[50] This may be simply a reminder of the relatively much greater quantity of Latin, of all kinds, being copied. Hoccleve, a Clerk of the Privy Seal, has a small part in Trinity R.3.2 as 'Scribe E', which may suggest that other government servants in similar positions may have supplemented their income by freelance work.

The means by which exemplars were acquired and made available for copying is another important question on which we are largely ignorant. It must be assumed that there was a certain amount of borrowing within the close circle of stationers and scriveners around Paternoster Row. It is altogether likely too that customers often supplied their own exemplars. Bennett says at one point: 'It can be shown that a number of manuscripts of the *Canterbury Tales* were made for relatives of a fortunate possessor of a copy.'[51] This is a shrewd guess of the way in which a fashion in literature, and the copying to cater for it, get established, but one wishes that Bennett had displayed his evidence. Scribes themselves, given the nature of their part in the production of manuscript books, are most unlikely to have retained exemplars, or to have noticed the differences between different exemplars in copying the same text. Two copies of the *Troy-Book*, Bodleian MS Digby 230 and MS Rawlinson C.446, were written by the same scribe: the former is characterised by the poem's editor as 'carelessly written [and] evidently copied from a comparatively late MS', while the latter is seen as an 'excellent MS'.[52] Similarly, the six complete copies of the *Confessio* made by Scribe D show no clear pattern of textual relationship, nor his two copies of the *Canterbury Tales* (though the latter are associated in decoration). Scribes seem to have been variously bewildered by and unaware of lacunae in their exemplars. Certain manuscripts of Lydgate's *Fall of Princes* clearly derive from an exemplar that lacked a gathering or some portion of one.[53] In the two manuscripts of Trevisa's *Polychronicon* copied by the 'delta scribe', a contemporary and emulator of Scribe D, one (BL Add. MS 24194) has a curious unremarked lacuna, with several chapters of text omitted, but no break in continuity of the writing,[54] while the other (Cambridge, St John's College, MS 204) has the complete text. One manuscript of the *Confessio* (Keswick Hall) has a lacuna in the text which corresponds exactly to the portion of text supplied in another manuscript (BL Harley 7184) from an exemplar of different textual affiliation.[55] Scribes of the *Canterbury Tales* seem often to have been receiving their exemplars piecemeal, and to have been uncertain how much or what was to come: the Hengwrt manuscript is the most famous example, but there are others.[56] The scribe of Cambridge, St John's College, MS L.1 seems not to have received his next portion of exemplar before he had to part with quire 7, upon which he wrote, rather plangently, 'her faileth thing þat is not yt made', thus giving rise to elaborate theories of authorial addition: there is no lacuna in the text, though.[57]

Doyle and Parkes suggest that by the middle of the century some stationers may have felt it worthwhile to retain exemplars in stock for some poetic texts.[58] There is some evidence to sustain this view, though it does not seem to have been a general practice. They point to two manuscripts of the *Confessio* in the same hand and with the same layout and decoration, BL MS Harley 7184 and Oxford, Magdalen College, MS 13, and to two similarly related manuscripts of the *Troy-Book*, BL MS Royal 18.D.vi and Oxford, Exeter College, MS 129. One might add to these a group of *Fall of Princes* manuscripts, BL MSS Harley 1245 and Add. 39659, and Longleat 254, which are textually related and may also be in the same hand.[59] But the most systematic evidence for the retention of exemplars seems to be in the work of the 'Lydgate scribe', in his four copies of Lydgate's *St Edmund* and (particularly) his two textually idiosyncratic copies of the *Fall of Princes*.[60] This may be an atypical case, in which local interest and possibly some direct connection with Lydgate himself may have given some particular impetus to the retention of master copies.

There is rather greater evidence of uniformity or standardisation in matters of layout of texts. It seems that particular poetic texts tended to settle into distinctive layouts relatively early in their histories. The most obvious example is probably the double column forty-six line copies of Gower's *Confessio*, which can be found in a number of copies by the D Scribe and elsewhere.[61] Copies of *Troilus and Criseyde* often employ a small book format, that at times becomes virtually a holster book, characterised by five spaced stanzas in a single column.[62] Most manuscripts of *Piers Plowman* use a single column format, some regularly employing forty lines to a column.[63] At least eighteen of the copies of Hoccleve's *Regement of Princes* adopt a single column format, with four stanzas to a page.[64] Length of text, as well as length of line (the *Confessio* line is shorter than the others) is obviously important in determining the nature of the layout, but one must assume that a factor in such standardisation was economic – the possibility of making realistic calculations of materials and time required for the execution of a manuscript, and also to allow the option of decoration.

Such exigencies of economy and space doubtless affected the *ordinatio* of poetic texts. Doyle and Parkes note the occurrence of a 'more "developed" stage' in manuscripts of the *Confessio Amantis* written by the D Scribe, where the Latin summaries are incorporated into the text column from the margins.[65] A similar development seems to have taken place in the manuscripts of Lydgate's *Siege of Thebes*. One notes, for instance, the text in BL MS Arundel 119, one of the earliest and best manuscripts. Here we see that an attempt has been made to impose upon the text an *ordinatio* remarkably like that of the Ellesmere manuscript. Lydgate's poem was written as a continuation of the

Canterbury Tales and appears with them in a number of manuscripts.[66] But elsewhere, the manuscripts of the poem reflect a tendency to compression of non-poetic matter, rubrics, summaries and the like, into the column. And this is possibly part of a general tendency in the copying of poetic texts.

One aspect of the *ordinatio* of these manuscripts is illustration. There is little evidence of systematic illustration. It can be found in a number of manuscripts by the Lydgate scribe of the *Life of St Edmund* which, as Dr Scott has shown, clearly derive from the same decorative models.[67] Lydgate's *Troy-Book* also developed a standardised sequence of miniatures, as did a number of manuscripts of the *Confessio Amantis*.[68] But such systematic illustration does not seem to extend beyond these poetic texts. Only seven of the *Canterbury Tales* manuscripts contain any miniatures at all, and only one, Ellesmere, any systematic programme of illustration.[69] Only four of the *Fall of Princes* contain any, and only two contain extensive illustration.[70] Only one manuscript of the *Siege of Thebes* has a sequence of miniatures, and that added in the early sixteenth century.[71] And other vernacular, secular poetic works generally contain only scattered illustration, where it occurs at all.[72]

Clearly, once again, the economic factor must have come into play, as well as other factors such as the availability of appropriate illustrative models. The nature and degree of elaborateness of any manuscript must ultimately be determined by the assurance that there was someone capable of paying for it. This fact raises in its turn the problem of the extent to which stationers or scribes, in addition to working to commission, may have engaged in the production of manuscripts on a speculative basis.

It is difficult to establish convincing criteria for identifying speculatively produced manuscripts. For example, Dr Scott in her excellent discussion of the various manuscripts of the 'Lydgate scribe' distinguishes Bodleian MS Laud misc. 673 from other manuscripts written by him on the basis of its lack of decoration, a characteristic which leads her to term it 'speculative'.[73] But it is doubtful whether the degree of decoration provides in itself a criterion for speculative production. It would seem at least as, if not more, likely that a scribe would execute specific commissions covering a decorative hierarchy of manuscripts from the very elaborate to the utilitarian, like Laud misc. 673.

The question of a scribe's willingness to undertake a wide range of types of copy, from the elaborately decorated to the plain, is evidenced in a different way by the activities of the 'hooked g scribe', so designated after the most distinctive feature of his hand.[74] He appears to have been a London-based scribe, active during the third quarter of the fifteenth century, who wrote at least four copies of Lydgate's *Fall*, three of the *Canterbury Tales*, two of the *Confessio*, and one of the Trevisa translation of the *Polychronicon*.[75] Like the Lydgate scribe, his productions range from the very elaborate, like the Devonshire manuscript of the *Canterbury Tales*, through those slightly less elaborate, like one of his copies of the *Confessio Amantis*, BL MS Harley 7184, which is nonetheless decorated in a systematic and relatively elaborate fashion, to BL Add. MS 21410 of Lydgate's *Fall of Princes*. This last contains no decoration at all. Space is left, however, for decorated initials at the beginning of each stanza, and guide letters are inserted; blanks have also been left for the insertion of larger initials at the beginning of running titles and of formal divisions. Such an absence of decoration could suggest that this manuscript was prepared 'for stock', to be completed according to a purchaser's specifications. But the massive speculative outlay in time and materials involved makes this an implausible assumption. It seems more probable that the *Fall of Princes* represents the scribe's characteristic way of preparing his copy, and that the purchaser elected for some reason not to have the decoration added.

There are other indications that owners were content to possess manuscripts that were unfinished in decorative terms. For example, BL MS Royal 18.D.II of Lydgate's *Troy-Book* and *Siege of Thebes* was executed in the mid-1450s or early 1460s for William Herbert, later earl of Pembroke. It was illuminated, but only a few of the spaces for miniatures were filled in – the initial presentation miniature and those marking the beginnings of the books of the *Troy-Book*. The remainder of the miniatures, some twenty-five (including all those for the *Siege of Thebes*) were not inserted until the first quarter of the sixteenth century. The reasons for this hiatus are unclear. But the growing stature of Herbert would seem to preclude the possibility that it was due to his poverty. And even in its unfinished state he seems to have felt it an appropriate gift for his son-in-law, Henry Percy, fourth earl of Northumberland. Possibly the failure to complete it was due to a lack of illustrative models, an hypothesis that gains some support from the lack of any other illustrative cycle for this poem.

Such perspectives may suggest some modification to the received view of the most famous unfinished poetic manuscript of the fifteenth century, Cambridge, Corpus Christi College, MS 61, Chaucer's *Troilus and Criseyde*, as that view is expressed by Parkes:

> The book seems to have been planned on a scale of magnificence which, although it must have reflected the taste of whoever commissioned the book in the first instance, was too ambitious in terms of what any other fifteenth-century patron in England was prepared to accept, either financially or in terms of literary and artistic taste.[76]

The fact that there are a large number of blank spaces in the manuscript, apparently left for miniatures, could imply that the person who commissioned it failed to produce the monies necessary for its completion, or that he died (Henry V has been suggested). There are many continental examples of such things happening, as well as examples of quality of decoration varying through a manuscript with the promptness of instalment payments.[77] No doubt there were many slips between cup and lip in the complex process of commissioning and producing books. But it is equally true that there are a remarkably large number of manuscripts in fifteenth-century England where the decoration has been left incomplete, and where it must be presumed that the customer was entirely satisfied to have it so, perhaps because he knew he could always have it completed (there are many examples) when it suited him. The blanks in Corpus 61 may therefore be due as much to artistic as to economic reasons – the inability to initiate or obtain an illustrative programme suitable to the content of the poem.

More complex questions raised by the problem of interpreting incompleteness are posed by a manuscript of Lydgate's *Troy-Book*, New York, PML MS 876.[78] This manuscript has one virtually complete miniature, at the end of Book I (fol. 6). There are blank spaces at the end of Book II (fols. 34r and 34v) presumably for miniatures, and smaller spaces throughout for decorated initials. But at other points (fols. 59 and 87, the ends of Books III and IV) large spaces have been filled in with pen and ink sketches.[79] These sketches indicate the failure to complete a manifest design and thus provide a more plausible basis for an assumption of some apparent breakdown in the relationship between producer and commissioner. Although this is not irrefutable evidence for such an assumption, the Morgan manuscript comes closest, among poetic manuscripts of the kind we have discussing, to indicating a failure due to economic cause, whether it was the prospective customer or the speculation that failed, since there are no other apparent obstacles to completion.

The last criterion adduced by Doyle and Parkes as a determinant of the existence of speculative book production is also hard to apply. They draw attention to a copy of the *Confessio*, Oxford, Corpus Christi College, MS 67, written by Scribe D, and to the blank in its first illuminated initial, where other manuscripts have an armorial shield. They also point to some manuscripts of Lydgate's *Troy-Book*, Bodleian MSS Rawlinson C.446 and Digby 230 (written by the same scribe), which have similar blanks;[80] one may add to these the Longleat and BL Add. MS 39659 copies of Lydgate's *Fall of Princes* (which may be in the same hand and appear textually related). Once again, the implications of the evidence are not altogether clear. For example, Rawlinson C.446 contains a number of contemporary miniatures by an artist associated with Scheere. It is not easy to reconcile such elaborate decoration with speculative manuscript production. The Corpus Gower also has miniatures. Possibly the shields were left blank in such cases either because the purchaser gave no instruction as to the way they should be filled in, or because he was not armigerous, as might be the case for the purchaser of even a relatively elaborate manuscript.

The two Lydgate manuscripts are less easy to assess. As we have noted earlier, there is some evidence to suggest that they derive from a common exemplar, possibly retained by a scribe or stationer to produce speculative copies. But since, by the third quarter of the fifteenth century when they were written, ownership of manuscripts, often very elaborate manuscripts, was clearly established among the merchant class,[81] it is not easy to place too much weight on the evidence of the blank shields.

A final question needs to be raised concerning non-metropolitan production. Most of the discussion here has, inevitably, centred on the development of book production in London, but it is important to ask whether there existed comparable centres of production outside London. Though we lack firm data, or even clear criteria for the determination of what is and is not provincial production, it can be said that there were during the fifteenth century a number of provincial centres producing copies of vernacular works, often on some scale. Dr Doyle, for instance, has pointed to the possibility of one such centre existing at Bristol in the 1420s and 1430s, and he mentions also York and Norwich.[82] GUL MS Hunterian U.1.1, of the *Canterbury Tales*, was certainly copied in Norwich.[83] The massive compilation of the works of Chaucer, CUL MS Gg.4.27, was equally certainly produced in East Anglia: it has many signs of provincialism, and may be an example of 'local production in which scribes worked in country houses or rectories to execute specific commissions'.[84] Many other manuscripts can be similarly localised in independent non-commercial centres. BL MS Harley 7333, a large compilation including works of Chaucer, Gower, Lydgate and Hoccleve, was made in Leicester for the Austin Canons there.[85] It seems that the provincial religious houses continued to provide centres for the ownership, and quite probably the copying of vernacular poetry. We know a great deal about the activities of John Capgrave as scribe and 'publisher' at the Austin friary in King's Lynn, Norfolk,[86] and it seems possible that several copies of Lydgate's *Fall of Princes* were produced in monasteries,[87] as well as some copies of *Piers Plowman*.[88] In connection with the broader issue, the majority of manuscripts of the A and C versions seem to be of provincial origin.[89]

A particularly interesting case of apparently provincial manuscript production is that of the 'Lydgate scribe'. His hand has been identified, as already noted, in at least nine manuscripts, all of which contain copies of works by Lydgate: two of his *Fall of Princes*, one of his *Troy-Book*, three of the *Secreta Secretorum* and four of the *Life of St Edmund*.[90] This distinctive focus on a single author, and particularly on his poem about St Edmund, the patron saint of Bury, suggests a Bury St Edmunds provenance for his work. There is support for this suggestion from the early provenances of some of these manuscripts, which suggest early owners in Suffolk. This scribe does not appear to have worked in collaboration. But, like the D Scribe, he does seem to have worked with a number of different artists to provide the often very elaborate programmes of miniatures in some his copies. His career may have been a lengthy one, possibly extending from the 1440s to the 1460s.

It is, however, difficult to pursue the question of provincial manuscript production very far in our present state of knowledge, since we often must perforce equate suggested provenance with presumed place of production.

The reasons for localising the Lydgate scribe at Bury remain circumstantial rather than truly evidential. But the evidence is, at least, rather more compelling than that used to localise other manuscripts at Bury. Until we have much more extensive dialect evidence available, and until more work has been done on such problems as regional variations in forms of abbreviations and in types of decoration, it is difficult to employ evidence other than provenance to localise production.

APPENDIX. *Some statistics for manuscripts containing major literary texts*

Text (no. of lines)	No. of MSS	Material			No. of scribes				Other contents		with mins.	Decoration		Average page area (cm²)
		Vellum	Paper	V+P	1	2	3	4+	add	coll		elabor-ate	minor or none	
Troilus (8,239)[1]	16	10	4	2	12	1	1	2	2	5	1	5	10	500
Canterbury Tales (c. 24,400)[1]	57	40	13	4	42	8	4	3	12	2	7	23	27	700
Regiment of Princes (5,463)	42	26	11	5	36	4	—	2	5	16	3	8	31	550
Confessio Amantis (33,444)	40	33	5	2	32	4	1	3	4[2]	1	16	10	14	940
Piers Plowman A (inc. A+C) (2,558)	18	10	7	1	17	1	—	—	1	8	1	1	16	530[3]
Piers Plowman B (7,302)	14	12	2	—	10	2	2	—	—	5	—	—	14	490
Piers Plowman C (7,338)	18	18	—	—	17	1	—	—	5	1	1	3	14	470
Troy-Book (30,117)	19	13	5	1	16	3	—	—	5	—	6	7	6	1030
Fall of Princes (36,365)	30	23	2	5	28	2	—	—	5	—	4	17	9	1180

The statistics are derived from the following sources:

Chaucer: Troilus and Criseyde, ed. B.A. Windeatt (London, 1984), pp. 68–75; Manly and Rickert, I, 29–544; M.C. Seymour, 'The Manuscripts of Hoccleve's *Regiment of Princes*', TEBS, 4 (7) (1974), 255–97; *The English Works of John Gower*, ed. G.C. Macaulay (Oxford, 1900), I, pp. cxxxviii–clxv; *Piers Plowman: The A Version*, ed. G. Kane (London, 1960), pp. 1–18; *Piers Plowman: The B Version*, ed. G. Kane and E.T. Donaldson (London, 1975), pp. 1–15; *Piers Plowman: The C Version*. Information derived from observation, library catalogues and other sources; *Lydgate's Troy-Book*, ed. H. Bergen, Part IV, EETS, ES, 126 (1935), pp. 1–54; *Lydgate's Fall of Princes*, ed. H. Bergen, Part IV, EETS, ES, 124 (1927), pp. 11–105.

Account is taken only of complete manuscripts or of fragments that may be presumed to have been once complete; excerpts are ignored. In the numbering of scribes, no account is taken of hands that make additions to the manuscript of an informal or significantly later kind. Such additions are likewise ignored in the indication of 'Other contents', which records either comparatively minor but integral and contemporary additions (add) or the existence of the whole manuscript as some kind of collection (coll). In the indication of the hierarchy of decoration, 'elaborate' is taken to require as a minimum the presence of illuminated (as distinct from rubricated or pen-flourished) initials and at least one decorated border.

Notes:

[1] Approximate figure, allowing 'real' verse equivalents for prose lines.

[2] With the addition of a further eight MSS in which short Latin and French pieces by Gower are included as addenda to the *Confessio Amantis*.

[3] If one ignored the presence of an A-text in the Vernon MS, this figure would go down to 450 cm^2.

NOTES

1 Literature is taken here to mean formal writing that gives or purports to give pleasure (with or without edification) and not merely pleasure-through-edification. It is not exclusively secular in spirit: *Piers Plowman*, however embarrassed its author may be at it, is 'literature', where the *Prick of Conscience* is not. The distinction was well understood in the Middle Ages. The works taken to epitomise vernacular 'literature' in this chapter are the long poems of Chaucer (*Canterbury Tales, Troilus and Criseyde*), Gower (*Confessio Amantis*), Langland (*Piers Plowman*), Hoccleve (*Regiment of Princes*) and Lydgate (*Troy-Book, Fall of Princes*).

2 Cf. Carleton Brown, who reports the conclusion of G.G. Coulton, who 'basing his opinion on his own general observations, once observed to me that for every one page of English written in the xiii, there were two or three in the xiv, and ten in the xv century. The *Index* confirms this statement' (*IMEV*, xi–xii), Coulton, of course, is talking about *all* manuscripts containing English.

3 None of these texts has been systematically studied in terms of their original production. The only clue we have therefore is provenance, where the evidence is incomplete and not necessarily to be equated with place of production. (It should be noted, however, that the Austin friars at least seem to have been regularly engaged in some form of commercial manuscript production in England during the fourteenth century; see L.F. Sandler, 'A Note on the Illumination of the Bohun Manuscripts', *Speculum*, 60 (1985), 372 and n. 25, and J.B. Friedman, 'Richard de Thorpe's Astronomical Kalendar and the Luxury Book Trade at York', *Studies in the Age of Chaucer*, 7 (1985), 147, 149.) Thus, thirty-nine manuscripts of the Main Version of the *Prick of Conscience* (out of a total of ninety-seven) have been dated from the fourteenth century (see Lewis and McIntosh). Of these, five appear to have been owned by religious houses: Arundel Castle, Sussex (possibly owned by a Franciscan Convent at York), BL Add. MS 22283 (the Simeon MS, possibly from a Cistercian house), BL Add. MS 24203 (from Fountains Abbey), Digby 99 (from a Cluniac Priory at Thetford) and Bodleian MS Eng.poet.a.1 (the Vernon MS – on which see n. 4 below). This last MS also includes the *South English Legendary*, the only copy of the thirteen complete and nine fragmentary MSS dating from before 1400 with any indications of early provenance. See further, M. Görlach, *The Textual Tradition of the South English Legendary*, Leeds Texts and Monographs, NS, 6 (University of Leeds, 1974), pp. 70–130. From among the *Northern Homily Cycle* MSS only the former Marquis of Bute MS has a clear religious provenance, having been owned by the abbey of St James and St Leonard of Franciscan nuns at Denny, Cambs.

4 On this MS, see A.I. Doyle, 'Vernon and Simeon Manuscripts'.

5 See C. Revard, 'Richard Hurd and MS Harley 2253', *NQ*, 204 (1979), 199–202.

6 See A.I. Doyle, 'The Manuscripts', p. 90.

7 See A. McIntosh, 'A New Approach to Middle English Dialectology', *English Studies*, 44 (1963), 5.

8 See the Introduction to the facsimile of the manuscript by D. Pearsall and I. Cunningham (London, 1974), and subsequently, T.A. Shonk, 'A Study of the Auchinleck Manuscript: Bookmen and Bookmaking in the Early Fourteenth

Century', *Speculum*, 60 (1985), 71–91, who analyses the scribal organisation in some detail, but does not reach any conclusions about the representativeness of Auchinleck in terms of fourteenth-century English book production.

9 The terms are Dr Doyle's; see his 'English Books In and Out of Court', p. 164. The original suggestion about the 'London bookshop' was made by L.H. Loomis, 'The Auchinleck Manuscript and a Possible London Bookshop, 1330–1340', *PMLA*, 57 (1942), 595–627.

10 Cf. A.I. Doyle, 'The extant manuscripts, by their language, suggest that the share of the capital in the making of copies of books in English may have been subsidiary to that of the provinces until the end of the century . . . ' ('English Books In and Out of Court', p. 166).

11 The most striking evidence appears in the early work of Scribes B and D of Cambridge, Trinity College, MS R.3.2, as identified by Doyle and Parkes. For further remarks on developments during this period see Doyle, 'English Books In and Out of Court', p. 169; and Parkes, '*Ordinatio* and *Compilatio*', pp. 133–4.

12 See further E. Salter, *Fourteenth Century Poetry* (Oxford, 1983), pp. 34–5.

13 See H.S. Bennett, *Books and Readers, 1475–1557* (Cambridge, 1952), p. 7.

14 See R.K. Root, 'Publication Before Printing', *PMLA*, 28 (1913), 417–32.

15 Macaulay's evidence would suggest that he kept close control over the revisions of the *Confessio Amantis*, especially as they are represented in Bodleian MS Fairfax 3, even to the extent of being in direct contact with the workshop where the copies were produced, and able to intervene in the copying process. See *Complete Works of John Gower*, ed. G.C. Macaulay (Oxford, 1901), ii, pp. clxvii, cxx. Though some of this evidence has been questioned by Peter Nicholson ('Gower's Revisions in the *Confessio Amantis*', *Chaucer Review*, 19 [1984], 123–42), the similar kind of evidence for his supervision of manuscripts of his Latin poem, the *Vox Clamantis*, looks secure. See *Complete Works*, ed. Macaulay (1902), iii, pp. lxiii–iv.

16 For details of Usk's borrowings, see Skeat's notes in his *Chaucerian and Other Pieces* (Oxford, 1897), pp. 451–84 *passim*.

17 See L.W. Patterson, 'Ambiguity and Interpretation: A Fifteenth Century Reading of *Troilus and Criseyde*', *Speculum*, 54 (1979), 297–330.

18 See G. Kane and E.T. Donaldson, *Piers Plowman: The B Version* (London, 1975), esp. pp. 1–2, 42, citing MSS BL Add. 10574, Cotton Caligula A.xi and Bodley 814. Note also the evidence of an early date for MS Bodley 851 put forward in *William Langland: Piers Plowman, the Z Version*, ed. A.G. Rigg and Charlotte Brewer, Toronto Pontifical Institute of Medieval Studies, Studies and Texts 59, pp. 2–6.

19 Walter de Bruges, a canon of York Minster, bequeathed a copy in 1396; see J.A. Burrow, 'The Audience of *Piers Plowman*', *Anglia*, 75 (1957), 373–84. A copy was owned by a London priest, William Palmere, in 1400; see R. Wood, 'A Fourteenth-Century London Owner of *Piers Plowman*', *Medium Aevum*, 53 (1984), 83–90.

20 Cf. the account of R.K. Root, *The Textual Tradition of Chaucer's Troilus* (London, 1916), pp. 256–7.

21 See B. Windeatt, 'The Text of the Troilus', in *Essays on Troilus and Criseyde*, ed. M. Salu (Cambridge, 1979), pp. 1–22; Manly and Rickert, i, p. 102, ii, pp. 421–3, 480, iv, p. 517.

22 See, e.g. R.K. Root, 'Publication Before Printing', *PMLA*, 28 (1913), 417–32, and H.S. Bennett, *Books and Readers*, pp. 2–3.

23 See P.J. Lucas, 'John Capgrave, O.S.A. (1393–1464), Scribe and Publisher', *TCBS*, 5 (1969), 1–35.

24 See further H.C. Schulz, 'Thomas Hoccleve, Scribe', *Speculum*, 12 (1937), 71–81; M.C. Seymour, 'The Manuscripts of Hoccleve's *Regiment of Princes*', *TEBS*, 4 (7) (1974), 255–8 and Doyle and Parkes, esp. pp. 198–9. Manly and Rickert (1, p. 168) link Fitzwilliam McClean 181 of the *Canterbury Tales* to Hoccleve and the Privy Seal.

25 See A.I. Doyle, 'New Light on John Shirley', *Medium Aevum*, 30 (1961), 93–101, and the references cited there for Shirley's career. The notion that Shirley was a 'publisher' has been challenged by R.F. Green in *Poets and Princepleasers* (Toronto, 1980), esp. p. 132; there is an attempted counterstatement by Edwards in Pearsall, *Manuscripts and Readers*, pp. 20–1; see also Ch. 12 below, pp. 284–91.

26 On this scriptorium see Scott, 'Lydgate's Lives'.

27 For example, BL Cotton Augustus A.iv and Bodleian Digby 230 and Rawlinson c. 446 of the *Troy-Book*, BL Arundel 119 of the *Siege of Thebes* and BL Add. 19252 of the *Life of Our Lady*.

28 See Bennett, 'Production and Dissemination', p. 174.

29 Viz. Bodley 693, Bodley 902, Fairfax 3, Cambridge, Trinity College, MS R.3.2, Keswick MS (now Geneva, Bodmer), Stafford MS (Huntington EL26.A.17), *olim* Phillipps 8192 (Princeton UL, Taylor Coll.), *olim* Wollaton Hall (Nottingham UL Mi LM 8), CUL Mm.2.21, GUL Hunterian S.i.7.

30 See further, J.J. Smith, 'Linguistic Features of Some Fifteenth-Century Middle English Manuscripts', in Pearsall, *Manuscripts and Readers*, pp. 104–12.

31 See M.B. Parkes, *English Cursive Book Hands*, rev. edn (London, 1979), p. xxiii.

32 The problems of lack of clear terminological distinctions between branches of the book-trade that we consider distinct are discussed in G. Pollard, 'The Company of Stationers', pp. 2–4.

33 See Ch. 4 above.

34 For details of the evidence for this claim see the Appendix, p. 270.

35 The nature of such demand in its relation to class is, in any case, difficult to be specific about, as Doyle points out ('English Books In and Out of Court', pp. 163–4).

36 E.g. the Ellesmere and Hengwrt manuscripts, BL Harley 7334, Lansdowne 851, and Oxford, Corpus Christi College, MS 198; see further Manly and Rickert, 1, pp. 565–9.

37 Viz. MSS Cambridge, Corpus Christi College, 61, CUL Gg.4.27, BL Harley 4912, Bodleian Rawl. poet. 163, Digby 181, Selden supra 56.

38 E.g. MSS Lincoln's Inn 150, CUL Dd.1.17, Bodleian Douce 320, NLW 733B, PML 818, Huntington HM 128. For examples of more elaborately decorated manuscripts of *Piers* cf. Cambridge, Trinity College, MS B.15.17, Bodleian Douce 104 and Oxford, Corpus Christi College, 201.

39 Cf. M.L. Samuels, 'Some Applications of Middle English Dialectology', *English Studies*, 44 (1963), 81–94.

40 Cf. e.g. their discussions of BL Egerton 2726, Harley 1758, Royal 18.C.ii, Sloane 1686 and *olim* Phillipps 8137 (now Rosenbach 1084/1), all of which are described as 'showing signs of supervision' or as 'supervised shop' manuscripts. It is possible

in at least some of these cases that the assertion may be correct insofar as it identifies a corrector as someone other than the scribe; e.g. BL Harley 1758, which contains a number of marginal and supralinear insertions probably not by the scribe.

41 See Manly and Rickert, I, pp. 570–1 (on the links between Petworth and Lichfield 2) and 577–9 (where Cambridge, Trinity College, R.3.3., Bodleian Rawlinson poet. 223 and the Devonshire MS, now Takamiya 8, are described as 'closely related in style and doubtless the product of the same shop'); see also Scott, 'A Mid-Fifteenth-Century English Illuminating Shop', who links a group of manuscripts (including a copy of Lydgate's *Life of Our Lady* and a fragment of his *Troy-Book*) to a shop on the basis of decoration.

42 See above, p. 259 and n. 17.

43 The other manuscripts of the *Confessio* are: Bodley 294 and 902 (part), Oxford, Corpus Christi College, 67, Oxford, Christ Church, 148, Columbia University, Plimpton 265, BL Egerton 1991 and the Robert H. Taylor manuscript in Princeton University Library (we are indebted for this last to Mr J.J. Griffiths); the *Canterbury Tales* manuscripts are BL Harley 7334 and Oxford, Corpus Christi College, MS 198; the 'Ilchester' manuscript of *Piers Plowman* is London University v.88; and the Trevisa manuscript is BL Add. 27944. See further, Doyle and Parkes, pp. 194–7.

44 See G.H. Putnam, *Books and Their Makers During the Middle Ages* (1896–97, repr. New York, 1962), pp. 65–7.

45 It seems to have occurred among some manuscripts of the *Confessio*: e.g. CUL Mm.2.21, where the copying by five different hands is non-sequential, and the Keswick Hall manuscript; see *Complete Works*, ed. Macaulay, pp. cxl–cxli and clxi–clxii. Macaulay links both these copies to early commercially produced exemplars: Mm.2.21 is 'closely connected to' Bodley 902 (see above, n. 43), and Keswick is described as 'corresponding column for column with [Fairfax 3] throughout'. There is no clear evidence of non-consecutive copying of exemplars among the manuscripts of the *Canterbury Tales* and virtually none among the manuscripts of Lydgate's major works: the only example is perhaps the Robert H. Taylor manuscript of the *Fall of Princes* (*olim* Wollaton Hall) where three different hands appear, one of which writes a single leaf and another gatherings ii–iii, xxvi–xxviii (see further *Fall of Princes*, ed. Bergen, IV, pp. 81–4).

46 A kind of error readily distinguishable from the auditory errors made by scribes memorising a line as they transfer it from their exemplar; on the distinction see H.J. Chaytor, *From Script to Print* (1945, repr. London, 1966), pp. 19–21.

47 See A. Hudson, 'Middle English', in *Editing Medieval Texts*, ed. A.G. Rigg (New York, 1977), p. 46.

48 See Chaytor, *From Script to Print*, p. 18, n. 2.

49 'The Complaint of the Black Knight', line 196 in *The Minor Poems of John Lydgate*, part II, ed. H.N. MacCracken, EETS, os, 192 (1934).

50 M.B. Parkes makes this point with reference to Cambridge, Corpus Christi College, 61 in *Troilus and Criseyde. A Facsimile* (Cambridge, 1978), p. 7, though there is abundant evidence of it in the manuscripts of Gower and Langland where there is, of course, extensive Latin.

51 Bennett, 'Production and Dissemination', p. 176.

52 *Troy-Book*, ed. Bergen, IV, pp. 26 and 13.

53 E.g. Princeton University, Garrett 139 (*olim* Phillipps 8117), and the University of Victoria manuscript, both of which have a gap in their text between III, 4872 and IV, 729, a total of 144 rhyme royal stanzas; see further *Manuscripta*, 22 (1978), 176–8.

54 The break comes in the middle of a column on fol. 227va without any break in the text; a portion of the text between Book VII, ch. viii and ch. ix is omitted, probably amounting to a single leaf.

55 See *Complete Works*, ed. Macaulay, II, pp. cxxxvi, clxiii.

56 The most striking instance is perhaps BL Harley 7333, where the text of the *Canterbury Tales* simply stops in mid-sentence at the bottom of a recto leaf (fol. 118), leaving the verso blank, and nothing else following. An equally interesting case, which clearly demonstrates the piecemeal circulation of exemplars, is Glasgow Hunterian U.1.1, a manuscript copied to within Fragment D directly from CUL Mm.2.5 by Geoffrey Spurling of Norwich and then from a different manuscript 'akin to Rawlinson poet. 224' (Manly and Rickert, I, 185). An example of a manuscript deriving from a defective exemplar, lacking a gathering, is Bodley 414; see Manly and Rickert, I, 60.

57 See *St John's College, Cambridge, Manuscript L.1: A Facsimile*, Introduction by R. Beadle and J.J. Griffiths (Norman, Okla., 1983), pp. xxvii–xxix.

58 Doyle and Parkes, p. 201.

59 See *Fall of Princes*, ed. Bergen, IV, esp. pp. 17–19.

60 See Scott, 'Lydgate's Lives', and A.S.G. Edwards, 'The McGill Fragment of Lydgate's *Fall of Princes*', *Scriptorium*, 28 (1974), 75–7.

61 See n.29 above.

62 Cf. e.g. BL Harley 3943 (in holster book form), BL Add. 12044, BL Harley 4912, PML M 817 (the Campsall manuscript), Cambridge, St John's College, L.1, and Bodleian Selden B.24.

63 In addition to the three *Piers Plowman* manuscripts apparently from the same shop (see above, n. 18) cf. also BL Add. 34779 and 35287.

64 E.g. MSS BL Arundel 38, Harley 116, Harley 4866, Royal 17.D.VI, Royal 17.D.XVIII, Royal 17.D.XIX; Bodleian Arch. Selden supra 53, Dugdale 45, Ashmole 40, Douce 158; CUL Gg.6.17, Hh.4.11, Cambridge, Magdalene College, Pepys 2101, Cambridge, St John's College, 223, Cambridge, Trinity College, R.3.22, Edinburgh University 202, Huntington EL 26.A.13, Huntington HM 135. A similar format for a text of comparable length and verse form appears with Lydgate's *Life of Our Lady* in a number of manuscripts: e.g. MSS BL Harley 3952, 4260, 5272, Cotton App. VIII, Sloane 1785; Cambridge, Trinity College, R.3.22, Bodleian 120, Hatton 73, Rawlinson poet. 140, GUL Hunterian 232 and University of Chicago 566.

65 Doyle and Parkes, pp. 194–5.

66 Viz. MSS BL Add. 5140, Egerton 2864, Oxford, Christ Church, 152, Longleat 257 and University of Texas 143 (*olim* Cardigan).

67 Scott, 'Lydgate's Lives', pp. 357–60.

68 See Lawton, 'Illustration of Late Medieval Secular Texts', and J.J. Griffiths, '*Confessio Amantis*: The Poem and Its Pictures', in *Gower's Confessio Amantis: Responses and Reassessments*, ed. A. Minnis (Cambridge, 1983), pp. 163–78.

69 Viz. the Ellesmere MS, CUL, Gg.4.27, Rylands English 63 + Rosenbach Foun-

dation 1084/2, Lansdowne 851, Bodley 686, Rawlinson poet. 223 and *olim* Devonshire; for discussion, see Manly and Rickert, I, 583–604.

70　Viz. MSS BL Harley 1766, McGill 143 (a fragment), Huntington HM 268 + BL Sloane 2452 and Rosenbach Foundation 439/16. Only the Harley and the Huntington manuscripts have extensive illustration.

71　BL MS Royal 18.D.II; for description see Warner and Gilson, II, 310.

72　See further, Lawton, 'Illustration of Late Medieval Secular Texts'.

73　Scott, 'Lydgate's Lives', p. 361; she characterises this manuscript as 'the lower range of the scribe's production . . . possibly made for sale across the board'.

74　The first discussion of this scribe was in Doyle and Parkes, p. 201 and Edwards, 'Lydgate Manuscripts', in Pearsall, *Manuscripts and Readers*, p. 19 and n. 19. In enlarging the list given there we have worked independently of an unpublished list prepared by Professor T. Takamiya; our list was arrived at by personal observation and may well differ in some particulars from Professor Takamiya's. We are grateful to Mr J.J. Griffiths for assistance.

75　The manuscripts of the *Fall* are BL Add. 21410, Lambeth 254, Bodleian Hatton 2 and Columbia University, Plimpton 255 (additional leaves from the last are in Philadelphia Free Library, Lewis 314 and Sotheby's Sale Catalogue, 6 December 1983, lot 20); the three *Canterbury Tales* manuscripts are Bodleian Rawlinson poet. 223, Cambridge, Trinity College, R.3.3. and the *olim* Devonshire manuscript; the *Confessio* manuscripts are BL Harley 7184 and Lyell 31; and the *Polychronicon* is in the Robert H. Taylor collection, Princeton University.

76　Parkes, *Troilus and Criseyde*, p. 13.

77　D.J.A. Ross points to a mid-fourteenth-century group of manuscripts done by the same group of illustrators, where variation in the treatment of the decoration in one of the manuscripts seems directly reponsive to instalment payments; see 'Methods of Book-Production in a XIVth Century French Miscellany (London, BM MS Royal 19.D.I)', *Scriptorium*, 6 (1952), 63–75.

78　The manuscript is bound with a copy of *Generides*, in the same hand, but codicologically distinct from the *Troy-Book*.

79　The same situation obtains in the manuscript of *Generides*; see the description in *Troy-Book*, ed. Bergen, IV, pp. 21–5.

80　Doyle and Parkes, pp. 209–10. For further discussion of the significance of the presence of armorial shields, see Ch. 8 above, pp. 167–9.

81　See Scott, *Mirroure of the Worlde*, p. 9 and n. 2, for a list of such manuscripts.

82　Doyle, 'English Books In and Out of Court', p. 173.

83　See above, n. 56.

84　See *Geoffrey Chaucer: Poetical Works: A Facsimile of Cambridge University Library Gg.4.27*, Intro. by M.B. Parkes and R. Beadle (Cambridge, 1980), p. 63.

85　Manly and Rickert, I, pp. 214–17.

86　See above, n. 23.

87　This may be to place an undue weight on provenance, but cf. e.g. BL Sloane 4031 (owned by the fifteenth century by Battle Abbey), Lambeth 254 (owned by Lanthony Priory).

88　See Parkes and Beadle, pp. 55–6, where this possibility is explored; cf. also Rawlinson poet. 137, a *Piers* manuscript owned by the Franciscan convent at Canterbury.

89 See Samuels, 'Some Applications'.
90 See Scott, 'Lydgate's Lives', pp. 342–3 for the fullest list: the two *Fall* manuscripts are BL Harley 1766 and McGill 143; the *Troy-Book* is Arundel 99; the three *Secreta* manuscripts are BL Sloane 2464, Bodleian Ashmole 46 and Laud misc. 673; the four *St Edmund* copies are BL Harley 4826 and Yates Thompson 47, the Castle Howard manuscript and Bodleian Ashmole 46 once more.

12 · ANTHOLOGIES AND MISCELLANIES: PRODUCTION AND CHOICE OF TEXTS

JULIA BOFFEY AND JOHN J. THOMPSON

FROM THE BEWILDERING VARIETY of manuscripts which might be considered in this chapter, we have selected for our focus those books least likely to feature elsewhere in this volume: anthologies of miscellaneously assorted texts, mainly in English, and mainly in verse, with imaginative and recreational rather than purely factual or spiritual functions. In the first half of the chapter we investigate the 'publication' of such material in carefully, often professionally organised and copied anthologies, looking at the impetus behind their compilation, and at some of the practices involved in their manufacture. Then we move on to consider methods of production involving less formal and less fully documented procedures.

English poetry appearing in anthologies before and during the fourteenth century kept various kinds of company. Large miscellanies like BL MS Harley 2253 included it with other material in a substantial volume where something to suit all tastes and needs might be found.[1] The huge Vernon and Simeon manuscripts (Bodleian Library MS Eng. poet.a.1 and BL Add. MS 22283 respectively) are closely related anthologies of more specifically religious texts, into which items (and groups of items) from many different sources were copied together, in planned sections, to make up large volumes which could have served both individual and corporate needs.[2] Preachers' manuals and 'commonplace books', sometimes produced in idiosyncratically personal ways, gathered up much English religious poetry, often together with Latin and prose texts.[3] It is hardly surprising that the focus here rests almost entirely on religious verse: there existed comparatively little secular poetry in English to be incorporated in anthologies. Apart from their dominance in major romance collections like the Auchinleck Manuscript (NLS MS Advocates' 19.2.1),[4] such English secular poems as were 'published' almost inevitably accompanied religious texts.

The great burgeoning of 'rym in Englyssh' during the late fourteenth and fifteenth centuries, however, encouraged the compilation of various new kinds of anthology. One noticeable innovation was the purely poetical collection.[5] Many manuscripts of this kind maintained a bias towards religious material, whether of a meditative, homiletic, or practical kind (examples include carol collections,[6] and works by individual poets, like the lyrics of

John Audelay, gathered together in Bodleian MS Douce 302)[7] – and some of
these anthologies of religious poetry achieved a semi-permanent form, apparently circulating in multiple copies.[8] Parallels can be drawn in the area of
predominantly secular 'collected works'. Chaucer's poems survive in a collected edition from the 1420s (CUL MS Gg.4.27); Hoccleve's autograph
manuscripts present selections of his own works; Lydgate's poems (especially
the shorter ones) were organised into collections.[9] Some of the procedures
involved in the production of anthologies can be usefully documented in those
collections which gather up examples of the minor poems of all these single
authors, volumes of Chaucerian and neo-Chaucerian poetry which concentrate particularly on works with secular, usually amorous themes.

A growing taste for such anthologies made itself felt in the second half of
the fifteenth century, seemingly generated by a small number of exemplars.
The nature of these volumes is best exemplified by one of the books listed
among the possessions of Sir John Paston, which gathered together *The Legend
of Good Women*, *La Belle Dame sans Merci*, *The Parliament of Fowls*, *The Temple of
Glass*, and some as yet unidentified works.[10] The nucleus of such manuscripts
was generally formed by an assortment of Chaucer's minor poems, around
which were fitted attempts to re-distil the influential 'aureat licour' – Lydgate's *Complaint of the Black Knight*, Clanvowe's *Cuckoo and Nightingale*, Hoccleve's *Letter of Cupid*.[11]

The textual relationships between these volumes suggest that the Chaucerian pieces in particular descended originally from independent groups of
gatherings (booklets), each containing a single longish work, or a group of
lyrics, from which anthologies of poetry could be made up and copied. The
appearance of some identical collocations of poems in different manuscripts
supports this hypothesis, which (apart from the fact of the somewhat surprising delay between the death of Chaucer and the general publication of his
minor poems) seems plausible enough.[12] Sometimes the origins of the texts in
small units of this kind are reflected in the make-up of the later fifteenth-
century manuscripts into which they were copied. Bodleian MS Fairfax 16,
which was produced by one main scribe, is made up of five distinct units,
each of which was foliated by a different hand. While the distinctness of the
units is reinforced by the large numbers of blank leaves which separate them,
it seems most unlikely that their combination should have been the fruit of
piecemeal or random collecting.[13] The completed volume was 'finished' with
care, to include a miniature and a scheme of decoration which incorporated
the prospective owner's coat of arms.[14] He perhaps selected his units from a
bookseller's existing stock of booklets with protective 'covers' of blank leaves,
and then specified the particular finishing details which would adapt the
collection to his own tastes and needs.

MS Tanner 346, related to Fairfax 16 by its contents, and probably
descended from similar exemplars, was also copied in units, this time by three

collaborating scribes.[15] Here, however, although the separate sections are again clearly differentiated, it seems that they were probably copied from the outset for some single, defined purpose, and furthermore that they were copied simultaneously. The processes involved can be tentatively reconstructed. Scribe A began with a stint on *The Legend of Good Women* (up to the end of *Ariadne*); he filled four gatherings, and needed an extra singleton at the end of the fourth to accommodate the final portion of his stint. B, meanwhile, might have been at work on a stint of roughly similar length (forty-two leaves, as opposed to the thirty-three copied by A) which completed *The Legend of Good Women*, and what is now the first unit in the manuscript; he filled five gatherings of eight leaves, and concluded with a bifolium. C could at this time have been working on his own individual section, which now forms the second unit of the manuscript, and includes *The Temple of Glass*, and *The Cuckoo and the Nightingale*. As this stint was a relatively short one, he might well have completed it quickly and have gone on to start another: the first gathering of *The Book of the Duchess*, which in its entirety now forms the third unit in the collection. B took over the rest of this, supplying one more gathering of eight leaves and a bifolium. A worked alone on *The Parliament of Fowls*, completing what is now the fourth and final unit in the manuscript, with one gathering of eight and one of four leaves. The coincidence of stints and gatherings here suggests that the units or booklets were a convenient device for apportioning work, enabling the scribes to use the 'leap-frogging' system of copying which has been observed in a Gower manuscript from the earlier fifteenth century, and necessitates no hypothesis of physical proximity of scribes in a formal scriptorium.[16] The exemplars used were obviously of an easily divisible kind, and may well themselves have been booklets or separate units.

MS Bodley 638, which duplicates some of the contents of MSS Tanner and Fairfax, in partially different order, reinforces the notion that individual texts, or groups of texts, were commonly available as exemplars in discrete sections.[17] Bodley 638, however, unlike its two earlier relatives, is not divisible into separate physical units. Items are regularly copied across breaks between gatherings, and the manuscript seems to have been planned and executed in the sequence in which its contents now exist. The single scribe, who names himself as 'Lyty',[18] could have made up his own copying sequence from a group of smaller exemplars, or he could perhaps have had access to a manuscript in which discrete textual and physical units had already been assembled in such a way that divisions between them were no longer noticeable, or not felt to be worth perpetuating. The same processes may well have influenced the final shape of Longleat MS 258, similar in content and appearance to Bodley 638, and also dating from later in the fifteenth century.[19]

Both Bodley 638 and Longleat 258 are carefully but economically made.

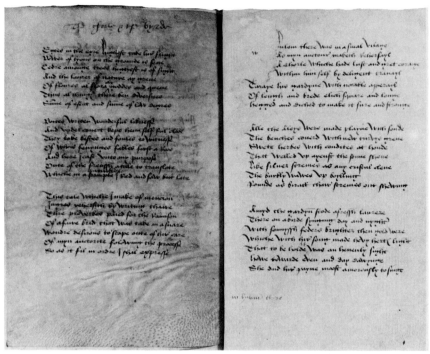

23   Longleat House, Warminster, Wiltshire, MS 258, fols. 137v–138r (Lydgate, *Churl and Bird*, lines 22–63). Fol. 137 forms part of an inner bifolium of parchment, slightly smaller than the paper leaves which makes up the rest of this gathering (average size 220 × 150 mm). Space was left for a decorated initial at the top of fol. 138r. The running title on fol. 137v was added by a later hand which annotated all the contents of the manuscript.

They are small volumes (about eight by six inches), and both are arranged generally in gatherings of sixteen leaves in which the innermost and outer-most bifolia are parchment, protecting an inner 'filling' of paper (see Ill. 23). They may well be amateur productions, copied by individuals for their own use. Neither has a sophisticated programme of ornamentation: Lyty ruled a frame, and supplied (or touched) his initials, headings and colophons in red; the Longleat scribe left spaces for ornamented capitals which were never completed. Tanner 346 and Fairfax 16, in contrast, are copied on parchment, with much more attention to visually pleasing detail. Tanner has a com-prehensive scheme of decoration (borders and capitals, with red and blue lombards), while Fairfax of course has its distinguished miniature, attributed to William Abell or to an artist connected with him.[20] Anthologies of this kind, it seems, were owned by both discerning, wealthy readers, and by those of lesser means. Furthermore, the obvious metropolitan connections of a manuscript like Fairfax 16 are not equally evident in all the volumes under consideration. The compilers of CUL MS Ff.1.6, who had access to at least one exemplar similar to if not the same as those used by the scribes of Tanner 346, seem to have been resident in the north Midlands,[21] and of course it is possible that John Paston's courtly anthologies may have been local rather than metropolitan productions.[22]

The kind of 'publication' enjoyed by texts such as those included in MS Fairfax 16 and its relatives – too small to form complete volumes on their own account, and yet too long to be categorised as mere makeweights – is neatly demonstrated by the different appearances in manuscripts of the English version of Alain Chartier's *La Belle Dame sans Merci*, attributed (in MS Harley 372) to Sir Richard Roos.[23] Both the French and English versions are of a length which would fill one large gathering, or a pamphlet-sized collection of several small ones, and the earliest readers of the work probably handled it in this flimsy form; one of the extant copies of the English translation, in BL MS Sloane 1710, preserves it as a single (now fragmentary) booklet. The layout and apparatus of the English version are remarkably similar in all six of the surviving manuscripts, and the company which the text keeps in the'five of these which qualify as anthologies is also of interest: particular items recur in conjunction with it (*Anelida and Arcite* and *The Letter of Cupid*, most noticeably), and the combinations suggest that *La Belle Dame* might have circulated as one of a series of items, or as part of a small collection, as well as in some independent form.

The textual affiliations of these six copies illustrate the co-existence of different manuscript traditions of single works among the material available to related London scribes. The manuscripts divide into two groups: an A group made up of CUL Ff.1.6, Cambridge, Trinity College, R.3.19, Longleat 258 and Sloane 1710 (the printed editions made by Pynson in *The Book of Fame*, 1526, and by Thynne in *The Workes of Geffray Chaucer*, 1532, are related to these), and a B group consisting of Fairfax 16 and Harley 372. The B group texts have descended from an exemplar in which some leaves were disarranged, and also preserve some textual idiosyncrasies.[24] MSS Harley 372 and Cambridge, Trinity College, R.3.19, however – one a B group and the other an A group text – may well have come from the same milieu, for the main scribe of R.3.19 worked elsewhere with the so-called 'Hammond scribe', a prolific London copyist who was responsible for *The Regiment of Princes* which now forms the second part of MS Harley 372.[25] That two scribes possibly related to the same commercial concern should have had access to such very different versions of the same text can only confirm suspicions that the organisation which supported them was a relatively informal, flexible one. The relationship of the Ff.1.6 text of *La Belle Dame* to the A group manuscripts is also revealing, for it shows that the scribes of this manuscript had access to a wider range of exemplars than those associated with the Fairfax 16/Tanner 346/Bodley 638 group, on which they relied for other texts.

Other features of the compilation and circulation of anthologies can be reconstructed from the practices of individual scribes or editors, such as John Shirley (c. 1366–1456), whose working methods are documented in a comparatively large group of surviving manuscripts.[26] The exact nature of Shirley's role in the history of book production is elusive, and attempts to define his activities have categorised him variously as a salesman, a literary agent, and simply a bibliophile.[27] Identification of the readership he envisaged for his collections has proved similarly problematical. We can at least be certain, however, that Shirley's bookish activities were varied: he was a man of letters himself, a 'litterateur' rather than merely a scribe or a middleman, and he read and translated and composed, as well as organising and copying. Works which he apparently read, and perhaps owned, included *Troilus and Criseyde* (Cambridge, Corpus Christi College, MS 61); a French translation of Vegetius's *De Re Militari* (BL MS Royal 20.B.xv); Chandos Herald's *Vie du Prince Noir* (London University Library MS 1); a volume of French treatises which included Jacques Legrand's *Livre de bonnes moeurs* (CUL MS Ff.1.33), and two anthologies, one containing works by Lydgate and Hoccleve (Huntington Library MS EL 26.A.13), the other collecting up extracts from the works of Richard Rolle and his followers (Cambridge, Gonville and Caius College, MS 669*/646). He perhaps also had access to a collection of the poems of Froissart (Bibliothèque Nationale MS f.fr.831) which was at some stage in the possession of his employer Richard Beauchamp.[28] This is a comprehensive selection, covering works in Latin, French, and English, in prose and in verse, and the different categories of devotional, historical, didactic and imaginative literature. Shirley's tastes, and his access to manuscripts, were wide-ranging.

His own compositions (mainly English prose translations of Latin and French works) indicate a further body of material on which he was able to draw. BL Add. MS 5467 contains three: a 'cronycle of the dethe and false murdure of James Stewarde last kynge of Scotys . . . translated oute of latyne into owre moders englisshe tong bi youre symple subget Johan Shirley in his last age' (fols. 72v, 84v);[29] 'les bones mures, in Englesshe the gode maners' (fol. 97r),[30] and an English prose translation of the *Secretum Secretorum*.[31] His poems, lame and halting as they confessedly are, confine themselves to semi-humorous introductory purposes. Two (*IMEV* 1426, 2598) act as contents tables for the manuscripts which they preface (BL Add. MS 16165, and the 'boke of John Sherley', perhaps Cambridge, Trinity College, MS R.3.20, from which Stow copied the 'Kalundare' of contents, and other material, onto fols. 132–79 of BL MS Add. 29729);[32] the other (*IMEV* 4260), possibly written for Shirley by Lydgate, or adapted from an existing Lydgatian envoy, forms a sort of bookplate, requesting the reader to return the volumes in which it is contained to their scribe-owner.[33]

These activities – reading, translating, composing – suggest a bookish environment, at the very least, and one in which Shirley was able to browse and select. He speaks in the 'Kalundare', albeit humorously, of seeking his materials 'in sondry place'. Although it may be purely an accident of manuscript survival which credits him with the copying of anthologies rather than volumes containing single works, nonetheless his most characteristic activity seems to have been the incorporation of his finds 'from sondry place' into edited collections. Almost all the surviving manuscripts copied in his hand are of this nature. Bodleian MS Ashmole 59, Cambridge, Trinity College, MS R.3.20, and BL Add. MS 16165 are the major anthologies.[34] A few leaves now forming part of BL MS Harley 78 (fols. 80–83) seem to be the tail-end of a similar collection.[35] Sion College MS Arc. L 40.2/E.44 (containing an English prose translation of Deguileville's *Pèlerinage de la vie humaine*) was almost certainly part of an anthology, in its original form.[36] Another lost volume, represented by a stray table of contents which is now bound up with MS Ashmole 59, was apparently also an anthology, including several poems by Lydgate.[37] Even the additions made by Shirley on a few blank leaves of the Huntington Lydgate/Hoccleve manuscript (EL.26.A.13) form a tiny anthology of their own.[38]

A variety of clues about Shirley's methods of tracing and acquiring material has survived. The 'Kalundare' and the metrical index offer hints, but no reliable evidence; their sense seems to have been determined all too often by constraints of rhyme and metre. In the manuscripts, though, are signs that he sometimes copied from written exemplars: marginal notes such as 'Shirley kouþe fynde no more of þis copye' suggest as much.[39] The rubrics and introductions to some items in his collections make great play of personal details, as if Shirley was directly claiming acquaintance with the authors of the works he copied, and it is of course possible that personal connections of some kind put various of the items in his way, in the form of manuscript exemplars, or as rough hand-written copies, or else (just conceivably) by oral transmission.[40]

The unreliable nature of some of the texts, and the carelessness of much of Shirley's copying, suggests that some of his output, at least, was written down from memory;[41] MS Ashmole 59, with its unusually poor texts, its laboured script, and the internal evidence which determines the date of copying as during Shirley's eighties, is a particular candidate. The Shirleian additions to Huntington MS EL.26.A.13 seem to be fragments which would be lodged in the mind rather than copied out from an exemplar – Shirley was familiar with most of these works, and used them elsewhere[42] – while the duplicated groupings of other short texts in some of his anthologies could well be the products of some kind of associative memorising.[43] In general, there is little evidence of attempts to arrange or order the manuscript contents in any coherent way, and the description of the main anthology section of MS Ashmole 59 as '[the] boke cleped þe Abstracte Brevyayre compyled of divers balades roundels virilayes tragedyes envoyes compleyntes moralites storyes

. . . ' (fol. 13r) would apply equally well to all of Shirley's collections, where distinctions between the works of different authors, between religious and secular material, between different literary forms, are generally unobserved.

The physical construction of Shirley's manuscripts, and the layout of their contents, are less eccentrically inconsistent than his texts. Most of the extant autograph copies are made on paper, although Shirley seems to have favoured the use of parchment for strengthening purposes at the beginnings and ends of his books.[44] The three major anthologies are similar in size – around ten by eight inches. Quiring is fairly consistent within individual manuscripts, but overall does not follow a characteristic pattern. BL Add. MS 16165 is made up predominantly of twelves, but occasionally tens and fourteens are used; an unusual arrangement of one regular twelve plus a singleton is adopted to accommodate the end of the prose *Gospel of Nicodemus*, but otherwise the 'odd' gatherings of ten and fourteen do not seem to serve any particular purpose, or correlate noticeably with contents. The Trinity manuscript is quired regularly throughout in eights, as is the Sion College volume; here, as with Add. MS 16165, items are generally copied across gatherings, and there is no evidence that Shirley organised his work in sections or booklets.[45] Further proof that he concentrated his copying activities on complete 'volumes' comes from his provision of running titles, designed – like the rhymed 'Kalundares', and the table of contents in MS Ashmole 59 – as 'reader-aids' of some kind; although Shirley apparently took no great pains to arrange his material, he at least provided some indication of what each volume would contain. The layout and ornamentation which he supplied are practised, but not in any way refined. Texts are usually laid out in single columns (apart from some of the very short notes and filler items), within a framework ruling. Shirley seems to have supplied his own rubrication and ornamentation, emphasising major initials with crude penwork flourishes, and sometimes providing the ascenders in the top line of text, and the descenders in the bottom line, with flourishes which extend out into the margins.[46]

The unsophisticated appearance of these volumes sits oddly with the reputation Shirley has gained as manager of a 'workshop' of busy London scribes.[47] That he had easy access to a wide range of manuscripts is proved both by his copying activities, and his ownership of the different volumes described above. His acquaintance with other members of the London book-trade is also amply documented,[48] and the fact that so many of his collections seem to have come into the hands of later manuscript-compilers (and probably survived in a relatively complete body until Stow's time) prompts speculation that his activities were more systematic than those of an antiquarian amateur.[49] If he ran a bookshop (or shops), though, or if he played some part in a more fluid and informal kind of book-production, it seems admittedly strange that the surviving volumes copied by him should be such unpolished artefacts – one wonders, for instance, why Shirley did not call upon a rubricator of his acquaintance, or in his employ, to 'finish off' his own copies, rather than supply crude ornamentation apparently on his own. The most plausible explanation, allowing simultaneously both for a professional rôle and for these amateurish productions, is that Shirley produced his autograph copies for limited circulation, either among close friends or among clients who would use them to make their personal choice of contents for better-produced volumes of their own. This would mean that the books were lent and consulted as 'stock copies', rather than owned by any of Shirley's potential audience, and would, coincidentally, explain the relative lack of ownership inscriptions and other marks of readership in them.[50]

Whether or not the surviving autograph anthologies served as direct exemplars for other collections, it is evident that manuscripts associated with Shirley were available to some other scribes, whose copies display their Shirleian connections in the characteristic rubrics and orthography which they preserve, or (more tenuously, in view of Shirley's own notorious textual unreliability) in their textual variants.[51] The provenance of one, BL MS Harley 7333 – from the Abbey of St Mary le Pratis, a house of Augustinian canons at Leicester – serves as an important reminder that Shirley's work enjoyed some kind of provincial circulation, but the associations of most of these manuscripts are with London. Moreover, Stow's knowledge of Shirley's collections testifies to their continuing availability in the metropolis.[52]

Among these different examples of material derived from Shirley's collections are two instances of the copying of one particularly prolific scribe who must have worked in London between the 1460s and 1480s. His name may have been 'Richard' or 'Richardown', but in the absence of conclusive evidence it seems safer to call him simply by Brusendorff's name of the 'Hammond scribe'.[53] His surviving work covers different kinds of material. He was involved in copying *The Canterbury Tales* and *The Regiment of Princes* at least twice each, and, in the case of the first of these, had access to different texts as exemplars. He also copied Fortescue's *Governance*, Lydgate's and Burgh's *Secrees*, the English prose *Merlin*, and at least part of *Piers the Ploughman's Creed*. He worked as sole scribe on two Shirley-derived Lydgate/Chaucer anthologies, on a collection of devotional and ecclesiastically informative material, and on a volume including medical treatises, and he contributed to an anthology of mainly religious and historical texts.[54]

Most of these manuscripts are undistinguished productions, copied onto paper, and unenlivened by anything but the most basic ornamentation.[55] To the extent that such characterisations are helpful, there is little about their appearance to distinguish them from obviously amateur compilations, and it is merely the range, habits, and associations of the scribe which brand them as commercial enterprises.[56] On occasions he worked with other copyists: with at least one more on MS Royal 17.D.xv, and with two others on

Cambridge, Trinity College, R.3.21, where the different scribes collaborated
in producing a series of booklets, individually foliated, which were eventually
bound together.[57] Elsewhere in his surviving work this scribe organised copy
in booklets for what must have been reasons of convenience,[58] but in R.3.21
the booklet format seems to have been deliberately adopted to produce a
number of reasonably small, independent – and perhaps independently
saleable – pamphlets. Their contents are, for the most part (other than *The
Life of Our Lady* and *The Court of Sapience*), items which would have been too
short to constitute whole, book-length volumes: religious and historical lyrics,
short prayers and devotional pieces, lives of saints. Some attempt has been
made to group them according to subject-matter: booklet v, for example, is
composed mainly of Marian lyrics, booklet VII mainly of complaints.

A puzzling feature of this collection is its duplicated material, particularly in booklets v and IX, in which Lydgate's *Ave Regina Celorum*, *Regina
Celi Letare*, *Ave Jesse Virgula* and the *Legend of Dan Joos* are copied in exactly
the same order, and with virtually the same layout.[59] A purchaser who
specified in advance the contents he required would hardly want duplication of this kind. The likeliest solution is that the booklets were produced
speculatively, and that a purchaser, in making his selection from existing
copies, would have had to tolerate a certain amount of duplication. Sir John
Paston obviously found himself with two copies of *La Belle Dame sans Merci*
and *The Parliament of Fowls* in this way.[60] In fact, some of the material in
MS R.3.21 seems to have been specially adapted, *after* the initial copying
stages, to suit the requirements of its purchaser. At the foot of the *Prayer for
Henry VI* (*IMEV* 2218) on fol. 245v, two extra stanzas have been added by
the scribe (a slightly fainter ink suggests that they were copied by him at a
different time from the main body of the poem), adapting it as a prayer for
'Edwardus 4', whose name is included in a medallion-like design; the
additions are rounded off with the colophon 'Explicit q*uod* Roger*us*
Thorney'. The decoration in various of these manuscript units was presumably arranged by or for Thorney, as if to upgrade the otherwise plain
booklets he was buying.

The hand of the main scribe of Cambridge, Trinity College, R.3.21, who
collaborated here with the Hammond scribe and with one other, can be
traced in another manuscript of London provenance, now Cambridge,
Trinity College, R.3.19 (Ill. 24).[61] This is closely related to R.3.21 in terms of
construction and execution, being largely copied by the one hand, and
similarly composed of individual booklets which have been separately
foliated by the same hand as that which foliated most of MS R.3.21. Its
contents are almost entirely – and most unusually – secular: perhaps its
component parts were designed to complement the religious bias of the
booklets making up MS R.3.21. Like R.3.21, it is copied on paper; some
decoration was planned, but never executed, and only guide-letters remain to

24   Cambridge, Trinity College, MS R.3.19 (599), fols. 161v–162r (the end of *O merciful and o merciable*, *IMEV* 2510; *The Judgement of Paris*, *IMEV* 3197; Lydgate's *Testament*, lines 241–275). This scribe also worked on MS R.3.21. Fol. 161 (modern foliation) constitutes the last leaf of the second of three gatherings of eight leaves (average size 265 × 200 mm) which make up what was originally the first booklet or section of the manuscript. Fol. 162 begins the third and final gathering of this booklet, and has been numbered '16' by the contemporary hand which supplied individual foliation to each booklet (and also foliated MS R.3.21): it is, of course, the seventeenth leaf of the booklet, but both the fourteenth and fifteenth leaves were mistakenly foliated as '14'. The plate shows the variable page layout used in this section, which contains many short poems, and the space left for a decorated initial letter to begin Lydgate's *Testament*. The later hand which attributes *The Judgement of Paris* to Chaucer appears elsewhere in the manuscript.

indicate the projected capitals. These booklets, unlike Thorney's in R.3.21, were never up-graded, and there have been no insertions or adaptations to suit the tastes of a purchaser. The outer leaves of some of the booklets are grubby and worn, as if the different parts did in fact remain in an unbound state for some time.[62] No precise indications of provenance remain in the manuscript, but a similar date and milieu to that of MS R.3.21 may be presumed.

These two Trinity volumes represent comparatively polished versions of the kind of composite anthology which dominated the field of English poetic manuscripts during the later fifteenth century. Production and circulation of material in booklets seems to have been a reality, here, with the booklets existing sometimes as recognisably separate components of a manuscript, and sometimes merely reflected in the make-up of collections which have been copied in a single unbroken sequence. While in many cases the booklets would be merely convenient portions of copy, divided up either into manageable stints, or to enable different scribes to work simultaneously, in some manuscripts, where material was grouped in sections according to source or to subject, their role in the anthologising process must have been a more positive one.

That few single booklets of this kind have survived is hardly surprising; their shelf-life must have been comparatively short. References in inventories and wills to small, unbound 'paper books', however, suggest that such units were available independently, and that – unlike Thorney's, or John Stanley's booklets in MS Fairfax 16, which seem to have been selected as a body, from one source – they were sometimes acquired singly, at different times, and from different places.[63] Lambeth Palace MS 306, from the later fifteenth century, is an amalgam of separate units – sometimes small anthologies in their own right – which came from different sources and yet were early on bound together to form a 'library' of sorts.[64] Five of the total ten booklets (I, III–V, VIII) must have come from the same source: they were copied by the same scribe (although kept in independent units by means of independent systems of leaf signatures), and they form a central core, an 'Everyman's Library' of practical, informative, devotional and entertaining material; they date from the reign of Edward IV. Booklets VI and IX, in different hands, but on the evidence of their leaf signatures perhaps originally related to each other, extend the range of the collection, supplying courtly and religious lyrics, carols, and a copy of *The Wright's Chaste Wife*. Together with these seven have been bound Caxton's printed edition of *The Life of Saint Winifred*, a seemingly independent booklet which contains poems by Lydgate, and some blank gatherings (possibly deliberately placed at the end of the historical material in booklet I) where John Stow was able to add copious notes.

Connections of provoking but often indefinable kinds between London-produced anthologies of this composite nature are inevitable. The hawking and hunting material in booklet VII of Lambeth MS 306, for example, reappears in various forms in numerous late fifteenth-century manuscripts, many of London provenance, but it is hard to trace direct textual or codicological relationship between any of them.[65] Some of the more unusual contents of Trinity College MS R.3.19 are also included in Bodleian MS Rawlinson c.86: *Piers of Fulham* (with its obvious London relevance) appears in both, as do different but related English translations of the story of *Guiscardo and Ghismonda* from the *Decameron*.[66] The concluding booklet of Rawlinson c.86, with its historically orientated contents (*The Expedition of Henry V*, *Verses on the Kings of England*, and the 'Tytle of France') has many further suggestive connections. Its 'Tytle of France' was also copied by John Colyns into BL MS Harley 2252, and the *Expedition of Henry V* reappears with other historical material in BL MS Harley 565, another volume of London provenance. The material was presumably in wide circulation and easily available to both professional and amateur scribes. We reach here a middle ground in which distinctions between 'systematic' and 'non-systematic', professional and non-professional book-production are impossible to observe. Rawlinson c.86 seems a kind of peculiar hybrid, the product of both professional and amateur copying;[67] Lambeth 306, in its incorporation of a printed section, introduces one further process. In this context, book production involves the amalgamation of the fruit of several originally independent and differently executed ventures.

An even greater sense of the multiplicity of possible ways of producing and using a miscellaneous book in the later Middle Ages can be gained by moving away now from those anthologies that are linked, however tenuously, by shared metropolitan origins and by networks of related texts or copyists to consider other more amorphous manuscript groupings. Although such scattered volumes frequently show telltale signs of their provincial origins, it is difficult to know whether such books and the items in them can comment usefully on specific patterns of regional book production in the period.[68]

In the face of these difficulties it is tempting to argue that all such collections are best considered *sui generis* and defy any easy classification in a history of book production. Nevertheless some general comments do seem worth making before a more detailed analysis of individual cases. For example, these manuscripts have provided a considerable number of items with a final – sometimes a unique – resting-place after a period of circulation elsewhere. Consequently, although literary texts might form only a small part of these collections, the books themselves play an important rôle for the literary historian seeking to consolidate an imperfect sense of the status or reputation of certain types of Middle English literature.[69] Moreover, despite the uncertain textual history of many pieces, and the notoriously protean nature of medieval literary genres, the fortunate survival of batches of material in a number of otherwise disparate collections does provide a useful preliminary indication of the appetites for certain types of reading material shared by many different late medieval book producers and their readers.[70] The voracious demands of these readers seem to have helped secure the contemporary reputation of John Lydgate, for example, whose didactic verse can be found in a multiplicity of manuscript settings in the miscellanies of the period.[71] It also ensured a continuing interest in older types of instructional writings which took on variously revitalised forms as they were set into new contexts, revised, dismantled and anthologised as they passed into the hands of new generations of compilers.[72]

The changing patterns of late medieval literary taste reflected by these developments remain unclear. It is fair to say, for example, that devotional miscellanies containing mystical writings were increasing in number and were being made available to some devout layfolk during the period.[73] At the same time too Middle English romance narratives seem to have remained the staple diet of another group of earnest-minded lay readers from the middle strata of medieval society whose interests were not so exclusively dominated by matters concerning the religious life. But the general requirements of this latter group for material that gives a relatively straightforward and un-ambiguous form of spiritual or moral instruction, as well as providing entertaining leisure-time reading, hardly amounts to a clearly defined literary preference for one type of writing over another.[74] Nevertheless, closer exam-ination of some of the miscellaneous collections being produced for this readership highlights the inadequacies of our knowledge about the multifa-rious nature of fifteenth-century reading habits and tastes, and suggests too the increasing number of uses to which a miscellaneous book and its contents might be put by an expanding reading audience who were requiring the written word for a complex of informational, devotional, and leisure-time purposes.

The term 'commonplace book' is frequently invoked to describe many such multi-purpose miscellanies.[75] Commonplace books, it is argued, are rather haphazard, amateur productions which have been compiled over a period according to the whims of their owners. In these miscellanies the book compiler's selection of material could be influenced by local, practical, domestic, or even political considerations, and the result is an intriguing and sometimes bizarre mélange where the modern reader gains some indication of the interests and habits of mind of an individual book producer. The term is broad enough to embrace most privately produced miscellanies and some institutional products, but frequently quoted examples which have been used to define this type of book include the mainly literary collection of Latin and English items in Cambridge, Trinity College, MS O.9.38 (a Glastonbury miscellany); the collection of mainly historical and political writings in Latin and English in Dublin, Trinity College, MS 516; and the rather more heterogeneous collections in Cambridge, Trinity College, MS O.2.53, Bod-leian MS Tanner 407, Dublin, Trinity College, MS 432, and Yale University Library MS 365 (the Brome manuscript).[76] Interestingly, however, many of these books that suggest themselves most naturally as private collections belong to the post-printing period, and even these are sometimes hybrid productions.[77] It is also important to be aware of the variety of different types of scribal interests, apparent intentions, activities, and even changes of plan which lurk behind some, but not all, of the so-called 'commonplace books', since these weaken any attempt to maintain a clear distinction between them and other types of miscellaneous collection. Thus, Trinity, MS O.2.53, which can be associated with the Ramston family in Essex, originally seems to have been formed from a series of independent physical units, but the previously independent existence of these units hardly contributed in any meaningful way to the eventual organisation of the miscellany.[78] On the other hand, a greater degree of selectivity and organisation does seem to underlie the collection assembled by a Glastonbury monk in Trinity MS O.9.38, despite the fact that this particular volume started life rather unpromisingly as an almost blank account book.[79]

The range of different types of reading interests that might be satisfied by a single miscellany is well illustrated by Bodleian MS Tanner 407, compiled in the last quarter of the fifteenth century by Robert Reynes of Acle in Norfolk.[80] Reynes played a leading rôle in the local affairs of his area and part of his collection represents his attempt to keep an official record of the activities of a local gild of St Anne. His chief literary interests would seem to have been in the drama since his collection includes the only extant copies of a speech assigned to a character Delight, an epilogue to another play, and fragments from a pageant on the Nine Worthies.[81] Nevertheless, the Reynes dramatic pieces are fragments, not complete texts, and can hardly be given the status of official records. This distinguishes the Reynes collection from the great drama anthologies of the period, where attempts were being made to stabilise a body of material which by its very nature was always liable to remain unfixed and open to change.[82] Instead, the survival of the Reynes dramatic scraps in such a modest setting might indicate that this particular scribe was also actively involved in the staging of local parish plays and simply used part of his paper stock to record his own acting parts. The status of the Reynes fragments might best be compared to that of the mid-fifteenth-century fragment of *Dux Moraud* in Bodleian MS Eng. poet. F.2 or to the fragments copied in the nearest available space in Bodleian MS Ashmole 750.[83] By contrast, the sheer diversity of formal and informal writing tasks attempted by Reynes serves to sharpen the difference between his collection and Shrewsbury School MS 6, an early fifteenth-century predominantly Latin anthology from the Lichfield area.[84] Here a carefully presented series of three Middle English speeches, complete with cues and interspersed with Latin passages, forms an integral part of a collection where the dramatic passages have clearly not strayed far from their liturgical origins.

The Reynes collection was made up of at least four separate units, three of which either began as or became note-books used for specific purposes. A broadly similar, very informal style of book production seems to have lain behind Dublin, Trinity College, MS 432, which contains the unique copy of the Northampton play of *Abraham and Isaac* and which seems to have belonged to the household of an active citizen of that town, and behind the Brome manuscript, which contains the unique copy of the Brome play of *Abraham and Isaac*.[85] Like the Reynes collection, both these miscellanies probably started life at some point in the second half of the fifteenth century as collections of unbound and unnumbered blank paper gatherings which began to be used for different writing purposes and so were gradually filled up with a very varied body of written material. In the case of the Brome manuscript it is still possible to use the sectional structure of the book to trace the activities of two scribe-compilers and to suggest at least two quite different stages by which this varied miscellany from the north Suffolk area came into existence. At the earliest stage the original Brome scribe seems to have copied his material into separate, sometimes only partially filled, irregularly sized gatherings. One of these (now the fifth and final quire) forms a 'legal' section and provided its earliest readers with appropriate legal models for imitation (complete with a serviceable vernacular translation) when deeds dealing with domestic issues were to be drawn up. Meanwhile, the first two surviving quires show that same copyist's interest in more edifying literature, despite the fact that the compilation of material in these incompletely filled quires seems to have proceeded rather intermittently and haphazardly, perhaps as the scribe came across scraps that interested him over a fairly lengthy period of time.[86] Moreover, the original Brome copyist need not be regarded as a book producer in the accepted sense of the word. Instead, it was a second copyist, Robert Melton of Stuston in Suffolk, who finally and irrevocably fixed the gatherings in the Brome manuscript into their present order by using some of the unfilled pages in the quires for his farm accounts for 1502–3 and 1507–8, his notes on local legal procedures, and for other brief devotional and medical snippets. Prior to Melton's interest in the collection the third and fourth gatherings had remained completely blank and each seems to have had a number of leaves removed, possibly for use in different types of writing tasks elsewhere.[87] Therefore, until the early years of the sixteenth century, the Brome manuscript hardly merited the title of 'book' but instead represented the remains of a single scribe's partly used paper stock where the unbound quires may have been kept within a single parchment wrapper. It is impossible to tell how much of this paper stock had been taken and used elsewhere before, finally, the surviving remnants became the Brome miscellany.[88]

Other collections which are also sometimes classed as commonplace books are perhaps better described as household miscellanies. National Library of Wales, Deposit MS Porkington 10, from the Welsh borders, contains an extraordinarily diverse collection of moral, medical, scientific and parodic items, some of which are shared by metropolitan collections and most of which might be found in an educated layman's private library.[89] Nevertheless, in comparison to the Reynes or Brome miscellanies, this seems a much more impersonal collection, and its mode of production has sometimes been misrepresented. Manchester, Chetham's Library MS 8009 was assembled in an incremental fashion by a large number of scribes over a considerable period of time, and it too hardly represents the personal reading tastes of a single owner.[90] Instead, its different portions give some indication of the clusters of material which seemed worth preserving and which became available – sometimes, perhaps, along with the scribes to copy them – in at least one regional household in the fifteenth century. The predominantly literary collection of polite reading material in CUL MS Ff.i.6, whose important metropolitan connections are discussed above, is another example of an informally produced miscellany which, by the sixteenth century, had ended up in the hands of the Finderns of South Derbyshire, but which, at the latest count, is the work of no fewer than forty different copyists.[91]

The composite nature of these regionally produced miscellanies confirms the view that the 'booklet' was a pragmatic mode of production as well as a relatively cheap means of marketing written material to an audience who did not want or could not afford more expensive books.[92] In the case of the Findern manuscript it seems probable that, like Topsy, the collection 'just grow'd' as suitable texts became available and as an existing sequence of loosely assembled, blank, or sometimes partly filled quires was supplemented by new material. Of particular interest here are the physical inserts in quires B and E which survive within composite quires yet may once have existed as separable portions of the larger collection.[93] The present physical state of this well-thumbed and fragmentary miscellany may itself represent successive scribal attempts to organise its contents and preserve items intact as the collection continued to grow as it was being read.

A similarly varied range of book-producing activities can be found in other regional literary collections, even when the bulk of the manuscript in question has been copied by just one or two scribes. NLS MS Advocates' 19.3.1, for instance, cannot claim to be a collection of genteel reading matter like the Findern collection, but this composite manuscript can still be associated with the same general north-east Midlands area (Ill. 25).[94] From at least the sixteenth century it too can be linked with a single household, in this case that of the Sherbrooke family of Oxton in Nottinghamshire.[95] Most of the items in MS Advocates' 19.3.1 are the work of just one copyist who frequently names himself as 'Heege' (fols. 6ov, 67v). Heege did work briefly with another scribe named 'John Hawghton', and the hand of another unnamed but contemporary scribe can also be found in the manuscript. Nevertheless, the degree of collaboration is strictly limited, and the actual organisation of the collection into discrete units may well have been Heege's responsibility. Some of the smaller units into which Heege's collection can be divided have even been signed independently from the rest, and their existence has been taken as an indication that they once formed a series of separately produced unbound volumes (a medieval 'library *in parvo*'). Taken in isolation, the grubby condition of the outer leaves of these small units might even suggest the hypothesis of a lending library of booklets produced by Heege and circulated around local readers before being bound up in a single volume.[96] The notion is an attractive one, suggesting simultaneously a non-commercial attitude to the circulation of texts, as well as a completely informal mode of regional 'publication' for small clusters of written material that recalls, perhaps, the metropolitan activities of John Shirley. This type of hypothesis

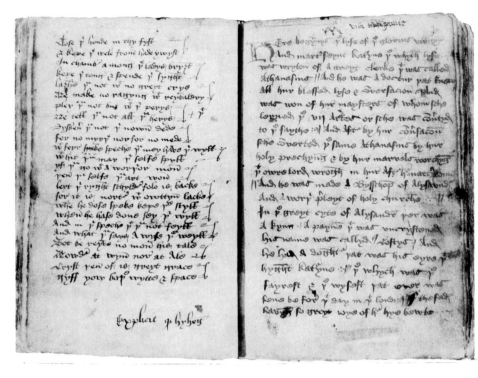

25   Edinburgh, National Library of Scotland, Advocates' MS 19.3.1, fols. 29v–30r (the end of
Stans Puer ad Mensam, 'Vrbanitas', *IMEV* 4153; opening lines of the ME prose *Life of St Catharine*).
The latter item is mistakenly entitled *Vita Margarite* on fol. 30r but correctly identified in the
damaged running titles later in this copy. *Stans Puer* is signed by the copyist, here 'hyheg', but
also 'heege' or 'heeg' elsewhere in the collection. Fol. 29v is the last leaf of the second quire unit
in the manuscript, numbered 'ixxx' on fol. 29r, and fol. 30r is the opening leaf of a third single
quire unit, numbered 'xxx' (average size of leaves 210 × 140 mm). This early system of foliation
runs from fol. 1 ('i') to fol. 40 ('xl'), thereby confirming the intended order of the first three
quires in the assembled collection.

would certainly go some way towards explaining how many clusters of items
seem to have circulated so widely and so well, in both geographical and social
terms, in the period before printing.[97]

On the other hand, of course, if MS Advocates' 19.3.1 did begin life as a
series of booklets, it is extremely fortunate that so many of them have
survived intact in a single collection. Indeed, the distribution of paper stocks
in different parts of Heege's collection, its organisation, and its lack of
duplicate items, all suggest that Heege may have merely used the booklet
form as a simple aid to his own editorial methods as he went about the task of
anthologising clusters of religious material, romance narratives, and short
lyric and comic items as they became available locally.[98] One obvious side
benefit of Heege's relatively unsophisticated production methods was that it

would allow the material Heege was copying to be used immediately by other readers while work on his unfinished collection was continuing. It must also be said that, despite any interim measures taken to group the material in various 'edited' or anthologised combinations, the unfilled pages in this collection eventually became fair game for those scribes – including, interestingly, at a later stage, Heege himself – who had access to the completed book and needed a blank space on which to jot down unrelated short extra 'filler' items. Several pages have now gone missing from the ends of Heege's original gatherings and some of these were probably blanks which were removed from Heege's general paper stock for use elsewhere, as similarly in the Brome manuscript.

Heege's chief long-term interest as a book-compiler seems to have been to produce his own collection of *domestitia* for his intended readers. This is an ambition shared by many regional book-producers of the period, and it can be assumed that the degree of personal literary selectivity sometimes shown in such miscellanies was directed either wholly or in large part by the suitability of the material available for family readership. Typical examples of these products include CUL MS Ff.2.38; Rate's collection in Bodleian MS Ashmole 61; the two 'Thornton' manuscripts (Lincoln Cathedral Library, MS 91 and BL Add. MS 31042); and perhaps BL MS Cotton Caligula A.II, and More's collection, now Naples, Biblioteca Nazionale, MS 13.B.29. In these relatively cheaply produced miscellanies the didactic writings of John Lydgate find a natural home alongside other morally improving material, including short poems lamenting the state of the world; edifying and exciting Middle English verse biographies; vernacular translations and paraphrases of familiar hymns, psalms and short prayers; and Middle English teaching texts which instruct the reader in the fundamental tenets of the Christian faith. It might be suspected that the producers of such collections could hardly have afforded to reject out of hand any promising material that came their way. But these are uncongenial surroundings for the fashionable and genteel reading-matter of the day, such as the works of Chaucer and Gower that were favoured by the compilers of the 'great works' anthologies, or items dealing with the intricacies of doctrinal controversies. These family collections are different in kind also from the well preserved 'family anthology' of carefully selected historical and exemplary material commissioned by Thomas Hopton of Swillington near Leeds,[99] or the anthology of polite literature with a strong moral interest such as that compiled by the scribe John Asloan for Thomas Ewen of Edinburgh in the early years of the sixteenth century.[100] Seen in this context, the 'homemade' literary miscellanies produced by Heege and others seem to mirror the rather less discriminating but no less avid reading interests of pragmatic owner-producers who had an eye for material with a utilitarian appeal, as well as for texts that reflected their own particular recreational interests.

Closer examination of some of these important literary collections also suggests the increasing number of ways in which some private book compilers were prepared to indicate their quasi-proprietorial regard for the material they were copying. In this respect, Heege's efforts to bring some kind of order to his collection can be conveniently contrasted with the activities of the scribe called Rate, again perhaps from the general north-east Midlands area, who gathered together a broadly similar collection of romances and other items of moral and religious instruction and entertainment in Bodleian MS Ashmole 61.[101] Rate's book belongs to that small group of miscellanies which, because of their long, narrow shape, are termed 'holster books'.[102] He originally seems to have copied his items continuously into an unbound series of gatherings, but the ordering of his material seems quite arbitrary and shows few signs of advance planning.[103] This is perhaps surprising since, like Heege, Rate shows a tendency to draw attention to his own identity at the end of many of his items, and it has been argued that some texts in his collection have been 'edited' for family consumption.[104] However, some sense of uniformity has been brought to Rate's book by his consistent use of a single column writing format (which seems sensible given the unusual shape of each page) and by a rather rudimentary, but nonetheless effective, programme of rubrication and decoration. Among other features, this makes sustained use of a fish and flower motif (see Ill. 26). These details, involving little technical expertise and no great expense, are obviously attempts to enhance the appeal of Rate's book for its intended readers. They reflect a conception of 'the whole book' and a concern for its visual attractiveness which are not always apparent in other non-systematic book productions of the period.[105]

Robert Thornton's two-volume collection, now surviving as Lincoln Cathedral Library, MS 91 (the Lincoln Thornton manuscript) and BL Add. MS 31042 (the London Thornton manuscript), represents a particularly interesting and ambitious attempt by a mid-fifteenth-century North Yorkshire gentleman to organise the mass of predominantly literary and devotional material available to him into some kind of manageable shape.[106] Many of the regional book producers so far discussed remain little more than names, but in Thornton's case the complex socio-literary milieu in which he lived and worked has already been established in some detail.[107] Thornton's activities as a book producer have been likened to the slightly earlier metropolitan career of John Shirley,[108] and the limited documentary evidence available certainly does not contradict the idea that, like Shirley, Thornton could have had access to a considerable range of reading material without leaving his own area, through links with family, friends, local religious houses and other contacts. Much of this material may have been made available to him in a number of different kinds of second-hand source, including perhaps more or less complete collections, commercially produced booklets, and even unbound quire units and stray leaves from dismembered manuscripts or

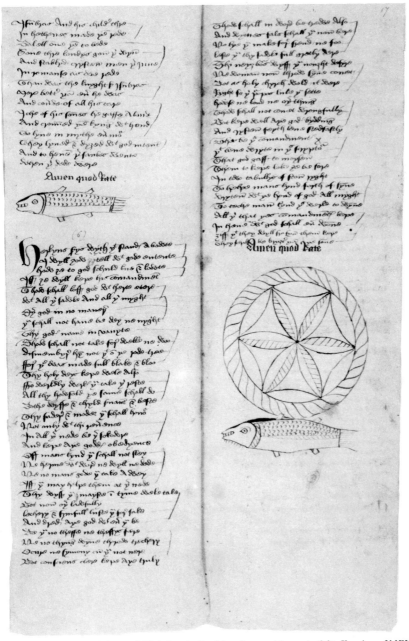

26   Oxford, Bodleian Library, MS Ashmole 61, fols. 16v–17r (the end of *Sir Ysumbras*, *IMEV* 1184; the 'Ten Commandments' from *Speculum Christiani*, *IMEV* 1111). Both items are signed by the copyist 'Rate' who also repeated the first eight lines of the latter item next to other material from *Speculum Christiani* on fol. 22v. Rate was probably responsible for the various decorative features in the manuscript as well. Faint creases in the centre of many of the leaves suggest that Rate's paper stock was already folded to form more conventional quires and that he then had to refold sheets, lengthwise, in order to make them conform to the 'holster book' format imposed on his collection (average size of leaves 418 × 138 mm).

work in progress by others.[109] This necessarily complicates many of the conclusions that might be drawn about the precise nature of Thornton's editorial instinct and methods. Like Heege, however, and unlike Shirley, Thornton can be shown to have retained a limited degree of control over the order in which some of his items might appear in his collection by copying them into manuscript units that were originally self-contained.[110] Moreover, the composite nature of his manuscripts suggests strongly that this is a privately produced two-volume compilation in which another regional book-producer has been keen to take immediate and maximum advantage of materials that only gradually and uncertainly became available for his use.

The present state of Thornton's manuscript offers many intriguing clues about the mixture of probable accident and possible design that characterises his working methods. For a time Thornton seems to have copied items that could have ended up in either one manuscript or the other, or in a single, very large collection. It was perhaps due mainly to a series of lucky finds in his exemplars that a 'romance' unit, a 'religious' unit, and a 'medical' unit evolved, to which he subsequently appended some additional items as they became available (these now form the Lincoln manuscript).[111] The core of the London manuscript was probably constructed in a similar kind of hit and miss fashion, and sometimes from the same stocks of paper as the Lincoln manuscript.[112] The evidence of these paper stocks and a mixture of physical and textual evidence suggest also that, at an even earlier stage in his compiling activities, Thornton copied texts like the *Northern Passion*, the alliterative *Morte Arthure*, the *Awntyrs of Arthure*, and the *Privity of the Passion* into separate quires or groups of quires. The *Northern Passion* was copied from a defective examplar, which Thornton evidently knew to be defective since on fols. 41rb and 41v in the London manuscript he left space in his own incomplete copy, so that the missing text could be supplied later from a different exemplar.[113] Such uncertainties of supply certainly proved a real problem for other scribes in the period, as they attempted to obtain 'best' texts of works like Hilton's *Scale of Perfection*, the *Prick of Conscience*, or the translation of Deguileville's *Pèlerinage de la Vie Humaine* attributed to Lydgate.[114] But Thornton's action here was born of desperation, although the present state of his manuscript may also argue for a degree of confidence on his part that was not matched by his ability to 'patch' the *Northern Passion* in the way he intended. Nevertheless, it is likely that this defective item was kept to one side for a time (perhaps alongside similarly incomplete texts), until it eventually formed part of the core of the London miscellany.[115] The three other items associated with this early stage in Thornton's career eventually ended up in the Lincoln manuscript.

There were, of course, many other private book producers in the period who collected quite different types of literary material. For example, it is possible to draw several important points of contrast between Thornton's relatively ambitious attempts to compile a collection of reading material in the vernacular with those of John Wilde, a fifteenth-century precentor of Waltham Abbey in Essex.[116] At some time after 1469 Wilde assembled a carefully written and profusely rubricated two-volume collection of predominantly Latin items that now survives as BL MS Lansdowne 763 (a musical anthology) and Bodleian MS Rawlinson B.214 (a varied collection of historical and 'Goliardic' items followed by an exposition of Ovid's *Metamorphoses*). These books share no items with Thornton's much less elegant collection, and, unlike Thornton, Wilde obviously maintained a much clearer distinction between the different types of anthology that he was trying to produce. Moreover, many of the texts in Wilde's collection have already been shown to share remarkably close links with similar items in a cluster of Latin miscellanies, including most notably BL MS Cotton Titus A.xx (a poetical miscellany compiled accretively in the London area after 1367, and sharing sixteen items in common with MS Rawlinson B.214); MS Bodley 851 (a late fourteenth-century composite miscellany with fifteenth-century additions, consisting of three discrete parts, of which at least the first part belonged to John Wells, monk of Ramsey, and sharing nine poems with the Rawlinson manuscript); and Bodleian MS Rawlinson G.109 (a composite miscellany dating from c. 1200, of unknown provenance, but in England, possibly Bury, from at least the fourteenth century, and sharing fourteen items with the Rawlinson manuscript). Therefore, unlike Thornton's case, where it is often necessary to assume a complex of different and ill-defined intermediary stages in the transmission of his texts, it was clearly in a learned clerical milieu, where certain types of material were more readily available and the practical conditions were perhaps more favourable, that Wilde's urge to anthologise was carefully nurtured.

Of course it was a similarly fertile ground that produced the many private devotional collections in the period which, in retrospect, seem to be the natural successors of more formal and ambitious collections like the Vernon and Simeon manuscripts.[117] In other respects, the more 'forward-looking' or 'humanist' aspects that have been associated with Wilde's interests and motives in producing his books might also profitably be compared to those displayed in the later monastic literary collection in BL Add. MS 60577 (the tri-lingual Winchester anthology).[118] Nevertheless, in spite of Wilde's undoubted advantages as a would-be compiler, he too sometimes resorted to the same kinds of unorthodox working methods that characterise, say, the achievements of Thornton and others. His pages are normally ruled only when he knew that he had the material to fill them, and a number of his irregularly sized gatherings and the pages in them were specifically tailored to fit the material they now contain. In addition, Wilde originally copied many of his items into quite separate manuscript units which, in his case, meant that these could be set to one side and returned to as additional suitable material became available. On at least two occasions, in the twelfth and fourteenth gatherings of Rawlinson B.214, Wilde (like Thornton) even seems to have resorted to turning his half-filled gatherings inside out in order to use the remaining space in them as appropriately as he could. Interestingly, Wilde's actions here have had the side-effect of blurring the distinction that he also seems, at one time, to have been trying hard to maintain between the 'historical' and 'satirical' sections of this collection. Such activity suggests that even Wilde's particular brand of discriminating literary intelligence was sometimes compromised by such mundanely practical and unpredictable considerations as a shortage of paper when he most needed it, or the limited and uncertain availability of certain exemplars.

In the absence of a strict sense of copyright, or of any form of direct supervision, it seems natural that the history of book production before printing should be full of examples of compilers like Shirley, Thornton, Heege, or Wilde, who may not have been 'professional' compilers any more than some writers were 'professional' authors, but who still found themselves making the types of decisions about their compilations now normally reserved for the publishing editor or even the author. In this sense, the varied interests and activities of these may go some way towards preparing us for the efforts of a figure like Humphrey Newton, a country gentleman, book producer and author from Newton and Pownall in East Cheshire.[119] Around 1500 Newton compiled for his family a cartulary which was gathered together with other legal details, genealogical notes and miscellaneous scraps (including a 'vision in a traunce of John Newton of Congleton, dreper and sherman 1492'). This collection forms the opening section of Bodleian MS lat. misc. c.66 (the former Capesthorne manuscript) and is followed by an apparently self-contained anthology of medical material written in a different hand. In turn, this is followed by a further motley assortment of informational and predominantly secular literary items (including a table of the planets, recipes for making inks and colours, a recipe for cooking rabbit, and extracts from a 'book of shrift'). This section also contains the only extant examples of what can be assumed to be final drafts of Newton's own literary compositions.[120] These poems demonstrate Newton's love of acrostics and his regard for the 'chanson d'aventure' as well as his particular interest in epistolary verse. Newton was hardly in the same league as writers like Hoccleve and Skelton (metropolitan bookmen for whom self-advertisement seems to have been a way of life), but his autograph copies do suggest something of the intriguing relationships that existed in the period between the home-based scribe and the literary material which interested him. While the Capesthorne manuscript is more like a series of miscellaneous and untidy notebooks than a 'great works' anthology on the Shirleian model, its contents suggest Newton's familiarity and ease with difficult verse forms as well as the fact that his experience of literature was not limited to the items contained in this single miscellany. The relatively modest but varied career of Newton as local landowner and family man, copyist, poet and reader (aware of the general literary trends of his day) might well be said to mirror the heterogeneous reading and writing habits of this age of informal book production.

NOTES

1 N.R. Ker, Introduction, *Facsimile of British Museum MS Harley 2253*, EETS, OS, 255 (London, 1965).

2 A.I. Doyle, 'Vernon and Simeon Manuscripts'; A.I. Doyle, 'University College, Oxford, MS 97, and its Relationship to the Simeon Manuscript (British Library Add. 22283)', and R.E. Lewis, 'The Relationship of the Vernon and Simeon Texts of the *Pricke of Conscience*', both in Benskin and Samuels, pp. 265–82, 251–64.

3 See, for example, E. Wilson, *A Descriptive Index of the English Lyrics in John of Grimestone's Preaching Book*, Medium Aevum Monographs, NS, 2 (Oxford, 1973, rpt 1977); S. Wenzel, *Verses in Sermons: the 'Fasciculus Morum' and its Middle English Poems* (Cambridge, Mass., 1978). For discussion of the term 'commonplace book', see below, pp. 292–3.

4 D.A. Pearsall and I.C. Cunningham, Introduction, *The Auchinleck MS: NLS Advocates' MS 19.2.1* (London, 1977).

5 See R. Woolf, *The English Religious Lyric in the Middle Ages* (Oxford, 1968), p. 375.

6 Such as BL MS Sloane 2593, and Bodleian MS Eng. Poet. e. 1, both described by R.L. Greene, *The Early English Carols*, 2nd edn (Oxford, 1977), pp. 306–7, 317–18.

7 *John Audelay: The Poems*, ed. E.K. Whiting, EETS, OS, 184 (London, 1931, rpt New York, 1971).

8 San Marino, California, Huntington Library MS HM 142, for example, seems to be a 'twin' to Longleat House MS 30; see H.C. Schulz, 'Middle English Texts from the "Bement" MS', *HLQ*, 3 (1939–40), 443–65, and R.A.B. Mynors, 'A Fifteenth-Century Scribe: T. Werken', *TCBS*, 1 (1950), 97–104.

9 In manuscripts such as BL Harley 2255; Cambridge, Jesus College, MS 56; Bodleian MS Laud misc. 683; and the closely related BL MS Lansdowne 699 and Leiden, MS Vossius 9, whose connections are described by J.A. Van Dorsten, 'The Leyden Lydgate Manuscript', *Scriptorium*, 14 (1960), 315–25. Such volumes have a place in the patterns of production instituted by or for original authors, as discussed in Chapter 11 above. The only surviving complete volume devoted to reading copies of English secular lyrics is BL MS Harley 682, containing English versions of some of the French poems of Charles of Orleans. See *Charles of Orleans: The English Poems*, ed. R. Steele and M. Day, EETS, OS, 215, 220 (London, 1941, 1946; rpt as one volume, with bibliographical supplement, 1970).

10 *The Paston Letters*, ed. N. Davis, 2 vols. (Oxford, 1971, 1976), I, pp. 517–18.

11 Surviving examples of such collections include Bodleian MSS Fairfax 16, Tanner 346, Bodley 638, Arch. Selden B.24, Digby 181; Cambridge, Magdalene College, MS Pepys 2006; CUL MS Ff.1.6, and Longleat House MS 258. See Hammond, *Chaucer*, pp. 325–405, and A. Brusendorff, *The Chaucer Tradition* (London, 1925), pp. 178–95.

12 *The Complaint of Mars* and *The Complaint of Venus* are almost invariably copied

together, while *Gentilesse, Lak of Stedfastnesse, Truth* and *The Complaint of Chaucer to his Purse* are frequently associated in various combinations. Sometimes the lyrics are run into each other, and copied as a continuous sequence, as in BL MS Cotton Cleopatra D.vii, fols. 188v–189v.

13 See J. Norton-Smith, Introduction, *Bodleian MS Fairfax 16* (London, 1979), for a facsimile and a bibliography of printed descriptions.

14 Fols. 14v–15r. The arms, quartering Stanley and Hooton, are those of John Stanley (d. by 1469), Usher of the Chamber to Henry VI from 1450 to 1455; see Norton-Smith, *Fairfax 16*, pp. xiii–xiv.

15 P.R. Robinson, Introduction, *MS Tanner 346* (Norman, Oklahoma, 1980).

16 See Doyle and Parkes, pp. 163–203.

17 P.R. Robinson, Introduction, *MS Bodley 638* (Norman, Oklahoma, 1981). A table illustrating the comparisons is provided by Hammond, *Chaucer*, p. 338.

18 On fols. 4v and 38r, for example.

19 Described by E.P. Hammond, 'MS Longleat 258: a Chaucerian Codex', *MLN*, 19 (1904), 196–8; E. Seaton, *Sir Richard Roos, Lancastrian Poet* (London, 1961), pp. 92–3; *The Flower and the Leaf and the Assembly of Ladies*, ed. D.A. Pearsall (London, 1962, rpt Manchester, 1980), pp. 7–8.

20 Alexander, 'William Abell', and 'Painting and Manuscript Illustration', p. 152; cf. Norton-Smith, *Fairfax 16*, p. xxi.

21 H.N. MacCracken, 'Two Chaucerian *Ballades*', *Archiv*, 127 (1911), 323–7; J. Boffey, 'The Manuscripts of English Courtly Love Lyrics', in Pearsall, *Manuscripts and Readers*, pp. 3–14 (p. 7); K.D. Harris, 'The Origins and Make-Up of Cambridge, University Library MS Ff.1.6', *TCBS*, 8 (1983), 299–333. For a facsimile of the manuscript, see R. Beadle and A.E.B. Owen, Introduction, *The Findern Anthology* (London, 1977). The probable circumstances in which MS Ff.1.6 was produced are discussed below, pp. 295–6.

22 The scribe William Ebesham, employed by Sir John Paston for various projects, worked for him in both London and Norfolk; see Doyle, 'William Ebesham', and G.A. Lester, *Sir John Paston's 'Grete Boke'* (Woodbridge, 1984), pp. 34–48.

23 *The Poetical Works of Alain Chartier*, ed. J.C. Laidlaw (Cambridge, 1974), pp. 39–41, 328–70. Seaton, *Richard Roos, passim*. The English version survives in MSS CUL Ff.1.6; Trinity R.3.19; BL Harley 372 and Sloane 1710; Bodleian Fairfax 16; Longleat 258. *The Oxford Chaucer*, ed. W.W. Skeat, 7 vols. (London, 1894–7), vii, pp. li–lv, gives a good account of most of the manuscripts, and of Thynne's edition; further information is provided by Hammond, *Chaucer*, pp. 432–4, and by J.E. Blodgett, 'Some Printer's Copy for William Thynne's 1532 Edition of Chaucer', *The Library*, 6th series, 1 (1979), 97–113.

24 These textual groupings were first established by Skeat, who seems not to have consulted MSS Sloane 1710 and Longleat 258, or Pynson's print. His opinion of the copy in CUL MS Ff.1.6 as the 'best' text probably stands: it seems generally superior to that in Trinity MS R.3.19, the only other complete text. Skeat does not note that a sixteenth-century reader appears to have collated the copy in the B-group MS Harley 372 with one of the A-group texts (possibly a print) and to have made appropriate emendations in the manuscript.

25 See M.C. Seymour, 'The Manuscripts of Hoccleve's *Regiment of Princes*', *TEBS*, 4 (1955–71, published 1974), 253–97, at 266–7.

26 The fullest biographical discussion is provided by A.I. Doyle, 'More Light on John Shirley', *Medium Aevum*, 30 (1961), 93–101 (continued in an unpublished lecture delivered at the 2nd York Conference on Fifteenth-Century Manuscript Studies, July 1983), and 'English Books In and Out of Court', pp. 176–8. See also R.F. Green, 'Three Fifteenth-Century Notes', *ELN*, 14 (1976–7), 14–17, and C. Greenberg, 'John Shirley and the English Book Trade', *The Library*, 6th series, 4 (1982), 369–80. For general discussions of Shirley's influence, see Brusendorff, *Chaucer Tradition*, pp. 207–36; E.P. Hammond, *English Verse between Chaucer and Surrey* (Durham, N.C., 1927, rpt New York, 1965), pp. 191–201, and *Chaucer*, pp. 515–17; D.A. Pearsall, *John Lydgate* (London, 1970), pp. 72–82, and *Old English and Middle English Poetry* (London, 1977), pp. 213–14; R.H. Robbins, 'The Chaucer Apocrypha', in *A Manual of the Writings in Middle English*, 4, ed. A.E. Hartung (New Haven, Conn., 1973), pp. 1061–101, 1285–306; R.F. Green, *Poets and Princepleasers: Literature and the English Court in the Late Middle Ages* (Toronto, 1980), pp. 130–3.

27 These different views are suggested respectively (see note 26) by Hammond; by Pearsall, and by A.S.G. Edwards, 'Lydgate Manuscripts: Some Directions for Future Research', in Pearsall, *Manuscripts and Readers*, pp. 15–26; by Doyle; and by Green.

28 Information on Shirley's ownership of these manuscripts is provided (in the order in which they are discussed above) by M.B. Parkes and E. Salter, Introduction, *Troilus and Criseyde: A Facsimile of Corpus Christi College, Cambridge, MS 61* (Cambridge, 1978), p. 11; Warner and Gilson, II, 367; D.B. Tyson, *'La Vie du Prince Noir' by Chandos Herald. Edited from the Manuscript in the University of London Library*, Beihefte zur Zeitschrift für romanische Philologie 147 (Tübingen, 1975), p. 4; *Secretum Secretorum*, I, ed. A. Manzalaoui, EETS, os, 276 (London, 1977), p. xxxviii; A.I. Doyle, 'English Books In and Out of Court', p. 177, and 'More Light', p. 42; *The Lyric Poems of Jehan Froissart*, ed. R.R. McGregor, North Carolina Studies in the Romance Languages and Literatures 143 (Chapel Hill, 1975), 18.

29 Also copied c. 1440 into BL MS Add. 38690; see L.M. Matheson, 'Historical Prose', in Edwards, *Middle English Prose*, pp. 211–47, at pp. 215–16.

30 See B. Lindström, 'The English Versions of Jacques Legrand's *Livre de Bonnes Meurs*', *The Library*, 6th series, 1 (1979), 247–54.

31 Manzalaoui, *Secretum*, pp. xxxvii–xxxviii. Shirley copied another translation of this work into Bodleian MS Ashmole 59; *ibid.*, pp. xxxiii–xxxvi.

32 Opinion has been divided as to whether this 'Kalundare' describes a volume which is now lost, or was designed to accompany the collection which survives as Trinity MS R.3.20 (perhaps with the addition of Sion College, MS Arc.L 40.2/ E.44; see below, n. 36). E.P. Hammond, 'The Lost Quires of a Shirley Codex', *MLN*, 36 (1921), 184–5, supported the connection between the 'Kalundare' and the Trinity MS, as do (despite some other differences of opinion) K. Walls, 'Did Lydgate Translate the *Pèlerinage de la Vie Humaine*?' *NQ*, 222 (1977), 103–5, and R.F. Green, 'Lydgate and Deguileville Once More', *NQ*, 223 (1978), 105–6. Brusendorff, *Chaucer Tradition*, pp. 226–7, doubted the possibility.

33 See Bodleian MS Ashmole 59 and Trinity MS R.3.20. Shirley's own compositions are edited by Brusendorff, *Chaucer Tradition*, pp. 453–60, and by Hammond, *English Verse*, pp. 194–201. Further bibliography is included in Robbins, 'Chaucer Apocrypha'.

34 Their contents are described by E.P. Hammond, 'Ashmole 59 and Other Shirley Manuscripts', *Anglia*, 3 (1907), 320–48.

35 The surviving contents are an English prose *Doctrina et Consilium Galiensis*, with Chaucer's *Pity*, and his *Complaint to his Lady*.

36 At present it consists of twelve gatherings, and lacks two leaves at the beginning and one at the end. It may originally have preceded Trinity MS R.3.20, whose quire signatures start with 'xiiij', or have been at some stage bound with Bodleian MS Ashmole 59, in which the first quire signature has been changed from 'j' to 'xiij'. For further discussion see N.R. Ker, *Medieval Manuscripts in British Libraries*, I (Oxford, 1977), 290–1, and the articles by Walls and Green cited above in n. 32.

37 Reproduced by Hammond, 'Ashmole 59', p. 321, and by Brusendorff, *Chaucer Tradition*, pp. 210–11.

38 Lines 6–7 of Lydgate's *Prayer for King Henry VI and his Queen and People* (*IMEV* Supplement 1955.5); *Halsham's Balade* (*IMEV* 3504 and 3437); the 'Whetstone' stanza from *Troilus and Criseyde*, I, 631–7, and the 'Cantus Troili' (*sic*), I, 400–6; lines on poverty (*IMEV* 2820) from Walton's *Boethius*. See H.N. MacCracken, 'More Odd Texts of Chaucer's *Troilus*', *MLN*, 25 (1910), 126–7. We are grateful to Kate Harris for information about this manuscript.

39 Trinity MS R.3.20, p. 356.

40 Cf. Green, *Poets and Princepleasers*, p. 130.

41 Hammond, 'Ashmole 59', and *English Verse*, p. 192.

42 The *Troilus* 'Whetstone' stanza appears also in Trinity MS R.3.20; interestingly, while in the Trinity copy it is correctly headed 'Pandar to Troylus', in the Huntington MS it is headed 'Gower'. *Halsham's Balade* and its companion-piece *Tied with a Line* appear also in BL MS Add. 16165, and seem to be indicated by two of the titles in the Ashmole 59 table of contents.

43 All three of Shirley's major collections contain examples of shared material of this kind. *On kissing at 'Verbum caro factum est'* and the *Complaint for my Lady of Gloucester and Holland* occur as a pair in MSS Trinity R.3.20 (p. 362–7) and Ashmole 59 (fols. 56v–58v). The second poem is incomplete in the Ashmole copy, perhaps because Shirley's memory failed him at this point. A chain of similar material continues in both manuscripts: in R.3.20, the *Complaint* is followed by *Chaucer's words to Adam*, part of *The Fall of Princes* (III, 1569–1638), and a list of Knights of the Garter. In MS Ashmole 59 it is followed by part of the same *Fall* extract (III, 1608–38), and by the same list of Knights of the Garter. In both manuscripts Shirley produced a peculiarly random assortment of fragments which might have emerged in roughly associated fashion from the recesses of his memory. Further material is shared by MSS Ashmole 59 and BL Add. 16165: Lydgate's *Invocation to Saint Anne*, his *Lover's Lament*, and *Doubleness*. In MS Add. 16165 the sequence is interrupted with *The Departing of Chaucer* and Pycard's *Devynayle*. The omission of these two pieces in MS Ashmole 59, the later manuscript, may indicate that it was compiled from memory – a memory which sometimes failed.

44 MS Add. 16165 has three parchment leaves at the beginning (one singleton and one bifolium), and a parchment singleton at the end. Trinity MS R.3.20 concludes with three parchment leaves and one parchment stub.

45 The only breaks in MS R.3.20 where divisions between gatherings and between texts coincide occur after pp. 32 (the end of gathering 2, 'Suffolk's' roundels) and

144 (the end of gathering 9, after Chaucer's *Truth*). In Add. 16165, there are breaks after *The Complaint of the Black Knight*, and after a series of filler items, after fols. 200v and 246v.

46 This feature has been described as characteristic of Shirley manuscripts, and influential on the appearance of later fifteenth-century collections; see Ker, *Medieval Manuscripts*, I, 290–1.

47 A hypothesis supported particularly by E.P. Hammond, 'A Scribe of Chaucer', *MP*, 27 (1930), 26–33, but disputed by Doyle, 'John Shirley', and by Green, *Poets and Princepleasers*.

48 Doyle, 'John Shirley', and Christianson, in Ch. 4 above.

49 Hammond, 'A Scribe of Chaucer', and 'Ashmole 59'.

50 A feature noted by R.H. Robbins, *Secular Lyrics of the Fourteenth and Fifteenth Centuries*, 2nd edn (Oxford, 1955), p. xxiv.

51 See, for example, BL Add. MS 5467, described by Hammond, 'Ashmole 59', p. 346, and Brusendorff, *Chaucer Tradition*, p. 213; BL MS Harley 7333, described by Manly and Rickert, I, pp. 207–9, and Seymour, 'Manuscripts of the *Regiment*', 269–71; BL MSS Add. 34360 and Harley 2251, predominantly Lydgatian anthologies, with much common material, described by E.P. Hammond, 'Two British Museum Manuscripts: A Contribution to the Bibliography of John Lydgate', *Anglia*, 28 (1905), 1–28 (where a table of the duplicated portions of the manuscripts is provided), and Brusendorff, *Chaucer Tradition*, pp. 222–3 (it is also worth remarking that the pairing of *Tied with a Line* (*IMEV* 3436) and *Right as the Crab Goeth Forward* (*IMEV* 3655), on fols. 37v–39v of MS Harley 2251, reflects the ordering of items in the Ashmole 59 table of contents, where 'a comedye of worldes variacon (*sic*)' is followed by 'A Refraide as þe crabbe goþe'). Fols. 61–207 of the composite BL MS Cotton Titus A.xxvi form a miscellany which includes a copy of Lydgate's *Fifteen Joys of Our Lady* with a Shirley-derived rubric (fol. 157v); a brief description of the manuscript (with no reference to its Shirley connections) is given by Greene, *Early English Carols*, p. 297. BL MS Harley 7578, according to Brusendorff, *Chaucer Tradition*, pp. 228–9, contain a text of Chaucer's *Pity* which follows that of Shirley's autograph copies, while Bodleian MS Hatton 73 is described by Brusendorff, *Chaucer Tradition*, p. 228, as containing Shirleian texts of Chaucer's *Truth* and *Lak of Stedfastnesse*; for a brief description, see Madan, *Summary Catalogue*, II (2), pp. 850–1. Harvard University Library MS 530, long thought to have been another autograph Shirley anthology, is *not* in Shirley's hand, although derived from his collections; its contents are described by F.N. Robinson, 'On Two Manuscripts of Lydgate's *Guy of Warwick*', *Harvard Studies and Notes in Philology and Literature*, 5 (1896), 117–220. The burnt BL MS Cotton Otho A.xviii, thought by Brusendorff, *Chaucer Tradition*, p. 299, to have perhaps included Shirley-derived material, most probably antedated Shirley's collections: see G.B. Pace, 'Otho A.xviii', *Speculum*, 26 (1951), 306–16. Connections between Shirley's manuscripts and BL Add. MS 29729 are discussed above, p. 285, and their relationship with BL MS Harley 367 below, in n. 52.

52 For connections between Shirley's manuscripts and Stow's collection, BL Add. MS 29729, see above, n. 51. BL MS Harley 367, also Stow's, shares the following texts with Shirley's anthologies: Lydgate's *Life of St Margaret*, also in MS R.3.20; lines from *The Fall of Princes* (II, 4460–586) which are both copied in Ashmole 59

and listed in its stray table of contents; Lydgate's *Prayer to St Edmund on Behalf of Henry VI*, also in MS Ashmole 59; one stanza from *Scogan's Moral Balade*, also in MS Ashmole 59; *The Lover's Lament*, also – with identical rubric – in MSS Ashmole 59 and Add. 16165.

53 See BL Add. MS 34360, fol. 59r, and Brusendorff, *Chaucer Tradition*, p. 181–2; E.P. Hammond, 'The Nine-Syllabled Pentameter Line in Some Post-Chaucerian Manuscripts', *MP*, 23 (1925–6), 129–52, 'A Scribe of Chaucer', and 'Two British Museum MSS'; A.I. Doyle, 'An Unrecognized Piece of *Piers the Ploughman's Creed* and Other Work by its Scribe', *Speculum*, 34 (1959), 428–35, and 'English Books', p. 177, n. 42; R.F. Green, 'Notes on Some Manuscripts of Hoccleve's *Regiment of Princes*', *BLJ*, 4 (1978), 37–41.

54 See the description of BL MS Royal 17.D.xv, and Royal College of Physicians, MS 13, fols. 167–301 (except for fol. 241r) in Manly and Rickert, I, 476–84, 439–46; and of BL MSS Arundel 59 and Harley 372, fols. 71r–112r, in Seymour, 'Manuscripts of the *Regiment*', pp. 264–7.

55 Usually limited to blue and red tinting of initials, when present. The single exception among these plain manuscripts in Trinity R.3.21.

56 Manly and Rickert note a few signs of supervision and correction in the *Canterbury Tales* manuscripts: I, 440, 478.

57 For Trinity MS R.3.21, see James, *Trinity College Manuscripts*, II, pp. 69–74. K. Scott, *The Mirroure of the Worlde*, pl. 8, reproduces some of the illustrations. James noted 15 booklets; Hammond, 'A Scribe of Chaucer', p. 33, noted 12; Brusendorff, *Chaucer Tradition*, p. 182, n. 1, found 13. The present authors locate 13: present fols. 1–32; 33–50; 51–84; 85–156; 157–72; 173–80; 181–204; 205–20; 221–48; 249–56; 257–73; 274–304; 305–21. The Hammond scribe worked on what now forms the second booklet, taking over from the main contributing scribe on fol. 34r to copy *Parce Mihi Domine*, and the most of the *Pety Job*, until the main scribe resumed copying on the fifth line of fol. 49v. Here, unusually, some decoration was incorporated: *Parce Mihi Domine* is prefaced by a miniature, and its initial letter is worked into a border. It seems probable that the booklet was designed from the outset as an individual unit: its first recto was left blank, no doubt for protective purposes.

58 As in BL Add. MS 34360.

59 *The Fifteen Joys and Sorrows of Mary* is also repeated in these booklets, although not in sequence with the other duplicated contents. Elsewhere in the manuscript, the *Birds' Matins* and the *Verses on the Kings of England* are also copied twice.

60 See Davis, *Paston Letters*, I, pp. 517–18, for details of the repeated material.

61 Described by James, *Trinity MSS*, II, pp. 83–95, and by B.Y. Fletcher, 'An Edition of MS R.3.19 in Trinity College, Cambridge: a Poetical Miscellany of c. 1480', Ph.D. thesis, University of Chicago, 1973.

62 Cf. booklet XII, beginning at fol. 274, in Trinity MS R.3.21.

63 See, for example, the will of Robert Norwich Esq. (d. 1443) in H. Harrod, 'Extracts from Early Wills', *Norfolk and Norwich Arch. Soc.*, 4 (1855), 32, with 'the little quire of paper, with the kings of England versified', and the will of John Goodyere of Monken Hadley (d. 1504) in F.C. Cass, 'Books in Wills and Inventories', *NQ*, 7th series, 9 (1890), 271, with 'a queyr of phisik of the secrets of women'. Cf. also the information in the Paston booklist referred to above, n. 10.

64 See M.R. James, *A Descriptive Catalogue of the Manuscripts in the Library of Lambeth Palace: the Medieval Manuscripts* (Cambridge, 1932), pp. 421–6; Guddat-Figge, pp. 218–26. The present binding of the manuscript appears to date from the early sixteenth century; see J.B. Oldham, *English Blind-Stamped Bindings* (Cambridge, 1952), p. 43, and *Lybeaus Desconus*, ed. M. Mills, EETS, os, 261 (London, 1969), pp. 2–3.

65 R. Hands, 'Juliana Berners and the *Boke of St Albans*', *RES*, ns, 18 (1967), 373–86, and *English Hawking and Hunting in the 'Boke of St Albans'* (Oxford, 1975), p. xlv.

66 The version in MS Rawl. c.86 is by Gilbert Banester, and survives in only one other manuscript, BL Add. 12524 (where it is interestingly 'anthologised' as part of *The Legend of Good Women*). The anonymous translation in MS R.3.19, according to its modern editor, was made with the help of Banester's version; see *Early English Versions of the Tales of Guiscardo and Gismonda and Titus and Gisippus from the Decameron*, ed. H.G. Wright, EETS, os, 205 (London, 1937, rpt New York, 1971), pp. xxxvii–xliii, and R.F. Green, 'The Date of Gilbert Banester's Translation of the Tale of Guiscardo and Ghismonda', *NQ*, 223 (1978), 299–300.

67 MS Rawl. c.86 is described by J.J. Griffiths, 'A Re-Examination of Oxford, Bodleian Library, MS Rawlinson c.86', *Archiv*, 219 (1982), 381–8.

68 See, however, Dr Doyle's discussion of the conditions under which Bodleian MS Douce 322 and BL MS Harley 1706 were produced, in his 'Books Connected with the Vere Family and Barking Abbey', *Transactions of the Essex Archaeological Society*, ns, 25 (1958), 222–43; C.A. Luttrell, 'Three North-West Midland Manuscripts', *Neophilologus*, 42 (1958), 38–50; and the groundwork laid by the publications of Professors Angus McIntosh and M.L. Samuels. The mundane but undoubtedly various activities of local copyists remain virtually unexplored, but see Doyle, 'William Ebesham', and C. Revard, 'Richard Hurd and MS Harley 2253', *NQ*, 224 (1979), 199–202, and 'Three More Holographs in the Hand of the Scribe of MS Harley 2253', *NQ*, 227 (1982), 62–3.

69 The extant corpus of Middle English alliterative poetry provides an example of such a 'type' of literature; see the study of the miscellanies containing this type of verse in A.I. Doyle, 'The Manuscripts'.

70 See, for example, the general accounts in Guddat-Figge, and J. Boffey, *The Manuscripts of English Courtly Love Lyrics in the Later Middle Ages* (Cambridge, 1985). For a useful general indication of the more ephemeral types of writing which lie on the periphery of literature itself, see the brief discussion in R.H. Robbins, 'Mirth in Manuscripts', *Essays and Studies*, 21 (1968), 1–28. Some sense of the difficulties of dealing with even a tiny sampling of this type of sub-literary material in any kind of inclusive or scholarly manner can be gained from H. Hargreaves, 'Some Problems in Indexing Middle English Recipes', in Edwards and Pearsall, pp. 91–113.

71 This successive recopying has meant that the textual affiliations of items like Lydgate's *Dietary* or his *Verses on the Kings of England* remain only half-uncovered and still present a formidable challenge to the Lydgate scholar. See, however, A. Renoir, 'A Note on the Third Redaction of John Lydgate's *Verses on the Kings of England*', *Archiv*, 216 (1979), 347–8, and the most recent listing of manuscripts containing these items by A. Renoir and C.D. Benson, 'John Lydgate', in *A Manual of the Writings in Middle English*, vi, gen. ed. A.E. Hartung (New Haven, Conn., 1980), 1827–8, 2092–4 (*Dietary*), and 1864–5, 2125–7 (*Verses on the Kings of England*).

      For further discussions of the circulation of Lydgate's writings, see above, Ch.
      11.

72 Particularly interesting examples include the tortuous fifteenth-century textual
    history of Rolle's works and of Rolle-related material, and of compilations such as
    the *South English Legendary* and the *Prick of Conscience*. Further examples, discussion,
    and bibliographical references are provided in Chapter 13 below.

73 The most useful discussion of this development remains A.I. Doyle, *Survey*.

74 It may be more than a mere accident of survival, however, that there are very few
    instances in which works by Rolle or Hilton, or associated mystical writings, are
    actually combined in miscellaneous collections with Middle English romances.
    The main example here is Lincoln Cathedral Library MS 91 (Robert Thornton's
    collection), where Rolle-related material and three short Hilton items, together
    with a Middle English version of St Edmund's *Speculum Ecclesie*, form part of a
    'religious' unit that accompanies 'romance' and 'medical' units in one miscellany.
    The examples provided by the Vernon and Simeon manuscripts are more appar-
    ent than real, given the pious nature of the 'romances' they contain. More
    surprising, perhaps, is the general failure of the *Speculum Ecclesie* to survive in
    manuscripts containing romances. The text survives in a number of different
    translations and adaptations, and seems to have had considerable appeal to both
    religious and lay readers as 'the great storehouse from which Rolle derived some of
    his favorite subjects and ideas' (C. Horstmann, *Yorkshire Writers*, I (London, 1895),
    p. 219). Yet it is only in the Vernon and Simeon collections, Thornton's 'religious'
    unit, and CUL MS Ff.2.38 that versions of the *Speculum* survive alongside roman-
    ces. For attempts to make Rolle's *Form* and St Edmund's *Speculum* more palatable
    to their intended late medieval audience, see N.F. Blake, '*The Form of Living* in
    Prose and Poetry', *Archiv*, 211 (1974), 300–8. For details of attempts to popularise
    meditative practices see Ch. 13 below.

75 For discussion and use of the term see Robbins, *Secular Lyrics*, pp. xxviii–xxx;
    A.G. Rigg, *A Glastonbury Miscellany* (Oxford, 1968), pp. 24–6; Guddat-Figge,
    pp. 25–8.

76 The list can be supplemented by non-literary miscellanies such as BL MSS Harley
    3362 and Sloane 3215, Bodleian MS Rawlinson D.1222, and CUL MS Ll.1.18.

77 Later examples include the extraordinary MS Lambeth 306 (whose earlier
    associations were discussed above); the second part of BL MS Harley 2386, which
    was organised around a fifteenth-century copy of 'the Boke of John Maundeuyle'
    (see M.C. Seymour, 'The English Manuscripts of *Mandeville's Travels*', *TEBS*, 4
    (1955–71, published 1974), 169–210, at 186–7; the composite Bodleian MS
    Ashmole 45, organized around a late copy of the *Erl of Toulous* (see Guddat-Figge,
    pp. 247–9); and BL MS Harley 2252, consisting of a nucleus of two romances
    which John Colyns, an early sixteenth-century London mercer, purchased or had
    copied, and around which he assembled his own body of written material (see
    C. Meale, 'Wynkyn de Worde's Setting-Copy for *Ipomydon*', *SB*, 35 (1982), 156–71,
    at 157, and 'The Compiler at Work: John Colyns and BL MS Harley 2252', in
    Pearsall, *Manuscripts and Readers*, pp. 82–103).

78 For MS O.2.53, see James, *Trinity MSS*, III, 169–74, and the useful comments in
    Meale, 'The Compiler at Work', p. 93, n. 12.

79 Rigg, *Glastonbury Miscellany*, pp. 5–7.

80 See further C. Louis, *The Commonplace Book of Robert Reynes of Acle: an Edition of Tanner MS 407* (New York and London, 1980).

81 Discussed along with other dramatic survivals from the period in *Non-Cycle Plays and Fragments*, ed. N. Davis, EETS, ss, 1 (London, 1970), and reproduced in facsimile by Davis, in *Non-Cycle Plays and the Winchester Dialogues*, Leeds Texts and Monographs, Medieval Drama Facsimiles (Leeds, 1979).

82 For discussion see the excellent Leeds Texts and Monographs, Medieval Drama Facsimiles series. This includes *The York Play* (BL Add. MS 35290), introd. Richard Beadle and Peter Meredith (1983); *The Towneley Cycle: a Facsimile of Huntington MS HM 1*, introd. A.C. Cawley and M. Stevens (1976); *The N-Town Plays: a Facsimile of British Library MS Cotton Vespasian D.VIII*, introd. P. Meredith and S.J. Kahrl (1977), which should be supplemented by S. Spector, 'The Composition and Development of an Eclectic Manuscript: Cotton Vespasian D.viii', *LSE*, ns, 9 (1977), 62–83, and 'Symmetry in Watermark Sequences', *SB*, 31 (1978), 162–78; *The Chester Mystery Cycle: a Facsimile of MS Bodley 175*, introd. R.M. Lumiansky and D. Mills (1973), and *The Chester Mystery Cycle: a Facsimile of MS Harley 2124*, introd. D. Mills (1984).

83 Davis, *Non-Cycle Plays and Fragments*, pp. c–cxi, cxviii–cxx.

84 Davis, *Non-Cycle Plays and Fragments*, pp. xiv–xxii.

85 The original quiring of Dublin, Trinity College, MS 432 has yet to be determined. For description of the contents see Davis, *Non-Cycle Plays and Fragments*, pp. xlvii–lviii. For the Brome manuscript, compare the account given here to those in *The Book of Brome: a Commonplace Book of the Fifteenth Century*, ed. L. Toulmin Smith (London, 1886), and Davis, *Non-Cycle Plays and the Winchester Dialogues*, pp. 49–50.

86 For example, the original Brome scribe used the leaves that now form the opening of this two-quire 'literary' unit to jot down a series of short moral pieces and cipher puzzles, rather as some medieval scribes used the flyleaves of some books for their own random scribbles. But the central portion of the same gathering now contains a copy of the Middle English *Ypotis*, with the scribe's copy of *Abraham and Isaac* added as a final item in the quire, and the last page of the gathering (fol. 22v) left blank. In the second gathering the Brome scribe seems to have used his paper stock in a similarly random fashion, often leaving blank leaves between items for no apparent reason. Some of these have remained blank and some were used by a later scribe for farm accounts. Compare also the irregular and puzzling use of paper that gives the manuscript containing the York plays an equally 'unfinished' appearance (Beadle and Meredith, *The York Play*, p. xvi).

87 Blank leaves in irregularly sized gatherings, or seemingly arbitrary cancellations, are quite common in miscellanies that have been produced over a lengthy period of time, and need not always be seen as a consequence of some form of fascicular book production. For example, letter-writing (whether for business matters or to maintain contacts with family and friends) is one of the many scribal pursuits for which a very limited amount of paper might have been required by the copyist who was also a potential book compiler. In this context, see G.A. Lester's brief account of the stock of watermarked paper shared by some of the Paston letters and part of the Paston 'Grete Boke', in *Sir John Paston's 'Grete Boke'*, p. 42.

88 Compare also the fate of other composite fifteenth-century miscellanies that are now wholly or partially dismembered. These include Bodleian MSS Douce 326

and Rawlinson poet. 34 (where a scribe called 'W.F.' copied the earliest items in each collection and a certain John Bygge then used the remaining space in W.F.'s quires for his own work). These are discussed further in P.R. Robinson, 'A Study of Some Aspects of the Transmission of English Verse Texts in Late Mediaeval Manuscripts', B.Litt. thesis, University of Oxford, 1972, pp. 220–4, and Guddat-Figge, pp. 267–8.

89 Described in A. Kurvinen, 'MS Porkington 10: Description with Abstracts', *NM*, 54 (1953), 33–67; the identification of scribal stints suggested here needs some revision.

90 This is a more earnest-minded late fifteenth-century anthology from the East Midlands (?), comprising a collection of English romance narratives and saints' lives, Marian items and courtesy texts, with later additions. The scribal stints which produced this collection are described in Guddat-Figge, pp. 238–40.

91 The estimate is made and the hands putatively identified in Harris, 'CUL MS Ff.1.6', Appendix III ('The Scribes'). See also n. 21 above.

92 Compare the 'convenience' arrangement of material into sections discussed above and the comments on this practice made by Doyle, 'The Manuscripts', and by N.F. Blake in his review of Robinson, *Tanner 346*, in *English Studies*, 63 (1982), 71–3.

93 These units contain respectively Clanvowe's *Boke of Cupide* and an extract from Chaucer's *Legend of Good Women*; see V.J. Scattergood, 'The Authorship of *The Boke of Cupide*', *Anglia*, 82 (1964), 137–49, at 141. The present anomalous position of *Sir Degrevant*, the only Middle English romance in the collection, copied by two scribes and straddled across two gatherings in a very composite section of the miscellany, may well, after future close scrutiny, permit the peeling away of additional layers of scribal activity.

94 Described by P. Hardman, 'A Mediaeval "Library In Parvo"', *Medium Aevum*, 47 (1978), 262–73.

95 For the beginnings of an attempt to draw together information about the ways in which some literary items circulated and books were produced and read in the north-east Midlands, see T. Turville-Petre, 'Some Medieval English Manuscripts in the North-East Midlands', in Pearsall, *Manuscripts and Readers*, pp. 125–41.

96 Despite certain points of similarity in their working methods, a distinction might still be maintained here between the type of booklet 'publication' enjoyed by literary material copied by someone with the interests and resources of the 'Hammond scribe' (to take the most obvious metropolitan example), and the booklets produced by someone like Heege, whose resources were much more limited and whose audience may well have been restricted to the same readership as that for which his completed volume was intended.

97 This quasi-philanthropic attitude towards the circulation of Middle English texts achieved more formal expression in the period in the activities of those pious London laymen who were engaged in the commissioning of specialised devotional miscellanies for 'a comyn profit' rather than for hard cash. Typical examples of such books, written so that they could pass 'from personne to personne, man or woman, as longe as þe book enduriþ', include BL MSS Harley 933, Harley 2336, Harley 6579; Bodleian MS Douce 25, and CUL MS Ff.6.31. For details of the association of these books with religious houses in London and elsewhere, see

Doyle, *Survey*, II, pp. 208–14, and the brief comments by M.B. Parkes, 'The Literacy of the Laity', p. 568.

98 Heege's use of his stocks of watermarked paper would certainly support this theory. For example, he used the same stock of paper for the first and second quires in his collection although these once seem to have formed two quite separate units. Another stock of paper was used for the fourth surviving quire (another separate booklet) and for all but two bifolia of the three-quire unit that now forms quires seven, eight, and nine in the miscellany.

99 Consisting of a Middle English *Brut* in prose, selections from Hoccleve, and a copy of the Middle English prose *King Ponthus of Galicia*. For the Hoptons' personal interest in this decorative volume (now Bodleian, MS Digby 185), see F.J. Mather, 'King Ponthus and the Fair Sidone', *PMLA*, 12 (1897), 1–150; Pächt and Alexander, III, 86.

100 See *The Asloan Manuscript: a Miscellany in Prose and Verse Written by John Asloan in the Reign of James the Fifth*, ed. W.A. Craigie, STS (1923). For an account of Asloan's various scribal activities, including the Ewan commission, see C.C. van Buuren-Veenenbos, 'John Asloan, an Edinburgh Scribe', *English Studies*, 47 (1966), 365–72, at 366–8.

101 For the dialect evidence supporting a north-east Midlands provenance for this collection see the discussion in *Sir Orfeo*, ed. A.J. Bliss, Oxford English Monographs (London, 1966), p. xvii. Rate shares with Heege an interest in *Sir Ysumbras* and *The Adulterous Falmouth Squire*, as well as in versions of *Stans Puer ad Mensam* and Maidstone's psalm paraphrases. For descriptions of MS Ashmole 61, see Bliss, *Sir Orfeo*, pp. xi–xiii, and Mills, *Lybeaus Desconus*, pp. 4–6.

102 Other examples of the 'holster book', which have helped perpetuate the idea that these books may once have been the portable property of minstrels, include Lincoln's Inn MS 150 (a well-used early fifteenth-century collection of four Middle English romances and an A-text of *Piers Plowman*); Bodleian MS Douce 228 (a fifteenth-century fragment of the Middle English *Richard Coeur de Lion* that has been practically read to pieces); Oxford, Balliol College, MS 354 (the sixteenth-century miscellany of 'dyuers tales and baletts and dyueris Reconynges' belonging to the London grocer Richard Hill), and BL MS Add. 27879 (the celebrated seventeenth-century Percy Folio manuscript). However, the example of Trinity MS O.9.38 (the Glastonbury miscellany discussed above) and other fifteenth-century manuscripts which share the agenda format would suggest that the term 'holster book' is valuable only insofar as it indicates an alternative method for folding paper sheets that could then be used for a variety of writing tasks. For discussion, see G.S. Ivy, 'The Bibliography of the Manuscript Book', in *The English Library before 1700*, ed. F. Wormald and C.E. Wright (London, 1958), pp. 32–65, at p. 64, n. 71; R.H. Robbins's review of Rigg, *A Glastonbury Miscellany*, in *Anglia*, 89 (1971), 141–2; and the excellent analysis in Guddat-Figge, pp. 30–3.

103 However, for the faulty early foliation of MS Ashmole 61 which suggests some disarrangement of Rate's quires, see Mills, *Lybeaus Desconus*, pp. 4–5.

104 Comments on Rate's idiosyncratic scribal tendencies include those of Bliss, *Sir Orfeo*, p. xvii; Parkes, 'Literacy of the Laity', p. 569, and P. Robinson and F. McSparran, Introduction, *Cambridge University Library MS Ff.2.38* (London,

1979), p. xvii. Note too the reservations expressed by M. Mills in his review of this facsimile in *Medium Aevum*, 51 (1982), 246–50.

105 See the discussion in P. de Wit, 'The Visual Experience of Fifteenth-Century English Readers', D.Phil. thesis, University of Oxford, 1977, pp. 50ff.

106 For the range of material which Thornton copied, and general descriptions of his manuscripts, see K. Stern, 'The London "Thornton" Miscellany', *Scriptorium*, 30 (1976), 26–37, 201–18; and D.S. Brewer and A.E.B. Owen, Introduction, *The Thornton Manuscript: Lincoln Cathedral Library MS 91*, 2nd edn (London, 1978).

107 See *The 'Liber de Diversis Medicinis'*, ed. M.S. Ogden, EETS, os, 207 (London, 1938), pp. viii–xv; G.R. Keiser, 'Lincoln Cathedral MS 91: Life and Milieu of the Scribe', *SB*, 32 (1979), 158–79, and 'More Light on the Life and Milieu of Robert Thornton', *SB*, 36 (1983), 111–19.

108 The comparison seems to create as many problems as it solves. See Stern, 'The London "Thornton" Miscellany', p. 213; Doyle, 'The Manuscripts', p. 95.

109 For the discussion of the secondhand nature of Thornton's sources see Doyle, *Survey*, 1, pp. 44, 199, and Keiser, 'More Light', pp. 116–17 (inappropriateness of the feminine forms in Thornton's copies of St Edmund's *Mirror* and Hilton's *Mixed Life* indicates that these versions were originally intended for an audience of female religious rather than for a family collection; see also n. 74 above); A. McIntosh, 'The Textual Transmission of the Alliterative *Morte Arthure*', in *English and Medieval Studies Presented to J.R.R. Tolkien*, ed. N. Davis and C.L. Wrenn (London, 1962), pp. 231–40 (a common Lincolnshire source for Thornton's copies of the *Alliterative Morte* and the *Privity of the Passion*). The Thornton collection is now the subject of a more detailed linguistic scrutiny, on the McIntosh model, by Professor Frances McSparran.

110 For a dual system of numeration in Thornton's 'medical' unit which permits the possibility that Thornton's copy of the *Liber de Diversis Medicinis* may have been used by readers before it was finally incorporated into his larger collection, see the note by John Thompson in *TCBS*, 8 (1982), 270–5. For brief discussion of Thornton's unorthodox compiling activities elsewhere in his collection, see Thompson's 'The Compiler in Action: Robert Thornton and the "Thornton Romances" in Lincoln Cathedral MS 91', in Pearsall, *Manuscripts and Readers*, pp. 113–24. For the network of manuscripts that are textually related to the Thornton 'religious' unit (consideration of which imposes important and necessary restrictions on the assumptions that can be drawn about Thornton's own compiling activities), see the analysis in Thompson, 'Robert Thornton and his Book Producing Activities', D.Phil. thesis, University of York, 1983, pp. 63–153.

111 For example, the idea behind Thornton's 'romance' unit may well have been inspired by a cluster of romances in one of his sources. Other 'romance' units to have survived from the period (either as complete collections or as textual clusters within larger miscellanies) include those in CUL MS Ff.2.38 (three romances in common with Thornton's collection); BL MS Egerton 2862 (three romances in common with MS Ff.2.38 and two with Thornton); PUL, R.H. Taylor Collection (*olim* Ireland–Blackburne, *olim* Bodmer; one romance shared with Thornton); Lincoln's Inn, MS 150 (one romance shared with MS Egerton 2862). A good sense of the detailed textual analysis required before any further conclusions can be drawn about the accident of the survival of these

items in multiple copies can be gained from N. Jacobs, 'The Processes of Scribal Substitution and Redaction: a Study of the Cambridge Fragment of *Sir Degarré*', *Medium Aevum*, 53 (1984), 26–48. However, for the tendency of the compilers of MS Ff.2.38 to absorb the ready-made textual sequences in their sources, see also the cluster of short religious pieces which the book shares with Cambridge, Magdalene College, MS Pepys 1548, outlined in J.R. Kreuzer, 'The Twelve Profits of Anger', *PMLA*, 53 (1938), 78–85, at 78–9, and in Robinson and McSparran, *CUL Ff.2.38*, p. ix.

112 A brief description, in need of some updating, can be found in S.M. Horrall, 'The Watermarks of the Thornton Manuscripts', *NQ*, 225 (1980), 385–6.

113 See *The Northern Passion*, ed. F.A. Foster, EETS, os, 147 (London, 1916), 13.

114 For the flotation of the 'Holy Name' passage (in chapter 44) and the 'Charity' passage (in chapter 70) in copies of Hilton's *Scale*, see Ch. 13 below; for the remarkable frequency with which survive copies of the *Prick of Conscience* reconstructed from a pastiche of different textual traditions, see Lewis and McIntosh. Compare too the situation in BL MS Cotton Vitellius C.xiii and MS Stowe 952, both containing the Middle English translation of Deguileville's *Pèlerinage de la vie humaine* attributed to Lydgate, where scribes waited in vain for a copy of Chaucer's *ABC to the Virgin* which was promised by the text (lines 19751–9) but not forthcoming in the exemplar; see the text and description in *The Pilgrimage of the Life of Man*, ed. F.J. Furnivall, EETS, es, 77, 83, 92 (London, 1899, 1901, 1904), lxvii*–lxix*, 528; and the brief account (erroneous in the case of MS Stowe 952) in Renoir and Benson, 'Lydgate', p. 2143.

115 For the London Thornton manuscript, see the revised account in John Thompson's *Robert Thornton and the London Thornton Manuscript* (Cambridge, 1987).

116 The discussion here is heavily indebted to A.G. Rigg, 'Medieval Latin Poetic Anthologies (1)', *Medieval Studies*, 39 (1977), 281–330, at 308–30. This article forms the first in an important series of studies of textually related 'Goliardic' anthologies continued in *Medieval Studies*, 40 (1978), 387–407; 41 (1979), 468–505; 43 (1981), 472–97.

117 Discussion of this development is beyond the scope of the present chapter, but see the comments in Ch. 13 below.

118 For discussion see E. Wilson, Introduction, *The Winchester Anthology: a Facsimile of British Library Additional MS 60577*, with an account of the music by Iain Fenlon (Cambridge, 1981). The accretion of material around an original 'core' in this collection is discussed by D. Pearsall in his review, *NQ*, 228 (1983), 161–5.

119 For Newton see R.H. Robbins, 'A Gawain Epigone', *MLN*, 58 (1943), 361–6, and 'The Poems of Humphrey Newton Esq., 1466–1536', *PMLA*, 65 (1950), 249–81.

120 For the tradition of versifying esquires to which Newton seems to belong, see Pearsall, *Old and Middle English Poetry*, p. 226.

13 · VERNACULAR BOOKS OF RELIGION

VINCENT GILLESPIE

At the end of the fourteenth century, 'the literate laity were taking the clergy's words out of their mouths'. By the reign of Elizabeth, 'the private citizen had become articulate in the presence of the deity'.[1] The major developments in the production of religious books in the period 1375 to 1475 are responses to, and catalysts of, the rapidly developing interest in and market for vernacular guides to godliness.[2] The fifteenth century witnessed an extensive and consistent process of assimilation by the laity of techniques and materials of spiritual advancement, which had historically been the preserve of the clerical and monastic orders. Some manuscripts also reveal increasingly sophisticated if often unsustained attempts to facilitate the use of books through the application to vernacular texts of learned techniques of layout and systems of apparatus. Texts which had originally been written for the limited needs of enclosed communities were adapted, translated and quarried to supply the needs of a wider clerical and lay audience, and classics of spirituality from the twelfth and thirteenth centuries enjoyed new leases of life in the fifteenth.

The ecclesiastical legislation of the thirteenth century had established a required syllabus of parochial instruction and a structural norm for manuals catering for it. During the same period most dioceses had developed networks for the distribution of legislation: archdeacons held the exemplars from which priests were expected to copy the decrees. The copies were, on occasion, to be brought to convocations where the texts would be corrected and updated, and where the priest might be examined in his knowledge of them.[3] The archdeacons acted in effect as diocesan 'stationers'. This network for text distribution and copying was perhaps used for the dissemination of Archbishop Thoresby's decrees (1357), and was in use in at least one English diocese in the fifteenth century.[4]

Wich's injunction that his priests should copy the legislation *in libellis suis* suggests that this system may have encouraged the development of a certain type of book – the clerical miscellany – into which material could be copied as it came to hand.[5] The predominance of Latin in these miscellanies, and the personal, practical and occasional nature of many of them, hardly encouraged the development of substantial lay interest in and demand for volumes of this type. But Thoresby's decision to publish in a vernacular translation his restatement and updating for the Northern province of Archbishop Pecham's earlier decrees reflects a growing awareness and exploitation of the vernacular in catechetic contexts. This facilitated lay access to such texts (although not as directly or deliberately as the Lollards suggested) and stimulated the production of vernacular miscellanies by analogy with the earlier Latin collections.[6]

Although the typical clerical miscellany of the period was still likely to contain more Latin than English, and Latin pastoral and contemplative texts continued to be produced in significant numbers, the surviving manuscripts suggest that the main impetus was towards copies of works in the vernacular.[7] This was not only because of the expanding lay audience but also because some priests realised the potential of such texts for pastoral work and for use by the less literate members of the clergy themselves. It was not just laymen who suffered from 'defaute of bokus and sympulnys of letture'.[8] The former awareness of a traditional distinction between the audience for works in Latin, French or English (well attested in the works of Rolle, for example) gave way to a new, more pragmatic view of the appropriate language for a religious text in the course of the fourteenth century. The *Speculum Vitae*, which was in circulation before 1384, rejects the use of Latin and French, preferring English 'þat es yhour kynde langage':

> For þat langage es mast schewed
> Als wele amonge lered als lewed.[9]

It is consistent with the new-found respectability of the vernacular in religious contexts that in the fourteenth century the most striking development in pastoral aids is the emergence of manuscripts in which a number of distinct vernacular texts have been brought together to form a sequence providing instruction in the fundamental beliefs and disciplines of the Church; in effect an *ad hoc* manual of pastoral and catechetic material, similar in kind but somewhat narrower in focus than the Latin miscellanies.[10] It seems probable that the widespread use of such collections in schools soon expanded into a wider market.[11] Significant numbers of manuscripts, both amateur and professional productions, testify to the popularity of these catechetic aids.[12]

Oxford, Bodleian Library, MS Rawlinson C.209, for example, begins with a Cross Row and a sequence covering the teaching syllabus, augmented by the Eight Tokens of Meekness (Jolliffe G.12), the Sixteen Conditions of Charity (Jolliffe G.4), the Four Tokens of Salvation, and texts on the Name of Jesus and on reading and listening to Scripture. These simple devotional texts expand the utility of the basic catechetic manual. The book is written in one hand and the separate items are unified by a standard apparatus, forming a collection of the sort that might well have been professionally produced for casual sale. Such collections are sometimes preserved in separate booklets in manuscripts containing other texts. A striking example of a *libellus* of syllabus material is preserved in Oxford, New College, MS 67, the bulk of which is occupied by an elaborate vernacular New Testament. It is preceded by a separate bifolium in a hand similar to, but not the same as, the main text hand, which contains the Sixteen Conditions of Charity and lists of the Decalogue, Bodily Virtues and Ghostly Wits, with consistent marginal rubrication, providing basic catechetic material in what might well have been a family Bible. Such small pamphlets containing material covering the teaching syllabus possibly circulated independently. But these texts could also be subsumed into larger collections.[13] In Harley 1706, the syllabus material, overlapping in part but never fully with that in other manuscripts, has been assembled from a variety of sources to form a didactic sequence.[14] Even copies of large, apparently self-sufficient texts often include an *ad hoc* manual to enhance the usefulness of the volume, as several copies of the *Prick of Conscience* show.[15]

Translation and adaptation remained primarily the responsibility of the clergy because of their inherited expertise. As Pecock puts it, they

kunnen write bookis groundly and fruytfully and formaly and treuly, vnwasstly and saverosely.

The continuing importance of clerical intermediaries, repeatedly stressed by Pecock, is demonstrated by the English translation of Suso's *Orologium Sapientie*, and the second translation of a Kempis's *De Imitacione Christi*. Both were made by clerics at the instigation of lay people.[16] As the laity began to extend the application of its literacy to religious and devotional texts, books moved more freely between clerical and lay readers.[17]

The precise extent of this movement remains unclear. The evidence of the surviving manuscripts points to extensive ownership of vernacular religious books by religious houses and the clergy. Similar evidence for lay ownership is patchier and more limited. However, this may owe something to the accidents of preservation and perhaps to a tendency among laymen to bequeathe or donate books to religious houses, churches and members of the clergy. Testamentary evidence and comments in vernacular texts suggest a developing interest in and ownership of vernacular religious books among the laity.[18]

Moreover, books were produced to order specifically for lay readers. Four manuscripts contain inscriptions explaining that they were made at the expense of particular individuals, all London merchants of the early fifteenth century, for 'a comyne profite'.[19] These books were to be circulated amongst acquaintances, and at the death of the instigator each book was to be left to another individual who would continue the circulation. A fifth manuscript contains the inscription without the name of an individual: the book is said to have been 'maad of þe goodis of a certeyne persoone' (see fig. 27).[20] This type

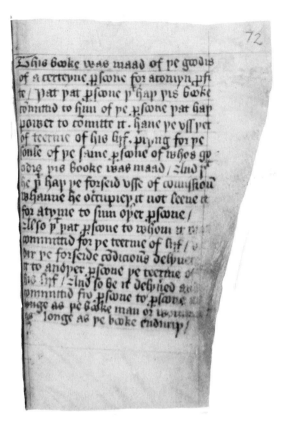

27   Oxford, Bodleian Library, MS Douce 25, fol. 72r, a 'common profit' inscription (see p. 319).

of purchase may have been so familiar to stationers that books were made in
advance of a specific order, although the anonymity may have been motivated by piety. The original purpose of the books seems to have been
frustrated in the case of BL MS Harley 993, which at some point came into
the possession of Syon, but this illustrates the characteristic tendency of
material of this kind to circulate as easily among religious as among lay
communities. Moreover, the evidence of Peter Idley's impressive command of
his Latin sources should remind us that the laity was capable of independent
access to and intelligent translation and interpretation of the *originalia*.[21]

The authors and compilers of vernacular texts responded to the extension
of the potential audience by referring explicitly to both priests and laymen as
possible users of their works. At the simplest level such references are not
more than formulaic invocation of *lered* and *lewed*. A version of David of
Augsburg's *De Exterioris et Interioris Hominis Compositione* explicitly sees the act
of translation opening the text to a new audience:

And thought yt so be that thys booke . . . towche principally the religious persons, neuer the later every seculer man or womman . . . may fynde here in sufficient instruccion.[22]

The versatility of particular religious texts was extended in another way. Not only was primarily monastic and clerical material being made available to the laity, but texts written for the particular circumstances of female religious (which had achieved, somewhat earlier, extension of their audience into the ranks of the pious noble and gentlewomen) were being addressed to laymen. Thus a treatise 'aʒence fleshly affeccions' emphasises its wider utility:

þouʒ þis tretis and writyng after þe maner of spech be made to women allonly and þat for certeyn causys yet every man havying discrecoun þat redis þerin may also take well hys lernyng and spirituall availe þerby as it had ben written to hem also specially as it is written to women.[23]

Five surviving copies of the *Ancrene Riwle* were made in the fourteenth century.[24] Adaptations in two of the manuscripts point toward audiences far beyond the anchoresses for whom it was originally composed: the Pepys text to a Lollard group, and the Vernon copy perhaps paid for by a secular patron, even if its ultimate destination may have been a religious house.[25]

A similarly extended readership evolved for the contemplative and mystical writings of Rolle and Hilton. The interests and abilities of the female religious for whom Rolle was writing in the fourteenth century are in some ways paradigmatic of those of the wider lay audience in the fifteenth. Moreover, there is ample evidence that clerical readers also came to value and exploit the resources of this vernacular tradition of spiritual guidance.

It is not surprising, therefore, that Rolle's vernacular epistles were rapidly disseminated throughout the country in the fifteenth century. Many, including even some that are of a very high textual quality, are copies in a non-northern dialect. Many can be shown to have been in secular possession, while a good proportion show signs of either clerical or religious use at some stage in their history.[26] Some copies replace the original addressee with the name of a new reader. The actual mechanics of the dissemination of the vernacular epistles are still unclear. It is possible that in Yorkshire a combination of clerical and secular interests contrived to make the hermit's English works readily available; six or seven copies conveniently bring together all three of the epistles. CUL MS Dd.5.64 looks like an attempt to collect together (in texts of unusual authority) Rolle's writings on the contemplative life. The manuscript, which preserves valuable information about the intended audience of the works, and detailed Latin colophons evincing respect for the author and knowledge of his life, was probably produced in Yorkshire early in the fifteenth century.[27]

Many of Hilton's writings were declaredly composed with a single addressee in mind: *Scale* 1, *Mixed Life* and the Latin letter to Adam Horsley appear to be responses to individual requests.[28] However, the vagueness of the address in the opening of *Scale* II suggests that its dedication may be a literary fiction. In the case of the longer English works, the frequency of their preservation is, curiously, in inverse proportion to the specificity of their dedication. *Scale* I survives in forty-five English copies, Scale II in only twenty-six; extracts from the first book are also very common, from the second rare.[29] The nature of the manuscripts suggests that dissemination was not organised: many are of relatively low quality, and there is considerable diversity of style in presentation of the text.[30] The textual evidence for book I suggests that the 'publication' may have been a good deal more complicated than the state of the manuscripts suggests, and that after the first text had been 'released' by Hilton some revisions and additions may have been supplied to early owners.[31]

Though the individual dedications found in several of Rolle's writings or in book I of Hilton's *Scale* were quickly superseded by their widespread dissemination, the author of *The Cloud of Unknowing* and its related treatises seems to have attempted to prevent such distribution and, to judge by the surviving evidence concerning ownership, to have been largely successful. In *The Cloud* itself and in the *Epistle of Privy Counselling* the author warns off inexpert readers, explicitly those in the active life, and directs the works to a primary audience of contemplatives.[32] Apart from four of the short texts which appear in one early printed book there seems to be no evidence of borrowing of material into anthologies or derivative works.[33] The signs are that the author's warnings were respected, and these warnings conditioned the appearance of copies and the preservation of the integrity of each work. Tighter control seems to have been exercised over the dissemination of the text known in its English version as *The Mirror of Simple Souls*, a translation of a French original composed by Margaret Porete, who was burnt at the stake in Paris in 1310 as a member of the sect of the Brethren of the Free Spirit.[34] Despite (perhaps because of) its dubious background, all the indications are that the text entered and circulated in England exclusively under Carthusian auspices: all three surviving manuscripts of the English version derive from Carthusian houses, and Richard Misyn, a Mount Grace Carthusian, translated the work again from English into Latin.[35] The English translator added notes to some obscure points of the difficult text, suggesting that he had perceived the heterodox nature of his original and was perhaps attempting to bring its imagery into the range familiar to readers of *The Cloud*. There is, by contrast with *The Cloud*, no internal prohibition on wide circulation, but it would seem that the Carthusians exercised some control over its dissemination.

Another Mount Grace text, Love's *Mirrour*, apparently the first complete rendering of the *Meditationes Vitae Christi*, was, by contrast, one of the most widely disseminated works of vernacular devotion.[36] A Latin memorandum preserved in a number, but by no means all, of the surviving manuscripts

28 Cambridge University Library MS Add. 6578, fol. 2v. Nicholas Love's *Mirrour of the Blessed Lyf of Jesu Christ*. Note the *ex libris* inscription of Mount Grace Carthusian house at the top, the added memorandum recording Arundel's approval, and the note at the foot (see p. 322).

explains that the translator's *originalis copia* was presented in London to Archbishop Arundel, who, having scrutinised it, returned it with his commendation and with his licence for its dissemination 'ad fidelium edificationem et hereticorum sive Lollardorum confutationem'.[37] The fact that over fifty manuscripts of the translation survive might led to the easy assumption that this is a text where licensed dissemination might most closely approximate to modern publication. But it has recently been suggested that the wording of the memorandum, its fluctuating position and occasional omission from the manuscripts, and its addition along with other marginalia in one important early copy, indicate that Arundel was authorising a text that had already been in existence for some years and had entered circulation before his inspection.[38] That the text itself was not stable is clear from the inclusion in two manuscripts of different versions (Love's and an earlier rendering) of the section describing Christ's passion; Love may have begun his work either as an expansion of that earlier translation or as a deliberate alternative to it.[39]

The presentation of the text to Arundel occurred in London, far from the northern area in which Love ended his life. To what extent the circulation of copies derived from a single northern exemplar is unclear: the note in the early manuscript, CUL Add. MS 6578, 'caue de istis verbis gude pro gode Item hir pro heere in pluralitate' (fol. 2v) (illustrated in Ill. 28) warns of the linguistic problems that might face a metropolitan scribe in copying from a northern exemplar, and implies that this manuscript, which belonged at one stage to the northern Carthusian house of Mount Grace, was prepared as an exemplar. But translation was early and complete in some cases, as is evident from the copy now in the Foyle collection; the language of the main scribe is localisable to Essex. The copy has the *ex libris* inscription of Sybilla de Felton, abbess of Barking, who died in 1419, and hence must have been made within a few years of Arundel's licence.[40] Copying of the *Mirrour* was not limited to any monastic order. One manuscript is in the hand of a scribe who also copied a number of long secular texts and who seems to have been a metropolitan freelance often working to commission.[41]

The release of a text by a medieval author did not necessarily mark the end of his involvement with it. Equally, once released, a text might be developed and changed beyond the author's control, without indication of non-authorial intervention in any one copy. Furthermore, regardless of the original intentions of authors (or compilers), or of later editors, the manuscripts of most religious texts are likely to suggest a range of identifiably different uses to which each was put. The vernacular *Visitacio Infirmorum* (Jolliffe L.5), for example, illustrates McFarlane's claim about the spiritual emancipation of the laity. The text is often found in copies of the *Manuale*, or of the *Missal*, suggesting that its admonitions to and preparations of the dying were being employed in pastoral contexts.[42] In BL Add. MS 32320, a *Manuale*, the *Visitacio* is the only vernacular text in the manuscript, and it is rubricated and divided by analogy with the liturgical texts. Cambridge, Gonville and Caius College, MS 209, another *Manuale*, includes the *Visitacio* (in a variant form) as part of a self-contained quire, inserted into the manuscript, which contains the *Forms of Absolution* for those on the point of death, the *Visitacio* in catechism form, a hymn in praise of God who raised Lazarus, the *De profundis*, and the *Requiem eternam*. The quire is just the sort of practical booklet that could well have circulated independently, containing a sequence of texts dealing in this case with the approach of and immediate sequel to death.

With the expansion of the lay market, and particularly the accelerating demand for *ars moriendi* material, the *Visitacio* soon moved out of the context of clerical and practical collections into the more ambiguous world of the devotional miscellany. BL Royal 17.A.xxvi, for example, uniformly quired and ruled, and written in one hand for most of its contents, appears to be a professionally produced collection for the vernacular market. It contains an extensive *ad hoc* manual, together with *Foure þingis þat neden to men* (Jolliffe I.9), *þe visitacioun of syk men*, and a glossed translation of the Apocalypse. The book caters for a man's needs from the cradle to the grave, and beyond to the Last Judgment. Its contents have been assembled with some care; the *Visitacio* is probably included for the reflexive value of its *contemptus mundi* theme and its encouragement to self-knowledge and self-assessment.

Miscellany manuscripts are frequently governed by an inscrutable internal logic and even more often by the random acquisition of material. Occasionally, however, a compiler explains his intentions as he marshals his material, indicating the rationale of the collection. In Manchester, John Rylands University Library, MS English 85, a sequence of didactic and devotional texts on the rudiments of the faith is provided with an introduction, exlaining that they are intended 'to helpe euery persoone þat þenkiþ to be saued'. After this initial exposition of the syllabus there is 'a prolog for more declaracioun of þingis þat goen bifore' (fol. 19r–v). This explains that, in the first sequence, the Commandments were 'but schortli declarid' and only the texts of the *Pater Noster* and Creed were provided. Therefore the texts following the prologue will discuss the Twelve Lettings of Prayer ('whereþoruȝ men moun knowe þe beter whi men ben not hered in her praier of god alwei'), provide a further exposition of the Creed, and 'for as moche as charite and loue comprehendiþ alle þe comaundementis', discuss the responsibilities of loving God and our neighbour. At the end of these texts, a peroration explains that this love is the end of 'al goddis lawe and al declaracioun þerof as in þis short co(m)pilacioun and all oþer tretiis'. The Rylands manuscript is in one professional book-hand throughout, with a uniform apparatus keying the texts into the editorial framework provided by the compiler, and although the manuscript had other texts added to it in the fifteenth century, the quiring suggests that the sequence was originally intended to be a self-contained structural unit.[43]

Such thematic cohesion is by no means the rule, however, even in well produced books. One way of 'reading' Bodleian Library, MS Laud misc. 210, for example, would be to regard it as a collection of 'forms of living'; it contains the *Book to a Mother*, the *Life of Soul*, and the *Abbey* and *Charter of the Abbey of the Holy Ghost* (explicitly aimed at an audience in the world wishing to live in some way under religious discipline). But it also contains the *Visitacio*, two decalogue treatises, discussion on the uses of tribulation (ubiquitous in such collections in the fifteenth century) and a confession formula. The collection was probably developed from a core of texts: the first, Rolle's *Form of Living*, occupies a booklet of its own in a hand and format different from those in the rest of the book, and the sequence of extant signatures begins with the quire after the Rolle; later additions include the *Abbey of the Holy Ghost* (perhaps to complement the *Charter* already copied). The book would be difficult to use casually; there is no consistent apparatus, and rubrics and titles are found variously at the beginnings or ends of texts (perhaps reflecting the characteristics of different exemplars). Yet scriptural texts have been carefully identified in the margins, and the book was carefully executed.

Whatever governed the process of selection, compilers and collectors felt little compunction when excerpting and rearranging material from other texts. As Pecock says:

for þe dyuers ententis of þe treter in oon book and in an oþer, þe ordris of þe same maters tretid bi hem in þe oon book in þe oþer may conueniently and allowabily be chaungid and dyuersid.[44]

The important criterion is not the integrity of the text, but its utility in context. Sermon manuscripts, for instance, regularly fail to distinguish between the original work and added material; Myrc's *Festial* is often excerpted or augmented without indication of a change of author, and the *Northern Homily Cycle* exists in three versions, variously altered and supplemented.[45] Thus Pecock, envisaging the criticism that his works will 'passe the capacity and þe receyuablenes of ful manye persoonys', recommends that:

summe extractis or out drauȝtis be maad into smaler bokis and treticis proporcianable and euere meete to ech mannys mesure of receyuablenesse.

An apparently random collection can represent a process of gradual collection or simply the accidental accretion of material, or may reflect the taste of a particular patron or collector, or the speculative activity of a bookseller. The detailed evidence at present available casts little light on the balance between professional copying and promotion of such collections, and the exercise of individual initiative in the acquisition and copying of texts.

Not surprisingly, the nature, contents and availability of exemplars could affect the order and contents of a collection. As Dr Doyle has shown in his account of the relationship between Oxford, University College, MS 97 and the Simeon manuscript, the contents of collections of this kind may tell us less about the interests of a particular collector than about the availability of certain texts in certain areas and in certain groupings.[46] The partial repetition of a series of texts in a group of manuscripts might be accounted for by the bringing together of distinct physical units (booklets or quires, for example, containing one or more complete texts) drawn from whatever source and variously combined to form collections. Any such collection could in turn become an exemplar itself, and could have further material added to it.

In a relatively closed literary, devotional, social or geographical environment, the repertoire of available texts may have been restricted. But even under such circumstances, selection and discrimination were not denied to the collector of such materials.[47] Manuscripts apparently derived from common exemplars do not always reproduce the texts in the order of the exemplar; nor do they necessarily reproduce all the texts of the exemplar.

These patterns may be observed in a group of metropolitan manuscripts containing copies of the *Book of the Craft of Dying* (Jolliffe L. 4(a)) and the *Treatise of Ghostly Battle* (Jolliffe H.3).[48] The grouping of the contents in manuscripts of both texts must have been derived from the exemplars.[49] Two manuscripts containing both texts are the work of the same scribe. One of these originally preserved the same contents in the same order as another manuscript by a different scribe.[50] Certain of these manuscripts were owned by members of the gentry and merchant classes of fifteenth-century London, and the cohesion of the contents, order and copying may be explained by their production to satisfy local demand.[51] In the case of the *Book of the Craft of Dying*, it is possible to trace the development of a pattern of dissemination, from its circulation as an independent text, through a grouping with other commonly associated texts into booklets, to the final stage of incorporating such groups of texts into larger and possibly more heterogeneous collections.[52]

It may be that Rolle's works also circulated quite extensively in booklet form. The *Form of Living*, the longest of the vernacular epistles, occupies a separate booklet added to the beginning of MS Laud misc. 210. Bodleian Library, MS Ashmole 1524 also preserves the text in a booklet from which unused pages at the end of the second quire have been cut away. MS Bodley 110 preserves the *Form* in a booklet preceded by a Latin *Disputacio inter Corpus et Animam*. Booklet circulation was also common for sequences of devotional texts. Rawlinson C.285 contains four booklets: the first and fourth contain books i and ii of *The Scale of Perfection*, the second and third the *Form of Living* and other short devotional texts.[53] Booklet ii opens with the *Form of Living*, in which the mode of address has been changed from the original Margaret to

Cicely, suggesting that it (or its exemplar) was made for a religious, or a devout laywoman. Later in the century the book belonged to a dominus Johannes Marchal, perhaps a Yorkshire secular priest. Two other manuscripts, CUL Ff.5.40 and CUL Dd.5.55, have texts in common with Rawlinson. Ff.5.40 does not have book II of the *Scale*, but adds material not in Rawlinson before and after book I of the *Scale*, which may have been derived from booklets not reproduced in, or lost from Rawlinson. Dd.5.55 is closer to Ff.5.40 than to Rawlinson. Both contain the *Commandment*, which is not in Rawlinson, and Ff.5.40 precedes the *Scale* with a booklet containing an English *Emendatio Vitae* and Hilton's *Mixed Life*. However, texts added later in Rawlinson were copied sequentially in the others; either their scribes copied what they wanted from Rawlinson (or from its constituent booklets before final arrangement), blurring the original booklet structure by continuous copying, or they had access to the texts from other sources.

Despite the widespread dissemination of the vernacular works of Rolle in miscellanies throughout the country, a large proportion of the extant copies of his vernacular works show an unusual respect for the structures in the texts: chapter divisions are usually preserved, paragraphing is extensively executed to divide the text into *sententiae*, and many of the scribes punctuate the texts in a way which suggests that some care was taken in the presentation of his works, even when they were emended for the needs of a new audience.[54]

Such care in the transmission of presentation was by no means commonplace in collections of vernacular texts. But efforts were made in some manuscripts to assist users to exploit more easily the resources of books by the provision of more explicit kinds of apparatus. These efforts were prompted by the increasing range of vernacular materials available to compilers and collectors and by the increasing sophistication of readers and of the demands they were likely to make on books. An early example is the Vernon manuscript, which has the distinct advantage over its sister compilation Simeon of a list of contents to the compendious collection of vernacular texts they both contain.[55] This transforms the book from a somewhat random collection into a working anthology. The list of *tituli* in Vernon has been added in a separate quire by a hand different from that responsible for the text. It may have been executed sometime shortly after the main task of copying, perhaps as a response to the demands of readers. The list of *tituli* gathers the incidental rubrics found within the texts in the manuscript, grouping them together under a numbered heading for each work. It not only facilitates reference to complete works but also allows access to sections of works containing matter of particular interest to a particular reader at a particular time, permitting the manuscript to be read thematically. In a sense, it becomes a spiritual encyclopaedia.

The development of the concept of *ordinatio* greatly increased the usefulness

Cheſt

of þt/ and he þt bi word is clepid
apreeſt of þt: knowe he & teche he
bi word & lyuynge þe lawe of his
lord/ leſt ellis þt he be oon of þo
þt ſeiþ poul ſpekiþ of: þt knowle-   tīm i·
chen bi mouþ & bi word þt þei kno
wen god. but þer dedis & lyuīg
þei denyen þe knowynge of hym/
of whiche man folk ſpekiþ ſeynt
ion ſeyinge/ he þt ſeiþ þt he knoiſ   ī iō 2·
god & kepiþ not his comaūdemeu-
tis: he is alier & þ is no truþe ī hī/
and ī anoþir place he ſeiþ/ he þt   ſeiī
he loueþ god & hatiþ his broþir: ī iō e
he is alier. Of ſiche manere he-
tis ſpekiþ ſeynt ambroſe. ſeyng
ī þis man Bruyerē þeꝛe leſynge: 22·q·ly c
foꝛ alle þat louen leſyngis. ben   caueте
ſones of þe deuyle/ not oonly ī falſe
woꝛdis: but ī feyned werkis is
leſynge/ ffoꝛ loue it is a leſynge

29   Oxford, Bodleian Library, MS Bodley 3, fol. 63r. *Pore Caitif*. Note the four marginal references, the first three biblical and the last to canon law (see p. 332).

of Latin compilations, and similar techniques were applied to the design of some vernacular compilations.[56] CUL Hh.1.12 is a spiritual miscellany made up of extracts from longer works (including the *Pore Caitif*, the vernacular *Stimulus Amoris* and the *Form of Living*), following an extremely popular pattern which began with texts related to the standard teaching syllabus and progressed to more advanced spiritual instruction. The compiler borrowed from his three main sources in sequential blocks, choosing material loosely related to the development of spiritual love (other sources include Hilton's *Eight Chapters on Perfection* and the *Prayer and Confession of St Brandan*). The text is preceded by a Kalendar 'that maketh mencyoun of all the chapettells þat ben in þe book'. This listing was executed after the main work of compilation had been completed and is preserved in a quire added at the beginning of the book. It is written in a hand somewhat later than the main hand of the text, and the division into chapters within the text has been indicated by marginal rubric chapter numbers, apparently added by this hand. Again this apparatus facilitates consultation, and non-sequential reading.[57]

Less versatile are lists of contents of a complete volume. Bodleian Library, MS Douce 322 'in whome is contente dyuers deuowte tretis and specyally þe tretis þat is callid ars moriendi' (fol. ir) has a list of contents in the first quire, which contains a donation note, and which may have been added to the volume after the rest had been copied and before it was presented to Pernelle Wrattisley a nun at the Dominican priory of Dartford, and *nece* of the donor, William Baron.[58] Baron was an officer in the Royal Exchequer and active in London affairs between 1430 and 1470; it seems to have been at his instigation that the anthology was put together. The manuscript's contents correspond to the first and major part of MS Harley 1706 (linked with Barking Abbey), and it seems likely that Harley was copied from Douce. Doyle has argued that Douce was put together in a professional scriptorium, using materials from various sources, and that the Harley copy was made from it after it had gone to Dartford. A complex network of associations existed between Dartford and the Essex nunnery at Barking that, typically, involves the movement of books and texts through family, and often lay, intermediaries.

In longer texts, apparatus could be an integral part of the design of the work. The Harley manuscript also contains the *Contemplations of the Dread and Love of God*, or *Fervor Amoris* (one of the texts it does not share with Douce). To judge by the ownership of copies, it circulated widely in religious use, although it seems to have been intended for lay people.[59] *Fervor Amoris* is extensively indebted (without acknowledgment) to Rolle and Hilton, although, once again typically, the prologue makes no attempt to dispel the illusion of a single author. The text is preceded by a Kalendar of the chapters, which in most copies are assigned a letter of the alphabet. The prologue makes it clear that the material has been carefully ordered:

30   London, British Library, MS Harley 2409, fols. 1v–2r. *Contemplations of the Dread and Love of God*, showing part of the alphabetical list of chapters and the secondary division into four degrees of love (see p. 330).

This shorte epystle that foloweth is dyuyded in sondry maters & eche mater by hymselfe in sondry tytles ... And þat thou mayst sone fynde what mater the pleaseth these tytles ben here in the Epystle marked with dyuerse lettres in maner of a table.[60]

The apparatus is an integral part of the work, and the compiler was envisaging users who would wish to refer to sections of the compilation (see Ill. 30). Although similarly elaborate apparatuses are found in other vernacular texts (like Love's *Mirrour*), it is noticeable that most copies of the *Fervor Amoris* are not de luxe manuscripts but rather unpretentious working books: the text is a sophisticated workhorse rather than a devotional thoroughbred.

In the case of Love's *Mirrour*, there is a considerable degree of similarity in layout and apparatus in the extent manuscripts. Most copies have the long chapter headings prominently displayed in red. Rubricated running titles indicate a double division of the material; conventionally by chapters, and by days of the week (a structuring of the text which is original to this version).[61] The authorities cited within the text are regularly identified in the margins, and Love enclosed his additions to the pseudo-Bonaventuran original between the initials N and B, as he explains in a note to the reader found in most copies:

Attende lector huius libri prout sequitur in anglico scripti quod vbicunque in margine ponitur litera. N: verba sunt translatoris siue compilatoris in anglico praeter illa que inseruntur in libro scripto secundum communem opinionem a venerabili doctore Bonauentura in latino de meditacione vite christi. Et quum peruenitur ad processum et verba eiusdem doctoris inseritur in margine litera.B.prout legenti siue intuenti istum librum speculi vite christi poterit apparere.[62]

Some manuscripts also note in the margin material in the text that might be used to argue against Lollard views. It has been suggested that these annotations may go back not to the earliest stages of the text's history, but rather to a stage after 1410, when someone took advantage of the implications of Arundel's licence that the *Mirrour* could be a substitute for the banned scriptural translations.[63]

The compiler of the *Pore Caitif* announces his intention of putting together a treatise to show 'symple men and wymmen of good wil' the way to heaven 'wiþouten multiplicacioun of manye bookis'.[64] Though there is an intelligible rationale for the ordering of the first half of the work, which parallels catechetic manuals, it is more difficult to see any logic in the ordering of the rest. Despite the heterogeneous origins of the compilation, the thirty surviving manuscripts that contain the whole assemblage of fourteen tracts are for the most part remarkably uniform in style of presentation and quality. The majority are uniformly small, pocket-sized volumes, written in single columns in professional book-hands, with running titles for each tract and marginal identification of the authorities cited in the text (see Ill. 29).[65] Sources are consistently identified only in the early sections of the work, possibly to signal the orthodoxy of the instruction in these catechetic tracts. This localised identification of sources may derive from the compiler's exemplar and perhaps in turn from the exemplars of the constituent texts.

Accurate scribal work might well have consisted not only in careful attention to the copying of the text but also in the perpetuation of the structures and layout of the text in the scribal exemplar. The lengths to which scribal imitation might go can be illustrated from manuscripts of the *Prick of Conscience*. Of the 115 manuscripts that may reasonably be presumed to have been originally complete, only fifteen are in a format other than a single column.[66] The octosyllabic metre of the long work would lead one to think that a double column arrangement would have been more suitable, producing an economic use of a leaf of regular shape; the result is that most of the manuscripts are of comparatively tall, narrow format.[67] Yet this uniformity cannot be the outcome of a centrally imposed decision: the linguistic evidence reveals that copying was geographically widely dispersed.

A similar case is provided by the *Speculum Vitae*, a re-ordering of material from the *Somme le Roi* into a grand synthetic double commentary on the *Pater Noster* some 16,000 lines long, often preserved on its own.[68] Given the size of the work, it is noticeable that generally no attempt is made to economise by employing double columns or stinting on provision for the apparatus. It is a paradoxical text. Although northern in origin, it achieved a national popularity, and in 1384 a Cambridge University court was convened:

propter defectus et haereses examinanda, ne minus litterati populum per eam negligenter fallant, et in varios errores fallaciter inducant,

a fact recorded in three copies as a kind of *nihil obstat*, similar to that provided by Arundel for Love's *Mirror*.[69] Although probably written for oral performance and for an audience of little theological sophistication, most manuscripts contain an elaborate Latin apparatus. The arrangement of the material may be derived from an earlier Latin *tabula* on the *Pater Noster*, traces of which seem to surface in the marginal apparatus which signposts the subdivisions of the text. The manuscripts are usually quarto-size but several are in holster book format. The invariable appearance of some form of apparatus suggests that it was an original feature of the work and not an accretion through use.[70] In many copies the page is prepared to accommodate the apparatus as an integral and important part of the text. In Bodley 446, for example, the written space is shifted over towards the gutter, and a separate ruled column provided in the outer margin for the apparatus (see Ill. 31). A second layer of apparatus in the manuscripts is provided by running titles in the top margin. Here the manuscripts divide three ways. A few have no running titles at all. Some have descriptive running titles which pinpoint material on a particular subject (e.g. *De Statu Religiosorum*). The most sophisticated manuscripts, including the largest copies, have a synthetic running title which, in the second commentary, provides an account of how the different heptads relate to each other.[71]

In a sense, the visual awareness shown by the copyists of the *Speculum Vitae* is a recognition that the work would be consulted as well as listened to, not merely in sequential sections but in a more random and selective way, a possibility which the text itself seems to confirm.[72] Most of the surviving copies date from the first half of the fifteenth century, suggesting that despite its somewhat dated criticisms of ballads and lewd songs, the work was flourishing in the new devotional environment. The interest shown in the text by religious might be explained by their natural inclination to collect works which would easily lend themselves to communal reading. Nevertheless, as the *Speculum* was the nearest thing to a vernacular *summa* produced in the period, the apparently extensive and careful production of copies was unlikely to have been solely in response to this demand. The importance of the apparatus and perhaps its usefulness is suggested by its retention in the manuscripts of the *derimage* version, *The Myrrour of Lewd Men and Women*.[73]

The different levels of the apparatus in copies of the *Speculum Vitae* may be tied to the textual affiliations of the manuscript groups; but the development of levels of apparatus of differing degrees of complexity and sophistication

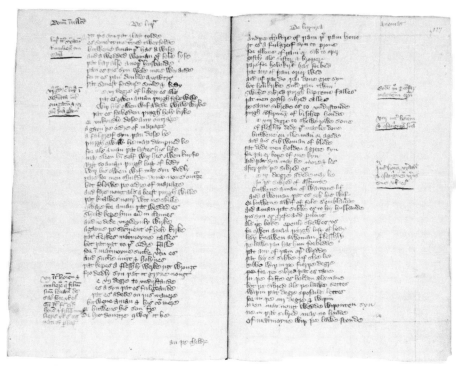

31   Oxford, Bodleian Library, MS Bodley 446, fols. 126v–127r. *Speculum Vitae*, showing the marginal annotation and running titles indicating the Deadly Sin, Gift of the Spirit and Petition of the *Pater Noster* under consideration (see p. 332).

suggests that thought was given to the range of demands which might be made upon the text. While the relatively uniform transmissions of the levels of apparatus may have depended upon faithful copying, their original generation cannot have done.

Yet it is by no means always the case that a complex textual apparatus was preserved in the dissemination of a substantial text, as the manuscripts of *Dives and Pauper* show.[74] The text has a clearly defined structure: it is a dialogue between Pauper the cleric and Dives, an educated layman, which is organised by topic through commentary on the ten commandments. The author took pains to indicate within the text the biblical, patristic or canonical authority for many of Pauper's observations. The material within each commandment was also divided into chapters, a detailed list of which is provided at the beginning of the work. But this organisation is not reflected in the ten surviving complete manuscripts. The presentation of the text in these copies is very diverse. Some manuscripts articulate the structures of the text by clearly differentiating speakers, providing chapter headings and running titles, and by marking authorities. Other copies fail to signal these features in any way, making the text very difficult to follow.[75] Presumably the circumstances at the early stages of dissemination of *Dives and Pauper* were quite different from those obtaining in the case of the *Pore Caitif*, the *Speculum Vitae* and other texts.

With characteristic, if idealistic perception, Pecock in the *Book of Faith* highlights the changed pastoral context in which books of religion were being produced in the fifteenth century:

> it is not ynouȝ that the seid bokis be writen and made and leid up or rest in the hondis of clerkis . . . but tho bokis musten be distributid and delid abroad to manye.[76]

Religious books did circulate among a wider readership, and changed to accommodate the needs and abilities of their audience. Attempts were made to increase the utility of some collections and compilations, but many, perhaps most, remained idiosyncratic in their organisation. Attempts were made to organise the circulation of some texts or groups of texts, but the transmission of many, perhaps most, remains unclear. The complexities and uncertainties in the production of religious books are such that those seeking for firmer answers must, in Pecock's words, 'take long leiser, forto sadli be wel aqueyntid with the bokis, and with the skills and motivis therynne writen'.[77]

NOTES

1 K.B. McFarlane, *Lancastrian Kings and Lollard Knights* (Oxford, 1972), p. 204; Louis B. Wright, *Middle Class Culture in Elizabethan England* (Chapel Hill, 1935), p. 241.

2 References for individual works are given in the footnotes below. P.S. Jolliffe, *A Check-list of Middle English Prose Writings of Spiritual Guidance* (Toronto, 1974) is a very useful guide to the anonymous texts that it covers, but it excludes the major writers and texts, much didactic writing, most compilations and all sermons or works tinged with Lollardy. R. Raymo, 'Works of Religious and Philosophical Instruction', in *A Manual of the Writings in Middle English*, ed. A.E. Hartung, 7 (Hamden, Conn., 1986), provides updated bibliographies and lists of manuscripts for many didactic and catechetical works. V.M. Lagorio and R. Bradley, *The 14th-Century English Mystics: A Comprehensive Annotated Bibliography* (New York and London, 1981) concentrates on Rolle, *The Cloud*, Hilton, Julian of Norwich and Margery Kempe, contains no details about manuscripts and is not exhaustive. P. Revell, *Fifteenth Century English Prayers and Meditations A Descriptive List of Manuscripts in the British Library* (New York and London, 1975) deals only with the one collection, but that haphazardly, omitting some texts that might be expected and including others that would not. On ownership, see the valuable recent thesis by Susan Cavanaugh, 'A Study of Books Privately Owned in England 1330–1450', unpublished Ph.D. thesis (University of Pennsylvania, 1980), soon to be published in Boydell and Brewer's *Manuscript Studies* series. Ownership by religious houses is ascertainable from N.R. Ker, *Medieval Libraries of Great Britain* (London, 2nd edn,

1964); Carthusian houses and some nunneries of several orders held a large number of vernacular works. One of the most useful discussions, to which the present chapter is deeply indebted, is the unpublished dissertation of Doyle, *Survey*.

3 See C.R. Cheney, *English Synodalia of the Thirteenth Century* (Oxford, 1941, rpt with new intro. 1968), pp. 45–7; 'Legislation of the Medieval Church', *EHR*, 50 (1935), 193–224, 385–417, at 208–17; *Councils and Synods*, II *(1205–1313)*, ed. F.M. Powicke and C.R. Cheney (Oxford, 1964), pp. 179, 319, 435. Several bishops published their own manuals to assist their parish clergy: *Councils and Synods*, pp. 214–26, 1059–77; *English Synodalia*, pp. 149–52.

4 D. Wilkins, *Concilia Magnae Britanniae et Hiberniae*, 4 vols. (London, 1737), III, p. 72. In 1435 a vernacular exposition of the Pechamite syllabus was promulgated for Bath and Wells, and archdeacons were to oversee its distribution: see *The Register of John Stafford, Bishop of Bath and Wells 1425–1443*, ed. T.S. Holmes, II, Somerset Record Society 32 (1916), pp. 173–80.

5 Statutes of Chichester I (1245 × 52), cap. 79, *Councils and Synods*, p. 467.

6 For the Lollard use of Thoresby's decision, see M. Deanesly, *The Lollard Bible* (Cambridge, 1920), p. 141; C. Bühler, 'A Lollard Tract: On Translating the Bible into English', *Medium Aevum*, 7 (1938), 167–83. On Latin pastoral miscellanies, see W.A. Pantin, *The English Church in the Fourteenth Century* (Cambridge, 1955), ch. 9, and Appendix II; V. Gillespie, 'The Literary Form of the Middle English Pastoral Manual, with Particular Reference to the *Speculum Christiani* and some related texts', unpublished D.Phil. thesis (Oxford, 1981), ch. 3.

7 The Latin tradition lies outside the scope of this chapter. On the Latin *pastoralia*, see L.E. Boyle, 'A Study of the Works attributed to William of Pagula with special reference to the *Oculis Sacerdotis* and *Summa Summarum*', unpublished D.Phil. thesis (Oxford, 1956); Pantin, *English Church*, ch. 9; Gillespie, 'Literary Form', *passim*. The religious orders continued to produce Latin mystical works, and even translated some vernacular treatises into Latin; Pantin, *English Church*, ch. 11; J.P.H. Clark, 'English and Latin in the *Scale of Perfection* – Theological Considerations', in *Spiritualität Heute und Gestern*, 1, Analecta Cartusiana 35 (1982), pp. 167–212; J. Hogg, 'The Latin *Cloud*', in *The Medieval Mystical Tradition in England: Dartington 1984*, ed. M. Glasscoe (Cambridge, 1984), pp. 104–15. On the currency of earlier monastic and spiritual writings in the later Middle Ages, see G. Constable, 'Twelfth-Century Spirituality and the Late Middle Ages', *Medieval and Renaissance Studies*, 5 (1971 for 1969), 27–60; 'The Popularity of Twelfth-Century Spiritual Writers in the late Middle Ages', in *Renaissance Studies in Honor of Hans Baron*, ed. A. Melho and J.A. Tobaschi (North Illinois, 1971), pp. 5–8. On translated devotional texts in Middle English, see the useful survey by M. Sargent, 'Minor Devotional Writings', in Edwards, *Middle English Prose*, pp. 147–75.

8 From the Prologue to Myrc's *Festial* (not printed by Erbe), BL Cotton Claudius A.II, fol. 3v. A vernacular exposition of Pecham's decree (Jolliffe A.2) *made in oure moder tunge for diuerse causes*, is intended for 'symple curates curales or upplandisshe', see P. Hodgson, '*Ignorantia Sacerdotum*: a Fifteenth-Century Discourse on the Lambeth Constitutions', *RES*, 24 (1948), 1–11. BL Sloane 1584 is a vernacular pastoral miscellany, linked with the Premonstratensian canons of Coverham (Ker, *Medieval Libraries*, p. 55).

9 BL Add. 33995, fol. 1r; cf. *Memoriale Credencium*, ed. J.H.L. Kengen (Nijmegen, 1979): 'taketh hede to þis litul tretys þat is y write in englisch tong for lewed men þat konne not vnderstonde latyne ne frenssche' (p. 37). For other examples, see V. Gillespie, 'Lukynge in haly bukes: *Lectio* in some late Medieval Spiritual Miscellanies', in *Spätmittelalterliche Geistliche Literatur in der Nationalsprache*, 2, Analecta Cartusiana 106 (1984), pp. 1–27, esp. p. 7.

10 Cf. A.I. Doyle, 'A Treatise of the Three Estates', *Dominican Studies*, 3 (1950), 351–8; C. Bühler, 'The Middle English Texts of Morgan MS. 861', *PMLA*, 69 (1954), 686–92.

11 On the presence of didactic material in Primers, see *The Prymer ab. 1400*, ed. H. Littlehales, II (London, 1892), esp. nos. II–IV, V, VI–VIII, XII–XIII; G.A. Plimpton, *The Education of Chaucer* (London, 1935), plates IX.1–IX.15. BL Add. MS 60577 contains a sequence of independent texts on the syllabus, preceded by a cross and alphabet (items 180–201). This section of the manuscript is clearly written on alternate lines of the ruling and may have been copied from or show the influence of a schoolbook: see *The Winchester Anthology: A Facsimile of B.L. Add. MS. 60577 with an introduction and list of contents by Edward Wilson and an account of the music by Iain Fenlon* (Cambridge, 1981).

12 The following list is illustrative and by no means exhaustive: Cambridge, Trinity College, MSS B.14.54 and R.3.21; CUL MSS Ii.6.43, Ff.6.55, Hh.1.12; BL MSS Harley 535, 1197, 2406, Royal 17. A.xxvi; Oxford, New College, MS 67; Oxford, Trinity College, MS E.6; Oxford, University College, MS 97; Bodleian Library, MSS Bodley 938, Add. B.6, Laud misc. 23, 174, Lyell 29, Rawlinson A.381, C.209, C.699, C.751, Tanner 336; Edinburgh UL MS 93. Some of these are discussed in greater detail below. Raymo, 24, prints an extensive list of manuscripts containing miscellaneous catechetic material.

13 E.g. Cambridge, Trinity College, MS R.3.21, where the first book (fols. 1–32) is an *ad hoc* sequence: A.I. Doyle, 'A Text attributed to Ruusbroec circulating in England', in *Dr. L. Reypens-Album*, Studien on Tekstuitgaven von Ons Geestelijk erf, 16 (1964), pp. 153–71, notes (p. 160) that the script and style resemble those of Douce 322, and that in some sections the same layout is used. On booklets, see P.R. Robinson, 'The Booklet'.

On a larger scale Harley 2406, possibly a Gilbertine volume, consists of three distinct sections containing catechetic texts. In its composite form the manuscript provides a useful compendium of pastoral and spiritual instruction, but each of the three sections is capable of independent circulation and was probably copied separately. Rawlinson A.381 has a catechetic booklet which ends *Explicit libellus de doctrina simplicium*; the other contents of the manuscript (Myrc's *Festial*) suggest that the booklet may have been in clerical hands; cf. Harley 535, where the *Memoriale Credencium* and vernacular prayers and meditations have had a set of episcopal constitutions added at the front.

14 The sequence is in verse: *IMEV* 3685, 2770, 469, 3041, 362, 1815, 1126, 505, 475, 1746. Harley 2339 has five items in common (3685, 2770, 3040, 1815, 1126) and adds 4200, 3555; Doyle, 'A Treatise of the Three Estates', p. 250. CUL Ff.2.38 has a similar sequence of verse texts: *IMEV* 3040, 3262, 1815, 1126, 2770, 4200; *Cambridge University Library MS.Ff.2.38, with an introduction by Frances McSparran and Pamela R. Robinson* (London, 1979), items 9–18. G.H. Russell, 'Vernacular Instruc-

tion of the Laity in the Later Middle Ages in England: Some Texts and Notes',
Journal of Religious History, 2 (1962–3), 98–119, prints two further verse sequences
from Bodley 549 and Hatton 12.

15 Lewis and McIntosh, *Descriptive guide*, pp. 42, 43, 56, 62, 81, 85.

16 *The Reule of Crysten Religioun by Reginald Pecock, D.D.*, ed. W.C. Greet, EETS, os, 171
(1927), p. 19. Cf. *The Folewer to the Donet by Reginald Pecock, D.D.*, ed. E.V.
Hitchcock, EETS, os, 164 (1924), p. 8; see C. Horstmann, '*Orologium Sapientie or The
Seven Poynts of Trewe Wisdom* aus MS Douce 114', *Anglia*, 10 (1888), 323–89, at 325,
line 1, and *The Earliest English Translations of the De Imitatione Christi*, ed. J.K.
Ingram, EETS, es, 63 (1893), p. 153, lines 1–9. The translations were made from
Latin rather than the respective original vernaculars: see R. Lovett, 'Henry Suso
and the Medieval Mystical Tradition in England', in *The Medieval Mystical Tradi-
tion in England*, ed. M. Glasscoe (Exeter, 1982), pp. 47–62; 'The *Imitation of Christ* in
Late Medieval England', *TRHS*, 5th series, 18 (1968), 97–121.

17 M.B. Parkes, 'The Literacy of the Laity'; M. Vale, *Piety, Charity and Literacy among
the Yorkshire Gentry, 1370–1480*, Borthwick Papers 50 (1976); Doyle, *Survey*, II,
302–22.

18 E.g., H.R. Plomer, 'Books Mentioned in Wills', *Transactions of the Bibliographical
Society*, 7 (1902–4), 14–21; M. Deanesly, 'Vernacular Books'; G.R. Owst, 'Some
Books and Book-owners of Fifteenth-Century St Albans', *St Albans and Herts.
Architectural and Archaeological Society Transactions* (1928), 176–95. For other refer-
ences, see S.L. Thrupp, *The Merchant Class of Medieval London* (Ann Arbor, 1948,
pbk 1962), pp. 161–3; J.I. Kermode, 'The Merchants of Three Northern Towns',
in *Profession, Vocation, and Culture in Later Medieval England*, ed. C.H. Clough
(Liverpool, 1983), pp. 7–49, esp. pp. 36–7. See below, n. 57.

19 BL Harley 993, Harley 2336, CUL Ff.6.31, Lambeth 472. See *The Minor Works of
Walter Hilton*, ed. D. Jones (London, 1929), pp. xi–xviii; M. Sargent, 'Walter
Hilton's *Scale of Perfection*: The London Manuscript Group Re-considered', *Medium
Aevum*, 52 (1983), 189–216, at 205–6. See also G.R. Keiser, 'Patronage and Piety in
Fifteenth-Century England: Margaret, Duchess of Clarence, Symon Wynter and
Beinecke MS 317', *Yale University Library Gazette*, 60 (1985), 32–46.

20 Bodleian MS Douce 25. In the *Book of Faith*, Pecock urges prelates and 'othere
my3ty men of good' to cause books 'to be writun in greet multitude, and to be wel
correctid, and thanne aftir to be sende, and to be govun or lende abroad amonge
the seid lay persoonys' (ed. J.L. Morison (Glasgow, 1909), p. 117). This is
described as a ghostly alms giving.

21 *Peter Idley's Instructions to his Son*, ed. Charlotte d'Evelyn (Oxford, 1935).

22 P.S. Jolliffe, 'Middle English Translations of the *De Exterioris et Interioris Hominis
Compositione*', *Mediaeval Studies*, 36 (1974), 259–77, at 274; see p. 274–5 for other
examples. Cf. *The Treatise of Ghostly Battle* (Jolliffe H.3) which invokes an audience
of priests and laymen, and the vernacular *Templum Domini*, an expansion and
reworking of Grossesteste's *tabula* on the pastoral care (*IMEV* 967), printed in R.D.
Cornelius, *The Figurative Castle* (Bryn Mawr, 1930), pp. 90–112.

23 Rawlinson C.894, fol. 98v (Jolliffe K.1); the text is incorporated into *Disce Mori*
(Jolliffe A.6) and the derivative *Ignorancia Sacerdotum* (Jolliffe A.2).

24 See the edition of BL MS Royal 8.C.1 by A.C. Baugh, EETS, os, 232 (1956), of
Cambridge, Magdalene College, MS Pepys 2498 by A. Zettersten, EETS, os, 274

(1976), and of the Latin text by C. d'Evelyn, EETS, os, 216 (1944); to these and the unprinted Vernon text should be added the printed material that derives from the *Ancrene Riwle* through a French intermediary in *The Tretyse of Loue*, ed. J.H. Fisher, EETS, os, 223 (1951).

25 On Pepys see E. Colledge, '*The Recluse*. A Lollard interpolated version of the *Ancrene Riwle*', *RES*, 15 (1939), 1–15, 129–45; on Vernon, see A.I. Doyle, 'Vernon and Simeon Manuscripts'; 'University College, Oxford, MS 97 and its relationship to the Simeon Manuscript (British Library Add. 22283)' in Benskin and Samuels, pp. 265–82, and 'English Books In and Out of Court', pp. 167–8.

26 See H.E. Allen, *Writings ascribed to Richard Rolle and Materials for his Biography* (New York and London, 1927); though this has been superseded in some particulars, and is obviously out of date for newly discovered manuscripts, it remains the standard guide. M. Deanesly 'Vernacular Books', gives some details about ownership particularly from wills; also A.I. Doyle, 'Carthusian Participation in the Movement of Works of Richard Rolle between England and Other Parts of Europe in the Fourteenth and Fifteenth Centuries', in *Kartäusermystik und -Mystiker*, 2, Analecta Cartusiana 55 (1981), pp. 109–20, and references. Much more detail about the textual affinities of Rolle's shorter works is now available in S. Ogilvie-Thomson's critical edition, EETS, OS, 293 (1988).

27 It is made up of three booklets in different hands, the second and third now deficient through loss of quires. The third booklet contains the English epistles and the attributed lyrics.

28 Book I of the *Scale* is being edited for EETS by A.J. Bliss, Book II for the same by S.S. Hussey; for some relevant material see S.S. Hussey, 'The Text of *The Scale of Perfection*, Book II', *NM*, 65 (1964), 75–92, and 'Editing the Middle English Mystics', in *Spiritualität Heute und Gestern*, 2, Analecta Cartusiana 35 (1983), pp. 160–73, esp. pp. 167–73; Sargent 'The London Group', pp. 189–216. For the shorter English writings see Lagorio and Bradley, *English Mystics*, nos. 442, 445, 465, 467–8, and C. Horstmann, *Yorkshire Writers* (London and New York, 1895–6), I, pp. 264–92; for the Latin writings see the notes to J.P.H. Clark, 'The "Lightsome Darkness" – Aspects of Walter Hilton's Theological Background', *Downside Review*, 95 (1977), 95–109.

29 The statement may well need modification when further late medieval anthologies have been studied; but *Disce Mori*, a compilation surviving in Bodleian, MS Laud misc. 99 and Oxford, Jesus College, MS 39, seems typical. Quotations from *Scale* I appear in the latter manuscript, pp. 169–70, 330–6, 613–20, 620–2, from the *Eight Chapters* on pp. 175–7 and a short extract from *Scale* II.30 on pp. 607–8. One fifteenth-century Latin compilation has extensive borrowings from the Latin *Scale* II, as well as from Rolle and the *Stimulus Amoris*: see V. Gillespie, 'The *Cibus Anime* Book 3: A Guide for Contemplatives?', in *Spiritualität Heute und Gestern*, 3, Analecta Cartusiana 35 (1983), pp. 90–119.

30 For instance CUL MS Dd.5.55; Cambridge, Trinity College, MS O.7.47; Cambridge, St John's College, MS G.35; BL MSS Harley 1022, 1035, 6573, 6579; Bodleian Library, MS Rawlinson C.285. Typical of the rather random appearance of many manuscripts is BL Harley 330: this is written in two columns, in a book-hand for the first 103 folios and thereafter in a rougher anglicana hand; it contains *Scale* I in English, followed by Rolle's *Oleum Effusum* and the *Scale* II in

Latin, but the change of hand does not coincide with the change in language. This copy, despite its roughness, is probably a professionally made manuscript; many others give the impression of being amateur productions, and were certainly designed only for private reading. Harley 330 also makes it absolutely plain that in dissemination the two books of Hilton's work were completely independent.

31 Sargent. 'The London Group', pp. 195–7. A comparable explanation would account for the variable number of chapters found in copies of the translation (whether by Hilton or not) of the *Stimulus Amoris*, and variation between those called for by the list of chapters, the numbering of chapters and the chapters actually present. There is now an edition of the text by H. Kane, *The Prickyng of Love*, Salzburg Studies in English Literature, Elizabethan and Renaissance Studies 92:10 (1983); the question of this discrepancy is considered by J.P.H. Clark, 'Walter Hilton and the *Stimulus Amoris*', *Downside Review*, 102 (1984), 79–118.

32 The standard editions are those by P. Hodgson, EETS, os, 218 (1944) and os, 231 (1955), more recently collected into a single volume without apparatus: *The Cloud of Unknowing and Related Treatises*, Analecta Cartusiana 3 (1982); references are to the EETS editions. For the warnings, see *Cloud*, pp. 1–2, 135.

33 See Hodgson, EETS 218, pp. ix–xxvii and EETS 231, pp. ix–xviii; for the printed edition, p. xiii. A summary is given in Anal. Cart., pp. xiv–xvii.

34 The text has been edited by M. Doiron in *Archivio italiano per la storia della pietà*, 5 (1968), 243–382, though for some reservations about the edition and about the comments of E. Colledge in the appendix see the review by A. Hudson, *RES*, ns, 20 (1969), 479–82.

35 The case of Carthusian transmission is accepted by M. Sargent in his otherwise somewhat cautious paper 'The Transmission by the English Carthusians of some Late Medieval Spiritual Writings', *Journal of Ecclesiastical History*, 27 (1976), 225–40, at 238–9.

36 The text was edited by L.F. Powell, *The Mirrour of the Blessed Lyf of Jesu Christ* (Oxford, 1908) using only three manuscripts; there is a study by E. Salter, *Nicholas Love's 'Myrrour of the Blesed Lyf of Jesu Christ'*, Analecta Cartusiana 10 (1974), and some comments and an updated list of manuscripts in her study of 'The Manuscripts'. See also M. Sargent, 'Bonaventura English: A survey of the Middle English Prose Translations of Early Franciscan Literature', in *Spätmittelalterliche Geistliche Literatur in der Nationalsprache*, 2, Analecta Cartusiana 106 (1984), pp. 145–76.

37 The manuscript used by Powell did not contain the licence; it is printed by Salter, pp. 1–2. It has been usual to connect the licence with Arundel's Constitutions (printed Wilkins, *Concilia*, III, pp. 314–19) in which biblical translation was forbidden and ownership, unless in an authorised version and by an approved person, of translations prescribed.

38 A.I. Doyle, 'Reflections'.

39 J. Reakes, 'The Middle English Prose Translation of the *Meditaciones de Passione Christi* and its Links with Manuscripts of Love's *Myrrour*', *NQ*, 225 (1980), 199–202. On the circulation of extracts from the *Mirrour*, see Salter, *Myrrour*, p. 9, and note particularly CUL Ii.4.9 where two separate extracts are found in different parts of the manuscript (fols. 69v and 95–6).

40 Doyle, 'Reflections', p. 86.

41 Oxford, Brasenose College, MS 9; Doyle and Parkes, pp. 206–8; the scribe copied Trevisa's translation of the *Polychronicon* more than once and Gower's *Confessio* amongst other works. A commission probably in London produced the most splendid surviving copy of the *Mirrour*, that now NLS, MS, Advocates' 18.1.7, made for Edmund, fourth Lord Grey of Ruthin following his marriage to Lady Katherine Percy, daughter of the second earl of Northumberland, in about 1460.

42 Doyle, *Survey*, I, pp. 219–24; Raymo, 215. Other copies have linked with religious houses (e.g. BL Harley 211: Norwich Carmelites) or secular clergy (e.g. Oxford, University College, MS 4: perhaps from Beverley Minster).

43 For recent descriptions of John Rylands Eng.85, see N.R. Ker, *Medieval Manuscripts in British Libraries*, III, (Oxford, 1983), p. 409 and G.A. Lester, *The Index of Middle English Prose Handlist II: Manuscripts containing Middle English Prose in the John Rylands and Chetham's Libraries, Manchester* (Cambridge, 1985), pp. 14–24. The decalogue treatise from the sequence has been discussed by A. Kellogg and E.W. Talbert, 'The Wycliffite *Pater Noster* and *Ten Commandments*, with special reference to English MSS 85 and 90 in the John Rylands Library', *BJRL*, 42 (1960), 345–77, and A. Martin 'The Middle English Versions of *The Ten Commandments* with special reference to Rylands English MS 85', *BJRL*, 64 (1981–2), 191–217. The sequence begins with a Cross Row (see n. 11 above). Other manuscripts including sections from the sequence are: Durham Cathedral MS A.IV.212, Bodleian Library, MS Laud misc. 23, BL Cotton Titus D.XIX, Cambridge, Trinity College, MSS R.3.21 and O.1.74. The process of fragmentation and emendation of the sequence to suit new contexts has yet to be investigated, so it is not clear whether the manuscripts, which all seem to be of metropolitan provenance, represent evidence of entrepreneurial variation of a repertoire of texts, or the exploitation of an organised compilation by selective recopying motivated by personal taste.

44 *Reule of Crysten Religioun*, ed. Greet, pp. 16, 22, cf. *Templum Domini*, pr. Cornelius, p. 112:

> To somme men is þis mater merke
> And to summe it is full clere'. (775–6)

45 A.J. Fletcher and S. Powell, 'The Origins of a Fifteenth-Century Sermon Collection: MSS Harley 2247 and Royal 18 B.xxv', *LSE*, NS, 10 (1978), 74–96; S. Powell, *The Advent and Nativity Sermons from a Fifteenth-Century Revision of John Mirk's Festial*, Middle English Texts 13 (Heidelberg, 1981). For other collections of diverse origins see, for instance, Lincoln Cathedral MS 133, Bodleian Library, MSS Greaves 54 and Hatton 96, CUL MS Gg.6.16. On the first two see A.J. Fletcher, 'Unnoticed Sermons from John Mirk's *Festial*', *Speculum*, 55 (1980), 514–22. See the brief introduction to S. Nevanlinna's edition of the expanded version of the *Northern Homily Cycle*, *Mémoires de la Société Néophilologique de Helsinki*, 38 (1972) and 431 (1973), 1–31.

46 See Doyle's papers listed in n. 25.

47 E.g. the environment in which Thornton's two collections were assembled; G.R. Keiser, 'Lincoln Cathedral Library MS.91: Life and Milieu of the Scribe', *SB*, 32 (1979), 158–79, and 'More Light on the Life and Milieu of Robert Thornton', *SB*, 36 (1983), 111–19.

48 Doyle, *Survey*, I, 219–24; Raymo, 216 (BCD) and 173; G.R. Morgan, 'A Critical Edition of Caxton's *The Art and Craft to know well to Die* and *Ars Moriendi* together

with the Antecedent Manuscript Material', unpublished D.Phil. thesis (Oxford, 1973); V.R. Murray, 'An Edition of *A Tretyse of Gostly Batayle* and *Milicia Christi*', unpublished D.Phil. thesis (Oxford, 1970).

49 Cf. the sequence of texts containing *The Mirror of Sinners* and the *Treatise of the Three Arrows* discussed by Doyle, *Survey*, I, pp. 165–70, and the group of manuscripts listed in n. 70, below.

50 Of the original eighteen items in BL Royal 17.C.xviii, the first five are found in the same order in Oxford, Corpus Christi College, MS 220 (which was written by the same scribe) and all eighteen are found in the same order in Bodleian Library, MS Rawlinson C.894 (written by a different scribe). Other manuscripts in the group include Bodleian Library, MS Douce 322, partly reproduced in BL MS Harley 1706 (see p. 330); CUL MS Ff.5.45, with four texts in common with Douce and Harley; Manchester, John Rylands University Library, MS English 94, with five texts in common with Douce, Harley, Royal, Corpus and Rawlinson; and Cambridge, Trinity College, MS R.3.21, the first booklet of which is similar in script and layout to Douce 322 (see n. 13 above).

51 In Corpus Oxford 220 appear the names of John and Isabell Manyngham whose associations were with the city of London; Bodleian Rawlinson C.894 belonged to the Roberts family of Middlesex.

52 Morgan, 'Critical Edition', pp. 92–8.

53 I: fols. 1–39v; II: fols. 40–63v; III: fols. 64–73v; IV: fols. 74–228v. The originally blank leaves at the ends of several booklets have been filled subsequently.

54 Cf. the evidence recorded by L.K. Smedick, 'Parallelism and Pointing in Rolle's Rhythmical Style', *Mediaeval Studies*, 41 (1979), 404–67, although her stylistic interpretation of this evidence is open to question.

55 M. Serjeantson, 'The Index of the Vernon Manuscript', *MLR*, 32 (1937), 224–61.

56 M.B. Parkes, '*Ordinatio* and *Compilatio*'. These efforts to improve reader access were unsystematic and erratic, and most manuscripts continued to offer little assistance to the casual user, particularly the products of *ad hoc* and amateur copying.

57 Cf. Pennsylvania MS English 8 (containing the *Scale*, vernacular *Stimulus Amoris* and the *Contemplations of the Dread and Love of God*) which provides running book numbers and chapter numbers for each text. BL Burney 356 is divided into 22 (originally 23) books, although it is a compilation of separate treatises.

58 On this manuscript, see A.I. Doyle, 'Books Connected with the Vere Family and Barking Abbey', *Essex Archaeological Society's Transactions*, NS, 25 (1958), 222–43. The hand responsible for the first quire is also found in the fourth (fols. 18r–20r), but quire 2 in the present arrangement has the donor Baron's shield in the top margin, suggesting that this was originally the beginning of the volume before it was prepared for donation. Although the first half of Harley 1706 is probably a copy of Douce, it has the list of contents at the end of the collection.

59 Cambridge, Trinity College, MS B.15.42 has a reference to Fr. Willelmus Caston dated 1448 on an endleaf, perhaps suggesting ownership by a friar; BL Harley 2409 was given by Maud Wade, prioress of Swyne (c. 1473–82) to Joan Hyltoft of Nuncoton, both Cistercian nunneries; BL MS Royal 17.A.xxv was owned by a friar early in the sixteenth century; the contents of Bodleian Ashmole 1286 seem to

point towards compilation for religious use; CUL MS Ii.6.40 has been adapted for monastic use.

60 Jolliffe H.15, pr. Horstmann, *Yorkshire Writers*, II, pp. 72–105 (this quotation p. 72); J. Krochalis, 'Contemplations of the Dread and Love of God: Two Newly Identified Pennsylvania Manuscripts', *University of Pennsylvania Library Chronicle*, 41–2 (1976–8), 3–22; Gillespie, 'Lukynge', 24–6.

61 Cf. Salter, *Myrrour*, p. 15. Typical examples are BL Add. MSS 19901, 21006, 30031, Royal 18.C.x; Bodleian Library, MSS Rawlinson A.387B, Bodley 207; Cambridge, Trinity College, MSS B.15.16 and B.15.32; CUL MSS Ll.4.3 and Mm.5.15.

62 Ed. Powell, p. [6]. For an alternative interpretation of this note, see P. O'Connell, 'Love's *Mirrour* and the *Meditationes Vitae Christi*', in *Collectanea Cartusiensia*, 2, Analecta Cartusiana 82.2 (1980), pp. 3–44.

63 Doyle, 'Reflections', pp. 82–3.

64 Jolliffe B; Bodleian Library, MS Bodley 3, fols. 1v–2r; M.T. Brady, '*The Pore Caitif*: An Introductory Study', *Traditio*, 10 (1954), 529–48. A number of studies have elucidated the sources of this interesting compilation: M.T. Brady, 'The Apostles and the Creed in Manuscripts of *The Pore Caitif*', *Speculum*, 32 (1957), 323–5; 'Rolle's "Form of Living" and "The Pore Caitif"', *Traditio*, 36 (1980), 426–35; 'The Seynt and His Boke: Rolle's Emendatio Vitae and The Pore Caitif', *Fourteenth-century English Mystics Newsletter*, 7 (1981), 20–31; 'Rolle and the Pattern of Tracts in "The Pore Caitif"', *Traditio*, 39 (1983), 456–65; M. Sargent, 'A Source of the *Pore Caitif* Tract "Of Man's Will"', *Medieval Studies*, 41 (1979), 535–9.

65 Typical are BL MSS Harley 953, 2322, 2336; Lambeth Palace MSS 484, 541; Bodleian Library, MSS Bodley 3, 288, Lyell 29, Rawlinson C.69; CUL MS Ff.6.34; Cambridge, St John's College, MS G.28; Cambridge, Trinity College, MS B.14.53. At the other end of the scale is Longleat 4, a large volume in two columns, where the text is preceded by a long set of sermons and followed by the *Abbey of the Holy Ghost* (Joliffe H.9(b)).

66 Two of the exceptions are the Vernon and Simeon manuscripts (Lewis and McIntosh, nos. MV 40 and MV 70) where the triple columns are the standard format in those vast volumes for rhyming verse. For the geographical locations see the map in Lewis and McIntosh, p. 171. For comments on the text of the *Pricke* in the two manuscripts see R.E. Lewis, 'The Relationship of the Vernon and Simeon Texts of the *Pricke of Conscience*', in Benskin and Samuels, pp. 251–64.

67 The 'economics' of parchment size and use is an obscure question, given the paucity of information on manuscript prices in the medieval period and our ignorance of the size of medieval sheep and cattle; for a brief discussion see H.E. Bell, 'The Price of Books in Medieval England', *The Library*, 4th series, 17 (1936), 313–32, and more recently C. Bozzolo and E. Ornato, *Pour une histoire du livre manuscrit au moyen âge: Trois essais de codicologie quantitative* (Paris, 1980), pp. 19–49.

68 *IMEV* 245; Raymo 7. BL MS Royal 17.C.viii now contains only the *Speculum Vitae*, but a flyleaf note suggests that this was not the intention of the compiler: 'Sir William I lat you wyt þai stond euen in ordour as þai shalle do in þe buk. And sett þe two qweres of Saynt Edmoundes lyff in þe latter end of þe buk' (fol. 1r).

69 Printed by H.E. Allen, 'The Speculum Vitae: Addendum', *PMLA*, 32 (1917),

133–62, at 147–8. Cf. the colophon in Cambridge, Fitzwilliam Museum, MS McClean 130: 'Explicit tractatus de oratione dominica scilicet de paternoster, in quo reprehenduntur multa vicia, et in quo continentur omnes virtutes que in hac vita degentibus sunt necessarie, et specialiter illiteratis docende ad dei honorem' (fol. 200r).

70 Cf. Bodleian Library, MSS Lyell 28, Rawlinson C.890; BL Add. 33995, Harley 435.

71 E.g. *No running titles*: Harley 435, Stowe 951, Greaves 43, Cotton Tiberius E.vii. *Descriptive*: Rawlinson C.890, Royal 17.C.viii. Harley 2260, BL Add. 8151. *Systematic*: BL Add. 33995, Hatton 18, Hatton 19, Lyell 28, Bodley 446, BL Add. 22558, Bodleian Eng. poet. d.5, Rawlinson C.884 (partial). Hatton 19 has a note to the corrector (*Incipe corrector*) at the beginning of quire 8 (fol. 59r).

72 Alle es wryten here on þis boke
Wha so wil rede it ouer a[n]d loke
It es na vertu vnnethes ne synne
þat he ne sal fynde it wryten þar inne . . .
þerfore lewed men has grete nede
þis boke oft to here or rede (BL Add. MS 33995, fol. 96r).

73 Raymo, 8; ed. V. Nelson, Middle English Texts 14 (Heidelberg, 1981), who unfortunately does not print the apparatus, although some of it is incorporated into her text. BL Harley 45 is ruled up to accommodate an extensive marginal apparatus.

74 Raymo, 45; text edited by P.H. Barnum, EETS, os, 275 and 280 (1976–80): her introduction gives references to previous discussion. The plates in the two volumes provide illustration of most of the complete copies.

75 Particularly difficult to follow would be BL Royal 17.C.xx, where none of the various scribes provides running titles, where chapters are marked only by number in the margins, and where no headings for new commandments are provided; some scribes underline Latin quotations; speakers are indicated only by *D* and *P*.

76 Ed. Morison, p. 116.

77 I am grateful to Dr Anne Hudson for her helpful comments on a draft of this chapter and for permission to use material on the longer religious texts, deriving from work she had undertaken at an earlier stage, when the chapter was envisaged as a collaborative project. The chapter as it stands and the opinions expressed are the sole responsibility of the author. Patricia Ingham, Malcolm Parkes and Jeremy Griffiths all made invaluable comments on versions of this chapter.

14 · SCIENTIFIC AND MEDICAL BOOKS

LINDA EHRSAM VOIGTS

SCIENTIFIC AND MEDICAL MANUSCRIPTS [1] from late medieval England survive in daunting numbers, and rarely have they been dealt with collectively.[2] This chapter cannot provide a definitive map of the scientific book production of that era; rather it is an attempt to give an overall survey in the hope that future research will bring into tighter focus aspects here treated cursorily. Such an overview seems not to have been attempted before, perhaps because of two formidable barriers to understanding the scientific and medical manuscripts of late medieval England created by twentieth-century scholarship: a concept of 'science' that derives from the scientific revolution; and misleading assumptions about the nature of the medieval scientific manuscript based on studies of the printed book. These two barriers must be overcome before the territory they barricade can be explored.

The first obstacle is largely one of nomenclature – how can we identify a 'scientific book' if what we call *science* is not what medievals understood as *sciencia*? It is a problem more vexing for science than it is for medicine. In practical terms, medicine, then as now, was largely perceived less as an attempt to understand the natural world than as a technology for maintaining or restoring health,[3] and the modern taxonomy of medical texts as dealing with diagnosis, prognosis, and therapy has proved useful, although it is not without problems.[4]

For the terms *science* and *sciencia*, however, the issues are more complex, for there are vastly differing definitions of what is meant by 'science' in the Middle Ages. One is the exclusive view that addresses only those aspects of medieval thought that are similar to the concerns of the modern sciences, and perhaps technology. That approach is well illustrated by A.C. Crombie's *Augustine to Galileo*, which concentrates on those medieval disciplines dealing with subjects similar to those of the modern physical and biological sciences, which omits consideration of music, magic, physiognomy and chiromancy, and which treats alchemy only briefly.[5] This approach is characteristic of many standard works on the history of medieval science,[6] although it differs from the principle of selection used in the monumental Thorndike and Kibre *Catalogue*.[7] There is no cause to question the value of the study of history of science that has contributed so much to our understanding of the Middle

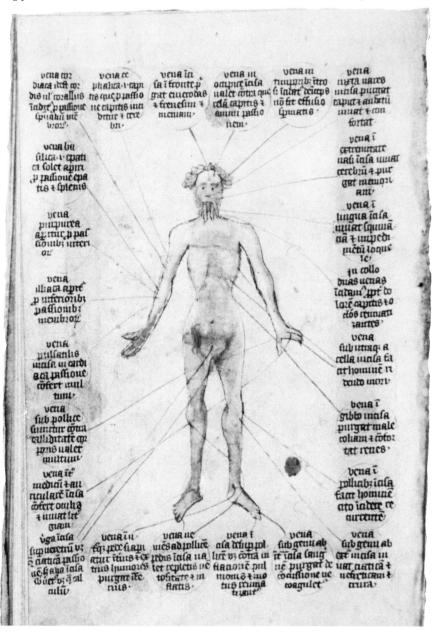

32   Los Angeles, Library of Irwin J. Pincus, M.D., Pincus *horae*, late 14th or early 15th century, fol. 31v.

Ages, but the fact remains that 'scientific manuscripts' written in England from 1375 to 1500 contain – in addition to the texts studied by historians of science – texts often excluded by the expectations of these historians.

Before examining the other extreme, a much more inclusive definition of medieval science, it is also important to acknowledge that much that is of interest to historians of science is found in writing that would be considered 'science' in neither the Middle Ages nor the twentieth century. Questions of physical science can be studied in theology and logic treatises, as for example in 'insolubilia',[8] and historians of science have found questions of interest in devotional[9] and belletristic texts as well.[10] In addition, encyclopedias contain voluminous material, some of which is of interest to historians of science,[11] and both medicine and science can be found in books of Hours (see Ill. 32).[12] Because these manuscripts are only incidentally 'scientific', they do not fall within the purview of this chapter, however valuable they have proved for the history of science.

Perhaps in part as a reaction against an understanding of science that excludes many of the texts, diagrams, and illustrations found in codices containing other, indisputably 'scientific' texts, the twentieth-century German study of *Fachliteratur* has provided a much more inclusive definition that represents the opposite extreme in this spectrum of assumptions.[13] This *Fachliteratur* tradition excludes only devotional and belletristic writing, and bases its inclusiveness on medieval classifications of knowledge. The classification of Hugh of St Victor, for example, included the mechanical sciences of fabric-making, armament, commerce, agriculture, hunting and theatrics. Another, that of Michael Scot, included among the practical sciences, agriculture, alchemy, necromancy, augury, the science of mirrors and navigation, among many others, and the complex system of Robert Kilwardby included, among the practical arts, ethics and mechanics, the latter embracing farming, cooking, tailoring, armament, architecture and commerce.[14] The application of this inclusive approach can be seen in Laurel Braswell's discussion of Middle English *Fachprosa* that surveys not only those texts that we would now call 'science' along with those that made up the quadrivium and occult and prognostic writings, but also manuals for conduct and for chivalric, military, and sporting endeavours; grammar books; recipe books for cooking and book production; guidebooks for travel; and miscellaneous treatises on such subjects as sailing, lacemaking, and the assize of bread and ale.[15] Although antedating the study of *Fachliteratur*, and less inclusive than it, Dorothea Waley Singer's net was also an extremely broad one.[16]

The dilemma posed by the extremes of these two approaches is that neither of them accurately describes the contents of 'scientific' books produced in England in the later Middle Ages. To be sure, a definition which identifies scientific texts in terms of modern science excludes many kinds of texts found in manuscripts cheek by jowl with what are unquestionably 'scientific' texts.

On the other hand, the capacious definition of *Fachliteratur* blurs the evidence of the similar content of most 'scientific' manuscripts. Although one does occasionally find information on agriculture (particularly arboriculture and viniculture) as companion texts to writings on astronomy, medicine, or alchemy, the other categories of Hugh of St Victor, Michael Scot and Robert Kilwardby that have to do with business (accounting, book-production, commerce), manners and sports, and domestic endeavours (cooking and lacemaking) are not commonly met with in the company of 'scientific' writings. Rather they are to be found in educational and business books[17] and in household books.[18]

Accordingly, one of the theses of this chapter is that – even if there is no agreement on a definition of 'medieval science' – it is possible to identify the medieval 'scientific book', both by its physical characteristics (aspects to be dealt with later in this chapter) and by the kinds of texts that it contains. These texts deal with more subjects than those addressed by many historians of science, but fewer than those studied by students of *Fachliteratur*, and there is a classification of medieval science that grew out of years of manuscript study and that reflects most of the actual content of those books. The classification, that of Mahmoud Manzalaoui, includes most of the kinds of texts found in the late medieval scientific codex in three categories:

1. activities that are experimentally sound, mathematically true, or empirically useful (geometry, astronomy, pharmacology, herbal lore)
2. pseudo-sciences or consistent logical systems involving study but which cannot now be substantiated by experimental fact (dream lore, lapidaries, judicial astrology, physiognomy)
3. the occult (alchemy, geomancy, chiromancy)[19]

If one adds to Manzalaoui's categories other kinds of medical writing and agricultural treatises, we have a useful description of the texts that characteristically make up the scientific and medical codices produced in England in the late medieval period.

To illustrate the kinds of texts actually found in the late medieval scientific book, three manuscripts can be cited as representative. While each of them illustrates some of the physical and linguistic features of the scientific manuscript (matters to be discussed later), they are important at this point because the texts they contain are typical. The first codex, BL MS Egerton 847, is a Latin manuscript containing, exclusive of the first booklet which was added later by J.O. Halliwell-Phillips, tables and treatises on the zodiac and planets, lunary material, a text on the interpretation of dreams, three physiognomy texts, two chiromancy texts (one attributed to 'Rodricum de Majoricis' of Oxford), a practical geometry, Grosseteste's *De sphaera*, the text of the same name by John of Sacrobosco, texts and tables on nativities and planetary influence, a 'theory of the planets' attributed to Walter Brytte, William Rede's canons on the Alfonsine tables, and the commentary of

33 London, British Library, MS Egerton 847, Latin astronomical, mathematical and prognostic compendium, middle of first half of 15th century, fol. 55r.

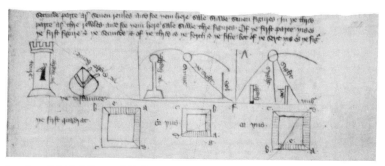

34 London, British Library, MS Sloane 213, Latin, English, French medical, mathematical and magical miscellany, end of 14th or beginning of 15th century, fol. 124r.

Walter Burley on Aristotle's *Libri Meteororum* (Ill. 33).[20] A second instance is BL MS Sloane 213, containing twenty-four texts in Latin, Middle English, and Middle French. It includes a number of medical recipe compilations, Macer's poem on the virtues of herbs, the *Isagoge* of Hunayn ibn Ishaq, a *regimen sanitatis*, medical texts attributed to Arnald of Villa Nova and John of St-Amand, a text on perilous days for bloodletting, an astrology treatise, a geometry text, *Imago Mundi* of Honorius of Autun, and a plague tract (Ill. 34).[21] The third example, a codex from a 'medical publishing house' to be discussed later, is Cambridge, Trinity College, MS O.1.77, containing fifteen Latin and Middle English texts. The texts include several on a variety of kinds of medicines, two uroscopy texts, a *regimen sanitatis*, three plague tracts, two texts on planets and one on zodiacal-lunary conjunctions, planetary tables, a treatise on the zodiac, a text on wine attributed to Arnald of Villa Nova, an anonymous text on wine, and an alchemical treatise.[22]

If one grants that the 'scientific' book in late medieval England is recognisable, on one level by the kinds of texts it contains, then we have surmounted

one barrier – the variety of interpretations of 'medieval science'. There is,
however, yet another barrier erected by the constraints of twentieth-century
scholarship that must be addressed, and that is a misunderstanding of the
handwritten scientific book by historians of the printed book, at least in the
English-language tradition.[23] These misconceptions are exemplified by
Elizabeth Eisenstein's *The Printing Press as an Agent of Change*.[24] In Part Three
of this important and influential study, 'The Book of Nature Transformed',
Eisenstein argues that the reason the Scientific Revolution came to pass 'was
not that men turned from books to nature, but rather that books went from
script to print' (p. 488). A number of the points made by Eisenstein in
arguing this thesis misrepresent the scientific codex. For example, she contrasts the handwritten with the printed book by comparing a fourteenth-
century Anglo-Norman verse 'algorism' with Simon Stevin's 1585 printed
work on fractions (pp. 467–8). Aside from the fact that neither text is
representative, the use of an Anglo-Norman example is curious in that
Eisenstein also credits printing with the rise of scientific writing in the
vernacular.

In particular, three of Eisenstein's generalisations concerning the scientific
manuscript reflect a lack of familiarity with the handwritten scientific book of
the preceding era, at least as regards England. The first is that scribal
transmission always represents deterioration in text (see pp. 499, 504–5). In
fact, a number of scholars have pointed out intelligent modification or
'improvement' of scientific texts in the course of scribal transmission,[25] and,
in the case of late medieval English manuscripts in particular, historians have
argued that surgery texts in this period show considerable advance and are to
be found in English as well as Latin.[26] A second assumption on the part of
Eisenstein is that widespread reliance on illustrations is peculiar to the
printed book[27] and that 'a sequence of hand-copied images will usually reveal
degradation and decay' (p. 479). In fact, as the survey presented below
reveals, the late medieval English manuscript is characterised by extensive
use of illustrations and diagrams, and not all illustrations uniformly deterio-
rated. For example, in the case of bloodletting diagrams, late medieval
illustrations of venesection points 'caught up' with the textual tradition in
their representation of five rather than three arm veins.[28] The third assumption has already been mentioned: it is Eisenstein's conclusion that vernacular
scientific writing developed because of printing.[29] Any examination of scientific and medical manuscripts produced in England before Caxton will belie
that assumption, witness the data in the survey presented below on the high
incidence of Middle English in sophisticated as well as popular scientific and
medical writing of the fifteenth century. In short, Eisenstein's conclusions
reflect a lack of familiarity with the late medieval scientific and medical
manuscript, and should not go unrefined.

Furthermore, although this is not the place to assess the impact of printing on science, it is important to point out that other scholars argue that printing had a retardative influence on the development of scientific thought, that because of the conservative and popularising nature of publication in the first century and a half of printing, innovation was unlikely to find an audience via the book.[30] This view is accurate for the scientific and medical texts printed in England in the three decades after Caxton set up his press in Westminster. Caxton printed 'scientific' material, including arithmetic, only in his translation of Vincent of Beauvais' thirteenth-century encyclopedia *Myrrour of the Worlde* (*STC* 24762) and the simplified *Regimen Sanitatis Salernitanum*, called *The Governal of Health* (*STC* 12138; also de Worde, *STC* 12139). Wynkyn de Worde printed Trevisa's translation of the thirteenth-century encyclopedia of Bartholomaeus Anglicus, *De Proprietatibus Rerum* (*STC* 1536), a tract on equine medicine (*STC* 20439.3), and Walter of Henley's thirteenth-century book of husbandry (*STC* 25007). William de Machlinia printed the plague tract attributed to Cnut (*STC* 4589, 4590, 4591; also van Doesborch in Antwerp, (*STC* 4593), and both the *Liber Aggregationis* (*STC* 258) and the *Secreta Mulierum* (*STC* 273) attributed to Albertus Magnus. The St Albans printer – the only publisher to address a more educated audience – published the *Liber Modorum Significandi* of Albertus Magnus (*STC* 268), Antonius Andrae, *Scriptum super Logica* (*STC* 582), and Joannes Canonicus, *Quaestiones super Octo Libros Phisicorum Aristotilis* (*STC* 14621), and Theodoric Rood printed a logic treatise in Oxford (*STC* 16693) in 1483.[31] These books printed from 1475 to 1505 reflect the interests and knowledge of 'scientists' (as inferred from the texts found in manuscripts) less than they do the expectations of commercial entrepreneurs as to what would sell in England at the end of the fifteenth century.

Although this chapter has thus far addressed two obstacles to our understanding of late medieval scientific and medical manuscripts, these barriers are more completely overturned by the evidence provided by a survey of such codices produced in England 1375–1500. Such a survey reveals that it is possible to come to a more accurate understanding of medicine and science by looking at the manuscripts themselves than it is via either a modern definition of science or an inclusive *Fachliteratur* approach; these manuscripts contain not only common patterns of texts as discussed above[32] illustrated by Egerton 847, Sloane 213, and Cambridge, Trinity College, MS O.1.77, but they also share physical features that set them off from belletristic, theological, philosophical, chronicle, legal, pedagogical and household manuscripts. Furthermore, such a survey reveals that these manuscripts are characterised by a dependence on illustrations and diagrams, and by the use of the vernacular, both features that have been wrongly credited to the scientific printed book.

This survey examined late medieval scientific and medical manuscripts produced in England that are now in the holdings of a number of American and British libraries.[33] Because the holdings of American collections are limited and – for the most part – random, I examined all relevant codices in those libraries, but in the case of the much larger British resources, I chose a representative sample from Dorothea Waley Singer's 101-box card file discussed above (see n. 2). From Singer's 'Hand-List of Scientific MSS in the British Isles Dating from before the Sixteenth Century', I chose what I hope were proportionate and representative examples of the various categories such as 'cosmology', 'alchemy', 'uroscopy', and the like for the period 1375–1500. The period beginning with 1375 is an arbitrary one, constrained by the subject of this book, but it is a convenient one, for the years 1375–1500 mark a fairly well-defined period of increasing use of the vernacular for medical and scientific writing; no codices containing science or medicine in Middle English other than remedy-books appear to have been written before 1375.[34] In the following century and a quarter, however, we can trace the rapid growth of the use of Middle English for medicine and science, even of the most sophisticated sort. The *terminus ad quem* I used in the survey, 1500, differs from the 1475 date used for the title of this volume. My decision to consider codices written in the last quarter of the century was based on the observation that many scientific and medical codices written in that period differed in kind from the popular and debased material that comprised contemporary printed scientific books.

Some qualification is necessary in selecting manuscript references from the Singer records. D.W. Singer had indexed encyclopedias and theological or devotional texts if they contained comments on cosmology or other elements of natural philosophy. While obiter dicta in non-scientific writings can prove valuable for historians of science,[35] their presence does not constitute a 'scientific' manuscript, and such citations were disregarded. Another element that affected my choice of manuscripts to examine was the fact that Singer often assigned earlier dates to manuscripts than do recent palaeographers. I selected manuscripts for examination on the assumption that Singer's dates for undated manuscripts should be reckoned at least twenty-five years too early, and my examination of the codices bore out that assumption.

Having selected the codices for study, I examined the manuscripts and recorded information on texts and languages and on the physical make-up of each book: binding, material, collation, booklet compilation, format and size, hands, decoration, illustration, diagrams, schematic representation and symbolic writing. I recorded information on 153 manuscripts, but a number of those were made up of formerly independent manuscripts arbitrarily bound together after the sixteenth century,[36] so the survey was in fact of 178 units that were treated as separate manuscripts in matters of text, language, and physical make-up. This information was entered in a data-base computer program to tabulate information on languages, binding, material, quiring, booklet compilation, column or page format, hands and the like. On the basis of the Singer card file, I cautiously estimate that more than 1,000 manuscripts that fit the definition I am using for 'scientific books' survive from late medieval England. If that is the case, then my survey was based on fifteen per cent or less of the surviving total. I believe that the Singer survey made possible the examination of a representative sample, but the conclusions to be drawn from a fraction of the total are tentative, hypotheses to be tested by further research.

To consider first the salient physical details of manuscripts surveyed, of those ninety-three codices where collation was feasible, nearly as many codices, forty-three, were quired in tens or more as were to be found in the more predictable gatherings of eights (fifty). In the matter of material, recorded by booklet so that the total count is inflated, there were 119 instances of parchment, fifty-nine of paper, and thirty mixed. As regards hands in the 178 units, Anglicana was most widely used: 79 codices contained only Anglicana hands. See Ills. 33, 34, 43, and 49 for instances of careful Anglicana hands, and Ills. 37, 40, 42, 47, 48, 51, 52, 55, 56, 57, 58 and 61 for much more informal forms of the hand. Fifty-one manuscripts contained only 'book' or textura hands. Ills. 46, 54, and 60 display instances of carefully executed textura, while 53 and 59 (rubrics) are less skilfully written, and 38 and 41 approach the careless. Only twelve instances of those surveyed were written exclusively in a secretary hand (see the writing in the roundels of Ill. 59); the remaining manuscripts contained a variety of hands or were written in hands best described as hybrid; see Ills. 44, and 45.

A striking feature of the manuscripts surveyed is the incidence of medieval booklet compilation.[37] Of the 178 manuscripts examined, thirty-eight were not written as entire books, but were assembled of discrete units before 1600. Of the thirty-eight, twenty-five are made up of booklets all dating from the fifteenth century, the most common kind of booklet compilation. A further eight codices were assembled as manuscripts in the sixteenth century, when they were still being consulted, and contain booklets from that century alongside the fifteenth-century ones; the data here reported do not include information from the later booklets. Particularly interesting was the group of five manuscripts where booklets from earlier centuries had been appropriated to make up manuscripts in the fifteenth century. Consider Ill. 35, an opening (fols. 248v–249) from Bodleian Library, MS Digby 235, a codex of Roger Bacon's *Opus majus*. On the left can be seen the last leaf of sixteen quires that were written in the last quarter of the fifteenth century to accompany two fourteenth-century quires of that text beginning on the right. Following the two fourteenth-century quires, fifteen more fifteenth-century quires follow. Note that the text is continuous and that catchword and text correspond, but that the layout and hand are different. There are other differences as well (red/green decoration in the older part instead of red/blue in the newer), but the match is nonetheless harmonious.[38]

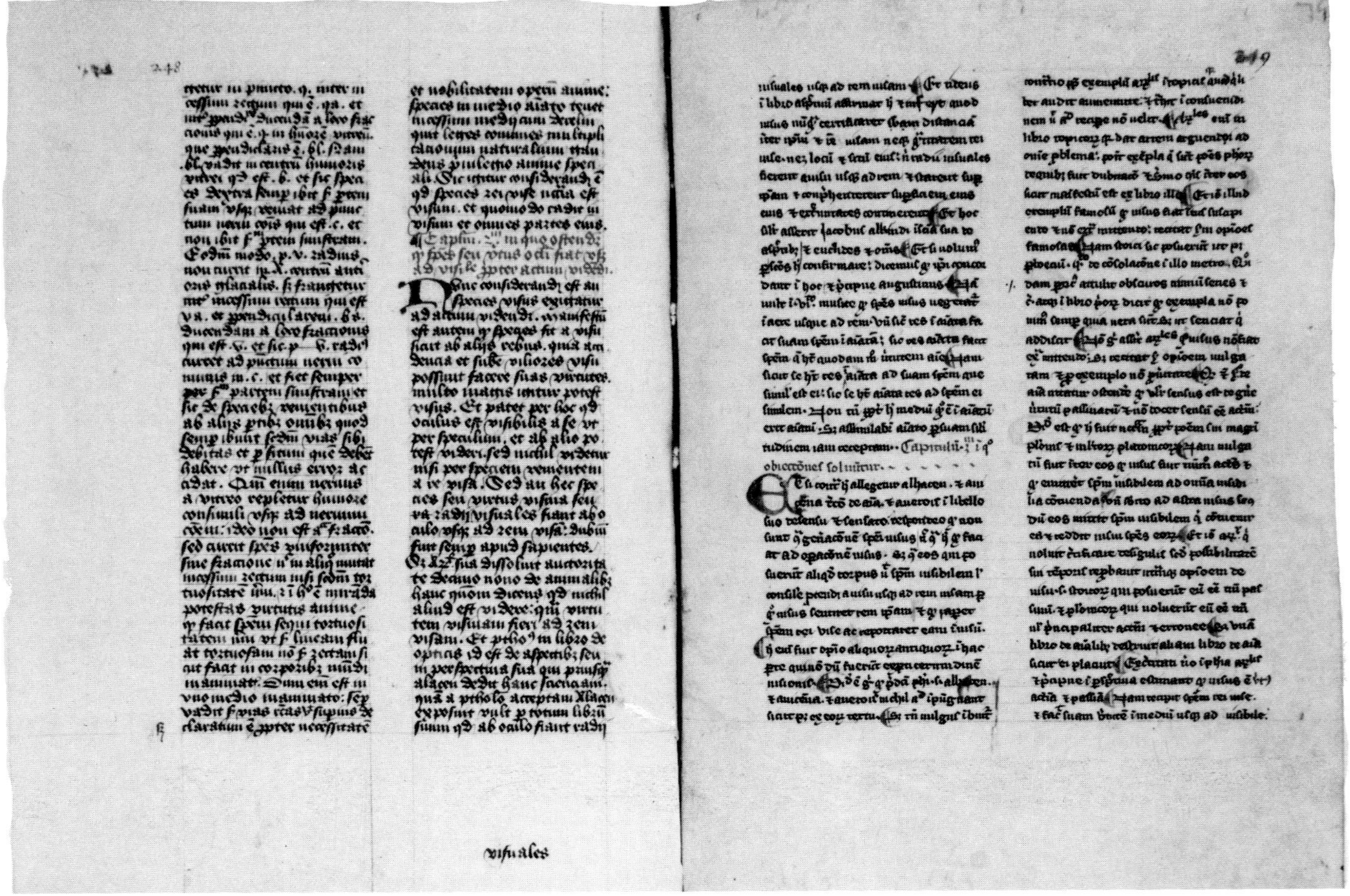

248
249
visuales

36 Oxford, Bodleian Library, MS Digby 98, Latin compendium of mathematics, astrology and natural philosophy, end of 12th and first half of 15th century, fols. 103v–104r.

Another fifteenth-century example of skillful integration of older booklets into manuscripts is illustrated by Bodleian Library, MS Digby 98, part 9, a manuscript where a booklet written at the end of the twelfth century forms the core of the much later mathematical codex. See Ill. 36, where, on the left, fol. 103v, can be seen the older booklet and on the right, the fifteenth-century continuation. The twelfth-century booklet contains, in addition to the text seen here, a Latin version of Euclid's geometry. On fols. 103v–104 can be seen the *De Arithmetice* of Boethius, where the fifteenth-century booklet appears to complete the Boethian text with the discussion of geometric, arithmetic, and harmonic proportions. This later completion was copied and signed by Peter Partridge (Partrich, d. 1451), professor of theology at Oxford and chancellor of Lincoln Cathedral. Also in Partridge's hand and following the Boethian text in the newer booklet, on fol. 109, is Simon de Bredon's commentary on that text.[39] Booklet compilation was clearly an important element in the late medieval production of scientific and medical manuscripts, for not only did it provide for the construction of anthologies, it also resulted in codices that combine older texts with more recent commentary.

A phenomenon related to booklets also bears mention. Small in size like the booklet, and even more portable, is the folded parchment compilation called the 'vade mecum', 'girdle book', or 'folding almanac', here illustrated by Bodleian Ashmole 6, fol. 13v (Ill. 37).[40] Many of these portable booklets survive from fourteenth- and fifteenth-century England.[41] They ordinarily contain, in addition to short medical and prognostic texts, calendrical material and planetary and zodiacal tables. In the case of Ill. 37, we see a table of lunar–zodiacal correspondences and a list of the qualities of parts of the body. These girdle books ordinarily also contained illustrations of zodiac and bloodletting men (Ills. 32 and 38 illustrate bloodletting and zodiac men of the sort frequently found in the vade mecum, although these instances are from books), and there is every reason to believe that they were written and illustrated as readily available tools for the peripatetic medical practitioner.

The last aspect of the survey of physical details that bears consideration is the incidence of visual material, ranging from schematic diagrams using words, through tables and instruments, to full-page miniatures. Again, the sample for this survey may be insufficient to extrapolate accurate numerical proportions for all scientific and medical manuscripts of the period, but it does indicate that this sort of book made extensive use of visual material, both conceptual and representational. Of the manuscripts examined, 164 of 178 contained some visual material, eighty-six instances of the 164 using words or numbers (in calendars, tables, charts, and schematic diagrams) and seventy-eight using pictures that range from marginal diagrams to full-page miniatures. A valuable historical survey of the visual dimension of scientific and medical manuscripts is John Murdoch's magisterial *Antiquity and the Middle Ages*.[42]

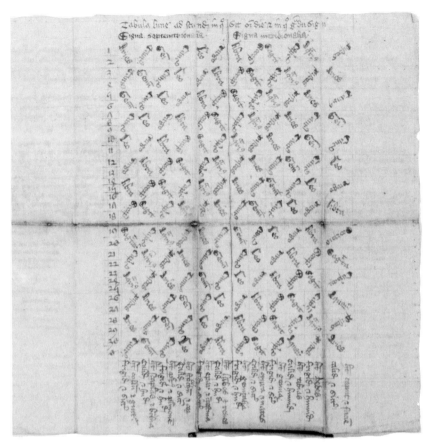

37 Oxford, Bodleian Library, MS Ashmole 6, Latin folding almanac, *vade medum*, or girdle-book, first half of 15th century, fol. 13v.

To begin by addressing visual depiction that is essentially conceptual is to acknowledge that illustrations can be both conceptual and representational. The zodiac man, for example (Ill. 38), depicts both the human body and concepts of astral influence, and geometry diagrams may fall into either category, but the division is a useful one nonetheless.[43] Conceptual depiction is sometimes simple, as, for example, in the case of Ill. 39, BL MS Sloane 1, fol. 313, where we see a schematic presentation from the discussion of things natural, unnatural, and 'contra naturum' from the *Isagoge* of Hunayn ibn Ishaq (Johannitius), a propaedeutic introduction to Galen usually found as the first text in the popular compendium called the Articella. Here, brackets lead the reader to the natural, spiritual, and animal subcategories in the first category of things natural, that of virtues. More complex relationships also

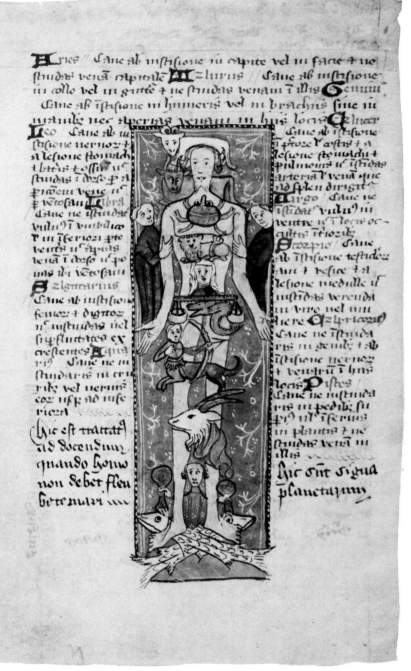

38   Cambridge, Trinity College, MS O.1.57, Latin and English medical and scientific miscellany, first half of 15th century, fol. 10v.

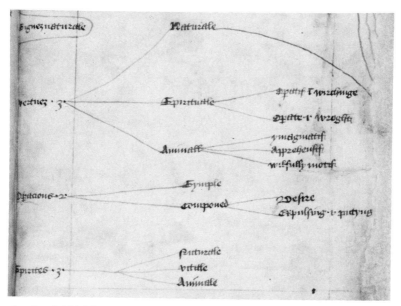

39   London, British Library, MS Sloane 1, English Surgery of Guy de Chauliac, middle of 15th century, fol. 313r.

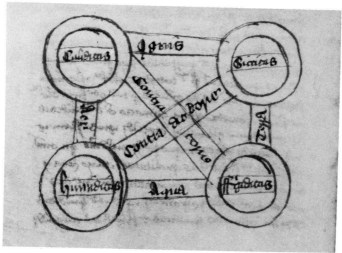

40   Oxford, Bodleian Library, MS Bodley 676, Latin compendium on natural philosophy, logic, and astronomy, middle of 15th century, fol. 156v.

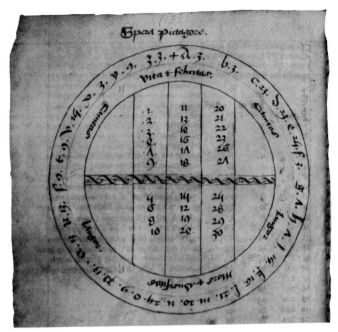

41   London, British Library, MS Harley 3719, predominantly Latin medical and astronomical
compendium, beginning of 15th century, fol. 175v.

are depicted in diagrams using words; for example, the contiguity and
contrariety of the four elements and four qualities can be seen in Ill. 40 from
Bodleian Library, MS Bodley 676, fol. 156v.[44] Another kind of schematic
depiction, in this case for the purpose of prognostication, is the Pythagorean
circle ('Spera Pictagora') as seen in BL MS Harley 3719, fol. 175v (Ill. 41).
To use this diagram, one adds the number equivalents of the letters in a
person's given name. To this sum one adds lunar and planetary components,
the age of the moon at the access of the illness and the number assigned to the
weekday on which the access occurred. The total is then divided by thirty,
and the remainder that cannot be divided is located in one of the number
columns to ascertain the outcome and duration of illness.[45] Approaching the
representational, but still largely conceptual, is the chiromancy diagram,
here illustrated by Wellcome MS 552, fol. 35r (Ill. 42). In this diagram signs
and inscriptions indicate the significance of parts of the palm.[46] Another
diagram, found in Bodleian Digby 97, fol. 280v (Ill. 43), illustrates one of the
six forms of horoscope or astrological reading for a particular date, in this
case that of an eclipse rather than the customary birth date.[47] This horoscope
illustrates the complex interrelationship between what we now consider the
concern of science, an eclipse, and what we now consider pseudo-science,
astrology.[48]

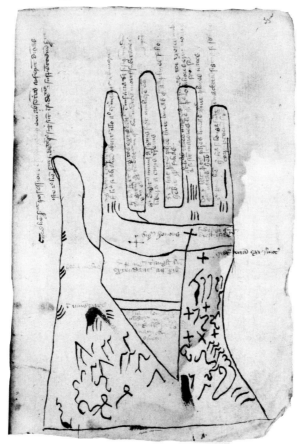

42 London, Wellcome Institute, MS 552, Latin and French chiromancy compendium, middle of 15th century, fol. 35r.

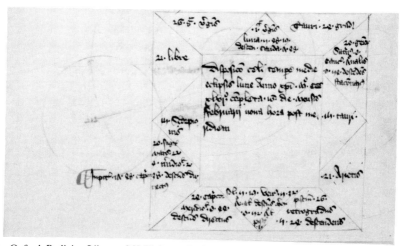

43 Oxford, Bodleian Library, MS Digby 97, Latin astronomical–astrological compendium, end of 14th century, fol. 280v.

44 Cambridge, University Library, MS Ee.3.61, Latin treatises and tables on mathematics, astronomy, and astrology, end of 15th century, fol. 62r.

45 Cambridge, University Library, MS Ee.3.61, Latin treatises and tables on mathematics, astronomy and astrology, end of 15th century, fol. 108v.

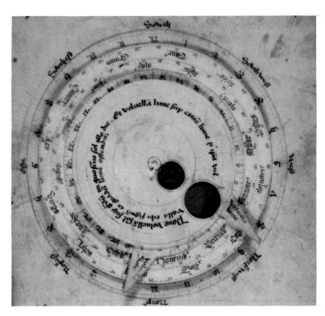

46   London, British Library, MS Harley 3719, predominantly Latin medical and astronomical compendium, beginning of 15th century, fol. 156.

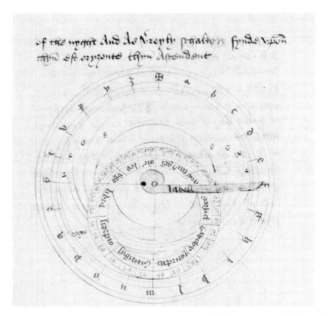

47   Cambridge, Trinity College, MS R.15.18, English and Latin astronomical treatises, middle of 15th century, p. 31.

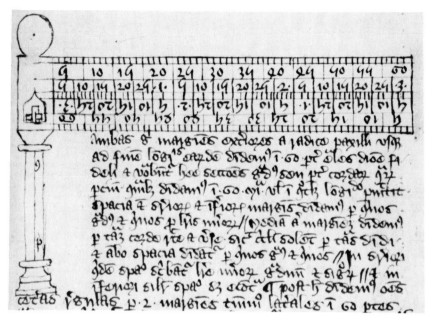

48 Oxford, Bodleian Library, MS Laud misc. 657, Latin astronomical treatises by Richard of Wallingford, end of 14th century, fol. 48r.

Closely related to these conceptual schemata are astronomical and mathematical relationships set forth in tables and charts; I recorded instances in fifty-two of the 178 manuscripts examined. The Alfonsine tables and their modifications bulk large in this count.[49] Illustrated in Ills. 44 and 45 are tables recorded by Lewis of Caerleon [d. 1494?] in CUL MS Ee.3.61, fols. 62 and 108v.[50] The first gives the ascension of signs by John de Lineriis (Lignères), and the second is associated with Humphrey, duke of Gloucester.[51] The less sophisticated astrological table in the vade mecum, Bodleian Library, MS Ashmole 6 (Ill. 37), was also common. Similar in purpose to tables, and as essential for astronomical–astrological calculation are instruments.[52] The lunar volvelle found in BL MS Harley 3719, fol. 156 (Ill. 46) is an instance where the codex actually becomes an instrument.[53] Manuscripts also contained diagrams to instruct the user in the manipulation of instruments. Codices containing Chaucer's well-known treatise on the astrolabe often contain such diagrams, as, for example, Cambridge, Trinity College, MS R.15.18, p. 31 (Ill. 47).[54] Bodleian Library, MS Laud misc. 657, fol. 48 (Ill. 48) illustrates one step in the construction of another instrument, the rectangulus, an easily constructed invention of Richard of Wallingford that served the purpose of an armillary sphere.[55]

Just as a lunar volvelle occupies an intermediate position between repre-

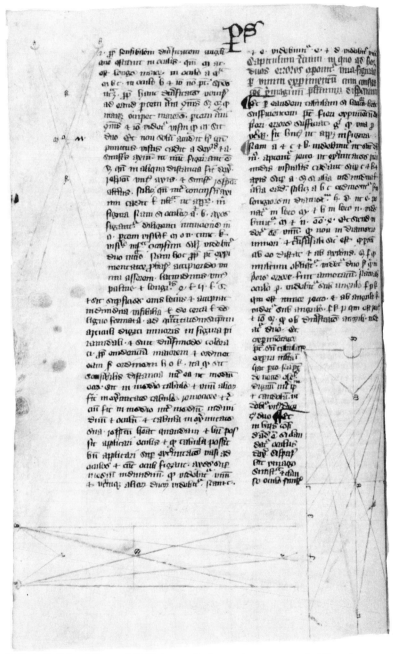

49   Oxford, Bodleian Library, MS Digby 77, Latin treatises on natural philosophy, most by English authors, end of 14th century, fol. 36v.

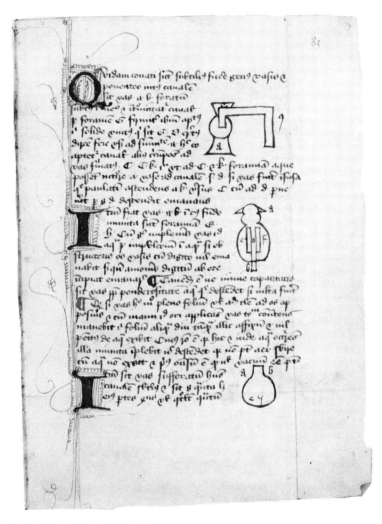

50   Cambridge, Trinity College, MS O.1.57, Latin and English medical miscellany, first half of
15th century, fol. 83r.

senting a concept and depicting an object, so too do mathematical and
geometrical illustrations.[56] Murdoch says of these drawings that 'their function was . . . almost always not to facilitate understanding, but to make it
possible'.[57] A drawing at the top of fol. 124 of BL MS Sloane 213, one of the
'typical' scientific manuscripts (Ill. 34), illustrates a Middle English
geometry text.[58] The drawings show the process and clarify the geometrical
basis for measuring heights by the calculation of triangles.[59] These aims
could be obscured, however. In another, a Latin practical geometry in

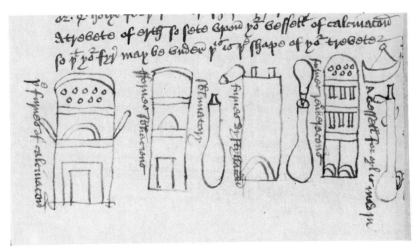

51 Cambridge, University Library, MS Kk.6.30, English and Latin alchemical and medical compendium, middle of second half of 15th century, fol. 11v.

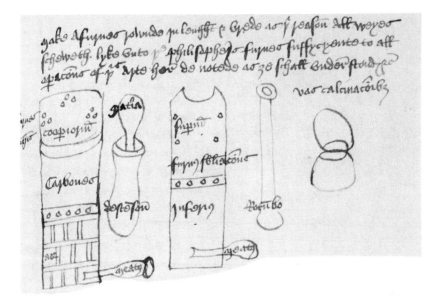

52 Cambridge, University Library, MS Kk.6.30, English and Latin alchemical and medical compendium, middle of second half of 15th century, fol. 17r.

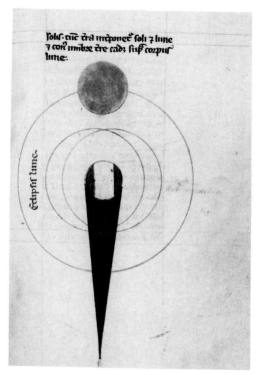

53   Oxford, St John's College, MS 205, Latin texts on mathematics and astronomy, middle of first half of 15th century, fol. 60r.

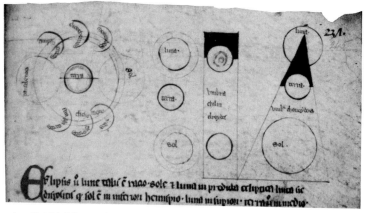

54   London, British Library, MS Harley 3719, predominantly Latin medical and astronomical compendium, beginning of 15th century, fol. 245.

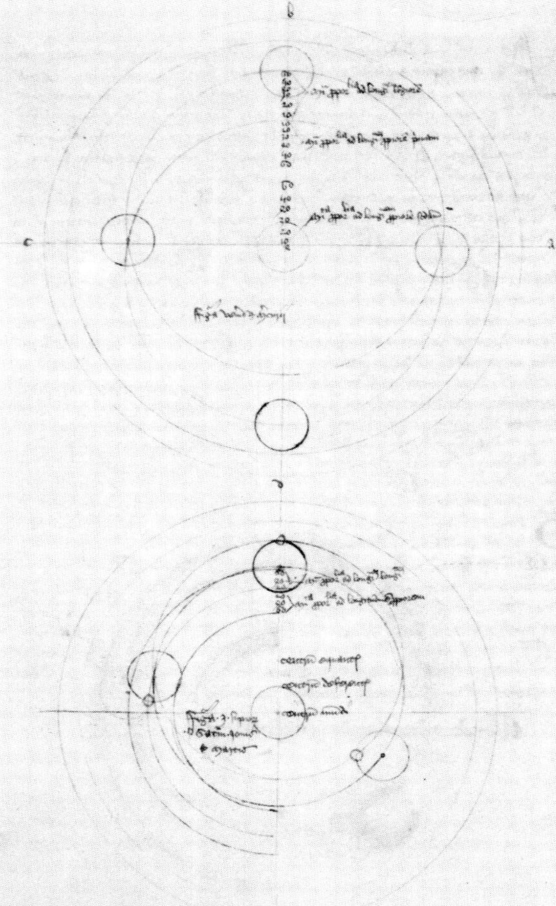

— pertinens 8 sphere Thome Werkworthe.

Nota pro motu octave spere quod ptholomeus posuit eam moveri conformiter ab occidente in orientem in 100 annis gradum unum. Et post eum Albategni fuit primus qui invenit errorem in positione illa. Eo quod invenit polos octave spere accedere sensibiliter ad polos none spere quando fecit consideracionem super hoc. Postea venit Thebit et sui sequaces scilicet Almeon et Arzachel qui posuerunt motum accessus et recessus octave spere secundum motum parvi circuli descripti a capite arietis octave spere circa caput arietis none spere quod posuerunt centrum illius circuli continue quiescere in capite arietis none spere. Et sic posuerunt motum octave spere esse difformem. Postea Alfonsus voluit concordare cum opinione ptholomei scilicet et Thebit posuit utrumque quia posuit centrum predicti circuli parvi continue moveri conformiter contra orientem. Posuit ergo motum augium planetarum esse conformem et propter hoc totum motum octave spere difformem propter eius accessionem et recessionem. Quia ista posicio contradictionem includit. Nam cum auges omnium planetarum moveantur ad motum octave spere contradictio est quod auges planetarum moveantur conformiter et spera octava difformiter. Et propter ista cum multi reputant tabulas Alfonsi magis falsas tabulis Arzachelis quamvis utreque fuerunt false propter processum temporis. Quia ad hunc tabule Alfonsi sint veriores fuerunt tamen magis false per longum processum temporis. Secundo tenent moderni quod polus octave spere accedit continue polo mundi in quinque annis minuto uno. Et quod octava spera movetur versus orientem modo scilicet anno Christi 1340 adquirendo in 60 annis gradum unum. Cum tamen tempore ptholomei scilicet 100 annis quesivit gradum unum. Secundo tamen iste motus octave spere versus orientem quam motus accessus poli eius ad polum mundi continue est velocior et velocior. Tamen 8 spera adquisivit per motum suum versus orientem a tempore ptholomei usque in hunc annum Christi 1340 18 gradus et 10 minuta sicut experta est Oxonie per multos valentes. Et polus octave spere adquisivit a tempore indorum usque ad tempus ptholomei nona minuta. Et a tempore ptholomei usque ad tempus Albategni 14 minuta. Et a tempore Albategni usque ad Arzachelem 8 minuta. Et ab Arzachele usque modo anno supradicto 4 minuta. Tamen maxima solis declinacio modo est 23 graduum 28 minutorum. Cum tamen fuit tempore indorum 24 gradus. Et ptholomeus fecit consideraciones suas per 138 annos post Christum. Et anno Christi 1316 addiderunt magistri Oxonie super loca stellarum fixarum in Almagesti ptholomei 16 gradus 20 minuta. Quia tantum processit 8 spera a tempore ptholomei. Nota ergo quod 25 gradus cancri in spera nona est modo in directo [illegible] stellarum fixarum [illegible] quarum directo fuit decimus gradus cancri tempore ptholomei. Nam octava spera a tempore ptholomei usque in annum Christi 1341 pertransivit 18 gradus 14 minuta. Quia modo in quolibet anno pertransit unum minutum. Ista patent per magistrum Simonem de Bredon qui circa annum Christi 1340 [illegible] motum 8 spere cum magna diligentia.

Stelle fixe alium habent motum precedentium. Sicut patet per observaciones veteres [illegible] stella Aldebaran invenit Hermes 24 gradus 14 minuta Tauri [illegible] a nodo [illegible] respectu ad nodum equinoctii. Quia quidam invenit Abrachis Tauri 10 gradus tempore. Et ptholomeus 12 gradus 20 minuta tempore. Et Albumazar 19 gradus 14 minuta tempore. Thebit 21 gradus 14 minuta tempore. Arzachel 23 gradus 20 minuta tempore. Albategni 25 gradus 30 minuta tempore. Domini Roberti Lincolniensis episcopi 28 gradus 20 minuta tempore. Et nos ut dicit Odyngton per observacionem Turketi et per computum invenimus eam Tauri 29 gradus tempore completo. Et ego Thomas Werkworth in anno Christi 1394 perfecte invenimus eam in geminis 0 gradus 28 minuta. Unde ut dicit Odyngton fit motus stellarum fixarum et augium planetarum in 80 annis

Mertonii Oxonie

Simon Bred[illegible]

Lincoln[illegible]

Odyngton

Thomas Werkworth

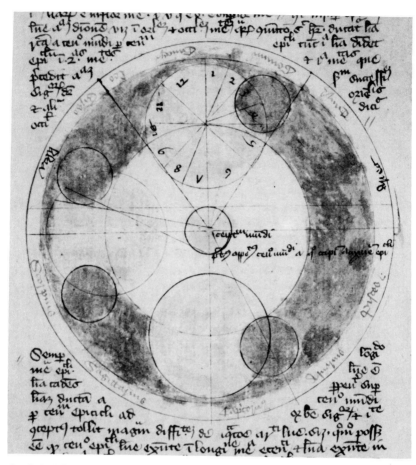

56 Oxford, Bodleian Library, MS Digby 98, Latin compendium of mathematics, astrology and natural philosophy, first half of 15th century, fol. 135v.

another of the 'typical' codices, BL MS Egerton 847, fol. 55 (Ill. 33), we see the visual emphasis less on the geometry involved or even on the instrument, the *quadrans vetus*, used in the calculation than on the towers and fenestration of the castles to be measured.

Like geometrical diagrams, illustrations of texts within what we now call the physical sciences are to some degree conceptual and display a close relationship to the text they illustrate, reflecting the medieval taxonomy that classified optics, statics, harmonics, and astronomy as 'scientiae mediae' between mathematics and natural philosophy.[60] In the Bodleian Digby 77 version of Roger Bacon's *De Perspectiva*, illustrated by fol. 36v (Ill. 49), three diagrams representing the refraction of light are designated by letters cited in the text, and space has been allowed at appropriate points in the text columns for the insertion of diagrams.[61] Another example from physical science of diagrams inserted in the text and keyed to the textual discussion is the drawing of siphons in Cambridge, Trinity College, MS O.1.57, fol. 83r (Ill. 50).[62]

Alchemy, another physical science,[63] is the subject-matter of a number of late medieval English codices with a high incidence of visual presentation. Many alchemical manuscripts survive from the fifteenth century in particular, and can be located with the Singer, Anderson and Addis three-volume *Catalogue*, an indispensable tool.[64] Visual material in alchemical manuscripts includes symbolic writing; emblematic representation of alchemical concepts and processes; and practical 'how-to' illustrations of apparatus and operations. Symbolic writing (see Ill. 61 and Murdoch, plate 79) will be addressed later. Emblematic alchemical iconography developed in the fourteenth century,[65] and is not frequently encountered in English medieval manuscripts, although late instances such as Cambridge, Trinity College, MS O.2.16 can be found. This manuscript is made up of three late fifteenth- and early sixteenth-century booklets and contains on fol. 27 a half-page illustration of the 'marriage of sol and luna' scene, as well as thirteen graceless marginal emblems of alchemical processes. Non-figural symbolic depictions of the relationship of metals, the so-called 'Lullian circles', are to be found on fols. 1v and 223, stiffened parchment leaves which originally made up the covers of the late fifteenth-century alchemical compendium that is now BL MS Sloane 1091.

Much more common than emblematic illustration in late medieval English alchemical codices are the more representational illustrations of alchemical equipment and processes. Ill. 51 and 52, both from CUL MS Kk.6.30 (fols. 11v and 17r), are perhaps typical. Ill. 51 displays unsophisticated drawings of furnaces for calcination, sublimation, distillation, and reverberation, and three vessels, one called a 'sublimatory'. Each is labelled in English. Ill. 52 from that manuscript depicts the distillation process in more detail, this time with Latin labels, although the text is English. For another fifteenth-century English example, see Jones, fig. 42 and for continental instances, Murdoch, plate 243.

Astronomical and astrological manuscripts from late medieval England were also frequently illustrated.[66] Eclipse diagrams are common, both simple ones such as Oxford, St John's College, MS 205, fol. 6or (Ill. 53), and more complex sets of the type that can be seen in Ill. 54 from BL MS Harley 3719, fol. 245, a manuscript with illustrations ranging from the learned – these eclipse diagrams and the lunar volvelle (Ill. 46) – to the popular Pythagorean Sphere (Ill. 41).[67] Much more sophisticated is Bodleian Digby 97, fols. 142v–143r (Ill. 55) where a diagram illustrating planetary orbits, epicycles, and eccentrics faces the text *De sphaera* of Thomas Werkwerth, which cites the Merton masters Walter of Odington and Simon de Bredon.[68] Bredon's treatise on planets, in Bodleian Digby 98, fol. 135v (Ill. 56) is illustrated within the text by a coloured diagram of planetary orbits and epicycles in relation to zodiacal positions, underscoring the inseparability of medieval astronomy and astrology.[69]

The links between astrology and medicine are typified by the ubiquitous zodiac man, a representation of celestial influence on the human body, here illustrated in Ill. 38 from Cambridge, Trinity College, MS O.1.57, fol. 10v.[70] Zodiac men are sometimes portrayed with the names of the zodiacal signs written on the parts of the body dominated by those signs,[71] but the zodiac man in Ill. 38 represents the tradition where the zodiacal symbols are painted on the body in the appropriate places.[72] It is also not uncommon to find both figures and words indicated on the human form,[73] or to find – instead of paired figures for zodiac and bloodletting men – a figure serving both functions.[74] Ill. 38 is from a codex that uses paired figures, however; the zodiac man on fol. 10v is matched by a bloodletting man on fol. 16v of that codex. Although less expertly painted, the phlebotomy man is presented in an identical format where text surrounds the miniature on three sides. In spite of the presence of a companion bloodletting figure, the text accompanying the zodiac man in Ill. 38 conveys information about the parts of the body from which bloodletting is to be eschewed under particular zodiacal signs; the two rubrics at the bottom of the page, 'Hic est tractatus ad docendum quando homo non debet fleubetemari', and 'Hic sunt signa planetarum', apply to texts rather than to the miniature.

Bloodletting or phlebotomy men, when they are not fused with zodiac men,[75] are more exclusively medical than zodiac figures, but that distinction is a modern one, and indeed, the two occur paired in medical manuscripts, girdle books, and even books of Hours, as is illustrated by Ill. 32 of fol. 31v in a late fourteenth-century *horae* produced in York, now owned by Irwin J. Pincus.[76] In this miniature we see lines extending from the appropriate bloodletting points to roundels containing the names of the veins and the disorders best treated by bleeding from those veins, information that reflects the anatomical organisation of most bloodletting texts, namely one based on a listing of veins from head to foot, each with the name of the ailment to be remedied by venesection from that point.[77] Information may be found in unenclosed lines of text surrounding the figures,[78] but the most popular format in English manuscripts encloses the specific vein information – whether in Latin or the vernacular – in roundels (or sometimes scrolls), as is illustrated by Ill. 32.[79]

Scenes of the actual process of letting blood are not common in late medieval English medical manuscripts, but instances can be cited.[80] While phlebotomy served, through hematoscopy, to provide prognostic and diag-

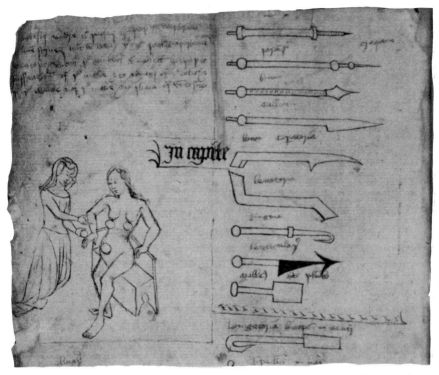

57   London, British Library, MS Sloane 6, predominantly English medical compendium, beginning of 15th century, fol. 177v.

nostic information, it was more often used for prophylaxis and therapy. A related therapy was cupping, the process whereby blood is withdrawn with the suction created by placing heated cups over scarified skin. That process, like venesection, is sometimes illustrated in English manuscripts of the fifteenth century. Ill. 57, a detail of fol. 177v of BL MS Sloane 6, an important medical manuscript, shows a woman applying cupping glasses to the body of a female patient.[81] The process of cautery, the application of heated irons to points of the body as a counter-irritant, was also occasionally depicted.[82] However, from the manuscript evidence, the claim cannot be made for the widespread popularity of either cautery or cupping that can be made for phlebotomy in late medieval English therapy. Anyone working with medical manuscripts of this period is struck by the relative paucity of cautery or cupping in texts and illustrations, in contrast to the ubiquitous Latin and English bloodletting texts and phlebotomy men in late fourteenth- and fifteenth-century manuscripts.[83]

   The form of therapy treated in lengthy texts, and the one which saw the greatest advance in the late Middle Ages, was surgery.[84] Many surgery texts

þe worche be þe benefice of enuyngꝰ mo
cꝰ ꝑuayle hym in þis cuꝝ ¶ Sic om
boici 9 do dissiplina stolaym̄ ffeble is þe
of dystrossyoñ þᵗ worche offiþ only þᵗ is fo
unde redy ⁊ not þᵗ is to be founde
Whanne þᵘ haft drawe ⁊ assayd cᵗ þᵗ pᵗ
⁊ þe brydell as it is aforesayd pame mayst
þᵘ chese wheryp þᵘ wolt titre · or titre cᵗ
þe nedle ¶ If þᵘ wolt titre þan þᵘ
shalt take þe boyd nedle ⁊ drawe it
þoroughꝰ þᵗ myddyll of þᵗ instrmeñt þᵗ is
callyd tondicle begynnynge at þᵗ grett
heed of þe tondicle ⁊ putte in porce
þᵗ myddyll þᵗ of in lengþe as it is afteward
frged pan take boþe heedys of þᵗ brydell
þᵗ be drawe þoroughꝰ þᵗ myddyll of þᵗ
cuꝝ ⁊ þᵗ heeys of þe fystule as it is aft
formed ⁊ in þᵗ myddyll of þᵗ instrmeñt
þᵗ shalbe an hole cᵗᵃ a worste be þᵗ coe
che þe sayd heeys of þᵗ brydell shulbe
drawe ⁊ sadly bownde to þᵗ hole of þᵗ
fystule ꝓꝑcyonally in lengþe off þᵗ sayd
brydell as it behouoþ ⁊ aft þᵗ dystance
of þᵗ hole of þᵗ tondicle pame take þᵗ
tondicle ⁊ putte in þᵗ hole of þᵗ nedle ⁊
to þᵗ hole of þᵗ fystule strongly prustyng
in aft take þᵗ worste cᵗ þe brydell ⁊
putte it in to þᵗ hole of þᵗ tondele þᵗ is
in þᵗ syde þᵗ of as it is frged ¶ And coþ
anne þᵘ haft putt it so in putte þy fyng
in to þᵗ luve ⁊ cᵗ þyn oþ hande prusto
strongly þᵗ tondicle cᵗ þᵗ hole aȝouþ
þy fyng ⁊ whan þᵘ seest tyme turne

58 Cambridge, Emmanuel College, MS 69, English versions of John of Arderne, *Liber Medicinarum* and *Practica*, beginning of 15th century, fol. 93v.

59   London, British Library, MS Sloane 2320, Latin and English medical, astrological, and
magical compendium, dated 1454, fol. 4v.

are illustrated only with depictions of surgeons' instruments of the sort that
accompany the cupping scene on fol. 177v of Sloane 6 (Ill. 57).[85] Such
instruments – along with cautery irons – are commonly illustrated in codices
containing the Middle English translation of the *Chirurgia* of Guy de Chauliac, for example.[86] Scenes of actual surgical operations in late medieval
English manuscripts – where the depictions are important to the text – are to
be found in the codices containing John of Arderne's *De Fistula in Ano*.[87] A
marginal diagram accompanying the Middle English version of Arderne's
text in Cambridge, Emmanuel College MS 69, fol. 93v (Ill. 58) portrays on
the left a snouted needle shielded by a *tendiculum* and on the right the
tightening of the ligature that cuts through the fistula.[88]

A final example of a common medical illustration, indeed perhaps the most
common, is the depiction of uroscopy flasks or jordans as seen, for instance, in
Ill. 59 from BL Sloane 2320, fol. 4v. These drawings are usually found in
groups of approximately twenty, with accompanying uroscopy text, as is the
case in Ill. 59, or without as, for example, in girdle books.[89] Although the
jordans are rarely executed with artistic expertise, their contents are ordinarily depicted with differing colors to illustrate the distinctions necessary for
the physician's visual analysis.[90] Ill. 59 is typical, not only because it repro-

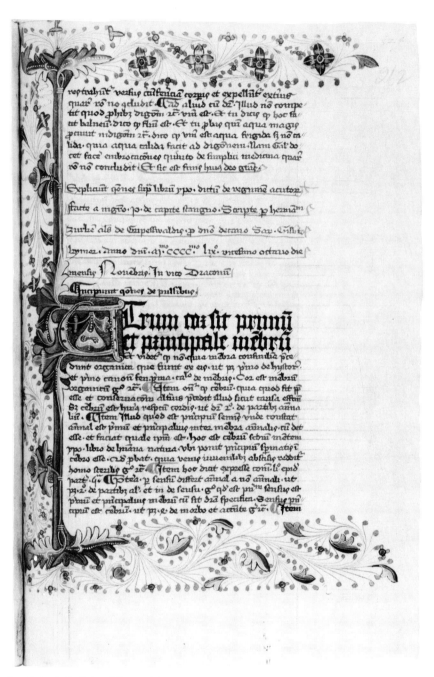

60   Oxford, Bodleian Library, MS Laud misc. 558, Latin medical compendium written by Hermann Zurke for Gilbert Kymer, dated 1459, fol. 262r.

61   Cambridge, University Library, MS Kk.6.30, English and Latin alchemical and medical compendium, middle of second half of 15th century, fol. 14r.

duces a 'mass-produced' illustration found in a group of closely related manuscripts to be discussed later, but also because it displays the use of roundels for information – in this case in Middle English in contrast to the Latin rubrics – in much the same way as the bloodletting man (Ill. 32). To be sure, such information could be presented without roundels,[91] in a circular format,[92] or in scrolls,[93] but the format illustrated by Ills. 59 and 32 is very common in late medieval English medical books. The high incidence of these drawings reflects the fact that analysis of urine was so essential to medical prognostication and diagnosis that the flask became the symbol of the physician in medieval iconography much as the stethoscope served that function in later years.[94]

Although the medical illustrations represented here by Ills. 32, 57, 58, and 59 exemplify the most common kinds of visual material in codices produced in England in the period under consideration, other, less common, medical pictures should also be noted, and the classes not characteristic of the era bear mention. Depictions of ancient medical authorities can be found,[95] although they – like the illustrated herbal in which they most frequently occur – are not typical of the late medieval English codex.[96] Anatomy illustrations, particularly the so-called 'Funfbilderserei' (a term used by Karl Sudhoff to label five companion figures illustrating bones, muscles, nerves, veins, and arteries),[97] are likewise not common in later English manuscripts, although a remarkable fifteenth-century English exception to this generalisation occurs in the 'Anatomia Copho' codex that is now London, Wellcome Institute, MS 290.[98] Gynaecological and obstetrical diagrams, particularly of fetal presentations, are occasionally also to be found, often drawn in the roundels that seem to be a favoured device for visual material in medical codices.[99]

Before leaving behind the visual presentation of scientific and medical texts, it should be pointed out that, as the schematic representation, tables, diagrams and miniatures discussed above make clear, late medieval English medical and scientific manuscripts are visual in an intensely practical, as opposed to decorative, way. To be sure, major artists may have produced anatomy illustrations and bloodletting and zodiac men,[100] but artistry in a medical or scientific manuscript is not the norm for this period. Of the 178 codices surveyed, 113 displayed painted initials and/or borders and/or sprays (five of which also had penwork initials) and eight contained penwork initials (in five of which painted initials also occur), but rarely was the decoration of high quality. Major exceptions to this generalisation are the manuscripts written for Gilbert Kymer by Hermann Zurke of Greifswald, illustrated by Bodleian Library, MS Laud misc. 558, fol. 262 (Ill. 60) and discussed below,[101] and the large de luxe surgery manuscripts, particularly those containing the Middle English version of the *Chirurgia* of Guy de Chauliac.[102]

In moving from an analysis of the visual material in the manuscripts I surveyed to a statistical breakdown of languages contained therein, it is appropriate to consider visual language – the symbolic language of alchemy and the related cryptography of esoteric writing. Of the 178 manuscripts surveyed, eleven contained symbolic alchemical writing of the sort seen in CUL MS Kk.6.30, fol. 14 (Ill. 61), where in the fourth line from the bottom, elements, such as gold and silver, are identified by planetary or other names and supplied with a symbol, as for example the sun and moon. This alchemical writing, where metals and other ingredients are represented by signs readily recognised by alchemists, serves as a form of shorthand and keeps the information from the eyes of outsiders.[103] Similar in function are cipher alphabets found in esoteric texts. Among the manuscripts surveyed, twenty-three contained some element of non-alchemical symbolic writing. A noteworthy example from the early fifteenth century is Cambridge, Trinity College, MS R.15.21 containing the *Liber Cosmographiae*, a compendium drawn together in Yorkshire by John de Foxton, who may have been the second scribe of the codex, responsible for 135 instances of ciphered words in the text, according to John Friedman.[104]

Most scientific and medical manuscripts from fourteenth- and fifteenth-century England are not, however, written in symbols or codes but in Latin, Middle English and/or French.[105] The statistical breakdown of languages in the manuscripts surveyed analyses 178 units, made up of discrete booklets as well as unified manuscripts, so it is possible that a booklet designated 'scientific' derives from a codex where the companion booklets are 'medical'. In this survey, in the category 'science' I recorded sixty-one booklets or unified manuscripts, of which thirty-six are exclusively Latin; fifteen, mixed Latin and Middle English; and ten, exclusively Middle English. In the category 'medicine' I recorded seventy-one entries, slightly more than for science. Of these, ten are exclusively Latin; thirty-seven, mixed Latin and Middle English (and sometimes Latin and Anglo-Norman, or all three); and twenty-four, exclusively Middle English. Of the forty-six entries for manuscripts or booklets containing both science and medicine, six are exclusively Latin; six, exclusively English; and thirty-four, bilingual or polyglot.

To reverse the emphasis and consider the language of the booklet or manuscript, of the 178 units we find fifty-two entries where the language is exclusively Latin, of which thirty-six are scientific manuscripts or booklets; ten, medical; and six contain both. There are forty exclusively English-language manuscripts, fewer than the exclusively Latin number. Of these, ten are entirely scientific, twenty-four are medical, and six are both. Neither the group of all-Latin entries nor the group of all-English entries is as numerous as the group of seventy-five manuscripts or discrete booklets containing *both* Latin and English texts, combined with the eleven instances containing the three languages Latin, Middle English, and Anglo-Norman or French. Of this total of eighty-six, fifteen are exclusively scientific, thirty-seven exclusively medical, and thirty-four contain both science and medicine.

The impression gained from such a survey is twofold. First, mixtures of languages are common in medical and scientific manuscripts, as can be seen in Ills. 52 and 59.[106] Second, the role of the vernacular both in science and in medicine should not be underestimated, although it was in medical writing that the vernacular clearly made greater inroads during this period (see Ills. 57 – where Middle English is found above the cupping scene, but the instrument labels are Latin – 58, and 59) than it did in purely scientific writing (but see Ills. 34, 47, 51, 52 and 61).[107] Of the manuscripts identified above as representative,[108] only Egerton 847 (Ill. 33) is monolingual, containing texts exclusively in Latin. Sloane 213 is polyglot,[109] and Cambridge, Trinity College, MS O.1.77 contains texts in both Latin and English.[110]

As valuable as it may be to make the case for the importance of the vernacular to late medieval English medicine and science through a statistical survey, the point can be made equally convincingly by citing significant and – in most cases – little known Middle English medical and scientific texts. A number of historians of medicine have argued that real advances took place in surgery during this era,[111] and many surgery texts are written in the vernacular. Not only were the surgeries of William of Saliceto, Lanfranc, and Guy de Chauliac translated 'in linguam maternam',[112] but it appears that composition of surgeries by Englishmen in their native tongues also occurred. Of the three Middle English surgeries that have been proffered as original compositions, one by an anonymous late fourteenth-century London surgeon, one attributed to Roger Marshall, and one attributed to Thomas Morstede, only the Morstede text has been published.[113]

However, the vernacularisation of medicine in the late medieval period was by no means confined to surgery, and it is easy to cite highly sophisticated and little known vernacular versions of medical texts associated with university learning, some of which suggest intelligent interaction with the text by the translator and the addition of commentary. Takamiya MS 60 contains, for example, the Middle English translation of *Liber prognosticorum seu de crisi et criticis diebus* of the Montpellier master Bernard of Gordon.[114] A compendium of vernacular texts is to be found in Sloane 6, a large codex (285×202 mm), equally remarkable for texts and illustration (see Ill. 57).[115] This manuscript contains English translations of a number of Latin texts from the university tradition: the *Isagoge* of Hunayn ibn Ishaq (fols. 1–9); a text on medicines 'after Richardine' (fols. 22–33v); the 'Speculum phebotomiae' (fols. 33–40v);[116] a short work on cupping (fols. 41–42v); material from Haly Abbas (fols. 43–50v); four of the five books of the surgery of William of Saliceto (fols. 51–140v); the treatise on the treatment of anal fistula by John of Arderne (fols. 140–174v); and a section of the influential *De Ingenio Sanitatis* of Galen (fols. 183–203v).

One final medical example is a manuscript of c. 1425, Cambridge, Gonville and Caius College, MS 176/97, a codex containing, *inter alia*, a Middle English translation of the full version of a thirteenth-century theoretical phlebotomy treatise, perhaps by Henry of Winchester, a Montpellier master (pp. 1–11),[117] and a long medical compendium (pp. 37–228). This compendium begins with a 'wisdom prologue' justifying the translation of the work for Thomas Plawdon/Ploudon (d. 1413), a London barber-surgeon. The compendium draws heavily on major *auctores*, – Hippocrates, Galen, Constantine, Avicenna, Isaac Israeli, Giles of Corbeil, Rhazes, and Walter Agilon – and contains sections on the origins of illness, humours, urines, fevers, and simple and compound medicines. The material is skillfully integrated. I have not succeeded in finding this text in Latin, and the possibility exists that the compendium was assembled from discrete Latin sources and translated by the 'Austin', who identifies himself in the prologue.[118]

Although the number of learned scientific treatises in the vernacular does not bulk so large as medical writings, there are also sophisticated scientific texts in Middle English, and many of the more learned texts remain unstudied.[119] As in the case of medical writings, the majority of the treatises are translations, but here too some of them contain commentary that may have been composed in the vernacular. Cambridge, Trinity College, MS R.14.52, for example, is a lengthy medical and scientific compendium written in 1458 by the 'prolific scribe', John Multon, a London stationer.[120] In addition to three Latin texts, the codex contains thirty Middle English treatises. Many of these thirty texts are medical – including the *De Retardatione Senectutis* of Roger Bacon (fols. 1–28), gynaecological writings (fols. 107–135v), John of Bourdeaux plague texts (fols. 153–58), a debased version of the long compendium in Gonville and Caius 176/97 (fols. 159–173dv), and short works on such varied subjects as sperm (fols. 28–40v), the brain (fols. 40v–44), and bloodletting (fols. 44v–46) – but the codex also contains a treatise on the seven liberal arts (fols. 244v–254), geometrical exercises (fol. 254rv), and a number of astronomical and astrological treatises of some sophistication as well as instructions for the construction of the 'newe quadraunt' (ten texts on fols. 215–244v, 255–262).

Middle English astronomical material is also to be found in two booklets in Bodleian Library, MS Ashmole 191: A (fols. 59–78v) contains the tables of William Rede and William Thirke in the vernacular; and D (fols. 197v–211) is comprised of tables for Easter and moveable feasts, tables of planets, eclipses and bissextile years (with commentary), and a discussion of the volvelle – all in English. The second group of texts in this codex is less distinguished than the first, resembling the interest in the prognostic uses of astrology seen in the Middle English translation of the *Exafrenon pronosticacionum temporis* by Richard of Wallingford in Bodleian Library, MS Digby 67, fols. 6–12v and five other codices.[121] More learned English texts are to be found in the first two booklets of Cambridge, Trinity College MS R.15.18. The first, illustrated, booklet (see Ill. 47), from the middle fifteenth century, contains Chaucer's 'Treatise on the Astrolabe' (pp. 1–80),[122] and tables of fixed stars and zodiacal positions for the year (pp. 83–8). The second, from the end of the fifteenth century, contains an English vernacular version of the *Ephemerides* of the Vienna mathematician Regiomontanus, who established in Nuremburg the first shop devoted to printing scientific writings (pp. 1–32). The *Ephemerides*, which gave the positions of heavenly bodies for every day from 1475 to 1506, also included astrological material on weather, cultivation, and therapy.[123] Regiomontanus printed the work in Nuremburg in 1474 and it circulated widely throughout Europe.[124] The Middle English version, which seems to include some commentary material, is likely a translation from the printed book, and it indicates the speed with which scientific material that was deemed useful made its way into the English vernacular manuscript.

The significance of the incidence of the vernacular in scientific and medical writing of late medieval England needs to be addressed in future scholarship, but one implication deserves comment. There has been a tendency to identify with the Middle Ages a mutual exclusivity of learned, Latin culture on one hand and popular, vernacular culture on the other, and to perceive that split as breaking down in the sixteenth century; a number of studies have examined the interpenetration of 'high' and popular cultures associated with the sixteenth century.[125] It appears, however, that, in England at least, the disjunction had been bridged in the fifteenth century by scientific and medical writings. Such a breakdown of traditional divisions is not surprising, for in the fourteenth century monastic and university cultures had merged in the scientific writings of such figures as Abbot Richard of Wallingford (see Ill. 48)[126] and Walter of Odington (see Ill. 55).[127] The incidence of Middle English in 'university' scientific and medical manuscripts in the fifteenth century reveals that the interaction of 'high' and 'low' culture was taking place in that era.[128] Cambridge, Gonville and Caius College, MS 84/166, for example, illustrates the mixture of levels of writing. The first (much earlier), pp. 1–172, third, pp. 227–42, and part of the fourth booklet, pp. 243–412, are made up of Latin texts that were the subject of university instruction. The second booklet, pp. 173–226, however, and part of the fourth are largely made up of unsophisticated calendrical, uroscopy, bloodletting and remedy material in the vernacular.[129] Yet the entire manuscript belonged to the Provost of King's College, Cambridge, John Argentine, one of the most learned physicians of fifteenth-century England, whose M.D. degree was from Padua (1465).[130]

The other side of the relationship is demonstrated by the presence of texts of apparently 'university' subject-matter in English – Roger Bacon's *De Retardatione Senectutis*, the treatises in Sloane 6 and Takamiya 60 discussed above,[131] and the long scholarly compendium Englished for a London barber surgeon,[132] to mention only a few. It has been claimed that in the fifteenth century English made few inroads in legal writing – which remained in

French – or in theology – because of the anti-Wycliffite reaction that bridled
the vernacular – and that significant learned English translation and composition took place only in the political philosophy of such writers as John
Fortescue.[133] To these writings it is necessary to add late Middle English
scientific and medical writing as another area in which learned expression of
the sort associated with university learning appeared in the vernacular.

It is clear, I trust, that medical and scientific handwritten books – particularly those containing vernacular texts – warrant more scholarly heed
than has been paid them in the past, if we are to understand the intellectual
milieu of the period 1375–1500. Before bringing this chapter to a close, I
should like to suggest that an important aspect of this history is the evidence –
at least by the mid-fifteenth century – of specialised production of medico-
scientific codices of the kind found in later printshops. This specialisation
may have had its beginnings in the specialisation of some scribes in prose,
particularly *Fachprosa*, in the early fifteenth century. Noteworthy in this
regard is the scribe designated *Delta* in the group of scribes identified by A.I.
Doyle and M.B. Parkes in their study of early *Canterbury Tales* and *Confessio
Amantis* manuscripts.[134] Doyle and Parkes ascribe five manuscripts to Delta:
Cambridge, St John's College, MS H.1 (204), the *Polychronicon* translated by
John Trevisa; BL Add. MS 24194, another *Polychronicon*; BL Royal MS
18.C.xxii, *Confessio Amantis*; Oxford, Brasenose College, MS 9, the *Mirrour* of
Nicholas Love; and Paris, BN MS ang.25, the *Cyrurgie* of Guy de Chauliac.
To this list Doyle adds Princeton, MS Garrett 151, another *Polychronicon*
codex, and a fragment of another *Confessio Amantis* manuscript recently
discovered at Trinity College, Cambridge.[135] It is striking that five of the
seven codices are prose and that four of the five – the three Trevisa and the
Chauliac codices – are *Fachprosa*. This concatenation may suggest a form of
specialisation; perhaps Delta can be differentiated from scribes A to D by his
expertise or interest in copying prose rather than verse.

Clearer evidence of scribal or workshop specialisation can be found by the
mid-fifteenth century in two groups of related manuscripts. This is not the
place for the extensive analysis of either group that I shall undertake elsewhere,[136] but the salient features of both groups lead to the conclusion that
medical and scientific 'publishing' could be found in the handwritten book in
England in the half-century before Caxton. The first group is made up of
eight medical, alchemical, and astrological codices (five) or booklets (three),
produced in London or Westminster in the 1450s and 1460s; Boston, Countway Library of Medicine, MS 19, written before 1468 by William Ebesham
for Sir John Paston;[137] Cambridge, Trinity College, MS O.1.77, dated 1460;
and six manuscripts in the Sloane Collection in the British Library: 1118,
1313 (dated 1458), 2320 (dated 1454; see Ill. 59 of fol. 4v), 2567, 2948 (dated
1462), and 3566.[138] Inasmuch as six of the eight codices are to be found in the
collection assembled by Sir Hans Sloane, I refer to them as the 'Sloane

Group'. The Group consists of five manuscripts c. 210 × 140 and three half that size or less. The same hands recur in the eight manuscripts, and most are written in a very yellowish ink. In the case of the larger sized codices, one finds identical layout. Four of the manuscripts share ten Latin and Middle English texts in the same sequence, all with illustrations in common (see Ill. 59). The three smaller codices are written on parchment, but the five larger manuscripts are written on paper (or on a combination of paper and parchment) and share common watermarks. The Sloane Group also had descendants, two later, closely related manuscripts. These larger, elaborately decorated parchment codices from the 1480s (Cambridge, Gonville and Caius College, MS 336/725 and Takamiya 33) share with the earlier group the core of ten texts and accompanying illustrations.[139]

The second example of specialisation in medical manuscript production can be seen in the Latin codices written by the scribe Hermann Zurke of Greifswald, a scrivener working in England who was responsible for six manuscripts dated from 1449 to 1460. While historians of the book have noted with interest the handsome manuscripts executed by this scribe (Ill. 60),[140] they have not considered the implications of the fact that five of the codices he signed are medical, nor of the peculiar nature of the texts contained in those manuscripts. The earliest of the medical manuscripts to be completed, a booklet in London, Lambeth Palace MS 444, was copied by Zurke in Oxford in 1451. The remaining four manuscripts were copied for Gilbert Kymer, twice chancellor of Oxford (1431–4; 1446–53), dean of Salisbury (1449–63), possible author of other medical texts,[141] and personal physician to Humphrey, duke of Gloucester.[142] These include Bodleian Library, MS Bodley 362 (copied 1448–55 in Oxford and Salisbury) and Bodley 361 (copied 1453–9 in Salisbury); Oxford, Merton College, MS 268 (copied 1458–9 in Salisbury); and Bodleian Library, MS Laud misc. 558 (copied 1459–60 in Salisbury; see Ill. 60 of fol. 262).

These five manuscripts represent a different kind of text and a wealthier audience than does the Sloane Group. A good deal of information about the scrivener can be derived from archival records in Oxford and London[143] and from the chatty colophons to each text in the codices he copied. What remains enigmatic, however, is the source of the exemplars for the twenty-nine medical texts he copied. These texts for the most part are university treatises, commentaries, and *questiones* from the fourteenth century, and seem to reflect the medical concerns of transalpine continental scholars. What is striking, however, is the fact that a third of the texts in the surviving manuscripts are uncommon and possibly unique, representing the sole citations in the Thorndike and Kibre *Catalogue*.[144] Where the exemplars for these texts were obtained and by whom is a question of considerable significance for our understanding of the transmission of medical knowledge in late medieval England, but the importance of Zurke for the present study is that his manuscripts provide a second clear-cut instance of the specialisation of medical and scientific book production in England before the introduction of printing.

In summary, it can be said that medical and scientific manuscripts produced in England between 1375 and 1500 are characterised by a number of features. These include frequent compilation from booklets; dependence upon visual material; and common use of English. These features, along with such identifiable groups of codices as the Sloane Group and the manuscripts written by Hermann Zurke of Griefswald, make it clear that a number of developments in science and medicine associated with the printed book – use of illustration, vernacular texts, and publishing specialisation – had, indeed, already occurred in England in the handwritten book. They also demonstrate that the interpenetration of learned and popular thought associated with the sixteenth century can be witnessed in some scientific and medical manuscripts of the preceding century.

NOTES

1 This chapter could not have been written without the kind assistance provided by the librarians of the many manuscript collections I consulted. I am also deeply grateful to P.M. Deery, A.I. Doyle, B.W. Hansen, P.M. Jones, G.R. Keiser, M.B. Parkes, K.L. Scott, and B.A. Shailor for their active participation in this study. These scholars should not, however, be held responsible for my errors and misjudgments.

2 The only scholar who could claim comprehensive familiarity with the content of these manuscripts was the indefatigable Dorothea Waley Singer, who, in the early years of this century, undertook to survey the entire body of medieval medical and scientific manuscripts contained in British and Irish libraries. The result of this endeavour is a collection of 101 boxes of paper slips now housed in the Department of Manuscripts of the British Library (CUP D.65; there is also a copy at the Warburg Institute), and widely available on microfilm. These boxes contain slips for texts arranged under a number of subject categories and a variety of kinds of indexes. Much of the material was obtained from catalogues, but Mrs Singer and her collegues also consulted manuscripts in their work. Some of the boxes at the British Library were damaged in the Second World War, but most of the slips survive. Mrs Singer described aspects of the undertaking in her 'Hand-list of Scientific MSS. in the British Isles Dating from before the Sixteenth Century', *Transactions of the Bibliographical Society*, 15 (1919) (rpt London, 1920), 1–7,. and in her 'Survey of Medical MSS. dating from before the Sixteenth Century', *Proceedings of the Royal Society of Medicine* (Section of the History of Medicine), 12 (1918–19), 96–107. Mrs Singer published two very useful catalogues from her survey: with Annie Anderson, *Catalogue of Latin and Vernacular Plague Texts in Great Britain* (London, 1950); and, with Annie Anderson and Robina Addis, *Catalogue of Latin and Vernacular Alchemical Manuscripts in Great Britain and Ireland Dating from Before the Sixteenth Century*, 3 vols. (Brussels, 1928–31). A helpful guide to the medical entries

in the handlist is R.H. Robbins, 'A Note on the Singer Survey of Medical Manuscripts in the British Isles', *Chaucer Review*, 4 (1969–70), 66–70.

3 In medieval hierarchies of learning, to be discussed in more detail below, *medicina* was frequently listed amongst the practical arts; see J. Murdoch, *Antiquity and the Middle Ages*, Album of Science (New York, 1984), plates 28–36. There were, however, schemata which gave it greater prominence; see, for example, B.S. Eastwood, 'The Place of Medicine in a Hierarchy of Knowledge', *Sudhoffs Archiv*, 66 (1982), 20–37.

4 This taxonomy was utilised, for example, in identifying Middle English medical texts by R.H. Robbins, 'Medical Manuscripts in Middle English', *Speculum*, 45 (1970), 393–415. It was also used for classifying medical manuscript illustration by Murdoch, *Antiquity and the Middle Ages*, ch. 23, and – to a large degree – by P.M. Jones, *Medieval Medical Miniatures* (London, 1984). Classification by diagnosis, prognosis and therapeutics is by no means entirely satisfactory, however. Astronomical–astrological calculation plays a medical role in diagnostic and prognostic assessment as well as in the administration of therapy. Similarly, phlebotomy was used for the diagnostic and prognostic exercises of hematoscopy and, of course, as a therapeutic and prophylactic procedure for many ailments. See L. Voigts, 'Editing Middle English Medical Texts: Needs and Issues', in *Editing Texts in the History of Science and Medicine*, ed. T.H. Levere (New York, 1982), pp. 41–2, and 'Medical Prose', in Edwards, *Middle English Prose*, pp. 321–2. An eight-fold division of the 'subject-matter of English vernacular medical literature 1486–1604' was proposed by Paul Slack in 'Mirrors of Health and Treasures of Poor Men', *Health, Medicine and Mortality in the Sixteenth Century*, ed. C. Webster (Cambridge, 1979), pp. 237–73.

5 *Science in the Middle Ages*. vol. I and *Science in the Later Middle Ages and Early Modern Times*. vol. II of *Augustine to Galileo* (London, 1979).

6 The important exception to this generalisation is Lynn Thorndike's magisterial *A History of Magic and Experimental Science*. See particularly vols. III and IV, *Fourteenth and Fifteenth Centuries* (New York, 1934). Thorndike deals comprehensively with astrology and alchemy, addresses chiromancy and geomancy, and argues convincingly that there were genuinely 'scientific' elements in physiognomy, even in the modern sense of *science* (IV, pp. 190–7). Thorndike's influence seems not to have been far-reaching, however, for physiognomy, chiromancy, and geomancy are ignored, and alchemy and astrology receive short shrift in more recent works such as *Science in the Middle Ages*, ed. D.C. Lindberg (Chicago, 1978), and *A Source Book in Medieval Science*, ed. E. Grant (Cambridge, Mass., 1974); indeed, in the latter work the only text on astrology included is Oresme's attack upon it, and more space is allotted to arguments against alchemy than to alchemical texts. Similarly, fewer than seven per cent of the total pages in C. Kren, *Medieval Science and Technology: A Selected, Annotated Bibliography* (New York, 1985), are allocated to a section headed 'Quasiscience' that includes astrology, alchemy, and magic and divination. A recent corrective, in the tradition of Thorndike, to this general view – for astrology at least – is S.J. Tester, *A History of Western Astrology* (Woodbridge, 1987).

7 L. Thorndike and P. Kibre, *A Catalogue of Incipits of Mediaeval Scientific Writings in Latin*, rev. edn (Cambridge, Mass., 1963).

8 See, for example, John Murdoch's 'Introduction', and Sec. 18 on logic in *A Source*

Book, ed. Grant, pp. 77–89; C. Wilson, *William Heytesbury: Medieval Logic and the Rise of Mathematical Physics*, University of Wisconsin Publications in Medieval Science 3 (Madison, 1956); and E.D. Sylla, 'Science for Undergraduates in Medieval Universities', *Science and Technology in Medieval Society*, ed. P.O. Long, Annals of the New York Academy of Science 441 (New York, 1985), pp. 171–86.

9 Singer, for example, includes writings of Julian of Norwich in her handlist, and astronomy and cosmology are the subject of J.R. Shackelford's 'The Apple/Candle Illustration in *The King's Mirror* and the *South English Legendary*', *Maal og Minne*, 1–2 (1984), 72–84.

10 Most important here are J.D. North, *Chaucer's Universe* (London, 1988) and 'Kalendares enlumyned ben they, *RES*, NS, 20 (1969), 129–54, 257–83, 418–44 (for an opposing point of view, see H.M. Smyser, 'A View of Chaucer's Astronomy', *Speculum*, 45 [1970], 369–73). Other studies, in which much of the focus is on Chaucer's literary – as opposed to scientific – works, include W.C. Curry, *Chaucer and the Mediaeval Sciences*, rev. edn (New York, 1960); F.M. Grimm, *Astronomical Lore in Chaucer*, University of Nebraska Studies in Language, Literature, and Criticism 2 (Lincoln, 1919); and C. Wood, *Chaucer and the Country of the Stars* (Princeton, 1970). See also G.G. Fox, *The Mediaeval Sciences in the Works of John Gower*, Princeton Studies in English 6 (Princeton, 1931).

11 See, for example, the entries under 'Encyclopedic Tradition', in Kren, *Medieval Science*, pp. 15–21, and 'The Latin Encyclopedists', in *A Source-Book*, ed. Grant, pp. 3–31.

12 Two studies of scientific material in *horae* are H. Bober, 'The Zodiacal Miniature of the *Très Riches Heures*', *JWCI*, 11 (1948), 1–34, and O. Neugebauer, 'Astronomical and Calendrical Data in the *Très Riches Heures*', in M. Meiss, *The Limbourgs and Their Contemporaries* (New York, 1974), pp. 421–31; rpt in Neugebauer, *Astronomy and History: Selected Essays* (New York, 1983). Also important is J.B. Friedman, 'Richard de Thorpe's Astronomical Kalendar and the Luxury Booktrade at York', *Studies in the Age of Chaucer*, 7 (1985), 137–59. For a study of non-astronomical material in *horae* see B. Yapp, *Birds in Medieval Manuscripts* (New York, 1982).

13 See, for example, P. Assion, *Altdeutsche Fachliteratur*, Grundlagen der Germanistik 13 (Berlin, 1973), and G. Eis, *Mittelalterliche Fachliteratur*, 2 Aufl., Sammlung Metzler, Abt. D, M 14 (Stuttgart, 1967).

14 These systems of classification have been extensively studied; see the bibliography in Kren, *Medieval Science*, pp. 41–4, and pp. 53–76 in *A Source Book*. I have found three studies particularly helpful: J.A. Weisheipl, 'Classification of the Sciences in Medieval Thought', *Mediaeval Studies*, 27 (1965), 54–90; G. Ovitt, Jr, 'The Status of the Mechanical Arts in Medieval Classifications of Learning', *Viator*, 14 (1983), 89–105; and Murdoch, *Antiquity and the Middle Ages*, plates 28–36.

15 'Utilitarian and Scientific Prose', in Edwards, *Middle English Prose*, pp. 337–87. A similar approach was taken by H.S. Bennett, 'Science and Information in English Writing of the Fifteenth Century', *MLR*, 39 (1944), 1–8, and by K. Bitterling, 'Chaucer and the Language of Science', Chaucer and Science, Section 11, New Chaucer Society Meeting, University of York, York, 8 August 1984.

16 Singer's forty-four main categories, listed in 'Hand-List of Scientific MSS.', p. 5, include 'Arts and Crafts', 'Geography' and 'Marvels'.

17 An example of an educational and 'business' book from fifteenth-century England

is Harvard Law Library, MS 43, which includes grammar exercises, legal forms, an extensive Latin–English nominale containing categories for book production, a treatise on accounting, and a dictaminal formulary. See L. Voigts, 'A Letter from a Middle English Dictaminal Formulary in Harvard Law Library MS 43', *Speculum*, 56 (1981), 575–80, and K. Gould, 'Terms for Book Production in a Latin–English Fifteenth-Century Nominale (Harvard Law Library MS 43)', *Publications of the Bibliographical Society of America*, 79 (1985), 75–99. A fifteenth-century codex containing a wide variety of materials reflecting the personal and business concerns of a village 'notary' is Bodleian Library, MS Tanner 407; it contains the assize of bread and ale, legal documents and records, charms and medical recipes, recipes for book production, devotional writings, numerology, weights and measures, and prognostications among its texts. See *The Commonplace Book of Robert Reynes of Acle: An Edition of Tanner MS 407*, ed. C. Louis (New York, 1980), and review by L. Voigts, *Speculum*, 56 (1981), 909–11.

18 An example of a fifteenth-century Latin and English institutional 'household book', apparently from Barking Abbey, is BL MS Cotton Julius D.VIII, which contains ecclesiastical and secular chronicle material; agricultural writings; instruction for bleaching linen; recipes for making medicines, soap, parchment and ink; instructions for cutting stones; a cookery treatise; and the charge to the celleress of the Abbey. Although medical recipes, both in collections and singly, can be found in business and household manuscripts, these manuscripts are not thereby considered 'medical' manuscripts for the purposes of the present study.

19 'Chaucer and Science', *Writers and their Background: Geoffrey Chaucer*, ed. D. Brewer (London, 1974), pp. 224–61. These categories provide an apt classification of the texts studied by Thorndike in vols. III and IV of his *History*, and of the illustrations, diagrams, and tables analysed by Murdoch, *Antiquity and the Middle Ages*. For a discussion of the Arabic, Latin, and Middle English traditions of a widely transmitted work containing scientific and occult material, see Manzalaoui's edition of the *Secreta Secretorum: Nine English Versions*, I, EETS, OS 276 (1977), pp. ix–l.

20 This codex, *olim* Cambridge, Trinity College, MS O.8.16, formerly contained even more texts which were removed from it at the time the first booklet was added. See D.A. Winstanley, 'Halliwell-Phillips and Trinity College Library', and 'Additional Notes' by R.W. Hunt, *The Library*, 5th series, 2 (1948), 250–82, and A.G. Watson, 'Thomas Allen of Oxford and His Manuscripts', *Medieval Scribes, Manuscripts and Libraries: Essays presented to N.R. Ker*, ed. M.B. Parkes and A.G. Watson (London, 1978), p. 310.

21 The booklet composition of this codex should be noted. The Middle English practical geometry text and following table, reproduced in Ill. 34, were printed as articles 7 and 8 by J.O. Halliwell-Phillips, *Rara Mathematica* (London, 1841).

22 The uroscopy illustrations contained in this codex are very similar to those in the sister codex BL MS Sloane 2320, reproduced in Ill. 59.

23 It should be pointed out that a rather different view is found in L. Febvre and H.-J. Martin, *The Coming of the Book: The Impact of Printing*, ed. G. Nowell-Smith and D. Wootton and trans. D. Gerard (London, 1976 (first published in 1958 as *L'Apparition du Livre*)), pp. 258–60, 276–7.

24 Two vols. printed as one (Cambridge, 1979).

25 Studies which deal with the 'improvement' of texts in the course of scribal
transmission in general include the following: W.C. Crossgrove, 'Textual Criticism in a Fourteenth Century Scientific Manuscript', in *Studies on Medieval Fachliteratur*, ed. W. Eamon, Scripta 6 (Brussels, 1982), pp. 45–58 (on the German
Macer Floridus); H. Sigerist, 'Zum Herbarius Pseudo-Apulei', *Sudhoffs Archiv*, 23
(1930), 197–204; and L. Voigts, 'Anglo-Saxon Plant Remedies and the Anglo-
Saxons', *Isis*, 70 (1979), 250–68.

26 On the progressive sophistication of writing on surgery in the later Middle Ages,
see Thorndike, *History*, IV, 614, and R.S. Gottfried, *Doctors and Medicine in Medieval
England, 1340–1530* (Princeton, 1986); the latter must be used with caution. Four
notable surgeons and authors of surgeries in late medieval England are (1) John
Arderne (see *De Arte Phisicali et De Cirurgia of Master John Arderne* trans. D'Arcy
Power (London, 1922), and, for the Middle English translation of his most famous
work, *Treatises of Fistula in Ano*, ed. D'Arcy Power, EETS, os, 139 (1910)); (2) an
anonymous late fourteenth-century London surgeon (Richard Grothé, 'Le ms.
Wellcome 564: deux traités de chirurgie en moyen-anglais', Ph.D. diss. Université
de Montréal (1982)); (3) the putative Thomas Morstede (see R.T. Beck, *The
Cutting Edge: Early History of the Surgeons of London* (London, 1974) for an edition of
'The Fair Book of Surgery'); and (4) Roger Marshall, to whom the 'Lantern of
Physicians' found in New York Academy of Medicine 13 is attributed (see B.
Wallner, *A Middle English Version of the Introduction to Guy de Chauliac's 'Chirurgia
magna' Edited from the MSS*. Acta Universitatis Lundensis Section 1, Theologica
Juridica Humaniora 12 (Lund, 1970), p. ix). All these surgeons save Arderne
wrote in the vernacular. On English surgery in this era, see, in addition to Beck,
C.H. Talbot, *Medicine in Medieval England* (London, 1967), and on the surgeons,
C.H. Talbot and E.A. Hammond, *The Medical Practitioners in Medieval England*
(London, 1965). For a surgical treatise written by a non-surgeon, see John of
Mirfield (d. 1407), *Surgery: A Translation of his Breviarium Bartholomei*, trans. J.B.
Colton (New York, 1969).

27 See, for example, p. 485. It may well be that the distortion in Eisenstein's
arguments regarding illustration result from the fact that she confines most of her
examples to botanical illustration.

28 Ill. 32 shows in the inner elbow the five arm veins plus *vena pulsatilis*, usually
indicated at the wrist or hand. On the introduction from Arabic sources of two
additional arm veins to the three from Greco-Roman tradition, see L. Voigts and
M. Rogers McVaugh, *A Latin Technical Phlebotomy and Its Middle English Translation*,
Transactions of the American Philosophical Society 74 (Philadelphia, 1984), p. 4,
and on the tradition of illustrations, see p. 5 and plates I–III.

29 See, for example, p. 541. Similarly, when Janel Mueller traces the development of
English prose style 1380–1580 in *The Native Tongue and the Word* (Chicago, 1984),
pp. 275–88, she ignores English medical and scientific writing in the fifteenth
century and considers it only as regards sixteenth-century prose.

30 Febvre and Martin, *The Coming of the Book*, pp. 258–60, 276–7.

31 This listing draws on E.G. Duff, *Fifteenth-Century English Books: A Bibliography*, The
Bibliographical Society Illustrated Monographs 18 (Oxford, 1917), and M.B.
Stillwell, *The Awakening Interest in Science During the First Century of Printing, 1450–*

1550: An Annotated Checklist (New York, 1970) (by no means complete for English books), as well as the *STC*.

32 And as accurately described by Manzalaoui and Thorndike: see above, n. 19.

33 Data were recorded from the late medieval scientific and medical manuscripts produced in England now held in libraries at Harvard University (Houghton and Countway Library of Medicine), Yale University (Beinecke and Yale Medical Library), the University of Pennsylvania (Van Pelt Library), Bryn Mawr College Library, and the New York Academy of Medicine, in the United States, and in England from the British Library, Wellcome Institute, Bodleian Library, Cambridge University Library, York Minster Library, and a number of Oxford and Cambridge college libraries.

34 In the original *Manual of the Writings in Middle English* by J.E. Wells (New Haven, 1916), a bibliography with a terminus of 1400, the only entries that are not remedy-books (the Middle English *Surgery* of Lanfranc and the Middle English versions of Arderne's writings) date from the very end of the fourteenth century.

35 See above, nn. 9–12.

36 These codices, where discrete medieval units have been bound together in modern times, are not to be confused with codices bearing evidence of assembly from booklets in the fifteenth and sixteenth centuries; the latter will be discussed at some length, pp. 353–6.

37 I have attempted to distinguish medieval manuscripts compiled from booklets, often identified by medieval contents lists or – less frequently – by medieval bindings, from the arbitrary joinings of unrelated medieval units by later collectors and binders, but one cannot always be certain when booklets were brought together. On the booklet component of the manuscript book, see P.R. Robinson, 'The Booklet'.

38 One can conjecture that the older core was never a part of a codex containing the entire *Opus majus*; it bears early pagination, pp. 25–71, on the two gatherings of twelve. A preceding gathering of twelve, pp. 1–24 (replaced in this codex by fifteenth-century quires of eight and four), and an appended four leaves (in the fifteenth-century addition, a gathering of four) are all that is necessary to contain the text of Book or Part v of the *Opus majus*, a text with diagrams that circulated independently as *De perspectiva*: see D.C. Lindberg, *A Catalogue of Medieval and Renaissance Optical Manuscripts*, Pontifical Institute of Mediaeval Studies, Subsidia Mediaevalia 4 (Toronto, 1975), pp. 40–2. On the hand of MS Digby 235, see M.B. Parkes, 'A Study of Certain Kinds of Scripts', B.Litt. Oxford, 1958, p. 114, and on the provenance, see Watson, 'Thomas Allen', pp. 291, 312.

39 Not only does the textual continuity make it clear that these booklets were assembled in the fifteenth century, a fifteenth-century contents list is also to be found on fol. 1 verso of Digby 98. On Peter Partridge, see *BRUO*, iii, p. 1430. For a discussion of the diagrammatic presentation of proportional relationships in the Boethian text, here seen on the right leaf of the opening (fol. 104) in Ill. 36, see plate 95 (Lambeth Palace MS 67, fol. 62v) and the accompanying discussion in Murdoch, *Antiquity and the Middle Ages*. As Ill. 36 here illustrates, the older core of this codex lacked diagrams. The lack of diagrams in the Euclid section may account for the presence, on fols. 129v–131v, of summary proofs for the first six

propositions of Book I of Euclid's *Elements*, followed by the figures alone for Propositions 7–47; Murdoch, *Antiquity and the Middle Ages*, Plate 111, reproduces a leaf of the figures alone, but does not associate it with the text earlier in the codex that lacks figures. Both the Euclid and Boethius were required study at Oxford, according to 1350 and 1431 statutes (see Sylla, 'Science for Undergraduates', pp. 173–4, n. 8) and are found in late fourteenth-century Merton College book lists (see N.R. Ker, 'The Books of Philosophy Distributed at Merton College in 1372 and 1375', (1981) rpt in Ker *Books, Collectors and Libraries*, ed. A.G. Watson (London, 1985), pp. 331–78).

40 On the folding almanac, see C.H. Talbot, 'A Mediaeval Physician's Vade Mecum', *Journal of the History of Medicine and Allied Sciences*', 16 (1961), 212–33; Jones, *Medieval Medical Miniatures*, pp. 67–9, and figs. 27, 28 of British Library examples; and Murdoch, *Antiquity and the Middle Ages*, plate 267, containing a photograph of the folded sheets and four views of unfolded sheets of the vade mecum Talbot described and partially edited, formerly owned by A. Dickson Wright (see also plate 93); Murdoch misleadingly cites the Wellcome Institute, which owns photographs of the girdle book used for four plates in the Talbot article but does not own the manuscript. A plate from that same girdle book was reproduced by S. Hindman and J.D. Farquhar, *Pen to Press; Illustrated Manuscripts and Printed Books in the First Century of Printing* (College Park, MD, 1977), plate 63. Ownership of the folding almanac is there attributed to A.A. Houghton, Jr, of Queenstown, Maryland. For a discussion of the pictorial tradition of what he calls 'folded medical calendars', see H. Bober, 'The Zodiacal Miniature', p. 26 and plate 11, containing views of opened sheets from three fifteenth-century girdle books in the British Library (two of which are represented in Jones, *Medieval Medical Miniatures*).

41 In addition to Ashmole 6 and the five girdle books reproduced in the works cited in the last note, Kathleen Scott has kindly called my attention to three other examples of the late medieval English vade mecum: Edinburgh, Royal Observatory, MS Cr.2.20 (2); New York, PML MS Glazier 47; and Philadelphia, Rosenbach Foundation, MS 1003/29.

42 See above, n. 3; Murdoch's discussion of medieval science as 'livresque', pp. 3–27, is particularly valuable.

43 What I treat as conceptual visual material, as opposed to representational, is addressed by Murdoch, *Antiquity and the Middle Ages*, in two separate sections: Part II, 'Standard Schemata and Techniques for the Visual Facilitation of Learning', pp. 29–84; and Part VI, 'Representation of Theories and Conceptions', pp. 275–368.

44 Cf. *ibid.*, plates 66, 67, and 284.

45 On the tradition and the texts that accompany this diagram, see my [Voigts] 'The Latin Verse and Middle English Prose Texts on the Sphere of Life and Death in Harley 3719', *Chaucer Review*, 21 (1986), 291–305. I am preparing an edition of a longer treatise in Middle English on two 'Pythagorean' circles and one square for *Practical and Popular Science of Medieval England*, ed. L. Matheson (East Lansing, forthcoming). For a full discussion of the related onomantic tradition of using tables to calculate victors and vanquished in combat and an edition of a number of texts, including four in Middle English, see C. Burnett, 'The Eadwine Psalter and

the Western Tradition of the Onomancy in Pseudo-Aristotle's *Secret of Secrets*', *Archives d'histoire doctrinale et littéraire du moyen âge* (forthcoming).

46 An edition of a Middle English chiromancy text from Bodleian Digby Roll 4 that reproduces the numerous drawings necessary to the text is *An Old Palmistry*, ed. D.J. Price (Cambridge, 1953). Palm diagrams were also used to explain finger reckoning and medieval musical theory (see Murdoch, *Antiquity and the Middle Ages*, plates 74–6), but in late medieval English codices they are most frequently chiromantic.

47 The definitive study of astrological calculation and the horoscope diagram is J.D. North, *Horoscopes and History*, Warburg Institute Surveys and Texts 13 (London, 1986). Of particular interest for the student of the late medieval English scientific manuscript are Secs. ii.12–22; see, for example, Secs. ii.20–1 on English royal horoscopes and Sec. ii.22 on the horoscopes of a mid-fifteenth-century London astrologer. The form of horoscope diagram illustrated here in Ill. 43, from MS Digby 97, is the most common of the six forms of the diagram; see fig. 1 in North. See also E. Poulle, *Les Sources Astronomiques (Textes, Tables, Instruments)*, Typologie des sources du moyen age occidental 39 (Turnhout, 1981), and H.M. Carey, 'Astrology at the English Court in the Later Middle Ages', in *Astrology, Science and Society: Historical Essays*, ed. P. Curry (Woodbridge, 1987), pp. 41–56, esp. pp. 49–55 on English royal horoscopes.

48 Also see the schematic presentation of mathematical proportions in Ill. 54 (see above, n. 39).

49 See *A Source Book*, ed. Grant, pp. 465–87; E. Poulle, *Les Tables Alphonsines avec les canons de Jean de Saxe: Edition, traduction et commentaire* (Paris, 1984); O. Gingerich, 'Alfonsine Tables', *Dictionary of the Middle Ages*, 1 (New York, 1982), pp. 159–69; and J.D. North, 'The Alfonsine Tables in England', in *Prismata: Festschrift für Willy Hartner*, ed. Y. Maeyama and W.G. Saltzer (Wiesbaden, 1977), pp. 269–301. On astronomical and calendrical tables, see Murdoch, *Antiquity in the Middle Ages*, plates 88–92, and the introductory discussion in *The Kalendarium of Nicholas of Lynn*, ed. S. Eisner (Athens, Ga., 1980), pp. 2–85.

50 On this manuscript, see North, *Horoscopes*, pp. 126–8, 130–1, 142–9. On this politically adroit physician and astronomer–astrologer, see P. Kibre, 'Lewis of Caerleon, Doctor of Medicine, Astronomy, and Mathematics', *Isis*, 43 (1952), 100–8, rpt, with same pagination, as ch. xv in P. Kibre, *Studies in Medieval Science* (London, 1984).

51 See North, 'Alfonsine Tables', pp. 285–9, 297, and Kibre, 'Lewis', p. 107. The table shown in Ill. 45 is one of a set associated with a Friar Ralph or Randolph, identified by Carey, 'Astrology at the English Court', pp. 50–1, as Friar John Randolf, O.F.M.

52 A brief introduction to the armillary sphere, the astrolabe, the quadrans vetus and quadrans novus, and the torquetum is to be found in Poulle, *Les Sources Astronomiques*. See also Murdoch, 'The Instruments of Science', pp. 261–74.

53 On lunar volvelles, see S. Lindberg, 'Mobiles in Books', *The Private Library*, 3rd series, 2 (1979), 49–82, Bober, 'Zodiacal Miniature', pp. 24–6 and plate 8, and Jones, *Medieval Medical Miniatures*, pp. 71–4 and plate 30, from the beautifully decorated BL MS Egerton 2572, fol. 51, the fifteenth-century guildbook of the barber surgeons of York. R.H. Robbins provides a list of a dozen Middle English

medical manuscripts containing volvelles in his 'Medical Manuscripts in Middle English', pp. 396–7.

54 On the instrument, see J.D. North, 'The Astrolabe', *Scientific American*, 230 (1) (January 1974), 96–106. For a discussion of twenty-three manuscripts containing this text, see P. Pintelon, *Chaucer's Treatise on the Astrolabe* (Antwerp, 1940). A codex not known to Pintelon is Harvard, Houghton MS Eng.920; see L. Voigts, 'Handlist of Middle English in Harvard Manuscripts', *Harvard Library Bulletin*, 33 (1985), 1–96.

55 *Richard of Wallingford: An Edition of his Writings*, intro., trans., and commentary by J.D. North (Oxford, 1976), I, 403–6, 428–31; II, 287–301. See also Murdoch, plate 240.

56 See above, n. 39.

57 P. 87.

58 The Middle English text was printed by Halliwell-Phillips, *Rara Mathematica* No. 7.

59 On practical geometry (planimetry, altimetry, and cosimetry), as well as theoretical and constructive geometry in the later Middle Ages, see L.R. Shelby, 'Geometry', *The Seven Liberal Arts in the Middle Ages*, ed. D.L. Wagner (Bloomington, 1983), pp. 196–217. See also Murdoch, *Antiquity and the Middle Ages*, plate 82; S.K. Victor, ed., *Practical Geometry in the High Middle Ages: Artis cuiuslibet consummatio and The Pratike de Geometrie*, Memoirs of the American Philosophical Society 134 (Philadelphia, 1979); the review of Victor by B. Hansen, *Speculum*, 57 (1982), 949–52; N.L. Hahn, *Medieval Mensuration: Quadrans vetus and geometrie due sunt partes principales*, Transactions of the American Philosophical Society 72 (Philadelphia, 1982); and the review of Hahn by B. Hall, *Speculum*, 60 (1985), 490–12.

60 See Murdoch, *Antiquity and the Middle Ages*, pp. 146–8.

61 *Ibid.*, plates 133, 134 and 214 for other diagrams from optics texts. On Bodleian Digby 77, see Watson, 'Thomas Allen', p. 311, and on the circulation of Bacon's *De perspectiva*, see above, n. 38.

62 The text, found on fols. 81–84v of this manuscript, 'Tractatus per quem cognoscitur ad deducendum aquam diversimode', begins 'Philosophi naturales dixerunt vas vacuum non esse', and is found in three other fifteenth-century manuscripts: see Thorndike and Kibre, *Catalogue*, 1040. The texts in this codex display a wide range of subject matter including zodiacal and bloodletting material (see Ill. 38). On medieval writings on the vacuum, see *A Source Book*, ed. Grant, pp. 324–60, and his *Much Ado about Nothing: Theories of Space and Vacuum from the Middle Ages to the Scientific Revolution* (Cambridge, 1981).

63 See Crombie, *Augustine to Galileo*, I, 139–49, and F.S. Taylor, *The Alchemists* (New York, 1949) *passim*.

64 See above, n. 2; there are still numerous textual problems to be sorted out regarding late medieval alchemical writings, but the *Catalogue* provides a helpful beginning. On alchemical manuscripts in American libraries, see W.J. Wilson, *Catalogue of Latin and Vernacular Alchemical Manuscripts in the United States and Canada*, *Osiris*, 6 (1939), 1–836, and L.C. Whitten, II, and R. Pachella, *Alchemy and the Occult: A Catalogue of Books and Manuscripts from the Collection of Paul and Mary Mellon Given to Yale University*, III, *Manuscripts 1225–1671* (New Haven, 1977).

65 See J. van Lennep, *Alchimie* (Brussels, 1984), and B. Obrist, *Les Debuts de l'imagerie alchimique (XIVe–XVe siècles)* (Paris, 1982). The Obrist volume, in calling attention

to the use of alchemical emblems in two fourteenth-century Dutch texts, is a useful reminder of the continental analogues to Middle English alchemical writing; see also the review of Obrist by W. Newman, *Speculum*, 60 (1985), 188–90, and Murdoch, *Antiquity and the Middle Ages*, plate 257.

66 For a general introduction to medieval European astronomy and astrology, see the entries under those two headings by O. Pedersen in vol. 1 of *Dictionary of the Middle Ages*, and O. Pedersen and P. Mogens, *Early Physics and Astronomy: A Historical Introduction* (New York, 1974), as well as C. Kren, 'Astronomy', in *The Seven Liberal Arts in the Middle Ages*, pp. 218–47 and Murdoch, *Antiquity and the Middle Ages*, pp. 240–60 and 288–93.

67 This codex also contains a brilliantly executed double-page combined zodiac and bloodletting man reproduced by Jones, *Medieval Medical Miniatures*, fig. 54, Murdoch, *Antiquity and the Middle Ages*, plate 265, and Bober, 'Zodiacal Miniature', plate 6c (note, however, that the photograph in Bober is identified by an incorrect manuscript number).

68 On Digby 97, see North, *Horoscopes*, pp. 119–22, 128, 130. On Walter of Odington, or Evesham, see Thorndike, *History of Magic*, III, 127–40; and on Walter and Simon de Bredon, see R.T. Gunther, 'The Merton School of Astronomy', *Early Science in Oxford*, II, pp. 45–73, Oxford Historical Society 78 (Oxford, 1923). On Simon de Bredon, see C.H. Talbot, 'Simon Bredon (c. 1300–1372): Physician, Mathematician and Astronomer', *British Journal for the History of Science*, 1 (1962), 19–30; the will of Simon de Bredon, important for the extensive list of books contained therein, was published by F.M. Powicke, *The Medieval Books of Merton College* (Oxford, 1931), pp. 82–6.

69 See the discussion above of Ill. 43, and n. 47.

70 On the history of the zodiac man, see C.C. Clark, 'The Zodiac Man in Medieval Medical Astrology', Ph.D. Diss., University of Colorado, 1979, and on the illustrative tradition, see Bober, 'Zodiacal Miniature', *passim*, Murdoch, *Antiquity and the Middle Ages*, plates 81, 265, and 266, and Jones, *Medieval Medical Miniatures*, pp. 69–71, and fig. 29. Most of these examples are English. To compare continental examples, see M.-J. Imbault-Huart, *La Médecine au moyen âge à travers les manuscrits de la Bibliothèque Nationale* (Paris, 1983), plates 14–18.

71 See, for example, Bober, 'Zodiacal Miniature', plates 4e, 4f, 10a, and 11a.

72 See, for example, *ibid.*, plates 5a, 5d, 5g, and 8b, and Jones, *Medieval Medical Miniatures*, fig. 29.

73 See, for example, Bober, 'Zodiacal Miniature', plates 4d, 5c, 5f, 8d, 8f, 9b, and 11d, and Murdoch, *Antiquity and the Middle Ages*, plates 264 (p. 316) and 267.

74 The most famous example of the combined zodiac and bloodletting man is that found on fol. 14v of the *Très Riches Heures* of Jean, duke of Berry (Musée Condé, Chantilly); see Bober, 'Zodiacal Miniature', plate 1. The fine fifteenth-century English example in Harley 3719 has been discussed above; see n. 67. See also *ibid.*, plates 6a, 6b, 7c, and 7d.

75 It is preferable to use the term 'bloodletting man' or 'phlebotomy man' rather than Bober's designation 'vein man', thereby reserving the term 'vein man' for the illustrative tradition, found mostly in later anatomical texts, depicting veins and arteries for instruction in anatomy rather than as a guide to bloodletting. On the illustrative tradition of bloodletting men, see Voigts and McVaugh, *A Latin*

Technical Phlebotomy, pp. 4–5, and plate II. For other reproductions of miniatures of phlebotomy men, see Bober, 'Zodiacal Miniature', plates 8a, 8c, 9a, 9c, 9d, 10b, 10c, 11b, and 11c; Murdoch, *Antiquity and the Middle Ages*, plates 265 and 267; and Jones, *Medieval Medical Miniatures*, fig. 54. For an early continental example, see Imbault-Huart, *La Médecine au moyen âge*, plate 46.

76 A zodiac man is to be found on the recto of that leaf, fol. 31. On the Pincus *horae*, see Friedman, 'Richard de Thorpe'.

77 See Voigts and McVaugh, *A Latin Technical Phlebotomy*, pp. 1–25. The Latin and Middle English texts edited by Voigts and McVaugh are not organised anatomically by bloodletting veins, however; they are organised by the more practical but less common principle of pathology.

78 As in Bober, 'Zodiacal Miniature', plate 11c and the Harley 3719 double-page combined figure (*ibid.*, plate 6c; Jones, *Medieval Medical Miniatures*, fig. 54; Murdoch, *Antiquity and the Middle Ages*, plate 265; and see above, n. 67). Yet another example, in an early fifteenth-century English manuscript of high artistry, is to be found on fol. 66v of Brussels, Bibliothèque Royale, MS 4862–69 (a companion zodiac man faces it on fol. 67); I am grateful to Kathleen Scott for information on this codex.

79 For other English examples where the text occurs in roundels, see Voigts and McVaugh, *A Latin Technical Phlebotomy*, plate II, Murdoch, *Antiquity and the Middle Ages*, plate 265 (second photograph), and Bober, 'Zodiacal Miniature', plates 8a and 9a. A variation on the roundels is the use of scrolls to contain the information: see, for instance, the example in Gonville and Caius MS 336/725, fol. 154, reproduced by Bober, *ibid.*, plate 10c. A sister codex, Takamiya MS 33, discussed below, contains a closely related phlebotomy man on fol. 50. Another variation, also conveyed to me by Kathleen Scott, is the presentation of the roundels containing information in a circle surrounding the figure; this format, unusual for fifteenth-century English manuscripts, can be seen in the folding almanac, Victoria, Australia, Ballarat, Fine Art Gallery, MS Crouch 4.

80 Such a scene, reproduced in Voigts and McVaugh, *A Latin Technical Phlebotomy*, plate I, can be seen in a mid-fifteenth-century Guy de Chauliac manuscript copied from a manuscript written in France for the duke of Bedford, Avon County Library, Reference Library, MS 10, fol. 230; see M.S. Ogden, ed. *The Cyrurgie of Guy de Chauliac*, I, Text, EETS, os, 207 (1969), p. viii. For a similar scene from another English manuscript, BL MS Egerton 2572, fol. 61, see Murdoch, plate 265, photo 3; photograph 4 of Murdoch's plate 265 shows a marginal drawing of the incision of an arm vein from the John Arderne *Practica* codex, BL Add. MS 29301, fol. 44v. For contemporary Flemish and German examples, see L.C. MacKinney, *Medical Illustrations in Medieval Manuscripts* (London, 1965), figs. 54 and 55, and pp. 57–8.

81 For reproductions of other scenes in Sloane 6, see Jones, *Medieval Medical Miniatures*, figs. 41 and 60 (ancient physicians), 49 (surgical instruments), and 56 (three scenes of a woman applying cups to male patients; in one a cautery iron is also applied). For a discussion of the Middle English texts in this codex, see the analysis below, following n. 115. For a fifteenth-century German cupping scene, see MacKinney, *Medieval Illustrations*, fig. 57, and for a fourteenth-century French example, Imbault-Huart, *La Médecine au moyen âge*, plate 28.

82 As indicated in n. 81, Jones, *Medieval Medical Miniatures*, fig. 56, reproduces a combined cautery and cupping scene from Sloane 6; that scene appears on fol. 177, the recto of fol. 177v, of which Ill. 57 is a detail. For earlier depictions of cautery points and cautery scenes, see Jones, *op cit.*, fig. 43, and Murdoch, *Antiquity and the Middle Ages*, plate 264.

83 See Voigts and McVaugh, *A Latin Technical Phlebotomy*.

84 See above, n. 26.

85 Additional surgical and cautery instruments from the lower portion of the same leaf, fol. 177v, can be seen in Jones, *Medieval Medical Miniatures*, fig. 49. Jones also reproduces (fig. 50) a miniature that combines surgery instruments and scenes from another manuscript containing Arderne texts, BL Add. 29301, fol. 25 (also Murdoch, *Antiquity and the Middle Ages*, plate 269).

86 For example, Paris, BN MS anglais 25 and New York Academy of Medicine, MS 12.

87 For Arderne manuscripts, see the list compiled by D'Arcy Power, pp. xxxiv–xxxv of *Treatises of Fistula in Ano*. On Arderne, see the works edited and translated by Power, above, n. 26; Talbot and Hammond; and – for a more recent evaluation – Jones, *Medieval Medical Miniatures*, pp. 110–13. See n. 80 for the Bristol illustrated Guy de Chauliac codex.

88 For other examples, in addition to the scene mentioned above, n. 85, see also fig. 87b (BL Sloane 56, fol. 44) in MacKinney, and Plate III in Power, ed., *Treatises of Fistula in Ano*.

89 See Jones, *op cit.*, pp. 56–9; the uroscopy flasks in Sloane 2320 accompany a Middle English text titled 'Practica urinarum' that begins 'Hit is to undirstond whoso will loke on uryne behoveth to considre iii thynges . . . '. This text, with standard illustrations and consistent companion texts is found in a group of closely related manuscripts discussed below, see nn. 137–9; it has been edited from Boston, Countway Library of Medicine MS 19 by M. Harley as 'The Middle English Contents of a Fifteenth-Century Medical Handbook', *Mediaevalia*, 8 (1985 for 1982), 171–88. For an example from a vade mecum where twenty jordans are crowded on one folded section, see Jones, *op cit.*, fig. 28.

90 See plate IV in Jones, *ibid.*, where the carefully coloured drawings illustrate a Middle English text in BL MS Sloane 7, fol. 59v.

91 As, for example, in the miniatures reproduced by Jones as fig. 28 and plate IV and Murdoch, *Antiquity and the Middle Ages*, fig. 260 (1), all fifteenth-century English codices.

92 As illustrated by Murdoch, *ibid.*, fig. 260 (1), and Talbot, 'A Mediaeval Physician's Vade Mecum', fig. 4. To be sure, roundels containing some of the written information are presented in the centre of the ring of flasks in both instances. In my experience, the ring of flasks is much less common than the set of twenty in fifteenth-century English manuscripts; it is to be found, however, on fol. 166 of York Minster Library, MS xvi.E.32, fol. 166, Cambridge, Gonville and Caius College, MS 336/725, fol. 76, conveys the information in a segmented ring (also containing roundels) with no depiction of flasks.

93 Two closely related manuscripts from the end of the fifteenth century, apparently descendants of the group represented by Ill. 59, substitute scrolls for the roundels containing the information of each flask. These are Tokyo, Takamiya MS 33, fols.

35v–37, and Gonville and Caius 336/725, fols. 137–9. The Cambridge manuscript, to be discussed below, also contains marginal depictions of jordans on fol. 67rv and the segmented ring of uroscopy information, mentioned above, on fol. 76.

94 For two representative miniatures in which the physician is depicted at work, viz., inspecting uroscopy flasks, see Murdoch, *Antiquity and the Middle Ages*, plate 183.

95 As, for example, in BL MS Sloane 6; see Jones, *Medieval Medical Miniatures*, figs. 41 and 60.

96 For reasons not altogether clear, the illustrated herbal was apparently much more popular on the continent in the fifteenth century than it was in England. See L. Voigts, 'Herbals, Western European', in *Dictionary of the Middle Ages*. VI, pp. 180–2, and, for an example of the continental herbal, *Livre des Simples Médecines, Codex Bruxellensis VI 1024: A 15th-century French Herbal*, ed. and commentary by C. Opsomer and W.T. Stearn and trans. by E. Roberts and W.T. Stearn, 2 vols. (Antwerp, 1984), as well as the review of the *Livre* by E. Patton deLuca in *Isis*, 76 (1985), 631–2.

97 *Tradition und Naturbeobachtung in den illustrationen medizinischer Handschriften und Frühdrucke vornehmlich des 15. Jahrhunderts*, Puschmann-Studien zur Geschichte der Medizin I (Leipzig, 1907). On some of the complexities of the accompanying textual tradition, see Y.V. O'Neill, 'The Fünfbilderserie Reconsidered', *Bulletin of the History of Medicine*, 43 (1969), 236–45. For four miniatures illustrating the series, see Murdoch, *Antiquity and the Middle Ages*, figs. 20 and 209.

98 I am grateful to Kathleen Scott for her comments on the illustrations in this manuscript.

99 See Jones, pp. 52–4, and figs. 19 and 20, from fifteenth-century English manuscripts, and B. Rowland, ed., *Medieval Woman's Guide to Health* (Kent, Ohio, 1981), pp. 39–48 and 124–33.

100 For example, the anatomy illustrations in Wellcome MS 290, mentioned above, the remarkable double-page combined zodiac and bloodletting man in BL MS Harley 3719, fols. 158v–159 (see above, n. 67), and the striking pair of bloodletting and zodiac men in Brussels, Bibliothèque Royale, MS 4862–9, fols. 66v and 67r. These last two miniatures, painted by a major artist, will be fully discussed by Kathleen Scott in her forthcoming study of fifteenth-century English illumination. I am grateful to her for sharing with me her discussion of this manuscript.

101 See nn. 140–4.

102 As, for example, Paris, BN MS anglais 25 and New York Academy of Medicine 12, mentioned above.

103 A helpful guide to alchemical symbols is F. Gettings, *Dictionary of Occult, Hermetic and Alchemical Sigils* (London, 1981). See also W.J. Wilson, *Catalogue of Latin and Vernacular Alchemical Manuscripts*.

104 'The Cipher Alphabet of John de Foxton's *Liber cosmographiae*', *Scriptorium*, 36 (1982), 219–35. For other studies of this manuscript by Friedman, see 'John de Foxton's Continuation of Ridwall's *Fulgentius metafloralis*', *Studies in Iconography*, 7–8 (1981–2), 65–79, and 'John Siferwas and the Mythological Illustrations in the *Liber cosmographiae* of John de Foxton', *Speculum*, 58 (1983), 391–418.

105 See comments above; on the languages of late medieval medical writing, see Voigts, 'Editing Middle English Texts', and 'Medical Prose'.

106 It is not uncommon to find medical remedies, for example, that begin in one language and carry on in another. Voigts reproduces as Plate 1 in 'Editing Middle English Medical Texts' a leaf from a remedy-book of c. 1400 (University of Missouri, *Fragmenta Manuscripta* No. 175v) where the initial remedy begins in English, changes to Latin, and concludes in French.

107 It is, perhaps, important to repeat that the distinction between science and medicine can blur, particularly in the case of medical manuscripts that contain a good deal of astronomical/astrological material.

108 See above, nn. 20–2.

109 In addition to Latin recipes and herbal and lapidary material, it contains short Latin texts by Johannitius, Avenzoar, Arnald of Villa Nova, John of St-Amand, and Honorius of Autun; an Old French lapidary; and anonymous Middle English remedies and texts on bloodletting, astrology and geometry (see Ill. 34).

110 Cambridge, Trinity College, MS O.1.77 begins with eleven texts on medicines, uroscopy, plague remedies, and planetary signs (fols. 1–101) found in a number of other related manuscripts (see below, nn. 137–9); of these eight are in Latin and three are in English. Following is a treatise on the planets (fols. 101v–136v), written partially in Latin and partially in English; two Latin texts on medicinal wines (fols. 137–73), one attributed to Arnald of Villa Nova; and a Latin alchemical–medical treatise (fols. 173–99v).

111 See above, n. 26.

112 A major portion of the surgery of William of Saliceto is to be found in a Middle English version, for example, in BL MS Sloane 6, fols. 51v–140v. Robert von Fleischhacker edited from two manuscripts *Lanfrank's 'Science of Cirurgie'*, EETS, os, 102 (1894), and Robbins, 'Medical Manuscripts', p. 406, has identified six additional codices. There are two editions from different manuscripts containing Middle English translations of the compendious 'Great Surgery' of Guy de Chauliac: that of Ogden (see above, n. 80) and that edited by Björn Wallner in the series Acta Universitatis Lundensis, Sectio 1, Theologica Juridica Humaniora, 5, 12, 23, 28, 39, 44 (Lund and Stockholm, 1964–85), not complete at this writing. There are, in addition, numerous other manuscripts containing Middle English surgeries, some apparently translations of Henry of Mondeville, which yet need to be studied, for example, London, Wellcome 564 (see n. 26), Cambridge, Peterhouse 118, and Glasgow, Hunterian 95.

113 See above, n. 26.

114 On the Latin textual tradition, see L.F. Demaitre, *Doctor Bernard de Gordon: Professor and Practitioner*, Pontifical Institute of Mediaeval Studies, Studies and Texts 51 (Toronto, 1980), pp. 189–90. On the basis of sample comparisons which Professor Demaitre and I have made of the Middle English version and the major Latin manuscripts, the English vernacular version appears to contain interpolated material not in the Latin manuscripts, but further study is needed.

115 See Jones, *Medieval Medical Miniatures*, figs 41, 49, 56, and 60.

116 Apparently a translation of the work of the same name by John Arderne; see D'Arcy Power, 'The Lesser Writings of John Arderne', *Seventeenth International Medical Congress*, Sec. 23, Hist. of Medicine, 1913 (London, 1914), pp. 108–9.

117 Ed. Voigts and McVaugh.

118 For a discussion of the work, and for the prologue dedication by Austin to the barber-surgeon Plawdon, see Voigts and McVaugh, *A Latin Technical Phlebotomy*, 'Introduction', pp. 14–16 and 24–5.

119 Braswell's 'Utilitarian and Scientific Prose', in Edwards, *Middle English Prose*, is a good place to begin, and – in spite of the title – a number of Middle English texts are listed in F.J. Carmody, *Arabic Astronomical and Astrological Sciences in Latin Translation: A Critical Bibliography* (Berkeley, 1956).

120 See Doyle, 'English Books In and Out of Court', p. 177.

121 See North, ed. *Richard of Wallingford*, I, xv–xvii, 179–243, II, 83–126; III, 15–17.

122 *The Works of Geoffrey Chaucer*, 2nd edn, ed. F.N. Robinson (Boston, 1957), pp. 544–63, 867–72; and the volume beginning with 'The House of Fame' in *The Complete Works of Geoffrey Chaucer*, 2nd edn, ed. W.W. Skeat (Oxford, 1900), pp. lvii–lxxx, 175–241, and especially the helpful diagrams, figs. 1–18; see also Pintelon, *Chaucer's Treatise on the Astrolabe*.

123 See Thorndike, *History*, IV, pp. 442–6.

124 E. Rosen, 'Regionomtanus', *Dictionary of Scientific Biography*, ed. C.C. Gillispie *et al.* (New York, 1970–80), XI, pp. 348–52.

125 See, for example, P. Burke, *Popular Culture in Early Modern Europe* (London, 1978), and – as regards medicine in England – two essays: P. Slack's 'Mirrors of Health and Treasures of Poor Men', pp. 237–73, and A. Chapman's 'Astrological Medicine', pp. 275–300, in *Health, Medicine and Mortality in the Sixteenth Century*, ed. Webster. For a sample of important studies dealing with the relation of learned and popular culture on the Continent during the sixteenth century, see M. Chrisman, *Lay Culture, Learned Culture: Books and Social Change in Strasbourg, 1480–1599* (New Haven, 1982); N.Z. Davis, *Society and Culture in Early Modern France: Eight Essays* (Stanford, 1975); and two works by C. Ginzburg: *The Night Battles: Witchcraft and Agrarian Cults in the Sixteenth and Seventeenth Centuries*, trans. J. and A. Tedeschi (Baltimore, 1983), and *The Cheese and the Worms: The Cosmos of a Sixteenth-Century Miller*, trans. J. and A. Tedeschi (Baltimore, 1980).

126 See 'The Life of Richard of Wallingford', in J.D. North, *Richard of Wallingford*, II, pp. 1–24. Sylla, 'Science for Undergraduates', pp. 175–7 discusses Wallingford as one of three figures, with Nicole Oresme and Walter Burley, who contributed to scientific thought in the fourteenth century from outside the university.

127 On Walter of Odington, or Evesham, see Thorndike, *History*, III, pp. 127–40 and 682–6. It should also be noted that the so-called 'university book' format of earlier centuries, well illustrated by Ill. 35 (where a fifteenth-century codex has been written in the style of the older core), does not characterise fifteenth-century scientific manuscripts written by Oxford scholars in Oxford; see Ills. 36, 55, 56, where the format resembles that of the vernacular texts seen in Ills. 34, 47 and 58, codices apparently produced outside the world of the university.

128 As we are reminded by the level of learning in 'A Treatise on the Astrolabe' by Geoffrey Chaucer, and Chaucer's putative authorship of 'The Equatorie'; see *The Equatorie of the Planetis*, ed. D.J. Price (Cambridge, 1955) and J.D. North, *Chaucer's Universe* (London, 1988).

129 The phlebotomy treatise on pp. 205–6, for example, is a simplified, 'popularised',

vernacular version of a longer 'university' treatise that circulated in Latin and was independently translated into the vernacular. For a discussion of this text, see Voigts and McVaugh, *A Latin Technical Phlebotomy*, pp. 28–9, and for an edition, Appendix A.

130 See Talbot and Hammond, *The Medical Practitioners*, and D.E. Rhodes, 'Provost Argentine of King's and His Books', *TCBS*, 2 (1956), 205–12.

131 See above, n. 114.

132 See above, n. 118.

133 See W. Matthews, *Later Medieval English Prose* (New York, 1963), pp. 166–87, and, on Fortescue, Mueller, *The Native Tongue and the Word*, pp. 132–3. It should be pointed out that Mueller, who does not address – or indeed acknowledge – the body of fifteenth-century scientific and medical writing, places much less importance for the rise of vernacular prose on political writers than she does on devotional writing and on the writings on doctrinal controversy of Reginald Pecock.

134 See Doyle and Parkes, pp. 206–8.

135 Letter, 28 September 1981. I have examined the St John's and the two British Library manuscripts, and have seen a microfilm of the Paris codex.

136 My study of Zurke was summarised in 'A Fifteenth-Century Medical Scribe', Annual Meeting, American Association for the History of Medicine, Duke University, 17 May 1985.

137 This identification was made by A.I. Doyle. I am most grateful for his comments on the codex. See the description of the manuscript in Sec. v., Francis A. Countway Library of Medicine, of L. Voigts, 'A Handlist of Middle English in Harvard Manuscripts'; a plate of fol. 16r is to be found on p. 88. For an edition of the Middle English texts in the manuscript, see Harley, 'Middle English Contents'.

138 I am deeply grateful to Peter Murray Jones, Librarian, King's College, Cambridge, for identifying MS Sloane 1118, and the booklets in MSS Sloane 2948 and 1313, as members of the group while he was Curator of Scientific and Medical Manuscripts at the British Library.

139 A number of the manuscripts share other common features, for example, the presence of the name 'Kyrkeby' cited as authority in texts and marginal notations.

140 See N.R. Ker, 'The Chaining, Labelling, and Inventory Numbers of Manuscripts Belonging to the Old University Library' (1955); rpt *Books, Collectors and Libraries*, pp. 321–6; G. Pollard, 'The Names of Some English Fifteenth-Century Binders', *The Library*, 5th series, 25 (1970), 193–218; and N. Barker, 'Quiring and the Binder', *Studies in the Book Trade in Honour of Graham Pollard*, ed. R.W. Hunt *et al.*, Oxford Bibliographical Society Publications, ns, 18 (Oxford, 1975), pp. 16–17, 25.

141 The dietary in BL Sloane 4, fols. 63–102, identified as having been written by Kymer in 1404 for Duke Humphrey, may be authentic, but the herbal beginning on fol. 6v of BL Sloane 770, with a marginal attribution to Kymer by a later hand, is a much less likely attribution.

142 See the entry on Kymer in *BRUO*, ii, pp. 1068–9.

143 For example, the Chancellor's Registry; see *Registrum Cancellarii Oxoniensis 1434–1469*, ed. H.E. Salter, Oxford Historical Society 93 (Oxford, 1932), I, p. 324.

144 Curiously enough, little additional material about these texts can be gleaned from materials at the Institut de Recherche et d'Histoire des Textes, but I am grateful to Professor Barbara Shailor for examining the incipit files there for me.

15 · MANUSCRIPT TO PRINT

N.F. BLAKE

IIT IS COMMON PRACTICE in major libraries today for manuscripts and printed books to be housed in different collections and to be catalogued separately. This division encourages users of either to think that they form disparate entities. While it is true that the development of the technology of printing may have had an important influence on our methods of thinking and organising intellectual and scholarly activity,[1] there are many points of contact between the two ways of committing language to paper. The continuity between the two media is often stressed in modern scholarship.[2] To those who were alive at the time, the two processes must have seemed similar; both could be referred to as *ars artificialiter scribendi* by contemporaries.[3] A not dissimilar situation in new technology exists today with the development of copying machines. A book made up of xerox sheets will not to the average reader seem very different except perhaps aesthetically from one made of printed or photo-offset pages. We should always bear in mind then that the beginning of printing was seen only as a different way of writing, and although it affected the number of copies that could be produced, it did not at first influence the way one wrote or made books.

It is now accepted that Johannes Gensfleisch zum Gutenberg invented printing in Mainz and that his first book appeared about 1455.[4] From Mainz, printing spread up and down the Rhine, and Ulrich Zell brought it to Cologne about 1464. Several printers were established in Cologne by 1471 when William Caxton arrived there to acquire a printing press and assistants. He joined forces with Johannes Veldener, and together they were responsible for publication of at least two books. With Veldener's help Caxton established a press at Bruges at the end of 1472 or beginning of 1473, where he published his translation of *History of Troy* (*STC* 15375) in 1473, the first book in English to be printed. In 1476, or possibly even in late 1475, he returned to England and set up a press at Westminster. There he continued operating his printing and publishing business until his death, probably in 1492.[5] In the meantime other printers started to operate presses in Oxford, St Albans and London, though most of these operations were shortlived.[6] Since this book is concerned with England I shall confine my remarks to what happened there in the fifteenth century, though parallels from other European countries may supplement the evidence available. In England I will concentrate on William Caxton, the first English printer and publisher, since his output spans most of the English incunable period.

The invention of printing did not change people's reading habits overnight. The texts which were printed in the fifteenth century were those which were also copied in manuscripts. Printing did bring with it greater commercial pressures, for the possibility of overextending oneself financially was much greater for a printer than for a scribe. Although commercial scriptoria which produced manuscript books speculatively were found in the fifteenth century, the manuscript trade was largely a bespoke trade. With printing the problem is one of disposing of multiple copies of the same text. This encouraged new methods of selling and distribution, and as a mass market developed it would lead to intervention by the state in the control of published work.[7] The printers, as is true of publishers still, looked for new texts which fell into established patterns. Caxton translated many French romances into English because he wanted to produce new reading matter in a familiar genre.[8] It is doubtful whether he would have translated those texts if printing had not been invented; and to that extent printing encouraged a great increase in the production of texts. On the other hand, in presenting his texts Caxton imitated the presentation and letter forms of manuscripts. For example, his vernacular texts are printed in a Flemish *bâtarde* type, while his liturgical and religious works are in a Gothic type; he did not employ title pages and only rarely did he include foliation; and his books were made up of quires marked with signature letters to ensure a correct binding sequence. It would be surprising if the technology used in the making of the manuscript book had not been taken over into the printed one, since manuscripts were the only models printers had available and they were still being produced side by side with printed books.

Books and manuscripts were not kept distinct in the fifteenth century in the way they are today. Libraries would shelve books and manuscripts together, as late fifteenth-century catalogues show.[9] Printed books were also bound together with manuscripts, as two examples of Caxton's books indicate. One of the three extant copies of his edition of *Saint Winifred* (*STC* 25853) is bound with manuscript religious and historical material in Lambeth Palace Library MS 306. The text has been provided with head-lines and marginalia by one of the manuscript's annotators. It occupies fols. 188–201v of the manuscript. One of the three extant copies of the *Propositio Johannis Russell* (*STC* 21458) is bound with mostly Latin religious material in an Ebesham manuscript, now Latin MS 395 in the John Rylands Library.[10] This behaviour is not surprising. Many manuscripts were little more than booklets, which were often grouped together in larger manuscript compilations. The inclusion of some printed books in this material, after printing was invented, is perfectly natural.

Printed books, particularly incunabula, often resemble manuscripts fairly closely. At first printing meant that only the text proper was produced by mechanical means. The technology to produce capitals or illumination mechanically did not exist. When a book was printed, it would be handed over to the rubricator and illuminator to be finished off, as had been the case with manuscripts. The printer would provide guide letters in the large initial gaps he left at the beginning of books and chapters so that the rubricator would know what letter to insert. The printer would also leave gaps to allow the rubricator to add paragraph marks where appropriate. In English printed books these were usually executed in red and blue ink alternately. It is much less common to find English incunabula which have been decorated by hand. It is often claimed that Caxton's edition of Gower's *Confessio Amantis* (*STC* 12142) has a space left for an illumination. On the folio which has the signature 1 2, in the first gathering, there is at the top of the leaf the heading *Prologus* and its number *Folio 2*. After that there is a gap and the prologue begins only halfway down the page and occupies the rest of the page. The top of the page appears to have been left deliberately blank as though it was going to contain some form of illumination. This is possible, though in this case it may have been a woodcut which was to fill the blank.[11] In one copy of Caxton's *History of Troy*, now at the Huntington Library, there is a frontispiece depicting the presentation of the book to its 'patron', Margaret of Burgundy. This frontispiece is a copper-plate engraving, and it was probably executed by the artist who is referred to as the Master of Mary of Burgundy, for its style resembles that found in manuscripts which he made for both Mary and Margaret of Burgundy.[12] However, as the frontispiece is found in only one copy, it may have been added specially to that copy. If so, it helps to make that copy like a manuscript, for one characteristic of manuscripts is that they are all different.

It is not common to find elaborate illustration in English incunabula. One copy of *Reynard the Fox* (*STC* 20919), Eton College MS 2.3.12, has initials painted floridly in gold, red and blue as far as fol. b1r, but it is possible that this ornamentation was executed only in the nineteenth century.[13] A more interesting example of decoration is the Cambridge University Library copy of the Oxford edition of *Expositio Symboli* of Rufinus printed in 1478 (*STC* 21433).[14] This copy contains the Goldwell arms, which probably belonged to James Goldwell, bishop of Norwich from 1472–1499. More importantly, the decoration in this copy, which consists of ornamentation and a miniature, is based on that found in British Library MS Sloane 1579, the manuscript which acted as copy-text for the printer, probably Theodoric Rood. The other ten extant copies of this edition are not decorated, and it may be that James Goldwell was the patron of the edition and was presented with a copy which was particularly elaborate. Sloane 1579 is an Italian manuscript which belonged at one time to Vespasiano da Bisticci, and its Italianate decoration may have been executed in Florence in the 1440s. Its use as a model in England is exceptional. The Pierpont Morgan copy of Caxton's first edition of the *Sarum Hours* (*STC* 15867), printed between 1476 and 1478, lacks the final eight folios. The rest that survives is printed on vellum and contains illumination which is modelled on that found in contemporary manuscript Books of Hours. The illumination is similar in style to that executed in Flanders in the second half of the fifteenth century. The edition is usually attributed to Caxton's Westminster period, though the illumination in this copy suggests that it may in fact belong to his Bruges period. The illumination of printed Books of Hours was not uncommon on the continent, though this is the only known example in a book published by an English printer.[15]

The illumination of printed books occurs most frequently in Latin texts, and a number of continental examples were catalogued by Olschki in 1914.[16] He noted the similarity between manuscripts and printed books, for the latter at first used the same letter forms, abbreviations, ligatures, punctuation and general disposition of the text. The signatures and capitals were introduced by hand, as was the decoration. As printed books at first had no title pages and could be printed on vellum, their similarity to manuscripts was considerable. After 1470 this similarity decreased as more of the printed book's layout, such as signatures and folio numbers, was executed in print. The illumination was the last feature added by hand to remain in printed books, and this included not only miniatures, but also decorations in the margins and elaborate initials. This type of illuminations was continued even after the use of woodcuts in printed books. Olschki was of the opinion that the addition of illuminations was designed to make printed books resemble manuscripts and perhaps even to deceive the buyers or owners; in some examples he noted that the printed colophon had been erased so that the evidence of printing was eradicated. Although there may have been isolated instances where printed books were passed off as manuscripts, it seems improbable that this was done on any regular basis. Illumination may have been added to make a book more valuable, and naturally this would apply to printed books as much as to manuscripts. Caxton himself adopted woodcuts for some of his texts, but even so they still in some cases had to be completed by hand. The woodcut illustrations in *Mirror of the World* (*STC* 24762) had to have the explanation of the symbols written in by hand.[17] Naturally, some texts like the *Indulgence* were more in the nature of modern forms, and these were completed in hand by the issuing officer.[18] In the case of the *Mirror of the World* the manuscript which Caxton made his translation from has been identified as BL MS Royal 19.A.ix.[19] The woodcuts in his edition were made by an English artist on the model of the illuminations in this manuscript. The edition illustrates how in printed books illumination by hand gave way to woodcuts modelled on manuscript illumination.

Although a number of exemplars for incunables have been identified, it is hardly surprising that only one of Caxton's exemplars has so far been identified with certainty: Vatican Library MS Latin 11441 acted as copy for his edition of *Nova Rhetorica* (*STC* 24188.5).[20] Many of Caxton's publications were his own translations of French originals. Presumably his translations were made on loose sheets and then used as copy-text by the compositor. When the printing was finished, it is likely that the sheets would be disposed of as waste. Second editions were more usually set up from printed copies than from manuscripts.[21] When Caxton issued his second edition of the *Canterbury Tales* (*STC* 5083), he claimed to have used a better manuscript to improve the text found in the first edition. Instead of printing direct from this manuscript, he made alterations in a copy of his own first edition, and that was then used as exemplar by the compositor.[22] When a book was printed, it is not likely that all sheets were bound up for sale immediately. Probably the publisher kept many sets of sheets in his office. When sales went well and he decided on a second edition, he probably took one of these sets of sheets to mark up for the compositor. When the new edition was finished, these sheets would again be disposed of as waste. Since the early printers seem to have co-operated quite extensively, it is possible that something similar happened when one printer re-issued a text that had been published first by a different one.

Vatican MS Latin 11441 is a large folio manuscript, mostly made up of paper, consisting of 538 folios. It consists of eighteen booklets, containing works written either by Lorenzo Guglielmo Traversagni (1425–1503), the author of *Nova Rhetorica*, or by his brother Giovanni Antonio. Lorenzo was a Franciscan from Saona who studied and taught at various places in Europe. Among other places, he stayed at Vienne, Toulouse, Cambridge, London and Paris. While he was in the university of Cambridge he wrote the *Nova Rhetorica*, and according to the colophon it was completed on 26 July 1478. It was a text book suitable for university use, and it is not surprising that someone thought it should be printed. The *Nova Rhetorica* occurs on folios 1 to 88 of Latin 11441. Although the printed version has no indication of printer or date or place of publication, the paper sorts and the type prove that it was issued by Caxton. The compositor copied the colophon found in the manuscript, except that by mistake he reproduced the scribe's 26 July 1478 as 6 July 1478. Recently a study of the paper used in Caxton's books has indicated that *Nova Rhetorica* was produced before the *Cordial* (*STC* 5758), which is dated 24 March 1479.[23] Hence the book was set up in print shortly after it was completed, and it is possible that Traversagni had Latin 11441 written to serve as exemplar for the compositors. The printed book consists of 124 leaves, so there is less on each of its pages than on those of the manuscript.

When a manuscript was copied it was possible for it to be written simultaneously by several scribes. To do this the manuscript was broken down into sections, usually of a quire each, and individual scribes were given their own

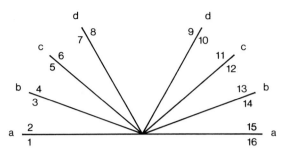

Fig. 3   Diagram showing the position of sheets in a gathering.

stint to complete. In such cases it was incumbent upon them to finish their
stint at the end of a folio or quire so that it could be joined without any blank
space to the stints written by other scribes.[24] In universities, texts were
similarly broken down into smaller portions so that separate parts could be
loaned out to students to make their own copies.[25] The technique of breaking
up a text for simultaneous copying was well understood in the medieval
period. The setting of printed books demanded a different method of organisation of the work, because it was usually neither economic nor technically
feasible to print a book in the sequence in which it was written or read. If a
printed book was made up of folio sheets of paper, each sheet would be folded
once to obtain four pages of text. As the sheets were collected into gatherings,
consisting usually of four sheets, the text which appeared as the four pages on
any one sheet would not be consecutive passages. As may be seen from the
diagram, the outer sheet of a gathering would have the first and second pages
on the recto and verso of one half, and then the penultimate and last pages of
the gathering on the recto and verso of the other half. If the gathering was a
quaternion, that is a gathering of four sheets, the pages on the outer sheet
would be 1, 2, 15 and 16. As the sheet was printed as a unit, it meant that
pages 1 and 16 would lie side by side in the forme and be printed at the same
time. The same applied to pages 2 and 15.

Most printers had only a limited supply of type and could not leave pages 1
and 2 set up in type until the compositor came round by natural sequence to
pages 15 and 16. It was necessary to be able to set up page 16 immediately
after page 1. Furthermore, it was usual for more than one compositor to work
on a text, because the pressman could pull off the required number of printed
sheets more quickly than a compositor could set up a sheet. Hence in order to
keep the press working continuously, it was necessary to have sufficient
compositors to keep the pressmen occupied. It was therefore essential to mark
off the text in some way so that the compositor would be able to set up page 16
before he had tackled pages 2 to 15. It is these signs of casting off which
usually provide the evidence that a manuscript has been used as a printer's

examplar.[26] This method of compositorial casting off may have been taken over from practices developed in scriptoria, since there is evidence that many manuscripts were written on sheets before they were folded and cut to produce the extant pages.[27]

Different printers had their own methods of working, and in the fifteenth century one cannot assume that what is true of one text applies to all others. In many cases the nature of the text or manuscript may have determined the way in which a compositor worked. A poetic text was likely to cause few problems in casting off, but a prose text was different, particularly if it had glosses or marginal notes. In such texts compositors tend to cast off each page with approximately the same number of lines rather than with the identical number. In Latin 11441 the usual number was twenty-eight lines of manuscript at first, though that seems to have been reduced later to about twenty-four lines. The number allowed for on page 19 of that quinternion is 25. It is difficult to account for this variation precisely, but the following points should be borne in mind. Handwriting may vary in size from page to page, even if it is all the work of one man. There were also numerous ways in which a scribe could reduce or expand his language, and many of these ways were available to the compositor as well. The most common was to use or alternatively to expand abbreviations. Another was simply to crowd letters in more closely or alternatively to spread them out very widely. Gaps between words could also be reduced or expanded. It was possible to vary the spelling of words in many languages so that they become longer or shorter. In English the addition or omission of final -*e* and the spelling of words ending in a single consonant with a double consonant with *e* to give the variants *ship: shippe* are well known. Finally it was always possible to adjust the language by adding or deleting words. This could be done either by simple addition or by substituting a phrase for a word. Hence the texts of early printed books are liable to be less accurate at the end of pages than they are elsewhere.[28] The text was not sacrosanct, and the compositor had no qualms about making minor adjustments to the language to accommodate the text on a given page. As a last resort it would always be possible for the compositor to have an extra line or part of a line of type at the bottom of his page, though that expedient was not often employed.

In Sloane 1579 the text is cast off in pages and the beginning of each page is indicated by a pattern or three or four small dots at the beginning of the marked-off page. This method is not common and it may have been used to make as little disfigurement of the manuscript as possible, for the illuminated manuscript was valuable and may not have belonged to the printer. In Vatican 11441 the casting off is much bolder. The printed book was set up in quinternions, that is, there were five folio sheets each folded once to give ten leaves and twenty pages in each gathering. The general rule the compositor followed was to mark the beginning of each page by its number in the quinternion, so that a series of numbers from 1 to 20 runs through the manuscript. This marking off commences with a series which runs only from 5 to 20, because there were some blanks at the beginning of the manuscript which were taken over as blanks in the printed edition as well. In fact in the Cambridge copy of the edition the blanks are missing, if there were any, and the first sixteen pages are divided up into a ternion (three folios folded once each to give twelve pages) and a single folio page folded once to give four sides. In the copies of the edition preserved at Uppsala and Turin there is an initial quinternion consisting of four blank and sixteen printed pages. It may be that the Cambridge system was adopted later to save paper. The manuscript finishes with a series of numbers that runs from 1 to 12, because the text finishes at that point. The copies all have a ternion at the end with no blank pages. To cast off the page the compositor must have either counted (not always accurately) a certain number of lines, or simply judged from the look of the text how much was to be included on the page. He then put the appropriate page number of that quinternion in either the left- or right-hand margin. Each page was normally expected to begin at the start of a line, though this did not happen when a word was divided between lines. Then the page commenced with the first complete word of that line. Occasionally, when there was a quotation of some other textual feature at the beginning of the line, this could also be placed on the previous page. When that happened there is usually some indication to this effect. The compositor when casting off also paid attention to new chapters or paragraphs which could be used as places to begin a new page. At the end of each cast-off page on the manuscript there is a little sign which resembles a tick. This is always placed in the right-hand margin. There are corrections in the manuscript, and these are incorporated in the text, such as the addition of *loquebat*.

An interesting feature of Latin 11441 is that it also contains immediately after the *Nova Rhetorica* a text of the *Epitome*, an abridged version of the earlier text (fols. 89–108). The colophon to the text notes that it was completed on 24 January 1480 under the protection of King Louis of France. The abridgement must have been composed during Traversagni's visit to Paris. Caxton also published an edition of this text, which, although undated, has been assigned to the period 1480–1 (*STC* 24190.3).[29] It must have been printed very shortly after it was completed, but Latin 11441 was not in this case used as the printer's exemplar. Presumably Traversagni had a copy made in Paris which he sent over to Westminster to be printed. It is interesting to think that he wanted the same printer to issue this second text, even though there were by 1480 enough printers in Paris to undertake this task. It may be that both texts were printed through the offices of Traversagni's Cambridge friends rather than because of his own efforts.

Other examples of manuscripts used as printer's copy have been identified and these are listed in the appendix. Although Wynkyn de Worde used a system similar to that found in Latin 11441, Pynson's method was somethat different. Of particular interest is a manuscript found in St John's College, Oxford (MS 266).[30] It occurs in a volume which is made up of printed texts and a manuscript text, and it is clear that these texts were meant to go together. The volume contains Caxton's *Troilus and Criseyde* (c. 1482; *STC* 5094), his second edition of the *Canterbury Tales* (c. 1482; *STC* 5083), his first edition of *Quattuor Sermones* (c. 1483; *STC* 17957 pt 2), and a manuscript version of Lydgate's *Siege of Thebes*. The Lydgate poem is written on paper, and the watermark evidence indicates that the paper was current from about 1476. The poem cannot have been copied until after 1482, because it was designed to fit in with the other texts. Each printed item in this collection is ruled by hand in red; and every page has full line and column ruling. The marginal lines are ruled right to the edges of the page so that they cross at the corners of the text. This ruling, which is uniform throughout, was obviously carried out after the pieces were collected together. But the ruling is continued on the pages which contain the text of the *Siege of Thebes*, although in this case it was executed before the text was copied since it continues beyond the end of the text for six leaves. There has been a conscious effort to unify the volume, even though it contains printed books and a manuscript text.[31] Gavin Bone, who published these details, also noted that the manuscript copy had been used as exemplar for Wynkyn de Worde's edition of *Siege of Thebes* (c. 1500; *STC* 17031), which survives only in an imperfect copy in the British Library. The two texts agree together against other manuscripts, and the St John's manuscript has the characteristic marks of compositorial casting off. Gavin Bone wondered whether the manuscript could have been copied from the printed text, but dismissed this possibility because of the compositor's marks and the date of the watermarks.

It may be that Gavin Bone dismissed the possibility that the St John's manuscript is a copy of a printed book too quickly; but if it is a copy, it is likely to be of a lost edition by Caxton rather than of the c. 1500 edition by de Worde. The *Siege of Thebes* is a continuation of the *Canterbury Tales* by Lydgate, for it contains the story that Lydgate the monk tells on the return journey from Canterbury. It would be a natural text for Caxton to publish at about the same time as the *Canterbury Tales*, which he re-issued c. 1482. In the prologue to that second edition he includes lavish praise of Chaucer. The language which Caxton uses for this eulogy is borrowed in part from the *Siege of Thebes*, which was evidently very familiar to Caxton at this period, since the passages from the poem he borrowed are taken from its middle and not from the beginning or end, which might indicate a superficial knowledge. It is also known that Caxton was very influenced by Lydgate, to whom he refers in his *History of Troy*, the first book he translated and printed.[32] Since the printed books in the St John's volume were issued by Caxton about 1482, it is possible to assume that he also printed an edition of *Siege of Thebes* at that time or a little earlier. It may well be that Roger Thorney, who owned this manuscript, could not acquire a copy of the printed version and so had a manuscript copy of it made for him to complete his volume. Attractive as this possibility is, for it has long puzzled Caxton scholars why he did not print any of Lydgate's longer poems, it is not possible to say that the evidence is strong enough to prove it. It should, however, be kept in mind as a distinct possibility. As we shall see, it was common to make manuscript copies of printed books, and there would be nothing untoward in Thorney having a copy made to complete a particular collection.

It may seem strange to modern readers that people would make manuscript copies of printed books, since it might easily be thought that the invention of printing would put an immediate end to copying.[33] A little reflection will suggest how improbable this is. Even in modern times, before the invention of the copying machine, a student at university, for example, who wanted a copy of an article had the option of buying the journal or copying out the article in full or in part. If the journal was no longer in print then the ways of getting one's own copy were restricted to the second-hand market or copying. As students often did not want the whole text, copying represented the quickest and cheapest method to use. The same would apply in the fifteenth century to all classes of reader. If you wanted a copy of a book, then you could have a copy made if you could not acquire a printed text. In the days when the book-trade was not so well developed throughout the country, it may well have been simpler and cheaper to have your own copy written out. Since this was what people had been accustomed to, it would be natural for them to continue employing this method even though the exemplar was a printed book. We do not know how the book distribution network operated or how effective it was, but if you lived in a small town in the Midlands you might have difficulty acquiring printed copies of texts. It is true that there is evidence that Caxton editions found their way to Scotland in the fifteenth century, where they were used by Henryson and other writers.[34] But it is not possible to tell how exceptional this was.

Another difficulty with printed books is that all copies of a given edition are virtually identical. The language in which they were written could not be adjusted for different parts of the country. Several of the copies of printed books that survive are in fact written in various northern dialects, and it may be that the owners preferred books in their own variety of English, though it may also be that it was more difficult to acquire the originals in these parts. Many people then as now made collections of writings which interested them and formed commonplace books. These more often contain matter copied from manuscripts or from oral sources. Inevitably some of the matter was also taken from printed books, for in scrap books of this kind there is no restriction on the source used. The rationale for the collection is usually the interest of the compiler. Inevitably with some books the printed version may have been the only source available to the person who wanted a copy. Even so it may seem surprising that some texts which were frequently printed, like the *Canterbury Tales*, were copied in whole or in part.

It is a common belief, though it is not supported by the evidence, that most collectors and many ordinary users preferred manuscripts to printed books, because the latter were more utilitarian. It is true that there are many manuscripts which are lavishly illuminated, but these form only a small proportion of the total manuscript output. The majority of manuscripts were as utilitarian as the average printed book. Even so, the belief that people appreciated manuscripts more has led many to assume that if a manuscript was made from a printed book it was to produce a de luxe version of the text, presumably for presentation to some patron. As we have seen, that was not strictly necessary, because a printed book could be illuminated to produce the same effect. With Caxton's output there is only one certain example of a de luxe manuscript produced from a printed book, though there is also one possible example.

The certain example is Lambeth Palace Library, MS 265, which is a copy of Caxton's *Dicts or Sayings* dated 1477. This is a manuscript made of vellum containing 109 folios. The verso of the first folio contains a presentation illumination. This illumination shows a well-dressed courtier, presumably Anthony Wydeville, Earl Rivers, presenting a book, which is bound in green with a single clasp, to Edward IV sitting on his throne and surrounded by his court, including the queen, Anthony Wydeville's sister, and the future Edward V. Next to Rivers there is another figure, also kneeling, who is dressed in black and has a tonsure. Although this figure has sometimes been interpreted as Caxton, it is more likely to be the scribe Haywarde, who signed the volume at the end of the epilogue. The illumination is frequently reproduced in modern books.[35] Underneath the picture is the rubric.:

> This boke late translate here in syght
> By Antony Erle   (*blank*)   the vertueux knyght

Although the name is either erased or not entered here and in other places in the book, the reference is clearly to Anthony Wydeville who translated the work from French into English and who, according to Caxton, requested that his translation should be printed. If this is so, then it is probable that Rivers also ordered the manuscript version of the translation to present to Edward IV. Why his name is erased is not clear, though he was beheaded by Richard III shortly after Edward's death.

Since the translation was made shortly before it was printed, and exists otherwise only in printed versions, this manuscript must have been made either from a printed version or from the copy-text which the compositor also used. The similarities in the text confirm this hypothesis. However, Haywarde's copy contains the passages added to the text by Caxton and Haywarde's colophon is modelled directly upon that found in some printed copy rather than from the manuscript copy-text.

The position is, however, rather more complicated than this because of the textual and printing history of the translation. The *Dicts or Sayings* was printed three times by Caxton. The first edition is dated to 1477, but it exists in two forms. The copy of the first edition in the John Rylands Library has a colophon which contains the words 'sette in forme and emprynted in this manere as ye maye here in this booke see Whiche was fynisshed the .xviij. day of the moneth of Novembre, the sevententh yere of the regne of kyng Edward the fourth' (i.e. 1477). The ten other extant copies do not have this colophon, though some lack the final folio. It has recently been suggested that this colophon was added to the Rylands copy after the book had been printed and that it consequently provides no evidence for the date of its printing; or rather it provides simply a *terminus ante quem*.[36] The second edition printed by Caxton contains this same colophon unchanged, although this edition must have been printed after 1477. The type of the second edition suggests a printing date after 1478 and the watermarks suggest a date of 1480. The second edition contains a corrected text, and many of these corrections have been entered in Lambeth 265 though in a way which does not call attention to them. In other words, the manuscript was copied from the first edition, but the scribe had access to the colophon added to one or more copies of that edition, and he also had access to the corrections incorporated in the second edition. The colophon of the manuscript echoes the words of the printed colophon quoted above as follows: 'sette in fourme & enprinted in right substanciale maner. And this boke was ffinisshed the xxiiij day of Decembre the xvij[th] yere of our liege lord king Edward þe iiij[th]'.

It is not easy to interpret this evidence. We may conclude that the copying of the manuscript was completed on 24 December 1477, but the illumination and corrections would probably have been inserted later, though we cannot say. Although the first printed edition was produced before 18 November 1477, its precise date of publication cannot be established. It is probable that the scribe of Lambeth 265 had more than a month to complete his copying; it was not a job that was rushed through. It is not clear whether the corrections in the manuscript or the second edition were made first. It is possible that a copy of the first edition was corrected and that this served as copy for both the manuscript corrections and the second edition. At all events what is clear is that there was considerable liaison between the scribe and the printing press. The scribe may have been a Benedictine at Westminster Abbey and so a near neighbour of Caxton, though we know little about Haywarde. What is even more difficult to assess is what role Earl Rivers played in all this.

Another manuscript which also has a close connection with Caxton's press is the Magdalene College, Cambridge, manuscript of his translation of Ovid's *Metamorphoses*. The translation, which is in fifteen books, became split up. The last six books were bequeathed to the college by Pepys in his will, dated 1703. The first nine books, which were thought to be lost, turned up in 1964 among the papers of Sir Thomas Phillipps and were ultimately reunited with the other half in the Pepys collection. The colophon of the manuscript reads:

Thus endeth Ouyde hys booke of Methamorphose translated & fynysshed by me William Caxton at Westmestre the xxij. day of Apryll. the yere of oure lord m^l.iiij^c.iiij^{xx}. And the xx yere of the Regne of kynge Edwarde the fourthe.

The work has been translated by Caxton, and several insertions in it show that he had taken some interest in the work. The manuscript was probably written shortly after 22 April 1480, for it is copied in a late fifteenth-century Flemish hand. The book itself contains a prologue which has been translated from the French version which Caxton used as his source, which was printed by Colard Mansion in Bruges in 1484. The prologue gives us no information about the translation or its possible printing. The manuscript contains illuminations at the beginning of each book, or rather provision is made for illuminations there. But the artist has completed only the first four illuminations, and the blanks still remain at the beginning of the last eleven books.[37] The completion of the manuscript was interrupted, though whether this was because the buyer was no longer willing to finance the venture or because the artist died we cannot tell. Since Earl Rivers is connected with the other illuminated manuscript copied from a Caxton print and since he was beheaded in 1483, at a time when the manuscript could have been written, it is tempting to think that he also had some link with the Magdalene manuscript. There is, however, no evidence to link him directly with it. The reasons for the copying of the manuscript and for the absence of some of the illuminations will never be known.

The more interesting question is whether the manuscript was copied from a printed edition or not, although no copy of a printed edition survives. Since Caxton made the translation, he must have made it for a printed edition, since there is otherwise no evidence that he made translations for scribal copying. Since the translation was completed in 1480 and since there is no known reason at that period which might have prevented him from printing the text, it is likely that it was printed. In his *Golden Legend*, which was finished on 20 November 1483, Caxton refers to several works which he had already 'parfourmed and accomplisshed'. This list includes 'the xv bookes of *Metamorphoseos* in whyche been conteyned the fables of Ovyde'. The other five works which are named had all been printed by Caxton, and so it would be reasonable to assume that the Ovid had also been printed by that time. The question whether Caxton had printed the text is of some importance, for if he did not then he must have taken an active hand in the organisation of the production of the manuscript, for it would have to be copied from his papers. If the book was printed, it remains possible that someone had the manuscript made without the printer's consent or knowledge, though how likely that is remains uncertain. The only way that this difficulty could be resolved is if there is something in the text which could indicate a printed exemplar such as the scribal copying of what is clearly a printing mistake. So far nothing has been found that is significant, though the whole manuscript has not yet been edited. Nevertheless, it is on balance reasonable to suppose that the manuscript is a copy of a printed book, and that Caxton did indeed issue a printed edition of the *Metamorphoses*.

When a manuscript has been used as copy for a printed book it usually contains tell-tale marks of casting off. When a manuscript is copied from a printed book, there are no such signs to help determine whether the exemplar was a printed book or a manuscript similar to the printed book. In those case where the translation was made to be printed, there is naturally an assumption that any surviving manuscript was made from a printed version, since the printed copies would form the only copies of the text available – apart that is from the papers used by the compositor himself. At times it can be shown that a manuscript was in a printing office, though in itself this would not prove that the manuscript had been used as a copy or was indeed a copy of a printed book. The Winchester Malory, now BL Add. MS 59678, has offsets of printed characters on some leaves, and these offsets have been identified as types used in combination in Caxton's workshop between 1480 and 1483.[38] There are no signs of casting off in the manuscript, and so it would seem that it was not used as the exemplar; in theory it is possible to think that it may have been copied from the printed text. However, the two copies vary so much textually that this is not a likely hypothesis. Bodleian Library, MS Fairfax 16, a collection of Chaucerian and other poetry, contains smudges which can be interpreted as printer's ink, probably from the fingers of a compositor. Again there is no sign of casting off in this manuscript, so it was probably not used as exemplar. Furthermore, the smudges cannot be dated. As it is known that John Stowe, the sixteenth-century antiquarian, owned the manuscript, it is likely that the smudges got on to it at that time rather than in the fifteenth century.[39] Sometimes layout and particular aspects of a text can give some evidence that a manuscript was copied from a printed book, though that evidence will not usually be foolproof. The best evidence probably comes from misprints which are taken over into the manuscript. The type of misprint which a compositor makes is different from the one a scribe will make, because the compositor may put his hand into the wrong compartment of characters whereas a scribe will confuse similar letter forms. In Bodleian Library, MS Hatton 51, which is a copy of Gower's *Confessio Amantis*, there is a reading which reflects a compositorial misprint. On fol. 131rb the last line but one reads 'Or otherwkse yf it stode'. In Caxton's printed edition of 1483 (*STC* 12142) there is the identical misprint in the line which reads 'Or otherwkse yf it so stode'. The misprint arises either from faulty distribution of type or because the *i* and *k* compartments of type were side by side and the compositor put his hand in the wrong one. It is unlikely that if the scribe was copying from a manuscript he would have confused *k* with *i* or *y*. In the case of this manuscript, the scribe has also tried to keep the pagination of the printed book, with its two columns per page. He wrote the text first in black ink leaving gaps for the Latin quotations, headings, and capitals so that they could be filled with red ink afterwards. Not all the gaps were subsequently filled. Either to save space or through carelessness, he did not always leave a gap for the Latin prose glosses, so the text of the manuscript differs from that of the printed edition considerably in some places. Nevertheless, even without the misprints which point to a printed exemplar it is beyond reasonable doubt that this manuscript was copied from Caxton's edition, for it includes his prologue but not his colophon.

The difficulty of deciding whether a manuscript comes from a printed edition may be illustrated by Cambridge, Trinity College, MS R.3.15, a copy of the *Canterbury Tales*. Apart from sixteenth-century additions, this is a paper manuscript of 306 folios made at the end of the fifteenth century. Some of the watermarks are said to be identical with those in Caxton's paper. In the Manly–Rickert account of manuscript affiliations this text was allocated to their group *b*, to which Caxton's first edition (*STC* 5082) also belongs. In fact these two texts form a small sub-group within group *b*. The manuscripts in group *b* descend vertically, rather than radially, from the archetype of the group, and R.3.15 was placed lower down the stemma than Caxton's edition.[40] It would, therefore, seem that textually it could be a copy of the printed version. It is unlikely that the printed copy comes from the manuscript because the former was issued c. 1476 and the latter is dated from c. 1480 to 1500, though the watermarks suggest a date c. 1485. Manly and Rickert describe R.3.15 as a twin of Caxton's edition, though the order of the tales has been disturbed somewhat in the manuscript.[41] This is because, they feel, the common ancestor used by both became distorted after the printed edition had been set up. But this variation in the tale order could have come about through the disruption of the printed sheets rather than through the disturbance of a manuscript. It will only be possible to tell what the relationship of these two texts is if they are subjected to closer study; at present one may accept the possibility that R.3.15 is a copy of Caxton's first edition.

An interesting manuscript copy of printed texts is BL MS Sloane 779. This is a paper manuscript of 155 folios written in 1484 by 'Dominus Grace' for 'Dame Margaret Wodward'; presumably the former is a cleric and the latter may have been a pious lady or semi-recluse. The manuscript contains copies of Caxton's first edition of *Game of Chess* (*STC* 4920), which was printed on 31 March 1474 in Bruges, and of his *Cordial* (*STC* 5758), printed on 14 March 1479 at Westminster. The *Game of Chess* was issued in a second edition with woodcuts about 1482 at Westminster. The manuscript copy of the *Game of Chess* omits Caxton's entire prologue, which referred to George, duke of

Clarence, and it begins with the main text proper. Caxton's epilogue is included, and although this refers to a lord, he is not named. The *Cordial* has no prologue in the printed version; it had a lengthy epilogue. This was substantially abbreviated by the scribe in Sloane 779, and all references to the translator, Anthony Wydeville, Earl Rivers, and the printer are omitted. The scribe very carefully copied parts of the epilogue but referred to Earl Rivers as 'the translatoure'. That the shortening was done by the scribe is suggested by various corrections. Where Caxton's edition reads 'Whiche werke present I begann', Sloane 779 has 'Whiche werke present [I *subsequently erased*] was begonne' (fol. 151r). The omission of all names would suggest that the scribe had no connection with Caxton or with the noblemen like Rivers. The names were omitted as irrelevant. Caxton may have included them to make the book appear more popular and fashionable, but that was of little interest to the scribe. Dame Margaret was presumably merely interested in the contents of the books, in their didactic material, and not in who else was reading it. The printed edition was simply a source for the text. Since the copy of the *Game of Chess* is from the first edition rather than the second, which being printed in 1482 was available in 1484, it is possible that the scribe was working outside London, where the printed text of the first edition, if not the second, would be easily obtainable. It does show that the edition printed in Bruges had made its way into many parts of England within a relatively short time. It also indicates how sensible Caxton was to concentrate on didactic works of this nature.

This last point is borne out by the number of manuscript copies made of the *Dicts or Sayings*. Caxton himself produced three editions of this work, but even so it often copied out by hand. Its attraction lay not only in its message, but also in its composite nature. It was easy to extract shorter or longer passages from it to include in a different volume. Dublin, Trinity College, MS 213, contains the Alexander section only on folios 70v–72r. BL Add. MS 60577 (the Winchester Anthology) has a different extract. Even those texts which apparently contain the full text have sometimes shortened it, as is true of the Chicago copy. Although there was much didactic literature copied in manuscripts in the fifteenth century, the flood of printed texts must have made printed editions particularly popular both for reading and as source material for copying.

Not all scribes were averse to referring to Caxton as the source of their material, and some may have found his editions convenient to make copies from. This probably applies to Cambridge, Peterhouse MS 190 which contains a copy of Warkworth's Chronicle detailing events in the late fifteenth century. This chronicle follows on from a copy of the *Brut*. In fact this earlier material (fols. 1–214v) is copied from Caxton, which is clearly indicated by the scribe who on fol. 214v wrote 'ffinysched and ended after the Copey of Caxton then in Westmynster'. The material copied from Caxton has turned out to consist partly of the first edition of the *Chronicles of England* (*STC* 9991) printed in 1480 (fols. 1–202r) and partly of the end of his edition of Higden's *Polychronicon* (*STC* 13438), printed in 1482 (fols. 202r–214v). The reasons for this mixture of printed editions are not known, though it is possible that the amalgamation of parts of two printed books occurred in the publisher's office. It is also possible that the scribe's copy of the first book was incomplete, and so he turned to the second one to finish off his preliminary matter. In this instance Warkworth was acting much like other scribes of the *Brut*, which had had a series of additions tacked onto it as the events it described receded further into the past. Many felt the need to bring it up to date. That Warkworth used a printed copy rather than a manuscript may be purely fortuitous, although he may well have felt that a printed history was more authentic and wider known than any manuscript copy would be.[42]

The transition to printed books was a gradual one, and the expertise that accumulated in scribal techniques over the centuries was not abandoned quickly. The presses could satisfy only some of the demand for written material which to an extent it helped to generate; and so scribes continued to supply the rest of the market. There was no conflict between the two means of production, for they complemented each other.

APPENDIX A

CAXTON PRINTS FOR WHICH A COPY-TEXT SURVIVES OR WHICH WERE USED AS COPY

1. CANTERBURY TALES, First Edition (*STC* 5082)

(i) Manly and Rickert, 1, p. 530 describe Cambridge, Trinity College, MS R.3.15 as a 'twin' of Caxton's print. They suggest that the two texts share a common exemplar, but the MS may be a copy of the print. It uses paper, dated c. 1485, also found in Caxton prints.

(ii) Manly and Rickert claim that in Cambridge, Trinity College, MS R.3.19 part of the General Prologue and all of the Monk's Tale (which is included in a book described as Lydgate's 'Bochas') were 'copied from the printed Caxton of c. 1478 rather than from the MS used by Caxton' (1, p. 533). The text is a composite of the *Fall of Princes* and the *Canterbury Tales*. The booklets are of various dates from late fifteenth to sixteenth centuries.

(iii) Bodleian Library, MS Laud 739 contains a late copy of the *Canterbury Tales*, c. 1470–90. Manly and Rickert think that 'in the first part of the text there are corrections in an early 16 C hand, which seem to come from a Caxton' (1, p. 319).

2. CANTERBURY TALES, Second Edition (*STC* 5083)

Manchester, Chetham's Library, MS 6709 is a collection of saints' lives and miracles copied by William Cotson in March 1490. It contains two tales from the *Canterbury Tales*: The Nun's Tale and the Prioress's Tale (fols. 157–75v). Manly and Rickert say 'Almost certainly copied from Caxton's second edition' (i, p. 83). See LIFE OF OUR LADY.

3. CHAUCERIAN MINOR POEMS

In his introduction to the facsimile of Cambridge, Magdalene College, MS Pepys 2006 (Norman, Oklahoma, 1985) A.S.G. Edwards suggests that the texts in the second part of the manuscript were possibly 'copied from a printed source, whether Caxton or Caxton derived' (p. xxix).

4. CHRONICLES OF ENGLAND, First Edition (*STC* 9991)

(i) Lambeth Palace Library, MS 264, fols. 143–69, dated from late fifteenth/early sixteenth century, contains a copy of Caxton's print: see Bühler, *Speculum*, 27 (1952), 178–83. M.R. James, *A Descriptive Catalogue of the Manuscripts in the Library of Lambeth Palace* (Cambridge, 1932), p. 411, writes: 'This last section is very likely from Caxton's printed edition' [i.e. the final continuation]. Other manuscripts in which the continuation was probably copied from Caxton's edition are Huntington HM 136 and Glasgow, MSS Hunterian 74 and 228, in which the continuation was never completed, and BL Cotton Claudius A. viii and Bodleian Library, MS Rawlinson poet. 32; see L. Matheson, *Speculum*, 60 (1985), 595–6. Matheson suggests that BL Add. 10099 may be a copy of Caxton's exemplar, which was completed as a presentation copy; and also that Caxton was the compiler of the continuation. See also POLYCHRONICON.

(ii) G. Raynaud, *Catalogue des manuscrits anglais de la Bibliothèque nationale* (Paris, 1884), no. 30, is a MS of the *Brut* which is described as 'Redaction incomplète de la *Chronique* dite de Caxton, dont la première édition est de 1480' (p. 11). The paper MS is of the fifteenth century, and it may contain a copy of Caxton's edition.

5. CONFESSIO AMANTIS (*STC* 12142)

Bühler, *Speculum*, 27 (1952), 178–83, notes that Bodleian Library, MS Hatton 51 (S.C. 4099) contains a copy of Caxton's print. The MS which contains the single work is dated c. 1500. It is written on parchment and contains 202 folios.

6. CORDIAL (*STC* 5758)

(i) Bühler, *Speculum*, 27 (1952), 178–83, notes that BL MS Sloane 779, fols. 76v–151r contain a copy of Caxton's print made by Dominus Grace for Dame Margaret Woodward in 1484; see also GAME OF CHESS.

(ii) CUL MS Nn.3.10, a quarto MS of paper from c. 1500 containing *Cordial* and Mirk's *Festial*. The former, on fols. 1–27, is imperfect at beginning and end. Bühler, *Speculum*, 27 (1952), 178–83, and *A Catalogue of the Manuscripts preserved in the Library of the University of Cambridge*, iv (Cambridge, 1861), p. 479.

(iii) Edinburgh, Scottish Record Office, MS GD 112/71/1 (1) is a manuscript consisting of two parts (i) a prose life of Edward II, and (ii) a copy of Rivers' *Cordial*. The latter text occurs on fols. 14r–79v. It is a copy of Caxton's edition with anglicised spellings which contain some Scottish variants. The watermarks, according to Dr Lyall, suggest a date of 1479 and certainly not later than 1485. Since Caxton's edition appeared in 1479, this copy, which was probably made in Scotland, must have been written shortly afterwards. On the final folio there is a note 'Iste liber pertinet Iohannes Cambell' in what is probably a fifteenth-century hand.

7. COURT OF SAPIENCE (*STC* 17015)

Bühler, *Speculum*, 27 (1952), 183 claims the BL Add. MS 29729 contains a copy of Caxton, though without saying which text. The MS contains a collection of English poems mostly by Lydgate, many of which were written by or for John Stowe from a Shirley manuscript. The most likely item to be a copy of a Caxton print is the *Court of Sapience* on fols. 87–122, though the British Library catalogue makes no reference to the possibility.

8. DICTS OR SAYINGS, First Edition (*STC* 6826, 6827)

(i) Lambeth Palace Library, MS 265, an illuminated MS on vellum written by Haywarde on 29 December 1477, was apparently intended for presentation to Edward IV. There are numerous references to it; see most recently L. Hellinga, *Caxton in Focus* (London, 1982), pp. 77–80. For a description of the MS see M.R. James, *A Descriptive Catalogue of Manuscripts in the Library of Lambeth Palace* (Cambridge, 1932), No. 264. See also C.F. Bühler, 'The Dictes and Sayings of the Philosophers', *The Library*, 4th series, 15 (1934–5), 316–29.

(ii) Chicago, Newberry Library, MS f.36 Ry 20, fols. 208–41 contains a shortened copy of the printed edition made by a North English scribe; C.F. Bühler, 'The Newberry Library Manuscripts of the *Dictes and Sayings of the Philosophers*', *Anglia*, 74 (1956), 281–91.

(iii) Columbia University Library, MS Plimpton 259 contains a shortened version of one of Caxton's editions, though certain identification of edition is impossible. C.F. Bühler, 'New Manuscripts of *The Dicts and Sayings of the Philosophers*', *MLN*, 63 (1948), 26–30.

(iv) BL Add. MS 60577 (Winchester Anthology), fols. 38–44v (written in Winchester after 1487) has an acephalous extract of Caxton's print containing some of the sayings attributed to Hermes. See *The Winchester Anthology. A Facsimile of British Library Additional Manuscript 60577*, with an Introduction by Edward Wilson (Cambridge, 1981).

9. DICTS OR SAYINGS, Second Edition (*STC* 6828)

(i) BL Add. MS 22718, a vellum MS in folio from late fifteenth/early sixteenth century which contains a text of the *Dicts or Sayings* including the colophon. The first folio is missing. See Bühler, *Speculum*, 27 (1952), 178–83 and Scott, *The Caxton*

Master, p. xi. For a full account, see Bühler, 'The Dictes and Sayings of the Philosophers'.

(ii) Dublin, Trinity College, MS 213, fols. 70v–72r, contains the Alexander extract from Caxton's print; the rest of the MS contains the *Wars of Alexander* and an A text of *Piers Plowman*. The MS is dated 1475–1500 and is associated with Durham Priory c. 1500. See T.K. Abbott, *Catalogue of the Manuscripts in the Library of Trinity College, Dublin* (London, 1900), No. 213; and Doyle, 'The Manuscripts', pp. 99–100.

(iii) Curt Bühler (New York) MS 11: see C.F. Bühler, 'New Manuscripts of *The Dicts and Sayings of the Philosophers*', *MLN*, 63 (1948), 26–30. This MS is in a fifteenth-century English hand.

10. ENEYDOS (*STC* 24796)

Princeton University Library, MS 128 contains a copy of Caxton's edition. The paper MS may be dated c. 1600. The copy has been given the title 'Caxton's translation of the Æneids out of French Dedicated to Prince Arthure Eldest sonne to King Henry the 7th'. It opens with Caxton's prologue. The colophon reads: 'Here finisheth the booke of Æneids, compiled by Virgill, wch hath beene translated out of Latine into French and out of French reduced into Englishe by mee William Caxton the xxij daie of June in the yeare of our Lord 1490 and in the fift yeare of kinge Henry the 7th.'

11. GAME OF CHESS, First Edition (*STC* 4920)

BL MS Sloane 779, fols. 1–76r, contains a copy of Caxton's print without prologue copied by Dominus Grace for Dame Margaret Woodward in 1484; see CORDIAL.

12. GOLDEN LEGEND (*STC* 24873)

(i) Bodleian Library, MS Bodley 952 contains a copy of the *Golden Legend* which is incomplete, but which was copied from Caxton's edition. The life of St Rock has the note 'The ffeste off saynt Rocke ys alwey holdyn on the morne after the day of Thassumpcion off owre lady whych lyff is traunslated owte off latyn in to englesche by me William Caxton' (fol. 219v). See M. Görlach, *The South English Legendary, Gilt Legende and Golden Legend* (Braunschweig, 1972), pp. 26–7, and C. Bühler, 'A New Middle English Life of Saint Winifred?' *Medieval Studies for Lillian Herlands Hornstein*, ed. J.B. Bessinger and R.R. Raymo (New York, 1976), p. 95. The MS is of the late fifteenth century and is incomplete at beginning and end.

(ii) New York, PML MS Bühler 26 contains *inter alia* a *Lyfe of St Weneffryde* written in the last quarter of the sixteenth century. Its colophon states that it is 'drawen out of an ould pryntinge boocke word by word'. Although it is not an exact copy of Caxton's version of the life in the *Golden Legend*, Bühler suggests that 'the most probable explanation' is that it is 'a free copy of the Caxton version, thus denying the very positive statement by the scribe and giving a fine example of the liberties which copyists were prepared to take with their exemplars'; see Bühler, *ibid.*, pp. 87–97.

13. HORSE, SHEEP AND GOOSE, Second Edition (*STC* 17018)

Huntington Library, MS HM 144, fols. 140v–144r, contains the second part of the poem copied from this edition: see C.F. Bühler's 'Lydgate's *Horse, Sheep and Goose* and Huntington MS. HM 144', *MLN*, 55 (1940), 563–9.

14. INDULGENCE 1476 (*STC* 14077 c. 106)

Queen's University Library, Belfast, has two MS copies of this indulgence, though both are a little damaged. They are included in a miscellaneous manuscript which may be dated to the end of the fifteenth century; the MS is Brett MS B50. See K. Povey, 'The Caxton Indulgence of 1476', *The Library*, 4th series, 19 (1938–9), 462–4.

15. JASON (*STC* 15383)

(i) Glasgow University Library, MS Hunterian 410, a paper MS of late fifteenth/early sixteenth century of 125 folios written in Flemish hand on same paper sorts as found in Caxton's prints. See Bühler, *Speculum*, 27 (1952), 178–83; and J. Young and P.H. Aitken, *A Catalogue of the Manuscripts in the Library of the Hunterian Museum in the University of Glasgow* (Glasgow, 1908), No. 410.

(ii) CUL MS Dd.3.45, partly paper and partly vellum, written in a slovenly hand of late fifteenth century, contains only *Jason* in its 102 fols. It is imperfect at beginning and end. See *A Catalogue of the Manuscripts preserved in the Library of the University of Cambridge*, 1 (Cambridge, 1856), pp. 101–2.

16. LIFE OF OUR LADY, First Edition (*STC* 17023)

(i) Manchester, Chetham's Library, MS 6709, a collection of saints' lives and miracles, copied by William Cotson in March 1490, contains on fols. 6v–156r a copy of Caxton's print: see R.A. Klinefelter, 'Lydgate's *Life of Our Lady* and the Chetham MS. 6709', *Publications of the Bibliographical Society of America*, 46 (1952), 396–7. See CANTERBURY TALES, second edition.

(ii) According to *Bibliotheca Anglo-Poetica; or, a descriptive catalogue of a rare and rich collection of early English Poetry: in the possession of Longman, Hurst, Rees, Orme and Brown* (London, 1815), No. 414, pp. 187–8, there is a paper MS made in 1602 which is 'a transcript from the edition by Caxton'. The MS opens: 'This booke was compiled by dan John Lydgate monke of Burye, at the excitacion and stirynge of the noble and victoryous Prince king Hary the fifthe in honour glory and reverence of the berth of our most Blessed Lady mayde wyf and Moder of our lord Jhesu, Chryst.' The *Life of our Lady* is followed by 'other metrical lines entitled "Lydgats testament and last will"'. The MS is now Liverpool Cathedral Library, MS Radcliffe 16.

17. NOVA RHETORICA (*STC* 24188.5, 24189)

This edition was set up from Vatican Library, MS Latin 11441 fols. 1–88: see J. Ruysschaert, 'Les manuscrits autographes de deux oeuvres de Lorenzo Guglielmo Traversagni imprimées chez Caxton', *BJRL*, 36 (1953–4), 191–7.

18. ORDER OF CHIVALRY (*STC* 3356.7)

BL MS Harley 6149, a paper MS of 174 folios, is a composite MS containing mainly matters of heraldry. It was compiled by Adam Loutfut, Kintyr Pursuivant, a Scottish scribe in the service of Sir William Cummyn, in 1494. It contains the *Order of Chivalry* copied from Caxton's print on fols. 83–109, probably after 29 September 1494. Loutfut's copy is in the Scots dialect and is edited in A.T.P. Byles, *The Book of Ordre of Chyualry*, EETS, os, 168 (1929). Loutfut's version was itself copied three times: (i) by M.R. Anderson at the end of the fifteenth century in Oxford, Queen's College, MS 161 fols. 65–82v; (ii) by John Scrymgeour about 1530 in Edinburgh, Advocates' Library MS 31.5.2; and (iii) by Sir David Lindsay in 1586 in Edinburgh, Advocates' Library MS 31.3.20.

19. OVID'S METAMORPHOSES

Caxton translated this book on 22 April 1480. It survives as MS 2124 in the Pepys Library, Magdalene College, Cambridge. It may be a copy of a printed edition, though no trace of such an edition has been discovered. See S. Gaselee and H.F.B. Brett-Smith, *Ovyde hys Booke of Methamorphose* (Oxford, 1924); and *The Metamorphoses of Ovid translated by William Caxton*, 2 vols. (New York, 1968).

20. POLYCHRONICON (*STC* 13438)

(i) It has been accepted that Cambridge, Peterhouse, MS 190 contained a copy of some Caxton material since the publication of J.O. Halliwell, *A Chronicle of the First Thirteen Years of the Reign of King Edward the Fourth by John Warkworth*. Camden Society, os, 10 (London, 1839). L.M. Matheson, *Speculum*, 60 (1985), 593–614, has now shown that Glasgow Hunterian 83 (T.3.21) and BL Harley 3730 are linked with Peterhouse 190. After a version of the *Brut* which in Peterhouse 190 may be copied from the St Albans *Chronicles of England* ending in 1419, there is a continuation from 1419 to 1461 consisting of sections of text copied at first from a Caxton edition of *Chronicles of England* and then from Caxton's *Polychronicon*. This compilation is followed by *Warkworth's Chronicle*. Hunterian 83 seems to be the original manuscript and Harley 3730 is a copy of it. For the period 1419 to 1461 Peterhouse 190 is probably a copy of Harley 3730. Three manuscripts were probably made for the fellows of Peterhouse about 1484, and may have been made in the College itself. See also CHRONICLES OF ENGLAND. Professor Matheson is compiling a book about these manuscripts; his article contains references to some previous discussions.

(ii) Two MSS have used Caxton's edition as the basis for a composite history from Adam to Hannibal, which makes use of a wide variety of sources; they are Oxford, Trinity College D 29 and Huntington MS HM 144. See K. Harris, 'John Gower's "Confessio Amantis" and the Virtues of Bad Texts', in Pearsall, *Manuscripts and Readers*, pp. 31ff, and C.W. Marx and J.F. Drennan (eds.), *The Middle English Prose Complaint of Our Lady and Gospel of Nicodemus* (Heidelberg, 1988), p. 13.

21. SIEGE OF JERUSALEM (*STC* 13175)

BL MS Royal 18.B.xxvi, a paper MS of 256 folios dated to the middle of the sixteenth century, contains *The History of Holy Ware*, part 2 of which is 'a condensation of Caxton's translation': see M.N. Colvin, *Godeffroy of Boloyne*, EETS, ES, 64 (1893), p. xvii.

22. STANS PUER (*STC* 17030)

A copy of Caxton's print is included in Richard Hill's commonplace book, now Oxford, Balliol College, MS 354, fols. 158v–60v, a paper MS of 248 fols. dating from the early sixteenth century. See R.A.B. Mynors, *Catalogue of the Manuscripts of Balliol College Oxford* (Oxford, 1963), pp. 352–4. R. Dyboski, *Songs, Carols and other Miscellaneous Pieces from the Balliol MS.354*, EETS, ES, 101 (1907), p. xxx, writes of *Stans Puer* that 'the Balliol text seems to be copied from Caxton's print'. On p. 179 Dyboski writes that *Salve Regina* and the rhyming rules which follow *Stans Puer* in the Balliol MS are also identical with Caxton 'so that we arrive at the conclusion, that the whole group of pieces, No. 60–3 in our catalogue table, were probably *transcribed in bulk from Caxton's quarto'*. The text of the *Book of Courtesy* in Balliol 354 is similar to that in Caxton's print, but it has not been identified as a copy of it. Balliol 354 also contains pieces copied from *Arnold's Chronicle* printed at Antwerp c. 1502–3 and at Southwark in c. 1521.

APPENDIX B

REJECTED CAXTON EXAMPLES

1. BOOK OF COURTESY (*STC* 3303)

Oriel College, MS 79 is listed by Bühler, *Speculum*, 27 (1952), 183, as a copy of Caxton's edition. The Caxton text and the Oriel MS were printed in F.J. Furnivall, *Caxton's Book of Courtesye*, EETS, ES, 3 (1868). It is clear that the Oriel text is different from Caxton's and cannot be copied from it.

2. BOOK OF GOOD MANNERS (*STC* 15394)

Bühler, *Speculum*, 27 (1952), 173–83, following Blades and the *Cambridge Bibliography of English Literature* I, p. 262, indicates that BL MS Harley 149 is a copy of Caxton's print. This is rejected by R.H. Wilson, in *A Manual of the Writings in Middle English*, II, edited by A.E. Hartung (New Haven, 1972), p. 943.

3. CONFESSIO AMANTIS (*STC* 12142)

G.C. Macaulay, *The English Works of John Gower*, EETS, ES, 81 (1900), p. clxiii, claimed that Oxford, Magdalen College, MS 213 was one of the three MSS used by Caxton as copy-text or else he used one so like Magd. 213 as to be indistinguishable from it. This position was supported by G. Bone, 'Extant Manuscripts Printed from by W. de Worde with Notes on the Owner, Roger Thorney', *The Library*, 4th series, 12 (1931–2), 285–6. He noted the similarity of the two texts and the occurrence in Magd. 213 of some indistinct crosses or circles which corresponded to the pages in Caxton's print. Bone did not think the proof for Magd. 213 as examplar for Caxton's edition conclusive, though he accepted it was very strong. This view was rejected by N.F. Blake, 'Caxton's Copytext and Gower's *Confessio Amantis*', *Anglia*, 85 (1967), 282–93, mainly on the grounds that the texts of the two were so different. Blake also claims that Caxton had only one MS of the poem.

4. CURIAL (*STC* 5057)

E.J. Hoffman, *Alain Chartier: His Work and Reputation* (New York, 1942), p. 162, indicates that there is a MS copy of Caxton's print in Bodley Rawlinson A338; and this information is repeated by R.H. Wilson in *A Manual of the Writings in Middle English 1050–1500* (New Haven, 1972) III, p. 938. Although this MS contains English translations of works by Chartier, it does not contain a copy of the *Curial*; for a description see M.S. Blayney, *Fifteenth-Century Translations of Alain Chartier's 'Le Traite de l'Esperance' and 'Le Quadrilogue Invectif'*, EETS, 281 (1980), II, pp. 4–9.

5. DICTS OR SAYINGS (*STC* 6826, 6827)

First Report of The Royal Commission on Historical Manuscripts (London, 1874), p. 60, col. 2, suggests that Lord Tollemache's MS (Helmingham Hall) is 'the same probably as that printed by Caxton'. C.F. Bühler, *The Dicts and Sayings of the Philosophers*, EETS, OS, 211 (1941), p. xxxix, dates the MS 'not after 1460' and so the text cannot be a copy of Caxton's. Bühler's book contains an edition of the text in this MS.

6. HOUSE OF FAME (*STC* 5087)

Bodleian Library, MS Fairfax 16 contains additional material to Chaucer's poems, including the *House of Fame*, which were added in Caxton's editions. These have been inserted in a seventeenth-century hand. The MS was listed by Bühler, *Speculum*, 27 (1952), 178–83 as a copy of a Caxton print. This extra material should be regarded as coming from a sixteenth-century edition of Chaucer rather than from Caxton.

APPENDIX C

OTHER INCUNABULA COPIED INTO MANUSCRIPTS OR FOR WHICH MANUSCRIPT COPYTEXTS EXIST IN ENGLAND

1. ASSEMBLY OF GODS (*STC* 17005, 17007)

According to G. Bone, 'Extant Manuscripts Printed from by W. de Worde with Notes on the Owner, Roger Thorney', *The Library*, 4th series, 12 (1931–2), 284–306, Wynkyn de Worde's c. 1498 edition of the *Assembly of Gods* (*STC* 17005), wrongly attributed to Lydgate, was printed from Cambridge, Trinity College, R.3.19, fols. 68r–98r; this MS text is edited in O.L. Triggs, *The Assembly of Gods*, EETS, ES, 69 (1896). In B.Y. Fletcher, 'The Textual Tradition of *The Assembly of Gods*', *PBSA*, 71 (1977), 191–4, it is claimed that this edition is later than *STC* 17007, traditionally dated c. 1500. The edition in *STC* 17007 was both copied in BL MS Royal 18.D.II, fols. 167a–180b (a manuscript made before 1520 which also includes a copy of Pynson's ?1515 edition of Lydgate's *Testament* (*STC* 17035)), and also served as the probable copytext of the c. 1498 edition, *STC* 17005.

2. BOKE OF ST ALBANS (*STC* 3308)

BL MS Lansdowne 762, fols. 16r–v contains various short items such as the properties of a horse, proverbs and various short verses which may have been copied from the *Boke of St Albans*; see C. Meale, 'The Social and Literary Contexts of a late Medieval Manuscript', D.Phil. diss., University of York, 1984, pp. 234–5.

3. CANTERBURY TALES (*STC* 5085)

Manly and Rickert, I, p. 416, say MS Phillipps 6570 was 'Probably used by Wynkyn de Worde to supplement his principal MS.' They do not offer any reasons for this statement. The MS is now Newberry Library, Silver MS 1, and a similar statement about its use by de Worde is made in C.O. Faye and W.H. Bond, *Supplement to the Census of Medieval and Renaissance Manuscripts in the United States and Canada* (New York, 1962), p. 176.

4. CHRONICLES OF ENGLAND (*STC* 9995)

According to L.M. Matheson, 'Historical Prose' in Edwards, *Middle English Prose*, pp. 224–5, Glasgow University Hunterian 83 contains at first a copy of the St Albans *Chronicles of England*: see also Appendix A.20 (i).

5. CONSOLATORIUM TIMORATE CONSCIENTIE

The Paris edition of 1478 of Johannes Nider's *Consolatorium Timorate Conscientie* (Hain–Copinger 11809) is copied in Dublin, Trinity College, MS 343, fols. 1–134: see T.K. Abbott, *Catalogue of the Manuscripts in the Library of Trinity College, Dublin* (London, 1900), No. 343.

6. DE PROPRIETATIBUS RERUM (*STC* 1536)

De Worde's edition c. 1495 used Columbia University Library, Plimpton MS 263 as copy-text; see Mitchner, 'Wynkyn de Worde's Use of the Plimpton Manuscript of *De Proprietatibus Rerum*', *The Library*, 5th series, 6 (1951–2), 7–18.

7. DIVES AND PAUPER (*STC* 19212)

Pynson's edition c. 1493 used Bodleian Library, MS Eng.th.d.36 as copy-text; see M.M. Morgan, 'Pynson's Manuscript of *Dives and Pauper*', *The Library*, 5th series, 8 (1953), 217–28.

8. FALL OF PRINCES (*STC* 3175)

The copy-text for Pynson's 1494 edition of this text has been identified as John Rylands Library MS English 2; see 'A Specimen of Early Printer's Copy: Rylands English 2', *BJRL*, 33 (1950–1), 194–6.

9. FESTIAL

Cambridge, St John's College, MS 187 (G 19) is a copy of Mirk's *Festial* and *Quattuor Sermones* printed at Rouen in 1499; the copy must have been made shortly after the book was printed. See Bühler, *The Fifteenth-Century Book*, p. 34; and M.R. James, *A Descriptive Catalogue of the Manuscripts in the Library of St John's College, Cambridge* (Cambridge, 1913), p. 224, no. 187.

10. LIFE OF ST EDITH

The extant copy of this work, BL Cotton Faustina B.iii fols. 199r–263r, contains marks probably from the late fifteenth century which may be interpreted as marking up for a printed edition; see J. Ayto, 'Marginalia in the Manuscript of the *Life of St Edith*: New Light on Early Printing', *The Library*, 5th series, 32 (1977), 28–36. No printed edition survives, if one was ever executed.

11. POLYCHRONICON (*STC* 13439)

Yale University Library, Beinecke Osborne Shelves MS 1.20 is a sixteenth-century paper manuscript contains an incomplete text of Wynkyn de Worde's 1495 edition of the *Polychronicon*. The MS contains only the prohemye, index to the whole work and an incomplete part of the first book. There are 25 paper leaves of text.

12. SIEGE OF THEBES (*STC* 17031)

A composite volume in St John's College, Oxford (MS 266), consisting of copies of Caxton editions and a manuscript version of Lydgate's *Siege of Thebes* was used as copy-text for de Worde's c. 1497 edition of *Siege of Thebes*; see G. Bone, 'Extant Manuscripts Printed from by W. de Worde with Notes on the Owner, Roger Thorney', *The Library*, 4th series, 12 (1931–2), 284–306.

13. SPECULUM AUREUM DECEM PRECEPTORUM DEI

A MS of this work in Latin by Henricus Harpius consisting of 320 vellum leaves was sold at Sotheby's on 6 December 1983 and is described in the sale catalogue. This MS was made in England, probably in London or Westminster, before 1492, when the donor William Morland, prebend of St Paul's, died. He bequeathed the MS to St Stephen's Chapel, Westminster Palace. The MS is copied from the first edition printed by Peter Schoeffer in Mainz in September 1474 (*Catalogue of Books Printed in the XVth Century now in the British Museum*, I, p. 30).

14. VITAS PATRUM (*STC* 14507)

BL Harley 2252, a commonplace book compiled by John Colyns, contains a section on the treachery of the English which was taken 'owte of A boke', and this is most likely to be de Worde's edition of *Vitas Patrum*, 1495.

15. THEODORIC WERKEN

This scribe copied Latin texts of Latin fathers for Christ Church, Canterbury, in 1477 and 1478 from editions printed in Italy; see R.A.B. Mynors, 'A Fifteenth-Century Scribe: T. Werken', *TCBS*, I (2) (1950), 97–104; and A.C. de la Mare, 'A Fragment of Augustine in the Hand of Theodoricus Werken', *TCBS*, 6 (1972–6), 285–90.

16. JOHN WHETHAM

John Whetham, monk of the Carthusian House at Sheen, copied in 1496 Chrysostom's *Homiliæ in evangelium S. Iohannis* for the Prior, Ralph Tracy, at the suggestion of the former Prior, J. Yngilby, then bishop of Llandaff. This MS, formerly in the possession of Mr W.L. Wood of Chandler's Cross, Hampshire, was sold at Sotheby's on 10 December 1969, lot 80. It appeared in the November 1974 catalogue of Charles Traylen, but its present owner is untraced. It was apparently copied from the 1470 or 1486 printed edition (Hain–Copinger 5036 and 5037). See N.R. Ker, *Medieval Libraries*, pp. 178, 305; and E.M. Thompson, *The Carthusian Order in England* (London, 1930), pp. 331–4.

APPENDIX D

REJECTED EXAMPLE

1. BOOK OF HUNTING (*STC* 3308)

Bühler, *The Fifteenth-Century Book*, p. 117, suggests that the *Book of Hunting* in the St Albans Printer's *Book of St Albans* may have been copied in Bodleian Library, MS Rawlinson poet.143 from the edition printed by de Worde in 1496. But Rachel Hands, *English Hawking and Hunting in the Boke of St Albans* (London, 1975), p. xxxiii, shows that the MS preserves an independent text from that of St Albans. Since de Worde's print was set up from the St Albans one, Rawl. poet.143 cannot be a copy-text of de Worde.

NOTES

1 E.L. Eisenstein, *The Printing Press as an Agent of Change. Communications and Cultural Transformations in Early-Modern Europe*, 2 vols. (Cambridge, 1979) emphasises how printing changed our attitudes and ways of thinking.

2 See, for example, Bühler, *The Fifteenth-Century Book*, and R. Hirsch, *Printing, Selling and Reading 1450–1550* (Wiesbaden, 1967).

3 A. Swierk, 'Was bedeutet "ars artificialiter scribendi"', *Der gegenwärtige Stand der Gutenberg-Forschung*, ed. H. Widmann, (Stuttgart, 1972), pp. 243–51, gives examples of the phrase being used by manuscript writers and masters.

4 For a brief introduction see V. Scholderer, *Johann Gutenberg, The Inventor of Printing* (London, 1963).

5 For Caxton see N.F. Blake, *Caxton and his World* (London, 1969); G.D. Painter, *William Caxton, a Quincentenary Biography of England's First Printer* (London, 1976); and H.M. Nixon, 'Caxton, his Contemporaries and Successors in the Book Trade from Westminster Documents', *The Library*, 5th series 31 (1976), 305–26.

6 A complete list of books is included in E.G. Duff, *Fifteenth Century English Books*, Bibliographical Society Illustrated Monographs 18 (London, 1917). For a general bibliography, though it is far from complete, see W.L. Heilbronner, *Printing and the Book in Fifteenth-Century England* (Charlottesville, 1967).

7 See W.M. Clyde, *The Struggle for the Freedom of the Press from Caxton to Cromwell* (London, 1934), and, more generally, Eisenstein, *The Printing Press as an Agent of Change*.

8 See N.F. Blake, 'William Caxton: his Choice of Texts', *Anglia*, 83 (1965), 289–307.

9 For example, Mary Bateson, *Catalogue of the Library of Syon Monastery, Isleworth* (Cambridge, 1898).

10 See C. Horstmann, 'Prosalegenden 1. Caxton's Ausgabe der h. Wenefrida', *Anglia*, 3 (1880), 293–319, and M.R. James, *A Descriptive Catalogue of the Manuscripts in the Library of Lambeth Palace* (Cambridge, 1932), No. 306 for Lambeth Palace Library, MS 306; and Doyle, 'William Ebesham', pp. 308–12, for a description of Rylands Latin MS 395.

11 W. Blades, *The Life and Typography of William Caxton* (London, 1861–3), I, pp. 140–1: 'This is the Author's prologue, which commences half-way down the page, the upper half being left blank for the insertion of an illuminator, as in several books printed by Colard Mansion.'

12 O. Pächt, *The Master of Mary of Burgundy* (London, 1948).

13 N.F. Blake, *The History of Reynard the Fox*, EETS 263 (London, 1970), pp. lxi–lxii.

14 For a full description see A.C. de la Mare and L. Hellinga, 'The First Book Printed in Oxford: the *Expositio Symboli* of Rufinus', *TCBS*, 8 (2) (1978), 184–244.

15 See *William Caxton: An Exhibition to Commemorate the Quincentenary of the Introduction of Printing into England* (London, 1976), p. 42.

16 L.S. Olschki, *Incunables illustrés imitant les manuscrits. Le passage du manuscrit au livre imprimé* (Florence, 1914), contains 49 examples of printed books made to resemble manuscripts: they are all Latin texts.

17 The text is edited and the woodcuts reproduced in Oliver H. Prior, *Caxton's Mirrour of the World*, EETS, ES, 110 (London, 1913). For a discussion of Caxton woodcuts

see Edward Hodnett, *English Woodcuts 1480–1535*, Bibliographical Society Illustrated Monographs 22 and 22a, rev. edn (Oxford, 1973).

18 For the earliest indulgence which has handwritten entries see A.W. Pollard, 'The New Caxton Indulgence', *The Library*, 4th series, 9 (1929), 87–9.

19 N.F. Blake, 'The "Mirror of the World" and M.S. Royal 19.A.IX', *NQ*, 212 (1967), 205–7.

20 For information about exemplars in English books see the appendices; for other exemplars see references in de la Mare and Hellinga, 'The First Book', p. 217.

21 See N.F. Blake, *Caxton: England's First Publisher* (London, 1976), pp. 85–119.

22 T.F. Dunn, *The Manuscript Source of Caxton's Second Edition of the Canterbury Tales* (Chicago, 1940).

23 L. Hellinga, *Caxton in Focus* (London, 1982), p. 82.

24 See Doyle and Parkes.

25 G. Pollard, 'The *pecia* System in the Medieval Universities', in *Medieval Scribes, Manuscripts and Libraries*, ed. M.B. Parkes and A.G. Watson (London, 1978), pp. 145–61.

26 L. Hellinga, 'Notes on the Order of Setting a Fifteenth-Century Book', *Quaerendo*, 4 (1974), 64–9.

27 For a study of the way in which medieval manuscripts were written before their sheets were folded and cut see L. Güssen, *Prolégomènes à la codicologie. Recherches sur la construction des cahiers et la mise en page des manuscrits médiévaux* (Ghent, 1977). This work contains a bibliography.

28 See L. Hellinga, 'Manuscripts in the Hands of Printers', *Manuscripts in the Fifty Years after the Invention of Printing*, ed. J.B. Trapp (London, 1983), pp. 3–11.

29 For a full description and edition see R.H. Martin, 'The *Epitome Margaritae Eloquentiae* of Laurentius Gulielmus de Saona', *Proceedings of the Leeds Philosophical and Literary Society: Literary and Historical Section*, 14 (4) (1971), 99–187.

30 G. Bone, 'Extant Manuscripts Printed from by W. de Worde with Notes on the Owner, Roger Thorney', *The Library*, 4th series, 12 (1931–2), 284–306.

31 For a similar instance in a Latin text see R.B. Haselden, 'A Scribe and Printer in the Fifteenth Century', *HLQ*, 2 (1939), 205–11.

32 N.F. Blake, 'Caxton and Chaucer', *LSE*, NS, 1 (1967), 19–36.

33 Attention has been given increasingly to this phenomenon. C.F. Bühler, 'The *Fasciculus Temporum* and Morgan Manuscript 801', *Speculum*, 27 (1952), 182–3, n. 29, provided a list of manuscript copies of Caxton prints which he supplemented in *The Fifteenth Century Book*, p. 34. Bühler has also written on copies of Latin manuscripts in that book and in 'An Unusual Fifteenth-Century Manuscript', *La Bibliofilia*, 42 (1940), 65–71. See also C.E. Lutz, 'Manuscripts copied from Printed Books', *Yale University Library Gazette*, 49 (1975), 261–7; S. Hindman and J.D. Farquhar, *Pen to Press. Illustrated Manuscripts and Printed Books in the First Century of Printing* (College Park, Md, and Baltimore, 1977), pp. 101ff.; and J.B. Trapp, *Manuscripts in the Fifty Years after the Invention of Printing* (London, 1983).

34 The evidence is disputed: for a discussion see D. Fox, 'Henryson and Caxton', *JEGP*, 67 (1968), 586–93.

35 For the most recent discussion of this manuscript with plates see Hellinga, *Caxton in Focus*, pp. 77–83.

36 *Ibid.*

37 For the illumination see Scott, *The Caxton Master*.

38 L. Hellinga, 'The Malory Manuscript and Caxton', *Aspects of Malory*, edited by T. Takamiya and D. Brewer (Cambridge, 1981), pp. 127–41.

39 For a description of the manuscript see *Bodleian Library MS Fairfax 16*, with an introduction by J. Norton-Smith (London, 1979).

40 Manly and Rickert, II, pp. 57–9.

41 *Ibid.*, I, p. 530.

42 See T. Takamiya, 'Print to Manuscript, or the Exemplars of Peterhouse MS 190', *TCBS* (forthcoming).

INDEX OF MANUSCRIPTS

Australia
Ballarat, Victoria, Fine Art Gallery, MS
  Crouch 4:396
Canberra, National Library of Australia, MS
  4052/2:159, 161
Melbourne, University of Victoria, MS of
  Lydgate:276

Austria
Vienna, Osterreichische Nationalbibliothek,
  Cod.1840:178, 194

Belgium
Brussels, Bibl. Royale, MS IV.1095:56
  MS 4862-9:57, 396, 398
  MS 9961-2:175

Denmark
Copenhagen, Kon.Bib.Thott 304:122

France
Boulogne-sur-Mer, Bibl.Municipale, MS
  93:56
Chantilly, Musée Condé, MS 65(1284):395
Paris, Bibl.Nationale, MS f.ang.25:58, 384,
  397-8
  MS f.ang.39:188
  MS f.fr.831:196, 284
  MS f.fr.10483-4:175
  MS f.lat.1158:196
  MS f.lat.1196:59, 108
  MS f.lat.1201:120-1
  MS f.lat.6276:56
  MS f.lat.13285:60
Rennes, Bibl.Municipale MS 22:56
Valenciennes, Bibl.Municipale MS 660:157

Germany
Wolfenbuttel, Herzog August-Bibliothek,
  Cod.Helmstedt 538:254

Ireland
Dublin, Royal Irish Academy, MS
  12.R.31:181

Dublin, Trinity College, MS 83:57
  MS 93 (B.3.3):56
  MS 213:418, 422
  MS 244:135
  MS 245:135
  MS 246:141
  MS 343:427
  MS 432:292-3, 311
  MS 505:62
  MS 516:174-5, 191, 292
  MS 523:229

Italy
Naples, Biblioteca Nazionale, MS 7.G.31:121
  MS 13.B.29:297
Rome, Biblioteca Apostolica Vaticana, MS
  lat.501:61
  MS lat.4681:191
  MS lat.11441:407-10, 411, 423
  Chig.H.VII.215:191

Japan
Tokyo, Takamiya Collection, MS 8 (*olim*
  Devonshire):275, 277
  MS 33:385, 396-7
  MS 60:381, 383

Netherlands
Leiden, University Library, MS Vossius
  9:303
  MS Scal.Hebr.8:175

Russia
Leningrad, Saltykov-Shahedrin Library, MS
  of Gudio delle Colonne:224

Spain
Madrid, Museo Lazaro-Galdiano MS
  15503:226

Sweden
Uppsala, University Library, MS
  C.193:121

Switzerland
Geneva, Bibl.Publique et Universitaire MS
   fr.166:181, 226
Geneva, Biblioteca Bodmeriana, Bodmer MS
   (*olim* Ireland-Blackburn, now in
   Princeton UL, Robert H. Taylor
   Collection):314
   olim Keswick Hall MS:263, 274–5

United Kingdom

Aberdeen, University Library
MS 21:62
MS 201:250–1
MS 214:249
MS 222:250
MS 257:248

Aberystwyth, National Library of Wales
MS 733B:274
MS 15537C:182
MS 17520:57
MS 21242C:58
Peniarth 392D:8, 263, 274
Peniarth 481D:209, 227
Porkington 10:294

Arundel Castle, Library of Duke of Norfolk
MS of Lydgate's *Life of St Edmund*:59, 61
Muniment M 534:158

Belfast, Queen's University Library
Brett B.50:423

Berkeley Castle, Gloucestershire
MS Book of Hours:108

Bristol, All Saints Church
MSS 1 and 2:27

Bristol, Avon County Library
Reference Library MS 10:396

Bute, see Rothesay

Cambridge, University Library
Add.2764:158
Add.4435:159–60
Add.5963:159, 161
Add.6684:140
Add.7071:174, 207, 228
Dd.1.27:61, 140
Dd.3.45:423
Dd.5.55:328, 339
Dd.5.64:321
Dd.8.2:108
Dd.9.15:60

Dd.12.69:189
Dd.14.30:138
Ee.2.17:236
Ee.3.61:60, 362–3, 365
Ff.1.6:8, 189, 234, 282, 283, 295–6,
   303–4
Ff.1.33:284
Ff.2.38:8, 297, 310, 314–15, 337
Ff.3.11:235
Ff.5.40:328
Ff.5.45:342
Ff.6.31:312, 338
Ff.6.34:343
Ff.6.55:337
Gg.2.6:15–16
Gg.4.27:8, 268, 276, 280
Gg.6.5:56, 62
Gg.6.16:341
Gg.6.17:276
Hh.1.12:330, 337
Hh.4.11:276
Ii.2.24:64
Ii.4.9:340
Ii.6.7:57
Ii.6.40:343
Ii.6.43:337
Kk.1.3:122
Kk.1.5:240
Kk.1.6:164
Kk.1.8:140
Kk.2.7:44, 60, 63–4
Kk.6.30:368, 372, 378, 380
Ll.1.13:140
Ll.1.18:310
Ll.4.3:343
Mm.2.5:276
Mm.2.15:140
Mm.2.21:274–5
Mm.3.14:63
Mm.5.15:343
Nn.3.10:420

Cambridge, College Libraries
Corpus Christi 61:8, 56, 188, 230, 266–7,
   274–5, 284
Corpus Christi 164:108, 190
Corpus Christi 285/1:223
Corpus Christi 496:189
Emmanuel 69 (I.3.17):375–6
Emmanuel I.3.18 (70):59
Emmanuel 1.4.13 (92):63
Gonville and Caius 196/102:55
Gonville and Caius 209/115:325
Gonville and Caius 17/133:108
Gonville and Caius 23/12:108
Gonville and Caius 84/166:383
Gonville and Caius 129/67:191

Gonville and Caius 148/198:61
Gonville and Caius 176/97:381–2
Gonville and Caius 247/473:107
Gonville and Caius 336/725:385, 396–8
Gonville and Caius 342/538:191
Gonville and Caius 492/261:108, 190
Gonville and Caius 669/646:284
Jesus 56:303
Kings 13:257
Kings 40:61
Kings, Charter 1446:107
Magdalene F.4.34:27
Magdalene, Pepys 15:140
Magdalene, Pepys 16:140
Magdalene, Pepys 1548:315
Magdalene, Pepys 1760:225
Magdalene, Pepys 2006:8, 218, 235, 238, 303, 420
Magdalene, Pepys 2073:140
Magdalene, Pepys 2101:276
Magdalene, Pepys 2124:27, 414–15, 424
Magdalene, Pepys 2498:338
Pembroke 204:73
Pembroke 236:122
Pembroke 237:140
Pembroke 307:170–1
Pembroke 314:159–60
Peterhouse 118:399
Peterhouse 190:418, 424
Sidney Sussex 2:58
St Catharine's 7:189
St John's 23 (B.1):62
St John's 223 (I.22):276
St John's 250 (N.17):122
St John's B.12 (34) 168, 189
St John's C.13 (63):86
St John's G.14 (182):60
St John's G.19 (187):428
St John's G.25 (193):135
St John's G.28 (195):343
St John's G.35 (202):339
St John's H.1(204):40, 263, 384
St John's H.5(208):60, 107
St John's L.1(235):8, 263–4, 276
Trinity B.5.25:136, 141
Trinity B.10.2:57, 60–1
Trinity B.10.5:160
Trinity B.10.12:58, 60
Trinity B.11.3:63, 177
Trinity B.11.7:57, 63, 98
Trinity B.11.13:63
Trinity B.11.20:57
Trinity B.11.34:160
Trinity B.14.17:237
Trinity B.14.50:135
Trinity B.14.53:343

Trinity B.14.54:337
Trinity B.15.16:343
Trinity B.15.17:274
Trinity B.15.32:343
Trinity B.15.42:342
Trinity O.1.57:358, 367, 372–3
Trinity O.1.74:341
Trinity O.1.77:349, 351, 381, 384, 399
Trinity O.2.16:372
Trinity O.2.53:292, 310
Trinity O.3.58:158
Trinity O.4.16:176–7
Trinity O.5.2:58, 236
Trinity O.7.47:339
Trinity O.8.16:389
Trinity O.9.1:60
Trinity O.9.38:292–3, 313
Trinity R.3.2:170, 262–3, 273–4
Trinity R.3.3:188, 275, 277
Trinity R.3.15:417, 419
Trinity R.3.19:283–4, 289–90, 304, 309, 419, 427
Trinity R.3.20:19–20, 285, 286, 305–7
Trinity R.3.21:107, 283, 288–9, 308, 337, 341–2
Trinity R.3.22:276
Trinity R.14.5:57, 60
Trinity R.14.52:107, 382
Trinity R.15.18:54, 364–5, 382
Trinity R.15.21:62, 380

Cambridge, Fitzwilliam Museum
Fitzwilliam 34:57
Fitzwilliam 57:178–9, 193–4
Fitzwilliam 329:60
Fitzwilliam 3–1979:56
Fitzwilliam 14–1950:55–6
Fitzwilliam 40–1950:180
Fitzwilliam 41–1950:180
Fitzwilliam McClean 90:63
Fitzwilliam McClean 130:344
Fitzwilliam McClean 181:274

Castle Howard
MS of Lydgate's *Life of St Edmund*:278

Durham, Cathedral Library
A.1.3:63
A.1.6:63
A.IV.212:341
Cosin v.iii.5:58
Cosin v.iii.9:2
Cosin v.iii.10:54
Cosin v.v.15:121
Cosin v.viii.6:134–5

Edinburgh, National Library of Scotland
Advocates 18.1.7:56–7, 60, 98, 187, 341
Advocates 18.3.10:249, 256
Advocates 18.3.11:249
Advocates 18.4.8:248–9, 256
Advocates 19.2.1:6, 8, 10, 234, 257, 272–3,
   279
Advocates 19.3.1:295–7
Advocates 25.4.10:244
Advocates 25.4.13:244
Advocates 25.5.10:245
Advocates 31.3.20:424
Advocates 31.5.2:424
Advocates 34.1.3 (A):247
Advocates 34.7.3:255

Edinburgh, Royal Observatory
Cr.1.2:54
Cr.2.20:392

Edinburgh, Scottish National Library of Medicine
MS 512:246

Edinburgh, Scottish Record Office
GD 112/71/1(1):242, 253, 420–1
GD 45/26/46:245–6

Edinburgh, University Library
MS 93:337
MS 169:56
MS 202:59, 276
MS 303:197
MS 308:57, 62
Laing iii.513:255

Eton College
MS 39 (Bk.4.3):101, 108
MS 101 (Bl.10):101, 108
Consolidation Charter:92, 98, 107

Exeter, Cathedral Library
MS 3529:27

Firle Place, Library of Lord Gage
Book of Hours:63

Glasgow, University Library
Hunterian 5 (S.1.5):27
Hunterian 7 (S.1.7):274
Hunterian 74 (T.3.12):420
Hunterian 83 (T.3.21):424, 427
Hunterian 95 (T.4.12):399
Hunterian 197 (U.1.1):189, 268, 276
Hunterian 228 (U.3.1):420
Hunterian 232 (U.3.5):276
Hunterian 270 (U.5.10):63
Hunterian 400 (V.2.20):242

Hunterian 410 (V.3.8):423
MS Gen.333:247–8
MS Gen.1130:187

Gloucester, Cathedral Library
Sel.3–21:82

Hatfield House
CP 308:54

Hertford, Hertfordshire Record Office
MS ref:57553:160

Leeds, University Library, Brotherton Collection
MS 15:63–4

Leicester, Wyggeston Hospital
MS of Leonardinus de Utino:82–3

Lichfield, Cathedral Library
MS 2:275

Lincoln, Cathedral Library
MS 91:8, 297–8, 300–1, 310, 314
MS 133:341
Gr.82:191

Liverpool, Cathedral Library
MS 6:56
Radcliffe 16:423

Liverpool, Merseyside Museum
MS 12009:197

London, British Library
Add.1698:96
Add.5140:188, 276
Add.5467:284, 307
Add.6173:70, 82
Add.6578:324
Add.7071:192
Add.8151:344
Add.10099:420
Add.10302:57
Add.10340:193
Add.10574:273
Add.11305:188
Add.12044:276
Add.12524:309
Add.14408:219
Add.15673:70, 82
Add.16165:16–19, 284–7, 306–8
Add.16998:108
Add.17012:206
Add.18111:244
Add.18850:223
Add.19252:274

Add.19901:343
Add.19909:103
Add.21006:343
Add.21410:266, 277
Add.22139:198, 240
Add.22283:272, 279, 301, 310, 327–8, 339, 343
Add.22558:344
Add.22718:421–2
Add.24057:82
Add.24194:263, 384
Add.24202:135
Add.24203:188, 272
Add.25588:57
Add.27879:313
Add.27924:64
Add.27944:63, 275
Add.28870:81
Add.29301:38, 40, 57, 60, 397
Add.29729:284, 307, 421
Add.30031:343
Add.30864:228
Add.30946:60
Add.31042:297–8, 300–1, 314–15
Add.32320:325
Add.32578:188
Add.33736:86
Add.33995:337, 344
Add.34360:107, 307–8
Add.34779:276
Add.34807:71, 83
Add.35181:161
Add.35287:276
Add.35288:235
Add.35290:311
Add.36983:123
Add.37049:56, 59
Add.37223:254
Add.37664:106
Add.38690:305
Add.39255:158
Add.39659:264, 267
Add.39810:175, 192
Add.40011B:147, 158
Add.40672:136
Add.41175:133–4, 136, 140–1
Add.41321:136
Add.42131:41, 54, 58–9, 61, 96, 108
Add.48976:59
Add.49597:160
Add.49622:147, 158
Add.50001:57, 63, 108
Add.54782:226
Add.57534:62
Add.57950:147, 151–5, 159–61
Add.58078:108
Add.59862:84

Add.59678:416
Add.60577:8, 72, 83, 301, 337, 418, 421
Add.60584:194
Add.65100:56
Arundel 20:123
Arundel 38:27, 59, 108, 168, 188, 230, 276
Arundel 59:107, 308
Arundel 99:278
Arundel 119:236, 264, 274
Arundel 203:56
Arundel 249:189
Burney 356:342
Cotton App.viii:276
Cotton Augustus A.iv:58, 164, 188, 236, 274
Cotton Caligula A.ii:297
Cotton Caligula A.xi:273
Cotton Claudius A.ii:336
Cotton Claudius A.viii:107, 420
Cotton Claudius B.i:58
Cotton Claudius E.viii:63
Cotton Cleopatra A.xiii:223
Cotton Cleopatra D.vii:304
Cotton Domitian A.xvii:223
Cotton Faustina B.iii:428
Cotton Faustina B.vi:56, 59
Cotton Faustina B.vii:56
Cotton Faustina B.ix:231
Cotton Julius A.iv:60
Cotton Julius D.viii:389
Cotton Julius E.iv:59, 213
Cotton Nero A.x:57, 60, 257
Cotton Nero D.xi:254
Cotton Otho A.xviii:307
Cotton Tiberius A.vii:60
Cotton Tiberius E.vii:344
Cotton Titus A.xx:301
Cotton Titus A.xxvi:307
Cotton Titus D.i:141
Cotton Titus D.xix:341
Cotton Vespasian A.xxiii:122
Cotton Vespasian D.viii:311
Cotton Vitellius C.xiii:315
Cotton Vitellius E.xi:246
Cotton vitellius F.ix:106
Egerton 615:59
Egerton 617–18:131
Egerton 847:348–9, 351, 371, 381
Egerton 1991:36, 108, 275
Egerton 2572:393, 396
Egerton 2726:261, 274
Egerton 2820:127, 138
Egerton 2862:314
Egerton 2864:276
Egerton 3307:154
Hargrave 274:58
Harley 45:344
Harley 53:233

Harley 78:19–20, 107, 285
Harley 116:276
Harley 149:425
Harley 211:341
Harley 219:208, 229
Harley 273:104, 174, 207, 228
Harley 326:58, 60, 210–12, 231
Harley 330:339–40
Harley 355:337
Harley 367:307
Harley 372:283–4, 304, 308
Harley 401:128
Harley 435:344
Harley 565:290
Harley 604:23–6
Harley 629:56
Harley 641:108
Harley 682:303
Harley 712:245–6
Harley 933:219, 312
Harley 953:343
Harley 993:320, 338
Harley 1022:339
Harley 1035:339
Harley 1197:337
Harley 1239:188
Harley 1245:264
Harley 1251:181
Harley 1706:309, 319, 330–1, 342
Harley 1758:274–5
Harley 1766:58, 60–1, 277–8
Harley 1776:209
Harley 1806:141
Harley 2124:311
Harley 2250:122
Harley 2252:235, 290, 310, 429
Harley 2253:257, 279
Harley 2255:303
Harley 2260:344
Harley 2278:56, 59, 223
Harley 2322:343
Harley 2324:138
Harley 2336:312, 338, 343
Harley 2339:337
Harley 2386:22–3, 310
Harley 2406:337
Harley 2409:331, 342
Harley 2887:57, 193
Harley 2915:107
Harley 2985:198
Harley 3352:205
Harley 3362:310
Harley 3490:168
Harley 3719:360, 364–5, 369, 372, 395, 398
Harley 3730:424
Harley 3903:140
Harley 3913:135

Harley 3943:216, 276
Harley 3952:276
Harley 3954:60
Harley 4011:123
Harley 4260:276
Harley 4431:189, 208, 229
Harley 4775:107
Harley 4826:56, 278
Harley 4866:27, 59, 276
Harley 4912:276
Harley 5272:276
Harley 5311:57
Harley 6041:169, 188
Harley 6149:424
Harley 6573:339
Harley 6579:312, 339
Harley 6613:138
Harley 7184:263–6, 277
Harley 7333:268, 276, 287, 307
Harley 7334:63, 274–5
Harley 7353:59
Harley 7578:307
Lansdowne 204:223
Lansdowne 285:198, 219–20
Lansdowne 699:303
Lansdowne 762:427
Lansdowne 763:301
Lansdowne 851:62, 274, 277
Royal 1.C.viii:131
Royal 1.E.ix:58, 61, 64, 108
Royal 2.A.xviii:56, 107–8
Royal 2.B.i:98
Royal 2.B.vii:124
Royal 2.B.x:63–4
Royal 5.C.iii:107, 190
Royal 8.C.i:338
Royal 8.D.x:107, 190
Royal 10.B.ix:27
Royal 12.E.xv:204–5
Royal 14.C.vii:175
Royal 14.E.ii:208
Royal 14.E.iii:174, 192, 207
Royal 15.D.ii:174, 191–2
Royal 15.E.v:225
Royal 15.E.vi:180, 187, 227
Royal 16.F.ii:205, 225
Royal 16.F.viii:206
Royal 17.A.xxv:342
Royal 17.A.xxvi:325, 337
Royal 17.B.xliii:56
Royal 17.C.viii:343–5
Royal 17.C.xviii:342
Royal 17.C.xx:344
Royal 17.C.xxxviii:60, 62
Royal 17.D.vi:27, 59, 233, 276
Royal 17.D.xv:107, 287, 308
Royal 17.D.xviii:276

Royal 17.D.xix:276
Royal 17.D.xx:254
Royal 17.D.xxi:233
Royal 17.E.v:236
Royal 18.A.xii:204, 219, 224
Royal 18.B.ix:137
Royal 18.B.xxvi:425
Royal 18.C.ii:274
Royal 18.C.x:343
Royal 18.C.xxii:384
Royal 18.C.xxvi:136, 141
Royal 18.D.i:141
Royal 18.D.ii:58, 188, 193-4, 215, 232, 236, 266, 277, 427
Royal 18.D.iv:169
Royal 18.D.vi:264
Royal 18.E.i:226
Royal 19.A.ix:406
Royal 19.A.xix:208
Royal 19.B.x:226
Royal 19.B.xviii:208, 229
Royal 19.C.i:174, 192
Royal 19.C.vi:178, 225
Royal 19.C.viii:178, 205
Royal 19.D.i:9
Royal 19.E.ii:225
Royal 19.E.iii:225
Royal 20.A.xix:226
Royal 20.B.i:230
Royal 20.B.ix:226
Royal 20.B.xv:284
Royal 20.D.xi:230
Royal 20.E.i-vi:178, 187
Sloane 1:357, 359
Slaone 4:401
Sloane 6:57, 374, 376, 381, 383, 396-9
Sloane 7:397
Sloane 56:397
Sloane 213:349, 351, 367, 381
Sloane 335:57
Sloane 770:401
Sloane 779:417-18, 420, 422
Sloane 1044:182
Sloane 1091:372
Sloane 1118:384, 401
Sloane 1313:384, 401
Sloane 1448A:63
Sloane 1579:405, 409
Sloane 1584:336
Sloane 1686:274
Sloane 1710:283-4, 304
Sloane 1785:276
Sloane 2002:56
Sloane 2027:216, 219, 234
Sloane 2320:376, 384, 389, 397
Sloane 2400:65, 81
Sloane 2452:209, 230, 277

Sloane 2464:278
Sloane 2567:384
Sloane 2593:303
Sloane 2948:384, 401
Sloane 3160:121
Sloane 3215:310
Sloane 3481:
Sloane 3566:384
Sloane 4031:237, 277
Stowe 16:108
Stowe 594:56
Stowe 951:344
Stowe 952:315
Yates-Thompson 47:59, 61, 278

London, College of Arms
Arundel 3:58
B.2.9:62
"Warwick MS":59

London, Company of Mercers
MS Ordinances:107

London, Company of Skinners
MS Fraternity Statutes, &c.:212-14, 224

London, Company of Tallow Chandlers
MS Patent of Arms:107

London, Dulwich College
MS 25:197

London, Gray's Inn
MS 8:107

London, Lambeth Palace Library
Lambeth 6:206, 216, 227
Lambeth 15:182
Lambeth 23:63
Lambeth 34:136, 141
Lambeth 67:391
Lambeth 69:58, 96, 98, 108
Lambeth 254:277
Lambeth 264:420
Lambeth 265:210, 212, 230-1, 413-14, 421
Lambeth 306:290-1, 310, 404, 430
Lambeth 444:385
Lambeth 472:108, 338
Lambeth 484:343
Lambeth 491:216, 234-5
Lambeth 541:343
MS Arundel:185
Reg.Whittlesey:159

London, Lincoln's Inn
MS 150:313-14

London, Royal College of Physicians
MS 13:107, 308

London, Sion College
Arc.L.40.2/E.44:19–21, 285, 286, 305
Arc.L.40.2/L.21:173, 191
Arc.L.40.2/L.28:175

London, Society of Antiquaries
MS 687:121

London, University of London Library
MS 1:284
MS V.88:275

London, Victoria and Albert Museum
L 2060–1948:173
Reid 7:181, 196
Reid 42:58
Reid 44–8:197

London, Wellcome Historical Medical Library
MS 290:57, 398
MS 552:360–1
MS 564:390, 399

London, Westminster Abbey, Library
MSS 34/2,34/5:27
MS 38 (*Liber Regalis*):57
MS 43:64
Liber Niger:161
Lytlington Missal:107–8
Muniment 12163:160

*Longleat House, Library of the Marquis of
    Bath*
MS 4:343
MS 9:191
MS 10:193
MS 30:303
MS 254:264, 267
MS 257:235–6, 276
MS 258:281–2, 283, 303–4
Misc.MS XIII:158

*Manchester, John Rylands University
    Library*
Eng.1:58, 60–1, 98, 168, 170, 236
Eng.2:428
Eng.63:276
Eng.85:138, 325–6, 341
Eng.90:138
Eng.94:342
Lat.22:174
Lat.165:58
Lat.211:81
Lat.395:404, 430

Manchester, Chetham's Library
Mun.A.3.131 (27929):81–2
Mun.A.4.104 (6709):419–20, 423
Mun.A.6.31 (8009):206–7, 234–5, 294
Mun.A.7.48 (6696):189

Norwich, Castle Museum
MS 158.926.4g3:141

Norwich, Cathedral Library
MS 2:27

Nottingham, University Library
Mi.LM.6:191
Mi.LM.8:274
Mi.LM.11:82
Wollaton Antiphonal:59, 164

Oxford, Bodleian Library
Add.B.6:337
Arch.Selden B.10:193
Arch.Selden B.24:;188, 240, 250–2, 276, 303
Arch.Selden supra 49:140
Arch.Selden supra 51:140
Arch.Selden supra 53:59, 276
Ashmole 6:356–7, 365, 392
Ashmole 40:276
Ashmole 45:310
Ashmole 46:278
Ashmole 59:20–1, 285–7, 305–8
Ashmole 61:297, 299, 313
Ashmole 191:382
Ashmole 750:293
Ashmole 764:57
Ashmole 765:107
Ashmole 1286:342
Ashmole 1474:253
Ashmole 1524:327
Ashmole 1827:104
Ashmole 1831:63
Auct.D.4.5:108
Barlow 5:63
Bodley 3:329, 343
Bodley 4:191
Bodley 95:82
Bodley 110:107, 190, 327
Bodley 120:276
Bodley 143:141
Bodley 175:311
Bodley 183:44, 140
Bodley 192:173
Bodley 198:173
Bodley 207:343
Bodley 243:136, 141
Bodley 263:56, 64
Bodley 264:56, 58, 60, 64, 96, 108, 175, 192
Bodley 277:64, 131, 223

Bodley 283:43
Bodley 288:141, 343
Bodley 294:108, 275
Bodley 316:120
Bodley 361:385
Bodley 362:385
Bodley 414:276
Bodley 423:188
Bodley 446:333–4, 344
Bodley 460:71, 82–3
Bodley 531:140
Bodley 540:141
Bodley 546:57
Bodley 549:122, 338
Bodley 596:60
Bodley 638:8, 281–2, 283, 303
Bodley 665:130–1, 140
Bodley 676:359–60
Bodley 686:62, 277
Bodley 690:227
Bodley 693:108, 274
Bodley 729:173
Bodley 814:273
Bodley 821:208
Bodley 851:189, 273, 301
Bodley 877:141
Bodley 902:108, 170, 274–5
Bodley 938:337
Bodley 943:60, 62
Bodley 952:422
Bodley 959:139
Digby 67:382
Digby 77:366, 371–2, 394
Digby 97:360–1, 370, 372–3, 395
Digby 98:173, 175, 191, 355–6, 371, 391
Digby 99:272
Digby 145:189
Digby 181:303
Digby 185:168, 188, 216, 233, 313
Digby 227:107
Digby 230:263, 267, 274
Digby 232:58, 218
Digby 233:58, 219
Digby 235:231, 353–4, 391
Digby Roll 4:393
Don.b.6:57
Don.b.31:159, 161
Don.b.32:159, 161
Don.d.85:37, 108
Douce 18:56
Douce 25:312, 320, 338
Douce 53:126, 138
Douce 104:59, 274
Douce 114:338
Douce 158:276
Douce 228:313
Douce 240:140

Douce 246:70, 82, 84
Douce 258:141
Douce 265:140
Douce 273–4:135
Douce 291:219, 237
Douce 302:280
Douce 320:274
Douce 322:309, 330, 342
Douce 324:235, 237
Douce 326:311
Douce 335:62
Douce 372:184
Dugdale 45:276
e Mus.65:188, 230
Eng.hist.c.775:194, 222
Eng.misc.c.291:158
Eng.poet.a.1:3, 8, 58, 60, 257, 259, 271–2,
    279, 301, 310, 328, 339, 343
Eng.poet.d.5:344
Eng.poet.e.1:303
Eng.poet.f.2:293
Eng.th.d.36:428
Eng.th.f.39:135
Ewelme Mun.VII.A.47:186, 229
Fairfax 3:273–5
Fairfax 4:231
Fairfax 11:140
Fairfax 16:8, 56, 218, 223, 280–4, 290, 303–4,
    416, 426
Fr.d.5:208
Gough Eccl.Top.5:140
Gough liturg.6:108
Gough liturg.10:196
Gough liturg.18:193
Greaves 43:344
Greaves 54:341
Hatton 2:277
Hatton 10:64
Hatton 12:338
Hatton 18:344
Hatton 19:344
Hatton 51:416–17, 420
Hatton 73:276, 307
Hatton 96:341
Hatton 111:140
Junius 29:140
Lat.liturg.b.19:158
Lat.liturg.f.2:57, 108
Lat.liturg.f.3:168
Lat.misc.c.66:302
Laud 416:219, 237
Laud 557:236
Laud 739:419
Laud misc.23:337, 341
Laud misc.99:339
Laud misc.100:244, 251
Laud misc.128:83

Laud misc.170:107
Laud misc.174:337
Laud misc.210:326–7
Laud misc.286:135, 141
Laud misc.321:141
Laud misc.414:107, 190
Laud misc.501:55
Laud misc.558:81, 377, 379, 385
Laud misc.570:208
Laud misc.609:64, 108
Laud misc.657:365
Laud misc.658:56
Laud misc.673:265, 278
Laud misc.683:303
Laud misc.701:70, 82, 84
Laud misc.706:120
Laud misc.724:57
Laud misc.730:62
Laud misc.733:60, 98
Laud misc.740:59, 61
Liturg.9:57
Liturg.Misc.400:197
Lyell 16:82
Lyell 22:56
Lyell 26:140
Lyell 28:344
Lyell 29:337, 343
Lyell 31:277
Lyell 33:195
Rawl.A.338:426
Rawl.A.381:337
Rawl.A.387B:343
Rawl.B.214:301–2
Rawl.C.69:343
Rawl.C.86:103, 108, 290–1, 309
Rawl.C.208:136
Rawl.C.209:318, 337
Rawl.C.259:140
Rawl.C.285:327, 339
Rawl.C.446:58, 263, 267, 274
Rawl.C.699:337
Rawl.C.751:136, 337
Rawl.C.884:344
Rawl.C.890:344
Rawl.C.894:338, 342
Rawl.D.913:107
Rawl.D.1222:310
Rawl.G.109:301
Rawl.liturg.f.36:206
Rawl.poet.14:235
Rawl.poet.32:420
Rawl.poet.34:312
Rawl.poet.118:123
Rawl.poet.137:189, 277
Rawl.poet.140:276
Rawl.poet.143:429
Rawl.poet.168:188

Rawl.poet.223:275, 277
Rawl.poet.224:276
Rolls 5:215
Tanner 16:141
Tanner 17:55, 59
Tanner 336:337
Tanner 346:8, 234, 280–4, 303
Tanner 407:292–3, 389

Oxford, College Libraries
All Souls 322:79
Balliol 183:173
Balliol 354:313, 425
Brasenose 9:341, 384
Campion Hall 3:197
Christ Church 148:168, 275
Christ Church 152:276
Corpus Christi 67:170, 227, 267, 275
Corpus Christi 82:173, 191
Corpus Christi 161:59
Corpus Christi 198:274–5
Corpus Christi 201:274
Corpus Christi 220:342
Exeter 129:264
Jesus 39:339
Jesus 124:203
Keble 14:56, 62
Lincoln lat.100:191
Lincoln lat.124:157
Magdalen 13:264
Magdalen 52:141
Magdalen 145:81
Magdalen 153:58
Magdalen 196:81
Magdalen 213:425–6
Magdalen 267:159, 161
Magdalen lat.15:173, 191
Magdalen, Fastolf Papers 43:186
Merton 23:62
Merton 268:81, 385
Merton 297B:64
Merton 319:62, 64
New College 37:191
New College 38:191
New College 67:319, 337
New College 91:191
New College 101:190
New College 104:190
New College 112:191
New College 122:191
New College 266:60
New College 288:57
New College 326:188–9
Oriel 15:138
Oriel 42:191
Oriel 75:64
Oriel 79:425

Queen's 161:424
Queen's 357:56
St John's 196:64
St John's 205:369, 372
St John's 266:411, 428
St John's 293:58
Trinity D.29:424
Trinity E.6:337
University College 4:341
University College 16:160
University College 74:141
University College 85:54, 58, 107
University College 91:108, 190
University College 97:327, 337
University College 188:235
University College 192:159

Petworth House, Sussex
MS of *Canterbury Tales*:275

Ripon, Cathedral Library
XVIII.H.9:82

Rothesay, Library of Marquess of Bute
MS of *Regiam Majestatem*:243–4
MS of *Northern Homily Cycle* (*olim* Bute):272
MS of Gower, etc.:244, 272

St Andrew's, University Library
PA 6295.A2A00:248
Muniments B54/7/1:28

Salisbury, Cathedral Library
MS 17:173
MS 99:70, 82
MS 103:122

Shrewsbury School
MS 6:293
B.III.24:82

Stonyhurst College, Lancashire
MS 60:206
MS *Summa de Officiis*:107

Stratford, Shakespeare Birthplace Trust
DR 37:160

Winchester College
Archives, Muniment 78:159

Woburn Abbey, Library of Duke of Bedford
MS 181:164

Worcester, Cathedral Library
F.10:120
F.172:107

York, Minster Library
Add.2:56
Add.256:59
XVI.D.2:141
XVI.E.32:397
XVI.L.12:135

United States and Canada
AUSTIN, University of Texas MS 143
    (Cardigan):261, 276
BALTIMORE, Walters Art Gallery, Walters
    239:197
BERKELEY, University of California MS
    150:34–5, 57
BOSTON, Countway Library of Medicine
    MS 19:384, 397
    MS deRicci 23:57
BOSTON, Public Library, MS f.med.94:240
CAMBRIDGE, Harvard University Library,
    Eng.530:307
    Eng.587:233
    Eng.752:218
    Eng.920:394
    Rich.35:216
    bMS.Typ.40:62
CAMBRIDGE, Harvard Law School
    Library, MS 25:204, 224
    MS 43:389
CHICAGO, Newberry Library, MS 254:237
    MS 566:276
    MS 32.9:189
    MS f.36 Ry 20:421
    MS Silver 1:427
CHICAGO, University Library, MS 254:237
    MS 566:276
LOS ANGELES, Library of Irwin J. Pincus,
    Horae:346, 373, 396
MALIBU, John Paul Getty Museum, MS
    Getty 17:64
MONTREAL, McGill University Library,
    MS 143:277–8
NEW HAVEN, Yale University, Beinecke
    Library, MS 27:59
    MS 317:122, 338
    MS 365:292–4, 311
    Osborne Shelves 1.20:428
NEW YORK, Academy of Medicine, MS
    12:390, 397–8
NEW YORK, Columbia University,
    Plimpton MS 255:277
    Plimpton MS 256:231
    Plimpton MS 259:421
    Plimpton MS 263:164, 427
    Plimpton MS 265:275
NEW YORK, Pierpont Morgan Library, MS
    Bühler 5:227
    MS Bühler 26:422

MS Glazier 9:36, 56, 224
MS Glazier 47:57, 392
M 105:180–1
M 124:188
M 126:60, 64, 107, 193
M 648:58, 60
M 775:56, 60, 193, 198, 219–20, 237
M 815:94, 205
M 817:62, 188, 223, 276
M 818:274
M 876:267
M 893:37, 39, 41, 58–9, 63, 98, 107, 193
M 1033:63
NEW YORK, Public Library, MS Spencer
    3:58, 63, 212, 231–2
MS Spencer 9:207, 228
MS Spencer 19:61
MS Spencer 193:215
PHILADELPHIA, Free Library, MS
    Widener 3:181
PHILADELPHIA, Museum of Art, MS
    45–65–6:57
PHILADELPHIA, Rosenbach Foundation,
    MS 439/16:58, 107, 209, 277
MS 1003/29:392
MS 1084/1:274
MS 1084/2:276–7
PHILADELPHIA, University of
    Pennsylvania, MS Eng.8:342
PRINCETON, University Library, MS
    Garrett 139:276
MS Garrett 140:217–18
MS Garrett 141:235

MS Garrett 150:216
MS Garrett 151:384
MS Garrett 168:206
MS 128:422
R. H. Taylor MSS:
    olim Ireland-Blackburn:235, 314
    of the Prick of Conscience:189
    of Trevisa's Polychronicon:277
    of Gower's Confessio Amantis:274–5
    of Lydgate's Fall of Princes:275
SAN MARINO, Huntington Library, MS
    EL 26.A.13:276, 284–6
MS EL 26.A.17:2, 168, 203, 274
MS EL 26.C.9:59, 61–2, 261, 264–5, 274,
    276
HM 1:311
HM 114:216
HM 128:274
HM 131:233
HM 132:62
HM 135:276
HM 136:420
HM 137:189, 261
HM 142:303
HM 144:423–4
HM 268:58, 61, 209, 230, 277
HM 503:138
HM 744:106
HM 19913:57–8
HM 19920:63
HM 39465:54, 108
URBANA, University of Illinois, MS
    DeRicci 70:63

GENERAL INDEX

Abbott, T.K., 422, 427
Abbey of the Holy Ghost, 326, 343
Abell, William, 91–2, 96–9, 101, 104, 106–7, 178, 188, 193, 203, 223, 282
Aberdeen, Cathedral and University, 239–40, 243, 250, 253
Abraham and Isaac, play of, 293
Acastre, John, stationer, 105
Actors, Peter, stationer, 77
Adams, A., 192
Adamson, J.W., 119
Addis, Robina, 372, 386
Aegidius di Columna, 58
Aiguebelle (Savoy), St Catherine's church, 144
Aitken, P.H., 28, 254, 423
Albertus Magnus, 68, 351
Alexander and Dindimus, 175
Alexander de Villa Dei, 80
Alexander of Hales, 79
Alexander, J.J.G., 54, 81, 98, 104, 106–7, 168, 179, 187, 192–4, 196, 221–4, 226, 229–31, 236–7, 304, 313
Aleyn, John, stationer, 105
Aleyn, John, canon, 148
Allan, A., 55, 59, 62, 179, 195
Allen, H.E., 121, 339, 343
Alliaco, Petrus de, 78
Amours, F.J., 253
Ancrene Riwle, 321, 339
Anderson, A., 372, 386
Anderson, D., 221, 230
Anderson, M.R., 424
Angles, H., 156
Anglo, S., 179, 195
Anne of Bohemia, 6, 168, 187
anthologies and miscellanies, production of, 279–315
Antonius Andrae, 351
Anys, John, limner, 96, 105–6
Aquinas, St Thomas, 83, 253
Arbuthnot, Alexander, 241
Arderne, John (of), 45, 54, 56, 60, 375–6, 381, 390–1, 396–7, 399

Arend, Z.M., 236
Argentine, John, provost of King's, 185, 383
Aristotle, 5, 253, 349
Arma Christi, 55
Armstrong, C.A.J., 226
Armstrong, Elizabeth, 103, 185, 197–8
Arnold, T., 141
Arthour and Merlin, 235
Arthur, Prince, son of Henry VII, 205
Arundel Castle, Sussex, 272
Arundel, secular college at, 114
Arundel, Thomas, archbishop of Canterbury, 116, 128, 131, 332–4
Asloan, John, scribe, 297, 313
Assembly of Gods, 426–7
Asshe, John, limner, 98, 106
Assion, P., 388
Astley, Sir John, 219–20, 237
Aston, John, 189
Aston, T.H., 120
Aston, Margaret, 138, 141, 234
atte Wode, Thomas, 105
Atwood, E. Bagby, 222
Aubert, H., 181, 196, 226
Audelay, John, 280
Augsburg, David of, 320
Augustine, St, 47, 54, 74, 77, 190
Aulus Gellius, 173
Avowinge of Arthur, 235
Awntyrs off Arthure, 235, 237, 300
Ayr, civic records, 243
Ayto, J., 428

Babbington, C., 142
Babyngton, Anthony, 228
Backhouse, J., 57, 63, 175, 193, 224–5
Bacon, John, 202
Bacon, Roger, 231, 353–4, 371, 382–3, 394
Balbus, Johannes, 203
Balfour, James, of Denmilne, 241, 254
Banester, Gilbert, 309
Banks, J., 122
Bannister, A.T., 157
Barber, G., 199

Barber, M.J., 221
Barbour, John, *Bruce*, 24, 253
Bardney abbey, 222
Barell, John, stationer, 97, 105
Barell, William, bookbinder, 100
Barkeby, John, stationer, 99
Barker, John, stationer, 105
Barker, N.J., 68, 70, 81–2, 401
Barker-Benfield, B.C., 190–1, 195–6, 221, 225, 233
Barking abbey, 330
Barnum, P.H., 122, 344
Baron, William, 330
Barough, William, stationer, 97, 105–6
Barron, C.M., 232
Bartholomaeus Anglicus, 54, 63
Bartle, R.H., 185, 190
Barwe, William, stationer, 97
Basing, P., 106
Bateson, M., 121, 430
Bathcom, William, 184
Battle abbey, 277
Baugh, A.C., 338
Beadle, R., 234, 276–7, 304, 311
Beauchamp, *see* Warwick
Beaufort, Henry, bishop of Winchester, 165, 185
Beaufort, Lady Margaret, 218, 235
Beauvale, Charterhouse, 116
Beccaria, Antonio, 248
Beck, R.T., 390
Bede, 239
Bedford, John, duke of, 170, 180–1, 186, 196, 202, 204, 221, 396
Bedford, Thomas, bookbinder, 78–9
Beets, J., 79
Belgrave, John, 141
Bell, H.E., 8, 10, 234, 343
Bell, S.G., 183, 232
Belle Dame sans Merci, *see* Chartier; Roos
Bellervu, John, stationer, 105
Benet, John, 174, 191
Bennett, H.S., 9–10, 103, 189, 260, 263, 273–5, 388
Bennett, J.A.W., 108
Benskin, M., 141, 303, 339, 343
Benson, C.D., 309, 315
Bent, M., 151, 153, 156–8, 160–1
Bergen, H., 168–9, 188, 230, 236, 271, 275–6
Berkeley, Elizabeth, 117
Berkeley, Thomas, Lord, 117, 219
Berliner, R., 55
Bermondsey priory, 114, 157
Bernard, William, 149
Berners, Dame Juliana, 235
Berry, Jean, duc de, 5, 192, 204, 219, 236, 395
Bertachinus, 86

Bessinger, J.B., 422
Biblia Pauperum, 54
Bischoff, B., 158
Bisticci, Vespasiano da, 10, 405
Bitterling, K., 388
Blades, W., 430
Blake, N.F., 8, 108, 233–4, 236, 310, 312, 426, 430–1
Blake, Raynold, bookseller, 100
Blayney, M.S., 228, 426
Bliss, A.J., 313, 339
Blodgett, T.E., 304
Bloomfield, M.W., 121–2
Blount, Walter, Baron Mountjoy, 212
Blundell, Robert, 165
Bober, H., 388, 392–3, 395–6
Boccaccio, 5, 9, 13, 27, 167, 209, 229, 257, 259, 290
Body, John, painter, 103
Boece, Hector, 250, 253
Boethius, 83, 122, 356, 391–2
Boffey, J., 228, 230, 304, 309
Bohun, Humphrey de, earl of Essex, 257
Bokebynder, Nicholas, 78
Bokenham, Osbern, 118–19, 123
Bologna, book trade in, 3
Bond, E.A., 120
Bond, W.H., 427
Bone, G., 411, 426–8, 431
Boke of St Albans, 427
Book of Courtesy, 425
Book of Good Manners, 425
Book of Hunting, 429
bookbinding, decorated English, 65–86
'booklets', their part in book production, 290–1, 293–6, 298, 312, 327–8, 353, 356, 380–6
books, coats of arms in, as evidence of ownership, 167–9; decoration of, classification of types of MS, 32–3; frequency of decoration, 31–4; decorative borderwork, 48–52; decoration of English poetic texts, 265–7; illustration, positioning of, 34–45; marginal positioning of, 43–5; content of, 45–8; patrons, buyers and owners, and evidence of book production, 163–99, 201–38; royal patrons and owners, 178–80, 202–6; price of books, 7, 10–12, 343; historical interests as a stimulus for book production, 215–19; production of books in monasteries and by the religious orders, 2–4, 13, 109–23, 257, 268; production of books for universities, the *pecia* system, 3–4, 8; production of religious books in the vernacular, 317–44; scientific and medical books, 32–3, 38, 45, 48, 54, 57, 345–402; definitions of such books,

345–8; physical make-up, 352–6; incidence of illustrative material, 356–79; languages contained in them, 379–84; evidence of specialised production of such books, 384–6; the 'Sloane group', 385–6; the book trade in general, second-hand books, 2, 6, 171–7; imports of books produced abroad, 180–3; *see also* paper; parchment; printed books; wills

Books of Hours, 32–9, 46–7, 143, 181–2, 347, 405–6

Boorman, S., 157

Bordeaux, John of, 382

Borell, John, stationer, 159

Bornstein, D., 226, 236

Bothwell, Richard, 244

Bothwell, John Ramsay, Lord, 246

Bourchier, Henry, earl of Essex, 216

Bourchier, Thomas, archbishop of Canterbury, 233

Bourchier, Sir Thomas, 216

Bourdichon, Jean, 225

Bourgain, P., 120

Bower, Walter, 245–6, 255

Bowers, R.H., 151, 157–9, 194

Bowland, Thomas, limner, 96, 98, 106

Boyle, L.E., 156, 336

Boys, John, textwriter, 96

Bozzolo, C., 8, 26–7, 144, 156, 167, 343

Bracy, John, scrivener, 105

Bradfelde, Ralph, 179, 194

Bradfelde, Robert, 203

Bradley, R., 335, 339

Bradshaw, Henry, 73

Brady, M.T., 343

Braidfut, Robert, 249, 256

Branca, V., 9

Brandeis, A., 122

Brandon, Nicholas, 233–4

Brandon, William, 219, 233–4, 237

Braswell, L., 347, 400

Bray, Catherine, 206

Bray, Sir Reginald, 206

Braybrook, bishop of London, 125

Braybrooke, Northants., 129

Bredon, Simon de, 356, 373, 395

Bredon, Walter de, 395

Brereton, William, stationer, 99, 106

Brett-Smith, H.F.B., 424

Brewer, C., 189, 273

Brewer, D.S., 61, 234, 314, 389, 432

Brewer, Thomas, 184

Brewster, Henry, 149

Brewyn (?), William, scribe, 123

Brie, F.W., 232

Brigit of Sweden, St, 116

Brinton, Thomas, 120

Briquet, C.M., 15–28, 233, 246, 248, 250–1, 255–6

Bristol, book production in, 13, 237, 268

Broke, Thomas, bookbinder, 97

Broune, John, limner, 96, 106

Brown, Agnes, 197

Brown, C., 272

Brown, John, merchant, 181

Brown, John, stationer, 190, 197

Brown, John, bishop of Glasgow, 253

Brown, R. Allen, 194, 222

Brown, T.J., 81

Bruges, 181

Bruges, Walter de, 273

Brunner, K., 235

Brusendorff. A., 159, 287, 303, 305–8

Brut, MSS of, 46, 68, 183, 198, 215–17, 233, 237, 313, 418–20

Brygon, William, 190

Brytte, Walter, 348

Buckingham, Humphrey, duke of, 149

Bühler, C., 6, 9, 55, 171, 189, 198, 229, 231, 336–7, 420–3, 425–6, 428–31

Buik of Alexander, 241

Bukofzer, M., 160

Bunch, Duncan, 253

Buren, A. van, 222

Burgh, Benedict, 209, 230

Burgh, Thomas, 118–19

Burgham, William, stationer, 106

Burgundy, book trade in, 202–9

Burke, P., 400

Burley, Simon, 10, 185–6

Burley, Walter, 70, 348–9, 400

Burner, John, 218

Burnett, C., 392

Burnham, John, 179, 194

Burrow, J.A., 273

Burton, John, 184

Burton, Robert, stationer, 100, 104, 106

Burton, Thomas, of Meaux, 111, 120

Bury St Edmund's, abbey, 117–18; book production at, 259–60, 268–9

Butrio, Antonius de, 82

Buttler, William, limner, 92, 106

Buuren-Veenenbos, C.C.van, 313

Buxton, John, 191

Bygge, John, scribe, 312

Byles, A.T.P., 229, 424

Bylton, Peter, stationer, 93, 96–7, 100–1, 104–6, 108

Caerleon, Lewis of, 365

Caesar, Julius, *Commentarii* and *De bello gallico*, 173, 249

Cambridge, book production in 143; bookbinding in, 68, 76

Cambridge, King's College, foundation of, 203

Cambridge, Richard, earl of, 229

Campbell, P.G.C., 228

Campsey, Suffolk, Augustinian nunnery, 118

Canonicus, Johannes, 351

Cant, Allan, 253

Canterbury. bookbinding in, 67, 72

Canterbury, Clement of, 191

Canterbury, Franciscan convent, 277

Capgrave, John, prior of Lynn, 55, 112, 118–19, 123, 259, 268

Carent family, 218

Carey, H.M., 393

Carlerius, Aegidius, 73

Carmelianus, Peter, 54, 86

Carmelite Missal, 52, 63

Carmody, F.J., 400

Carpenter, John, town clerk of London, 184

Carpenter, K.E., 190

Carraria, Milo de, 202, 221

Cary, G., 230

Cass, F.C. 308

Catherine, queen of Henry V, 223

Catherine of Siena, St, 116

Cato, *Distichs*, 6, 83

Cattley, S.R., 137

Catto, J., 223

Cavanaugh, S., 107–8, 183–4, 335

Cawley, A.C., 311

Caxton, William, 3, 67, 73, 104, 108, 143, 192, 198, 207–8, 228, 290, 350–1, 384, 403–7, 410–26, 428, 430–1

'Caxton Master', the, 202, 212, 221

Cecily of York, daughter of Edward IV, 192

Chalons family, 232

Chancery, clerks and scribes, 89, 103

Chandos Herald, *Vie du Prince Noir*, 284–5

Chapman, A., 400

Charles V, of France, 5, 204, 219, 224, 236

Charles VI, of France, 192

Charles the Bold, of Burgundy, 206

Charles of Orleans, 112–14, 120, 205, 219, 236, 303

Charlton, Lewis, bishop of Hereford, 150, 190

Charlton, Thomas, scrivener, 105

Charlton, Sir Thomas, Speaker of Commons, 186

Chartier, Alain, 55, 58, 228, 283, 426

Chastellaine, George, binder, 79

Chaucer, Geoffrey, 8, 14, 32–3, 48, 55, 218, 240, 242, 257, 260, 268, 280, 283, 287, 297, 400, 420; *ABC to the Virgin*, 315; *Adam Scriveyn*, 259; *Anelida*, 18, 217, 283; *Astrolabe*, 54, 365, 382; *Boece*, 16–19, 258–9; *Book of the Duchess*, 281; *Canterbury Tales*, 7, 43,

46–7, 61–3, 125, 168–9, 217, 235, 258–63, 268, 270–2, 274–7, 287, 308, 384, 407, 411, 413, 417, 419–20, 427; *Complaint of Mars*, 218, 220, 303; *Complaint of Venus*, 220, 303; *Complaint to his Lady*, 306; *Complaint to his Purse*, 304; *Complaint to Pity*, 306–7; *Envoy to Bukton*, 258;*Gentillesse*, 304; *House of Fame*, 258, 426; *Lak of Stedfastnesse*, 304, 307; *Legend of Good Women*, 6, 10, 258, 280–1, 309, 312; *Parliament of Fowls*, 219, 280–1, 288; *Troilus and Criseyde*, 56, 62, 137, 168, 188, 223, 230, 251–2, 258–9, 261, 264, 266, 270–2, 284, 306, 411; *Truth*, 304, 307

Chauliac, Guy de, *Chirurgia*, 58, 376, 379, 381, 384, 390, 396–7, 399

Chaundler, Thomas, Chancellor of Oxford, 35, 46

Chaunt, William, stationer, 104

Chaworth family, 218

Chaworth, Sir Thomas, 164–5, 184, 188

Chaytor, H.J., 9–10, 275

Cheney, C.R., 159, 336

Chepman, Walter, 253

Chesney, K., 229

Chester abbey, 112, 114

Chestre, Richard, chaplain to Henry VI, 107, 172

Chetham, Thomas, of Nuthurst, 169, 189

Chichele, Archbishop, 125

Childern, William, stationer, 92, 97, 103, 106

Chirche, Robert, stationer, 92, 97, 99, 104, 106, 108

Chrisman, M., 400

Christianson, C.P., 53, 73, 80, 83–4, 122, 138, 307

Christine de Pizan, 5–6, 9, 55, 208, 224, 228

Chronicles of England, 419–20, 424, 427

Chrysostom, St John, 70, 429

Church, Robert, 106

Cicero, 72, 83, 236, 248, 259

Clanchy, M.T., 157

Clanvowe, Sir John, 280–1, 312

Clare, Austin friary, 112

Clare, countess of, 2

Clarence, duchess of, 113, 116–17

Clarence, George, duke of, 417–18

Clarence, Thomas, duke of, 151–2

Clark, C.C, 395

Clark, J.P.H., 336, 339–40

Clark, L.G., 226

Clark, P., 185

Clarke, M.V., 222

Claveryng, John, 149

Claydon, John, skinner, 125–6, 134, 137

Clement of Hungary, 192

Clement of Lanthony, 135

Clerk, John, grocer, 104, 192, 207, 228

Clifton, Robert, 184
Cloud of Unknowing, 113, 322, 335, 340
Clough, C.H., 183–4, 189, 229, 338
Clyde, W.M., 430
Cockerell, Sydney, 186
Cok, Edmund, stationer, 92, 96, 99, 106, 108
Cok, Edward, stationer, 96, 106
Cok, Margaret, 99
Cok, Thomas, limner, 103
Coke, Christopher, binder, 71,78
Colin, G., 81
Colins, Richard, 132
Colker, M.L., 191
Colledge, E., 121, 123, 197, 339–40
Collins, H.B., 160
Collop, Richard, parchmener, 100, 108
Cologne, Carthusian house, at, 114
Colton, J.B., 390
Coluccio Salutati, 68
Colville, Anne, nun of Syon, 219
Colvin, H.M., 194, 222
Colvin, M.N., 425
Colyns, John, mercer, 290, 310, 429
'commonplace books', 292–5
Common Profit books, 312–13, 319–20
Company of Stationers, London, 6–7
Conlon, D.J., 196, 228
Constable, G., 336
Contemplations of the Dread and Love of God,
   330–1, 342
Cony, Henry, binder, 74
Cooke, John (Richard ?), composer, 152, 160
Cooper, C.H., 235–6
Corbet, John, stationer, 92, 106
Corbridge, Thomas of, 191
Cordial, see Rivers
Cornelius, R.D., 338, 341
Cornewalle, Roger, limner, 105
Cornysh, Thomas, 191
Corsten, S., 26
Cotson, William, 420, 423
Coulton, G.G., 272
Court of Sapience, 288, 421
Courtenay family, 230
Cowan, I.B., 254
Coxe, H.O., 237
Craft of Dying, 327
Craigie, W.A., 313
Cranley, Thomas, archbishop of Dublin,
   190–1
Crombie, A.C., 345, 394
Crome, Walter, 191
Crompton, J., 139
Cross, C., 140
Crossgrove, W.C., 390
Crow, M.M., 105
Crowland, Godfrey of, 175

Cummyn, Sir William, 424
Cunningham, I.C., 234, 272, 255, 303
Curial, 426
Curry, P., 393
Curry, W.C., 388
Cursor Mundi, 55

Dalton, R., 123
Darby, Richard, stationer, 99
Dartford, Dominican priory, 330
Dauntsey, Ambrose, 177, 193
Dauntsey, William, mercer, 193
Davenport, C., 81
Davies, R.G., 184
Davis, N., 158, 186, 227, 234, 237–8, 303,
   308, 311, 314
Davis, N.Z., 400
Day, M., 121, 303
Deane, Henry, 188
Deanesly, M., 7, 10, 163, 184, 336, 338–9
Dearden, J.S., 186
decoration, *see* books, decoration of
Deery, P.M., 386
Deguileville, Guillaume de, *Pélerinages*, and
   English translations, 5, 46–7, 55, 259, 285,
   300, 315
Dekyn, Thomas, Dominican friar, 137
Delaissé, L.M.J., 8
de la Mare, A.C., 54–5, 59, 62, 185, 190–1,
   195–6, 221, 233, 429–31
Delisle, L., 192, 221, 224, 236
Demaitre, L.F., 399
Dempster, G., 159
Denholm-Young, N., 146, 157
Dennis, R., 55
Denny, Cambs., nunnery, 272
Dent, Giles, 190
Depden, John, 185
Desert of Religion, 59
Desrolez, A., 190
D'Evelyn, C., 338–9
Devereux, Anne, wife of William Herbert,
   187, 215
Devon, Frederick, 107
Dickens, A.G., 232
Dicts or Sayings of the Philosophers, 59–60, 183,
   198, 210, 231, 236, 412–14, 418, 421–2,
   426; *see* Rivers
Dijk, S.J.P. van, 8, 159
Dillon, Viscount, 222, 232, 237
Disce Mori, 338–9
Dittmer, L., 160
Diverres, A., 192
Dives and Pauper, 63, 115, 122, 334–5, 428
Doiron, M., 340
Donaldson, E.T., 27, 188, 261, 271, 273
Donatus Devocionis, 114, 121

Dondaine, A., 157
Donne, Elizabeth, 226
Donne, John, 226
Dorsten, J.A. van, 303
Doutrepont, G., 222
Doyle, A.I., 6, 8, 10, 28, 53, 55, 60, 72, 81,
    83, 85, 102–8, 121–2, 140–1, 150, 155–6,
    166, 169–70, 186, 188–90, 193, 197–9, 216,
    222–4, 230–1, 233–7, 261–2, 264, 267–8,
    272–7, 303–5, 307–10, 312–14, 327, 330,
    336–43, 384, 386, 400–1, 422, 430–1
Drennan, J.F., 424
Driver, M.W., 230
Du Boulay, F.R.H., 234
Duff, E.G., 84, 103–4, 198, 390, 430
Dunce, Roger, bookbinder, 96
Dunfermline, book production in, 244, 246–8
Dunion, Ralph, 179, 194
Dunn, T.F., 431
Dunning, John, vicar of Perth, 253
Duns Scotus, 54, 86
Durandus, *Rationale Divinorum Officiorum*, 244
Durham, bookbinding in, 72
Durkan, J., 253–4
Dux Moraud, 147, 293
Dyboski, R., 236, 425
Dykkes, Robert, scrivener, 139
Dymmock, Roger, 134

Eamon, W., 390
Easton, Adam, monk of Norwich, 120
Eastwood, B.S., 387
Ebesham, William, scribe, 2, 107, 206, 220,
    237, 304, 384, 404
Edinburgh, Cathedral, 182
Edmund, St, *Mirror*, 310, 314
Edward II, 195
Edward III, 202, 219, 223, 236
Edward IV, 117–18, 167–8, 173, 179–80, 187,
    192, 202–6, 208, 212–13, 219–20, 226, 232,
    236, 290, 413–14, 421
Edward V, 205, 413
Edwards, A.S.G., 122, 224, 230, 233, 235–7,
    274, 276–7, 305, 309, 387–8, 400, 420, 427
Egbert, D.D., 191
Eggebrecht, H.H., 156
Eglyston, Thomas, stationer, 99
Einhard, *Vita Karoli Magni*, 173
Eis, G., 388
Eisenstein, E.L., 9–10, 108, 156, 172, 177,
    350, 390, 430
Eisner, S., 393
Elgin Cathedral Library, 240
Elizabeth of York, daughter of Edward IV,
    179, 192
Elizabeth (Woodville, Wydville), queen of
    Edward IV, 192, 213, 232, 413

Elmham, Thomas, of St Augustine's,
    Canterbury, 111
Elphinstone, William, bishop of Aberdeen,
    240–1, 250, 253
Eltham palace, 179, 222
Elys, John, 108
Elys, Richard, stationer, 97, 103, 106, 108
Emden, A.B., 160
Emendatio Vitae, 328
Eneydos, 422
Engelbert of Nassau, Count, 205
Enseignement de Vraie Noblesse, 181
Epistle of Privy Counselling, 322
Erfurt, Carthusian house at, 114
Erl of Tolous, 310
Ermengau, Matfre, 192
Erskine, Sir Robert, 255
Eston, Richard, 106
Eton College, foundation of, 203
Euclid, 356, 392
Eutropius, *Historia romana*, 249
Everett, D., 141
Evesham abbey, 113
Ewen, Thomas, 297
Expedition of Henry V, 290

Fabian, B., 199
Fachliteratur, 347–8
Fallows, D., 156
Farmer, H., 120
Farne, cell of Durham, 112
Farnely, William, clerk of Edinburgh, 254
Farquhar, J.D., 53, 62, 181, 197, 392, 431
Fastolf, Sir John, 186, 208, 219, 229, 236
"Fastolf Master", the, 181, 192, 201, 221, 224
Faulfiš, Mikuláš, 129
Fawkys, Thomas, rector, 104
Faye, C.O., 427
Febvre, L., 9, 26, 120, 389–90
Felton, Sybilla de, abbess of Barking, 324
Fenlon, I., 157, 225, 315, 337
Fenn, J., 237
Fervor Amoris, 330
Fetypace, William, mercer, 218, 220
Ficino, Marsilio, 76
Finchale, cell of Durham, 112
Fines, J., 140
Fisher, J.H., 103, 339
Fitch, M., 102
Fitch Lytle, G., 194, 225
FitzAlan, William, earl of Arundel, 233
FitzHugh, Thomas, 237
Fitzjohn, Robert, apprentice limner, 92, 106
Flanders, book trade in, 6–7
Fleet, John, Keeper of the Wardrobe, 223
Fleischhacken, Robert von, 399
Flemmyng, Robert, 191

Fletcher, A.J., 341
Fletcher, B.Y., 308, 427
Floretum, Wycliffite compilation, 128–9, 139
Follegh, William, of Devizes, 132, 140
Foot, M.M., 80–1, 83–4, 86
Fordoun, John of, *Chronicle*, 239–41, 246,
    253–4
Forshall, J., 139
Fortescue, Sir John, 113, 287, 384, 401
Foster, F.A., 315
Foulis, Alexander, of Linlithgow, 244, 255
Fountains abbey, 272
Fox, D., 431
Fox, G.S., 388
Fox, Richard, of St Albans, 164, 184–5
Fox, Richard, bishop, 80
Foxton, John de, *Liber Cosmographiae*, 57, 62,
    380
Frampton, Richard, scribe, 107, 223
France, book trade in, 202–9
Franciscus, Ricardus, scribe, 107, 178, 193,
    202, 209, 221
François, Maitre, 205–6, 225
Fraser, William, 254
Fraunkeleyn, Roger, carpenter, 94
Frederick III, Emperor, 206
French MSS in England, 207–9
Fridner, E., 141
Friedman, J.B., 63, 272, 380, 388, 396, 398
Froissart, Jean, 6, 209, 219, 226, 285
Frosten, Robert, stationer, 99
Fuller, John, 126
Furnivall, F.J., 123, 224, 228, 230, 315, 425
Fyslake, Thomas, Carmelite friar, 113
Fysshe, Thomas, limner, 92, 96–9, 106

Gagnebin, Bernard, 196
Gairdner, J., 10
Galbraith, V.H., 120, 122, 191
Game of Chess, 417–18, 422
Ganz, P., 159
Gardner, H.L., 121
Gascoigne, Thomas, Chancellor of Oxford,
    190
Gaselee, S., 424
Gaspar, C., 192
Gasquet, Abbot, 238
Gaunt, John of, 155, 165
Gawain and the Green Knight, 46, 57, 257
Generides 277
Genet, J.P., 122, 141
Geoffrey of Monmouth, 239
Gerard, D., 9, 26, 389
Gerardy, T., 21, 28–9
Gerhard von Wesel, of Cologne, 197
Germany, bookbinding in, 66
Gerould, G.H., 122

Gerson, Jean, 28, 77
Gettings, F., 398
Gibson, M.T., 81
Gibson, S., 70, 78–9, 82, 85
Giles, P.M., 196
Giles of Rome, 219
Gilles de Bretagne, 145–6, 157
Gillespie, V., 336–7, 339, 343
Gillisen, L., 159
Gilson, J., 187, 190–2, 196, 222, 225–6,
    228–30, 232–3, 277, 305
Gilte Legende, 123, 184
Gingerich, O., 393
Ginzburg, C., 400
Glade, Thomas, goldsmith, 105
Glahn, H., 160
Glasgow Cathedral library, 239–40
Glasgow, university, 240
Glasscoe, M., 336, 338
Gloucester, Eleanor Bohun, duchess of, 165
Gloucester, Humphrey, duke of, 68, 117–18,
    172, 175, 185, 195, 201, 204, 209, 219, 221,
    236, 365, 385, 401
Gloucester, Thomas of Woodstock, duke of,
    10, 111, 131, 175, 186, 193, 202, 219, 236
Glym, Thomas, haberdasher, 105
Godman, S., 254
Golden Legend, 415, 422
Goldwell, James, bishop of Norwich, 405
Goldwell, James, envoy, 182
Gollancz, I., 224
Goodman, A., 222
Goodyere, John, 308
Gordon, Bernard of, 381
Gordon, J.D., 228
Görlach, M., 122, 272, 422
Gospel of Nicodemus, 286
Gottfried, R.S., 390
Gould, K., 389
Governal of Health, 351
Gower, John, 2, 8, 14, 33, 39, 47, 58, 240,
    242, 257, 259–60, 268, 273, 275, 281, 297;
    Confessio Amantis, 6, 46, 55, 64, 168–70, 183,
    187, 198, 203, 240, 257, 260–5, 267, 270–2,
    275, 277, 341, 384, 405, 416, 420, 425–6;
    Vox Clamantis 273
Grace, Dominus, 422
Gradon, P., 223
Gransden, A., 120, 195, 232–4
Grant, E., 387–8, 393–4
Gravell, W., scribe, 123
Gray, D., 56, 59, 142, 196, 221
Gray, G.J., 159
Gray, James, rubricator, 245, 256
Gray, William, bishop of Ely, 180, 187, 190
Green, R.F., 107, 194, 222, 274, 305–9
Greenberg, C., 107, 305

Greene, R.L., 303, 307
Greet, W.C., 338, 341
Gregory, St, *Homilies*, 173; *Moralia*, 190, 203
Grey, of Ruthin, Edmund, Lord, 187, 341
Griffiths, J.J., 55, 58, 60, 103, 184, 188, 194, 275–7, 309, 344
Griffiths, R.A., 195, 228
Grimm, F.M., 388
Grinberg, H., 230–1
Grisdale, D.M., 120
Grocyn, William, vicar, 227
Grose, Francis, 194
Grosseteste, Robert, 190, 207, 348
Grothe, Richard, 390
Gryme, John, scribe, 126, 138
Guddat-Figge, G., 231, 233–5, 309–10, 312–13
Guescelin d' Euse, Cardinal, 175
Guido delle Colonne, 224
Guiscardo and Ghismonda, 290
Gumbert, J.P., 27, 159
Gunther, R.T., 395
Gunthorp, John, dean of Wells, 173, 190–1
Güssen, L., 431
Gutenberg, Johannes Gensfleisch zum, 403
Gybbe, William, priest, 123

Hackett, M.B., 121, 123
Halasey, S., 140
Hall, B., 394
Halliwell-Philips, J.O., 348, 389, 394, 424
Halsham's Balade, 306
Hamel, C.F.R. de, 8, 73, 78, 80, 84–5, 187, 197
Hamer, Robert, stationer, 106
Hamm, C., 157–8
Hammond, E.A., 228, 390, 397, 401
Hammond, E.P., 107, 303–8
"Hammond scribe", the, 283, 287–90, 308, 312
Hands, R., 309, 429
Hanna, R.W., 28, 234
Hansen, B.W., 386, 394
Hardman, P., 235, 312
Hardyng, John, 254; *Chronicle*, 223, 227, 242
Hargreaves, H., 139–40, 309
Harley, M., 397, 401
Harpenden, John, scribe, 99
Harpius, Henricus, 428–9
Harrington, J.H., 120
Harris, K.D., 55, 58, 184, 188–9, 193–4, 230, 234, 304, 306, 312, 424
Harrison, F.Ll., 156–7, 159
Harriss, G.L. and M.A., 191
Harrod, H., 308
Hartel, H., 187
Harthan, J., 54, 63

Hartung, A.E., 425
Harvey, B.F., 120
Harvey, E.R., 231
Haselden, R.B., 431
Hastings, William, Lord, 180, 196, 204, 206, 219, 226
Hatley, Walter, stationer, of Cambridge, 76
Hausknecht, E., 235
Hay, D., 178
Hay, Sir Gilbert, 72, 252, 256; *Alexander*, 241
Haymo, on the Pauline Epistles, 190
Haywarde, scribe, 413, 421
Hector, L.C., 120
Heege, scribe, 295–8, 300, 302, 312–13
Heilbronn, W.L., 430
Hellinga, L., 78, 104, 108, 182, 187, 189, 229, 421, 430–2
Henley, Walter of, 351
Henry III, 179, 222
Henry IV, 2, 6 (as earl of Derby), 174, 179, 192, 203, 208, 222–3
Henry V, 100, 117, 152, 179, 188, 195, 203–4, 218, 223, 230, 266
Henry VI, 28, 117–18, 131, 172, 179–80, 187, 203–4, 207, 213, 223, 304
Henry VII, 74, 131, 178–9, 187, 192, 203, 205–6, 208, 215, 225–6, 235
Henry VIII, 215, 225
Henryson, Robert, 240, 412
Herbert, J.A., 191, 228
Herbert, William, *see* Pembroke, earl of
Herman, H.J., 225
Hert, Thomas, stationer, 99
Hesewell, John, 164
Hethe, John, clerk of the Privy Seal, 223
Heyworth, P.L., 196, 221
Hicks, M.A., 232
Higden, Ranulph, *Polychronicon*, 47–8, 54, 64, 111–12, 114, 203, 419, 424, 428
Hildesheim, John of, 16, 230, 248
Hill, A.A., 222
Hill, Richard, grocer, 313, 425
Hilton, Walter, 113, 115, 121, 310, 321, 330, 335, 340; *Scale of Perfection*, 113–14, 219, 300, 315, 321–2, 327–8, 339, 342; *Of Mixed Life*, 314, 328
Hindman, S., 9, 53, 62, 229, 392, 431
Hinton abbey, 112
Hirsch, R., 9, 166, 430
Historia de preliis, 209, 230
History of Troy, 405, 411
Hitchcock, E.V., 338
Hobson, G.D., 67, 70, 72–4, 76, 79–80, 82–6
Hoccleve, Thomas, 2, 33, 56, 89, 97, 103, 218, 224, 240, 259, 263, 268, 274, 280, 285, 302, 313; *Letter of Cupid*, 280, 283; *Regiment*

of Princes, 13–14, 43, 61, 168–9, 230, 233, 264, 270–2, 283, 287
Hodgson, P., 336. 340
Hodnett, E., 431
Hoffman, E.J., 426
Hogg, J., 122, 336
Hokyns, Thomas, bookbinder, 70
Holand, John, earl of Huntingdon, 28
Holland, John, duke of Exeter, 186
Holmes, T.S., 336
Holywode, Thomas, bookbinder, 99
Honeybourne, M.B., 105
Honorius of Autun, 349
Hoo family, 169
Hoo, Eleanor, 196
Hoo, Sir Thomas, 181, 196
Hook, Robert, priest at Braybrooke, 129
Hopton family, of Swillington, 233, 313
Hopton, Richard, London rector, 101
Hopton, Thomas, 297
Hopton, Sir William, 216
Horner, P.J., 120
Horrall, S.M., 230, 315
Horsle, Roger, limner, 98, 106
Horsley, Adam, Carthusian, 113, 121, 321
Horstmann, C., 122–3, 310, 338–9, 343, 430
Hotersall, John, stationer, 99, 106
Houghton, A.A., 392
Howton, Marmaduke, stationer, 106
Hudson, A., 10, 122, 137–42, 223, 275, 340, 344
Hughes, A., 156
Hughes, M.J., 160, 224
Humphrey, duke of Gloucester, *see* Gloucester
Hun, John, stationer, 98, 105–6
Hunayn ibn Ishaq, *Isagoge*, 349, 357, 381
Hungerford, Lady, 209
Hungerford, Walter, Lord, 230
Hunt, John, artist, 96
Hunt, R.W., 120, 190–1, 195–6, 221, 237, 389, 401
Hunt, Thomas, stationer, 70, 77–8
Hussey, S.S., 121, 339
Hutton, Henry, stationer, 99
Huws, D., 237
Hyhelm, Thomas, limner, 96, 98, 106
Hyltoft, Joan, nun of Nuncoton, 342

Idley, Peter, *Instructions to his Son*, 320, 338
Ignorancia Sacerdotum, 338
Ile, Thomas, of Braybrooke, 141
Ilias Latina, 248
illustration *see* books, illustration of
Imbault-Huart, M.-J., 395–6
Infeld, Richard, stationer, 97
Ingham, P., 344
Ingram, J.K., 338

Innes, Thomas, 245
Ipomydon, 235
Isabeau de Bavière, 189
Isabeau of France, 208
Isabella of Castille, 205
Isabella of France, queen of Edward II, 179, 236
Irwin, R., 9–10
Ives, E.W., 189, 229
Ivy, G.S., 29, 313

Jacob, E.F., 138
Jacobs, N., 315
Jacob's Well, 115
James, M.R., 28, 121, 175, 191–4, 221, 231, 235, 237, 253, 256, 308–10, 420–1, 428, 430
James III, of Scotland, 244, 246
James IV, of Scotland, 250–2
Jaquette de Luxembourg, 170
Jason, 423
Jayne, S., 198
Jean d'Angoulême, brother of Charles of Orleans, 113–14, 188
Jenkins, Dafydd, 189
Jerome, St, 47, 54
Jervaulx abbey, bookbinding at, 67
Joan of Navarre, queen of Henry IV, 174
"Johannes", London scribe, 108, 175
Johannes de Giglis, 54
John IV, duke of Brittany, 145–6
John of Gaunt, *see* Gaunt
Jolliffe, P.S., 324–5, 327, 335–6, 338, 343
Joly, Richard, textwriter, 100
Jones, D., 338
Jones, P.E., 102
Jones, P.M., 54, 57, 60, 62, 372, 386, 392–3, 395–9, 401
Joseph, P.M., 387
Josephson, D.S., 159
Julian of Norwich, 335, 388

Kahrl, S.J., 311
Kane, G., 14, 23–5, 27, 29, 188, 261, 271, 273
Kane, H., 340
Kauffman, C.M., 187
Kays, Henry, keeper of the Hanaper, 103
Kebell, Thomas, lawyer, 208–9, 219
Keiser, G., 314, 338, 341, 386
Kekewich, M., 223
Kellogg, A.L., 138, 341
Kemerton, Gloucestershire, 129
Kempe, Margery, 335
Kempston, Nicholas, 191
Kemsyn, John, bookbinder, 72
Kendall, William, stationer, 97
Kengen, J.H.L., 337
Kennedy, A.J., 228

Ker, N.R., 12, 27–8, 66, 72, 81, 83, 139, 165, 186, 190–1, 194, 196–7, 221, 236, 247, 253, 255, 303, 306–7, 335–6, 341, 392, 401, 429
Kerling, N.J.M., 103, 197
Kermode, J.I., 184, 338
Keyle, John, painter, 103
Kibre, P., 345, 385, 387, 393–4
Kightley, C., 222
Kildare, Gerald Fitzgerald, earl of, 227
Kilwardby, Robert, 347–8
King, J.N., 198
King Ponthus, 313
Kinghorn, Robert, chaplain, 244–5, 255
Kingis Quair, 240, 250–1, 256
Kingsford, C.L., 105, 232–4
Kipling, G., 178, 194, 222, 225–6
Kirchberger, C., 121
Kleinhenz, C., 9, 60, 221
Klinefelter, R., 423
Kněhnič, Jiři, 129
Knighton, Henry, 111–12
Knowles, D., 1, 8, 119–20
Knyvet family, 218
Kolve, V.A., 47, 61–2
König, Ebehard, 182
Kren, T., 196, 225–6, 387–8, 395
Kreuzer, J.R., 315
Krochalis, J., 55, 343
Kurvinen, A., 312
Kylfoull, Richard, butcher, 92
Kymer, Gilbert, 68, 377, 379, 385, 401
Kyngeston, William, scrivener, 105

Labarre, A., 185
Lacy, Edmund, bishop of Exeter, 149
Lacy, James, stationer, 106
Laet, Jasper, of Borchloen, 246, 255
Lagorio, V., 335, 339
Laidlaw, J.C., 228, 304
Laing, M., 141
Lampe, G.W.H., 19
Lancaster, R. Kent, 194
Lancelot, in French, 257
Landshut, Franciscan house in, 114
Lanfranc, *Surgery*, 381, 391
Langland, William, *Piers Plowman*, 14, 23–6, 43, 48, 55, 137, 169, 188, 257–62, 264, 268, 270–2, 274–6, 313, 422
Langton, Stephen, 54, 65
Lantern of Light, The, 126, 137
Lanthony priory, 277
Lascelles, Roger de, of Richmond, 193
Latimer, Sir Thomas, 129, 139
Lavenham, Richard, Carmelite friar, 114–15
Lawlor, H.J., 254
Lawton, D., 186, 188

Lawton, L., 55, 58, 60–1, 122, 187, 232, 236, 276–7
Leconfield house, 179
Ledbury, Thomas, monk of Worcester, 120
Lefferts, P.M., 158
Legnano, John of, 174
Legrand, Jacques, 284
Leicester abbey, 113
Leicester, house of Austin canons, 268, 287
Lennep, J. van, 394
Leroquais, V., 187, 192
Leroy, A., 157
Lester, G.A., 8, 122, 193, 198, 227, 237, 304, 311, 341
Lesyngham, Thomas, stationer, 106
Lettou, John, 73–4
Lewis, R.E., 27, 188, 233, 272, 303, 315, 338, 343
Libel of English Policy, 123
Liber de Bestiis, 48
Liber de Diversis Medicinis, 314
Liber Pluscardensis, 246
Lidston, John, stationer, 97
Lieftinck, G.I., 192
Lilleshall abbey, 123
Lindberg, C., 139
Lindberg, D.C., 387, 391, 393
Lindsay, Sir David, 424
Lindstrom, B., 305
Lineriis, John de, 365
Littlehales, H., 226, 337
Littleton, *Tenores novelli*, 73, 86
Livres du Graunt Chaam, 46, 175
Lloyd-Morgan, C., 230
Lokton, Thomas, scribe, 108
Lollard book production, 6, 18–19, 125–42; Lollard 'Glossed Gospels', 132–4; Lollard homily cycles, 115
Lollards, Twelve Conclusions of the, 134
Lombardus, Petrus, *Sentences*, 78
London, book artisans in, 88–108; bookbinding in 66–8, 72–3; book painters in, 89; book production in, 14, 87–108, 143, 257–68, 284, 286–91, 327; book trade in 6, 87–108, 172–3; centred on Paternoster Row, 89, 92–9, 126, 263
Long, P.O., 388
Longland, bishop of Lincoln, 132, 136–7, 140
Loomis, L.H., 10, 273
Loomis, R.S., 222
Lough, J., 9
Louis, C., 311, 389
Louis XII, of France, 225
Louis of Bruges, Seigneur de Gruthuyse, 219, 236
Louis of Luxembourg, bishop of Ely, 145–6, 157

Lourdaux, W., 140
Loutfut, Adam, 424
Louvain, university, 240, 250
Love, Nicholas, *Myrrour of the Blessed Lyf of Jesu Christ*, 38, 46, 55, 58, 61, 115–16, 168–9, 183, 189, 198, 233, 322–4, 331–3, 341, 384
Lovell, Thomas, 227
Lovett, R., 338
Lowes, Patrick, bookbinder, 72
Lucas, P.J., 120, 123, 183, 224, 274
Lucius Annius, 249
Luders, A. 157
Lumby, J.R., 139
Lumiansky, R.M., 311
Lutolf, M., 156
Lutterworth, 128
Luttrell, C.A., 189, 309
Lutz, C.E., 431
Luxton, I., 140
Lyall, R.J., 254–5, 421
Lydgate, John, 6, 14, 20, 33, 39, 43–4, 46–7, 55, 117, 188, 213, 215, 218, 220, 240, 242, 259, 262, 268, 280, 283, 284–7, 288–91, 297, 306, 310, 412, 421, 427; *Churl and Bird*, 282; *Complaint of the Black Knight* 18, 280, 307; *Dietary*, 309; *Fall of Princes*, 27, 58, 64, 117, 169, 209, 230, 261, 263–6, 268, 270–2, 275–8, 306–7, 419, 428; *Horse, Sheep and Goose*, 423; *Life of Our Lady*, 56, 58, 117, 260, 274–6, 288, 423; *Life of St Alban*, 118, 122; *Life of St Edmund*, 43, 56, 117, 223, 264–5, 268, 278; *Life of St Margaret*, 20; *Pilgrimage of the Life of Man*, 19–21, 300, 315; *Secrees of the olde Philosoffres*, 21, 216, 219, 278, 287; *Siege of Thebes*, 187, 215, 219, 235, 236, 240, 260, 264–6, 274, 412, 428; *Temple of Glass*, 18–19, 258, 280–1; *Testament*, 427; *Troy-Book*, 58, 117, 164, 168, 170, 183–4, 187, 198, 215, 218, 230, 260–1, 263, 265–8, 270–2, 274–5, 277–8; *Verses on the Kings of England*, 309
'Lydgate scribe', the, 264–5, 268–9
Lyenel, David, stationer, 190
Lyle, Marion, of Houston, 240
Lymnour, John, barber, 105
Lympnour, Thomas, of Bury, 220
Lyna, F., 192
Lyncoln, Guy, painter, 103
Lyndwood, William, canonist, 126
Lynn, Austin friary, 118, 268
Lynne, Richard, stationer of Oxford, 190
Lyonhill, David, scribe, 108
Lyra, Nicholas of, 48, 54, 63, 78, 82
Lyty, scribe, 281–2

Mably, William, parchemener, 139

Macaulay, G.C., 8, 55, 222, 227, 271, 273, 275–6, 425–6
MacCracken, H.N., 28, 232, 275, 304, 306
McDiarmid, M.P., 253
Macfarlane, L.J., 254, 256
MacFarlane, K.B., 139, 186, 222, 226, 324, 335
McGregor, R.R., 305
Machaut, Guillaume de, 5–6
Machlinia, William de, bookbinder, 74, 351
McIntosh, A., 27, 188, 233, 272, 309, 314–15, 338, 343
McKenzie, D.F., 199
McKerrow, R.B., 28
MacKinney, L.C., 54, 396–7
McKinnon, J.W., 158
McKisack, M., 222
MacNulty, J., 121
Macrae-Gibson, O.D., 235
Macray, W.D., 193
McRoberts, D., 256
McSparran, F., 313–15, 337
McVaugh, M.R., 390, 395–7, 400–1
Madden, F., 139
Maghinardo dei Cavalcanti, 5
Magninus Mediolanensis, *Regimen sanitatis*, 82, 246, 351
Maidstone, Richard, Carmelite friar, 313–15
Mainz, Carthusian house at, 114
Makculloch, Magnus, notary public, 245–7
Malmesbury, William of, 191
Malory, Sir Thomas, 207, 228, 416
Mandeville's *Travels*, 7, 13–14, 22–3, 46, 48, 55, 61
Manion, M.M., 197
Manly, J.M., 62, 168, 184, 188, 235, 261, 271, 273–7, 307–8, 417, 419–20, 427, 432
Mansion, Colard, 415
manuals, of pastoral and catechetic instruction, 317–44
Manyngham family, 342
Manzaloui, M., 305, 348, 389, 391
Marchal, Johannes, 328
Marco Polo, *Travels*, 48, 64
Margaret of Anjou, queen of Henry VI, 180, 187, 203, 207–8, 213, 221, 232
Margaret of Burgundy, 405
Margaret, queen of Scotland, 205
Marks, R., 55, 193
Marleburgh, Thomas, stationer, 96–7, 105, 108, 190, 203, 222
Marliano, Raimundus de, 249
Marshall, Roger, 381, 390
Marston, T.E., 122
Martin, A., 138, 341
Martin, H.-J., 9, 26, 120, 389–90
Martin le Franc, *Champion des Dames*, 9

Martin, R.H. 431
Martyn, Richard, draper, 105
Marx, C.W., 424
Master of Game, see York, Edward, duke of
Mather, F.J., 233, 313
Matheson, L.M.,232–3, 237, 305, 392, 420, 424, 427
Matthews, W., 228, 401
Mauleverer family, 228
Meale, C.M., 188, 192, 194, 224, 227, 230, 235, 310, 427
Meditationes Vitae Christi, 7, 116, 322
Meiss, M., 194, 221, 388
Melton, Gilbert, stationer, 97, 107
Melton, Robert, scribe, 294
Memoriale Credencium, 337
Meredith, P, 311
Merlin, English prose, 235, 287
Metcalfe, W., 253
Metham, John, *Amoryus and Cleopes*, 235
Meyer, P., 228
Michael of Hungary, *Sermones*, 82
Middleton, A., 188
Middleton, B., 81
Millar, E.G., 226
Mills, D., 311
Mills, M., 237, 309, 313–14
Minio-Paluello, L., 138
Ministris in the Church, Of, 135
Minnis, A.J., 58, 276
Mirfield, John of 390
Mirk, John, 55; *Festial*, 115, 326, 336–7, 420, 428; *Instructions to Parish Priests*, 115
Mirror of Simple Souls, 322
Mirror of the World, 43, 406
Mirror to Devout People, 116
Misyn, Richard, 322
Mitchell, J., 224
Mitchell, James, priest of Exeter, 149
Mitchell, R.J., 221
Mitchell, W.S., 83
Mogens, P. 395
Molett, James, fruiterer, 92
monasteries, book production in, *see* books, production of
Mondeville, Henry of, 399
Monimail, Thomas, 247, 255
Moore, N., 104, 106
Moore, S., 9
Moore, S.N., 231
Moran, J.A. Hoeppner, 189
Morand, K., 192
More, John, bookbinder of Oxford, 70
More, Richard, bookbinder of London, 96, 104
Morgan, G.R., 341–2
Morgan, M.M., 428
Morgan, N., 193

Morise, William, alderman, 103
Morison, J.L., 338, 344
Morland, William, prebend of St Paul's, 429
Morstede, Thomas, 381, 390
Morte Arthure, alliterative, 300, 314
Morte Arthur, stanzaic, 235
Mortimer, Edmund, earl of March, 28
Mount Grace, Carthusian priory, 114, 116
Mueller, J., 321–3, 390, 401
Multon, John, stationer, 99, 106–7, 382
Multon, Robert, stationer, 97
Munby, A.N.L., 107, 172, 174, 185–6, 190
Mundy, Sir John, goldsmith, 170
Murdoch, J. 356–7, 367, 372, 387–9, 391–8
Murray, V.R., 342
music, production of books of 143–61; characteristics and distribution of books of music, 144–8; institution collections of books of music, 148–50; structure of books of music, 150–5
Myers, A.R., 194
Myllar, Andrew, 253
Mynors, R.A.B., 107, 180, 190, 196, 303, 425, 429
Myrc, *see* Mirk
Myrrour of Lewed Men and Women, 333

Neckham, Alexander, 63
Needham, P., 21, 28, 81
Nelson, V., 344
Nepos, Cornelius, 249
Nessefylde, William de, scribe, 108
Netherlands, bookbinding in, 66–7
Netter, Thomas of Walden, *Doctrinale*, 47, 64, 125
Neugebauer, O., 388
Neuton, John, prior of Battle abbey, 237
Nevanlinna, S., 341
Nevill, bishop of Salisbury, 132
Neville, Alice, 237
Neville, Anne, wife of Humphrey, earl of Stafford, 212
Neville, Anne, wife of Richard Beauchamp, earl of Warwick, 213
Neville, Joan, 233
Newman, W., 395
Newton, Humphrey, 302–3, 315
Newton, John, treasurer of York, 185, 302
Nichols, John, 185
Nicholson, P., 273
Nicolas, N.H., 194, 230
Nicolettus, P., *Summa naturalium*, 82
Nider, Johannes, *Consolatorium*, 79, 427
Nixon, H.M., 73–4, 80–1, 83–5, 198, 430
Nolcken, C. von, 139
Norfolk, John Howard, duke of, 220
Norfolk, John Mowbray, duke of, 168

North, J.D., 388, 393–5, 400
Northern Homily Cycle, 257, 272, 326
Northern Passion, 300
Norton, Thomas, *Ordinall of Alchemy*, 57
Norton-Smith, J., 223, 235, 256, 304, 432
Norwich, Robert, 308
Norwich, book production in, 268
Norwich Cathedral priory, 111-12
Nova Rhetorica, 407, 410, 423
Nova Statuta, MSS of, 64, 183, 198, 233
Nowell-Smith, G., 389
Nuremburg, Benedictine abbey, 114

O'Brien, R., 121
Obrist, B., 394–5
O'Connell, P.343
Ogden, M.S., 314, 396, 399
Ogilvie-Thomson, S., 339
Okewell, Richard, limner, 97, 99, 106
Oldcastle, Sir John, 129, 134, 224
Oldham, J.B., 67–86, 309
Olschki, L.S., 406, 430
Olson, C.C., 105
Olson, G. 234
O'Neill, Y.V. 398
Opsomer, C., 398
Opus Arduum, 136
Order of Chivalry, 424
ordinatio, increasing attention to, in book
    production, 328–35
Oresme, Nicole, 5, 387, 400
Orgel, S., 194, 225
Orme, N., 120
Ornato, E., 8, 26–7, 143, 156, 343
Orosius, 249
Osney, abbey, bookbinding in, 67
Otterburne, Thomas, chronicler, 122
Ouy, G. 121
Overall, W.H., 107
Ovid, 13, 27; *Metamorphoses*, 301, 414–16, 424
Ovitt, G., 388
Owen, A.E.B., 234, 304, 314
Owst, G.R., 184, 338
Oxford, book trade in, 3–4; bookbinders in,
    66–8, 70–3, 77, 80; book production in, 143,
    190; printing at, 403; All Souls College,
    150, 179; Magdalen College, 150, 155
Oxneye, Solomon, goldsmith, 105

Pace, G.B., 307
Pachella, R., 394
Pächt, O., 54, 187, 192–3, 196, 222, 225–6,
    229–31, 236–7, 313, 430
Page, John, carpenter, 94
Page, C., 155
Painter, G.D., 198, 430
Palliser, D.M., 198

Palmer, William, precentor, of Crediton, 190
Palmere, William, priest, of London, 273
Pantin, W.A., 119–20, 336
paper, introduction of, 7, 11–15; price of, 26;
    use of, 353; value of, for evidence of date,
    etc. 15–26, 251–2; *see also* watermarks
parchment, use of, for books, 11–15
Parchmener, William, Lollard, 129
Paris, book trade, 3–4
Paris, G., 229
Paris, Matthew, 63
Parker, Duncan, of Dundee, 244
Parker, Robert, priest, of Calais, 236
Parkes, M.B., 6, 8, 10, 53, 55, 60, 102–3,
    105–6, 150, 155–6, 170, 189–90, 196,
    198–9, 216, 221–2, 234, 243, 254–5, 261–2,
    264, 266–7, 273–7, 304–5, 313, 338, 341–2,
    344, 384, 386, 389, 391, 401, 431
Parshull, P.W., 226
Partridge (Partriche), Peter, Chancellor of
    Lincoln, 174, 191, 356, 391
Partonope of Blois, 235
Paston, Sir John, 2, 7, 122, 186, 198, 206,
    219–20, 237–8, 280, 283, 288, 304, 308,
    311, 384
Paston, Sir John III, 206
Paston Letters, 10
Patterson, L.W., 273
Patton de Luca, E., 398
Paul, J.Balfour, 255
Paulus Diaconus, *Historia Langobardum*, 173,
    239, 249
Payne, A., 55
Pearl, 46
Pearsall, D., 55, 58, 60–2, 122–3, 166, 184,
    186–8, 194, 232, 234–6, 272, 274, 277,
    303–5, 309–10, 312, 314–15, 424
Pecham, John, archbishop of Canterbury,
    318, 336
Pecock, Reginald, 5, 137, 259, 319, 326, 335,
    338, 401
Pedersen, O., 396
Peeke, Nicholas, coppersmith, 105
Peeris, William, Percy family poet, 215
Pembroke, William Herbert, earl of, 187,
    215, 218, 266
Pepys, Samuel, 415
Perceforest, 225
Percy family, 213, 215
Percy, Lady Catherine, 187
Percy, Henry, 4th earl of Northumberland, 266
Percy, Henry, 5th earl of Northumberland, 215
Percy, Katherine, wife of Lord Grey, 341
Periegetes, Dionisius, 248
Perth, Carthusian house at, 245
Peter of Blois, 4
Petrarch, 5, 9, 257, 259

Phebus, Gaston, *Livre de la Chasse*, 223, 236
Philip IV, of France, 192
Philip the Bold, duke of Burgundy, 204
Philip the Good, duke of Burgundy, 9, 192, 219, 236
Phillipps, Sir Thomas, 415
Phip, John, 136, 142
Piccard, G. 15–28, 251, 255–6
Pickering, F.P., 61
Piers of Fulham, 290
Piers Plowman, see Langland
Piers the Ploughman's Creed, 287
Pintelon, P., 394, 400
Plawdon (Ploudun), Thomas, 382, 400
Pleshey, Essex, 111
Plimpton, G.A., 337
Plomer, H.R., 84, 103, 105, 159, 163, 184, 190, 197, 226, 338
Ploughman's Tale, 136
Plummer, J., 196, 221, 224–5
Poitiers, Peter of, 42, 54
Pollard, A.W., 431
Pollard, G., 6–8, 10, 67–8, 70–4, 76–87, 102, 106, 189–90, 195, 198, 274, 401, 431
Poole, R.L., 139
Pore Caitif, 136, 329–30, 332, 335, 343
Porete, Margaret, 322
Porter, Sir William, 181
Postan, M.M., 156
Poulet, Quentin, 179, 203, 205, 222
Poulle, E. 393
Povey, K., 423
Powell, L.F., 340, 343
Powell, Roger, 81
Powell, S., 122, 341
Power, D'Arcy, 156, 390, 397, 399
Power, Lionel, composer, 151–2
Powicke, F.M., 159, 336, 395
Praier and Complaynte of the Ploweman, 136
Prentot, Simon, waxchandler, 105
Preston, John, 107
Price, D.J., 393, 400
Prick of Conscience, The, 14, 55, 125, 169, 213, 215, 257, 272, 300, 310, 315, 319, 332, 343
printing, influence of introduction of 350–1, 403–32; printed books, relation and resemblance to MSS, 405–6; printed books, manuscript exemplars for, 406–11, 419–29; printed books, manuscripts copied from, 411–19, 429; printed books, illumination of, 405–6
Prior, O.H., 430
Privity of the Passion, 46, 58, 300, 314
Propositio of John Russell, 404
Pucelle, Jean, 192
Pupilla Oculi, 54
Purches, Margaret, 227

Purches, Sir William, Lord Mayor of London, 206, 227
Putnam, G.H., 9, 275
Pycard, John, 161
Pycmore, Thomas, 254
Pye, John, stationer, 99, 101, 103–4, 106–8, 172–3, 190
Pynson, Richard, printer, 74, 76, 82, 100, 284, 304, 411, 427–8

Quaritch, B., 226
Quattuor Sermones 411, 428
Quintus Curtius, 173

Raabe, P., 199
Raine, J.,184–6
Ralegh, Thomas, rector, 70
Ramsbotham, A., 160
Ramston family, of Essex, 292
Randolph, Friar John, 393
Raoul de Mortet, bookseller, 5
Rastell, John, printer, 93
Rate, scribe, 298–9, 313
Ravescot, Ludovicus, printer, of Louvain, 78
Rawson, Avery, mercer, 227
Raymo, R.R., 335, 337, 341, 343–4, 422
Raynaud, G., 420
Reading abbey, 112
Reakes, J., 340
Rede, William, 348, 382
Reed, R., 26–7
Regiam majestatem, 243–5
Regiomontanus, 383
Regula Sacerdotalis, 18–19
René d'Anjou, 209
Renoir, A., 309, 315
Renson, J., 9
Repingdon, Philip, Austin canon, 115
Reuchlin, *Vocabularius*, 74
Revard, C., 272, 309
Reve, Johannes, scrivener, 103
Revell, P., 335
Reynard the Fox, 405
Reynes, Robert, of Acle, 293–4
Rhodes, D.E., 78, 85, 198, 401
Ricci, P.G., 9
Richard II, 6, 117, 179, 185, 187, 192, 202, 207
Richard III, 203, 216, 219, 224, 236, 413
Richard Coeur de Lyon, 235, 313
Richard de Bury, *Philobiblon*, 4, 7, 9
Richardson, M., 103–4
Richmond, C., 188, 233
Rickert, E., 62, 105, 168, 184, 188, 222, 235, 261, 271, 273–7, 307–8, 417, 419–20, 427, 432
Rickert, M., 59, 62–4, 175, 186, 192, 229
Rider, Richard, stationer, 97

Riddy, F., 255
Rigg, A.G., 10, 189, 273, 275, 310, 313, 315
Riley, H.R., 102
Ringbom, S., 55
Rivers, Anthony Wydville, 2nd Earl Rivers, 193, 212, 231, 236, 413–15, 418; *Cordial*, 242, 407, 417, 420–1
Rivers, Richard Woodville, 1st Earl Rivers, 175
Robard, John, stationer, 223
Robbins, R.H., 55, 305, 307, 309–10, 313, 315, 387, 393, 399
Robert, John, stationer, 96, 100, 104
Roberts, E., 398
Robinson, F.N., 307, 400
Robinson, P., 28, 158, 234, 304, 312–13, 315, 337, 391
Rogers, D., 79, 86
Rogers, N.J., 156, 196–7
Rolf, Thomas, scribe, 108
Rolle, Richard, 55, 62, 113, 284, 310, 318, 321–2, 328, 330, 335, 339; *Form of Living*, 326–8, 330; Psalter commentary, 134–5, 141
Rood, Theodoric, bookbinder, 77–8, 351, 405
Roos, Margaret, wife of Sir Richard, 207
Roos, Matilda, wife of Thomas, 229
Roos, Sir Richard, 174, 207, 228; *La Belle Dame sans Merci*, 280, 283–4, 288, 304
Roos, Thomas Manners, Lord, 174
Roos, Thomas, Lord Clifford, 229
Root, R.K., 9, 168, 273–4
Ros, Robert de, archdeacon, 93
Rosarium Theologiae, 128–9, 135
Rosen, E., 400
Rosenthal, J.T., 184
Ross, A., 253
Ross, C., 55, 195, 232
Ross, D.J.A., 9, 230, 277
Roth, F., 123
Roulande, John, textwriter, 96
Rous Rolls, 42–3
Rouse, M.A., 139
Rouse, R.H., 139, 147, 157
Rowland, B., 398
Rowland, John, stationer, 99
Rowse, Robert, parson, of London, 122
Rufinus, *Expositio symboli*, 405
Russell, G.H., 337
Russell, J.C., 119
Russell, John, *Boke of Nurture*, 216
Russell, John, envoy to Bruges, 182
Russell-Smith, J.M., 121
Ruysschaert, J., 423
Rymer, Thomas, 185
Rymyngton, William, monk of Sawley, 112, 114

Sabellicus, M.A., *Rerum Venetarum decades*, 76
Sacrobosco, John of, 348
Saenger, P., 141–2
saints' lives (Middle Scots), 15–16, 240, 253
St Albans abbey, 115; printing at, 351, 403
St Albans, Roger of, 195
St-Amand, John of, 349, 399
St Andrews, Austin canons at, 239
St Andrews, University, 16, 240, 245, 253, 255
St Edith, Life of, 428
St John Hope, W.H., 222, 232
St Victor, abbey of, 114
St Victor, Hugh of, 347–8
St Winifred, Life of, 290, 422, 404
Saliceto, William of, 381, 399
Salisbury, book production in, 385; bookbinding in, 67–8, 70, 72
Salisbury, John of, *Policraticus*, 83
Salisbury, Thomas Montagu, earl of, 181
Salle, Richard, painter, 103
Salter, E., 10, 60–2, 64, 122, 180, 188, 196, 227, 230, 233, 273, 305, 340, 343
Salter, H.E., 106, 402
Salu, M.B., 273
Sammut, A., 185, 192, 195, 221, 225
Sampson, John, scribe, 108
Samuels, M.L., 141, 274, 278, 303, 309, 339, 343
Sanders, Alice, of Amersham 132
Sandler, L.F., 8, 192–3, 272
Sargent, M.G., 121, 237, 336, 338–40, 343
Saxoferrato, Bartolus de, *Digestum novum*, 79
Scala Mundi, 54
Scattergood, V.J., 167, 184, 186, 221–2, 227, 312
Schaefer, O., 78
Scheerre, Herman, 96, 98, 105–8, 201, 221, 267
Scheves, William, 241, 245–8, 255
Schoeffer, Peter, 429
Scholderer, V., 430
Schrader, C.R., 236
Schramm, W.L., 10, 234
Schulz, H.C., 8, 103, 274, 303
Science, M., 122
scientific and medical books, *see* books, scientific, etc.
Scone, Austin canons at, 245
Scot, John, 104, 106
Scot, Michael, 347–8
Scot, Thomas, scribe, of Braybrooke, 139
Scotland, book production in, 242–53: books and book owners in, 239–56; book trade in, 240–1; notaries public, importance of in book production, 242–6; scribes, characteristics of hands of, 243, 249

Scott, K.L., 6, 8, 10, 53, 55, 57, 61, 102, 104–5, 108, 122, 188, 193, 195, 197–9, 212, 221, 224, 227, 231–3, 238, 265, 274–8, 308, 386, 392, 396, 398, 421, 432
Scotte, William, stationer, 97
Scrivener, Michael, Lollard, 129
Scriveners' Company, 89, 103–4, 242
Scrope, Anne, wife of John, Lord Scrope, 208
Scrope, archbishop of York, 10
Scrope family, 193
Scrope, Henry, Lord, of Masham, 164–5, 186
Scrope, John, Lord, of Masham, 116
Scrope, Sir John, 229
Scrope, Stephen, *Epistle of Othea*, 46, 55
Scrymgeour, John, 424
Seaton, E., 228, 304
Secreta Secretorum, 54, 58, 205, 284
Sellyng, William, prior, 68
Selwyn, D.G., 198
Seres, Robert, clerk of Dundee, 254
Serjeantson, M.S., 123, 342
Severs, J.B., 235
Seward, John, schoolmaster, 173
Seymour, M.C., 13, 22, 27, 29, 233, 236, 271, 274, 304, 307–8, 310
Seyssel, Claude de, French ambassador, 187, 205, 225
Shackelford, J.R., 388
Shailor, B., 386, 402
Sharnebrook, Edward, canon of St Paul's, 227
Sharpe, R.R., 102
Shaw, D., 254
Sheen Charterhouse, 112–14, 116, 121–2, 429
Shelby, L.R., 394
Sherborne, J.W., 184, 186, 221–2
Sherbrooke family, of Oxton, Notts., 295
Shirley, John, 10, 16–21, 26, 107, 230, 259, 274, 284–8, 295, 298, 300, 302, 305–7, 421
Shonk, T.A., 272
Shuldham, Edward, Magister, 184
Siege of Jerusalem, 425
Siferwas, John, 108
Sigerist, H., 390
Silagi, G., 157
Silkesteade, Thomas, prior of Winchester, 74
Silverton, Nicholas, stationer, 97, 106
Simpson, G.C., 254
Sinclair, Henry, Lord, 241, 250, 252
Sinclair, Sir William, 250
Singer, D.W., 347, 352–3, 372, 386, 388
Sir Amadace, 235
Sir Degrevant, 312
Sir Orfeo, 313
Sir Ysumbras, 313
Skeat, W.W., 27, 188, 228, 273, 304, 400
Skelton, John, 215, 302

Skene, W.F., 253
Skereueyn, Herman, artist, 96, 98, 105–6
Skinners' Company, 204
Skirlaw, Walter, bishop of Durham, 165
Skryvener, Thomas, of Amersham, 139
Slack, P., 387, 400
Sloane, Sir Hans, 384
"Sloane group" of scientific and medical MSS, 385–6
Smedick, L.K., 342
Smetana, C., 123
Smith, J. Challenor C., 102
Smith, J.J., 274
Smith, K.L., 235; *see* Scott, K. L.
Smith, L. Toulmin, 311
Smith, William, Lollard, 129
Smyser, H.M., 388
Somerset, Charles, 206
Somerset, John, physician, 104
Somerville, R., 107, 223
Somme le Roi, 332
South English Legendary, 43, 122, 257, 272, 310
Southern, R.W., 227
Southwark priory, 114
Sowdone of Babylon, 217–18
Spayne, Robert, legal scrivener, 104
Spector, S., 21, 28, 311
Speculum Humanae Salvationis, 42, 54, 63
Speculum Spiritualium, 114, 121
Speculum Vitae, 318, 332–5, 343
Spencer, E., 205
Spencer, H.L., 122
Spirleng (Spurling), Geoffrey, scribe of Norwich, 169, 276
Spirleng, Thomas, scribe of Norwich, 169
Spriggs, G.M., 105–6, 221
Sprottesburgh, Geoffrey, parchmener, 99
Spyny, William, 253
Stafford, Anne, 28
Stanley, E.G., 142
Stanley, John, of Hooton, 218, 290, 304
Stans Puer ad Mensam, 425
Stapilton, Agnes, 230
Stapilton, Sir Brian, 230
Stapleton, Catherine de la Pole, wife of Sir Miles, 235
Stapleton, Sir Miles, 235
Statutes, MSS of, 12, 220
Stearn, W.T., 398
Steele, R., 303
Steer, F.W., 103, 186
Stern, K., 192, 314
Stevens, M., 311
Stevenson, A., 26–9
Stevenson, A.H., 233
Stevenson, J.A.C., 253
Stevenson, J.H., 83

Stevin, Simon, 350
Stillwell, M.B., 390
Stimulus Amoris, 330, 340, 342
Stokes family, 233
Stone, L., 185
Stones, M.A., 9, 60, 221
Stow, G.B., 120
Stow (Stowe), John, 105, 232, 284, 287, 290, 307, 416, 421
Strasbourg, printing in, 16
Stratford, J., 186, 221, 224
Strecche, John, of Kenilworth, 111
Strohm, R., 143, 156
Strong, P. and F., 195, 223
Strong, R., 225
Sudbury, William, monk of Westminster, 117, 122
Sudhoff, K., 379
Suetonius, *De vita Caesarum*, 173, 249
Suffolk, Alice de la Pole, duchess of, 186, 208, 236
Suffolk, William de la Pole, duke of, 20, 28, 236
Suggett, H., 227
Sulyard, Anne, later Bourchier, 233
Sulyard, Sir John, 233
Suso, *Horologium Sapientiae*, 116, 319
Sutherland, L.S., 222
Swerbreke, Thomas, stationer, 106
Swetenham, legal scrivener, 103
Swierk, A., 430
Swinburn, L.M., 138
Sylla, E.D., 388, 392, 400
Symond, Thomas, stationer, 100
Syon abbey, 112–14, 116, 121
Sywardby, Elizabeth, 186

Taillour, John, textwriter, 100, 103–4
Takamiya, T., 277, 432
Talbert, E.W., 138, 341
Talbot, C.H., 10, 228, 390, 392, 395, 397, 401
Talbot, George, earl of Shrewsbury, 226
Talbot, Sir Gilbert, 206
Talbot, John, earl of Shrewsbury, 180, 187, 196, 202, 207, 208, 221
Talbot, Margaret Beauchamp, wife of Lord Talbot, 180
"Talbot Master", the, 196
Tanner, N., 138, 140
Tanselle, T.G., 29
Tattershall castle, Lincs., 149, 159
Tavistock abbey, 117; bookbinding in, 67, 70
Taylor, A.J., 194, 222
Taylor, E., 187, 194
Taylor, F.S., 394
Taylor, J., 120
Taylor, L., 85

Taylor, William, Lollard, 141
Temple, E., 54
Templum Domini, 338, 341
Terence, *Vulgaria*, 75–6
Tester, S.J., 387
Thetford priory, 272
Thirke, William, 382
Thirty-Seven Conclusions, 136
Thomas à Kempis, 319
Thomas, A.H., 102
Thomas, E.C., 9
Thomas, M., 9
Thompson, D.V., 26
Thompson, E.M., 429
Thompson, F., 225
Thompson, J.J., 234, 314–15
Thompson, J.W., 222
Thomson, D., 169
Thomson, J.A.F., 195
Thomson, W.R., 138
Thoresby, archbishop of York, 317–18, 336
Thorndike, L., 345, 385, 387, 389–91, 394–5, 400
Thorney, Roger, mercer, 236, 288–90, 412
Thornton, Robert, 16, 26, 234, 297–302, 310, 314, 341
Thorold Rogers, J.E., 138
Three Kings of Cologne, The, 56
Three Kings' Sons, The, 46, 55, 210–11, 227
Thrupp, S.L., 105, 156, 184, 232, 234, 338
Thwaites family, 218
Thwaytes, Sir Thomas, treasurer of Calais, 187
Thynne, William, 283
Tilliol, Maud de, 177, 193
Tilliol, Robert de, of Scaleby, Cumberland, 193
Tiptoft, John, earl of Worcester, 167–9, 173, 180, 191, 196–7, 201, 221, 236
Tito Livio Frulovisi, 223
Todd, H.J., 197
Torbok, Richard, 191
Torrent of Portyngale, 234
Tractatus de Regibus, 135
Tracy, Ralph, prior of Sheen, 429
Trapp, J.B., 108, 197, 431
Traversagni, Giovanni, Antonio, 407, 410
Traversagni, Lorenzo Guglielmo, 407, 410
Treatise of Ghostly Battle, 327, 338
Tresswell, Robert, 105–6
Tresswell, Thomas, limner, 97, 104, 106
Tretyse of Loue, The, 339
Trevisa, John, 236; translation of *Gospel of Nicodemus*, 16–19; of Bartholomaeus *De proprietatibus rerum*, 164, 236, 262, 351; of *De regimine principum*, 219; of Higden's *Polychronicon*, 263, 265, 341, 384

Trier, Carthusians, etc. in, 114
Triggs, O.L., 427
Tristan, in French, 257
Trivet, Nicholas, 83
Tudenham, Sir Thomas, 118
Tudor-Craig, P., 224, 226
Tunstall, Brian, 237
Tunstall, Cuthbert, 237
Tunstall, Thomas, 237
Turba Philosophorum, 43
Turner, D.H., 196, 226
Turville-Petre. T., 184, 312
Tyes, John, 161
Tynemouth priory, 112, 193
Tyson, D.B., 305
Tyssens, M., 9

Uffyngton, Thomas, of Oxford, bookbinder, 78
Unwin, G., 232
Upton, John de, canon of Wells, 184
Upton, Nicholas, 54; *De officio militari*, 60
Urbino, Bartholomeus de, 83
Urswick, Sir Thomas, Recorder of London, 186
Usk, Thomas, *Testament of Love*, 258, 273
Uthred of Boldon, monk of Durham, 112, 114
Utino, Leonardus de, *Sermones*, 71, 82

Vae Octuplex, 135
Valla, Laurentius, *Elegantiae*, 83, 250
Vale, J., 184, 194, 222–3, 236
Vale, M.G.A., 184, 338
Varty, K., 192
Vaus, John, 253
Veale, E.M., 232
Vegetius, *De re militari*, 55, 117, 204, 216, 218–20, 236–7, 284
Veldner, Johannes, of Louvain, printer, 78, 403
Verard, Antoine, 206, 226
Verhelst, D., 140
Verses on the Kings of England, 43, 59, 290, 308
Veysy, Thomas, scribe, 108, 190
Vickers, K.H., 221
Victor, S.K., 394
Villa Nova, Arnald of, 349, 399
Vinaver, E., 192, 228
Vincent of Beauvais, 74, 240, 351
Vines, V., 197
Visitacio Infirmorum, 324–6
Vitas Patrum, 2, 429
Voigts, L.E., 233, 387, 389–90, 392, 394–401
Voragine, Jacobus da, *Legenda Aurea*, 240
Vrelant, Guillaume, 181

Wade, Maud, prioress of Swyne, 342

Wadmore, J.F., 224
Wagner, A.R., 55
Wagner, D.L., 394
Wakelin, M.F., 122
Wakeryng, John 104
Walcote, John, limner, 100
Walcote, William de, priest, 186
Walden, John, grocer, 104
Waleys, Henry le, mayor of London, 92–4
Walker, Richard, grocer, 104
Walker, Thomas, grocer, 104
Wallingford, Richard of, 365, 382–3, 400
Wallner, B., 390, 399
Walls, K., 305–6
Walmisley, C.A., 102
Walsingham, Thomas, of St Alban's, 111–12, 117, 122
Walter of Odington (or Evesham), 373, 383, 395, 400
Walton, John, canon of Osney, 117, 122, 219, 306
Ward, H.L.D., 191, 196, 225, 228
Ward, W., 73
Warkworth's *Chronicle*, 418–19
Warmynstre, William, 174
Warner, G.F., 123, 187, 190–2, 196, 222, 225–6, 228–30, 232–3, 277, 305
Wars of Alexander, 422
Warwick, Richard Beauchamp, earl of, 18, 213, 284; *Pageants*, 46
Warwick, Richard Neville, earl of, 181, 206
watermarks, use of, in dating, etc. 15–26
Waters, P., 81
Wathey, A., 156–61, 222
Watson, A.G., 8, 12, 26, 83, 123, 195, 389, 391–2, 394, 431
Watson, R., 197
Watt, D.E.R., 254–5
Weale, W.H.J., 85
Weber, O., 26
Webster, C., 387
Weisheipl, J.A., 388
Weiss, R., 194–5, 221, 227
Welles, Leo, Lord, 186
Wellewyk, John, stationer, 106
Wells, John, monk of Ramsey, 301
Wells, J.E., 391
Wenzel, S., 303
Werken, Theodoric, scribe, 107, 429
Werkwerth, Thomas, 373
Wessington, John, of Durham, 111
West Dereham, abbey, 118
Westfalia, John of, printer, of Louvain, 77–8
Westhuizen, J.E. van der, 122
Westminster abbey, 155; chronicler, 111–12
Westminster, press at, 403